INTERNATIONAL POLITICAL ECONOMY

INTERNATIONAL POLITICAL ECONOMY

State-Market Relations in the Changing Global Order

EDITED BY

C. Roe Goddard
John T Passé-Smith
John G. Conklin

LYNNE
RIENNER
PUBLISHERS

BOULDER
LONDON

Published in the United States of America in 1996 by
Lynne Rienner Publishers, Inc.
1800 30th Street, Boulder, Colorado 80301

Library of Congress Cataloging-in-Publication Data
International political economy : state-market relations in the
    changing global order / edited by C. Roe Goddard, John T Passé-
    Smith, John G. Conklin.
        p.   cm.
    Includes bibliographical references and index.
    ISBN 1-55587-585-8 (pbk.) (alk. paper)
    1. International finance. 2. International economic relations.
3. Economic assistance. I. Goddard, C. Roe, 1956–   . II. Passé-
Smith, John T. III. Conklin, John G., 1939–
HG3881.I5769   1995
332'.042—dc20   95-21263
                                                     CIP

Published and distributed outside the Americas, Japan, and Australasia by
MACMILLAN PRESS LTD
Houndmills, Basingstoke, Hampshire RG21 2XS and London
Companies and representatives throughout the world

ISBN 0-333-64625-8

A catalogue record for this book is available from
the British Library

Printed and bound in the United States of America

∞   The paper used in this publication meets the requirements
     of the American National Standard for Permanence of
     Paper for Printed Library Materials Z39.48–1984.

5 4

CONTENTS

ACKNOWLEDGMENTS

The idea for a reader combining theoretical and institutional approaches to international political economy began in 1991 when we, the editors, collaboratively and collegially taught a course at Thunderbird, the American Graduate School of International Management. In the early discussions that took place between classes we decided that the volume would combine readings that reflect both the classical and the contemporary, bringing together disparate styles, methodologies, perspectives, and passions. We sought to include a blend of empiricism and advocacy that would be both challenging in terms of the level of difficulty and rewarding in terms of the conceptual tools and substantive knowledge gained. Tough editing decisions became even more difficult as time passed and also as one of the editors, John Passé-Smith, moved to a position at the University of Central Arkansas. After all of the meetings, conference calls, cross-country trips, and overnight mailings, the decisions are made, and we are happy with the final product.

Many of our friends and colleagues offered assistance along the way and we would be remiss if we did not acknowledge them. We are particularly indebted to those who have shared in the task of teaching the Introduction to International Political Economy course in the International Studies Department at Thunderbird: Marty Sours, Glenn Fong, Karen Walch, Earl Gibbons, Roy Nelson, and Dick Mahoney. These colleagues helped us shape the final content of the IPE course and this reader. So too have other colleagues in the Department of International Studies and World Business, including Beverly Springer, Femi Babarinde, Min Chen, Byron Jackson, Shoshona Tancer, Joaquim Duarte, Dale Vorderlandwehr, Jim Mills, and Francisco Carrada Bravo, who teach regional politics courses and international trade and finance.

Colleagues outside of Thunderbird also have contributed. We want to thank Robert Gilpin, Lorraine Eden, and Bob Denemark for their suggestions. We would also like to thank those who contributed original chapters to this volume: Barry Hughes, K. Sarwar Lateef, David Rapkin, Jonathan Strand, and Beverly Springer.

The Department of International Studies at Thunderbird, the Department of Political Science at the University of Central Arkansas, and the administrations of both schools provided important and welcome logistical support. Betsy Bryant and Diane O'Brien at Thunderbird and Marlene LeDuc at the University of Central Arkansas provided valuable clerical assistance and moral support. Judy Max and Cristine Bullert at the Center for Authoring and Presentation Support at Thunderbird were instrumental in assisting us with this project. Lynne Rienner and her staff were particularly helpful and patient in bringing this project to press.

We would also like to thank our Thunderbird students, both past and present, for making this class so enjoyable for us to teach. Each semester about 350 students register for this required, and perhaps even feared, course. The proceedings are coordinated across multiple sections and a common exam is given twice per semester. Since almost all first-semester students are taking the course, virtually the entire campus comes to a standstill as the students make their way to the largest auditorium on campus (a refurbished aircraft hangar) on exam days. For most Thunderbird students, this class is considered a rite of passage. In the end, we hope that they enjoy taking it as much as we enjoy teaching it.

Finally, and most important, we would like to thank our spouses. They share our work, endure our moods, and act like we are worth putting up with.

C. Roe Goddard
John T Passé-Smith
John G. Conklin

INTRODUCTION

John T Passé-Smith,
C. Roe Goddard,
and John G. Conklin

Momentous historical events are occurring so rapidly in the post–World War II era that in 1995 the pace rivals that of technological innovations in the computer industry. In the early 1970s, the world was faced with the collapse of the international economic system—the Bretton Woods system—that many thought had provided for a virtual explosion in the volume of global trade. The mid-1970s brought an oil embargo and a quadrupling of the price of petroleum, sparking one of the greatest transfers of wealth in human history. Petrodollars flowed out of oil-consuming countries into the oil-rich members of the Organization of Petroleum Exporting Countries (OPEC). This in turn gave way to a second and smaller oil shock that ushered in an extended and worldwide recession. Oil-exporting countries found an outlet for their wealth in the banks of the industrialized, developed world. Political leaders in the developed countries, fearing inflation, encouraged a diversion of the petrodollars to developing countries in the form of loans for development projects. By the early 1980s, Mexico had become the first on a long list of developing countries awash in international debt and unable to meet their financial obligations. For Mexico and other debtor countries, the 1980s became known as the lost decade. As the developed and developing countries and international financial institutions struggled to stabilize the global economy, another series of events unfolded that ultimately ended in the collapse of communism and placed even greater strains on international political and economic institutions.

In the decades prior to the 1970s, the study of international political economy had faded and was rarely offered as a field of study; the maelstrom of events enumerated above, however, aided in its revitalization. Many of these crises were symptoms of the disintegration of the post–World War II era of international financial stability and prosperity. At

1

the war's conclusion, the world turned from what many thought of as the "high" politics of warfare and destruction to the economics of rebuilding what had been destroyed. The United States finally accepted its leadership role, and, with the aid of international institutions created at Bretton Woods, economic growth exceeded most analysts' expectations. About a quarter of a century after the Bretton Woods system's inauguration, President Richard Nixon cut the tie between the U.S. dollar and gold, ending the system that had brought the conditions for rapid economic growth and financial stability. The death of the Bretton Woods era and the international hostility generated by the oil embargo marked the overt politicization of international economic relations. As the U.S. economy stumbled and issues of inflation, unemployment, and wages became more bitterly contested, politics focused increasingly on economic issues. Thus, both domestically and internationally, the economy was growing more politicized, and political systems were focusing their energies on economic problems.

International political economy also reemerged because the more salient issues of the day could not be explained adequately by those using models devised by scholars remaining within the narrow confines of the disciplines of political science or economics. Prior to this century it would have been considered odd to divorce things economic from things political. In trying to understand and explain society, Adam Smith, Alexander Hamilton, Karl Marx, and other writers of their eras assumed that economics was political and that politicians attempted to control economic outcomes. Around the turn of the twentieth century, the development of the academic disciplines of political science and economics separated the two topics. Economists developed rather elegant models of markets and market behavior, and political scientists explained the behavior of individuals and groups in seeking political organization and advantage. Independently, each discipline made great strides in gaining an understanding of its chosen area, but each was weakened by the exclusion of the subject matter that had become the domain of the other. The events of the post–World War II era made scholars painfully aware of this problem. Issues such as the oil embargo were neither wholly economic nor totally political. International political economy, which seeks to explain the intersection of politics and economics, thus reemerged as an important field of study. Its return has involved melding the work of the masters of previous centuries with the developments made in political science, sociology, and economics in the present century.

In this volume we have sought to include the contributions of those influential people who, in their attempts to understand the workings of the international system, have succeeded in creating a core literature around which subsequent ideas cluster. More contemporary thinkers who are intellectually indebted to these paradigm creators are also included. The first section of the book offers a very brief historical treatment of the rise and expansion of modern capitalism over the past four hundred years. These roots gave rise to three pools of knowledge that form the conceptual perspectives of liberalism, nationalism, and Marxism, the tenets of which provide the basic conceptual foundation of international political economy. Adam Smith provides the basic precepts of liberalism in his discussion of the workings of the market, with particular attention to the reasons for international trade. Alexander Hamilton's influential "Report on Manufactures" illustrates nationalist thought. Hamilton urged the U.S. Congress to intervene in the economy to encourage manufacturing; without such intervention, he thought, the United States would be unable to industrialize and would fail to become a country of consequence. The absolutely brutal conditions imposed on the workforce by the owners of the means of production in the early years of the industrial revolution inform Karl Marx's view of the world. His focus on conflict and the clash of classes in the unfolding of history remain popular in many areas. Each of these selections lends context and texture to the more contemporary discussions of the politics of the international economic system that are provided in the remaining chapters of the book's first section.

The second section offers a history of the international financial system and examines the important and controversial role played by the International Monetary Fund (IMF). At the outset of the post–World War II era, the countries that joined the Bretton Woods system pegged their currency to the U.S. dollar, and the United States tied the dollar to gold at $35 per ounce. The value of currencies was then allowed to fluctuate within a 1 percent band. One of the jobs of the IMF was to monitor this fixed-flexible exchange rate system to ensure compliance with the band. Proponents argue that this system provided the global financial stability that allowed unprecedented rates of economic growth; however, by the late 1960s many countries were experiencing difficulty in remaining within the established band, which in part prompted the crisis that sparked Nixon's withdrawal from the Bretton Woods system. With the collapse of the peg-and-band system, many critics called for a floating exchange rate system whereby the value of a currency is set by the currency market. Even though today most countries maintain a form of the floating exchange rate system, the debate is far from settled. With the U.S. dollar at its weakest since World War II against the Japanese yen, and with political hackles being raised within the European Monetary Union—in part because of the volatility of the exchange rates of member countries—the issue is more relevant than ever.

Students often become impatient with theory because it seems so removed from the headlines that grab their attention. However, the reader should note that both the criticisms and the defense of the policies and programs of the IMF, as well as those of the World Bank and the World Trade Organization, flow from the worldviews of the individuals and the leaders of these institutions. Developing countries often point to the rich countries' control of the IMF as evidence of the rich gaining authority over their economies or diminishing the sovereignty of their countries. In the past decade two *golpes de estado* were attempted in Venezuela. Some of the military conspirators offered a classic nationalist argument to justify their actions, claiming their behavior was proper because the Venezuelan government had surrendered its sovereignty when it agreed to IMF austerity plans. The core of the conspirators' nationalist defense was that political leaders are no longer legitimate when their decisions undermine the sovereignty of the country. Because the political leaders had given up control of the country to an international, or a foreign, institution, the leaders of the *golpe* were justified in attempting to overthrow the government.

Perhaps not surprisingly, the contemporary Marxist-oriented response would be little different. The core of the Marxist critique would be to accuse the rich nations of using the IMF to strip Venezuela of its natural resources, exploit its labor, and violate its sovereignty. Both the nationalist and the Marxist-oriented responses would probably express concern over the loss of sovereignty, but the Marxist orientation would isolate the economic motivation of the institutions (and the powers behind those institutions) that were acting *against* the developing country. Even neoliberals could dig back into the wealth of wisdom offered by Adam Smith to rationalize a Venezuelan response to the previously mentioned IMF austerity plans. As is seen in Chapter 3, Smith supported the Navigation Acts for reasons that seemingly boil down to economic advantage and nationalism.

The third section of the book concerns global economic development and the role of the World Bank. Conceived at the Bretton Woods Conference and formed in the aftermath of World War II, the Bank's initial responsibility was to aid in the reconstruction and development of Western Europe. By 1950 the U.S. Marshall Plan had surpassed the World Bank in the effort to restore Europe, so the Bank turned its attention to developing countries. One of the areas of interest to both the World Bank and international political economists is the impact of the transfer of technology from the developed to the developing world. Economic historians have surmised that poor countries have tremendous potential for rapid economic growth because of the lack of widespread use of sophisticated technology in production. As they adopt new technologies and utilize labor more efficiently, their growth rates should exceed those of the rich countries. This section takes stock of global economic growth and presents some potential lessons that might be utilized in the transition of the formerly communist countries of Eastern Europe.

Global trade relations is the theme of the fourth section. In the modern capitalist era, trade remains one of the most important economic ties between countries. The events of the past decade indicate that trade relations are as important in international political economy today as they have ever been. The policies the more powerful countries follow in the years ahead have been significantly affected by the results of the Uruguay Round of trade talks, the movement toward European union, and the North American Free Trade Agreement and its possible extension to the southern cone. One of the achievements of these agreements has been to reduce the taxation imposed on trade in the form of tariffs; however, numerous voices have protested the impact of this freer trade on the position of domestic labor, as well as on the sovereignty of the state. Nationalist complaints about free trade sometimes go beyond these concerns. For instance, Republican presidential hopeful and media personality Patrick Buchanan has complained that the U.S. government has not been forceful enough in seeking a trade advantage for its producers. As this section reveals, the debate is far from settled, and the eventual outcome will profoundly shape international political and economic relations for generations.

Part 5 examines the increasing significance of transnational corporations (TNCs) in international trade and politics. Praised by some and vilified by others, TNCs have evolved into one of the most important nongovernmental linkages between states. They stand accused of both creating and destroying the potential for Third World economic growth. Also important is the fact that an increasing percentage of world trade is conducted within TNCs. Rhys Jenkins estimates that intra-firm trade, which in this case refers to a transfer of goods to or from a corporation to its majority-owned foreign affiliates, constitutes 20 percent of U.S. exports and just over 30 percent of U.S. imports. Although this section is devoted to the role of transnationals in the international system, their influence has become so vast that a discussion of TNCs flows through every section of the book.

For the concluding section we wanted to select issues we believed would be at the heart of the international political economy debate in the coming decades. Global environmental policy and the communications revolution top the list. Neither will pass quietly from the scene because both transcend state borders and challenge state control. This section looks to the next century, provides a framework for understanding how each of the issues has evolved, and anticipates where the issues are heading.

As all teachers say of their areas of interest, this is a very complex and sophisticated field that cannot be digested in the course of a semester or even two. This statement may be especially true of international political economy because the latter blends political science with economics with sociology with history and so on. All of these disciplines bring their own terminology and their own interests and emphases, often leaving students to find their own way. It is our hope that this book, taken as a whole, provides a sound foundation for understanding the processes, institutions, and conflicts that arise in the international system.

PART 1

CONTENDING VIEWS OF INTERNATIONAL POLITICAL ECONOMY

1

THE NATURE OF POLITICAL ECONOMY

Robert Gilpin

Robert Gilpin presents a definition of international political economy (IPE) and discusses the scope of this field of study. According to Gilpin, the tensions and interactions between politics and the economy constitute the stuff of political economy. Although the relative influence of politics and the market changes over time, the two forces are forever linked; neither exists independent of the other. In this initial chapter, Gilpin discusses the parameters of the study of IPE and traces the concurrent rise of the modern state system and the global expansion of capitalism. He poses three questions to guide thinking about the subject: What are the causes and effects of the world market economy? What is the relationship between economic and political change? And what is the significance of the world economy for states? He concludes with an exploration of the rise of the market as a force that revolutionizes both societal and political relations within and among communities.

The parallel existence and mutual interaction of "state" and "market" in the modern world create "political economy"; without both state and market there could be no political economy. In the absence of the state, the price mechanism and market forces would determine the outcome of economic activities; this would be the pure world of the economist. In the absence of the market, the state or its equivalent would allocate economic resources; this would be the pure world of the political scientist. Although neither world can ever exist in a pure form, the relative

Reprinted with permission of the publisher from *The Political Economy of International Relations* by Robert Gilpin (Princeton: Princeton University Press, 1987): pp. 8–14, 18–24.

influence of the state or the market changes over time and in different circumstances. Therefore, the conceptions of "state" and "market" in the following analysis are what Max Weber has called ideal types.

The very term "political economy" is fraught with ambiguity. Adam Smith and classical economists used it to mean what today is called the science of economics. More recently, a number of scholars, such as Gary Becker, Anthony Downs, and Bruno Frey, have defined political economy as the application of the *methodology* of formal economics, that is, the so-called rational actor model, to all types of human behavior. Others who use the term political economy mean employment of a specific economic *theory* to explain social behavior; game, collective action, and Marxist theories are three examples. The public choice approach to political economy draws upon both the methodology and theory of economics to explain behavior. Still other scholars use political economy to refer to a set of *questions* generated by the interaction of economic and political activities, questions that are to be explored with whatever theoretical and methodological means are readily available (Tooze, 1984).

Although the approaches to political economy based on the application of the method and theory of economic science are very helpful, they are as yet inadequate to provide a comprehensive and satisfactory framework for scholarly inquiry. Concepts, variables, and causal relations have not yet been systematically developed; political and other noneconomic factors are frequently slighted. In fact, a unified methodology or theory of political economy would require a general comprehension of the process of social change, including the ways in which the social, economic, and political aspects of society interact. Therefore, I use the term "political economy" simply to indicate a set of questions to be examined by means of an eclectic mixture of analytic methods and theoretical perspectives.

These questions are generated by the interaction of the state and the market as the embodiment of politics and economics in the modern world. They ask how the state and its associated political processes affect the production and distribution of wealth and, in particular, how political decisions and interests influence the location of economic activities and the distribution of the costs and benefits of these activities. Conversely, these questions also inquire about the effect of markets and economic forces on the distribution of power and welfare among states and other political actors, and particularly about how these economic forces alter the international distribution of political and military power. Neither state nor market is primary; the causal relationships are interactive and indeed cyclical. Thus, the questions to be explored here focus on the mutual interactions of very different means for ordering and organizing human activities: the state and the market. . . .

The relationship of state and market, and especially the differences between these two organizing principles of social life, is a recurrent theme in scholarly discourse. On the one hand, the state is based on the concepts of territoriality, loyalty, and exclusivity, and it possesses a monopoly of the legitimate use of force. Although no state can long survive unless it assures the interests and gains the consent of the most powerful groups in society, states enjoy varying degrees of autonomy with respect to the societies of which they are a part. On the other hand, the market is based on the concepts of functional integration, contractual relationships, and expanding interdependence of buyers and sellers. It is a universe composed mainly of prices and quantities; the autonomous economic agent responding to price signals provides the basis of decision. For the state, territorial boundaries are a necessary basis of national autonomy and political unity. For the market, the elimination of all political and other obstacles to the operation of the price mechanism is imperative. The tension between these two fundamentally different ways of ordering human relationships has profoundly shaped the course of modern history and constitutes the crucial problem in the study of political economy.[1] . . .

The Issues of Political Economy

The conflict between the evolving economic and technical interdependence of the globe and the continuing compartmentalization of the world political system composed of sovereign states is a dominant motif of contemporary writings on international political economy.[2] Whereas powerful market forces in the form of trade, money, and foreign investment tend to jump national boundaries, to escape political control, and to integrate societies, the tendency of government is to restrict, to channel, and to make economic activities serve the perceived interests of the state and of powerful groups within it. The logic of the market is to locate economic activities where they are most productive and profitable; the logic of the state is to capture and control the process of economic growth and capital accumulation (Heilbroner, 1985, pp. 94–95).

Debate has raged for several centuries over the nature and consequences of the clash of the fundamentally opposed logic of the market and that of the state. From early modern writers such as David Hume, Adam Smith, and Alexander Hamilton to nineteenth-century luminaries such as David Ricardo, John Stuart Mill, and Karl Marx to contemporary scholars, opinion has been deeply divided over the interaction of economics and politics. The conflicting interpretations represent three fundamentally different ideologies of political economy. . . .

The inevitable clash gives rise to three general and interrelated issues that pervade the historic controversies in the field of international political economy. Each is related to the impact of the rise of a world market economy on the nature and dynamics of international relations.[3] Each is found in the treatises of eighteenth-century mercantilists, in the theories of classical and neoclassical economists over the past two centuries, and in the tomes of nineteenth-century Marxists and contemporary radical critics of capitalism and the world market economy. This long tradition of theorizing and speculation is crucial to an understanding of contemporary problems in trade, finance, and monetary relations.

The first issue is concerned with the economic and political causes and effects of the rise of a market economy. Under what conditions does a highly interdependent world economy emerge? Does it promote harmony or cause conflict among nation-states? Is a hegemonic power required if cooperative relations among capitalist states are to be ensured, or can cooperation arise spontaneously from mutual interest? On this issue theorists of different schools of thought have profoundly conflicting views.

Economic liberals believe that the benefits of an international division of labor based on the principle of comparative advantage cause markets to arise spontaneously and foster harmony among states; they also believe that expanding webs of economic interdependence create a basis for peace and cooperation in the competitive and anarchical state system. Economic nationalists, on the other hand, stress the role of power in the rise of a market and the conflictual nature of international economic relations; they argue that economic interdependence must have a political foundation and that it creates yet another arena of interstate conflict, increases national vulnerability, and constitutes a mechanism that one society can employ to dominate another. Although all Marxists emphasize the role of capitalist imperialism in the creation of a world market economy, they divide between the followers of V. I. Lenin, who argue that relations among market economies are by nature conflictual, and those of Lenin's chief protagonist, Karl Kautsky, who believe that market economies (at least the dominant ones) cooperate in the joint exploitation of the weaker economies of the globe. The alleged responsibility of the market system for peace or war, order or disorder, imperialism or self-determination, is embedded in this important issue, as is the crucial question of whether the existence of a liberal international economy requires a hegemonic economy to govern the system. The challenge to the United States and Western Europe from Japan and other rising economic powers at the end of this century dramatically highlights the importance of these matters.

The second issue pervading the subject of international political economy is the relationship between economic change and political change. What are the effects on international political relations and what problems are associated with structural changes in the global locus of economic activities, leading economic sectors, and cyclical rates of economic growth? And, vice versa, how do political factors affect the nature and consequences of structural changes in economic affairs? For example, one may question whether or not major economic fluctuations (business cycles) and their political effects are endogenous (internal) to the operation of the market economy, or whether economic cycles are themselves due to the impact on the economic system of exogenous (external) factors such as major wars or other political developments. It is also necessary to ask whether or not economic instabilities are the cause of profound political upheavals such as imperialist expansion, political revolution, and the great wars of the past several centuries.

[International political economy] is thus concerned in part with the effects of economic changes on international political relations. These economic changes undermine the international status quo and raise profound political problems: What will be the new basis of economic order and political leadership? Can or will adjustment to the changed economic realities, for example, new trading and monetary relations, take place? How will the inevitable clash between the desire of states for domestic autonomy and the need for international rules to govern change be reconciled? These issues of transition between historical epochs have again arisen with the global diffusion of economic activities and the profound shifts in the leading economic sectors taking place in the late twentieth century. It is important to probe the relationship between these structural changes and the crisis of the international political economy.

The third issue with which [international political economy is concerned] is the significance of a world market economy for domestic economies. What are its consequences for the economic development, economic decline, and economic welfare of individual societies? How does the world market economy affect the economic development of the less developed countries and the economic decline of advanced economies? What is its effect on domestic welfare? How does it affect the distribution of wealth and power among national societies? Does the functioning of the world economy tend to concentrate wealth and power, or does it tend to diffuse it?

Liberals and traditional Marxists alike consider the integration of a society into the world economy to be a positive factor in economic development and domestic welfare. Trade, most liberals argue, constitutes an "engine of growth", although the domestic sources of growth are more important, the growth process is greatly assisted by international flows of trade, capital, and productive technology. Traditional Marxists believe that these external forces promote economic development by breaking the bonds of conservative social structures. On the other hand, economic nationalists in both advanced and less developed countries believe that the world market economy operates to the disadvantage of the economy and domestic welfare. Trade, in their view, is an engine of exploitation, of underdevelopment, and, for more advanced economies, of economic decline. This controversy over the role of the world market in the global distribution of wealth, power, and welfare constitutes one of the most intensely debated and divisive questions in political economy.

These three issues, then—the causes and effects of the world market economy, the relationship between economic and political change, and the significance of the world economy for domestic economies—constitute the major theoretical interests of [international political economy]. . . .

The Importance of the Market

The study of political economy focuses on the market and its relationship to the state because the world market economy is critical to international relations in the modern era; even in socialist societies the key issue in economic debates is the appropriate role for internal and external market forces. As Karl Polanyi said in his classic study of the transformation of modern society:

> the fount and matrix of the [modern economic and political] system was the self-regulating market. It was this innovation which gave rise to a specific civilization. The gold standard was merely an attempt to extend the domestic market system to the international field; the balance-of-power system was a superstructure erected upon and, partly, worked through the gold standard; the liberal state was itself a creation of the self-regulating market. The key to the institutional system of the nineteenth century [as well as our own] lay in the laws governing market economy (Polanyi, 1957, p. 3).

Karl Marx, on the other hand, stressed capitalism or the capitalist mode of production as the creator and unique feature of the modern world. The defining characteristics of capitalism, as defined by Marx and his collaborator, Friedrich Engels, and which I accept, are the private ownership of the means of production, the existence of free or wage labor, the profit motive, and the drive to amass capital. These features provide capitalism with its dynamism; the dynamic character of the capitalist system has in turn transformed all aspects of modern society. As Gordon Craig has pointed out, the revolutionary nature of capitalism lay in the fact that, for the first time, the instinct to accumulate wealth became incorporated in the productive process; it was this combination of the desire for wealth with the economic system that changed the face of the earth (Craig, 1982, pp. 105–106). . . .

The dynamism of the capitalist system is due precisely to the fact that the capitalist, driven by the profit motive, must compete and survive in a competitive market economy. Competition weeds out the inefficient while rewarding efficiency and innovation; it encourages rationality. In the absence of a market, capitalism loses its creativity and essential vigor (McNeill, 1982). The distinctive features of the capitalistic mode of production, as defined by Marxists, would not have led to economic progress without the spur of market competition. In the presence of a market, however, even socialist or nationalized firms must strive to become profitable and competitive. The advent of socialism may not necessarily alter the underlying dynamics, provided that market competition or its functional equivalent survives. There is, as John Rawls reminds us, "no essential tie between the use of free markets and private ownership of the instruments of production" (Rawls, 1971, p. 271). Capitalism and the market exchange system are not necessarily connected.

The concept of "market" is thus broader than that of "capitalism." The essence of a market, defined in greater detail below, is the central role of relative prices in allocative decisions. The essence of capitalism, as noted above, is the private ownership of the means of production and the existence of free labor. Theoretically, a market system could be composed of public actors and unfree labor as envisioned in the concept of market socialism. The increasing role of the state and public actors in the market has recently led to a mixed economy of public and private enterprise. In practice, however, the market system has tended to be associated with international capitalism.

In summary, although the connection between the market exchange system and the capitalist mode of production is close, these terms are not the same—even though they will sometimes be used interchangeably in this [chapter]. Capitalism is too ambiguous a label to be used as an analytical category. There are in fact many varieties of capitalism that function differently. Is France truly capitalist, with 90 percent of its financial sector and much of its heavy industry nationalized and in state hands? How is one to categorize Japanese capitalism, with the central role of its state in guiding the economy? The contemporary world is composed largely of mixed economies that at the international level are forced to compete with one another.

Other scholars have identified industrialism, industrial society, and/or the development of scientific technology as the defining characteristics of modern economic life.[4] The development of both industrial technology and modern science are obviously important for the prosperity and character of the modern world. One cannot account for the Industrial Revolution and the advent of modern science simply as a response to market forces; without science-based technology the modern market economy could not have progressed very far.

The scientific breakthroughs of the seventeenth and eighteenth centuries that laid the foundations for modern industry and technology are not reducible to the operation of economic motives. Science is an intellectual creation resulting from human curiosity and the search for understanding of the universe. Yet without market demand for greater efficiencies and new products, the incentive to exploit science and develop innovations in technology would be greatly reduced. Although the advance of science increases the potential supply of new industries and technology, the market creates the demand necessary to bring the technologies into existence. Thus the crucial role of the market in propelling and organizing economic life is the reason for our focus here on the market and the implications of economic interdependence for international relations.

The concept of market or economic interdependence is a highly ambiguous term, and many different definitions exist.[5] In this [chapter] the *Oxford English Dictionary* definition of economic interdependence favored by Richard Cooper [is] used; it defines interdependence as "the fact or condition of depending each upon the other; mutual dependence" (Cooper, 1985, p. 1196). In addition, as Robert Keohane and Joseph Nye (1977) have noted, economic interdependence can refer to a power relationship, that is, to what Albert Hirschman (1945) calls vulnerability interdependence. Economic interdependence can also mean sensitivity interdependence, that is, changes in prices and quantities in different national markets respond readily to one another. . . .

If by increasing economic interdependence one means the operation of the "law of one price," that is, that identical goods will tend to have the same price, then global interdependence has reached an unprecedented level. The conclusions to be drawn from this fact, however, are not readily obvious. Although the integration of national markets into an expanding interdependent global economy is occurring, the effects that this growing interdependence is alleged to have upon international relations are uncertain. Interdependence is a phenomenon to be studied, not a ready-made set of conclusions regarding the nature and dynamics of international relations.

The Economic Consequences of a Market

Although a market is an abstract concept, a market economy can be defined as one in which goods and services are exchanged on the basis of relative prices; it is where transactions are negotiated and prices are determined. Its essence, as one economist has put it, is "the making of a price by higgling between buyers and sellers" (Condliffe, 1950, p. 301). *Market* Phrased in more formal terms, a market is "the whole of any region in which buyers and sellers are in such free intercourse with one another that the prices of the same goods tend to equality easily and quickly" (Cournot, quoted in Cooper, 1985, p. 1199). Its specific characteristics are dependent upon its degree of openness and the intensity of the competition among producers and sellers. Markets differ with respect to the freedom of participants to enter the market and also the extent to which individual buyers or sellers can influence the terms of the exchange. Thus, a perfect or self-regulating market is one that is open to all potential buyers or sellers and one in which no buyer or seller can determine the terms of the exchange. Although such a perfect market has never existed, it is the model of the world implicit in the development of economic theory.

A market economy is a significant departure from the three more traditional types of economic exchange. Although none of these forms of exchange has ever existed to the exclusion of the others, one type or another has tended to predominate. The most prevalent economic system throughout history, one that is still characteristic of many less developed economies, is localized exchange, which is highly restricted in terms of available goods and geographic scope. The second type of exchange is that of command economies, such as those of the great historic empires of Assyria and, to much lesser extent, Rome, or of the socialist bloc today; in these planned economies, the production, distribution, and prices of commodities tend to be controlled by the state bureaucracy. Third, there is, or rather there was, long-distance trade in high-value goods. The caravan routes of Asia and Africa were the principal loci of this trade. Although this trade was geographically extensive, it involved only a narrow range of goods (spices, silks, slaves, precious metals, etc.). For a number of reasons, markets tend to displace more traditional forms of economic exchange.

One reason for the primacy of the market in shaping the modern world is that it forces a reorganization of society in order to make the market work properly. When a market comes into existence, as Marx fully appreciated, it becomes a potent force driving social change. As one authority has put it, "once economic power is redistributed to those who embrace the productive ideal, their leverage as buyers, investors, and employers is seen as moving the rest of society. The critical step in establishing a market momentum is the alienation of land and labor. When these fundamental components of social existence come under the influence of the price mechanism, social direction itself passes to economic determinants" (Appleby, 1978, pp. 14–15).

In the absence of social, physical, and other constraints, a market economy has an expansive and dynamic quality. It tends to cause economic growth, to expand territorially, and to bring all segments of society into its embrace. Groups and states seek to restrain the operation of a market because it has the potential to exert a considerable force on society; efforts to control markets give rise to the political economy of international relations.

Three characteristics of a market economy are responsible for its dynamic nature: (1) the critical role of relative prices in the exchange of goods and services, (2) the centrality of competition as a determinant of individual and institutional behavior, and (3) the importance of efficiency in determining the survivability of economic actors. From these flow the profound consequences of a market for economic, social, and political life.

A market economy encourages growth for both static and dynamic reasons. A market increases the efficient allocation of existing resources. Economic growth occurs because the market fosters a reallocation of land, labor, and capital to those activities in which they are most productive. Also, since market competition forces the producer (if it is to prosper or even merely survive) to innovate and move the economy to higher levels of productive efficiency and technology, the market dynamically promotes technological and other types of innovation, thus increasing the power and capabilities of an economy. Although both the static and dynamic aspects of markets have encouraged economic growth throughout history, the dynamic factor has become of decisive importance since the advent of modern science as the basis of productive technology.

A market economy tends to expand geographically, spilling over political boundaries and encompassing an ever-increasing fraction of the human race (Kuznets, 1953, p. 308). The demand for less expensive labor and resources causes economic development to spread (Johnson, 1965b, pp. 11–12). Over time, more and more of the nonmarket economic periphery is brought within the orbit of the market mechanism. The reasons for this expansionist tendency include efficiencies of scale, improvements in transportation, and growth of demand. Adam Smith had this in mind when he stated that both the division of labor and economic growth are dependent on the scale of the market (Smith, 1937 [1776], p. 17). In order to take advantage of increased efficiencies and to reduce costs, economic actors try to expand the extent and scale of the market.

Yet another characteristic of a market economy is a tendency to incorporate every aspect of society into the nexus of market relations. Through such "commercialization," the market generally brings all facets of traditional society into the orbit of the price mechanism. Land, labor, and other so-called factors of production become commodities to be exchanged; they are subject to the interplay of market forces (Heilbroner, 1985, p. 117). Stated more crudely, everything has its price and, as an economist friend is fond of saying, "its value *is* its price." As a consequence, markets have a profound and destabilizing impact on a society because they dissolve traditional structures and social relations (Goldthorpe, 1978, p. 194).

At both the domestic and international levels a market system also tends to create a hierarchical division of labor among producers, a division based principally on specialization and what economists call the law of comparative advantage (or costs). As a consequence of market forces, society (domestic or international) becomes reordered into a dynamic core and a dependent periphery. The core is characterized principally by its more advanced levels of technology and economic development; the periphery is, at least initially, dependent on the core as a market for its commodity exports and as a source of productive techniques. In the short term, as the core of a market economy grows, it incorporates into its orbit a larger and larger periphery; in the long term, however, due to the diffusion of productive technology and the growth process, new cores tend to form in the periphery and then to become growth centers in their own right. These tendencies for the core to expand and stimulate the rise of new cores have profound consequences for economic and political affairs (Friedmann, 1972).

The market economy also tends to redistribute wealth and economic activities within and among societies. Although everyone benefits in absolute terms as each gains wealth from participation in a market economy, some do gain more than others. The tendency is for markets, at least initially, to concentrate wealth in particular groups, classes, or regions. The reasons for this tendency are numerous: the achievement of economies of scale, the existence of monopoly rents, the effects of positive externalities (spillovers from one economic activity to another) and feedbacks, the benefits of learning and experience, and a host of other efficiencies that produce a cycle of "they who have get." Subsequently, however, markets tend to diffuse wealth throughout the system due to technology transfer, changes in comparative advantage, and other factors. It may also produce in certain societies a vicious cycle of decline, depending on their flexibility and capacity to adapt to changes. A diffusion of wealth and growth, however, does not take place evenly throughout the system; it tends to concentrate in those new cores or centers of growth where conditions are most favorable. As a consequence, a market economy tends to result in a process of uneven development in both domestic and international systems.

A market economy, if left to its own devices, has profound effects on the nature and organization of societies as well as on the political relations among them. Although many of these consequences may be beneficial and much desired by a society, others are detrimental to the desires and interests of powerful groups and states. The resulting tendency, therefore, is for states to intervene in economic activities in order to advance the effects of markets beneficial to themselves and to counter those that are detrimental.

Market Effects and Political Responses

In the abstract world of economists, the economy and other aspects of society exist in separate and distinct spheres. Economists hypothesize a theoretical universe composed of autonomous, homogeneous, and maximizing individuals who are free and able to respond to market forces in terms of their perceived self-interest. They assume that economic structures are flexible and behaviors change automatically and predictably in response to price signals (Little, 1982, ch. 2). Social classes, ethnic loyalties, and national boundaries are assumed not to exist. When once asked what was missing from his classic textbook, Nobel laureate Paul Samuelson is reported to have responded, "the class struggle." This puts the point well, although he could have added, without undue exaggeration or violation of the spirit of the text, "races, nation-states, and all the other social and political divisions."

The essence of economics and its implications for social and political organization, as viewed by economists, are contained in what Samuelson has called "the most beautiful idea" in economic theory, namely, David Ricardo's law of comparative advantage. The implication of this simple concept is that domestic and international society should be organized in terms of relative efficiencies. It implies a universal division of labor based on specialization, in which each participant benefits absolutely in accordance with his or her contribution to the whole. It is a world in which the most humble person and the most resource-poor nation can find a niche and eventually prosper. A fundamental harmony of interest among individuals, groups, and states is assumed to underlie the growth and expansion of the market and of economic interdependence.

In the real world, divided among many different and frequently conflicting groups and states, markets have an impact vastly different from that envisaged by economic theory, and they give rise to powerful political reactions. Economic activities affect the political, social, and economic well-being of various groups and states differentially. The real world is a universe of exclusive and frequently conflicting loyalties and political boundaries in which the division of labor and the distribution of its benefits are determined as much by power and good fortune as they are by the laws of the market and the operation of the price mechanism. The assumption of a fundamental harmony of interest is most frequently invalid, and the growth and expansion of markets in a socially and politically fragmented globe have profound consequences for the nature and functioning of international politics. What then are these consequences that give rise to political responses?

One consequence of a market economy for domestic and international politics is that it has highly disruptive effects on a society; the introduction of market forces and the price mechanism into a society tends to overwhelm and even dissolve traditional social relations and institutions. The competition of the efficient drives out the inefficient and forces all to adapt to new ways. As noted earlier, markets have an inherent tendency to expand and bring everything into their orbit. New demands are constantly stimulated and new sources of supply sought. Further, markets are subject to cyclical fluctuations and disturbances over which the society may have little control; specialization and its resulting dependencies increase vulnerabilities to untoward events. In short, markets constitute a powerful source of sociopolitical change and produce equally powerful responses as societies attempt to protect themselves against market forces (Polanyi, 1957). Therefore, no state, however liberal its predilections, permits the full and unregulated development of market forces.

Another consequence of a market economy is that it significantly affects the distribution of wealth and power within and among societies. In theory, all can take advantage of market opportunities to better themselves. In practice, however, individuals, groups, or states are differently endowed and situated to take advantage of these opportunities and therefore the growth of wealth and the spread of economic activities in a market system tends to be uneven, favoring one state or another. Thus, states attempt to guide market forces to benefit their own citizens, resulting, at least in the short run, in the unequal distribution of wealth and power among the participants in the market and the stratification of societies in the international political economy (Hawtrey, 1952).

Another important consequence of a market economy for states is due to the fact that economic interdependence establishes a power relationship among groups and societies. A market is not politically neutral; its existence creates economic power which one actor can use against another. Economic interdependence creates vulnerabilities that can be exploited and manipulated. In the words of Albert Hirschman, "the power to interrupt commercial or financial relations with any country . . . is the root cause of the influence or power position which a country acquires in other countries" through its market relations (Hirschman, 1945, p. 16). In varying degrees, then, economic interdependence establishes hierarchical, dependency, and power relations among groups and national societies. In response to this situation, states attempt to enhance their own independence and to increase the dependence of other states.

A market economy confers both benefits and costs on groups and societies. On the one hand, economic specialization and a division of labor foster economic growth and an increase in the wealth of market participants. Although gains are unevenly distributed, in general everyone benefits in absolute terms. Therefore few societies choose to absent themselves from participation in the world economic system. Yet, on the other hand, a market economy also imposes economic, social, and political costs on particular groups and societies, so that in relative terms, some benefit more than others. Thus, states seek to protect themselves and limit the costs to themselves and their citizens. The struggle among groups and states over the distribution of benefits and costs has become a major feature of international relations in the modern world.

Conclusion

The central concerns of [international political economy], then, are the impact of the world market economy on the relations of states and the ways in which states seek to influence market forces for their own advantage. Embedded in this relationship of state and market are three closely related issues of importance to the student of politics. The first is the way in which market interdependence affects and is affected by international politics and in particular by the presence or absence of political leadership. The second is the interaction of economic and political change that gives rise to an intense competition among states over the global location of economic activities, especially the so-called commanding heights of modern industry. The third is the effect of the world market on economic development and the consequent effort of states to control or at least to be in a position to influence the rules or regimes governing trade, foreign investment, and the international monetary system as well as other aspects of the international political economy.

Behind seemingly technical issues of trade or international money lurk significant political issues that profoundly influence the power, independence, and well-being of individual states. Thus, although trade may well be of mutual benefit, every state wants its own gains to be disproportionately to its advantage; it wants to move up the technological ladder to reap the highest value-added return from its own contribution to the international division of labor. Similarly, every state wants to have its say in decision making about the rules of the international monetary system. In every area of international economic affairs, economic and political issues are deeply entwined.

Scholars and other individuals differ, however, on the nature of the relationship between economic and political affairs. Although many positions can be identified, almost everyone tends to fall into one of three contrasting perspectives, ideologies, or schools of thought. They are liberalism, nationalism, and Marxism. . . .

Notes

1. The concepts of state and market used in this book are derived primarily from Max Weber (1978, vol. I, pp. 56, 82, and passim) .

2. Perhaps the first writer to address this theme systematically was Eugene Staley (1939).

3. Obviously, the choice of these three issues as the central ones will not meet with the approval of everyone in the field of international political economy. Many would quite rightly come up with another set. These issues exclude, for example, such topics as the making and substance of foreign economic policy. Although this subject is important, the principal focus of this book is on the structure, functioning, and interaction of the international economic and political systems. A parallel and not invidious distinction can be and usually is made between the study of the foreign policies of particular states and the study of the theory of international relations. Although these subjects are closely related, they ask different questions and are based on different assumptions. Gaddis (1982) and Waltz (1979) are respectively excellent examples of each approach.

4. Goldthorpe (1984, ch. 13); Giddens (1985), and Rostow (1975) are representative of these positions.

5. An excellent analysis of these various meanings is Cooper (1985, pp. 1196–1200).

References

Appleby, Joyce Oldham. 1978. *Economic Thought and Ideology in Seventeenth-Century England.* Princeton: Princeton University Press.
Condliffe, J. B. 1950. *The Commerce of Nations.* New York: W. W. Norton.

Cooper, Richard. 1985. "Economic Interdependence and Coordination of Economic Policies." In Jones and Kenen, Vol. 2, Chapter 23.

Craig, Gordon A. 1982. *The Germans*. New York: G. P. Putnam's Sons.

Friedmann, John. 1972. "A General Theory of Polarized Development." In Niles M. Hansen, ed., *Growth Centers in Regional Economic Development*. New York: Free Press.

Gaddis, John Lewis. 1982. *Strategies of Containment: A Critical Appraisal of Postwar American National Security Policy*. New York: Oxford University Press.

Giddens, Anthony. 1985. *A Contemporary Critique of Historical Materialism*. Vol. 2, *The Nation-State and Violence*. Berkeley: University of California Press.

Goldthorpe, John H. 1978. "The Current Inflation: Towards a Sociological Account." In Fred Hirsch and John H. Goldthorpe, eds., *The Political Economy of Inflation*. Cambridge: Harvard University Press.

Goldthorpe, John H., ed. 1984. *Order and Conflict in Contemporary Capitalism: Studies in the Political Economy of Western European Nations*. Oxford: Clarendon Press.

Hawtrey, Ralph G. 1952. *Economic Aspects of Sovereignty*. London: Longmans.

Heilbroner, Robert L. 1980. *Marxism: For and Against*. New York: W. W. Norton.

Heilbroner, Robert L. 1985. *The Nature and Logic of Capitalism*. New York: W. W. Norton.

Hirschman, Albert O. 1945. *National Power and the Structure of Foreign Trade*. Berkeley: University of California Press.

Johnson, Harry G. 1965b. *The World Economy at the Crossroads: A Survey of Current Problems of Money, Trade, and Economic Development*. New York: Oxford University Press.

Keohane, Robert O., and Joseph S. Nye, Jr., 1977. *Power and Interdependence: World Politics in Transition*. Boston: Little, Brown.

Kuznets, Simon. 1953. *Economic Change: Selected Essays in Business Cycles, National Income, and Economic Growth*. New York: W. W. Norton.

Little, Ian M. D. 1982. *Economic Development: Theory, Policy and International Relations*. New York: Basic Books.

McNeill, William H. 1982. *The Pursuit of Power: Technology, Armed Force, and Society since A.D. 1000*. Chicago: University of Chicago Press.

Polanyi, Karl. 1957. *The Great Transformation: The Political and Economic Origins of Our Time*. Boston: Beacon Press.

Rawls, John. 1971. *A Theory of Justice*. Cambridge: Harvard University Press.

Rostow, W. W. 1975. *How It All Began: Origins of the Modern Economy*. New York: McGraw-Hill.

Smith, Adam. 1937 [1776]. *An Inquiry into the Nature and Causes of the Wealth of Nations*. New York: Modern Library.

Staley, Eugene. 1939. *World Economy in Transition: Technology vs. Politics, Laissez-Faire vs. Planning, Power vs. Welfare*. New York: Council on Foreign Relations.

Tooze, Roger. 1984. "Perspectives and Theory: A Consumers' Guide." In Susan Strange, ed., *Paths to International Political Economy*. London: George Allen and Unwin.

Waltz, Kenneth N. 1979. *Theory of International Politics*. Reading, Mass.: Addison-Wesley.

Weber, Max. 1978. *Economy and Society: An Outline of Interpretive Sociology*. 2 vols. Guenther Roth and Claus Wittich, eds. Berkeley: University of California Press.

2

INTERNATIONAL POLITICS
AND INTERNATIONAL ECONOMICS

—— *Jeffry A. Frieden and David A. Lake* ——

*In the previous chapter, Robert Gilpin discussed the scope of international po-
litical economy and described the evolution of the state system and capitalism.
This contribution by Jeffry Frieden and David Lake outlines the historical
and philosophical foundations of liberalism, realism, and Marxism, which constitute the three paradigms or worldviews devised to interpret the international system and the behavior of the institutions and organizations created to
govern it. Understanding the tenets and assumptions of these worldviews aids
the student of international political economy in understanding why countries
and institutions act the way they do, and why conflicts emerge between and
among them.*

Three Perspectives on International Political Economy

Nearly all studies in International Political Economy can be classified
into one of three mutually exclusive perspectives: Liberalism, Marxism,
and Realism. Each of the three perspectives has a unique set of simplifying assumptions used to render the world less complex and more
readily understandable. Assumptions are assertions accepted as true for
purposes of further investigations. The value of an assumption lies in
the ability of the theory built upon it to explain observed phenomena.
Thus, assumptions are neither true nor false, only useful or not useful.

Reprinted with permission from *International Political Economy: Perspectives on
Global Power and Wealth* by Jeffry A. Frieden and David A. Lake (New York: St.
Martin's Press). Copyright © 1990.

The assumptions upon which each of these three perspectives is based lead international political economists to view the world in very different ways. Many Liberals regard foreign direct investment in less developed countries, for instance, as a mutually rewarding exchange between entrepreneurs. Many Marxists, on the other hand, see the foreign firm as exploiting the less developed country. Consequently, a first step in studying International Political Economy is to understand the assumptions made by each of the three perspectives.

Liberalism

The Liberal perspective is drawn primarily from the field of economics and can be traced to the writings of Adam Smith (1723–1790) and David Ricardo (1772–1823). Smith and Ricardo were reacting to the pervasive economic controls that existed under mercantilism between the sixteenth and nineteenth centuries. In this period, the domestic and international economies were tightly regulated by governments in order to expand national power and wealth. Smith, Ricardo, and their followers argued that the philosophy underlying this practice was mistaken. Rather, these Liberals asserted that national wealth was best increased by allowing free and unrestricted exchange among individuals in both the domestic and international economies. As their ideas gained adherents in the early nineteenth century, many of the mercantilist trade restrictions were dismantled.

Smith and the nineteenth-century Liberals were the economic reformers of their era. In International Political Economy, advocates of free trade and free markets are still referred to as Liberals. In twentieth-century American domestic politics, on the other hand, the term has come to mean just the opposite. In the United States today, "Conservatives" generally support free markets and less government intervention, while "Liberals" advocate greater governmental intervention in the market to stimulate growth and mitigate inequalities. These contradictory uses of the term "Liberal" may seem confusing, but in the readings below and elsewhere, the context usually makes the author's meaning clear.

Three assumptions are central to the Liberal perspective. First, Liberals assume that individuals are the principal actors within the political economy and the proper unit of analysis. While this may seem obvious, as all social activity can ultimately be traced back to individuals, this first assumption gains its importance by comparison with Marxism and Realism, each of which makes alternative assumptions (see below).

Second, Liberals assume that individuals are rational, utility-maximizing actors. Rational action means that individuals make cost-benefit calculations across a wide range of possible options. Actors are utility maximizers when, given a calculated range of benefits, they choose the option which yields the highest level of subjective satisfaction. This does not imply that individuals actually gain from every utility-maximizing choice. In some circumstances, utility maximization implies that the individual will choose the option that makes him or her least worse off.

Third, Liberals assume that individuals maximize utility by making trade-offs between goods. Consider the trade-off between clothing and jewelry. At high levels of clothing and low levels of jewelry some individuals—depending upon their desires for these two goods—might be willing to trade some of their wearing apparel for more jewelry. Likewise, if an individual possesses a great deal of jewelry but little clothing, he or she might be willing to trade jewelry for apparel. Individuals thus increase their utility, according to Liberals, by exchanging goods with others. Those who desire jewelry more strongly than clothing will trade the latter for the former. Others who prefer clothing over jewelry will trade jewelry for apparel. This process of exchange will occur until each individual, given the existing quantities of jewelry and clothing, is as well off as possible without making someone else worse off. At this point, all individuals in society will have maximized their uniquely defined utilities. Some will possess jewelry but no clothing. Others will possess only clothing. The vast majority of us, on the other hand, will possess varying mixes of both.

The Liberal argument has traditionally been applied primarily to the economy, in which it implies that there is no basis for conflict in the marketplace. Because market exchanges are voluntary, and if there are no impediments to trade among individuals, Liberals reason, everyone can be made as well off as possible given existing stocks of goods and services. All participants in the market, in other words, will be at their highest possible level of utility. Neo-classical economists, who are generally Liberals, believe firmly in the superiority of the market as the allocator of scarce resources.

Liberals therefore believe that the economic role of government should be quite limited. Many forms of government intervention in the economy, they argue, intentionally or unintentionally restrict the market and thereby prevent potentially rewarding trades from occurring.

Liberals do generally support the provision by government of certain "public goods," goods and services that make society better off but that would not be provided by private markets.[1] The government, for example, plays an important role in supplying the conditions necessary for the maintenance of a free and competitive market. Governments must provide for the defense of the country, protect property rights, and prevent unfair collusion or concentration of power within the market. The government should also, according to most Liberals, educate its citizens, build infrastructure, and provide and regulate a common currency. The proper role of government, in other words, is to provide the necessary foundation for the market.

At the level of the international economy, Liberals assert that a fundamental harmony of interests exists between as well as within countries. As Richard Cobden argued in the fight against trade protection in Great Britain during the early nineteenth century, all countries are best off when goods and services move freely across national borders in mutually rewarding exchanges. If universal free trade were to exist, Cobden reasoned, all countries would enjoy the highest level of utility and there would be no economic basis for international conflict and war.

Liberals also believe that governments should manage the international economy in much the same way as they manage their domestic economies. They should establish rules and regulations—often referred to as "international regimes"—to govern exchanges between different national currencies and ensure that no country or domestic group is damaged by "unfair" international competition.

Liberals realize, of course, that governments often do far more than this at both the domestic and international levels, and they have applied their theoretical tools to analyze patterns of government activity. As might be expected, the principal Liberal approach—known generally as "public choice" or "rational choice"—thinks of the political arena as a marketplace. Politicians compete among each other for the privilege of holding office; individuals and groups compete among each other to get support for their preferred policies from office-holders—with votes, campaign contributions, and lobbying. This view, closely related to long-standing theories of interest-group pluralism, sees government action as the result of competition among politicians, and among their constituents.

Marxism

Marxism originated with the writings of Karl Marx, a nineteenth-century political economist and perhaps capitalism's severest critic. Just as Liberalism emerged in reaction to mercantilism, Marxism was a response to the spread of Liberalism in the nineteenth century. Where for Liberals the market allows individuals to maximize their utility, Marx saw capitalism and the market creating extremes of wealth for capitalists and poverty for workers. While everyone may have been better off than before, the capitalists were clearly expanding their wealth more rapidly than all others. Marx rejected the assertion that exchange between individuals necessarily maximizes the welfare of the whole society. Accordingly, Marx perceived capitalism as an inherently conflictual system that both should and will be inevitably overthrown and replaced by socialism.

Marxism makes three essential assumptions. First, Marxists believe that classes are the dominant actors in the political economy and are the appropriate unit of analysis. Marxists identify two economically determined aggregations of individuals, or classes, as central: capital, or the owners of the means of production, and labor, or workers.

Second, Marxists assume that classes act in their material economic interests. Just as Liberals assume that individuals act rationally to maximize their utility, Marxists assume that each class acts to maximize the economic well-being of the class as a whole.

Third, Marxists assume that the basis of the capitalist economy is the exploitation of labor by capital. Marx's analysis began with the labor theory of value, which holds that the value of any product is determined by the amount of past and present labor used to produce it. Marx believed that under capitalism the value of any product could be broken down into three components: constant capital, or past labor as embodied in plant and equipment or the raw materials necessary to produce the good; variable capital, the wages paid to present labor to produce the item; and surplus value—defined as profits, rents, and interest—which was expropriated by or paid to the capitalist. The capitalists' expropriation of surplus value, according to Marx, denies labor the full return for its efforts.

This third assumption leads Marxists to see the political economy as necessarily conflictual, because the relationship between capitalists and workers is essentially antagonistic. Surplus value is not the capitalist's "reward" for investment, but something that is taken away from labor. Because the means of production are controlled by a minority within society—the capitalists—labor does not receive its full return; conflict between the classes will thus occur because of this exploitation. For Marx, the relationship between capital and labor is zero-sum; any gain for the capitalist must come at the expense of labor, and vice versa.

Starting with these three assumptions, Marx constructed a sophisticated theory of capitalist crisis. Such crisis would, Marx believed, ultimately lead to the overthrow of capitalism by labor and the erection of a socialist society in which the means of production would be owned jointly by all members of society and no surplus value would be expropriated.

While Marx wrote primarily about domestic political economy, or the dynamics and form of economic change within a single country, Lenin extended Marx's ideas to the international political economy to explain imperialism and war. Imperialism, Lenin argued, was endemic to modern capitalism. As capitalism decayed in the most developed

Imperial

nations, these nations would attempt to solve their problems by exporting capital abroad. As this capital required protection from both local
and foreign challengers, governments would colonize regions to safeguard the interests of their foreign investors. When the area available
for colonization began to shrink, capitalist countries would compete for
control over these areas and intracapitalist wars would eventually occur.

Today, Marxists who study the international political economy
are primarily concerned with two sets of analytical and practical issues.
The first concerns the fate of labor in a world of increasingly interna-
tionalized capital. With the growth of multinational corporations and
the rise of globally integrated financial markets, the greater international mobility of capital appears to have weakened the economic and
political power of labor. If workers in a particular country demand
higher wages or improved health and safety measures, for example, the
multinational capitalist can simply shift production to another country
where labor is more compliant. As a result, many Marxists fear that
labor's ability to negotiate with capital for a more equitable division of
surplus value has been significantly undermined. Understanding how
and in what ways labor has been weakened and how workers should respond to the increased mobility of capital is thus an important research
agenda.

Second, Marxists are concerned with the poverty and continued
underdevelopment of the Third World. Some Marxists argue that development is blocked by domestic ruling classes who pursue their own
narrow interests at the expense of national economic progress. "Dependency" theorists, on the other hand, extend Marx's class-analytic framework to the level of the international economy. According to these
Marxists, the global system is stratified into an area of autonomous self-
sustaining growth, the "core" or First World, and a region of attenu-
ated inhibited growth, the "periphery" or Third World. International
capitalism, in this view, extracts surplus value from the periphery and
concentrates it in the core, just as capitalists exploit workers within a
single country. The principal questions here focus on the mechanisms
of exploitation—whether they be multinational corporations, international financial markets and organizations, or trade—and the appropriate strategies for stimulating autonomous growth and development in
the periphery.

While Liberals perceive the political economy as inherently harmonious, Marxists believe conflict is endemic. Marxists adopt different
assumptions and derive a very different understanding of the world. For
Marxists, economics determines politics. The nature of politics and the
fundamental cleavages within and between societies, in other words, are
rooted in economics.

Realism

Realism has perhaps the longest pedigree of the three principal perspectives in International Political Economy, starting with Thucydides's writings in 400 B.C. and including Niccolo Machiavelli, Thomas Hobbes, and the mercantilists Jean-Baptiste Colbert and Friedrich List. Discredited with the rise of Liberalism in the nineteenth century, Realism reemerged as an important perspective only in the aftermath of the Great Depression of the 1930s as scholars sought to understand the causes of the widespread economic warfare of "beggar-thy-neighbor" policies initiated in 1929. Realists believe that nation-states pursue power and shape the economy to this end. Unlike Liberals and Marxists, Realists perceive politics as determining economics.

Realism is based upon three assumptions. First, Realists assume that nation-states are the dominant actors within the international political economy and the proper unit of analysis. According to Realists, the international system is anarchical, a condition under which nation-states are sovereign, the sole judge of their own behaviors, and subject to no higher authority. If no authority is higher than the nation-state, Realists also believe that all actors are subordinate to the nation-state. While private citizens can interact with their counterparts in other countries, Realists assert that the basis for this interaction is legislated by the nation-state. Thus, where Liberals focus on individuals and Marxists on classes, Realists concentrate on nation-states.

Second, Realists assume that nation-states are power maximizers. Because the international system is based upon anarchy, the use of force or coercion by other nation-states is always a possibility and no other country or higher authority is obligated to come to the aid of a nation-state under attack. Nation-states are thus ultimately dependent upon their own resources for protection. For Realists, then, each nation-state must always be prepared to defend itself to the best of its ability. It must always seek to maximize its power; the failure to do so threatens the very existence of the nation-state and may make it vulnerable to others. Power is a relative concept. If one nation-state (or any other actor) expands its power over another, it can do so only at the expense of the second. Thus, for Realists, politics is a zero-sum game and by necessity conflictual. If one nation-state wins, another must lose.

Third, Realists assume that nation-states are rational actors in the same sense that Liberals assume individuals are rational. Nation-states are assumed to perform cost-benefit analyses and choose the option which yields the greatest value, in this case, the one which maximizes power.

It is the assumption of power maximization that gives Realism its distinctive approach to International Political Economy. While economic

all about Power

considerations may often complement power concerns, the former are—in the Realist view—subordinate to the latter. Liberals and Marxists see individuals and classes, respectively, as always seeking to maximize their economic well-being. Realists, on the other hand, allow for circumstances in which nation-states sacrifice economic gain to weaken their opponents or strengthen themselves in military or diplomatic terms. Thus, trade protection—which might reduce a country's overall income by restricting the market—may be adopted for reasons of national political power.

Given its assumptions, Realist political economy is primarily concerned with how changes in the distribution of international power affect the form and type of international economy. The best known Realist approach to this question is the "theory of hegemonic stability," which holds that an open international economy—that is, one characterized by the free exchange of goods, capital, and services—is most likely to exist when a single dominant or hegemonic power is present to stabilize the system and construct a strong regime. For Realists, then, politics underlies economics. In the pursuit of power, nation-states shape the international economy to best serve their desired ends.

Each of these three perspectives adopts different assumptions to simplify reality and render it more explicable. Liberals assume that individuals are the proper unit of analysis, while Marxists and Realists make similar assumptions for classes and nation-states, respectively. The three perspectives also differ on the inevitability of conflict within the political economy. Liberals believe economics and politics are largely autonomous spheres, Marxists maintain that economics determines politics, and Realists argue that politics determines economics.

These three perspectives lead to widely different explanations of specific events and general processes within the international political economy. Their differences have generated numerous debates in the field, many of which are contained in the readings herein. Overlying these perspectives are two additional debates on the relative importance of international and domestic factors, and of social or state forces, in determining economic policy. . . .

Note

1. More specifically, a public good is one that, in its purest form, is *nonrival in consumption* and *nonexcludable*. The first characteristic means that consumption of the good by one person does not reduce the opportunities for others to consume the good: clean air can be breathed by one without reducing its availability to others. The second characteristic means that nobody can

be prevented from consuming the good—those who do not contribute to pollution control are still able to breathe clean air. These two conditions are fully met only rarely, but goods that come close to them are generally considered public goods.

Contending Views of International Political Economy: Liberalism, Interdependence, and Sovereignty-at-Bay

3

EXCERPTS FROM
THE WEALTH OF NATIONS

Adam Smith

Adam Smith's The Wealth of Nations (1776), *along with the later works of David Ricardo, established the central concepts that are now recognized as classic liberalism. In this excerpt from* The Wealth of Nations, *Smith makes his case for free trade, arguing that goods should be purchased from the most efficient producer, regardless of the country of origin. The advantage of this type of trade is not only seen in the savings obtained for individuals and societies as a result of encouraging production by the most efficient producers; in addition, jobs will be shifted to the most efficient sectors of the economy. Unlike some contemporary proponents of free trade, Smith does not champion unconditional or unilateral free trade. Here he explains how national-security concerns led him to sympathize with the Navigation Acts. He also concedes that in some cases it may be wise to neutralize the advantages some foreign governments give to their producers. Such actions, Smith warns, may backfire and damage long-term trade relations.*

The importation of gold and silver is not the principal, much less the sole benefit which a nation derives from its foreign trade. Between whatever places foreign trade is carried on, they all of them derive two distinct benefits from it. It carries out that surplus part of the produce of their land and labour for which there is no demand among them, and brings back in return for it something else for which there is a demand. It gives a value to their superfluities, by exchanging them for something else, which may satisfy a part of their wants, and increase their enjoyments. By means of it, the narrowness of the home market does not hinder the division of labour in any particular branch of art or manufacture from being carried to the highest perfection. By opening a more extensive market for whatever part of the produce of their labour may exceed the home consumption, it encourages them to improve its productive powers, and to augment its annual produce to the utmost, and thereby to increase the real revenue and wealth of the society. These great and important services foreign trade is continually occupied in performing, to all the different countries between which it is carried on. They all derive great benefit from it, though that in which the merchant resides generally derives the greatest, as he is generally more employed in supplying the wants, and carrying out the superfluities of his own, than of any other particular country. To import the gold and silver which may be wanted, into the countries which have no mines, is, no doubt, a part of the business of foreign commerce. It is, however, a most insignificant part of it. A country which carried on foreign trade merely upon this account, could scarce have occasion to freight a ship in a century.

It is not by the importation of gold and silver, that the discovery of America has enriched Europe. By the abundance of the American mines, those metals have become cheaper. A service of plate can now be purchased for about a third part of the corn, or a third part of the labour, which it would have cost in the fifteenth century. With the same annual expence of labour and commodities, Europe can annually purchase about three times the quantity of plate which it could have purchased at that time. But when a commodity comes to be sold for a third part of what had been its usual price, not only those who purchased it before can purchase three times their former quantity, but it is brought down to the level of a greater number of purchasers, perhaps to more than ten, perhaps to more than twenty times the former number. So that there may be in Europe at present not only more than three times, but more than twenty or thirty times the quantity of plate which would have been in it, even in its present state of improvement, had the discovery of the American mines never been made. . . . By opening a new and inexhaustible market to all the commodities of Europe, [the American colonies] gave occasion to new divisions of labour and improvements of art, which, in the narrow circle of the ancient commerce, could never have taken place for want of a market to take off the greater part of their produce. The productive powers of labour were improved, and its produce increased in all the different countries of Europe, and together with it the real revenue and wealth of the inhabitants. . . .

The discovery of a passage to the East Indies, by the Cape of Good Hope, which happened much about the same time, opened, perhaps, a still more extensive range to foreign commerce than even that of America, notwithstanding the greater distance. There were but two nations in America, in any respect superior to savages, and these were destroyed almost as soon as discovered. The rest were savages. But the empires of China, Indostan, Japan, as well as several others in the East Indies, without having richer mines of gold or silver, were in every other respect much richer, better cultivated, and more advanced in all arts and manufactures than either Mexico or Peru, even though we should credit, what plainly deserves no credit, the exaggerated accounts of the Spanish writers, concerning the ancient state of those empires. But rich and civilized nations can always exchange to a much greater value with one another, than with savages and barbarians. Europe, however, has hitherto derived much less advantage from its commerce with the East Indies, than from that with America. The Portuguese monopolized the East India trade to themselves for about a century, and it was only indirectly and through them, that the other nations of Europe could either sent out or receive any goods from that country. When the Dutch, in the beginning of the last century, began to encroach upon them, they vested their whole East India commerce in an exclusive company. The English, French, Swedes, and Europe has ever yet had the benefit of a free commerce to the East Indies. No other reason need be assigned why it has never been so advantageous as the trade to America, which, between almost every nation of Europe and its own colonies, is free to all its subjects. . . .

What is prudence in the conduct of every private family, can scarce be folly in that of a great kingdom. If a foreign country can supply us with a commodity cheaper than we ourselves can make it, better buy it of them with some part of the produce of our own industry, employed in a way in which we have some advantage. The general industry of the country, being always in proportion to the capital which employs it, will not thereby be diminished, no more than that of the above-mentioned artificers; but only left to find out the way in which it can be employed with the greatest advantage. It is certainly not employed to the greatest advantage, when it is thus directed towards an object which it can buy cheaper than it can make. The value of its annual produce is certainly more or less diminished, when it is thus turned away from producing commodities evidently of more value than the commodity which it is directed to produce. According to the supposition, that commodity could be purchased from foreign countries cheaper than it can be made at home. It could, therefore, have been purchased with a part only of the commodities, or, what is the same thing, with a part only of the price of the commodities, which the industry employed by an equal capital would have produced at home, had it been left to follow its natural course. The industry of the country, therefore, is thus turned away from a more, to a less advantageous employment, and the exchangeable value of its annual produce, instead of being increased, according to the intention of the lawgiver, must necessarily be diminished by every such regulation.

By means of such regulations, indeed, a particular manufacture may sometimes be acquired sooner than it could have been otherwise, and after a certain time may be made at home as cheap or cheaper than in the foreign country. But though the industry of the society may be thus carried with advantage into a particular channel sooner than it could have been otherwise, it will by no means follow that the sum total, either of its industry, or of its revenue, can ever be augmented by any such regulation. The industry of the society can augment only in proportion as its capital augments, and its capital can augment only in proportion to what can be gradually saved out of its revenue. But the immediate effect of every such regulation is to diminish its revenue, and what diminishes its revenue is certainly not very likely to augment its capital faster than it would have augmented of its own accord, had both capital and industry been left to find out their natural employments.

Though for want of such regulations the society should never acquire the proposed manufacture, it would not, upon that account, necessarily be the poorer in any one period of its duration. In every period of its duration its whole capital and industry might still have been employed, though upon different objects, in the manner that was most advantageous at the time. In every period its revenue might have been the greatest which its capital could afford, and both capital and revenue might have been augmented with the greatest possible rapidity.

The natural advantages which one country has over another in producing particular commodities are sometimes so great, that it is acknowledged by all the world to be in vain to struggle with them. By means of glasses, hotbeds, and hotwalls, very good grapes can be raised in Scotland, and very good wine too can be made of them at about thirty times the expence for which at least equally good can be brought from foreign countries. Would it be a reasonable law to prohibit the importation of all foreign wines, merely to encourage the making of claret and burgundy in Scotland? But if there would be a manifest absurdity in turning towards any employment, thirty times more of the capital and industry of the country, than would be necessary to purchase from foreign countries an equal quantity of the commodities wanted, there must be an absurdity, though not altogether so glaring, yet exactly of the same kind, in turning towards any such employment a thirtieth, or even a three hundredth part more of either. Whether the advantages which one country has over another, be natural or acquired, is in this respect of no consequence. As long as the one country has those advantages, and the other wants them, it will always be more advantageous for the latter, rather to buy of the former than to make. It is an acquired advantage only, which one artificer has over his neighbour, who exercises another trade; and yet they both find it more advantageous to buy of one another, than to make what does not belong to their particular trades.

Merchants and manufacturers are the people who derive the greatest advantage from this monopoly of the home-market. The prohibition of the importation of foreign cattle, and of salt provisions, together with the high duties upon foreign corn, which in times of moderate plenty amount to a prohibition, are not near so advantageous to the graziers and farmers of Great Britain, as other regulations of the same kind are to its merchants and manufacturers. Manufactures, those of the finer kind especially, are more easily transported from one country to another than corn or cattle. It is in the fetching and carrying manufactures, accordingly, that foreign trade is chiefly employed. In manufactures, a very small advantage will enable foreigners to undersell our own workmen, even in the home market. It will require a very great one to enable them to do so in the rude produce of the soil. If the free importation of foreign manufactures were permitted, several of the home manufactures would probably suffer, and some of them, perhaps, go to ruin altogether, and a considerable part of the stock and industry at present employed in them, would be forced to find out some other employment. But the freest importation of the rude produce of the soil could have no such effect upon the agriculture of the country.

If the importation of foreign cattle, for example, were made ever so free, so few could be imported, that the grazing trade of Great Britain could be little affected by it. Live cattle are, perhaps, the only commodity of which the transportation is more expensive by sea than by land. By land they carry themselves to market. By sea, not only the cattle, but their food and their water too, must be carried at no small expence and inconveniency. The short sea between Ireland and Great Britain, indeed, renders the importation of Irish cattle more easy. But though the free importation of them, which was lately permitted only for a limited time, were rendered perpetual, it could have no considerable effect upon the interest of the graziers of Great Britain. Those parts of Great Britain which border upon the Irish sea are all grazing countries. Irish cattle could never be imported for their use, but must be drove through those very extensive countries, at no small expence and inconveniency, before they could arrive at their proper market. Fat cattle could not be drove so far. Lean cattle, therefore, only could be imported, and such importation could interfere, not with the interest of the feeding or fattening countries, to which, by reducing the price of lean cattle, it would rather be advantageous, but with that of the breeding countries only. The small number of Irish cattle imported since their importation was permitted, together with the good price at which lean cattle still continue to sell, seem to demonstrate that even the breeding countries of Great Britain are never likely to be much affected by the free importation of Irish cattle. The common people of Ireland, indeed, are said to have sometimes opposed with violence the exportation of their cattle. But if the exporters had found any great advantage in continuing the trade, they could easily, when the law was on their side, have conquered this mobbish opposition.

Feeding and fattening countries, besides, must always be highly improved, whereas breeding countries are generally uncultivated. The high price of lean cattle, by augmenting the value of uncultivated land, is like a bounty against improvement. To any country which was highly improved throughout, it would be more advantageous to import its lean cattle than to breed them. The province of Holland, accordingly, is said to follow this maxim at present. The mountains of Scotland, Wales and Northumberland, indeed, are countries not capable of much improvement, and seem destined by nature to be the breeding countries of Great Britain. The freest importation of foreign cattle could have no other effect than to hinder those breeding countries from taking advantage of the increasing population and improvement of the rest of the kingdom, from raising their price to an exorbitant height, and from laying a real tax upon all the more improved and cultivated parts of the country.

The freest importation of salt provisions, in the same manner, could have as little effect upon the interest of the graziers of Great Britain as that of live cattle. Salt provisions are not only a very bulky commodity, but when compared with fresh meat, they are a commodity both of worse quality, and as they cost more labour and expence, of higher price. They could never, therefore, come into competition with the fresh meat, though they might with the salt provisions of the country. They might be used for victualling ships for distant voyages, and such like uses, but could never make any considerable part of the food of the people. The small quantity of salt provisions imported from Ireland since their importation was rendered free, is an experimental proof that our graziers have nothing to apprehend from it. It does not appear that the price of butcher's-meat has ever been sensibly affected by it.

Even the free importation of foreign corn could very little affect the interest of the farmers of Great Britain. Corn is a much more bulky commodity than butcher's-meat. A pound of wheat at a penny is as dear as a pound of butcher's-meat at fourpence. The small quantity of foreign corn imported even in times of the greatest scarcity, may satisfy our farmers that they can have nothing to fear from the freest importation. The average quantity imported one year with another, amounts only, according to the very well informed author of the tracts upon the corn trade, to twenty-three thousand seven hundred and twenty-eight quarters of all sorts of grain, and does not exceed the five hundredth and seventy-one part of the annual consumption. But as the bounty upon corn occasions a greater exportation in years of plenty, so it must of consequence occasion a greater importation in years of scarcity, than in the actual state of tillage would otherwise take place. By means of it, the plenty of one year does not compensate the scarcity of another, and as the average quantity exported is necessarily augmented by it, so must likewise, in the actual state of tillage, the average quantity imported. If there were no bounty, as less corn would be exported, so it is probable that, one year with another, less would be imported than at present. The corn merchants, the fetchers and carriers of corn between Great Britain and foreign countries, would have much less employment, and might suffer considerably; but the country gentlemen and farmers could suffer very little. It is in the corn merchants accordingly, rather than in the country gentlemen and farmers, that I have observed the greatest anxiety for the renewal and continuation of the bounty.

Country gentlemen and farmers are, to their great honour, of all people, the least subject to the wretched spirit of monopoly. The undertaker of a great manufactory is sometimes alarmed if another work of the same kind is established within twenty miles of him. The Dutch undertaker of the woollen manufacture at Abbeville stipulated, that no work of the same kind should be established within thirty leagues of that city. Farmers and country gentlemen, on the contrary, are generally disposed rather to promote than to obstruct the cultivation and improvement of their neighbours' farms and estates. They have no secrets, such as those of the greater part of manufacturers, but are generally rather fond of communicating to their neighbours, and of extending as far as possible any new practice which they have found to be advantageous. *Pius Questus*, says old Cato, *stabilissimusque, minimeque invidiosus; minimeque male cogitantes sunt, qui in eo studio occupati sunt*. Country gentlemen and farmers, dispersed in different parts of the country, cannot so easily combine as merchants and manufacturers, who being collected into towns, and accustomed to that exclusive corporation spirit which prevails in them, naturally endeavour to obtain against all their countrymen, the same exclusive privilege which they generally possess against the inhabitants of their respective towns. They accordingly seem to have been the original inventors of those restraints upon the importation of foreign goods, which secure to them the monopoly of the home-market. It was probably in imitation of them, and to put themselves upon a level with those who, they found, were disposed to oppress them, that the country gentlemen and farmers of Great Britain so far forgot the generosity which is natural to their station, as to demand the exclusive privilege of supplying their countrymen with corn and butcher's-meat. They did not perhaps take time to consider, how much less their interest could be affected by the freedom of trade, than that of the people whose example they followed.

To prohibit by a perpetual law the importation of foreign corn and cattle, is in reality to enact, that the population and industry of the country shall at no time exceed what the rude produce of its own soil can maintain.

There seem, however, to be two cases in which it will generally be advantageous to lay some burden upon foreign, for the encouragement of domestic industry.

The first is, when some particular sort of industry is necessary for the defence of the country. The defence of Great Britain, for example, depends very much upon the number of its sailors and shipping. The act of navigation, therefore, very properly endeavours to give the sailors and shipping of Great Britain the monopoly of the trade of their own country, in some cases, by absolute prohibitions, and in others by heavy burdens upon the shipping of foreign countries. The following are the principal dispositions of this act.

First, all ships, of which the owners, masters, and three-fourths of the mariners are not British subjects, are prohibited, upon pain of forfeiting ship and cargo, from trading to the British settlements and plantations, or from being employed in the coasting trade of Great Britain.

Secondly, a great variety of the most bulky articles of importation can be brought into Great Britain only, either in such ships as are above described, or in ships of the country where those goods are produced, and of which the owners, masters, and three-fourths of the mariners, are of that particular country; and when imported even in ships of this latter kind, they are subject to double aliens duty. If imported in ships of any other country, the penalty is forfeiture of ship and goods. When this act was made, the Dutch were, what they still are, the great carriers of Europe, and by this regulation they were entirely excluded from being the carriers to Great Britain, or from importing to us the goods of any other European country.

Thirdly, a great variety of the most bulky articles of importation are prohibited from being imported, even in British ships, from any country but that in which they are produced; under pain of forfeiting ship and cargo. This regulation too was probably intended against the Dutch. Holland was then, as now, the great emporium for all European goods, and by this regulation, British ships were hindered from loading in Holland the goods of any other European country.

Fourthly, salt fish of all kinds, whale-fins, whale-bone, oil, and blubber, not caught by and cured on board British vessels, when imported into Great Britain, are subjected to double aliens duty. The Dutch, as they are still the principal, were then the only fishers in Europe that attempted to supply foreign nations with fish. By this regulation, a very heavy burden was laid upon their supplying Great Britain.

When the act of navigation was made, though England and Holland were not actually at war, the most violent animosity subsisted between the two nations. It had begun during the government of the long parliament, which first framed this act, and it broke out soon after in the Dutch wars during that of the Protector and of Charles the Second. It is not impossible, therefore, that some of the regulations of this famous act may have proceeded from national animosity. They are as wise, however, as if they had all been dictated by the most deliberate wisdom. National animosity at that particular time aimed at the very same object which the most deliberate wisdom would have recommended, the diminution of the naval power of Holland, the only naval power which could endanger the security of England.

The act of navigation is not favourable to foreign commerce, or to the growth of that opulence which can arise from it. The interest of a nation in its commercial relations to foreign nations is, like that of a merchant with regard to the different people with whom he deals, to buy as cheap and to sell as dear as possible. But it will be most likely to buy cheap, when by the most perfect freedom of trade it encourages all nations to bring to it the goods which it has occasion to purchase; and, for the same reason, it will be most likely to sell dear, when its markets are thus filled with the greatest number of buyers. The act of navigation, it is true, lays no burden upon foreign ships that come to export the produce of British industry. Even the ancient aliens duty, which used to be paid upon all goods exported as well as imported, has, by several subsequent acts, been taken off from the greater part of the articles of exportation. But if foreigners, either by prohibitions or high duties, are hindered from coming to sell, they cannot always afford to come to buy; because coming without a cargo, they must lose the freight from their own country to Great Britain. By diminishing the number of sellers, therefore, we necessarily diminish that of buyers, and are thus likely not only to buy foreign goods dearer, but to sell our own cheaper, than if there was a more perfect freedom of trade. As defence, however, is of much more importance than opulence, the act of navigation is, perhaps, the wisest of all the commercial regulations of England.

The second case, in which it will generally be advantageous to lay some burden upon foreign for the encouragement of domestic industry, is, when some tax is imposed at home upon the produce of the latter. In this case, it seems reasonable that an equal tax should be imposed upon the like produce of the former. This would not give the monopoly of the home market to domestic industry, nor turn towards a particular employment a greater share of the stock and labour of the country, than what would naturally go to it. It would only hinder any part of what would naturally go to it from being turned away by the tax, into a less natural direction, and would leave the competition between foreign and domestic industry, after the tax, as nearly as possible upon the same footing as before it. In Great Britain, when any such tax is laid upon the produce of domestic industry, it is usual at the same time, in order to stop the clamorous complaints of our merchants and manufacturers, that they will be undersold at home, to lay a much heavier duty upon the importation of all foreign goods of the same kind.

This second limitation of the freedom of trade according to some people should, upon some occasions, be extended much farther than to the precise foreign commodities which could come into competition with those which had been taxed at home. When the necessaries of life have been taxed in any country, it becomes proper, they pretend, to tax not only the like necessaries of life imported from other countries, but all sorts of foreign goods which can come into competition with any thing that is the produce of domestic industry. Subsistence, they say, becomes necessarily dearer in consequence of such taxes; and the price of labour must always rise with the price of the labourers subsistence. Every commodity, therefore, which is the produce of domestic industry, though not immediately taxed itself, becomes dearer in consequence of such taxes, because the labour which produces it becomes so. Such taxes, therefore, are really equivalent, they say, to a tax upon every particular commodity produced at home. In order to put domestic upon the same footing with foreign industry, therefore, it becomes necessary, they think, to lay some duty upon every foreign commodity, equal to this enhancement of the price of the home commodities with which it can come into competition.

Whether taxes upon the necessaries of life, such as those in Great Britain upon soap, salt, leather, candles, &c. necessarily raise the price of labour, and consequently that of all other commodities I shall consider hereafter, when I come to treat of taxes. Supposing, however, in the mean time, that they have this effect, and they have it undoubtedly, this general enhancement of the price of all commodities, in consequence of that of labour, is a case which differs in the two following respects from that of a particular commodity, of which the price was enhanced by a particular tax immediately imposed upon it.

First, it might always be known with great exactness how far the price of such a commodity could be enhanced by such a tax: but how far the general enhancement of the price of labour might affect that of every different commodity about which labour was employed, could never be known with any tolerable exactness. It would be impossible, therefore, to proportion with any tolerable exactness the tax upon every foreign, to this enhancement of the price of every home commodity.

Secondly, taxes upon the necessaries of life have nearly the same effect upon the circumstances of the people as a poor soil and a bad climate. Provisions are thereby rendered dearer in the same manner as if it required extraordinary labour and expence to raise them. As in the natural scarcity arising from soil and climate, it would be absurd to direct the people in what manner they ought to employ their capitals and industry, so is it likewise in the artificial scarcity arising from such taxes. To be left to accommodate, as well as they could, their industry to their situation, and to find out those employments in which, notwithstanding their unfavourable circumstances, they might have some advantage either in the home or in the foreign market, is what in both cases would evidently be most for their advantage. To lay a new tax upon them, because they are already overburdened with taxes, and because they already pay too dear for the necessaries of life, to make them likewise pay too dear for the greater part of other commodities, is certainly a most absurd way of making amends.

Such taxes, when they have grown up to a certain height, are a curse equal to the barrenness of the earth and the inclemency of the heavens; and yet it is in the richest and most industrious countries that they have been most generally imposed. No other countries could support so great a disorder. As the strongest bodies only can live and enjoy health, under an unwholesome regimen; so the nations only, that in every sort of industry have the greatest natural and acquired advantages, can subsist and prosper under such taxes. Holland is the country in Europe in which they abound most, and which from peculiar circumstances continues to prosper, not by means of them, as has been most absurdly supposed, but in spite of them.

As there are two cases in which it will generally be advantageous to lay some burden upon foreign, for the encouragement of domestic industry; so there are two others in which it may sometimes be a matter or deliberation; in the one, how far it is proper to continue the free importation of certain foreign goods; and in the other, how far, or in what manner, it may be proper to restore that free importation after it has been for some time interrupted.

The case in which it may sometimes be a matter of deliberation how far it is proper to continue the free importation of certain foreign goods, is, when some foreign nation restrains by high duties or prohibitions the importation of some of our manufactures into their country. Revenge in this case naturally dictates retaliation, and that we should impose the like duties and prohibitions upon the importation of some or all of their manufactures into ours. Nations accordingly seldom fail to retaliate in this manner. The French have been particularly forward to favour their own manufactures by restraining the importation of such foreign goods as could come into competition with them. In this consisted a great part of the policy of Mr. Colbert, who, notwithstanding his great abilities, seems in this case to have been imposed upon by the sophistry of merchants and manufacturers, who are always demanding a monopoly against their countrymen. It is at present the opinion of the most intelligent men in France that his operations of this kind have not been beneficial to his country. That minister, by the tariff of 1667, imposed very high duties upon a great number of foreign manufactures. Upon his refusing to moderate them in favour of the Dutch, they in 1671 prohibited the importation of the wines, brandies and manufactures of France. The war of 1672 seems to have been in part occasioned by this commercial dispute. The peace of Nimeguen put an end to it in 1678, by moderating some of those duties in favour of the Dutch, who in consequence took off their prohibition. It was about the same time that the French and English began mutually to oppress each other's industry, by the like duties and prohibitions, of which the French, however, seem to have set the first example. The spirit of hostility which has subsisted between the two nations ever since, has hitherto hindered them from being moderated on either side. In 1697 the English prohibited the importation of bonelace, the manufacture of Flanders. The government of that country, at that time under the dominion of Spain, prohibited in return the importation of English woollens. In 1700, the prohibition of importing bonelace into England, was taken off upon condition that the importation of English woollens into Flanders should be put on the same footing as before.

There may be good policy in retaliations of this kind, when there is a probability that they will procure the repeal of the high duties or prohibitions complained of. The recovery of a great foreign market will generally more than compensate the transitory inconveniency of paying dearer during a short time for some sorts of goods. To judge whether such retaliations are likely to produce such an effect, does not, perhaps, belong so much to the science of a legislator, whose deliberations ought to be governed by general principles which are always the same, as to the skill of that insidious and crafty animal, vulgarly called a statesman or politician, whose councils are directed by the momentary fluctuations of affairs. When there is no probability that any such repeal can be procured, it seems a bad method of compensating the injury done to certain classes of our people, to do another injury ourselves, not only to those classes, but to almost all the other classes of them. When our neighbours prohibit some manufacture of ours, we generally prohibit, not only the same, for that alone would seldom affect them considerably, but some other manufacture of theirs. This may no doubt give encouragement to some particular class of workmen among ourselves, and by excluding some of their rivals, may enable them to raise their price in the home-market. Those workmen, however, who suffered by our neighbours' prohibition will not be benefited by ours. On the contrary, they and almost all the other classes of our citizens will thereby be obliged to pay dearer than before for certain goods. Every such law, therefore, imposes a real tax upon the whole country, not in favour of that particular class of workmen who were injured by our neighbours' prohibition, but of some other class.

The case in which it may sometimes be a matter of deliberation, how far, or in what manner, it is proper to restore the free importation of foreign goods, after it has been for some time interrupted, is, when particular manufactures, by means of high duties or prohibitions upon all foreign goods which can come into competition with them, have been so far extended as to employ a great multitude of hands. Humanity may in this case require that the freedom of trade should be restored only by slow gradations, and with a good deal of reserve and circumspection. Were those high duties and prohibitions taken away all at once, cheaper foreign goods of the same kind might be poured so fast into the home market, as to deprive all at once many thousands of our people of their ordinary employment and means of subsistence. The disorder which this would occasion might no doubt be very considerable. It would in all probability, however, be much less than is commonly imagined, for the two following reasons:

First, all those manufactures, of which any part is commonly exported to other European countries without a bounty, could be very little affected by the freest importation of foreign goods. Such manufactures must be sold as cheap abroad as any other foreign goods of the same quality and kind, and consequently must be sold cheaper at home. They would still, therefore, keep possession of the home market, and though a capricious man of fashion might sometimes prefer foreign wares, merely because they were foreign, to cheaper and better goods of the same kind that were made at home, this folly could, from the nature of things, extend to so few, that it could make no sensible impression upon the general employment of the people. But a great part of all the different branches of our woollen manufacture, of our tanned leather, and of our hard-ware, are annually exported to other European countries without any bounty, and these are the manufactures which employ the greatest number of hands. The silk, perhaps, is the manufacture which would suffer the most by this freedom of trade, and after it the linen, though the latter much less than the former.

Secondly, though a great number of people should, by thus restoring the freedom of trade, be thrown all at once out of their ordinary employment and common method of subsistence, it would by no means follow that they would thereby be deprived either of employment or subsistence. By the reduction of the army and navy at the end of the late war, more than a hundred thousand soldiers and seamen, a number equal to what is employed in the greatest manufactures, were all at once thrown out of their ordinary employment; but, though they no doubt suffered some inconveniency, they were not thereby deprived of all employment and subsistence. The greater part of the seamen, it is probable, gradually betook themselves to the merchant-service as they could find occasion, and in the meantime both they and the soldiers were absorbed in the great mass of the people, and employed in a great variety of occupations. Not only no great convulsion, but no sensible disorder arose from so great a change in the situation of more than a hundred thousand men, all accustomed to the use of arms, and many of them to rapine and plunder. The number of vagrants was scarce anywhere sensibly increased by it, even the wages of labour were not reduced by it in any occupation, so far as I have been able to learn, except in that of seamen in the merchant-service. But if we compare together the habits of a soldier and of any sort of manufacturer, we shall find that those of the latter do not tend so much to disqualify him from being employed in a new trade, as those of the former from being employed in any. The manufacturer has always been accustomed to look for his subsistence from his labour only: the soldier to expect it from his pay. Application and industry have been familiar to the one; idleness and dissipation to the other. But it is surely much easier to change the direction of industry from one sort of labour to another, than to turn idleness and dissipation to any. To the greater part of manufactures besides, it has already been observed, there are other collateral manufactures of so similar a nature, that a workman can easily transfer his industry from one of them to another. The greater part of such workmen too are occasionally employed in country labour. The stock which employed them in a particular manufacture before, will still remain in the country to employ an equal number of people in some other way. The capital of the country remaining the same, the demand for labour will likewise be the same, or very nearly the same, though it may be exerted in different places and for different occupations. Soldiers and seamen, indeed, when discharged from the king's service, are at liberty to exercise any trade, within any town or place of Great Britain or Ireland. Let the same natural liberty of exercising what species of industry they please, be restored to all his majesty's subjects, in the same manner as to soldiers and seamen; that is, break down the exclusive privileges of corporations, and repeal the statute of apprenticeship, both which are real encroachments upon natural liberty, and add to these the repeal of the law of settlements, so that a poor workman, when thrown out of employment either in one trade or in one place, may seek for it in another trade or in another place, without the fear either of a prosecution or of a removal, and neither the public nor the individuals will suffer much more from the occasional disbanding some particular classes of manufacturers, than from that of soldiers. Our manufacturers have no doubt great merit with their country, but they cannot have more than those who defend it with their blood, nor deserve to be treated with more delicacy.

To expect, indeed, that the freedom of trade should ever be entirely restored in Great Britain, is as absurd as to expect that an Oceana or Utopia should ever be established in it. Not only the prejudices of the public, but what is much more unconquerable, the private interests of many individuals, irresistibly oppose it. Were the officers of the army to oppose with the same zeal and unanimity any reduction in the number of forces, with which master manufacturers set themselves against every law that is likely to increase the number of their rivals in the home market; were the former to animate their soldiers, in the same manner as the latter enflame their workmen, to attack with violence and outrage the proposers of any such regulation; to attempt to reduce the army would be as dangerous as it has now become to attempt to diminish in any respect the monopoly which our manufacturers have obtained against us. This monopoly has so much increased the number of some particular tribes of them, that, like an overgrown standing army, they have become formidable to the government, and upon many occasions intimidate the legislature. The member of parliament who supports every proposal for strengthening this monopoly, is sure to acquire not only the reputation of understanding trade, but great popularity and influence with an order of men whose numbers and wealth render them of great importance. If he opposes them, on the contrary, and still more if he has authority enough to be able to thwart them, neither the most acknowledged probity, nor the highest rank, nor the greatest public services, can protect him from the most infamous abuse and detraction, from personal insults, nor sometimes from real danger, arising from the insolent outrage of furious and disappointed monopolists.

The undertaker of a great manufacture, who, by the home markets being suddenly laid open to the competition of foreigners, should be obliged to abandon his trade, would no doubt suffer very considerably. That part of his capital which had usually been employed in purchasing materials and in paying his workmen, might, without much difficulty, perhaps, find another employment. But that part of it which was fixed in workhouses, and in the instruments of trade, could scarce be disposed of without considerable loss. The equitable regard, therefore, to his interest requires that changes of this kind should never be introduced suddenly, but slowly, gradually, and after a very long warning. The legislature, were it possible that its deliberations could be always directed, not by the clamorous importunity of partial interests, but by an extensive view of the general good, ought upon this very account, perhaps, to be particularly careful neither to establish any new monopolies of this kind, nor to extend further those which are already established. Every such regulation introduces some degree of real disorder into the constitution of the state, which it will be difficult afterwards to cure without occasioning another disorder.

How far it may be proper to impose taxes upon the importation of foreign goods, in order, not to prevent their importation, but to raise a revenue for government, I shall consider hereafter when I come to treat of taxes. Taxes imposed with a view to prevent, or even to diminish importation, are evidently as destructive of the revenue of the customs as of the freedom of trade.

4

REALISM AND COMPLEX
INTERDEPENDENCE

⎯⎯ Robert O. Keohane and Joseph S. Nye ⎯⎯

In this classic work, Robert Keohane and Joseph Nye offer a neoliberal critique of the realist worldview. They assert that in the post–World War II era countries have become more and more intertwined economically. The explosive growth in the size and number of transnational corporations has blurred state boundaries, rendering traditional realist assumptions about the centrality of the state questionable. Realists contend that the state is the dominant actor in world politics and that military force and violence are the primary means by which states achieve their goals. Keohane and Nye propose an alternative ideal type—complex interdependence—that emphasizes cooperation rather than conflict. While the authors caution that violence and conflict have not disappeared, they point to the growing importance of nonsecurity-related issues such as international monetary relations and global environmental concerns. To them the day-to-day affairs of states have more to do with promoting cooperative economic interactions than with military and security matters.

One's assumptions about world politics profoundly affect what one sees and how one constructs theories to explain events. We believe that the assumptions of political realists, whose theories dominated the postwar period, are often an inadequate basis for analyzing the politics of interdependence. The realist assumptions about world politics can be seen as defining an extreme set of conditions or ideal type. One could also imagine very different conditions. In this chapter, we shall construct another ideal type, the opposite of realism. We call it *complex interdependence*. After establishing the differences between realism and complex interdependence, we shall argue that complex interdependence sometimes comes closer to reality than does realism. When it does, traditional explanations of change in international regimes become questionable and the search for new explanatory models becomes more urgent.

For political realists, international politics, like all other politics, is a struggle for power but, unlike domestic politics, a struggle dominated by organized violence. . . . Three assumptions are integral to the realist vision. First, states as coherent units are the dominant actors in world politics. This is a double assumption: states are predominant; and they act as coherent units. Second, realists assume that force is a usable and effective instrument of policy. Other instruments may also be employed, but using or threatening force is the most effective means of wielding power. Third, partly because of their second assumption, realists assume a hierarchy of issues in world politics, headed by questions of military security: the "high politics" of military security dominates the "low politics" of economic and social affairs.

These realist assumptions define an ideal type of world politics. They allow us to imagine a world in which politics is continually characterized by active or potential conflict among states, with the use of force possible at any time. Each state attempts to defend its territory and interests from real or perceived threats. Political integration among states is slight and lasts only as long as it serves the national interests of the most powerful states. Transnational actors either do not exist or are politically unimportant. Only the adept exercise of force or the threat of force permits states to survive, and only while statesmen succeed in adjusting their interests, as in a well-functioning balance of power, is the system stable.

Each of the realist assumptions can be challenged. If we challenge them all simultaneously, we can imagine a world in which actors other than states participate directly in world politics, in which a clear hierarchy of issues does not exist, and in which force is an ineffective instrument of policy. Under these conditions—which we call the characteristics of complex interdependence—one would expect world politics to be very different than under realist conditions.

The Characteristics of Complex Interdependence

Complex interdependence has three main characteristics:

1. *Multiple channels* connect societies, including: informal ties between governmental elites as well as formal foreign office arrangements; informal ties among nongovernmental elites (face-to-face and through telecommunications); and transnational organizations (such as multinational banks or corporations). These channels can be summarized as interstate, transgovernmental, and transnational relations. *Interstate* relations are the normal channels assumed by realists. *Transgovernmental* applies when we relax the realist assumption that states act coherently as units; *transnational* applies when we relax the assumption that states are the only units.

2. The agenda of interstate relationships consists of multiple issues that are not arranged in a clear or consistent hierarchy. This *absence of hierarchy among issues* means, among other things, that military security does not consistently dominate the agenda. Many issues arise from what used to be considered domestic policy, and the distinction between domestic and foreign issues becomes blurred. These issues are considered in several government departments (not just foreign offices), and at several levels. Inadequate policy coordination on these issues involves significant costs. Different issues generate different coalitions, both within governments and across them, and involve different degrees of conflict. Politics does not stop at the waters' edge.

3. Military force is not used by governments toward other governments within the region, or on the issues, when complex interdependence prevails. It may, however, be important in these governments' relations with governments outside that region, or on other issues. Military force could, for instance, be irrelevant to resolving disagreements on economic issues among members of an alliance, yet at the same time be very important for that alliance's political and military relations with a rival bloc. For the former relationships this condition of complex interdependence would be met; for the latter, it would not.

Traditional theories of international politics implicitly or explicitly deny the accuracy of these three assumptions. Traditionalists are therefore tempted also to deny the relevance of criticisms based on the complex interdependence ideal type. We believe, however, that our three conditions are fairly well approximated on some global issues of economic and ecological interdependence and that they come close to characterizing the entire relationship between some countries. One of our purposes here is to prove that contention. In [*Power and Interdependence: World Politics in Transition* we] examine complex interdependence in oceans policy and monetary policy and in the relationships of the United States to Canada and Australia. In this chapter, however, we shall try to convince you to take these criticisms of traditional assumptions seriously. . . .

The Political Processes of Complex Interdependence

The three main characteristics of complex interdependence give rise to distinctive political processes, which translate power resources into power as control of outcomes. As we argued earlier, something is usually lost or added in the translation. Under conditions of complex interdependence the translation will be different than under realist conditions, and our predictions about outcomes will need to be adjusted accordingly.

In the realist world, military security will be the dominant goal of states. It will even affect issues that are not directly involved with military power or territorial defense. Nonmilitary problems will not only be subordinated to military ones; they will be studied for their politico-military implications. Balance of payments issues, for instance, will be considered at least as much in the light of their implications for world power generally as for their purely financial ramifications. . . .

In a world of complex interdependence, however, one expects some officials, particularly at lower levels, to emphasize the *variety* of state goals that must be pursued. In the absence of a clear hierarchy of issues, goals will vary by issue, and may not be closely related. Each bureaucracy will pursue its own concerns; and although several agencies may reach compromises on issues that affect them all, they will find that a consistent pattern of policy is difficult to maintain. Moreover, transnational actors will introduce different goals into various groups of issues.

Linkage Strategies

Goals will therefore vary by issue area under complex interdependence, but so will the distribution of power and the typical political processes. Traditional analysis focuses on *the* international system, and leads us to anticipate similar political processes on a variety of issues. Militarily and economically strong states will dominate a variety of organizations and a variety of issues, by linking their own policies on some issues to other states' policies on other issues. By using their overall dominance to prevail on their weak issues, the strongest states will, in the traditional model, ensure a congruence between the overall structure of military and economic power and the pattern of outcomes on any one issue area. Thus world politics can be treated as a seamless web.

Under complex interdependence, such congruence is less likely to occur. As military force is devalued, militarily strong states will find it more difficult to use their overall dominance to control outcomes on issues in which they are weak. And since the distribution of power resources in trade, shipping, or oil, for example, may be quite different, patterns of outcomes and distinctive political processes are likely to vary from one set of issues to another. If force were readily applicable, and military security were the highest foreign policy goal, these variations in the issue structures of power would not matter very much. The linkages drawn from them to military issues would ensure consistent dominance by the overall strongest states. But when military force is largely immobilized, strong states will find that linkage is less effective. They may still attempt such links, but in the absence of a hierarchy of issues, their success will be problematic.

Dominant states may try to secure much the same result by using overall economic power to affect results on other issues. If only economic objectives are at stake, they may succeed: money, after all, is fungible. But economic objectives have political implications, and economic linkage by the strong is limited by domestic, transnational, and transgovernmental actors who resist having their interests traded off. Furthermore, the international actors may be different on different issues, and the international organizations in which negotiations take place are often quite separate. Thus it is difficult, for example, to imagine a militarily or economically strong state linking concessions on monetary policy to reciprocal concessions in oceans policy. On the other hand, poor weak states are not similarly inhibited from linking unrelated issues, partly because their domestic interests are less complex. Linkage of unrelated issues is often a means of extracting concessions or side payments from rich and powerful states. And unlike powerful states whose instrument for linkage (military force) is often too costly to use, the linkage instrument used by poor, weak states—international organization—is available and inexpensive.

Thus as the utility of force declines, and as issues become more equal in importance, the distribution of power within each issue will become more important. If linkages become less effective on the whole, outcomes of political bargaining will increasingly vary by issue area.

The differentiation among issue areas in complex interdependence means that linkages among issues will become more problematic and will tend to reduce rather than reinforce international hierarchy. Linkage strategies, and defense against them, will pose critical strategic choices for states. Should issues be considered separately or as a package? If linkages are to be drawn, which issues should be linked, and on which of the linked issues should concessions be made? How far can one push a linkage before it becomes counterproductive? For instance, should one seek formal agreements or informal, but less politically sensitive, understandings? The fact that world politics under complex interdependence is not a seamless web leads us to expect that efforts to stitch seams together advantageously, as reflected in linkage strategies, will, very often, determine the shape of the fabric.

Agenda Setting

Our second assumption of complex interdependence, the lack of clear hierarchy among multiple issues, leads us to expect that the politics of agenda formation and control will become more important. Traditional analyses lead statesmen to focus on politico-military issues and to pay little attention to the broader politics of agenda formation. Statesmen assume that the agenda will be set by shifts in the balance of power, actual or anticipated, and by perceived threats to the security of states. Other issues will only be very important when they seem to affect security and military power. In these cases, agendas will be influenced strongly by considerations of the overall balance of power.

Yet, today, some nonmilitary issues are emphasized in interstate relations at one time, whereas others of seemingly equal importance are neglected or quietly handled at a technical level. International monetary politics, problems of commodity terms of trade, oil, food, and multinational corporations have all been important during the last decade; but not all have been high on interstate agendas throughout that period.

Traditional analysts of international politics have paid little attention to agenda formation: to how issues come to receive sustained attention by high officials. The traditional orientation toward military and security affairs implies that the crucial problems of foreign policy are imposed on states by the actions or threats of other states. These are high politics as opposed to the low politics of economic affairs. Yet, as the complexity of actors and issues in world politics increases, the utility of force declines and the line between domestic policy and foreign policy becomes blurred: as the conditions of complex interdependence are more closely approximated, the politics of agenda formation becomes more subtle and differentiated.

Under complex interdependence we can expect the agenda to be affected by the international and domestic problems created by economic growth and increasing sensitivity interdependence. . . . Discontented domestic groups will politicize issues and force more issues once considered domestic onto the interstate agenda. Shifts in the distribution of power resources within sets of issues will also affect agendas. During the early 1970s the increased power of oil-producing governments over the transnational corporations and the consumer countries dramatically altered the policy agenda. Moreover, agendas for one group of issues may change as a result of linkages from other groups in which power resources are changing; for example, the broader agenda of North-South trade issues changed after the OPEC price rises and the oil embargo of 1973–74. Even if capabilities among states do not change, agendas may be affected by shifts in the importance of transnational actors. The publicity surrounding multinational corporations in the early 1970s, coupled with their rapid growth over the past twenty years, put the regulation of such corporations higher on both the United Nations agenda and national agendas.

Transnational and Transgovernmental Relations

Our third condition of complex interdependence, multiple channels of contact among societies, further blurs the distinction between domestic and international politics. The availability of partners in political coalitions is not necessarily limited by national boundaries as traditional analysis assumes. The nearer a situation is to complex interdependence, the more we expect the outcomes of political bargaining to be affected by transnational relations. Multinational corporations may be significant both as independent actors and as instruments manipulated by governments. The attitudes and policy stands of domestic groups are likely to be affected by communications, organized or not, between them and their counterparts abroad.

Thus the existence of multiple channels of contact leads us to expect limits, beyond those normally found in domestic politics, on the ability of statesmen to calculate the manipulation of interdependence or follow a consistent strategy of linkage. Statesmen must consider differential as well as aggregate effects of interdependence strategies and their likely implications for politicization and agenda control. Transactions among societies—economic and social transactions more than security ones—affect groups differently. Opportunities and costs from increased transnational ties may be greater for certain groups—for instance, American workers in the textile or shoe industries—than for others. Some organizations or groups may interact directly with actors in other societies or with other governments to increase their benefits from a network of interaction. Some actors may therefore be less vulnerable as well as less sensitive to changes elsewhere in the network than are others, and this will affect patterns of political action.

The multiple channels of contact found in complex interdependence are not limited to nongovernmental actors. Contacts between governmental bureaucracies charged with similar tasks may not only alter their perspectives but lead to transgovernmental coalitions on particular policy questions. To improve their chances of success, government agencies attempt to bring actors from other governments into their own decision-making processes as allies. Agencies of powerful states such as the United States have used such coalitions to penetrate weaker governments in such countries as Turkey and Chile. They have also been used to help agencies of other governments penetrate the United States bureaucracy.[1] . . .

The existence of transgovernmental policy networks leads to a different interpretation of one of the standard propositions about international politics—that states act in their own interest. Under complex interdependence, this conventional wisdom begs two important questions: which self and which interest? A government agency may pursue its own interests under the guise of the national interest; and recurrent interactions can change official perceptions of their interests. . . .

The ambiguity of the national interest raises serious problems for the top political leaders of governments. As bureaucracies contact each other directly across national borders (without going through foreign offices), centralized control becomes more difficult. There is less assurance that the state will be united when dealing with foreign governments or that its components will interpret national interests similarly when negotiating with foreigners. The state may prove to be multifaceted, even schizophrenic. National interests will be defined differently on different issues, at different times, and by different governmental units. States that are better placed to maintain their coherence (because of a centralized political tradition such as France's) will be better able to manipulate uneven interdependence than fragmented states that at first glance seem to have more resources in an issue area.

Role of International Organizations

Finally, the existence of multiple channels leads one to predict a different and significant role for international organizations in world politics. Realists in the tradition of Hans J. Morgenthau have portrayed a world in which states, acting from self-interest, struggle for "power and peace." Security issues are dominant; war threatens. In such a world, one may assume that international institutions will have a minor role, limited by the rare congruence of such interests. International organizations are then clearly peripheral to world politics. But in a world of multiple issues imperfectly linked, in which coalitions are formed transnationally and transgovernmentally, the potential role of international institutions in political bargaining is greatly increased. In particular, they help set the international agenda, and act as catalysts for coalition-formation and as arenas for political initiatives and linkage by weak states.

Governments must organize themselves to cope with the flow of business generated by international organizations. By defining the salient issues, and deciding which issues can be grouped together, organizations may help to determine governmental priorities and the nature of interdepartmental committees and other arrangements within governments. The 1972 Stockholm Environment Conference strengthened the position of environmental agencies in various governments. The 1974 World Food Conference focused the attention of important parts of the United States government on prevention of food shortages. The September 1975 United Nations special session on proposals for a New International Economic Order generated an intragovernmental debate about policies toward the Third World in general. The International Monetary Fund and the General Agreement on Tariffs and Trade have focused governmental activity on money and trade instead of on private direct investment, which has no comparable international organization.

By bringing officials together, international organizations help to activate potential coalitions in world politics. It is quite obvious that international organizations have been very important in bringing together representatives of less developed countries, most of which do not maintain embassies in one another's capitals. Third World strategies of solidarity among poor countries have been developed in and for a series of international conferences, mostly under the auspices of the United Nations.[2] International organizations also allow agencies of governments, which might not otherwise come into contact, to turn potential or tacit coalitions into explicit transgovernmental coalitions characterized by direct communications. In some cases, international secretariats deliberately promote this process by forming coalitions with groups of governments, or with units of governments, as well as with nongovernmental organizations having similar interests.[3]

International organizations are frequently congenial institutions for weak states. The one-state-one-vote norm of the United Nations system favors coalitions of the small and powerless. Secretariats are often responsive to Third World demands. Furthermore, the substantive norms of most international organizations, as they have developed over the years, stress social and economic equity as well as the equality of states. Past resolutions expressing Third World positions, sometimes agreed to with reservations by industrialized countries, are used to legitimize other demands. These agreements are rarely binding, but up to a point the norms of the institution make opposition look more harshly self-interested and less defensible. . . .

Complex interdependence therefore yields different political patterns than does the realist conception of the world. (Table 4.1 summarizes these differences.) Thus, one would expect traditional theories to fail to explain international regime change in situations of complex interdependence. But, for a situation that approximates realist conditions, traditional theories should be appropriate. . . .

Table 4.1   Political Processes Under Conditions of Realism and Complex Interdependence

	Realism	Complex Interdependence
Goals of actors	Military security will be the dominant goal.	Goals of states will vary by issue area. Transgovernmental politics will make goals difficult to define. Transnational actors will pursue their own goals.
Instruments of state policy	Military force will be most effective, although economic and other instruments will also be used.	Power resources specific to issue areas will be most relevant. Manipulation of interdependence, international organizations, and transnational actors will be major instruments.
Agenda formation	Potential shifts in the balance of power and security threats will set the agenda in high politics and will strongly influence other agendas.	Agenda will be affected by changes in the distribution of power resources within issue areas; the status of international regimes; changes in the importance of transnational actors; linkages from other issues and politicization as a result of rising sensitivity interdependence.
Linkages of issues	Linkages will reduce differences in outcomes among issue areas and reinforce international hierarchy.	Linkages by strong states will be more difficult to make since force will be ineffective. Linkages by weak states through international organizations will erode rather than reinforce hierarchy.
Roles of international organizations	Roles are minor, limited by state power and the importance of military force.	Organizations will set agendas, induce coalition-formation, and act as arenas for political action by weak states. Ability to choose the organizational forum for an issue and to mobilize votes will be an important political resource.

Notes

1. For a more detailed discussion, see Robert O. Keohane and Joseph S. Nye, Jr., "Transgovernmental Relations and International Organizations," *World Politics* 27, no. 1 (October 1974): 39–62.

2. Branislav Gosovic and John Gerard Ruggie, "On the Creation of a New International Economic Order: Issue Linkage and the Seventh Special Session of the UN General Assembly," *International Organization* 30, no. 2 (Spring 1976): 309–46.

3. Robert W. Cox, "The Executive Head," *International Organization* 23, no. 2 (Spring 1969): 205–30.

5

TRADE LESSONS
FROM THE WORLD ECONOMY

Peter F. Drucker

Peter Drucker has been a major contributor to the genre of neoliberalism that asserts that the power of the state has been eclipsed by the transnational corporation (TNC), a perspective that is sometimes called "sovereignty at bay." In the 1970s Raymond Vernon noted that innovations in communications and transportation had accelerated and allowed for an explosion in the number of TNCs. In fact, TNCs had become so numerous and were such an important part of so many countries' economies that they had diminished the importance of the state. In this chapter, Drucker attempts to show that as the global economy transforms everyday life, traditional policies and remedies attempted by states are no longer operable. The proper response to this transformation, according to Drucker, is to abandon the ways of thinking that have dominated policy since 1945 and to move toward a global economic policy.

All Economics Is International

In recent years the economies of all developed nations have been stagnant, yet the world economy has still expanded at a good clip. And it has been growing faster for the past 40 years than at any time since modern economies and the discipline of economics emerged in the eighteenth century. From this seeming paradox there are lessons to be learned, and they are quite different from what practically everyone asserts, whether they be free traders, managed traders or protectionists.

Reprinted by permission of *Foreign Affairs* (January/February 1994, vol. 73, no. 1). © 1994 by the Council on Foreign Relations, Inc.

Too many economists, politicians and segments of the public treat the external economy as something separate and safely ignored when they make policy for the domestic economy. Contrary lessons emerge from a proper understanding of the profound changes in four areas—the structure of the world economy, the changed meaning of trade and investment, the relationship between world and domestic economies, and the difference between workable and unworkable trade policies.

The segments that comprise the world economy—the flows of money and information on the one hand, and trade and investment on the other—are rapidly merging into one transaction. They increasingly represent different dimensions of cross-border alliances, the strongest integrating force of the world economy. Both of these segments are growing fast. The center of world money flows, the London Interbank Market, handles more money in one day than would be needed in many months—perhaps an entire year—to finance the real economy of international trade and investment. Similarly, the trades during one day on the main currency markets of London, New York, Zurich and Tokyo exceed by several orders of magnitude what would be needed to finance the international transactions of the real economy.

Today's money flows are vastly larger than traditional portfolio investments made for the sake of short-term income from dividends and interest. Portfolio money flows were once the stabilizers of the international economy, flowing from countries of low short-term returns to countries of higher short-term returns, thus maintaining an equilibrium. They reacted to a country's financial policy or economic condition. Driven by the expectation of speculative profits, today's world money flows have become the great destabilizers, forcing countries into precipitous interest rate hikes that throttle business activity, or into overnight devaluations that drag a currency below its trade parity or purchasing-power parity, thus generating inflationary pressures. These money flows are a pathological phenomenon. They underline the fact that neither fixed nor flexible foreign exchange rates (the only two known systems) really work. Contemporary money flows do not respond to attempted government restrictions such as taxes on money-flow profits; the trading just moves elsewhere. All that can be done as part of an effective trade policy is to build resistance into the economy against the impact of the flows.

Information flows in the world economy are probably growing faster than any category of transactions in history. Consisting of meetings, software, magazines, books, movies, videos, telecommunications and a host of new technologies, information flows may already exceed money flows in the fees, royalties and profits they generate. Unlike money flows, information flows have benign economic impacts. In fact, few things so stimulate economic growth as the rapid development of information, whether telecommunications, computer data, computer networks or entertainment media. In the United States, information flows—and the goods needed to carry them—have become the largest single source of foreign currency income. But just as we do not view medieval cathedrals economically—although they were once Europe's biggest generators of economic activity next to farming, and its biggest nonmilitary employer—information flows have mostly social and cultural impacts. Economic factors like high costs restrain rather than motivate information flows.

The first lesson is that these two significant economic phenomena—money flows and information flows—do not fit into any theory or policy. They are not even transitional; they are nonnational.

What Trade Deficit?

For practically everyone international trade means merchandise trade, the import and export of manufactured goods, farm products and raw materials. But international trade is increasingly services trade, little reported and largely unnoticed. The United States has the largest share of the trade in services among developed countries, followed by the United Kingdom. Japan is at the bottom of the list. The services trade of all developed countries is growing fast, and it may equal or overtake their merchandise trade within ten years. Knowledge is the basis of most service exports and imports. As a result, most service trade is based on long-term commitments, which makes it—excluding tourism—impervious to foreign exchange fluctuations and changes in labor costs.

Even merchandise trade is no longer confined to the sale and purchase of individual goods. Increasingly it is a relationship in which a transaction is only a shipment and an accounting entry. More and more merchandise trade is becoming "structural" and thereby impervious to short-term (and even long-term) changes in the traditional economic factors. Automobile production is a good example. Plant location decisions by manufacturers and suppliers are made at the time of product design. Until the model is redesigned, say in ten years, the plants and the countries specified in the original design are locked in. There will be change only in the event of a catastrophe such as a war or fire that destroys a plant. Or take the case of a Swiss pharmaceutical company's Irish plant. Rather than sell a product, it ships chemical intermediates to the company's finished product plants in countries on both sides of the Atlantic. For this the company charges a "transfer" price, which is a pure accounting convention having as much to do with taxes as with production costs. The traditional factors of production are also largely irrelevant to what might be called "institutional" trade, in which businesses, whether manufacturers or large retailers, buy machinery, equipment and supplies for new plants or stores, wherever located, from the suppliers of their existing plants, that is, those in their home countries.

Markets and knowledge are important in these types of structural and institutional trade decisions; labor costs, capital costs and foreign exchange rates are restraints rather than determinants. More important, neither type of trade is foreign trade, except in a legal sense, even when it is trade across national boundaries. For the individual business—the automobile manufacturer, the Swiss pharmaceutical company, the retailer—these are transactions within its own system.

Accounting for these developments, US trading activity is more or less in balance. The trade deficit bewailed in the media and by public and private officials is in merchandise trade, caused primarily by an appalling waste of petroleum and a steady decline in the volume and prices of farm exports. The services trade account has a large surplus. According to little-read official figures, published every three months, the services trade surplus amounts to two thirds of the merchandise trade deficit. Moreover, government statisticians acknowledge gross underreporting of service exports, perhaps by as much as 50 percent.

The Coming of Alliances

Traditional direct investment abroad to start or acquire businesses continues to grow. Since the 1980s direct investment in the United States by Europeans, Japanese, Canadians and Mexicans has grown explosively. But the action is rapidly shifting to alliances such as joint ventures, partnerships, knowledge agreements and out-sourcing arrangements. In alliances, investment is secondary, if there is any at all. A recent example is the dividing up of design and production of an advanced microchip between Intel, a US-based microchip designer, and Sharp, the Japanese electronics manufacturer. Both will share the final product. There are alliances between scores of university research labs and businesses—pharmaceutical, electronic, engineering, food processing and computer firms. There are alliances in which organizations outsource support activities; a number of American hospitals, and some in the United Kingdom and Japan, let independent suppliers do their maintenance, housekeeping, billing and data processing, and increasingly let them run the labs and the physical therapy and diagnostic centers. Computer makers now outsource the data processing for their own businesses to contractors like Electronic Data Systems, the company

Ross Perot built and sold to General Motors. They are also entering alliances with small, independent software designers. Commercial banks are entering alliances with producers and managers of mutual funds. Small and medium-sized colleges are entering alliances with one another to do paperwork jointly.

Some of these alliances involve substantial capital investment, as in the joint ventures of the 1960s and 1970s between Japanese and US companies to produce American-designed goods in Japan for the Japanese market. But even then the basis of the alliance was not capital but complementary knowledge—technical and manufacturing knowledge supplied by the Americans, marketing knowledge and management supplied by the Japanese. More and more, investment of whatever size is symbolic—a minority share in each other's business is regarded as "bonding" between partners. In many alliances there is no financial relationship between the partners. (There is apparently none between Intel and Sharp.)

Alliances, formal and informal, are becoming the dominant form of economic integration in the world economy. Some major companies, such as Toshiba, the Japanese electronics giant, and Corning Glass, the world's leading maker of high-engineered glass, may each have more than 100 alliances all over the world. Integration in the Common Market is proceeding far more through alliances than through mergers and acquisitions, especially among the middle-sized companies that dominate most European economies. As with structural institutional trade, businesses make little distinction between domestic and foreign partners in their alliances. An alliance creates a relationship in which it does not matter whether one partner speaks Japanese, another English and a third German or Finnish. And while alliances increasingly generate both trade and investment, they are based on neither. They pool knowledge.

The Vital Link

For developed economies, the distinction between the domestic and international economy has ceased to be a reality, however much political, cultural or psychological strength remains in the idea. An unambiguous lesson of the last 40 years is that increased participation in the world economy has become the key to domestic economic growth and prosperity. Since 1950 there has been a close correlation between a country's domestic economic performance and its participation in the world economy. The two major countries whose economies have grown the fastest in the world economy, Japan and South Korea, are also the two countries whose domestic economies have grown the fastest. The same correlation applies to the two European countries that have done best in the world economy in the last 40 years, West Germany and Sweden. The countries that have retreated from the world economy (most notably the United Kingdom) have consistently done worse domestically. In the two major countries that have maintained their participation rate in the world economy within a fairly narrow range—the United States and France—the domestic economy has put in an average performance, neither doing exceptionally well nor suffering persistent malaise and crisis like the United Kingdom.

The same correlation holds true for major segments within a developed economy. In the United States, for instance, services have tremendously increased their world economy participation in the last 15 years; finance, higher education and information are examples. American agriculture, which has consistently shrunk in terms of world economy participation, has been in continual depression and crisis, masked only by ever-growing subsidies.

Conversely, there is little correlation between economic performance and policies to stimulate the domestic economy. The record shows that a government can harm its domestic economy by driving up inflation. But there is not the slightest evidence that any government policy to stimulate the economy has an impact, whether it be Keynesian, monetarist, supply-side or neoclassical. Contrary to what some economists confidently promised 40 years ago, business cycles have not been abolished. They still operate pretty much the way they have for the past 150 years. No country has been able to escape them. When a government policy to stimulate the economy actually coincided with cyclical recovery (which has been rare), it was by pure coincidence. No one policy shows more such coincidences than any other. And no policy that "worked" in a given country in recession A showed any results when tried again in the same country in recession B or recession C. The evidence not only suggests that government policies to stimulate the economy in the short term are ineffectual but also something far more surprising: they are largely irrelevant. Government, the evidence shows clearly, cannot control the economic weather.

The evidence of the past four decades does show convincingly that participation in the world economy has become the controlling factor in the domestic economic performance of developed countries. For example, a sharp increase in manufacturing and service exports kept the US economy from slipping into deep recession in 1992, and unemployment rates for adult men and women never reached the highs of earlier post–World War II recessions. Similarly, Japan's sharply increased exports have kept its current recession from producing unemployment figures at European levels of eight to ten percent.

What Works, What Does Not

The evidence is crystal clear that both advocates of managed trade and conventional free traders are wrong in their prescriptions for economic growth. Japan's industrial policy of attempting to select and support "winning" business sectors is by now a well-known failure. Practically all the industries the Japanese Ministry of International Trade and Industry (MITI) picked—such as supercomputers and pharmaceuticals—have been at best also-rans. The Japanese businesses that succeeded, like Sony and the automobile companies, were opposed or ignored by MITI. Trying to pick winners requires a fortune-teller, and the world economy has become far too complex to be outguessed. Japan's economy benefited from a competency—an extraordinary ability to miniaturize products—that was virtually unknown to MITI. Pivotal economic events often take place long before we notice their occurrence. The available data simply do not report important developments such as the growth of the service trade, of structural and institutional trade, of alliances.

Still, the outstanding overall performance of Japan and other Asian countries cannot be explained away as merely a triumph of conventional free trade. Two common economic policies emerge from a recent World Bank study of eight East Asian "superstars"—Japan, South Korea, Hong Kong, Taiwan, Singapore, Malaysia, Thailand and Indonesia. First, they do not try to manage short-term fluctuations in their domestic economies; they do not try to control the economic weather. Moreover, not one of the East Asian economies took off until it had given up attempts to manage domestic short-term fluctuations. All eight countries focus instead on creating the right economic climate. They keep inflation low. They invest heavily in education and training. They reward savings and investment and penalize consumption. The eight started modernizing their economies at very different times, but once they got going, all have shown similar growth in both their domestic and international economies.

Together they now account for 21 percent of the world's manufactured goods exports, versus nine percent 30 years ago. Five percent of their populations live below the poverty line, compared with about 40 percent in 1960, and four of them—Japan, Hong Kong, Taiwan and Singapore—rank among the world's richest countries. Yet the eight are totally different in their culture, history, political systems and tax policies. They range from laissez-faire Hong Kong to interventionist Singapore to statist Indonesia.

The second major finding of the World Bank study is that these eight countries pursue policies to enhance the competitiveness of their industries in the world economy with only secondary attention to domestic effect. These countries then foster and promote their proven successes in the world economy. Though MITI neither anticipated nor much encouraged Japan's world market successes, the whole Japanese system is geared to running with them. Japan offers its exporters substantial tax benefits and credits, which remain scarce and expensive for domestic businesses, and it deliberately keeps prices and profits high in a protected domestic market in order to generate cash for overseas investment and market penetration.

The same lessons were being taught until recently by the two countries in the West that showed similar growth: West Germany and Sweden. These countries, too, have very different domestic policies. But both created and maintained an economic growth climate, and through the same measures: control of inflation, high investment in education and training, a high savings rate obtained by high taxes on consumption and fairly low taxes on savings and investment. Both also gave priority to the world economy in governmental and business decisions. The moment they forgot this—when the trade unions a few years back began to subordinate Germany's competitive standing to their wage demands, and the Swedes subordinated their industries' competitive standing to ever-larger welfare spending—their domestic economies went into stagnation.

An additional lesson of the world economy is that investment abroad creates jobs at home. In both the 1960s and the 1980s, expanded US business investments overseas spurred rapid domestic job creation. The same correlation held for Japan and Sweden, both of which invested heavily in overseas plants to produce goods for their home markets. In manufacturing—and in many services, such as retailing—investment per worker in the machinery, tools and equipment of a new facility is three to five times annual production. Most of this productive equipment comes from institutional trade (that is, from the home country of the investor), and most of it is produced by high-wage labor. The initial employment generated to get the new facility into production is substantially larger than the annual output and employment during its first few years of operation.

The last 40 years also teach that protection does not protect. In fact, the evidence shows quite clearly that protection hastens decline. Less-protected US farm products—soybeans, fruit, beef and poultry—have fared a good deal better on world markets than have the more subsidized traditional crops, such as corn, wheat and cotton. Equally persuasive evidence suggests that the American automobile industry's share of its domestic market went into a precipitous decline as soon as the US government forced the Japanese into "voluntary" export restraints. That protection breeds complacency, inefficiency and cartels has been known since before Adam Smith. The counter-argument has always been that it protects jobs, but the evidence of the last 40 years strongly suggests that it does not even do that.

Free Trade Is Not Enough

The world economy has become too important for a country not to have a world-economy policy. Managed trade is a delusion of grandeur. Outright protectionism can only do harm, but simply trying to thwart protectionism is not enough. What is needed is a deliberate and active—indeed, aggressive—policy that gives the demands, opportunities and dynamics of the external economy priority over domestic policy demands and problems. For the United States and a number of other countries, it means abandoning ways of thinking that have dominated American economics perhaps since 1933, and certainly since 1945. We still see the demands and opportunities of the world economy as externalities. We usually do not ask whether domestic decisions will hurt American competitiveness, participation and standing in the world economy. The reverse must become the rule: will a proposed domestic move advance American competitiveness and participation in the world economy? The answer to this question determines what are the right domestic economic policy and business decisions. The lessons of the last 40 years teach us that integration is the only basis for an international trade policy that can work, the only way to rapidly revive a domestic economy in turbulence and chronic recession.

Contending Views of International Political Economy: Mercantilism, Nationalism, and Hegemonic Stability

6

EXCERPTS FROM
REPORT ON MANUFACTURES

—————————— *Alexander Hamilton* ——————————

Classic mercantilism involved extensive state regulation of the economy in the interest of national strength and development. At its core, it advocated policies of political and economic self-reliance and the building of wealth through trade policies that encouraged exports and discouraged imports. The strength of a country, according to the mercantilists, could be measured by its gold horde; because trade debts were resolved in gold, a successful trade policy would swell government coffers and thus the strength of the government. As this excerpt from the Report on Manufactures (1791) *shows, Alexander Hamilton does not call for building a gold horde to demonstrate governmental strength, but he does make the classic call for government action to aid in the development of the economy and the promotion of national self-reliance. Hamilton worries that during the war of independence the colonies had to rely upon foreign trade and armaments to maintain the war. If the United States wanted to be a country of consequence, Hamilton argues, it would have to spend public funds to encourage the emergence of manufactures and to protect these nascent domestic industries from foreign competition.*

The Secretary of the Treasury, in obedience to the order of ye House of Representatives, of the 15th day of January, 1790, has applied his attention, at as early a period as his other duties would permit, to the subject of Manufactures; and particularly to the means of promoting such as will tend to render the United States, independent on foreign nations for military and other essential supplies. And he thereupon respectfully submits the following Report.

The expediency of encouraging manufactures in the United States, which was not long since deemed very questionable, appears at this time to be pretty generally admitted. The embarrassments, which have obstructed the progress of our external trade, have led to serious reflections on the necessity of enlarging the sphere of our domestic commerce: the restrictive regulations, which in foreign markets abridge the vent of the increasing surplus of our Agricultural produce, serve to beget an earnest desire, that a more extensive demand for that surplus may be created at home: And the complete success, which was rewarded manufacturing enterprise, in some valuable branches, conspiring with the promising symptoms, which attend some less mature essays, in others, justify a hope, that the obstacles to the growth of this species of industry are less formidable than they were apprehended to be, and that it is not difficult to find, in its further extension, a full indemnification of any external disadvantages, which are or may be experienced, as well as an accession of resources, favorable to national independence and safety.

There still are, nevertheless, respectable patrons of opinions, unfriendly to the encouragement of manufactures. The following are, substantially, the arguments by, which these opinions are defended.

"In every country (say those who entertain them) Agriculture is the most beneficial and *productive* object of human industry. This position, generally, if not universally true, applies with peculiar emphasis to the United States, on account of their immense tracts of fertile territory, uninhabited and unimproved. Nothing can afford so advantageous an employment for capital and labour, as the conversion of this extensive wilderness into cultivated farms. Nothing equally with this, can contribute to the population, strength and real riches of the country.

"To endeavor, by the extraordinary patronage of Government, to accelerate the growth of manufactures, is, in fact, to endeavor, by force and art, to transfer the natural current of industry from a more, to a less beneficial channel. Whatever has such a tendency must necessarily be unwise. Indeed it can hardly ever be wise in a government, to attempt to give a direction to the industry of its citizens. This under the quick sighted guidance of private interest, will, if left to itself, infallibly find its own way to the most profitable employment: and 'tis by such employment, that the public prosperity will be most effectually promoted. To leave industry to itself, therefore, is, in almost every case, the soundest as well as the simplest policy. . . . "

It has been maintained that Agriculture is, not only, the most productive, but the only productive, species of industry. The reality of this suggestion in either aspect, has, however, not been verified by any accurate detail of facts and calculations; and the general arguments, which are adduced to prove it, are rather subtle and paradoxical, than solid or convincing. . . .

It might also be observed, with a contrary view, that the labor employed in Agriculture is in a great measure periodical and occasional, depending on seasons, liable to various and long intermissions; while that occupied in many manufactures is constant and regular, extending through the year, embracing in some instances night as well as day. It is also probable, that there are among the cultivators of land, more examples of remissness, than among artificers. The farmer, from the peculiar fertility of his land, or some other favorable circumstance, may frequently obtain a livelihood, even with a considerable degree of carelessness in the mode of cultivation; but the artisan can with difficulty effect the same object, without exerting himself pretty equally with all those who are engaged in the same pursuit. And if it may likewise be assumed as a fact, that manufactures open a wider field to exertions of ingenuity than agriculture, it would not be a strained conjecture, that the labour employed in the former, being at once more *constant*, more uniform and more ingenious, than that which is employed in the latter, will be found, at the same time more productive. . . .

The foregoing suggestions are *not designed to inculcate an opinion that manufacturing industry is more productive than that of Agriculture.* They are intended rather to show that the reverse of this proposition is not ascertained; that the general arguments which are brought to establish it are not satisfactory; and, consequently that a supposition of the superior productiveness of Tillage ought to be no obstacle to listening to any substantial inducements to the encouragement of manufactures, which may be otherwise perceived to exist, through an apprehension; that they may have a tendency to divert labour from a more to a less profitable employment. . . .

It is now proper to proceed a step further, and to enumerate the principal circumstances, from which it may be inferred that manufacturing establishments not only occasion a positive augmentation of the Produce and Revenue of the Society, but that they contribute essentially to rendering them greater than they could possibly be, without such establishments. These circumstances are—

1. The division of labour.
2. An extension of the use of Machinery.
3. Additional employment to classes of the community not ordinarily engaged in the business.
4. The promoting of emigration from foreign Countries.
5. The furnishing greater scope for the diversity of talents and dispositions which discriminate men from each other.
6. The affording a more ample and various field for enterprize.
7. The creating in some instances a new, and securing in all, a more certain and steady demand for the surplus produce of the soil.

Each of these circumstances has a considerable influence upon the total mass of industrious effort in a community: Together, they add to it a degree of energy and effect, which are not easily conceived. . . .

It is a primary object of the policy of nations, to be able to supply themselves with subsistence from their own soils; and manufacturing nations, as far as circumstances permit, endeavor to procure from the same source, the raw materials necessary for their own fabrics. This disposition, urged by the spirit of monopoly, is sometimes even carried to an injudicious extreme. It seems not always to be recollected, that nations who have neither mines nor manufactures, can only obtain the manufactured articles, of which they stand in need, by an exchange of the products of their soils; and that, if those who can best furnish them with such articles are unwilling to give a due course to this exchange, they must of necessity, make every possible effort to manufacture for themselves; the effect of which is that the manufacturing nations abridge the natural advantages of their situation, through an unwillingness to permit the Agricultural countries to enjoy the advantages of theirs, and sacrifice the interests of a mutually beneficial intercourse to the vain project of *selling every thing and buying nothing*.

But it is also a consequence of the policy, which has been noted, that the foreign demand for the products of Agricultural Countries is, in a great degree, rather casual and occasional, than certain or constant. To what extent injurious interruptions of the demand for some of the staple commodities of the United States, may have been experienced from that cause, must be referred to the judgment of those who are engaged in carrying on the commerce of the country; but it may be safely affirmed, that such interruptions are at times very inconveniently felt, and that cases not unfrequently occur, in which markets are so confined and restricted as to render the demand very unequal to the supply.

Independently likewise of the artificial impediments, which are created by the policy in question, there are natural causes tending to render the external demand for the surplus of Agricultural nations a precarious reliance. The differences of seasons, in the countries, which are the consumers, make immense differences in the produce of their own soils, in different years; and consequently in the degrees of their necessity for foreign supply. Plentiful harvests with them, especially if similar ones occur at the same time in the countries, which are the furnishers, occasion of course a glut in the markets of the latter. . . .

The foregoing considerations seem sufficient to establish, as general propositions, that it is the interest of nations to diversify the industrious pursuits of the individuals who compose them—that the establishment of manufactures is calculated not only to increase the general stock of useful and productive labour; but even to improve the state of Agriculture. . . .

If the system of perfect liberty to industry and commerce were the prevailing system of nations, the arguments which dissuade a country, in the predicament of the United States, from zealous pursuit of manufactures, would doubtless have great force. It will not be affirmed, that they might not be permitted, with few exceptions, to serve as a rule of national conduct. In such a state of things, each country would have the full benefit of its peculiar advantages to compensate for its deficiencies or disadvantages. If one nation were in a condition to supply manufactured articles on better terms than another, that other might find an abundant indemnification in a superior capacity to furnish the produce of the soil. And a free exchange, mutually beneficial, of the commodities which each was able to supply, on the best terms, might be carried on between them, supporting in full vigour the industry of each. And though the circumstances which have been mentioned and others, which will be unfolded hereafter render it probable, that nations merely Agricultural would not enjoy the same degree of opulence, in proportion to their numbers, as those which united manufactures with agriculture; yet the progressive improvement of the lands of the former might, in the end, atone for an inferior degree of opulence in the meantime; and in a case in which opposite considerations are pretty equally balanced, the option ought perhaps always to be, in favor of leaving Industry to its own direction.

But the system which has been mentioned, is far from characterising the general policy of Nations. The prevalent one has been regulated by an opposite spirit. The consequence of it is, that the United States are to a certain extent in the situation of a country precluded from foreign Commerce. They can indeed, without difficulty obtain from abroad the manufactured supplies of which they are in want; but they experience numerous and very injurious impediments to the emission and vent of their own commodities. Nor is this the case in reference to a single foreign nation only. The regulations of several countries, with which we have the most extensive intercourse, throw serious obstructions in the way of the principal staples of the United States.

In such a position of things, the United States cannot exchange with Europe on equal terms; and the want of reciprocity would render them the victim of a system which should induce them to confine their views to Agriculture, and refrain from Manufactures. A constant and increasing necessity, on their part, for the commodities of Europe, and only a partial and occasional demand for their own, in return, could not but expose them to a state of impoverishment, compared with the opulence to which their political and natural advantages authorise them to aspire.

Remarks of this kind are not made in the spirit of complaint. 'Tis for the nations, whose regulations are alluded to, to judge for themselves, whether, by aiming at too much, they do not lose more than they gain. It is for the United States to consider by what means they can render themselves least dependent on the combinations, right or wrong, of foreign policy.

It is no small consolation, that already the measures which have embarrassed our Trade, have accelerated internal improvements, which upon the whole have bettered our affairs. To diversify and extend these improvements is the surest and safest method of indemnifying ourselves for any inconveniences, which those or similar measures have a tendency to beget. If Europe will not take from us the products of our soil, upon terms consistent with our interest, the natural remedy is to contract as fast as possible our wants of her. . . .

The remaining objections to a particular encouragement of manufactures in the United States now require to be examined.

One of these turns on the proposition, that Industry, if left to itself, will naturally find its way to the most useful and profitable employment: whence it is inferred that manufactures without the aid of government will grow up as soon and as fast, as the natural state of things and the interest of the community may require. . . .

Experience teaches, that men are often so much governed by what they are accustomed to see and practise, that the simplest and most obvious improvements, in the most ordinary occupations, are adopted with hesitation, reluctance, and by slow gradations. . . . To produce the desirable changes as early as may be expedient, may therefore require the incitement and patronage of government. . . .

The superiority antecedently enjoyed by nations, who have preoccupied and perfected a branch of industry, constitutes a more formidable obstacle . . . to the introduction of the same branch into a country in which it did not before exist. To maintain between the recent establishments of one country and the long matured establishments of another country, a competition upon equal terms, both as to quality and price, is in most cases impracticable. The disparity, in the one or in the other, or in both, must necessarily be so considerable as to forbid a successful rivalship, without the extraordinary aid and protection of government.

But the greatest obstacle of all to the successful prosecution of a new branch of industry in a country, in which it was before unknown, consists, as far as the instances apply, in the bounties premiums and other aids which are granted, in a variety of cases, by the nations, in which the establishments to be imitated are previously introduced. It is well known . . . that certain nations grant bounties on the exportation of particular commodities, to enable their own workmen to undersell and supplant all competitors in the countries to which those commodities are sent. Hence the undertakers of a new manufacture have to contend not only with the natural disadvantages of a new undertaking, but with the gratuities and remunerations which other governments bestow. To be enabled to contend with success, it is evident that the interference and aid of their own governments are indispensable. . . .

There remains to be noticed an objection to the encouragement of manufactures, of a nature different from those which question the probability of success. This is derived from its supposed tendency to give a monopoly of advantages to particular classes, at the expense of the rest of the community, who, it is affirmed, would be able to procure the requisite supplies of manufactured articles on better terms from foreigners, than from our own Citizens, and who, it is alleged, are reduced to the necessity of paying an enhanced price for whatever they want, by every measure, which obstructs the free competition of foreign commodities.

It is not an unreasonable supposition, that measures, which serve to abridge the free competition of foreign Articles, have a tendency to occasion an enhancement of prices and it is not to be denied that such is the effect, in a number of Cases; but the fact does not uniformly correspond with the theory. A reduction of prices has, in several instances immediately succeeded the establishment of a domestic manufacture. Whether it be that foreign manufactures endeavour to supplant, by underselling our own, or whatever else be the cause, the effect has been such as is stated, and the reverse of what might have been expected.

But though it were true, that the immediate and certain effect of regulations controling the competition of foreign with domestic fabrics was an increase of Price, it is universally true, that the contrary is the ultimate effect with every successful manufacture. When a domestic manufacture has attained to perfection, and has engaged in the prosecution of it a competent number of Persons, it invariably becomes cheaper. Being free from the heavy charges which attend the importation of foreign commodities, it can be afforded, and accordingly seldom or never fails to be sold Cheaper, in process of time, than was the foreign Article for which it is a substitute. The internal competition which takes place, soon does away [with] every thing like Monopoly, and by degrees reduces the price of the Article to the *minimum* of a reasonable profit on the Capital employed. This accords with the reason of the thing, and with experience.

Whence it follows, that it is the interest of a community, with a view to eventual and permanent economy, to encourage the growth of manufactures. In a national view, a temporary enhancement of price must always be well compensated by a permanent reduction of it. . . .

[T]he uniform appearance of an abundance of specie, as the concomitant of a flourishing state of manufactures, and of the reverse, where they do not prevail, afford a strong presumption of their favorable operation upon the wealth of a Country.

Not only the wealth, but the independence and security of a Country, appear to be materially connected with the prosperity of manufactures. Every nation, with a view to those great objects, ought to endeavour to possess within itself all the essentials of national supply. These comprise the means of *Subsistence, habitation, clothing,* and *defence.*

The possession of these is necessary to the perfection of the body politic; to the safety as well as to the welfare of the society; the want of either is the want of an important Organ of political life and Motion; and in the various crises which await a state, it must severely feel the effects of any such deficiency. The extreme embarrassments of the United States during the late War, from an incapacity of supplying themselves, are still matter of keen recollection: A future war might be expected again to exemplify the mischiefs and dangers of a situation to which that incapacity is still too great a degree applicable, unless changed by timely and vigorous exertion. To effect this change, as fast as shall be prudent, merits all attention and all the Zeal of our Public Councils; 'tis the next great work to be accomplished.

The want of a Navy, to protect our external commerce, as long as it shall Continue, must render it a peculiarly precarious reliance, for the supply of essential articles, and must serve to strengthen prodigiously the arguments in favour of manufactures. . . .

In order to a better judgment of the Means proper to be resorted to by the United States, it will be of use to Advert to those which have been employed with success in other Countries. The principal of these are—

I. Protecting Duties—or Duties on Those Foreign Articles Which Are the Rivals of the Domestic Ones Intended to Be Encouraged

Duties of this nature evidently amount to a virtual bounty on the domestic fabrics since by enhancing the charges on foreign articles, they enable the National Manufacturers to undersell all their foreign Competitors. The propriety of this species of encouragement need not be dwelt upon, as it is not only a clear result from the numerous topics which have been suggested, but is sanctioned by the laws of the United States, in a variety of instances; it has the additional recommendation of being a resource of revenue. Indeed all the duties imposed on imported articles, though with an exclusive view to Revenue, have the effect in Contemplation, and except where they fall on raw materials wear a beneficent aspect toward the manufactures of the Country.

II. Prohibitions of Rival Articles, or Duties Equivalent to Prohibitions

Considering a monopoly of the domestic market to its own manufacturers as the reigning policy of manufacturing Nations, a similar policy on the part of the United States in every proper instance, is dictated, it might almost be said, by the principles of distributive justice; certainly, by the duty of endeavoring to secure to their own Citizens a reciprocity of advantages.

III. Prohibitions of the Exportation of the Materials of Manufactures

The desire of securing a cheap and plentiful supply for the national workmen, and where the article is either peculiar to the Country, or of peculiar quality there, the jealousy of enabling foreign workmen to rival those of the nation with its own Materials, are the leading motives to this species of regulation. It ought not to be affirmed, that it is in no instance proper, but it is, certainly one which ought to be adopted with great circumspection, and only in very plain Cases. . . .

IV. Pecuniary Bounties

This has been found one of the most efficacious means of encouraging manufactures, and, is in some views, the best. Though it has not yet been practiced upon by the Government of the United states (unless the allowance on the exportation of dried and pickled Fish and salted meat could be considered as a bounty), and though it is less favored by public Opinion than some other modes. . . .

A Question has been made concerning the Constitutional right of the Government of the United States to apply this species of encouragement, but there is certainly no good foundation for such a question. The National Legislature has express authority "To lay and Collect taxes, duties, imposts, and excises, to pay the Debts, and provide for the *Common defence* and *general welfare*." . . .

V. Premiums

These are of a nature allied to bounties, though distinguishable from them in some important features.

Bounties are applicable to the whole quantity of an article produced, or manufactured, or exported, and involve a correspondent expense. Premiums serve to reward some particular excellence or superiority, some extraordinary exertion or skill, and are dispensed only in a small number of cases. But their effect is to stimulate general effort, contrived so as to be both honorary and lucrative, they address themselves to different passions; touching the chords as well of emulation as of Interest. They are accordingly a very economical means of exciting the enterprise of a whole Community. . . .

VI. The Exemption of the Materials of Manufactures from Duties

The policy of that Exemption as a general rule particularly in reference to new Establishments is obvious. It can hardly ever be advisable to add the obstructions of fiscal burthens to the difficulties which naturally embarrass a new manufacture; and where it is matured and in condition to become an object of revenue it is generally speaking better that the fabric than the Material should be the subject of Taxation. . . .

VII. Drawbacks of the Duties Which Are Imposed on the Materials of Manufactures

It has already been observed as a general rule that duties on those materials ought with certain exceptions, to be forborne. Of these exceptions, three cases occur, which may serve as examples—one, where the material is itself an object of general or extensive consumption, and a lit and productive source of revenue: Another, where a manufacture of a simpler kind, the competition of which with a like domestic article is desired to be restrained, partakes of the Nature of a raw material, from being capable, by a further process to be converted into a manufacture of a different kind, the introduction or growth of which is desired to be encouraged; a third where the Material itself is a production of the country, and in sufficient abundance to furnish a cheap and plentiful supply to the national Manufacturers. . . .

VIII. The Encouragement of New Inventions and Discoveries, at Home, and of the Introduction into the United States of Such as May Have Been Made in Other Countries; Particularly Those Which Relate to Machinery

This is among the most useful and unexceptionable of the aids, which can be given to manufactures. The usual means of that encouragement are pecuniary rewards, and, for a time, exclusive privileges. The first must be employed according to the occasion, and the utility of the invention or discovery. For the last, so far as respects "authors and inventors," provision has been made by Law. But it is desirable, in regard to improvements, and secrets of extraordinary value, to be able to extend the same benefit to Introducers, as well as Authors and Inventors; a policy which has been practiced with advantage in other countries. . . .

IX. Judicious Regulations for the Inspection of Manufactured Commodities

This is not among the least important of the means by which the prosperity of manufactures may be promoted. It is indeed in many cases one of the most essential. Contributing to prevent frauds upon consumers at home and exporters to foreign countries, to improve the quality and preserve the character of the national manufactures, it cannot fail to aid the expeditious and advantageous sale of them, and to serve as a guard against successful competition from other quarters. . . .

X. The Facilitating of Pecuniary Remittances from Place to Place

—is a point of considerable moment to trade in general, and to manufactures in particular; by rendering more easy the purchase of raw materials and provisions and the payment for manufactured supplies. A general circulation of Bank paper, which is expected from the institution lately established will be most valuable mean to this end. But much good would also accrue from some additional provisions respecting inland bills of exchange. If those drawn in one state payable in another were made negotiable, everywhere, and interest and damages allowed in case of protest, it would greatly promote negotiations between the Citizens of different states, by rendering them more secure; and, with it the convenience and advantage of the Merchants and manufacturers of each.

XI. The Facilitating of the Transportation of Commodities

Improvements favoring this object intimately concern all domestic interests of a community; but they may without impropriety be mentioned as having an important relation to manufactures. There is perhaps

scarcely anything which has been better calculated to assist the manufacturers of Great Britain than the amelioration of the public roads of
that Kingdom, and the great progress which has been of late made in
opening canals. . . .

[After discussing the importance of a number of raw materials
and industries—iron, copper, lead, fossil coal, wood, skins, grain, flax
and hemp, cotton, wool, silk, glass, gunpowder, paper, printed books,
refined sugars, and chocolate—Hamilton concludes his *Report on Manufactures.—Eds.*]

The foregoing heads comprise the most important of the several
kinds of manufactures, which have occurred as requiring, and, at the
same time, as most proper for public encouragement; and such measures for affording it, as have appeared best calculated to answer the
end, have been suggested.

The observations, which have accompanied this delineation of
objects, supersede the necessity of many supplementary remarks. One
or two however may not be altogether superfluous.

Bounties are in various instances proposed as one species of
encouragement.

It is a familiar objection to them, that they are difficult to be
managed and liable to frauds. But neither that difficulty nor this danger
seems sufficiently great to countervail the advantages of which they are
productive, when rightly applied. And it is presumed to have been
shown, that they are in some cases, particularly in the infancy of new
enterprises, indispensable.

It will however be necessary to guard, with extraordinary circumspection, the manner of dispensing them. The requisite precautions
have been thought of; but to enter into the detail would swell this report, already voluminous, to a size too inconvenient.

If the principle shall not be deemed inadmissable the means of
avoiding an abuse of it will not be likely to present insurmountable obstacles. There are useful guides from practice in other quarters.

It shall therefore only be remarked here, in relations to this
point, that any bounty, which may be applied to the *manufacture* of an
article, cannot with safety extend beyond those manufactories, at which
the making of the articles is a *regular trade*. . . .

The possibility of a diminution of the revenue may also present
itself, as an objection to the arrangements, which have been submitted.

But there is no truth, which may be more firmly relied upon,
than that the interests of the revenue are promoted, by whatever promotes an increase of National industry and wealth.

In proportion to the degree of these, is the capacity of every
country to contribute to the public Treasury; and where the capacity
to pay is increased, or even is not decreased, the only consequence of

measures, which diminish any particular resource is a change of the object. If by encouraging the manufacture of an article at home, the revenue, which has been wont to accrue from its importation, should be lessened, an indemnification, can easily be found, either out of the manufacture itself, or from some other object, which may be deemed more convenient.

The measures however, which have been submitted, taken aggregately, will for a long time to come rather augment than decrease the public revenue.

There is little room to hope, that the progress of manufactures, will so equally keep pace with the progress of population, as to prevent, even, a gradual augmentation of the product of the duties on imported articles.

As, nevertheless, an abolition in some instances, and a reduction in others of duties, which have been pledged for the public debt, is proposed, it is essential, that it should be accompanied with a competent substitute. In order to this, it is requisite, that all the additional duties which shall be laid, be appropriated in the first instance, to replace all defalcations, which may proceed from any such abolition or diminution. It is evident, at first glance, that they will not only be adequate to this, but will yield a considerable surplus.

This surplus will serve:

First. To constitute a fund for paying the bounties which shall have been decreed.

Secondly. To constitute a fund for the operations of a Board to be established, for promoting Arts, Agriculture, Manufactures and Commerce. Of this institution, different intimations have been given, in the course of this report. An outline of a plan for it shall now be submitted.

Let a certain annual sum, be set apart, and placed under the management of Commissioners, not less than three, to consist of certain Officers of the Government and their Successors in Office.

Let these Commissioners be empowered to apply the fund confided to them to defray the expenses of the emigration of Artists and Manufacturers in particular branches of extraordinary importance—to induce the prosecution and introduction of useful discoveries, inventions, and improvements, by proportionate rewards, judiciously held out and applied—to encourage by premiums both honorable and lucrative the exertions of individuals, and of classes, in relation to the several objects they are charged with promoting—and to afford such other aids to those objects as may be generally designated by law.

The Commissioners to render to the Legislature an annual account of their transactions and disbursements; and all such sums as shall not have been applied to the purposes of their trust, at the end of every three years, to revert to the Treasury. It may also be enjoined upon them not to draw out the money, but for the purpose of some specific disbursement.

It may, moreover, be of use to authorize them to receive voluntary contributions, making it their duty to apply them to the particular objects for which they may have been made, if any shall have been designated by the donors.

There is reason to believe that the progress of particular manufactures has been much retarded by the want of skilful workmen. And it often happens, that the capitals employed are not equal to the purposes of bringing from abroad workmen of a superior kind. Here, in cases worthy of it, the auxiliary agency of Government would, in all probability, be useful. There are also valuable workmen in every branch, who are prevented from emigrating solely by the want of means. Occasional aids to such persons properly administered might be a source of valuable acquisitions to the country.

The propriety of stimulating by rewards, the invention and introduction of useful improvements, is admitted without difficulty. But the success of attempts in this way must evidently depend much on the manner of conducting them. It is probable, that the placing of the dispensation of those rewards under some proper discretionary direction, where they may be accompanied by *collateral expedients*, will serve to give them the surest efficacy. It seems impracticable to apportion, by general rules, specific compensations for discoveries of unknown and disproportionate utility.

The great use which may be made of a fund of this nature, to procure and import foreign improvements is particularly obvious. Among these, the article of machines would form a most important item.

The operation and utility of premiums have been adverted to; together with the advantages which have resulted from their dispensation, under the direction of certain public and private societies. Of this some experience has been had, in the instance of the Pennsylvania Society for Promotion of Manufactures and useful Arts; but the funds of that association have been too contracted to produce more than a very small portion of the good to which the principles of it would have led. It may confidently be affirmed that there is scarcely any thing which has been devised, better calculated to excite a general spirit of improvement than the institutions of this nature. They are truly invaluable.

In countries where there is great private wealth, much may be effected by the voluntary contributions of patriotic individuals; but in a community situated like that of the United States, the public purse must supply the deficiency of private resource. In what can it be so useful, as in prompting and improving the efforts of industry?

All which is humbly submitted.
Alexander Hamilton, Secy of the Treasury.

7

THE THEORY OF HEGEMONIC STABILITY AND CHANGES IN INTERNATIONAL ECONOMIC REGIMES, 1967–1977

Robert O. Keohane

When attempting to describe the neorealist version of hegemonic stability theory, scholars often cite this work by Robert Keohane because it offers a clear explanation of the tenets and assumptions of the theory. Neorealists, such as Robert Gilpin, believe the state is the most important actor in the international system and that states need a powerful leader to ensure compliance with the rules. If the hegemonic leader chooses to enforce a set of neoliberal rules, the international system will be characterized by monetary and exchange stability, free trade, and a high potential for global economic growth. When challengers to the hegemon arise, the system, according to neorealist thought, becomes economically unstable and violent. Keohane found some support for this theory. One of his primary criticisms surrounds the measurement of power. Hegemonic stability theorists, Keohane believes, lean too heavily upon tangible resources (gross domestic product, oil import dependence, and similar factors) in their measurements of power, whereas intangibles—such as confidence in a currency or in some political positions relative to others—receive too little attention or weight.

Europe and Japan had recovered impressively from World War II and during the 1960s the United States had been enjoying strong, sustained

Reprinted with permission from "The Theory of Hegemonic Stability and Changes in International Regimes, 1967–1977," in *Changes in the International System*, eds. Ole Holsti, Randolph Siverson, and Alexander George. Boulder: Westview Press, 1980, pp. 131–132, 136–149, 151–152, 154–155.

economic growth as well. Both unemployment and inflation in seven major industrialized countries stood at an average of only 2.8 percent. International trade had been growing even faster than output, which was expanding at about 5 percent annually; and direct investment abroad was increasing at an even faster rate.[1] The Kennedy Round of trade talks was successfully completed in June 1967; in the same month, the threat of an oil embargo by Arab countries in the wake of an Israeli-Arab war had been laughed off by the Western industrialized states. Fixed exchange rates prevailed; gold could still be obtained from the United States in exchange for dollars; and a prospective "international money," Special Drawing Rights (SDRs), was created in 1967 under the auspices of the International Monetary Fund (IMF). The United States, "astride the world like a colossus," felt confident enough of its power and position to deploy half a million men to settle the affairs of Vietnam. U.S. power and dynamism constituted the problem or the promise; "the American challenge" was global. Conservative and radical commentators alike regarded U.S. dominance as the central reality of contemporary world politics, although they differed as to whether its implications were benign or malign (Liska, 1967; Servan-Schreiber, 1969; Magdoff, 1969).

A decade later the situation was very different. Unemployment rates in the West had almost doubled while inflation rates had increased almost threefold. Surplus capacity had appeared in the steel, textiles, and ship-building industries, and was feared in others (Strange, 1979). Confidence that Keynesian policies could ensure uninterrupted growth had been undermined if not shattered. Meanwhile, the United States had been defeated in Vietnam and no longer seemed to have either the capability or inclination to extend its military domination to the far corners of the world. The inability of the United States to prevent or counteract the oil price increases of 1973–1974 seemed to symbolize the drastic changes that had taken place. . . .

Explaining Changes in International Regimes

A parsimonious theory of international regime change has recently been developed by a number of authors, notably Charles Kindleberger, Robert Gilpin, and Stephen Krasner. According to this theory, strong international economic regimes depend on hegemonic power. Fragmentation of power between competing countries leads to fragmentation of the international economic regime; concentration of power contributes to stability.[2] Hegemonic powers have the capabilities to maintain international regimes that they favor. They may use coercion to enforce adherence to rules; or they may rely largely on positive sanctions—the provision of benefits to those who cooperate. Both hegemonic power and the smaller states may have incentives to collaborate in maintaining a regime—the hegemonic power gains the ability to shape and dominate its international environment, while providing a sufficient flow of benefits to small middle powers to persuade them to acquiesce. Some international regimes can be seen partially as collective goods, whose benefits (such as stable money) can be consumed by all participants without detracting from others' enjoyment of them. Insofar as this is the case, economic theory leads us to expect that extremely large, dominant countries will be particularly willing to provide these goods, while relatively small participants will attempt to secure "free rides" by avoiding proportionate shares of payment. International systems with highly skewed distributions of capabilities will therefore tend to be more amply supplied with such collective goods than systems characterized by equality among actors.[3]

The particular concern of this chapter is the erosion of international economic regimes. The hegemonic stability theory seeks sources of erosion in changes in the relative capabilities of states. As the distribution of tangible resources, especially economic resources, becomes more equal, international regimes should weaken. One reason for this is that the capabilities of the hegemonial power will decline—it will become less capable of enforcing rules against unwilling participants, and it will have fewer resources with which to entice or bribe other states into remaining within the confines of the regime. Yet the incentives facing governments will also change. As the hegemonial state's margin of resource superiority over its partners declines, the costs of leadership will become more burdensome. Enforcement of rules will be more difficult and side payments will seem less justifiable. Should other states—now increasingly strong economic rivals—not have to contribute their "fair shares" to the collective enterprise? The hegemon (or former hegemon) is likely to seek to place additional burdens on its allies. At the same time, the incentives of the formerly subordinate secondary states will change. They will not only become more capable of reducing their support for the regime; they may acquire new interests in doing so. On the one hand, they will perceive the possibility of rising above their subordinate status, and they may even glimpse the prospect of reshaping the international regime in order better to suit their own interests. On the other hand, they may begin to worry that their efforts (and those of others) in chipping away at the hegemonial power and its regime may be too successful—that the regime itself may collapse. This fear, however, may lead them to take further action to hedge their bets, reducing their reliance on the hegemonial regime and perhaps attempting to set up alternative arrangements of their own.

As applied to the last century and a half, this theory—which will be referred to as the "hegemonic stability" theory—does well at identifying apparently necessary conditions for strong international economic regimes, but poorly at establishing sufficient conditions. International economic regimes have been most orderly and predictable where there was a single hegemonic state in the world system: Britain during the mid-nineteenth century in trade and until 1914 in international financial affairs; the United States after 1945. Yet although tangible U.S. power resources were large during the interwar period, international economic regimes were anything but orderly. High inequality of capabilities was not, therefore, a sufficient condition for strong international regimes; there was in the case of the United States a lag between its attainment of capabilities and its acquisition of a willingness to exert leadership, or of a taste for domination depending on point of view.[4]

The concern here is not with the validity of the hegemonic stability theory throughout the last 150 years, but with its ability to account for changes in international economic regimes during the decade between 1967 and 1977. Since the United States remained active during those years as the leading capitalist country, the problem of "leadership lag" does not exist, which raises difficulties for the interpretation of the interwar period. Thus the theory should apply to the 1967–1977 period. Insofar as "potential economic power" (Krasner's term) became more equally distributed—reducing the share of the United States—during the 1960s and early to mid-1970s, U.S.-created and U.S.-centered international economic regimes should also have suffered erosion or decline.

The hegemonic stability thesis is a power-as-resource theory, which attempts to link tangible state capabilities (conceptualized as "power resources") to behavior. In its simplest form, it is what James G. March calls a "basic force model" in which outcomes reflect the potential power (tangible and known capabilities) of actors. Basic force models typically fail to predict accurately particular political outcomes, in part because differential opportunity costs often lead competing actors to use different proportions of their potential power. Yet they offer clearer and more easily interpretable explanations than "force activation models," which incorporate assumptions about differential exercise of power.[5] Regarding tendencies rather than particular decisions, they are especially useful in establishing a baseline, a measure of what can be accounted for by the very parsimonious theory that tangible resources are directly related to outcomes, in this case to the nature of international regimes. The hegemonic stability theory, which is systemic and parsimonious, therefore seems to constitute a useful starting point for analysis, on the assumption that it is valuable to see how much can be learned from simple explanations before proceeding to more complex theoretical formulations.

Ultimately, it will be necessary to integrate systemic analysis with explanations at the level of foreign policy. Domestic forces help to explain changes in the international political structure; changes in the international political structure affect domestic institutions and preferences (Gourevitch, 1978: 881–912). This chapter focuses only on one part of the overall research problem: the relationship between international structure and international regimes. It examines to what extent changes in recent international economic regimes can be accounted for by changes in international power distributions within the relevant issue areas.

Changes in International Economic Regimes, 1967–1977

The dependent variable in this analysis is international regime change between 1967 and 1977 in three issues areas: international monetary relations, trade in manufactured goods, and the production and sale of petroleum. These are not the only important areas of international economic activity—for example, foreign investment is not included—but they are among the most important.[6] Descriptive contentions about international regime change in the three chosen areas are that (1) all three international regimes existing in 1967 became weaker during the subsequent decade; (2) this weakening was most pronounced in the petroleum area and in monetary relations, where the old norms were destroyed and very different practices emerged—it was less sudden and less decisive in the field of trade; and (3) in the areas of trade and money, the dominant political coalitions supporting the regime remained largely the same, although in money certain countries (especially Saudi Arabia) were added to the inner "club," whereas in the petroleum issue area, power shifted decisively from multinational oil companies and governments of major industrialized countries to producing governments. Taking all three dimensions into account, it is clear that regime change was most pronounced during the decade in oil and least pronounced in trade in manufactured goods, with the international monetary regime occupying an intermediate position.

These descriptive contentions will now be briefly documented and then interpreted, inquiring about the extent to which the hegemonic stability theory accounts for these changes in international economic regimes.

The international trade regime of the General Agreement on Tariffs and Trade was premised on the principles of reciprocity, liberalization, and nondiscrimination. Partly as a result of its success, world trade had increased since 1950 at a much more rapid rate than world production. Furthermore, tariff liberalization was continuing: in mid-1967 the Kennedy round was successfully completed, substantially reducing tariffs on a wide range of industrial products. Yet despite its obvious successes, the GATT trade regime in 1967 was already showing signs of stress. The reciprocity and nondiscrimination provisions of GATT were already breaking down. Tolerance for illegal trade restrictions had grown, few formal complaints were being processed, and by 1967 GATT did not even require states maintaining illegal quantitative restrictions to obtain formal waivers of the rules. The "general breakdown in GATT legal affairs" had gone very far indeed, largely as a result of toleration of illegal restrictions such as the variable levy of the European Economic Community (EEC), EEC association agreements, and export subsidies (Hudec, 1975: 256; Patterson, 1965). In addition, nontariff barriers, which were not dealt with effectively by GATT codes, were becoming more important. The trade regime in 1967 was thus strongest in the area of tariff liberalization, but less effective on nontariff barriers or in dealing with discrimination.

In the decade ending in 1967 the international monetary regime was explicit, formally institutionalized, and highly stable. Governments belonging to the International Monetary Fund were to maintain official par values for their currencies, which could be changed only to correct a "fundamental disequilibrium" and only in consultation with the IMF. During these nine years, the rules were largely followed; parity changes for major currencies were few and minor.[7] In response to large U.S. deficits in its overall liquidity balance of payments, the U.S. government introduced an Interest Equalization Tax in 1963 and voluntary capital controls in 1965; in addition, a variety of ingenious if somewhat ephemeral expedients had been devised, both to improve official U.S. balance of payments statements and to provide for cooperative actions by central banks or treasuries to counteract the effects of destabilizing capital flows. Until November 1967 even British devaluation (seen by many as imminent in 1964) had been avoided. Nevertheless, as in trade, signs of weakness in the system were apparent. U.S. deficits had to a limited extent already undermined confidence in the dollar; and the United States was fighting a costly war in Vietnam which it was attempting to finance without tax increases at home. Consequently, inflation was increasing in the United States (Shapiro, in Krause and Salant, 1977).

The international regime for oil was not explicitly defined by inter-governmental agreement in 1967. There was no global international organization supervising the energy regime. Yet, as mentioned above, the governing arrangements for international oil production and trade were rather clear. With the support of their home governments, the major international oil companies cooperated to control production and, within limits, price. The companies were unpopular in the host countries, and these host country governments put the companies on the defensive on particular issues, seeking increased revenue or increased control. However, as Turner puts it, "the critical fact is that the companies did not really lose control of their relationship with host governments until the 1970s, when the concessionary system finally came close to being swept away. The long preceding decade of the 1960s had seen only minimal improvement for the host governments in the terms under which the majors did business with them" (Turner, 1978: 70). The companies retained superior financial resources and capabilities in production, transportation, and marketing that the countries could not attain. Furthermore, the companies possessed superior information: "Whatever the weakness of company defences which is apparent in retrospect, the host governments did not realize it at the time. Their knowledge of the complexities of the industry was scanty, their experience of serious bargaining with the companies was limited and their awe of the companies was great" (Turner, 1978: 94–95).

In addition, and perhaps most important, the feudal and semi-feudal elites that controlled many oil-producing countries until the end of the 1960s were more often concerned with their personal and family interests than with modernization or national interests on a larger scale.

Although the U.S. government did not participate directly in oil production or trade, it was the most influential actor in the system. The United States had moved decisively during and after World War II to ensure that U.S. companies would continue to control Saudi Arabian oil (Kolko, 1968: 294–307; Krasner, 1978: 190–205; Feis, 1944, 1947: 104; Shwadran, 1955: 302–309; U.S. GPO, 1943, 1944: v. 4: 941–948; v. 3: 94–111). Later, when the Anglo-Iranian Oil Company became unwelcome as sole concessionaire in Iran, the United States sponsored an arrangement by which U.S. firms received 40 percent of the consortium established in the wake of the U.S.-sponsored coup that overthrew Premier Mossadegh and restored the shah to his throne (Krasner, 1978: 119–128; Kolko, 1972: 413–420; Blair, 1976: 43–47, 78–80; U.S. Congress, 1974b). U.S. tax policy was changed in 1950 to permit U.S. oil companies to increase payments to producing governments without sacrificing profits, thus solidifying the U.S. position in the Middle East and Venezuela (U.S. Congress, 1974a: 84–110; Jenkins and Wright, 1975; Krasner, 1978: 205–213). The United States had provided military aid and political support to the rulers of Saudi Arabia and Iran, maintaining close relations with them throughout the first two postwar decades (except for the Mossadegh period in Iran). And in case of trouble—as in 1956–1957—the United States was willing to use its own reserves to supply Europe with petroleum (U.S. Congress, 1957; OECD,

1958; Eisenhower, 1957: 124). The governing arrangements for oil thus reflected the U.S. government's interests in an ample supply of oil at stable or declining prices, close political ties with conservative Middle Eastern governments, and profits for U.S.-based multinational companies.

The international economic regime of 1977 looked very different. Least affected was the trade regime, although even here important changes had taken place. Between 1967 and 1977, nontariff barriers to trade continued to proliferate, and the principle of nondiscrimination was further undermined. Restrictions on textile imports from less developed countries, originally limited to cotton textiles, were extended to woolen and manmade fabrics in 1974 (GATT, 1974; UNCTAD, 1977).[8] Nontariff barriers affecting world steel trade in the early 1970s included import licensing, foreign exchange restrictions, quotas, export limitations, domestic-biased procurement, subsidies, import surcharges, and antidumping measures (MacPhee, 1974). During the 1970s, "voluntary" export restraints, which had covered about one-eighth of U.S. imports in 1971, were further extended (Bergsten, 1975b). In late 1977, the United States devised a "trigger price system" to help protect the U.S. steel industry from low-priced imports. Contemporaneously, the European Economic Community launched an ambitious program to protect and rationalize some of its basic industries afflicted with surplus but relatively inefficient capacity, such as steel and shipbuilding. On the basis of a general survey, the GATT secretariat estimated tentatively in 1977 that import restrictions introduced or seriously threatened by industrially advanced countries since 1974 would affect 3–5 percent of world trade—$30 to $50 billion. The stresses on the international trade system, according to the director-general of GATT, "have now become such that they seriously threaten the whole fabric of postwar cooperation in international trade policy" (IMF Survey, 12 Dec. 1977: 373).

Nevertheless, the weakening of some aspects of the international trade regime had not led, by the end of 1977, to reductions in trade or to trade wars; in fact, after a 4 percent decline in 1975, the volume of world trade rose 11 percent in 1976 and 4 percent in 1977 (IMF Survey, 20 Mar. 1978: 81, and 18 Sept. 1978: 285). Furthermore, by 1977 the Tokyo round of trade negotiations was well underway; in 1979 agreement was reached on trade liberalizing measures that not only would (if put into effect) reduce tariffs on industrial products, but that would also limit or prohibit a wide range of nontariff barriers, including export subsidies, national preferences on government procurement, and excessively complex import licensing procedures (New York Times, 12 Apr. 1979). The weakening of elements of the old regime was therefore accompanied both by expanding trade (although at a lower rate than before 1973) and by efforts to strengthen the rules in a variety of areas.

By 1977 the international monetary regime had changed much more dramatically. The pegged-rate regime devised at Bretton Woods had collapsed in 1971, and its jerry-built successor had failed in 1973. Since then, major currencies had been floating against one another, their values affected both by market forces and frequently extensive governmental intervention. In 1976 international agreement was reached on amendments to the Articles of Agreement of the International Monetary Fund, yet this did not return the world to stable international exchange rates or multilateral rule making but merely provided for vaguely defined "multilateral surveillance" of floating exchange rates. Exchange rates have fluctuated quite sharply at times, and have certainly been more unpredictable than they were in the 1960s. Substantial secular changes have also taken place; nominal effective exchange rates on 15 May 1978, as a percentage of the rates prevailing in March 1973, ranged from 58.6 for Italy to 130.0 for Germany and 154.2 for Switzerland (Morgan Guaranty Trust Co., 1978).

In the oil area, the rules of the old regime were shattered between 1967 and 1977, as power shifted dramatically from the multinational oil companies and home governments (especially the United States and Britain), on the one hand, to producing countries' governments, on the other. The latter, organized since 1960 in the Organization of Petroleum Exporting Countries, secured a substantial price rise in negotiations at Teheran in 1971, then virtually quadrupled prices without negotiation after the Yom Kippur War of October 1973. Despite some blustering and various vague threats the United States could do little directly about this, although high rates of inflation in industrial countries and the decline of the dollar in 1977 helped to reduce substantially the real price of oil between 1974 and 1977 (Morgan Guaranty Trust Co., 1978).[9] By 1977 the United States had apparently conceded control of the regime for oil pricing and production to OPEC, and particularly to its key member, Saudi Arabia. OPEC made the rules in 1977, influenced (but not controlled) by the United States. Only in case of a crippling supply embargo would the United States be likely to act. The United States was still, with its military and economic strength, an influential actor, but it was no longer dominant.

Reviewing this evidence about three international economic regimes supports the generalizations offered earlier. Although all three old regimes became weaker during the decade, this was most pronounced for oil and money, least for trade. In oil, furthermore, dominant coalitions changed as well, so that by 1977 the regime that existed, dominated by OPEC countries, was essentially a *new regime*. The old petroleum regime had disappeared. By contrast, the 1977 trade regime was still a recognizable version of the regime existing in 1967; and the international monetary regime of 1977, although vastly different than in 1967, retained the same core of supportive states along with the same international organization, the IMF, as its monitoring agent. Since the rules had changed, the function of the IMF had also changed; but it persisted as an element, as well as a symbol, of continuity. In the oil area, the emergence of the International Energy Agency (IEA) after the oil embargo symbolized discontinuity: only after losing control of the pricing-production regime did it become necessary for the industrialized countries to construct their own formal international organization.

The Theory of Hegemonic Stability and International Regime Change

It should be apparent from the above account that a theory purporting to explain international economic regime change between 1967 and 1977 faces two tasks: first, to account for the *general pattern* of increasing weakness, and second, to explain why the oil regime experienced the most serious changes, followed by money and trade. Furthermore, hegemonic stability theory must show not only a correspondence between patterns of regime change and changes in tangible power resources, but it must be possible to provide at least a plausible account of how those resource changes could have caused the regime changes that we observe.

The most parsimonious version of a hegemonic stability theory would be that changes in the *overall* international economic structure account for the changes in international regimes that we have described. Under this interpretation, a decline in U.S. economic power (as measured crudely by gross domestic product) would be held responsible for changes in international economic regimes. Power in this view would be seen as a fungible set of tangible economic resources that can be used for a variety of purposes in world politics.

There are conceptual as well as empirical problems with this parsimonious overall structure theory. The notion that power resources are fungible—that they can be allocated to issues as policymakers choose, without losing efficacy—is not very plausible in world political economy. . . . A second problem with the overall structure version of the hegemonic stability thesis is itself contextual: since we have to account not only for the general pattern of increasing weakness but also for differential patterns by issue area, focusing on a single independent variable will clearly not suffice. Changes in the overall U.S. economic position will clearly not explain different patterns of regime change in different issue areas.

Table 7.1 indicates the gross domestic product of the United States and the five other major market economy countries. As the last column indicates, the U.S. share of gross domestic product (GDP) of all five countries fell between 1960 and 1975 from about two-thirds to about one-half of the total five-country GDP. This is consistent with the hegemonic stability thesis, although one can question whether such a moderate decline (leaving the United States more than triple the economic size of its nearest competitor) accounts very convincingly for the regime changes that have been observed. . . .

Table 7.2 summarizes the evidence about changes in the distribution of economic power resources in the areas of trade, money, and petroleum. For trade and money the same comparative measures are used, similar to those used in Table 7.1: the U.S. proportion of resources is compared to that of the top five market-economy countries taken as a group. This measure can be justified on the grounds that only Germany, Britain, France and Japan were strong enough during this period to consider challenging the United States or attempting to thwart it in significant ways; they are the potential rivals against whom it is significant to measure U.S. resources. The measures have to be somewhat different for petroleum. The relevant resources here appear to be U.S. imports vs. excess production capacity (since in 1956–1957 and 1967 the United States helped to maintain the existing regime by shipping oil to Europe from its own wells), and oil imports as a percentage of energy supply, giving a measure of relative U.S. and European dependence on imports.[10]

None of these measures of "economic power" is perfect; indeed, they are quite crude. Often the composition of exports, for instance, may be as important as the amount; and the balance of trade may in some cases weigh as heavily as the combinations of imports and exports. Probably most deficient is the monetary measure, since reserves are not

Table 7.1 Distribution of Overall Economic Resources Among the Five Major Market-Economy Countries, 1960–1975
(gross domestic product in billions of current U.S. dollars)

Year	United States	Germany	Britain	France	Japan	U.S. Percent of Top Five Countries
1960	507	72	71	61	43	67
1963	594	95	85	83	68	64
1970	981	185	122	141	197	60
1975	1526	419	229	335	491	51

Source: United Nations Statistical Yearbook, 1977, pp. 742–744. Last column calculated from these figures.

Table 7.2   Distribution of Economic Resources, by Issue Area, Among the Five Major Market-Economy Countries, 1960–1975

A. Trade Resources (exports plus imports as percentage of world trade)

Year	United States	Germany	Britain	France	Japan	U.S. as Percent of Top Five Countries
1960	13.4	8.1	8.7	4.9	3.3	35
1965	14.4	9.4	8.0	5.7	4.2	35
1970	15.0	11.0	6.9	6.3	6.2	33
1975	13.0	10.0	5.8	6.4	6.6	31

Source: Kenneth N. Waltz, *Theory of International Politics* (Reading, Mass.: Addison-Wesley, 1979), Appendix Table IV, p. 215. Last column calculated from these figures.

B. Monetary Resources (reserves as percentage of world reserves)

Year	United States	Germany	Britain	France	Japan	U.S. as Percent of Top Five Countries
1960	32.4	11.8	6.2	3.8	3.3	56
1965	21.8	10.5	4.2	9.0	3.0	45
1970	15.5	10.7	3.0	5.3	5.2	39
1975	7.0	13.6	2.4	5.5	5.6	21

Source: Calculated from *International Financial Statistics* (Washington, D.C.: IMF), Volume XXXI-5 (May, 1978), 1978 Supplement, pp. 34–35. Last column calculated from these percentages.

C. Petroleum Resources
   1. United States imports and excess production capacity in three crisis years

Year	U.S. Oil Imports as Percent of Oil Consumption	U.S. Excess Production Capacity as Percent of Oil Consumption	Ratio of U.S. to European Position
1956	11	25	+14
1967	19	25	+6
1973	35	10	−25

Source: Joel Darmstadter and Hans H. Landsberg, "The Economic Background," in Raymond Vernon, ed., *The Oil Crisis*, special issue of *Daedalus*, Fall 1975 (pp. 30–31).

   2. Oil imports as percentage of energy supply

Year	United States	Western Europe	Japan	Ratio of U.S. to European Dependence
1967	9	50	62	.18
1970	10	57	73	.18
1973	17	60	80	.28
1976	20	54	74	.37

Source: Kenneth N. Waltz, *Theory of International Politics* (Reading, Mass.: Addison-Wesley, 1979) Appendix Table X, p. 221. Last column calculated from these figures.

necessarily an indicator of a country's *net* positions. Measures of the U.S. net liquidity position, however, would also show a sharp decline (U.S. GPO, 1971: 40; *International Economic Report of the President*, 1977: 161).[11]

The figures on economic resources provide prima facie support for the hegemonic stability thesis. The U.S. proportion of trade, for the top five market-economy countries, fell only slightly between 1960 and 1975—much less than its proportion of gross domestic product, reflecting the rapid increases during these years in U.S. trade as a proportion of total product. As we saw, the international trade regime—already under pressure in 1967—changed less in the subsequent decade than the regimes for money and oil. U.S. financial resources in the form of reserves fell sharply, reflecting the shift from U.S. dominance in 1960 to the struggles over exchange rates of the 1970s. In view of the continued ability of the United States to finance its deficits with newly printed dollars and treasury bills rather than with reserves, Table 7.2, B should not over interpreted: it does *not* mean that Germany was "twice as powerful as the United States" in the monetary area by 1975. Yet it does, as indicated above, signal a very strong shift in the resource situation of the United States. Finally, the petroleum figures—especially in Table 7.2, C-1—are dramatic: the United States went from a large positive position in 1956 and a small positive position in 1967 to a very large petroleum deficit by 1973. The hegemonic stability theory accurately predicts from this data that U.S. power in the oil area and the stability of the old international oil regime would decline sharply during the 1970s.

These findings lend plausibility to the hegemonic stability theory by not disconfirming its predictions. They do not, however, establish its validity, before concluding that the theory accounts for the observed changes, to see whether plausible causal sequences can be constructed linking shifts in the international distribution of power to changes in international regimes. The following sections of this [chapter] therefore consider the most plausible and well-founded particular accounts of changes in our three issue areas, to see whether the causal arguments in these accounts are consistent with the hegemonic stability theory. The ensuing discussion begins with oil, since it fits the theory so well, and then addresses the more difficult cases. . . .

Interpreting Changes in the Petroleum Regime

The hegemonic stability model leads us to expect a change in international petroleum arrangements during the mid-1970s: The dominance of the United States and other industrialized countries was increasingly being undermined, as OPEC members gained potential power resources at their expense. What the Yom Kippur War did was to make the Arab members of OPEC willing to take greater risks. When their actions succeeded in quadrupling the price of oil almost overnight, mutual confidence rose that members of the cartel who cut back production would not be "double-crossed" by other producers, but would rather benefit from the externalities (high prices as a result of supply shortages) created by others' similar actions. Calculations about externalities became positive and risks fell. A self-reinforcing cycle of underlying resource strength leading to success, to increased incentives to cooperate, and to greater strength was launched. . . .

Interpreting Changes in the International Monetary Regime

On the basis of the hegemonic stability theory, one would predict that the major financial powers would have had great difficulty reconstructing the international monetary regime after the events of 1971. Yet the theory's precise prediction would have been ambiguous. As Table 7.1 indicates, in the early 1970s the gross domestic product of the United States still exceeded the combined total of the four next largest market-economy countries. Unilateral U.S. actions, furthermore, had strengthened the U.S. position and made its weak official reserve position less relevant. Thus there was some reason to believe that it might have been possible to reconstruct a stable international monetary regime under U.S. leadership in 1971.

This, of course, failed to occur. The exchange rates established at the Smithsonian Institution in December 1971 collapsed within fifteen months. The United States was no more willing after 1971 to play a responsible, constrained international role than it had been during the six years before the destruction of the Bretton Woods regime. Indeed, the U.S. monetary expansion of 1972, which helped to secure Richard Nixon's reelection, implied a decision by the administration to abandon that role.[12] Had its own economic policies been tailored to international demands, the United States could probably in 1971 have resumed leadership of a reconstructed international monetary system; but the United States did not have sufficient power to compel others to accept a regime in which only it would have monetary autonomy. Between 1971 and 1976, the United States was the most influential actor in international monetary negotiations, and secured a weak flexible exchange rate regime that was closer to its own preferences than to those of its partners; but given its own penchant for monetary autonomy, it could not construct a strong, stable new regime. . . .

Interpreting Changes in the International Trade Regime

As has been seen, changes in the trade regime between 1967 and 1977 were broadly consistent with changes in potential power resources in the issue area. Power resources (as measured by shares of world trade among the industrialized countries) changed less in trade than in money or oil; and the regime changed less as well. So once again, the hegemonic stability theory is not disconfirmed.

The causal argument of the hegemonic stability theory, however, implies that the changes we do observe in trade (which are less than those in money and oil but are by no means insignificant) should be ascribable to changes in international political structure. Yet this does not appear to be the case. Protectionism is largely a grass-roots phenomenon, reflecting the desire of individuals for economic security and stability and of privileged groups for higher incomes than they would command in a free market. Adam Smith excoriated guilds for protecting the wages of their members at the expense of society (although to the advantage, he thought, of the towns) (Smith, 1776). Officials of the GATT now criticize labor unions and inefficient industries for seeking similar protection and attempt to refute their arguments that such actions would increase national as well as group income. Most governments of advanced capitalist states show little enthusiasm for protectionist policies, but have been increasingly goaded into them by domestic interests. . . .

To some extent, difficulties in maintaining liberal trade among the OECD countries do reflect erosion of U.S. hegemony, although this is more pronounced as compared with the 1950s than with the late 1960s. In the 1950s the United States was willing to open its markets to Japanese goods in order to integrate Japan into the world economic system, even when most European states refused to do so promptly or fully. This has been much less the case in recent years. Until the European Common Market came into existence, the United States dominated trade negotiations; but since the EEC has been active, it has successfully demanded numerous exceptions to GATT rules. Relative equality in trade-related power resources between the EEC and the United States seems to have been a necessary, if not sufficient, condition for this shift.

On the whole, the hegemonic stability theory does not explain recent changes in international trade regimes as well as it explains changes in money or oil. The theory is not disconfirmed by the trade evidence, and correctly anticipates less regime change in trade than in money or oil; but it is also not very helpful in interpreting the changes that we do observe. Most major forces affecting the trade regime have little to do with the decline of U.S. power. For an adequate explanation of changes in trade, domestic political and economic patterns, and the strategies of domestic political actors, would have to be taken into account.

Hegemonic Stability and Complex Interdependence: A Conclusion

A structural approach to international regime change, differentiated by issue area, takes us some distance toward a sophisticated understanding of recent changes in the international politics of oil, money, and trade. Eroding U.S. hegemony helps to account for political reversals in petroleum politics, to a lesser extent for the disintegration of the Bretton Woods international monetary regime, and to a still lesser extent for the continuing decay of the GATT-based trade regime.

Table 7.3 summarizes the results of the analysis. There is a definite correspondence between the expectations of a hegemonic stability theory and the evidence presented here. Changes in tangible power resources by issue area and changes in regimes tend to go together. In terms of causal analysis, however, the results are more mixed. In the petroleum area a plausible and compelling argument links changes in potential economic power resources directly with outcomes. With some significant caveats and qualifications, this is also true in international monetary politics; but in trade, the observed changes do not seem causally related to shifts in international political structure.

On the basis of this evidence, we should be cautious about putting the hegemonic stability theory forward as a powerful explanation of events. It is clearly useful as a first step; to ignore its congruence with reality, and its considerable explanatory power, would be foolish. Nevertheless, it carries with it the conceptual difficulties and ambiguities characteristic of power analysis. Power is viewed in terms of resources; if the theory is to be operationized, these resources have to be tangible. Gross domestic product, oil import dependence, international monetary reserves, and share of world trade are crude indicators of power in this sense. Less tangible resources such as confidence (in oneself or in a currency) or political position relative to other actors are not taken into account. Yet these sources of influence would seem to be conceptually as close to what is meant by "power resources" as are the more tangible and measurable factors listed above. Tangible resource models, therefore, are inherently crude and can hardly serve as more than first-cut approximations—very rough models that indicate the range of possible behavior or the probable path of change, rather than offering precise predictions.

Table 7.3   Hegemonic Stability and International Economic Regimes 1966–1977: An Analytic Summary

| | Issue Area | | |
	Oil	Money	Trade
Correspondence between changes in power resources and changes in international regimes:			
Extent of change in tangible power resources, 1965–1977 (rank orders)	1	2	3
Extent of change in regime, 1967–1977 (rank orders)	1	2	3
Causal links:			
Plausibility of causal argument linking tangible resource changes to changes in the regime	high	medium	low

Notes

1. For figures relating to these points, see McCracken et al. (1977) esp. pp. 41–42. Cited below as "McCracken Report."
2. For analysis along these lines, see the following: Kindleberger (1974); Gilpin (1975); and Krasner (1976) pp. 317–347.
3. Kindleberger relies most heavily on the theory of collective goods. See his "Systems of International Economic Organization," in Calleo (1976) pp. 19–20; and Kindleberger, *The World in Depression*, chap. 14. It is necessary to be cautious in viewing international regimes as "collective goods," since in many cases rivalry may exist (everyone may benefit from stable money but not everyone can benefit noncompetitively from an open U.S. market for imported electronic products) and countries can be excluded from many international regimes (as the debate over whether to give most-favored-nation status to the Soviet Union illustrates). On the provision of collective goods, a useful article is Olson and Zeckhauser (1966) 48:266–279, reprinted in Russett (1968). See also Ruggie (1972) 66. September: 874–893.
4. Both Krasner, "State Power," and Kindleberger, *World in Depression*, make this admission. The hegemonic stability theory is criticized by Calleo (1976) in his concluding essay in Rowland. Calleo dislikes hegemony and seems reluctant to admit its association with economic order; he therefore seeks both to reinterpret the pre-1914 period as not "imperial," and to characterize the bloc system of the 1930s as having "worked relatively well." Harold van B.

Cleveland and Benjamin Rowland make better differentiated arguments in the same volume that critique or qualify the hegemonic stability thesis.

5. The problem with "force activation models" is that such models can "save" virtually any hypothesis, since one can always think of reasons, after the fact, why an actor may not have used all available potential power. See March, in Easton (1966), esp. pp. 54–61. See also Harsanyi (1962): 67–80.

6. Recent work on foreign investment indicates that international regimes in this area have also changed since 1967. See Krasner (1978); and Lipson (forthcoming).

7. For good discussions, see Cohen (1977); Bergsten (1975a); Eckes, Jr. (1975); and Hirsch (1967).

8. This was accomplished by the Arrangement Regarding International Trade in Textiles, known as the "Multifiber Agreement," or MFA. For the text, see "Arrangement Regarding International Trade in Textiles" (GATT publication, 1974). UNCTAD has commented on implementation of the agreement in "International Trade in Textiles," Report by UNCTAD secretariat, 12 May 1977.

9. On the basis of an index with 1974 as 100, OPEC's terms of trade had declined by 1977 to 91.0 (and by 1978 to 81.0). In 1977 this reflected import prices that were 25 percent higher, compared with oil prices that had only increased by 14 percent. Morgan Guaranty Trust Company, *World Financial Markets*, December 1978.

10. Since excess U.S. capacity fell between 1967 and 1976, the figures in Table 7.2, part C-2, actually understate the increase in U.S. dependence on foreign oil during that nine-year period. In 1967 the United States could have withstood a complete embargo quite comfortably (apart from any obligations or desire it might have had to export oil), simply by increasing production from shut-in wells. In a sense, then, its real energy dependence increased from zero to 20 percent during the 1967–1976 period.

11. U.S. liquid liabilities to all foreigners began to exceed reserve assets in 1959 (not alarming for a country acting in many ways like a bank), and had reached five times reserve assets by 1971. U.S. Government Printing Office, *The United States in the Changing World Economy*, statistical background material (1971), chart 53, p. 40. However, total U.S. assets abroad remained about 50 percent higher than foreign assets in the United States in 1975 [*International Economic Report of the President* (January 1977), p. 161].

12. For a discussion of President Nixon's manipulation of U.S. monetary policy for electoral purposes in 1971–1972, see Tufte (1978), pp. 45–55.

References

Bergsten, C. Fred. 1975a. *Dilemmas of the Dollar*. New York: New York University Press.
———. 1975b. "On the Non-Equivalence of Import Quotas and 'Voluntary' Export Restraints," in Bergsten, ed., *Toward a New World Trade Policy: The Maidenhead Papers*. Lexington, Mass.: Lexington Books.
Blair, John M. 1976. *The Control of Oil*. New York: Pantheon Books, pp. 43–47, 78–80.
Calleo, David P. 1976. in Rowland, ed., *Balance of Power or Hegemony: The Interwar Monetary System*. New York: New York University Press, published for the Lehrman Institute.

Cohen, Benjamin J. 1977. *Organizing the World's Money: The Political Economy of International Monetary Relations.* New York: Basic Books.

Eckes Jr., Alfred E. 1975. *A Search for Solvency: Bretton Woods and the International Monetary System, 1941–1971.* Austin: University of Texas Press.

Eisenhower, Dwight D. 1957. *Public Papers of the President. News Conference of President Eisenhower.* Washington, D.C.: Government Printing Office, p. 124. 6 February.

Feis, Herbert. 1947. *Seen From E.A.:Three International Episodes.* New York: Alfred A. Knopf, pp. 104ff.

———. 1944. *Petroleum and American Foreign Policy.* Stanford, Calif.: Food Research Institute, Stanford University, March.

Gilpin, Robert. 1975. *U.S. Power and the Multinational Corporation.* New York: Basic Books.

Gourevitch, Peter A. 1978. "The Second Image Reversed," *International Organization* 32 Autumn: 881–912.

Harsanyi, John C. 1962. "Measurement of Social Power, Opportunity Costs, and the Theory of Two-Person Bargaining Games," *Behavioral Science* 7: 67–80.

Hirsch, Fred. 1967. *Money International.* London: Penguin Press.

Hudec, Robert E. 1975. *The GATT Legal System and World Trade Diplomacy* New York: Praeger Publishers, p. 256.

IMF Survey, 12 December 1977, p. 373; 20 March 1978, p. 81; and 18 September 1978, p. 285.

International Economic Report of the President (January 1977), p. 161.

Jenkins, Glenn P. and Brian D. Wright. 1975. "Taxation of Income of Multinational Corporations: The Case of the United States Petroleum Industry," *Review of Economics and Statistics* 17. February.

Kindleberger, Charles P. 1976. "Systems of International Economic Organization," in Calleo, ed., *Money and the Coming World Order.* New York: New York University Press for the Lehrman Institute, pp. 19–20

———. 1974. *The World in Depression, 1929–1939.* Berkeley: University of California Press, chap 14.

Kolko, Gabriel. 1968. *The Politics of War: 1943–45.* New York: Vintage Books, pp. 294–307.

Kolko, Joyce and Gabriel. 1972. *The Limits of Power: The World and American Foreign Policy, 1946–1954.* New York: Harper and Row, pp. 413–420.

Krasner, Stephen D. 1978. *Defending the National Interest: Raw Materials Investment and U.S. Foreign Policy.* Princeton, N.J.: Princeton University Press. pp. 119–128, 190–213.

———. 1976. "State Power and the Structure of International Trade," *World Politics* 28. April: pp. 317–347.

Lipson, Charles. forthcoming. *Standing Guard: The Protection of Foreign Investment.* Berkeley: University of California Press.

Liska, George. 1967. *Imperial America: The International Politics of Primacy,* no. 2. Washington, D.C.: Johns Hopkins Studies in International Affairs.

MacPhee, Craig R. 1974. *Restrictions on International Trade in Steel.* Lexington, Mass.: Lexington Books.

Magdoff, Harry. 1969. *The Age of Imperialism.* New York: Monthly Review Press.

March, James G. 1966. "The Power of Power," in Easton, ed., *Varieties of Political Theory.* New York: Prentice-Hall, esp. pp. 54–61.

McCracken, Paul et al. 1977. *Towards Full Employment and Price Stability.* Paris: Organization for Economic Cooperation and Development.

Morgan Guaranty Trust Company, *World Financial Markets*, May and December 1978.

New York Times, 12 April 1979.

OECD. 1958. *Europe's Need for Oil: Implications and Lessons of the Suez Crisis.* Paris.

Olson, Jr., Mancur and Richard Zeckhauser. 1966. "An Economic Theory of Alliances," *Review of Economics and Statistics* 48:266–279, reprinted in Russett, ed., 1968. *Economic Theories of International Politics.* Chicago: Markham Publishing Co.

Patterson, Gardner C. 1965. *Discrimination in International Trade.* Princeton, N.J.: Princeton University Press.

Ruggie, John Gerard. 1972. "Collective Goods and Future International Collaboration," *American Political Science Review* 66. September: 874–893.

Servan-Schreiber, J. J. 1969. *The American Challenge*, trans. Ronald Steel. New York: Avon Books.

Shapiro, Harold T. 1977. "Inflation in the United States," in Krause and Salant, eds., *Worldwide Inflation: Theory and Recent Experience.* Washington, D.C.: Brookings Institution.

Shwadran, Benjamin. 1955. *The Middle East, Oil and the Great Powers.* New York: Praeger Publishers, pp. 302–309.

Smith, Adam, 1776. *An Inquiry into the Nature and Causes of the Wealth of Nations*, book 1, part 2, chap. 10

Strange, Susan. 1979. "The Management of Surplus Capacity," *International Organization* 33. Summer.

Tufte, Edward R. 1978. *Political Control of the Economy.* Princeton, N.J.: Princeton University Press, pp. 45–55.

Turner, Louis. 1978. *Oil Companies in the International System.* London: George Allen and Unwin for the Royal Institute of International Affairs, p. 70, 94–95.

U.S. Congress: Senate, Committee on Foreign Relations, Subcommittee on Multinational Corporations. 1974a. *The International Petroleum Cartel, The Iranian Consortium and U.S. National Security*, Committee Print, 93rd Cong., 2d sess., 21 February.

———. 1974b. *Multinational Corporations and United States Foreign Policy*, Part 4, Hearings, 93rd Cong., 2d sess., 30 January, pp. 84–110.

U.S. Congress: Senate, Committee on the Judiciary and on Interior and Insular Affairs. 1957. *Emergency Oil Lift Program*, Hearings, 85th Cong., 1st sess., February.

U.S. Government Printing Office. 1971. *The United States in the Changing World Economy.* Washington, D.C.: U.S. GPO, chart 53, p. 40.

———. 1943 and 1944. *Foreign Relations of the United States.* Washington, D.C.: U.S. GPO. Vol. 4, pp. 941–948; vol.3, pp. 94–111.

8

IS INTERNATIONAL COMPETITIVENESS A MEANINGFUL CONCEPT?

David P. Rapkin and Jonathan R. Strand

Competitiveness has become a familiar slogan for politicians and government leaders interested in rallying support for greater national efforts to succeed in the global economy. This raises questions as to whether the world's leading states are involved in economic competition to any important degree and whether major domestic economic problems can be attributed to a failure to compete internationally. Rapkin and Strand review the notion of competitiveness in both its economic and political contexts. They find that from an economic perspective the term has little meaning. Nevertheless, competitiveness is "real" in the arena of politics because it is believed to translate into military, diplomatic, and knowledge-related capabilities. Thus, economic competitiveness is perceived as a determinant of the relative position of states within the hierarchy of the international political economy; from a political perspective, it encourages stronger state action to ensure economic success and has become an umbrella concept and a shorthand instrument for asking how we are doing.

In the 1980s mounting awareness of and concern about national decline seemed to diminish the U.S. commitment to the open international economic order it had been instrumental in creating just a few decades earlier. The view of the world economy as a positive-sum game—in which all participants, including the United States, stood to benefit—seemed to recede in the face of nationalistic conceptions of a zero-sum realm in which the United States was losing ground to East Asian and European competitors. Since the mid-1980s, questions about international competitiveness have become a regular part of the public discourse on U.S. domestic and foreign economic policies.[1] Has the

United States lost economic competitiveness to other countries, especially Japan? If so, why, and what, if anything, should be done about it? Is there a constructive role for government policy in the creation, maintenance, or restoration of competitiveness? Or is competitiveness a property of firms—rather than countries—and thus a matter best left for determination by private choices and the operation of markets?

To address these questions, U.S. politicians, corporate leaders, scholars, and business analysts have held hearings, convened conferences and seminars, and published a large body of books, reports, articles, and op-ed pieces on competitiveness issues. The messages thus conveyed have typically bemoaned the loss of competitiveness, expounded on the societal and governmental shortcomings alleged to have brought this loss about, and proposed public policies or private strategies to arrest or reverse the adverse trend. In the process of debate, competitiveness has become a "motherhood and apple pie" political issue: Although differences exist in diagnosis and remedy, no one is opposed to improving U.S. competitiveness. As such, it has been a bipartisan concern, with both Republicans and Democrats couching their respective policy agendas in its rhetoric. In consequence, the term is now used so ubiquitously and in such a diffuse and imprecise manner as to confound whatever descriptive or explanatory value the competitiveness concept may offer in principle. But the debate over competitiveness is more than an esoteric scholarly duel or a rhetorical contest among politicians. Changes made in U.S. foreign and domestic economic policies by recent Republican and Democratic administrations have been intended explicitly to improve national competitiveness.

As this chapter demonstrates, competitiveness exhibits all of the features of an "essentially contested concept": a variety of meanings, or connotations, with disagreement over which are correct and how to weight or combine them; difficulties in applying the concept, particularly in specifying the real-world objects (e.g., firms or countries) the concept denotes; and differences in the way the concept is appraised, insofar as conflicting values and divergent preferences are embedded in its use (Connolly, 1993: chapter 1). If, as W. E. Connolly contended, collectively hashing out the meaning of contested concepts is itself a form of politics, then observers should be neither surprised nor alarmed by the use of competitiveness as a political slogan, a kind of broad rubric under which different societal and governmental actors—for example, firms, unions, parties and their candidates, government agencies—attempt to advance their own self-interested agendas. Political sloganeering, although perhaps muddying the definitional waters for those who aim to make social scientific use of the concept, would seem to be a rather common and ultimately harmless purpose for the term.

But P. Krugman (1994a, 1994b), in several recent polemical assaults on the concept and its advocates (including President Clinton and several of his senior economic advisers), has argued forcefully not only that national competitiveness is meaningless but also that concerns about competitiveness amount to a "dangerous obsession." The danger, according to Krugman, arises because pursuit of competitiveness is likely to lead to misallocation of government resources, heightened trade conflict and possibly a world trade war, and wrongheaded economic policies. In Krugman's (1994a: 43–44) terms, "A government wedded to the ideology of competitiveness is as unlikely to make good economic policy as a government committed to creationism is to make good science policy."

Krugman's polemics have the virtues of illuminating some sloppy, politicized uses of the economic competitiveness concept and of framing a number of important issues that have received inadequate attention in the debates over competitiveness. This chapter contends, contrary to Krugman, that a broader version of competitiveness is indeed a meaningful concept. Broadening the definition of competitiveness first involves taking into account its institutional and ideological, as well as economic, components. The discussion then turns to two unresolved denotative issues: whether competitiveness is a property of countries as well as firms, and how the assessment of national competitiveness is confounded by the transnationalization of the world economy. The heart of the chapter develops the argument that competitiveness should be understood as an international *political* economy concept, rather than a narrowly economic concept, that is closely linked to the notion of relative gains and position among states. Because policymakers cannot afford to ignore relative gains, they will continue to find some version of the competitiveness concept indispensable.

Problems of Connotation:
What Does Competitiveness Mean?

The most widely accepted definition of competitiveness, first developed by the President's Commission on Industrial Competitiveness (1985: 1), is stated in succinct, plain language: "A nation's competitiveness is the degree to which it can, under free and fair market conditions, produce goods and services that meet the tests of international markets while simultaneously expanding the real incomes of its citizens." The three main elements of the definition are, in effect, variables: conditions in a country's export markets, the ability to produce and sell goods and services in those markets, and the real incomes, or standards of living, of its citizens.

The first element, the openness and fairness of markets among a country's trading partners, is an environmental variable few countries are large or powerful enough to affect directly through national policies. Most, therefore, must take this aspect of their international environment as it exists in the short to medium term.[2] Discrimination against foreign products or firms can distort the assessment of competitiveness. To the extent that a country closes its markets to protect an industry from international competition, it may be able to artificially sustain competitiveness, or at least the appearance of it, for a time. As a corollary, "genuinely" competitive firms or countries—that is, those that would best meet the definition's criteria in the absence of the discrimination—will appear less competitive.

The ability to sell goods and services in world markets, the second element of the definition, is the outcome of a complex array of causal forces, alternatively referred to in the literature as sources, determinants, or ingredients of competitiveness. This is the area in which much of the confusion over different connotations arises: Definitions of competitiveness based on its sources—such as productivity growth, savings and investment rates, research and development (R&D) efforts, and human resource development—do not necessarily yield the same results as operational definitions based on attempts to measure outcomes, such as trade balances and shares of world trade in manufactures or high-tech goods.

Even if the focus is limited to sources of competitiveness, enormous connotational complexity is evident. At the extreme, consider the World Competitiveness Report produced by the World Economic Forum in Switzerland, which ranks the competitiveness of forty-one countries as determined by no fewer than 381 criteria (*Economist*, September 10, 1994: 81). M. Porter's (1990: chapter 3) catalog of the determinants of national competitive advantage is also unwieldy. It begins with four national attributes that shape competitiveness: factor conditions, demand conditions, related and supporting industries, and firm strategy, structure, and rivalry. Factor conditions are broken down into factor endowments, hierarchies among factors, factor creation, and selective factor disadvantages. Narrowing the focus further, the factor endowments category alone consists of five components—human resources, physical resources, knowledge resources, capital resources, and infrastructure. Each of these five is then described in terms of numbers of indicators, which are only illustrative rather than exhaustive. A full description of all of the determinants would likely fill a volume larger than Porter's 855-page tome.

Some authors slice the competitiveness literature more parsimoniously. R. Nelson (1992) collapsed the different approaches to the competitiveness debate into three main clusters, each of which emphasizes different connotations: microeconomic (focusing on the firm), macroeconomic (e.g., costs of capital, aggregate savings and investment rates, productivity growth), and activist industrial policies, such as subsidized R&D and home-market protection. Taking a different tack, S. D. Cohen (1995) identified seven different schools of thought on U.S. competitiveness, arrayed along a "continuum of concern" according to the severity of the problem in the view of each school. If the variables included in Nelson's three and Cohen's seven approaches were enumerated, however, more lengthy lists would soon result.

Another way to summarize the different approaches to the meaning of competitiveness is through disciplinary orientation. Economists naturally tend to focus on economic ingredients of competitiveness, such as savings and investment rates, capital and labor costs, employment levels, and productivity growth. Even if only economic variables were used to define competitiveness, considerable internal complexity would be apparent. Other social scientists, however, broaden the concept's connotation by emphasizing such factors as sociopolitical institutions and ideology. J. A. Hart (1992), for example, contended that the form of state-society relations (linking government, business, and labor) influences a country's capacity for creating and diffusing new technologies; this capacity is the principal determinant of international competitiveness. I. Nakatani (1995) pointed to U.S.-Japan institutional differences, specifically the organization of capital markets and the structure of interfirm relations, as the sources of competitive asymmetries between the two countries. An even more comprehensive institutional approach compared "national systems of innovation," defined as "the network of institutions in the public and private sectors whose activities and interactions initiate, import, modify and diffuse new technologies" (Freeman, 1987: 1).[3]

Sociopolitical institutions are internally complex and are less amenable to precise measurement than are the economic variables typically used to define competitiveness. This "soft" characteristic of institutional approaches is even more evident in ideological approaches to competitiveness. S. Reich (1995), for example, examined the ideologies underlying the Japanese government's propensity to intervene and the noninterventionary tendencies of its U.S. counterpart and argued that the competitive differences in the markets for automobiles and semiconductors that arose in the 1980s can be traced to this ideological disparity. E. Vogel (1987) emphasized instead Japan's "adaptive communitarianism" as the key ideological ingredient of the country's competitive success. Suffice it to say that the addition of institutional and ideological connotations to the economic ones pushes the internal complexity of the competitiveness concept to intractable proportions.

Economists and noneconomists alike, however, agree that the most important source of competitiveness is productivity growth—that is, increases in the amount produced per worker.[4] Productivity growth is viewed as necessary both for the ability to meet the test of international markets and for the expansion of real incomes (the third element in the definition of competitiveness). But rather than representing a straightforward, unproblematic variable that can be readily inserted into measurement models of competitiveness, measures of productivity growth are "very complex syntheses" that themselves need explanation (Cohen, 1994: 196).

Yet another connotational dispute turns on whether the competitiveness of a large economy for which trade is a relatively small component, such as that of the United States, reduces to domestic productivity growth. In Krugman's (1994a: 32) terms, "For an economy with very little international trade, 'competitiveness' would turn out to be a funny way of saying 'productivity' and would have nothing to do with international competition."[5] Compare this assertion with the more conventional view, as expressed by A. J. Lenz (1987: 33): "Improving a nation's international competitiveness depends fundamentally on productivity growth rates. That does not mean just increasing productivity; in an integrated world economy, rates of productivity increase must compare favorably with those of major foreign competitors." It follows, then, that "for the most part . . . international competitiveness is a contest of productivity increases" (Lenz, 1991: 17).

This difference spills over into the definitional stipulation that rising standards of living must accompany the ability to meet the test of international markets. A country that preserved its ability to sell goods and services in world markets only by means of reduced wage levels or currency devaluations would not satisfy this requirement—that is, it would not have maintained its competitiveness. For Krugman (1994a: 32), because improvements in U.S. living standards are "determined almost entirely by domestic factors, primarily . . . domestic productivity growth . . . not productivity growth relative to other countries," the link between performance in world markets and living standards is spurious at best. In sum, Krugman's solution to the connotational problem is to dismiss it as having no valid meaning because "it is simply not the case that the world's leading nations are to any important degree in economic competition with each other, or that any of their major economic problems can be attributed to failures to compete on world markets" (1994a: 30). To examine Krugman's claim more closely, the issue of denotation needs to be addressed.

Problems of Denotation:
To What Does Competitiveness Refer?

To what real-world objects does the concept of national competitiveness refer? Do the rules concerning application of the concept enable clear demarcation between those entities to which it applies (e.g., firms, industries, sectors, cities, countries, regions) and those to which it does not? Krugman (1994a: 31) contended that competitiveness is a meaningful property of corporations but not of countries because whereas uncompetitive firms will "cease to exist," countries "have no well-defined bottom line [and] do not go out of business." Although this distinction might be sufficient to deflate President Clinton's rhetorical suggestion that a country is "like a big corporation competing in the global marketplace" (cited in Krugman, 1994a: 29), there is more to the concept of national competitiveness. In our view, Krugman focused too narrowly on a definition of competitiveness that denotes only firms. Although competition among firms is clearly and only economic, competition among countries is more complex and multifaceted. Hence, there is no reason to limit our conception of the competitiveness of countries to a straightforward extension of the competitiveness of firms. Various other forms of competition do not require that "losers" cease to exist— for example, sports, school admissions, beauty contests—and these, like business competition, may also be partly analogous to aspects of competition among countries.

More serious denotational problems arise from the processes by which the different steps involved in the production of any given product are increasingly spread over multiple firms, or branches of the same firm, operating in different countries. These transnationalization processes—which may be either global(ization) or regional(ization) in scope—have been spurred by a number of convergent developments: a relaxed regulatory environment; the increased managerial control enabled by time- and distance-shrinking information and communication technologies; a proliferation of organizational innovations—corporate alliances, tie-ups, technology sharing, marketing agreements, and so on—of varying formality and duration; the scale and complexity of developing new technologies; and exchange rate movements and political pressures that, primarily in the case of Japan, have encouraged offshore relocation of production facilities. The consequences of these developments include increased difficulty in identifying specific firms or products with particular countries, a problem that is well expressed by the title of R. Reich's (1991) article, "Who Is Us?" The fundamental implication of Reich's question is that fewer and fewer issues of trade and investment policy permit an appeal to an unequivocal national interest.[6]

This is more than simply a matter of frustrated consumers discovering the futility of "buy American" campaigns. The phenomenon of transnational production confounds the measurement and interpretation of international economic flows and national accounts by which national economic performance has traditionally been tallied. Consider the example of Sangshin Electric presented in M. Bernard and J. Ravenhill's (1995b) analysis of the regionalization of production in East Asia. Sangshin is a Korean-Japanese joint venture that is headquartered in Korea and managed by Koreans but that relies on key inputs from Japan to produce electronic components that are then exported to manufacturers in North America, Europe, and elsewhere in Asia, as well as sold to Korean producers of consumer electronics. Sangshin also operates a manufacturing plant in Malaysia, where it relies on Japanese management and on procurement from Korea and Japan to produce lower-end electronics for export back to Korea and to other destinations. Suppose, for example, that a U.S. firm purchases components from Sangshin's Malaysian plant. This transaction would be registered as a Malaysian export to the United States but would hardly be reflective of Malaysian competitiveness vis-à-vis the United States. But which country's national competitiveness does it reflect? Does the fact that a decade ago the same product would likely have been imported from Japan or perhaps Korea mean that the former exporting country is now less competitive? How would our calculations of U.S. competitiveness be affected if a U.S. firm, operating either at home or abroad, is involved at some point in Sangshin's production network?

These questions do not exhaust the difficulties involved in reckoning national competitiveness in a world economy in which production is increasingly transnationalized. Nor is Sangshin an exceptional example.[7] In fact, for more complex products (e.g., finished rather than intermediate goods or, at the extreme, a Boeing commercial aircraft) production networks tend to be even more far-flung, involving firms from a wider array of national origins. Although it is possible in principle to sort out issues of national competitiveness in these circumstances, the exercise would involve unraveling at the microlevel networks of firms on virtually a product-by-product or a transaction-by-transaction basis. The value of aggregated measures of national accounts such as trade balances—already fairly problematic indicators of national competitiveness—is diminished further by the transnationalization of production.

In sum, even if complete agreement on the meaning(s) connoted by the competitiveness concept were reached, it would still suffer from vague denotation. Does competitiveness pertain to firms or to transnational networks of firms? Is it useful to speak of competitiveness as a property of nation-states or of regions, such as East Asia? And if transnationalization confounds the measurement of competitiveness, will further transnationalization eventually make the concept an imponderable?

The Appraisive Dimension:
Competitiveness as Political Slogan

The connotational and denotational disputes surveyed so far are compounded by appraisive differences over the practical purposes to which the concept is put. Politicians seeking hard-line trade policies blame Japan or other countries for the loss or denial of U.S. competitiveness. Those who advocate more extensive government involvement in development of new technologies rationalize their proposals in terms of competitiveness, as do those seeking deregulation and a reduced government role. Labor supporters construe issues such as health insurance, child care, and worker retraining as crucial to competitiveness. As E. J. Rollins (1987: 122) pointed out, "When you talk to labor groups about competitiveness, they think you want them to work more hours for less pay." At the same time, corporate leaders attempt to justify laying off workers and closing factories—"downsizing" or "re-engineering," in currently fashionable lingo—as necessary for maintaining or regaining competitiveness.

Different groups appraise competitiveness differently, but the main problem is not that some people appraise competitiveness positively whereas others regard it negatively. Rather, the problem arises because everyone appraises the concept positively as long as they are able to frame their economic and social agenda in competitiveness terms. In short, the concept has proven to be rather malleable. N. Ornstein's (in Keene et al., 1987: 131) observations in this regard are worth quoting at some length:

> Using the word "competitiveness" is a way of taking an issue that does not resound for the public and making it resound. We want to be competitive in everything. We are sports fans. We watch horse races and political contests. The notion of appealing to patriotism by suggesting that it's us against them does get juices flowing. We can take an issue of that sort and make it all things to all people. We can talk about competitiveness in education and not necessarily make it the onerous burden for students or teachers of working longer. Instead Democrats can talk about increasing federal involvement in education and frame it in terms of competitiveness. In the same way, by framing it in terms of competitiveness, Republicans can talk about unleashing industry without having to take the flak of being for big business. To whatever degree it can be cloaked as a patriotic

issue that nobody can be against, everybody can gain some benefits from it.

It is easy to understand Krugman's (1994a) exasperation with the
appropriation of competitiveness, by what he termed "policy entrepreneurs," for use as a kind of political slogan. Moreover, it cannot be denied that the concept's connection to normative purposes makes more
difficult the task of assessing its scientific—that is, descriptive and explanatory—usefulness. From a different perspective, however, it is
precisely this normative "contamination" that makes the concept of
competitiveness especially interesting. Although these appraisive differences, as well as the connotational and denotational problems discussed
earlier, may reduce the usefulness of competitiveness as an *economic* concept, it does not follow that the political baby should be thrown out
with the economic bathwater. By adding the more explicitly political
consideration of relative gains among states, the next section develops
competitiveness as an international political economy concept.

Competitiveness as an Index of Relative Gains

If a strictly economic conception of competitiveness is plagued by the
kinds of imprecision described in previous sections, what is gained by
reconstruing it in political terms? A political perspective will not necessarily bring the ambiguous connotations and vague denotations into
sharp focus. Indeed, in certain ways a political interpretation makes the
concept even more complex and unwieldy, but, in our view, the additional insight it provides makes this a worthwhile trade-off.
    The argument for a political interpretation is simple: We con-
tend that because it is believed to affect the military, political, and
knowledge-related capabilities of nation-states, economic competitiveness is regarded as a determinant of these states' relative positions in the
international political economy. Policymakers use some construct of
competitiveness—even if it is termed something else and no matter how
crudely measured—to estimate the trajectory of their own and other
countries as they ascend, decline, or maintain their position in a hier-
archically structured international system. Position within that hierarchy is seen as intrinsically related to states' abilities to attain their core
goals of security, welfare, and the preservation of sovereignty: "Even if
nation-states do not fear for their physical survival, they worry that a
decrease in their power relative to those of other nation-states will compromise their political autonomy, expose them to the influence attempts

of others, or lessen their ability to prevail in political disputes with allies and adversaries" (Mastanduno, 1991: 78).

The relative gains argument claims simply that states are more concerned with how well they perform in relation to one another than with how well they perform themselves.[8] But to claim that policymakers assess national competitiveness as a kind of index of relative gains is not to say that their decisions are always driven by relative gains considerations.[9] They may or may not be willing to trade absolute welfare gains for relative gains or, more likely, to avoid relative loss. Such tradeoffs arise in situations in which policymakers face a choice "between maximizing America's economic welfare and maximizing its political power (sacrificing mutual economic benefits to ensure an advantageous relative distribution of economic benefits, so as to enhance the nation's ability to influence others), or between maximizing economic welfare and minimizing the nation's vulnerability to being coerced by others" (Moran, 1993: 3). This approach raises the questions of when and under what circumstances relative gains concerns are likely to weigh more heavily than absolute gains in the policy calculus.

Several developments appear to have made relative gains more salient to U.S. citizens and their political leaders during the 1980s and early 1990s; they also help to explain the emergence, subsequent popularization, and wide usage of the competitiveness concept. These developments include the public debate over the extent and meaning of the long-term U.S. decline from its formerly hegemonic position and the largely unexpected end of the Cold War. Decline seemed manifest in a number of adverse trends that beset the United States in the 1980s, inter alia, mounting budget and trade deficits, losses of domestic market share to imports in politically sensitive industries such as automobiles, and the rapid transformation from the world's largest creditor to its largest debtor. Furthermore, the litany of U.S. economic problems seemed to coincide with, and provide a striking contrast to, the success and apparent buoyancy of the Japanese economy. After four unreflective decades at the apex of the international political economy, the developments of the 1980s compelled U.S. citizens to begin thinking of their country's position and trajectory relative to those of other countries.

Perceptions of long-term U.S. decline may have made relative gains concerns more salient, but the language of decline proved to be a politically ineffective way to broach the matter, probably because the term *relative decline* (or just plain *decline*) sounds like inexorable macrohistorical forces grinding along beyond human agency or control—an intractable problem unlikely to be ameliorated in the foreseeable future. Additionally, any policy proposal or political campaign premised on the idea that the United States has declined is easily criticized as excessively negative and defeatist. The competitiveness rubric, in contrast, seems to reduce the same issues to more manageable and politically palatable proportions and to a shorter-term time frame. When presented as a lack of competitiveness, however defined, the problem is perceived as one that allows U.S. citizens to roll up their sleeves, take corrective steps, and expect positive results within the short to medium term.

The end of the Cold War has also increased the perceived importance of relative gains, especially vis-à-vis allies, to U.S. policymakers. As long as security imperatives stemming from the Soviet threat were dominant, "U.S. policy makers . . . paid little attention to the possibility that a loss of power vis-à-vis friends could present serious and unforeseen difficulties, either because friends can become enemies or because managing the international system may be more difficult in a world in which power has become more evenly distributed" (Krasner, 1986: 787). But as the Soviet threat receded, relative gains by Japan and Germany, for example, were no longer discounted so readily. A stronger version of this reasoning holds that gains by allies during the Cold War may well have been tallied as relative gains for the U.S.-led alliance vis-à-vis the Soviet bloc. After the Cold War, however, such aggregated calculations of gains quickly lost relevance.

These hypotheses linking U.S. decline and the end of the Cold War to the emergence of relative gains considerations have stimulated some interesting research. M. Mastanduno (1991: 75), for example, reported that in the latter half of the 1980s, relative gains considerations crept into the U.S. policymaking *process* on three issues involving U.S.-Japan high-technology competition, but they had an uneven impact on policy *outcomes*. Relative gains concerns were reflected "fully and unambiguously" in satellite trade policy; altered the course of U.S. policy in relation to codevelopment of the FSX fighter but were not reflected in the final outcome; and affected U.S. policy only modestly, if at all, in the case of high-definition television. Overall, Mastanduno (1991: 109, 108) concluded that these cases "provide strong though not unconditional support . . . for the hypothesis that as relative economic power declines and external security threats diminish, a hegemonic state is likely to pursue relative gains more forcefully in economic relations with its allies."

As an illustration of the prevalence of relative gains concerns, consider another question posed by Robert Reich: "Which of these futures do you prefer," one in which by the year 2000 "the American economy grows by a respectable 25 percent, but the Japanese economy grows a whopping 75 percent," or one which "the American economy grows only 10 percent and the Japanese economy grows an anemic 10.3 percent" (*Wall Street Journal*, June 18, 1990: A10). Reich asked this question in informal surveys of different types of audiences, including corporate leaders, investment bankers, State Department officials, economists, graduate students, and lay people. Only one group, economists, preferred the scenario that maximizes absolute gains.[10] Why would the majority of people faced with Reich's hypothetical situation choose to have the United States forego 15 percent in economic growth rather than have a long-standing ally experience a growth rate that is significantly higher? Reich concluded that the survey results imply that most U.S. citizens, at least in 1990, think of the U.S. relationship with Japan (and other competitors) in terms of relative, not absolute, gains. What seemed to matter to those selecting the first scenario was not the absolute rate of U.S. economic growth but how that rate compared with the rates of other major powers.

Numerous changes in U.S. economic policies since the early 1980s can be interpreted from a relative gains perspective. Beginning in the early 1980s, for example, the otherwise laissez-faire–oriented Reagan administration began to block acquisition by Japanese companies of certain U.S. high-technology firms, ostensibly because of their importance to defense-related industries.[11] In 1984, in response to the competitive challenge posed by government-sponsored collaborative projects in Japan, U.S. antitrust law was revised to allow collaborative research among consortia of U.S. firms. By 1986, with Japanese semiconductor producers having surpassed U.S. firms' world market share and after numerous U.S. chip manufacturers had bowed out of the competition, U.S. officials had pressured the Japanese government into an agreement that established targets for the share of foreign firms in Japan's semiconductor market. The following year, taking advantage of the earlier relaxation of antitrust laws, the U.S. government matched the $100 million put up by a consortium of fourteen U.S. chip makers to fund Sematech, a collaborative project aimed at developing leading-edge technologies for manufacturing chips. Throughout this period and into the 1990s, the U.S. government championed the cause of Motorola, a U.S. telecommunications firm, in its bid to gain entry to Japanese markets, especially the cellular phone market. The Clinton administration—influenced by the ideas of Laura d'Andrea Tyson, Robert Reich, and others who advocated more activist high-technology policies—has tried unsuccessfully to expand the managed trade arrangements pioneered in the 1986 semiconductor agreement. This brief survey is far from exhaustive, but it shows that U.S. foreign and domestic economic policies changed in the 1980s and early 1990s in ways consistent with the relative gains hypothesis.

A hypothetical scenario further illustrates the relative gains interpretation of competitiveness, as well as the concept's distinctiveness vis-à-vis productivity. Consider that Japan achieved a much less impressive economic gain during the post–World War II period and that by the mid-1980s its major productive activities were textiles, light manufactures, and low-end consumer electronics. Suppose also that U.S. and European economic growth and industrial evolution had proceeded according to the historical record. Would the United States in the 1980s have then perceived that it had a competitiveness problem? Probably not. Western European countries had challenged the United States in various industries and sectors, but they did not seem poised to surpass the United States in any significant dimension of economic vitality or importance (except for aggregated market size). Thus, without Japan as an economic powerhouse, and with the relative U.S. position in the world economy unchallenged, it is reasonable to conjecture that the competitiveness debate would not have emerged or at least that it would not have become such a prominent political issue. Yet even if there had been no perception of a loss of competitiveness, the United States in the 1980s did not lack serious economic problems, not the least of which were sagging rates of productivity growth. In both the actual and the counterfactual scenarios, the U.S. productivity problem slows absolute gains in U.S. standards of living regardless of other countries' economic performance. But because of the difference in relative gains, the actual scenario's competitiveness problem would not likely arise in the counterfactual scenario.

Does the strong preference for absolute gains characteristic of most economists blind them to consideration of relative gains? Overall, Krugman's (1994a: 35) arguments do not acknowledge the political significance of relative gains and position or their relation to economic capabilities, but he did allow that "there is always a rivalry for status and power—countries that grow faster will see their political rank rise. So it is always interesting to *compare* countries." Rather than considering either the implications of this observation or the basis on which countries might be compared, Krugman's (1994a: 35) next sentence dispenses with the issue by means of false attribution to a straw man: "But asserting that Japanese growth diminishes U.S. status is very different from saying that it reduces the U.S. standard of living—and it is the latter that the rhetoric of competitiveness asserts." The first objection is that, as it is hoped the preceding section made clear, there are multiple "rhetorics of competitiveness," not just one. The second is that Krugman not only collapsed these into a single voice, he also attributed to this voice a claim made by few who use the competitiveness concept. No doubt there are politicians or scholars, reflecting polemical excess or intellectual error, who claim that Japan's growth has occurred at the expense of U.S. welfare. But such a simplistic zero-sum proposition does not derive from an interest in competitiveness per se; nor does it characterize accurately or fairly the preponderance of the work on the subject.

There are other points at which Krugman, perhaps inadvertently, approached recognition of the concept of national competitiveness, as, for example, when he acknowledged that "the United States has some real problems in international competition" (1994b: 286). How is this statement to be interpreted? Suppose that at a certain point in time the United States was beset by many more (fewer) such "real problems" than had been the case at an earlier point. Would it be reasonable to conclude that the United States had lost (gained) competitiveness? Or suppose that both Japan and the United States—or, more accurately, firms headquartered in the two countries—were competing in the same sectors, industries, and product markets and that U.S. firms had many more problems in this international competition than did their Japanese counterparts. Can one infer from these circumstances that Japan enjoyed an edge in international competitiveness vis-à-vis the United States? Suppose further that at a subsequent point in time the United States had reduced the number and severity of its problems in international competition whereas Japan's had increased. Would these developments provide an adequate basis to claim that the United States had gained and Japan had lost competitiveness (at least vis-à-vis each other)?

It is no surprise that we answer affirmatively for all three of these hypothetical scenarios—(1) one country over time, and (2) static and (3) dynamic comparisons of two countries. In each case, the competitiveness concept provides meaningful and useful information about the relative position, and changes therein, of countries in the world economy. Furthermore, and to move the issue from the hypothetical realm, the static and dynamic scenarios sketched here describe in rough-and-ready fashion recent trends in the competitiveness of the United States and Japan. In the late 1980s and into the early 1990s Japanese industries seemed virtually invincible, with little prospect of U.S. firms recapturing the home and third-country markets lost to Japanese competitors. Heavy capital investment and technological development in the second half of the 1980s seemed to ensure that Japan's competitive advantages would persist for the indefinite future.

A surprisingly rapid and largely unanticipated U.S. comeback became evident by late 1993; U.S. firms have regained competitiveness across a range of products, including automobiles and other traditional manufacturing industries, such as machine tools, but especially in various industries based on information and communication technologies (ICT). To some extent, this turnaround is attributable to the continued weakening of the U.S. dollar against the Japanese yen and to the protracted recession in Japan. But in many of the ICT industries associated with the information revolution—including, among others, software, microprocessors, telecommunications, multimedia, and networking—

innovation and creation of new products have enabled firms not only to open wide technological leads over their Japanese counterparts but also to define new markets and redefine old ones on terms advantageous to U.S. strengths.

By early 1994, Japanese media, business leaders, and government officials were expressing alarm at the perceived loss of competitiveness to U.S. firms such as Microsoft and Intel and were suggesting that Japan was becoming a U.S. "colony" or "subcontractor." To be sure, there is an element of hyperbole in these expressions of alarm, just as the competitive demise and prowess of U.S. and Japanese firms, respectively, were exaggerated only a few short years ago. Japan retains considerable advantages in different kinds of manufacturing, and these and other strengths will no doubt be reasserted. Appreciation of the dollar vis-à-vis the yen could quickly erase some of the gains made by U.S. firms.

Nonetheless, it is evident that some set of important variables has undergone significant change. No one can specify with certainty the variables that constitute this set or how to join them in a system of causal relationships. Indeed, the regionalization and globalization processes discussed earlier are further confounding these already difficult tasks of theorization and measurement. Were it not for the sensitivity to relative gains that infuses a comparative (international) dimension to these issues, it would be easier to accept Krugman's (1994a: 32) claim that they are coterminous with "domestic productivity growth, period."[12] Instead, we find more useful S. S. Cohen's (1994: 197) contention that competitiveness provides a better organizing concept for "reconsideration of a broad set of indicators, none of which tells the whole story but that together provide a highly legitimate focus."

To conclude, the point is not that relative gains always, or even usually, dominate absolute gains in the calculus of foreign policymakers. But these policymakers cannot afford to ignore relative gains considerations, which weigh more heavily in consequence of hegemonic decline and the end of the Cold War. In this context, competitiveness has served as a kind of umbrella concept within which the following kinds of questions are addressed: "How are we doing as an economy? . . . How are we doing compared to the other guys? And why?" (Cohen, 1994: 197). As suggested earlier, foreign policymakers regularly seek answers to these kinds of questions because of their perceived importance to states' capabilities and, thus, also to the relative position and trajectory of their state in the international political economy. Although policymakers obviously lack a comprehensive, logically consistent, well-measured concept of national competitiveness, it nevertheless occupies a critical place in their implicit models of how the world works.

Conclusion

We have argued that competitiveness is a useful and, for some purposes, a necessary concept. Although the concept is fraught with the problems of meaning, reference, and values associated with essentially contested concepts, a class of questions exists for which some version of competitiveness is indispensable. From the standpoint of neoclassical economics and its emphasis on absolute gains, competitiveness may indeed nearly reduce to productivity growth. An international political economy perspective, however, compels consideration of relative gains across states. In this context, assessing competitiveness—construed as an organizing framework for addressing the questions "How are we doing compared to the other guys? And why?"—becomes a necessary, albeit imprecise, endeavor.

The most problematic aspect of this endeavor is the denotational morass created by the processes of transnationalization (or globalization or regionalization). Put simply, answers to "How are we doing?" presuppose that "Who is us?" has been answered satisfactorily. And, as argued earlier, it is difficult to deny that the latter question is becoming harder, rather than easier, to address. But regardless of whether scholars are able to formulate and agree on a more valid, reliable, and operationalizable version of competitiveness, foreign policymakers will continue to assess it by whatever imperfect means are available. Insofar as this expectation holds, the concept cannot be discarded by those interested in the behavior of states and the operation of the international political economy.

Notes

1. We do not mean to suggest that anxieties about competitiveness are unique to the United States. To the contrary, such concerns are ubiquitous among states, at least among the so-called great powers. For example, see Sandholtz's (1995) discussion of the evolution of competitiveness concerns in post-war Europe. The focus of this chapter, however, is on the evaluation of the competitiveness concept in the U.S. context.

2. The United States, because of the still considerable weight it is able to bring to bear in bilateral settings, is the glaring exception in both principle and practice. Focus on this aspect of a country's competitive status—the openness of others' markets—is, unfortunately, susceptible to a kind of scapegoating in which it is easy to externalize blame for competitive failings while avoiding those politically painful measures that would follow from more critical self-scrutiny of internal shortcomings. From an East Asian perspective, this description fits the United States and its resort since the late 1980s to unilateral

methods of prying open the markets of countries deemed—according to U.S.-defined and-applied criteria—to be unreasonably closed or unfair. For various perspectives on the infamous "super 301" provision of U.S. trade law as an instrument of aggressive unilateralism, see the selections in Bhagwati and Patrick (1990). The emphasis on other countries' alleged unfairness as a source of U.S. competitiveness woes also seems to have led to an inordinate reliance on trade policy solutions, which most economists regard as unlikely to help solve the problem; see Lenz (1991: 198–203) for the limitations of trade policy approaches to competitiveness.

3. For alternative institutional approaches, see Best (1990) and Lazonick (1990).

4. It is important to note that productivity "not only means churning out more units of a good or service for each unit of input, but also improving quality and creating innovative new products" (Lenz, 1991: 16).

5. For the argument that Krugman's (1994a, 1994b) narrow reliance on a simple export/gross domestic product (GDP) test—while ignoring the effects of imports, as well as flows of investment, technology, and human resources—leads to a gross underestimation of the impact of the world economy on that of the United States, see Preeg (1994).

6. Reich has been secretary of labor from the outset of the Clinton administration. His argument, briefly, is that the U.S. national economic interest can no longer be directly equated with the interests of U.S. corporations; foreign firms that bring technology and provide high-wage employment could contribute more to U.S. competitiveness than their U.S. counterparts, especially footloose firms that move their manufacturing operations away from the United States. One response to "Who is us?" was an article entitled "They Are Not Us: Why American Ownership Still Matters" by Laura D'Andrea Tyson, who later became chairperson of President Clinton's Council of Economic Advisers. Tyson (1991: 1) acknowledged with Reich that globalization has been proceeding apace, but she is less ready to dissolve the distinction between U.S. and foreign corporations: "The economic fate of nations is still tied closely to the success of their domestically based corporations." For a fuller exposition of her arguments—which seem to have influenced Clinton administration trade and industrial policies—advocating certain kinds of government intervention to maintain competitiveness in high-technology industries, see Tyson (1992).

7. Additional examples of the regionalization of production in East Asia, as well as a fuller theorization of this phenomenon, can be found in Bernard and Ravenhill (1995a).

8. For a strong version of the relative gains argument, see Grieco (1990), especially pages 40–49. For a very useful and highly readable discussion of relative and absolute gains, see Stein (1990: chapter 5).

9. Snidal (1991) argued that the effect of relative gains in impeding cooperation attenuates as the number of states involved increases but is still present in bilateral situations. This important qualification to the relative gains argument does not diminish its consistency with the interpretation that U.S. relative gains concerns arose primarily in relation to Japan. On this last point, see Mastanduno (1991).

10. This result is not surprising in light of what Moran (1993: 2) characterized, perhaps too strongly, as the economics discipline's "scorn for relative rather than mutual gains."

11. For a very useful account and interpretation of these interventions, as well as other instances of U.S. "techno-nationalism," see Kohno (1995).

Kohno is skeptical of the security motivations ostensibly underlying these actions.

12. Consider Francis's (1992: 66) treatment of the distinction between productivity and competitiveness, which is entirely consistent with this chapter's relative gains argument: "While it is easy to demonstrate one nation's low and slow-growing productivity it is harder to measure lack of competitiveness. . . . Partly this is because it is much more difficult to define competitiveness than productivity. Whereas the performance of an economy can be measured in absolute terms (e.g., in terms of GDP per capita) competitiveness is a relative quality. Competitiveness implies the presence of a competition. It is a zero-sum game."

References

Bernard, M., and J. Ravenhill. 1995a. "Beyond Product Cycles and Flying Geese: Regionalization, Hierarchy, and the Industrialization of East Asia." *World Politics* 47, no. 2 (January): 171–209.

———. 1995b. "The Pursuit of Competitiveness in East Asia: Regionalization of Production and Its Consequences," in D. P. Rapkin and W. P. Avery, eds., *National Competitiveness in a Global Economy*, pp. 103–132. Boulder: Lynne Rienner Publishers.

Best, M. H. 1990. *The New Competition: The Institutions of Industrial Restructuring*. Cambridge: Harvard University Press.

Bhagwati, J., and H. T. Patrick, eds. 1990. *Aggressive Unilateralism: America's 301 Trade Policy and the World Trading System*. Ann Arbor: University of Michigan Press.

Cohen, S. D. 1995. "Does the United States Have an International Competitiveness Problem?" in D. P. Rapkin and W. P. Avery, eds., *National Competitiveness in a Global Economy*, pp. 21–40. Boulder: Lynne Rienner Publishers.

Cohen, S. S. 1994. "Speaking Freely." *Foreign Affairs* 73, no. 4 (July–August): 194–197.

Connolly, W. E. 1993. *The Terms of Political Discourse* (3rd ed.). Princeton: Princeton University Press.

Francis, A. 1992. "The Process of National Industrial Regeneration and Competitiveness." *Strategic Management Journal* 13: 61–78.

Freeman, C. 1987. *Technology Policy and Economic Performance: Lessons from Japan*. London: Pinter Publishers.

Grieco, J. M. 1990. *Cooperation Among Nations: Europe, America, and Non-Tariff Barriers to Trade*. Ithaca: Cornell University Press.

Hart, J. A. 1992. *Rival Capitalists: International Competitiveness in the United States, Japan, and Western Europe*. Ithaca: Cornell University Press.

Keene, K. H., P. G. Kirk Jr., N. Ornstein, E. J. Rollins, and J. H. Makin. 1987. "The Meaning of Competitiveness," in C. E. Barfield and J. H. Makin, eds., *Trade Policy and U.S. Competitiveness*, pp. 131–135. Washington, D.C.: American Enterprise Institute.

Kennedy, P. 1987. *The Rise and Fall of the Great Powers: Economic Change and Military Conflict, 1500–2000*. New York: Random House.

Kohno, M. 1995. "Ideas and Foreign Policy: The Emergence of Techno-Nationalism in U.S. Policies Toward Japan," in D. P. Rapkin and W. P.

Avery, eds., *National Competitiveness in a Global Economy*, pp. 199–224. Boulder: Lynne Rienner Publishers.

Krasner, S. D. 1986. "Trade Conflicts and the Common Defense: The United States and Japan." *Political Science Quarterly* 101, no. 5: 787–806.

Krugman, P. 1994a. "Competitiveness: A Dangerous Obsession." *Foreign Affairs* 73, no. 2: 28–44.

———. 1994b. *Peddling Prosperity: Economic Sense and Nonsense in the Age of Diminished Expectations*. New York: W. W. Norton.

Lazonick, W. 1990. *Competitive Advantage on the Shop Floor*. Cambridge: Harvard University Press.

Lenz, A. J. 1987. "Overview of the U.S. Competitiveness Position Today," in C. E. Barfield and J. H. Makin, eds., *Trade Policy and U.S. Competitiveness*, pp. 27–35. Washington, D.C.: American Enterprise Institute.

———. 1991. *Beyond Blue Economic Horizons: U.S. Trade Performance and U.S. International Competitiveness in the 1990s*. New York: Praeger.

Mastanduno, M. 1991. "Do Relative Gains Matter?" *International Security* 16, no. 1: 73–113.

Moran, T. H. 1993. *American Economic Policy and National Security*. New York: Council on Foreign Relations.

Nakatani, I. 1995. "Sources of Competitive Asymmetries Between the United States and Japan," in D. P. Rapkin and W. P. Avery, eds., *National Competitiveness in a Global Economy*, pp. 41–54. Boulder: Lynne Rienner Publishers.

Nelson, R. 1992. "Recent Writings on Competitiveness: Boxing the Compass." *California Management Review* (Winter): 127–137.

Porter, M. 1990. *The Competitive Advantage of Nations*. New York: The Free Press.

Preeg, E. H. 1994. "Krugman's Competitiveness: A Dangerous Obfuscation." *Washington Quarterly* 17, no. 4: 111–122.

President's Commission on Industrial Competitiveness. 1985. *Global Competition: The New Reality*. Washington, D.C.: U.S. Government Printing Office.

Rapkin, D. P. 1990. "The Contested Concept of Hegemonic Leadership," in D. P. Rapkin, ed., *Hegemony and World Leadership*, pp. 1–19. Boulder: Lynne Rienner Publishers.

Reich, R. 1991. "Who Is Us?" *Harvard Business Review* (January–February): 53–59.

Reich, S. 1995. "Ideology and Competitiveness: The Basis for U.S. and Japanese Economic Policies," in D. P. Rapkin and W. P. Avery, eds., *National Competitiveness in a Global Economy*, pp. 55–102. Boulder: Lynne Rienner Publishers.

Rollins, E. J. 1987. "A Republican's View," in C. E. Barfield and J. Makin, eds., *Trade Policy and U.S. Competitiveness*, pp. 122–126. Washington, D.C.: American Enterprise Institute.

Sandholtz, W. 1995. "Cooperating to Compete: The European Experiment," in D. P. Rapkin and W. P. Avery, eds., *National Competitiveness in a Global Economy*, pp. 225–242. Boulder: Lynne Rienner Publishers.

Sandholtz, W., M. Borrus, J. Zysman, K. Conca, J. Stowsky, S. Vogel, and S. Weber. 1992. *The Highest Stakes: The Economic Foundations of the Next Security System*. New York: Oxford University Press.

Snidal, D. 1991. "Relative Gains and the Pattern of International Cooperation." *American Political Science Review* 85, no. 3 (September): 701–726.

Stein, A. A. 1990. *Why Nations Cooperate: Circumstance and Choice in International Relations*. Ithaca, N.Y.: Cornell University Press.

Tyson, L. d'A. 1991. "They Are Not Us: Why American Ownership Still Matters." *American Prospect* (Winter): 37–49.

————. 1992. *Who's Bashing Whom? Trade Conflict in High-Technology Industries*. Washington, D.C.: Institute for International Economics.

Viner, J. 1948. "Power vs. Plenty as Objectives of Foreign Policy in the Seventeenth and Eighteenth Centuries." *World Politics* 1: 1–29.

Vogel, E. 1987. "Japan: Adaptive Communitarianism," in G. C. Lodge and E. F. Vogel, eds., *Ideology and National Competitiveness: An Analysis of Nine Countries*, pp. 141–171. Boston: Harvard Business School Press.

9

A NEW ECONOMIC GAME

Lester Thurow

*Lester Thurow has gained recent notoriety for cautioning against pushing for-
ward with a free trade agenda when most countries are not playing by these
rules. In this chapter Thurow argues that with the collapse of communism and
the success of the General Agreement on Tariffs and Trade–Bretton Woods
system, the new international economic system is in dire need of direction. Both
Japan and Europe, led by Germany, have risen to challenge U.S. hegemony,
but none of the leaders has established new rules. In the absence of a "communist menace," new competition exists between an individualistic, Anglo-Saxon
capitalist model, evidenced in the United States and Great Britain, and the
communitarian model of Europe and Japan. Unlike the previous system, which
was characterized by conditions that allowed countries at different levels of development to occupy niches that did not threaten other states, the modern world
is moving toward head-to-head competition for seven vital industrial sectors:
microelectronics, biotechnology, the new materials-science industries, telecommunications, civilian aviation, robotics and machine tools, and computers
and software. In this new competitive world, some countries will win and some
will lose.*

In the spring of 1991 British prime minister Margaret Thatcher lost
her job. She had not lost an election. It was not obvious that she would.
She lost her job because she insisted on playing the old twentieth-century
economic game. She simply would not recognize that the world had
changed and that she would have to change with it. She would not play
the twenty-first century's economic game. Having lost touch with

Excerpts from "A New Economic Game," in *Head to Head: The Coming Economic
Battle Among Japan, Europe, and America* (pp. 27–37, 39, 55–56) are reprinted
with permission from William Morrow & Co. (New York), 1992.

reality, she had to be pushed aside by those who were previously her allies.

Her downfall arose over the issue of European integration. Her stated purpose was to preserve the powers of the Bank of England to control money supplies and set British interest rates. She saw losing these powers as "the greatest abdication of national and parliamentary sovereignty in our history" (*Economist*, June 29, 1991, 27). She did not understand that these economic powers were no longer within her national power. In the new world economy what Mrs. Thatcher wanted to do could not be done—even though it had always been done in the past.

As of January 1, 1993, any European bank will be able to place an office in any other European city without government permission. When this happens, everyone will borrow in the country where interest rates were lowest and lend in the country where interest rates were highest—making interest rates the same everywhere in Europe. Mrs. Thatcher's only real choice was to join the European Monetary System (EMS) and have the power to appoint some of the members of a new European central bank, or refuse to do so and watch the German Bundesbank, in the absence of any British votes, gradually become the effective central bank for Europe. To retain any economic power over interest rates for the United Kingdom, she had to participate. . . .

New Competitors

Looking backward, future historians will see the twentieth century as a century of niche competition and the twenty-first century as a century of head-to-head competition. In 1950 the United States had a per capita GNP four times that of West Germany and fifteen times that of Japan. What were high-wage products from the Japanese perspective were low-wage products in West Germany. What were high-wage products in West Germany were low-wage products in America. As a result, imports from West Germany or Japan were not seen as threatening the good jobs that Americans wanted. Conversely, America's exports did not threaten good jobs in West Germany or Japan. The United States exported agricultural products that they could not grow, raw materials that they did not have, and high-tech products, such as civilian jet airliners, that they could not build.

The 1990s start from a very different place. In broad terms there are now three relatively equal contenders—Japan; the European Community, centered around its most powerful country, Germany; and the United States. Measured in terms of external purchasing power (how much can be bought if one's income is spent abroad), the per capita

GNPs of Japan and Germany are slightly larger than that of the United States. The exact amount depends upon the precise value of the dollar, mark, and yen when the measurements are made. . . .

What was an era of niche competition in the last half of the twentieth century will become an era of head-to-head competition in the first half of the twenty-first century. Niche competition is win-win. Everyone has a place where they can excel; no one is going to be driven out of business. Head-to-head competition is win-lose. Not everyone will get those seven key industries [microelectronics, biotechnology, the new materials-science industries, telecommunications, civilian aviation, robotics and machine tools, and computers and software]. Some will win; some will lose.

The shift to head-to-head competition can be seen in the language of current economic discourse. In the Japanese, but not the American, version of the book *The Japan That Can Say No*, Mr. Ishihara states that the superpower military warfare of the twentieth century will be replaced by economic warfare in the twenty-first century, and that Japan will be the winner of the twenty-first century's economic wars (1991, 50). In the American version he talks about "the Pacific age." Normura Securities sees a world where "competition in the marketplace could well become extremely intense" (Ishihara 1991, 50).

Similar views exist in Germany. On German television in February 1990, Chancellor Helmut Kohl of West Germany issued his counterdeclaration of economic war: "The 1990s will be the decade of the Europeans and not that of the Japanese" (*The Boston Globe* February 9, 1990, 2). Implicitly, Chancellor Kohl sees an America already out of the game. The same point has been bluntly put by the prime minister of France, Edith Cresson: "There is a world economic war on" (*Toronto Globe and Mail* May 16, 1991, A16). The rotating head of the EEC and foreign minister of Italy, Gianni De Michelis, thinks that "all this points to Europe recovering its role as the core of the world economy. The next ten years will make evident Japan's big short comings" (*International Herald Tribune* March 26, 1990, 2).

Today's tough talk is merely a prelude to tomorrow's tough economic competition. Conflicts in economic self-interest will also be sharper than they otherwise would have been because of the disappearance of the Soviet military bear. In the next half century no one has to moderate economic positions to preserve the military alliances that were necessary to contain the USSR. In the past half century military needs prevented economic conflicts from getting out of hand. From now on, economic cooperation will have to stand on its own, and economic arrangements will not be held together with military glue.

On one level a prediction that economic warfare will replace military warfare is good news. Vigorous competition may spur economic growth. There is nothing morally wrong with an aggressive invasion of well-made, superbly marketed German or Japanese products. Being bought is not the same thing as being militarily occupied. At the same time the military metaphor is fundamentally incorrect. The economic game that will be played in the twenty-first century will have cooperative as well as competitive elements. As we shall later see, a cooperative macroeconomic locomotive will have to be built to prevent the cycles that are inherent in capitalism. The world's common environment will require global cooperation if it is to be livable for anyone.

Economics abhors a vacuum no less than Mother Nature. The economic competition between communism and capitalism is over, but another competition between two different forms of capitalism is already under way. Using a distinction first made by George C. Lodge, a Harvard Business School professor, the individualistic Anglo-Saxon British-American form of capitalism is going to face off against the communitarian German and Japanese variants of capitalism . . . (Lodge 1991, 15–16).

America and Britain trumpet individualistic values: the brilliant entrepreneur, Nobel Prize winners, large wage differentials, individual responsibility for skills, easy to fire and easy to quit, profit maximization, and hostile mergers and takeovers—their hero is the Lone Ranger. In contrast, Germany and Japan trumpet communitarian values: business groups, social responsibility for skills, teamwork, firm loyalty, industry strategies, and active industrial policies that promote growth. Anglo-Saxon firms are profit maximizers; Japanese business firms play a game that might better be known as "strategic conquest." Americans believe in "consumer economics;" Japanese believe in "producer economics."

In the Anglo-Saxon variant of capitalism, the individual is supposed to have a personal economic strategy for success, and the business firm is supposed to have an economic strategy that is a reflection of the wishes of its individual shareholders. Since shareholders want income to maximize their lifetime consumption, their firms must be profit maximizers. For the profit-maximizing firm, customer and employee relations are merely a means to the end of higher profits for the shareholders. Wages are to be beaten down where possible, and when not needed, employees are to be laid off. Lower wages equal higher profits. Workers in the Anglo-Saxon system are expected to change employers whenever opportunities arise to earn higher wages elsewhere. They owe their employer nothing. In contrast, many Japanese firms still refer to voluntary quits as "treason" . . . (*Financial Times* April 8, 1991, 4).

The communitarian business firm has a very different set of stakeholders who must be consulted when its strategies are being set. In Japanese business firms employees are seen as the number one stakeholder, customers number two, and the shareholders a distant number three.

Since the employee is the prime stakeholder, higher employee wages are a central goal of the firm in Japan. Profits will be sacrificed to maintain either wages or employment. Dividend payouts to the shareholders are low.

Communitarian societies expect companies to invest in the skills of their work forces. In the United States and Great Britain, skills are an individual responsibility. Firms exist to promote efficiency by hiring skills at the lowest possible wage rates. Labor is not a member of the team. It is just another factor of production to be rented when it is needed, and laid off when it is not.

Beyond personal and firm strategies, communitarian capitalism believes in having strategies at two additional levels. Business groups such as the Mitsui group or the Deutsche Bank group are expected to have collective strategies. Companies should be financially interlocked and work together to strengthen each other's activities. The Japanese break up into vertical *keiretsu* made up of suppliers, producers, and retailers, and horizontal *keiretsu* made up of firms in different industries. At the top of the pyramid of Japanese business groups are the major former *zaibatsu* groups: Mitsui group (23 member firms), Mitsubishi group (28 member firms), Sumitomo group (21 member firms), Fuji group (29 member firms), Sanwa group (39 member firms), Dai-Ichi Kangyo group (45 member firms) . . . (Yoshitomi 1990, 10).

Similar patterns exist in Germany. . . . In March 1990 the two biggest business groups in the world (the Mitsubishi group from Japan and the Daimler Benz-Deutsche Bank group from Germany) held a secret meeting in Singapore to talk about a global alliance (*The Japan Economic Journal* 1990, 1; *The Economist*, March 10, 1990, 72). Among other things, both were interested in expanding their market share in civilian aircraft production. From an American perspective everything about that Singapore meeting was criminally illegal. It violated both antitrust and banking laws. In the United States banks cannot own industrial firms and businesses cannot sit down behind closed doors to plan joint strategies. Those doing so get thrown into jail for extended periods of time. Yet in today's world Americans cannot force the rest of the world to play the economic game as Americans think it should be played. The game will be played under international, not American rules.

Both Europe and Japan believe that government has a role to play in economic growth. Airbus Industries, a civilian aircraft manufacturer owned by the British, French, German, and Spanish governments, is an expression of a pan-European strategy. It was designed to break the American monopoly and get Europe back into civilian aircraft manufacturing. Today it is a success, as it has captured 20 percent of the aircraft market and announced plans to double production and capture one third of the worldwide market by the mid-1990s. . . .

Germany, the dominant European economic power, sees itself as having a *"social-market"* economy and not just a "market" economy. Codetermination is required to broaden the ranks of corporate stakeholders beyond that of the traditional capitalistic owners to include workers. German governments (state and federal) own more shares in more industries (airlines, autos, steel, chemicals, electric power, transportation—some outright, some partially) than any noncommunist country on the face of the globe. Public investments such as Airbus Industries are not controversial political issues. Privatization is not sweeping across Germany as it did across Great Britain.

Government is believed to have an important role in insuring that everyone has the skills necessary to participate in the market. Germany's socially financed apprenticeship system is the envy of the world. Social-welfare policies are seen as a necessary part of a market economy. Unfettered capitalism is believed to generate levels of income inequality that are unacceptable.

In contrast, in the United States social-welfare programs are seen as regrettable necessities, since people will not provide for their own futures (old age, unemployment, ill health), but there are continual reminders that the higher taxes necessary to pay for social-welfare benefits will reduce work incentives for those paying taxes and that the benefits will undercut work incentives for those receiving them. In the ideal Anglo-Saxon market economy, social-welfare policies would not be necessary. . . .

In America's economic theology, government has no role in investment funding and a *legitimate* one only in basic R&D. These rules are sometimes violated in practice, but the theology is clear. In the Anglo-Saxon view governments should protect private-property rights, then step back, get out of the way, and let individuals do their thing. Profit maximization will lead capitalism in the right directions. . . .

While very different histories have led to very different systems, today those very different systems face off in the same world economy. Let me suggest that the military metaphors now so widely used should be replaced by the language of football. Despite its competitive element—the desire to win—football also has a cooperative element. Everyone has to agree on the rules of the game, the referees, and how to split the proceeds. One can want to win yet still remain friends both during and after the game. But what the rest of the world knows as football is known in America as soccer. What Americans like about American football—frequent time-outs, lots of huddles, and unlimited substitutions—is not found in world football. It is a faster game. So too is the economic game ahead. All sides will call themselves capitalists, but participants will be playing two very different games. . . .

New Rules for Playing the Game

The late 1920s and early 1930s began with a series of worldwide financial crashes that ultimately spiraled downward into the Great Depression. As GNPs fell, the dominant countries each created trading blocks (the Japanese Co-Prosperity Sphere, the British Empire, the French Union, Germany plus eastern Europe, America with its Monroe Doctrine) to minimize imports and preserve jobs. If only one country had kept imports out, limiting imports would have helped it avoid the Great Depression, but with everyone restricting trade, the downward pressures were simply magnified. In the aggregate, fewer imports must equal fewer exports. Eventually, those economic blocks evolved into military blocks, and World War II began.

In the aftermath of World War II, the GATT–Bretton Woods trading system was built to prevent a repetition of these events. Trade restrictions and tariff barriers were gradually reduced in a series of trading rounds such as the Kennedy round or the Tokyo round. Under the rules, each country had to treat all other countries in exactly the same way—the most-favored-nation principle. The best deal (the lowest tariffs, the easiest access, the fewest restrictions) given to anyone must be given to everyone—effectively prohibiting trading blocks.

This system has been described as "unilateral global Keynesianism" (Mead 1989, 3, 10, 26). It was unilateral in that the United States was "single-handedly prepared to direct and maintain the system." The dollar was the medium of exchange and the standard of value. America was the manager of the system. It practiced "global Keynesianism" (tightening monetary and fiscal policies when inflation threatened; loosening monetary and fiscal polices when recession threatened) so that it could be an economic locomotive for the rest of the world. It provided a "market of first resort" where countries could export relatively easily and the United States did not insist on strict reciprocity in its commercial dealings with other countries. The system was also very Anglo-Saxon—a universal rule-driven system as opposed to a deal-driven system.

America performed these functions not because it was altruistic, although it might have been, but because, as the world's biggest economy, it had more to gain from an open global economy than anyone else. America believed that it could not be prosperous unless the world was prosperous and everyone had equal access to raw materials and markets.

History will record that the GATT–Bretton Woods trading system was one of the world's all-time great successes. In the forty years after it was adopted, the world economy grew faster than it had grown in all of human history. That growth was also much more widely shared. With the exception of a handful of countries, mostly in Africa, everyone had much higher real per capita incomes in 1990 than they had in 1945. Where the United States was once much richer than the rest of the world, by the late 1980s it had become just one of a number of approximately equally wealthy countries. As America's position shifted from one of effortless economic superiority to one of equality, America's share of the world's GNP necessarily fell from far more than half of the world's total in the 1940s to 22–23 percent of the total in the late 1980s (IMF 1991, 1).

This success makes evolution along the previous track impossible. Economic arrangements that work in a unipolar world simply do not work in a multipolar world.

In the first three decades after World War II, everyone played a win-win economic game. Imports that looked small to the United States (3 to 5 percent of GNP) provided large markets to the rest of the world because of America's great wealth and giant size. Export opportunities were abundant for anyone who wanted to sell in the U.S. market, and the jobs that were associated with these exports were high-wage jobs by the standards of the exporting countries. Viewed from the American perspective, these imports were not threatening. Foreign market shares were small, and import penetration came in what were in America labor-intensive, low-wage industries that were being phased out anyway.

These imports were just an expression of what came to be known as the "product cycle." America would invent a new high-tech product and learn to mass produce it. Gradually, the product would shift to being a mid-tech product best produced in mid-wage countries such as Japan or Europe, from whence it would eventually move as a low-tech product to low-wage countries in the Third World.

Balancing America's trading accounts was not a problem. America could grow farm products that the rest of the world could not grow, supply raw materials such as oil that the rest of the world did not have, and manufacture unique high-tech products such as the Boeing 707 that the rest of the world could not build. America's exports did not compete with products from the rest of the world. They filled gaps that the rest of the world could not fill. In the jargon of today's strategic planners, each country had a noncompetitive niche where it could be a winner. America grew rapidly; the rest of the world grew even more rapidly.

Because of its size, America served as a locomotive for the world economy. When the system was established, memories of the Great Depression were still sharp. Whenever the world sank into a recession, to prevent it from becoming a depression the United States would use its fiscal and monetary policies to stimulate demand—benefiting both

American and foreign producers. Foreign exports to America would rise, pulling the exporting countries out of their economic slump. With higher export earnings, these countries would buy more unique American products.

But with success, the American locomotive gradually grew too small to pull the rest of the world. The last gasp of the old macroeconomic locomotive was seen in the aftermath of the 1981–1982 recession. American macroeconomic stimulus, starting in the fall of 1982, pulled the industrial world out of its sharpest post–World War II recession. In 1983 and 1984 most of the growth in both Europe and Japan could be traced to exports to the American market. But for the first time the United States found itself burdened with a large trade deficit as a consequence. Its exports did not automatically rise to balance its imports.

America's effortless exports were a thing of the past. The green revolution in the developed and underdeveloped world had sharply curtailed foreign markets for American farm products. America had gradually shifted from being a large exporter of raw materials, such as oil, to being a large importer. The unique high-tech products that the rest of the world could not build had disappeared in a world of technical parity. They could be gotten many other places. What in the past had been a temporary cyclical trade deficit became a permanent structural trade deficit.

A successful noncompetitive niche-export environment had evolved gradually into an intensely competitive head-to-head export environment. Head-to-head competition is never win-win; at best it is win-lose (Dudley 1991, 1). In America, with imports $162 billion greater than exports in 1987, politically there were simply many more American losers than winners (Council of Economic Advisers 1991, 402). Abroad, the elimination of America's trade deficit (the loss of all of those exports) threatened the jobs of millions of workers.

The nature of the problem can be seen in the maneuvering over high-definition television (HDTV). Europe, Japan, and the United States are all deliberately setting different technical standards for HDTV to insure that producers from other regions cannot dominate their market (U.S. Congress 1989). The spirit of GATT would call for common standards to set a level playing field. But no one wants a level playing field. Everyone wants an edge.

In response, slowly but surely, trade is increasingly being managed by governments. Nontariff import barriers are rising everywhere. In the United States the percentage of American imports subject to nontariff restriction has doubled to 25 percent in the past decade (*The Economist* July 7, 1990, 13). At the leading edge of technology, the Japanese-American semiconductor pact effectively turns semiconductor chips into a managed sector, and at the lagging edge of technology, the ever-expanding multifiber agreement keeps textiles in the managed sector. Autos, an intermediate technology, have for more than a decade been in the managed sector. The door to the market of first resort is slowly but surely closing.

The trends are clear. America makes special arrangements with Canada and is negotiating special arrangements with Mexico. Europe talks about associate memberships in the European Community for the remaining nonmember countries in Western Europe and some of Middle Europe. Migration pressures from North Africa are leading it to a Mexican-style agreement with the countries of North Africa whereby it will become Europe's preferential low-wage manufacturing area. Bilateral negotiations, prohibited under GATT and leading to principles very different from that of most-favored-nation, are under way everywhere.

Most of them are held under the cover of setting up a "common market." Technically, the common market escape clause from the most-favored-nation principle is only supposed to be used if the ultimate objective of the common market is a real political union. Europeans can argue that this is the case in Europe, but in North America there is not even a pretense that the Canadian, Mexican, and American economic talks are a prelude to political union. The Structural Impediment Talks between Japan and America didn't even bother with this legal "fig leaf." The world has forgotten what it learned in the 1920s. Bilateral negotiations cannot lead to a stable trading system.

To work, a multipolar, integrated, open world economy requires fiscal and monetary coordination among the major countries—Germany, Japan, and the United States. A common locomotive is needed, and it can only exist if the major countries stimulate or restrict their economies in unison. There is no doubt that coordination can work. The world witnessed a demonstration of this effectiveness in 1988. In 1988 almost every developed country grew faster than it had in 1987, faster than it was predicted to grow in November 1987. The coordinating event was, of course, the stock market crash of October 1987. In the aftermath of that crash, every government thought that its economy would tumble into a recession, and all took prompt actions to stimulate their economies. In concert, the stimulation worked—forward momentum was almost instantaneous.

In normal times, however, coordination has proved illusive. Within two days in February 1991, the U.S. Federal Reserve Board announced that it was lowering interest rates, while the German Bundesbank announced that it was raising interest rates. In early 1991 America had a recession and wanted to stimulate demand; it needed lower interest rates. Germany had a boom and wanted to cut back on consumer demands. Higher interest rates were necessary to attract capital to pay for investments in eastern Germany. No agreement was possible.

Coordination is one of those words that is easy to say but hard to do. It means that each country must occasionally take actions that it does not want to take. The reasons for the resistance to coordination are easy to understand. In February 1991 Germany and America would have had to agree on whether the world's major problem was recession or inflation. Coordination would have required the United States to balance its budget to allow the world to move to lower real interest rates. The world needs more savings to handle the investment demands of the Second World and Third World and to repair the damage in Kuwait. America should not be the world's biggest borrower. But Americans neither want to raise taxes nor cut government services. That is what they voted for in November 1988, when they elected a Republican read-my-lips, no-new-taxes president and a Democratic no-cuts-in-government-services Congress.

If American budget balancing is not to depress world aggregate demand and instigate a recession, coordination requires Germany to grow much faster over an extended period of time. In the 1980s, West Germany was unwilling to do so. It faced negative demography and a falling German labor force in the 1990s. It did not want to grow faster and suck in hundreds of thousands of guest workers. All of those desires were reversed at the end of the decade because of events in East Germany, but the shifts in German policies were not brought about by desires to build an efficient world locomotive. The German interest in growth arose because of the desperate need to bring east German income levels up to those of western Germany just as soon as possible to prevent everyone in eastern Germany from moving to western Germany.

While the events in eastern Germany provide a window of opportunity to reduce the world's structural trade imbalances (the German trade surplus will fall from 135 billion marks in 1990 to about 30 billion marks in 1991), fortunate circumstances are not a permanent substitute for deliberate macroeconomic coordination (Fisher 1991, 13). They give the world economy a little breathing room and the prospect of faster growth in the 1990s, but in the long run, accidental coordination is not a good substitute for planned coordination.

If the 1991 Anglo-Saxon recession were to spread to the rest of the world, the United States could not do in 1992 what it did a decade earlier. It entered the recession with an already large trade deficit—not the surplus of 1981. Instead of being the world's largest net creditor, which could borrow at will, it would be the world's largest net debtor and a shaky credit risk. It could not compound its already large internal government deficit with further tax cuts or increased expenditures. It simply could not set its macroeconomic policies to grow faster than the rest of the world so as to provide an export market to pull everyone one else back to prosperity.

The need to construct a new macroeconomic locomotive has gotten a lot of attention, if not much action, but a market of first resort is no less important. All of the successful developing countries in the past half century have gone through a phase where they sent most of their exports to the United States. The United States has effectively been the open market of first resort on which any country that wished to join the industrial world focused its attention during the takeoff phase of economic growth. Between 1981 and 1986, 42 percent of Korea's growth and 74 percent of Taiwan's growth could be traced to exports to the American market (*Journal of Japanese Trade and Industry* 1988, 11). While America represents only 23 percent of world GNP, in 1987 it took 48 percent of the manufactured exports from all of the Third World countries combined (World Bank 1989, A36–A37). In contrast, the European Economic Community (EEC) took 29 percent and Japan, 12 percent. Yet the aggregate EEC GNP is larger than that of the United States, and Japan's GNP is only 40 percent smaller. Earlier, during the dollar-shortage era of the 1950s, Europe was equally dependent upon access to the U.S. market for its success. The United States has been the market where successful developing countries earned the foreign exchange they needed to grow.

The American market cannot forever absorb most of the exports from the Third World. At some point in the future, the United States will have to generate a trade surplus to pay interest on its accumulated international debts. When it does so, it will cut back on its foreign purchases and go through a period where its market is effectively closed to developing countries.

The system also needs a manager if it is to work (*The Economist*, September 22, 1990, 5). That need can be seen in the failure of the Uruguay round of GATT trade negotiations to meet their deadlines. Freer trade in agricultural products heads the Uruguay negotiating list, but this is an area where little progress is possible, since millions of farmers and the land they now farm would have to leave farming (*The Economist*, September 22, 1990, 30). The world can simply produce more than those who have money to pay for it want to eat. No government is going to sign an agreement that forces large numbers of its farmers and much of its land to leave agriculture.

Services are second on the Uruguay negotiating list, but they are just not worth fighting about (*The Economist*, September 22, 1990, 36). Less than 10 percent of America's exports are real services (returns on American investments abroad are counted as service exports in the official statistics) and real services have not been growing in importance in recent years. Service industries can be owned by foreigners, but most services have to be produced where they are consumed. Leaving travel and license fees aside, America's 1990 service exports to foreigners amounted to only twenty-seven billion dollars (Sinai and Sofianou, 1991, 13). Financial services were seen as a boom area, but U.S. exports never exceeded five billion dollars.

Although Third World countries firmly believe the opposite, they might even be the big beneficiaries from freer trade in services. With modern telecommunications, American computer-software factories have, for example, been opened up in India, and the Caribbean is increasingly being used for processing insurance forms. The developed world's clerical functions could well move to the Third World with free trade in services. But the Third World doesn't see it that way. These countries think their future growth industries, the services, will be captured by companies from the First World.

With the United States opting out of its leadership role to look after its own narrow self-interests, bilateral negotiations (the Japanese-American Structural Impediment Talks) and special bilateral trade agreements (United States-Canada and United States-Mexico) have replaced multilateral negotiations as the place where real concessions are made. But this automatically leads to a trading-block mentality. The semiconductor agreement between the United States and Japan guarantees the United States more than 20 percent of the Japanese market, but no provision is made for the Europeans (Kehoe, 1991, 5). Outsiders do not have equal access, and the special privileges given to one are not given to all.

Everyone is now unilaterally judging their own trade disputes—no one more so than the United States. One of the GATT–Bretton Woods institutions, the International Trade Organization, was never created. The need to do what it was designed to do—judge trade disputes and enforce decisions resolving those disputes—has only become more obvious in recent years. Increasingly, countries are making themselves judges of their own trade disputes. When this happens, multilateralism ceases to have any real meaning.

To make an open world economy work, everyone must feel that they have an equal chance to win—what is known as "a level playing field" in America; "reciprocity" in Europe; or "equal opportunity, not equal outcomes," in Japan. But if the economic game is to be seen as fair, there must be broadly similar taxes, regulations, and private modes of operation. "Economic life-style variables" such as fringe benefits must be harmonized. German firms cannot give three years leave to new mothers unless the rest of the world is willing to match its generosity (Goodhard, 1991, 2).

In theory, exchange-rate differences could compensate for differences in macroeconomic systems. Those countries less open to imports or with lower social-welfare payments would have higher currency values than they would have had if their systems had been more open or more generous. But in fact, currency values don't automatically handicap the players in the required manner. Currency values are often dominated by other factors, such as capital flows.

Even if exchange rates did work as theory predicts, they would not solve the problem. The players in the market would every day see an unfair game and would not notice the offsetting changes in currency values. Consider the Japanese business groups (Mitsui, Mitsubishi, etc.) and their interlocking ownership. They hold monthly meetings to plot strategy in the Japanese and American markets. American CEOs holding such a meeting would find themselves in jail regardless of whether they were talking about the Japanese or the American market. The opportunity to work out common strategies of conquest in home or foreign markets cannot be permitted to only one side, even if a lower value of the dollar would theoretically compensate the American side for its inability to form such strategic alliances. If distribution systems are owned or controlled by producers in one country (Japan) but open in another (Holland), one set of exporters finds it much easier to get his products on store shelves than another. Philips, a Dutch firm, not surprisingly complains that it does not have equal access to the Japanese market for its consumer products.

In the real economic world the game must be roughly similar to be seen as fair. Complicated opaque compensatory factors are not a satisfactory political answer, even if they are a theoretical economic answer.

In an open world economy the high minimum wages of Europe are threatened by the low minimum wages of the United States. Long European vacations (thirty days in Germany) are not viable given short vacations in the Pacific Rim (eleven days in Japan) (Protzman, 1991, f6). Production simply moves to those parts of the world where such benefits don't have to be paid, thereby forcing the benefits to be eliminated. Benefits that are now hidden in prices have to become overt in wages. Economists think markets become more efficient when hidden benefits become visible benefits, but average voters have very different preferences.

In an open world economy, everyone, not just unskilled American workers, has to be willing to live with factor price equalization. The capitalist who is willing to work for the lowest rate of return in the world sets the maximum rate of return for everyone else. If the Japanese capitalist will accept a 3 percent return, Americans cannot have 15 percent.

The GATT–Bretton Woods trading system is dead. It died not in failure but at the normal end of a very successful life. Logically, a new

Bretton Woods conference should now be under way. But politically, it cannot be called. Such a conference can only occur if there is a dominant political power that can force everyone to agree. In 1944 the United States was such a power (Germany and Japan were not even represented). Today there is no such power. If the Uruguay round cannot succeed, much more fundamental negotiations certainly could not succeed.

The required economic changes cannot, however, wait for the right political moment to call such a conference. Success is forcing the rules of the game to change, even if no one formally writes a new set of rules. In this case the rules of the new game will be informally written in Europe. Those who control the world's largest market get to write the rules. That is as it always has been. When the United States had the world's largest market, it got to write the rules. As the Europeans negotiate the rules for their internal common market and decide how outsiders relate to their market, they will effectively be writing the rules for the world trade in the next century. Everyone else will gradually adopt Europe's rules as the world's de facto operating system.

The Europeans are going to write the rules for a system of "managed trade" and "quasi trading blocks." Management agreements, such as those now governing semiconductors, will spread, and the countries within any one block, such as Canada within the American market, will get special trading privileges not given to outsiders. I will call the blocks quasi trading blocks to distinguish them from the trading blocks of the 1930s. The quasi trading blocks of the 1990s will attempt to manage trade, but they will not attempt to reduce or eliminate it as the trading blocks of the 1930s did.

New Opportunities

At temperatures near absolute zero, and now at much higher temperatures in some ceramic materials, superconductivity occurs. The rules that govern the propagation of electricity suddenly change. Old constants are no longer constant. New rules suddenly apply. Resistance disappears, and electrical devices that could not previously be built can now be built, but the currents that are unleashed are difficult to control.

Much the same is happening in the world economy. New players, technologies, and rules are coming together to generate an economic form of superconductivity. Old constants will have to be discarded. Suddenly, new rules will emerge in a very different game. Potentially, much more productive economies can be built, but controlling the currents that will be unleashed will be equally difficult.

References

Boston Globe. 1990. "Kohl to Reassure Soviets on Unification," February 9.

Council of Economic Advisors. 1991. *Economic Report of the President*, Washington, D.C., GPO.

Dudley, William, ed. 1991. *Trade Opposing Views*, San Diego, Greenhaven Press.

The Economist. 1990. "A Tokyo Stuttgart Axis?," March 10.

The Economist. 1990. "Mercantilists in Houston," July 7.

The Economist. 1990. "Nothing to Lose but Its Chains," September 22.

The Economist. 1991. "She Makes Her Stand," June 29.

Financial Times. 1991. "Graduates Take Rites of Passage into Japanese Corporate Life," April 8.

Fisher, Andrew. 1991. "Home Thoughts Rather Than Abroad," *Financial Times*, July 26.

Goodhard, David. 1991. "Germany Raises Child Care Leave to 3 Years," *Financial Times*, August 15.

International Herald Tribune. 1990. "Europe: A Golden Opportunity Not to Be Missed," March 26.

International Monetary Fund. 1991. *International Financial Statistics*, Washington, D.C., April.

Ishihara, Shintaro. 1991. *The Japan That Can Say No: Why Japan Will Be First Among Equals*, New York, Simon and Schuster.

The Japan Economic Journal. 1990. March 17.

Journal of Japanese Trade and Industry. 1988. "Helping the NICs Help the World Economy," no. 4.

Kehoe, Louise. 1991. "Chip Pact Gives Letter to the Spirit of U.S. Hopes," *Financial Times*, June 6.

Lodge, George C. 1991. *Perestroika for America*. Boston, Harvard Business School Press.

Mead, Walter Russell. 1989. "From Bretton Woods to the Bush Team," *World Policy Journal*, Summer.

Protzman, Ferdinand. 1991. "Greetings from Fortress Germany," *The New York Times*, August 18.

Sinai, Allen, and Zaharo Sofianou. 1991. "U.S. Service Exports: 'Who Buys What?'" *The Service Economy*. Washington, D.C.: Coalition of Service Industries.

Toronto Globe and Mail. 1991. "France's New Prime Minister a Socialist Battler," May 16.

U.S. Congress. 1989. *Prospects for Development of a U.S. HDTV Industry: Hearings before Committee on Government Affairs*. U.S. Senate, 101st Congress, 1st sess., August.

World Bank. 1989. *Handbook of International Trade and Development Statistics*, Washington, D.C., The Bank.

Yoshitomi, Masaru. 1990. "Keiretsu: An Insider's Guide to Japan's Conglomerates," *International Economic Insights*, Sept/Oct.

CONTENDING VIEWS OF INTERNATIONAL POLITICAL ECONOMY: MARXISM, DEPENDENCY, AND WORLD SYSTEMS THEORY

10

EXCERPTS FROM *CAPITAL* AND *COMMUNIST MANIFESTO*

Karl Marx and Friedrich Engels

The following excerpts from the classic works of Karl Marx focus on Marx's critique of the nature of capitalism in the workplace and in society. In the selection from Capital *(1867), Marx outlines the division and specialization of labor under capitalistic conditions and the conversion of labor to commodity status. Marx contends that this division impoverishes and brutalizes the worker—the foundation of the notion of estrangement, or alienation, an enduring concept of the Marxist literature. The excerpt from the* Manifesto *(1848) focuses on the capitalist class (the bourgeoisie) and its powerful and revolutionary impact on society, providing a summary glimpse of the Marxist view of the dialectical forces of history. The contradictions of capitalism become apparent in the pauperization of all classes except the capitalists and in the persistence of ever deeper crises in the impending clash of historical forces—the capitalist and proletarian classes. Many of Marx's ideas about capitalism, such as his analysis of alienation and of the distributional impact of capitalism, remain timely on the cusp of the twenty-first century.*

Capital, Karl Marx

The Detail Labourer and His Implements

If we now go more into detail, it is, in the first place, clear that a labourer who all his life performs one and the same simple operation, converts his whole body into the automatic, specialised implement of

that operation. Consequently, he takes less time in doing it, than the artificer who performs a whole series of operations in succession. But the
collective labourer, who constitutes the living mechanism of manufacture, is made up solely of such specialised detail labourers. Hence, in
comparison with the independent handicraft, more is produced in a
given time, or the productive power of labor is increased. Moreover,
when once this fractional work is established as the exclusive function of
one person, the methods it employs become perfected. The workman's
continued repetition of the same simple act, and the concentration of
his attention on it, teach him by experience how to attain the desired effects with the minimum of exertion. But since there are always several
generations of labourers living at one time, and working together at the
manufacture of a given article, the technical skill, the tricks of the trade
thus acquired, become established, and are accumulated and handed
down. Manufacture, in fact, produces the skill of the detail labourer, by
reproducing, and systematically driving to an extreme within the workshop, the naturally developed differentiation of trades, which it found
ready to hand in society at large. On the other hand, the conversion of
fractional work into the life-calling of one mall, corresponds to the tendency shown by earlier societies, to make trades hereditary; either to
petrify them into castes, or whenever definite historical conditions
beget in the individual a tendency to vary in a manner incompatible
with the nature of castes, to ossify them into guilds. . . .

An artificer, who performs one after another the various fractional operations in the production of a finished article, must at one
time change his place, at another his tools. The transition from one operation to another interrupts the Row of his labour, and creates, so to
say, gaps in his working-day. These gaps close up so soon as he is tied
to one and the same operation all day long; they vanish in proportion as
the changes in his work diminish. The resulting increased productive
power is owing either to an increased expenditure of labour-power in a
given time—i.e., to increased intensity of labour—or to a decrease in
the amount of labour-power unproductively consumed. The extra expenditure of power, demanded by every transition from rest to motion,
is made up for by prolonging the duration of the normal velocity when
once acquired. On the other hand, constant labour of one uniform kind
disturbs the intensity and flow of a man's animal spirits, which had
recreation and delight in mere change of activity. . . .

Early in the manufacturing period, the principle of lessening the
necessary labour-time in the production of commodities, was adopted
and formulated: and the use of machines, especially for certain simple
first processes that have to be conducted on a very large scale, and with
the application of great force, sprang up here and there. Thus, at an
early period in paper manufacture, the tearing up of the rags was done

by paper-mills; and in metal works, the pounding of the ores was effected by stamping mills. The Roman Empire had handed down the elementary form of all machinery in the water-wheel.

The handicraft period bequeathed to us the great inventions of the compass, of gunpowder, of type-printing, and of the automatic clock. But, on the whole, machinery played that subordinate part which Adam Smith assigns to it in comparison with division of labour. The sporadic use of machinery in the 17th century was of the greatest importance, because it supplied the great mathematicians of that time with a practical basis and stimulant to the creation of the science of mechanics.

The collective labourer, formed by the combination of a number of detail labourers, is the machinery specially characteristic of the manufacturing period. The various operations that are performed in turns by the producer of a commodity, and coalesce one with another during the progress of production, lay claim to him in various ways. In one operation he must exert more strength, in another more skill, in another more attention; and the same individual does not possess all these qualities in an equal degree. After Manufacture has once separated, made independent, and isolated the various operations, the labourers are divided, classified, and grouped according to their predominating qualities. If their natural endowments are, on the one hand, the foundation on which the division of labour is built up, on the other hand, Manufacture, once introduced, develops in them new powers that are by nature fitted only for limited and special functions. The collective laborer now possesses, in an equal degree of excellence, all the qualities requisite for production, and expends them in the most economical manner, by exclusively employing all his organs, consisting of particular labourers, or groups of labourers, in performing their special functions. The one-sidedness and the deficiencies of the detail labourer become perfections when he is a part of the collective labourer. The habit of doing only one thing converts him into a never failing instrument, while his connection with the whole mechanism compels him to work with the regularity of the parts of a machine. Since the collective labourer has functions, both simple and complex, both high and low, his members, the individual labour-powers, require different degrees of training, and must therefore have different values. Manufacture, therefore, develops a hierarchy of labour-powers, to which there corresponds a scale of wages. If, on the one hand, the individual labourers are appropriated and annexed for life by a limited function; on the other hand, the various operations of the hierarchy are parcelled out among the labourers according to both their natural and their acquired capabilities. Every process of production, however, requires certain simple manipulations, which every man is capable of doing. They too are now severed from their connection with the more pregnant moments of activity, and ossified into exclusive functions of specially appointed laborers. Hence, Manufacture suggests, ill every handicraft that it seizes upon, a class of so-called unskilled labourers, a class which handicraft industry strictly excluded. . . .

Section 4: Division of Labour
in Manufacture, and Division of Labour in Society

Division of labour in a society, and the corresponding tying down of individuals to a particular calling, develops itself, just as does the division of labour in manufacture, from opposite starting-points. Within a family, and after further development with a tribe, there springs up naturally a division of labour, caused by differences of sex and age, a division that is consequently based on a purely physiological foundation, which division enlarges its materials by the expansion of the community, by the increase of population, and more especially, by the conflicts between different tribes, and the subjugation of one tribe by another. On the other hand, as I have before remarked, the exchange of products springs up at the points where different families, tribes, communities, come in contact; for, in the beginning of civilisation, it is not private individuals but families, tribes, &c., that meet on an independent footing. Different communities find different means of production, and different means of subsistence in their natural environment. Hence, their modes of production, and of living, and their products are different. It is this spontaneously developed difference which, when different communities come in contact, calls forth the mutual exchange of products, and the consequent gradual conversion of those products into commodities. . . .

The foundation of every division of labour that is well developed, and brought about by the exchange of commodities, is the separation between town and country. It may be said, that the whole economic history of society is summed up in the movement of this antithesis. We pass it over, however, for the present.

Just as a certain number of simultaneously employed labourers are the material pre-requisites for division of labour in manufacture, so are the number and density of the populations, which here correspond to the agglomeration in one workshop, a necessary condition for the division of labour in society. Nevertheless, this density is more or less relative. A relatively thinly populated country, with well-developed means of communication, has a denser population than a more numerously populated country, with badly-developed means of communication; and in this sense the Northern States of the American Union, for instance, are more thickly populated than India.

Since the production and the circulation of commodities are the general pre-requisites of the capitalist mode of production, division of labour in manufacture demands, that division of labour in society at large should previously have attained a certain degree of development. Inversely, the former division reacts upon and develops and multiplies the latter. Simultaneously, with the differentiation of the instruments of labour, the industries that produce these instruments, become more and more differentiated. If the manufacturing system seize upon an industry, which, previously, was carried on in connection with others, either as a chief or as a subordinate industry, and by one producer, these industries immediately separate their connection, and become independent. If it seize upon a particular stage in the production of a commodity, the other stages of its production become converted into so many independent industries. It has already been stated, that where the finished article consists merely of a number of parts fitted together, the detail operations may re-establish themselves as genuine and separate handicrafts. In order to carry out more perfectly the division of labour in manufacture, a single branch of production is, according to the varieties of its raw material, or the various forms that one and the same raw material may assume, split up into numerous, and to some extent, entirely new manufactures. Accordingly, in France alone, in the first half of the 18th century, over 100 different kinds of silk stuffs were woven, and, in Avignon, it was law, that "every apprentice should devote himself to only one sort of fabrication, and should not learn the separation of several kinds of stuff at once." The territorial division of labour, which confines special branches of production to special districts of a country, acquires fresh stimulus from the manufacturing system, which exploits every special advantage. The Colonial system and the opening out of the markets of the world, both of which are included in the general conditions of existence of the manufacturing period, furnish rich material for developing the division of labour in society. It is not the place, here, to go on to show how division of labour seizes upon, not only the economic, but every other sphere of society, and everywhere lays the foundation of that all engrossing system of specialising and sorting men, that development in a man of one single faculty at the expense of all other faculties, which caused A. Ferguson, the master of Adam Smith, to exclaim: "We make a nation of Helots, and have no free citizens."

But, in spite of the numerous analogies and links connecting them, division of labour in the interior of a society, and that in the interior of a workshop, differ not only in degree, but also in kind. The analogy appears most indisputable where there is an invisible bond uniting the various branches of trade. For instance the cattle-breeder produces hides, the tanner makes the hides into leather, and the shoemaker, the leather into boots. Here the thing produced by each of them is but a step towards the final form, which is the product of all their labours combined. There are, besides, all the various industries that supply the cattle-breeder, the tanner, and the shoemaker with the means of production. Now it is quite possible to imagine, with Adam Smith, that the difference between the above social division of labour, and the division in manufacture, is merely subjective, exists merely for the observer, who, in a manufacture, can see with one glance, all the numerous operations being performed on one spot, while in the instance given above, the spreading out of the work over great areas, and the great number of people employed in each branch of labour, obscure the connexion. But what is it that forms the bond between the independent labours of the cattle-breeder, the tanner, and the shoe-maker? It is the fact that their respective products are commodities. What, on the other hand, characterises division of labour in manufactures? The fact that the detail labourer produces no commodities. It is only the common product of all the detail labourers becomes a commodity. Division of labour in society is brought about by the purchase and sale of the products of different branches of industry, while the connection between the detail operations in a workshop, is due to the sale of the labour-power of several workmen to one capitalist, who applies it as combined labour-power. The division of labour in the workshop implies concentration of the means of production in the hands of one capitalist; the division of labour in society implies their dispersion among many independent producers of commodities. . . .

The same bourgeois mind denounces with equal vigour every conscious attempt to socially control and regulate the process of production, as an inroad upon such sacred things as the rights of property, freedom and unrestricted play for the bent of the individual capitalist. It is very characteristic that the enthusiastic apologists of the factory system have nothing more damning to urge against a general organisation of the labour of society, than that it would turn all society into one immense factory.

If, in a society with capitalist production, anarchy in the social division of labour and despotism in that of the workshop are mutual conditions the one of the other, we find, on the contrary, in those earlier forms of society in which the separation of trades has been spontaneously developed, then crystallised, and finally made permanent by law, on the one hand, a specimen of the organisation of the labour of society, in accordance with an approved and authoritative plan, and on the other, the entire exclusion of division of labour in the workshop, or at all events a mere dwarf-like or sporadic and accidental development of the same.

Those small and extremely ancient Indian communities, some of which have continued down to this day, are based on possession in common of the land, on the blending of agriculture and handicrafts, and on an unalterable division of labour, which serves, whenever a new community is started, as a plan and scheme ready cut and dried. . . . The law that regulates the division of labour in the community acts with the irresistible authority of a law of Nature, at the same time that each individual artificer, the smith, the carpenter, and so on, conducts in his workshop all the operations of his handicraft in the traditional way, but independently, and without recognising any authority over him. The simplicity of the organisation for production in these self-sufficing communities that constantly reproduce themselves in the same form, and when accidentally destroyed, spring up again on the spot and with the same name—this simplicity supplies the key to the secret of the unchangeableness of Asiatic societies, an unchangeableness in such striking contrast with the constant dissolution and refounding of Asiatic States, and the never-ceasing changes of dynasty. The structure of the economic elements of society remains untouched by the storm-clouds of the political sky. . . .

While division of labour in society at large; whether such division be brought about or not by exchange of commodities, is common to economic formulations of society the most diverse, division of labour in the workshop, as practised by manufacture, is a special creation of the capitalist mode of production alone.

Section 5: The Capitalistic Character of Manufacture

An increased number of labourers under the control of one capitalist is the natural starting-point, as well of co-operation generally, as of manufacture in particular. But the division of labour in manufacture makes this increase in the number of workmen a technical necessity. The minimum number that any given capitalist is bound to employ is here prescribed by the previously established division of labour. On the other hand, the advantages of further division are obtainable only by adding to the number of workmen, and this can be done only by adding multiples of the various detail groups. But an increase in the variable component of the capital employed necessitates an increase in its constant component, too, in the workshops, implements, &c., and, in particular, in the raw material, the call for which grows quicker than the number of workmen. The quantity of it consumed in a given time, by a given amount of labour, increases in the same ratio as does the productive power of that labour in consequence of its division. Hence, it is a law, based on the very nature of manufacture, that the minimum amount of capital, which is bound to be in the hands of each capitalist, must keep increasing; in other words, that the transformation into capital of the social means of production and subsistence must keep extending.

In manufacture, as well as in simple co-operation, the collective working organism is a form of existence of capital. The mechanism that is made up of numerous individual detail labourers belongs to the capitalist. Hence, the productive power resulting from a combination of labours appears to be the productive power of capital. Manufacture proper not only subjects the previously independent workman to the discipline and command of capital, but, in addition, creates a hierarchic gradation of the workmen themselves. While simple co-operation leaves the mode of working by the individual for the most part unchanged, manufacture thoroughly revolutionises it, and seizes labour-power by its very roots. It converts the labourer into a crippled monstrosity, by forcing his detail dexterity at the expense of a world of productive capabilities and instincts; just as in the States of La Plata they butcher a whole beast for the sake of his hide or his tallow. Not only is the detail work distributed to the different individuals, but the individual himself is made the automatic motor of a fractional operation, and the absurd fable of Menenius Agrippa, which makes man a mere fragment of his own body, becomes realised. If, at first, the workman sells his labour-power to capital, because the material means of producing a commodity fail him, now his very labour-power refuses its services unless it has been sold to capital. Its functions can be exercised only in an environment that exists in the workshop of the capitalist after the sale. By nature unfitted to make anything independently, the manufacturing labourer develops productive activity as a mere appendage of the capitalist's workshop. . . .

In manufacture, in order to make the collective labourer, and through him capital, rich in social productive power, each labourer must be made poor in individual productive powers. "Ignorance is the mother of industry as well as of superstition. Reflection and fancy are subject to err; but a habit of moving the hand or the foot is independent of either. Manufactures, accordingly, prosper most where the mind is least consulted, and where the workshop may . . . be considered as an engine, the parts of which are men." As a matter of fact, some few manufacturers in the middle of the 18th century preferred for certain operations that were trade secrets, to employ half-idiotic persons.

"The understandings of the greater part of men," says Adam Smith, "are necessarily formed by their ordinary employments. The man whose whole life is spent in performing a few simple operations . . . has no occasion to exert his understanding. . . . He generally becomes as stupid and ignorant as it is possible for a human creature to become." After describing the stupidity of the detail labourer he goes on: "The uniformity of his stationary life naturally corrupts the courage of his mind. . . . It corrupts even the activity of his body and renders him incapable of exerting his strength with vigour and perseverance in any other employments than that to which he has been bred. His dexterity at his own particular trade seems in this manner to be acquired at the expense of his intellectual, social, and martial virtues. But in every improved and civilised society, this is the state into which the labouring poor, that is, the great body of the people, must necessarily fall." For preventing the complete deterioration of the great mass of the people by division of labour, A. Smith recommends education of the people by the State, but prudently, and in homeopathic doses. . . .

Some crippling of body and mind is inseparable even from division of labour in society as a whole. Since, however, manufacture carries this social separation of branches of labour much further, and also, by its peculiar division, attacks the individual at the very roots of his life, it is the first to afford the materials for, and to give a start to, industrial pathology.

"To subdivide a man is to execute him, if he deserves the sentence, to assassinate him if he does not. . . . The subdivision of labour is the assassination of a people."

Communist Manifesto, Karl Marx and Friedrich Engels

A spectre is haunting Europe—the spectre of Communism. All the Powers of old Europe have entered into a holy alliance to exorcise this spectre: Pope and Czar, Metternich and Guizot, French Radicals and German police-spies.

Where is the party in opposition that has not been decried as Communistic by its opponents in power? Where the Opposition that has not hurled back the branding reproach of Communism, against the more advanced opposition parties, as well as against its reactionary adversaries?

Two things result from this fact.

I.   Communism is already acknowledged by all European Powers to be itself a Power.

II. It is high time that Communists should openly, in the face of the whole world, publish their views, their aims, their tendencies, and meet this nursery tale of the Spectre of Communism with a Manifesto of the party itself.

To this end, Communists of various nationalities have assembled in London, and sketched the following Manifesto, to be published in the English, French, German, Italian, Flemish and Danish languages.

I. Bourgeois and Proletarians

The history of all hitherto existing society is the history of class struggles.

Freeman and slave, patrician and plebeian, lord and serf, guild-master and journeyman, in a word, oppressor and oppressed, stood in constant opposition to one another, carried on an uninterrupted, now hidden, now open fight, a fight that each time ended, either in a revolutionary re-constitution of society at large, or in the common ruin of the contending classes.

In the earlier epochs of history, we find almost everywhere a complicated arrangement of society into various orders, a manifold gradation of social rank. In ancient Rome we have patricians, knights, plebeians, slaves; in the Middle Ages, feudal lords, vassals, guild-masters, journeymen, apprentices, serfs; in almost all of these classes, again, subordinate gradations.

The modern bourgeois society that has sprouted from the ruins of feudal society has not done away with class antagonisms. It has but established new classes, new conditions of oppression, new forms of struggle in place of the old ones.

Our epoch, the epoch of the bourgeoisie, possesses, however, this distinctive feature: it has simplified the class antagonisms: Society as a whole is more and more splitting up into two great hostile camps, into two great classes directly facing each other: Bourgeoisie and Proletariat.

From the serfs of the Middle Ages sprang the chartered burghers of the earliest towns. From these burgesses the first elements of the bourgeoisie were developed.

The discovery of America, the rounding of the Cape, opened up fresh ground for the rising bourgeoisie. The East-Indian and Chinese markets, the colonisation of America, trade with the colonies, the increase in the means of exchange and in commodities generally, gave to commerce, to navigation, to industry, an impulse never before known, and thereby, to the revolutionary element in the tottering feudal society, a rapid development.

The feudal system of industry, under which industrial production was monopolised by closed guilds, now no longer sufficed for the growing wants of the new markets. The manufacturing system took its place. The guild-masters were pushed on one side by the manufacturing middle class; division of labour between the different corporate guilds vanished in the face of division of labour in each single workshop.

Meantime the markets kept ever growing, the demand ever rising. Even manufacture no longer sufficed. Thereupon, steam and machinery revolutionised industrial production. The place of manufacture was taken by the giant, Modern Industry, the place of the industrial middle class, by industrial millionaires, the leaders of whole industrial armies, the modern bourgeois.

Modern industry has established the world-market, for which the discovery of America paved the way. This market has given an immense development to commerce, to navigation, to communication by land. This development has, in its turn, reacted on the extension of industry; and in proportion as industry, commerce, navigation, railways extended, in the same proportion the bourgeoisie developed, increased its capital, and pushed into the background every class handed down from the Middle Ages.

We see, therefore, how the modern bourgeoisie is itself the product of a long course of development, of a series of revolutions in the modes of production and of exchange.

Each step in the development of the bourgeoisie was accompanied by a corresponding political advance of that class. An oppressed class under the sway of the feudal nobility, an armed and self-governing association in the mediaeval commune; here independent urban republic (as in Italy and Germany), there taxable "third estate" of the monarchy (as in France), afterwards, in the period of manufacture proper, serving either the semi-feudal or the absolute monarchy as a counterpoise against the nobility, and, in fact, corner-stone of the great monarchies in general, the bourgeoisie has at last, since the establishment of Modern Industry and of the world-market, conquered for itself, in the modern representative State, exclusive political sway. The executive of the modern State is but a committee for managing the common affairs of the whole bourgeoisie.

The bourgeoisie, historically, has played a most revolutionary part.

The bourgeoisie, wherever it has got the upper hand, has put an end to all feudal, patriarchal, idyllic relations. It has pitilessly torn asunder the motley feudal ties that bound man to his "natural superiors," and has left remaining no other nexus between man and man than naked self-interest, than callous "cash payment." It has drowned the most heavenly ecstasies of religious fervour, of chivalrous enthusiasm, of philistine sentimentalism, in the icy water of egotistical calculation. It has resolved personal worth into exchange value, and in place of the numberless indefeasible chartered freedoms, has set up that single, unconscionable freedom—Free Trade. In one word, for exploitation, veiled by religious and political illusions, it has substituted naked, shameless, direct, brutal exploitation.

The bourgeoisie has stripped of its halo every occupation hitherto honoured and looked up to with reverent awe. It has converted the physician, the lawyer, the priest, the poet, the man of science, into its paid wage-labourers. The bourgeoisie has torn away from the family its sentimental veil, and has reduced the family relation to a mere money relation. The bourgeoisie has disclosed how it came to pass that the brutal display of vigour in the Middle Ages, which Reactionists so much admire, found its fitting complement in the most slothful indolence. It has been the first to show what man's activity can bring about. It has accomplished wonders far surpassing Egyptian pyramids, Roman aqueducts, and Gothic cathedrals; it has conducted expeditions that put in the shade all former Exoduses of nations and crusades.

The bourgeoisie cannot exist without constantly revolutionising the instruments of production, and thereby the relations of production, and with them the whole relations of society. Conservation of the old modes of production in unaltered form, was, on the contrary, the first condition of existence for all earlier industrial classes. Constant revolutionising of production, uninterrupted disturbance of all social conditions, everlasting uncertainty and agitation distinguish the bourgeois epoch from all earlier ones. All fixed, fast-frozen relations, with their train of ancient and venerable prejudices and opinions, are swept away, all new-formed ones become antiquated before they can ossify. All that is solid melts into air, all that is holy is profaned, and man is at last compelled to face with sober senses, his real conditions of life, and his relations with his kind.

The need of a constantly expanding market for its products chases the bourgeoisie over the whole surface of the globe. It must nestle everywhere, settle everywhere, establish connexions everywhere.

The bourgeoisie has through its exploitation of the world-market given a cosmopolitan character to production and consumption in every country. To the great chagrin of Reactionists, it has drawn from under the feet of industry the national ground on which it stood. All old-established national industries have been destroyed or are daily being destroyed. They are dislodged by new industries, whose introduction becomes a life and death question for all civilised nations, by industries that no longer work up indigenous raw material, but raw material drawn from the remotest zones; industries whose products are consumed, not only at home, but in every quarter of the globe. In place of the old wants, satisfied by the productions of the country, we find new wants, requiring for their satisfaction the products of distant lands and climes. In place of the old local and national seclusion and self-sufficiency, we have intercourse in every direction, universal inter-dependence of nations. And as in material, so also in intellectual production. The intellectual creations of individual nations become common property. National one-sidedness and narrow-mindedness become more and more impossible, and from the numerous national and local literatures, there arises a world literature.

The bourgeoisie, by the rapid improvement of all instruments of production, by the immensely facilitated means of communication, draws all, even the most barbarian, nations into civilisation. The cheap prices of its commodities are the heavy artillery with which it batters down all Chinese walls, with which it forces the barbarians' intensely obstinate hatred of foreigners to capitulate. It compels all nations, on pain of extinction, to adopt the bourgeois mode of production; it compels them to introduce what it calls civilisation into their midst, i.e., to become bourgeois themselves. In one word, it creates a world after its own image.

The bourgeoisie has subjected the country to the rule of the towns. It has created enormous cities, has greatly increased the urban population as compared with the rural, and has thus rescued a considerable part of the population from the idiocy of rural life. Just as it has made the country dependent on the towns, so it has made barbarian and semi-barbarian countries dependent on the civilised ones, nations of peasants on nations of bourgeois, the East on the West.

The bourgeoisie keeps more and more doing away with the scattered state of the population, of the means of production, and of property. It has agglomerated population, centralised means of production, and has concentrated property in a few hands. The necessary consequence of this was political centralisation. Independent, or but loosely connected provinces, with separate interests, laws, governments and systems of taxation, became lumped together into one nation, with one government, one code of laws, one national class-interest, one frontier and one customs-tariff.

The bourgeoisie, during its rule of scarce one hundred years, has created more massive and more colossal productive forces than have all preceding generations together. Subjection of Nature's forces to man, machinery, application of chemistry to industry and agriculture, steam-navigation, railways, electric telegraphs, clearing of whole continents for cultivation, canalisation of rivers, whole populations conjured out of the ground—what earlier century had even a presentiment that such productive forces slumbered in the lap of social labour?

We see then: the means of production and of exchange, on whose foundation the bourgeoisie built itself up, were generated in feudal society. At a certain stage in the development of these means of production and of exchange, the conditions under which feudal society produced and exchanged, the feudal organisation of agriculture and manufacturing industry, in one word, the feudal relations of property became no longer compatible with the already developed productive forces; they became so many fetters. They had to be burst asunder; they were burst asunder.

Into their place stepped free competition, accompanied by a social and political constitution adapted to it, and by the economical and political sway of the bourgeois class.

A similar movement is going on before our own eyes. Modern bourgeois society with its relations of production, of exchange and of property, a society that has conjured up such gigantic means of production and of exchange, is like the sorcerer, who is no longer able to control the powers of the nether world whom he has called up by his spells. For many a decade past the history of industry and commerce is but the history of the revolt of modern productive forces against modern conditions of production, against the property relations that are the conditions for the existence of the bourgeoisie and of its rule. It is enough to mention the commercial crises that by their periodical return put on its trial, each time more threateningly, the existence of the entire bourgeois society. In these crises a great part not only of the existing products, but also of the previously created productive forces, are periodically destroyed. In these crises there breaks out an epidemic that, in all earlier epochs, would have seemed an absurdity—the epidemic of overproduction. Society suddenly finds itself put back into a state of momentary barbarism; it appears as if a famine, a universal war of devastation had cut off the supply of every means of subsistence; industry and commerce seem to be destroyed; and why? Because there is too much civilisation, too much means of subsistence, too much industry, too much commerce. The productive forces at the disposal of society no longer tend to further the development of the conditions of bourgeois property; on the contrary, they have become too powerful for these conditions, by which they are fettered, and so soon as they overcome these fetters, they bring disorder into the whole of bourgeois society, endanger the existence of bourgeois property. The conditions of bourgeois society are too narrow to comprise the wealth created by them. And how does the bourgeoisie get over these crises? On the one hand by enforced destruction of a mass of productive forces; on the other, by the conquest of new markets, and by the more thorough exploitation of the old ones. That is to say, by paving the way for more extensive and more destructive crises, and by diminishing the means whereby crises are prevented. The weapons with which the bourgeoisie felled feudalism to the ground are now turned against the bourgeoisie itself.

But not only has the bourgeoisie forged the weapons that bring death to itself; it has also called into existence the men who are to wield those weapons—the modern working class—the proletarians.

In proportion as the bourgeoisie, i.e., capital, is developed, in the same proportion is the proletariat, the modern working class, developed—a class of labourers, who live only so long as they find work and who had work only so long as their labour increases capital. These labourers, who must sell themselves piece-meal, are a commodity, like every other article of commerce, and are consequently exposed to all the vicissitudes of competition, to all the fluctuations of the market.

Owing to the extensive use of machinery and to division of labour, the work of the proletarians has lost all individual character, and consequently, all charm for the workman: He becomes an appendage of the machine, and it is only the most simple, most monotonous, and most easily acquired knack, that is required of him. Hence, the cost of production of a workman is restricted, almost entirely, to the means of subsistence that he requires for his maintenance, and for the propagation of his race. But the price of a commodity, and therefore also of labour, is equal to its cost of production. In proportion, therefore, as the repulsiveness of the work increases, the wage decreases. Nay more, in proportion as the use of machinery and division of labour increases, in the same proportion the burden of toil also increases, whether by prolongation of the working hours, by increase of the work exacted in a given time or by increased speed of the machinery, etc.

Modern industry has converted the little workshop of the patriarchal master into the great factory of the industrial capitalist. Masses of labourers, crowded into the factory, are organised like soldiers. As privates of the industrial army they are placed under the command of a perfect hierarchy of officers and sergeants. Not only are they slaves of the bourgeois class, and of the bourgeois State; they are daily and hourly enslaved by the machine, by the over-looker, and, above all, by the individual bourgeois manufacturer himself. The more openly this despotism proclaims gain to be its end and aim, the more petty, the more hateful and the more embittering it is.

The less the skill and exertion of strength implied in manual labour, in other words, the more modern industry becomes developed, the more is the labour of men superseded by that of women. Differences of age and sex have no longer any distinctive social validity for the working class. All are instruments of labour, more or less expensive to use, according to their age and sex.

No sooner is the exploitation of the labourer by the manufacturer, so far, at an end, that he receives his wages in cash, than he is set upon by the other portions of the bourgeoisie, the landlord, the shopkeeper, the pawnbroker, etc.

The lower strata of the middle class—the small tradespeople, shopkeepers, and retired tradesmen generally, the handicraftsmen and peasants—all these sink gradually into the proletariat, partly because their diminutive capital does not suffice for the scale on which Modern Industry is carried on, and is swamped in the competition with the large capitalists, partly because their specialised skill is rendered worthless by new methods of production. Thus the proletariat is recruited from all classes of the population. . . .

The essential condition for the existence, and for the sway of the bourgeois class, is the formation and augmentation of capital; the condition for capital is wage-labour. Wage-labour rests exclusively on competition between the labourers. The advance of industry, whose involuntary promoter is the bourgeoisie, replaces the isolation of the labourers, due to competition, by their revolutionary combination, due to association. The development of Modern Industry, therefore, cuts from under its feet the very foundation on which the bourgeoisie produces and appropriates products. What the bourgeoisie, therefore, produces, above all, is its own grave-diggers. Its fall and the victory of the proletariat are equally inevitable.

11

THE STRUCTURE OF DEPENDENCE

Theotonio dos Santos

In this chapter, Theotonio dos Santos, a Brazilian economist, crafts what is probably the most cited definition of dependence. Although some scholars argue that there is no such thing as a coherent dependency "theory," dos Santos presents many of the most commonly held tenets. He argues that dependence is difficult to define because it is conditioned by the characteristics of the dependent country and it has changed over time. Three basic forms of dependence have appeared: (1) colonial, (2) financial-industrial, and (3) multinational corporate. Dos Santos focuses on how the latest form, that arising out of the linkage between dependent countries and multinational corporations, limits the developmental potential of newly industrializing nations and is blamed for restricting the size of local markets and contributing to income inequality. Ultimately, according to dos Santos, dependent development will culminate in revolutionary movements of the left or the right.

This chapter attempts to demonstrate that the dependence of Latin American countries on other countries cannot be overcome without a qualitative change in their internal structures and external relations. We shall attempt to show that the relations of dependence to which these countries are subjected conform to a type of international and internal structure which leads them to underdevelopment or more precisely to a dependent structure that deepens and aggravates the fundamental problems of their peoples.

Reprinted with permission from *The American Economic Review*, vol. 60 (May 1970): 231–236.

I. What Is Dependence?

By dependence we mean a situation in which the economy of certain countries is conditioned by the development and expansion of another economy to which the former is subjected. The relation of interdependence between two or more economies, and between these and world trade, assumes the form of dependence when some countries (the dominant ones) can expand and can be self-sustaining, while other countries (the dependent ones) can do this only as a reflection of that expansion, which can have either a positive or a negative effect on their immediate development (dos Santos, 1968b; p. 6).

The concept of dependence permits us to see the internal situation of these countries as part of world economy. In the Marxian tradition, the theory of imperialism has been developed as a study of the process of expansion of the imperialist centers and of their world domination. In the epoch of the revolutionary movement of the Third World, we have to develop the theory of laws of internal development in those countries that are the object of such expansion and are governed by them. This theoretical step transcends the theory of development which seeks to explain the situation of the underdeveloped countries as a product of their slowness or failure to adopt the patterns of efficiency characteristic of developed countries (or to "modernize" or "develop" themselves). Although capitalist development theory admits the existence of an "external" dependence, it is unable to perceive underdevelopment in the way our present theory perceives it, as a consequence and part of the process of the world expansion of capitalism—a part that is necessary to and integrally linked with it.

In analyzing the process of constituting a world economy that integrates the so-called "national economies" in a world market of commodities, capital, and even of labor power, we see that the relations produced by this market are unequal and combined—unequal because development of parts of the system occurs at the expense of other parts. Trade relations are based on monopolistic control of the market, which leads to the transfer of surplus generated in the dependent countries to the dominant countries; financial relations are, from the viewpoint of the dominant powers, based on loans and the export of capital, which permit them to receive interest and profits, thus increasing their domestic surplus and strengthening their control over the economies of the other countries. For the dependent countries these relations represent an export of profits and interest which carries off part of the surplus generated domestically and leads to a loss of control over their productive resources. In order to permit these disadvantageous relations, the dependent countries must generate large surpluses, not in such a way as to create higher levels of technology but rather creating super-exploited manpower. The result is to limit the development of their internal market and their technical and cultural capacity, as well as the moral and physical health of their people. We call this combined development because it is the combination of these inequalities and the transfer of resources from the most backward and dependent sectors to the most advanced and dominant ones which explains the inequality, deepens it, and transforms it into a necessary and structural element of the world economy.

II. Historic Forms of Dependence

Historic forms of dependence are conditioned by: (1) the basic forms of this world economy which has its own laws of development; (2) the type of economic relations dominant in the capitalist centers and the ways in which the latter expand outward; and (3) the types of economic relations existing inside the peripheral countries which are incorporated into the situation of dependence within the network of international economic relations generated by capitalist expansion. It is not within the purview of this chapter to study these forms in detail but only to distinguish broad characteristics of development.

Drawing on an earlier study, we may distinguish: (1) Colonial dependence, trade export in nature, in which commercial and financial capital in alliance with the colonialist state dominated the economic relations and the colonies by means of a trade monopoly, (2) Financial-industrial dependence, which consolidated itself at the end of the nineteenth century, characterized by the domination of big capital in the hegemonic centers, and its expansion abroad through investment in the production of raw materials and agricultural products for consumption in the hegemonic centers. A productive structure grew up in the dependent countries devoted to the export of these products (which I.V. Levin labeled export economies [Levin, 1964]; other analysis in other regions [Myrdal, 1968; Nkrumah, 1966]), producing what the Economic Commission for Latin America (ECLA) has called "foreign-oriented development" (desarrollo hacia afuera) (Cepal, 1968). (3) In the postwar period a new type of dependence has been consolidated, based on multinational corporations which began to invest in industries geared to the internal market of underdeveloped countries. This form of dependence is basically technological-industrial dependence (dos Santos, 1968a).

Each of these forms of dependence corresponds to a situation which conditioned not only the international relations of these countries but also their internal structures: the orientation of production, the forms of capital accumulation, the reproduction of the economy, and, simultaneously, their social and political structure.

III. The Export Economies

In forms (1) and (2) of dependence, production is geared to those products destined for export (gold, silver, and tropical products in the colonial epoch; raw materials and agricultural products in the epoch of industrial-financial dependence); i.e., production is determined by demand from the hegemonic centers. The internal productive structure is characterized by rigid specialization and monoculture in entire regions (the Caribbean, the Brazilian Northeast, etc.). Alongside these export sectors there grew up certain complementary economic activities (cattle-raising and some manufacturing, for example) which were dependent, in general, on the export sector to which they sell their products. There was a third, subsistence economy which provided manpower for the export sector under favorable conditions and toward which excess population shifted during periods unfavorable to international trade.

Under these conditions, the existing internal market was restricted by four factors: (1) Most of the national income was derived from export, which was used to purchase the inputs required by export production (slaves, for example) or luxury goods consumed by the hacienda- and mine-owners, and by the more prosperous employees. (2) The available manpower was subject to very arduous forms of superexploitation, which limited its consumption. (3) Part of the consumption of these workers was provided by the subsistence economy, which served as a complement to their income and as a refuge during periods of depression. (4) A fourth factor was to be found in those countries in which land and mines were in the hands of foreigners (cases of an enclave economy): a great part of the accumulated surplus was destined to be sent abroad in the form of profits, limiting not only internal consumption but also possibilities of reinvestment (Baran, 1967). In the case of enclave economies the relations of the foreign companies with the hegemonic center were even more exploitative and were complemented by the fact that purchases by the enclave were made directly abroad.

IV. The New Dependence

The new form of dependence, (3) above, is in process of developing and is conditioned by the exigencies of the international commodity and capital markets. The possibility of generating new investments depends on the existence of financial resources in foreign currency for the purchase of machinery and processed raw materials not produced domestically. Such purchases are subject to two limitations: the limit of resources generated by the export sector (reflected in the balance of payments, which includes not only trade but also service relations); and the limitations of monopoly on patents which leads monopolistic firms to prefer to transfer their machines in the form of capital rather than as commodities for sale. It is necessary to analyze these relations of dependence if we are to understand the fundamental structural limits they place on the development of these economies.

· 1. Industrial development is dependent on an export sector for the foreign currency to buy the inputs utilized by the industrial sector. The first consequence of this dependence is the need to preserve the traditional export sector, which limits economically the development of the internal market by the conservation of backward relations of production and signifies, politically, the maintenance of power by traditional decadent oligarchies. In the countries where these sectors are controlled by foreign capital, it signifies the remittance abroad of high profits, and political dependence on those interests. Only in rare instances does foreign capital not control at least the marketing of these products. In response to these limitations, dependent countries in the 1930s and 1940s developed a policy of exchange restrictions and taxes on the national and foreign export sector; today they tend toward the gradual nationalization of production and toward the imposition of certain timid limitations on foreign control of the marketing of exported products. Furthermore, they seek, still somewhat timidly, to obtain better terms for the sale of their products. In recent decades, they have created mechanisms for international price agreements, and today the United Nations Conference on Trade and Development (UNCTAD) and ECLA press to obtain more favorable tariff conditions for these products on the part of the hegemonic centers. It is important to point out that the industrial development of these countries is dependent on the situation of the export sector, the continued existence of which they are obliged to accept.

2. Industrial development is, then, strongly conditioned by fluctuations in the balance of payments. This leads toward deficit due to the relations of dependence themselves. The causes of the deficit are three:

a. Trade relations take place in a highly monopolized international market, which tends to lower the price of raw materials and to raise the prices of industrial products, particularly inputs. In the second place, there is a tendency in modern technology to replace various primary products with synthetic raw materials. Consequently, the balance of trade in these countries tends to be less favorable (even though they show a general surplus). The overall Latin American balance of trade from 1946 to 1968 shows a surplus for each of those years. The same thing happens in almost every underdeveloped country. However, the losses due to deterioration of the terms of trade (on the basis of data from ECLA and the International Monetary Fund), excluding Cuba, were $26,383 million for the 1951–66 period, taking 1950 prices as a base. If Cuba and Venezuela are excluded, the total is $15,925 million.

b. For the reasons already given, foreign capital retains control over the most dynamic sectors of the economy and repatriates a high volume of profit; consequently, capital accounts are highly unfavorable to dependent countries. The data show that the amount of capital leaving the country is much greater than the amount entering; this produces an enslaving deficit in capital accounts. To this must be added the deficit in certain services which are virtually under total foreign control—such as freight transport, royalty payments, technical aid, etc. Consequently, an important deficit is produced in the total balance of payments; thus limiting the possibility of importation of inputs for industrialization.

c. The result is that "foreign financing" becomes necessary, in two forms: to cover the existing deficit, and to "finance" development by means of loans for the stimulation of investments and to "supply" an internal economic surplus which was decapitalized to a large extent by the remittance of part of the surplus generated domestically and sent abroad as profits.

Foreign capital and foreign "aid" thus fill up the holes that they themselves created. The real value of this aid, however, is doubtful. If overcharges resulting from the restrictive terms of the aid are subtracted from the total amount of the grants, the average net flow, according to calculations of the Inter-American Economic and Social Council, is approximately 54 percent of the gross flow (Interamerican Economic and Social Council, 1969).

If we take account of certain further facts—that a high proportion of aid is paid in local currencies, that Latin American countries make contributions to international financial institutions, and that credits are often "tied"—we find a "real component of foreign aid" of 42.2 percent on a very favorable hypothesis and of 38.3 percent on a more realistic one (Interamerican Economic and Social Council, 1969, II, p. 33). The gravity of the situation becomes even clearer if we consider that these credits are used in large part to finance North American investments, to subsidize foreign imports which compete with national products, to introduce technology not adapted to the needs of underdeveloped countries, and to invest in low-priority sectors of the national economies. The hard truth is that the underdeveloped countries have to pay for all of the "aid" they receive. This situation is generating an enormous protest movement by Latin American governments seeking at least partial relief from such negative relations.

3. Finally, industrial development is strongly conditioned by the technological monopoly exercised by imperialist centers. We have seen that the underdeveloped countries depend on the importation of machinery and raw materials for the development of their industries. However, these goods are not freely available in the international market; they are patented and usually belong to the big companies. The big companies do not sell machinery and processed raw materials as simple merchandise: they demand either the payment of royalties, etc., for their utilization or, in most cases, they convert these goods into capital and introduce them in the form of their own investments. This is how machinery which is replaced in the hegemonic centers by more advanced technology is sent to dependent countries as capital for the installation of affiliates. Let us pause and examine these relations in order to understand their oppressive and exploitative character.

The dependent countries do not have sufficient foreign currency, for the reasons given. Local businessmen have financing difficulties, and they must pay for the utilization of certain patented techniques. These factors oblige the national bourgeois governments to facilitate the entry of foreign capital in order to supply the restricted national market, which is strongly protected by high tariffs in order to promote industrialization. Thus, foreign capital enters with all the advantages: in many cases, it is given exemption from exchange controls for the importation of machinery; financing of sites for installation of industries is provided; government financing agencies facilitate industrialization; loans are available from foreign and domestic banks, which prefer such clients; foreign aid often subsidizes such investments and finances complementary public investments; after installation, high profits obtained in such favorable circumstances can be reinvested freely. Thus it is not surprising that the data of the U.S. Department of Commerce reveal that the percentage of capital brought in from abroad by these companies is but a part of the total amount of invested capital. These data show that in the period from 1946 to 1967 the new entries of capital into Latin America for direct investment amounted to $5,415 million, while the sum of reinvested profits was $4,424 million. On the other hand, the transfers of profits from Latin America to the United States amounted to $14,775 million. If we estimate total profits as approximately equal to transfers plus reinvestments we have the sum of $18,983 million. In spite of enormous transfers of profits to the United States, the book value of the United States's direct investment in Latin America went from $3,045 million in 1946 to $10,213 million in 1967.

From these data it is clear that: (1) Of the new investments made by U.S. companies in Latin America for the period 1946–67, 55 percent corresponds to new entries of capital and 45 percent to reinvestment of profits; in recent years, the trend is more marked, with reinvestments between 1960 and 1966 representing more than 60 percent of new investments. (2) Remittances remained at about 10 percent of book value throughout the period. (3) The ratio of remitted capital to new flow is around 2.7 for the period 1946–67; that is, for each dollar that enters $2.70 leaves. In the 1960s this ratio roughly doubled, and in some years was considerably higher.

The *Survey of Current Business* data on sources and uses of funds for direct North American investment in Latin America in the period 1957–64 show that, of the total sources of direct investment in Latin America, only 11.8 percent came from the United States. The remainder is, in large part, the result of the activities of North American firms in Latin America (46.4 percent net income, 27.7 percent under the heading of depreciation), and from "sources located abroad" (14.1 percent). It is significant that the funds obtained abroad that are external to the companies are greater than the funds originating in the United States.

V. Effects on the Productive Structure

It is easy to grasp, even if only superficially, the effects that this dependent structure has on the productive system itself in these countries and the role of this structure in determining a specified type of development, characterized by its dependent nature.

The productive system in the underdeveloped countries is essentially determined by these international relations. In the first place, the need to conserve the agrarian or mining export structure generates a combination between more advanced economic centers that extract surplus value from the more backward sectors and internal "metropolitan" centers on the one hand, and internal interdependent "colonial" centers on the other (Frank, 1968). The unequal and combined character of capitalist development at the international level is reproduced internally in an acute form. In the second place the industrial and technological structure responds more closely to the interests of the multinational corporations than to internal developmental needs (conceived of not only in terms of the overall interests of the population, but also from the point of view of the interests of a national capitalist development). In the third place, the same technological and economic-financial concentration of the hegemonic economies is transferred without substantial alteration to very different economies and societies, giving rise to a highly unequal productive structure, a high concentration of incomes, underutilization of installed capacity, intensive exploitation of existing markets concentrated in large cities, etc.

The accumulation of capital in such circumstances assumes its own characteristics. In the first place, it is characterized by profound differences among domestic wage-levels, in the context of a local cheap labor market, combined with a capital-intensive technology. The result, from the point of view of relative surplus value, is a high rate of exploitation of labor power. (On measurements of forms of exploitation, see Casanova, 1969.)

This exploitation is further aggravated by the high prices of industrial products enforced by protectionism, exemptions and subsidies given by the national governments, and "aid" from hegemonic centers. Furthermore, since dependent accumulation is necessarily tied into the international economy, it is profoundly conditioned by the unequal and combined character of international capitalist economic relations, by the technological and financial control of the imperialist centers by the realities of the balance of payments, by the economic policies of the state, etc. The role of the state in the growth of national and foreign capital merits a much fuller analysis than can be made here. Using the analysis offered here as a point of departure, it is possible to understand the limits that this productive system imposes on the growth of the internal markets of these countries. The survival of traditional relations in the countryside is a serious limitation on the size of the market, since industrialization does not offer hopeful prospects. The productive structure created by dependent industrialization limits the growth of the internal market.

First, it subjects the labor force to highly exploitative relations which limit its purchasing power. Second, in adopting a technology of intensive capital use, it creates very few jobs in comparison with population growth, and limits the generation of new sources of income. These two limitations affect the growth of the consumer goods market. Third, the remittance abroad of profits carries away part of the economic surplus generated within the country. In all these ways limits are put on the possible creation of basic national industries which could provide a market for the capital goods this surplus would make possible if it were not remitted abroad.

From this cursory analysis we see that the alleged backwardness of these economies is not due to a lack of integration with capitalism but that, to the contrary, the most powerful obstacles to their full development come from the way in which they are joined to this international system and its laws of development.

VI. Some Conclusions: Dependent Reproduction

In order to understand the system of dependent reproduction and the socioeconomic institutions created by it, we must see it as part of a system of world economic relations based on monopolistic control of large-scale capital, on control of certain economic and financial centers over others, on a monopoly of complex technology that leads to unequal and combined development at a national and international level. Attempts to analyze backwardness as a failure to assimilate more advanced models of production or to modernize are nothing more than ideology disguised as science. The same is true of the attempts to analyze this international economy in terms of relations among elements in free competition, such as the theory of comparative costs which seeks to justify the inequalities of the world economic system and to conceal the relations of exploitation on which it is based (Palloix, 1969).

In reality we can understand what is happening in the underdeveloped countries only when we see that they develop within the framework of a process of dependent production and reproduction. This system is a dependent one because it reproduces a productive system whose development is limited by those world relations which necessarily lead to the development of only certain economic sectors, to trade under unequal conditions (Emmanuel, 1969), to domestic competition with international capital under unequal conditions, to the imposition of relations of superexploitation of the domestic labor force with a view to dividing the economic surplus thus generated between internal and external forces of domination. (On economic surplus and its utilization in the dependent countries, see Baran, 1967.)

In reproducing such a productive system and such international relations, the development of dependent capitalism reproduces the factors that prevent it from reaching a nationally and internationally advantageous situation; and it thus reproduces backwardness, misery, and social marginalization within its borders. The development that it produces benefits very narrow sectors, encounters unyielding domestic obstacles to its continued economic growth (with respect to both internal and foreign markets), and leads to the progressive accumulation of balance-of-payments deficits, which in turn generate more dependence and more superexploitation.

The political measures proposed by the developmentalists of ECLA, UNCTAD, Inter-American Development Bank (BID), etc., do not appear to permit destruction of these terrible chains imposed by dependent development. We have examined the alternative forms of development presented for Latin America and the dependent countries under such conditions elsewhere (dos Santos; 1969). Everything now indicates that what can be expected is a long process of sharp political and military confrontations and of profound social radicalization which will lead these countries to a dilemma: governments of force, which open the way to fascism, or popular revolutionary governments, which open the way to socialism. Intermediate solutions have proved to be, in such a contradictory reality, empty and utopian.

References

Paul Baran, *Political Economy of Growth* (Monthly Review Press, 1967).

Thomas Balogh, *Unequal Partners* (Basil Blackwell, 1963).

Pablo Gonzalez Casanova, *Sociología de la explotación, Siglo XXI* (Mexico, 1969).

Cepal, *La CEPAL y el Análisis del Desarrollo Latinoamericano* (1968, Santiago, Chile).

Consejo Interamericano Economico Social (CIES) O.A.S., Interamerican Economic and Social Council, External Financing for Development in L.A. *El Financiamiento Externo para el Desarrollo de América Latina* (Pan-American Union, Washington,1969).

Theotonio dos Santos, *El nuevo carácter de la dependencia*, CESO (Santiago de Chile, 1968a).

———, *La crisis de la teoría del desarrollo y las relaciones de dependencia en América Latina*, Boletin del CESO, 3 (Santiago, Chile, 1968b).

———, *La dependencia económica y las alternotivas de cambio en América Latina*, Ponencia al IX Congreso Latinoamericano de Sociología (México, Nov., 1969).

A. Emmanuel, *L'Echange Inégal* (Maspero, Paris, 1969).

Andre G. Frank, *Development and Underdevelopment in Latin America* (Monthly Review Press, 1968).

I. V. Levin, *The Export Economies* (Harvard Univ. Press, 1964).

Gunnar Myrdal, *Asian Drama* (Pantheon, 1968).

K. Nkrumah, *Neocolonialismo, última etapa del imperialismo*, (Siglo XXI, Mexico, 1966).

Cristian Palloix, *Problemes de la Croissance en Economie Ouverte* (Maspero, Paris, 1969).

12

DEPENDENCE IN AN INTERDEPENDENT WORLD

—————————— *Immanuel Wallerstein* ——————————

Immanuel Wallerstein is generally considered the driving intellectual force behind the "world system" school of thought, and he argues that dependency theory is a subset of his world system perspective. Wallerstein states that countries fall into one of three groups, which are related to each other in a three-tiered hierarchical formation. The rich, industrialized, and militarily stronger countries constitute the core of the capitalist world system. The poorest, often agrarian, countries belong to the periphery, the weakest tier in the hierarchy. The semiperiphery is characterized by an economic base that combines core industrialization and peripheral agriculture. In this chapter, Wallerstein reviews three strategies—seizing the chance, promotion by invitation, and self-reliance—a country might use to move from the periphery or the semiperiphery to the next highest tier. Unlike some of the earlier dependency theorists, Wallerstein does not suggest that these growth strategies are hopeless, but neither does he view development as inevitable. According to Wallerstein, the success of some countries comes at the expense of others. With its roots in Marxist thought, world systems theory assumes that the relationship among the tiers is one of conflict and exploitation.

We live in a capitalist world-economy, one that took definitive shape as a European world-economy in the sixteenth century (see Wallerstein

Reprinted with permission of the author from "Dependence in an interdependent world: the limited possibilities of transformation within the capitalist world-economy," in *The Capitalist World Economy: Essays by Immanuel Wallerstein,* by Immanuel Wallerstein, pp. 66–93. New York: Cambridge University Press, 1979.

1974a) and came to include the whole world geographically in the nineteenth century. Capitalism as a system of production for sale in a market for profit and appropriation of this profit on the basis of individual or collective ownership has only existed in, and can be said to require, a world-system in which the political units are not coextensive with the boundaries of the market economy. This has permitted sellers to profit from strengths in the market whenever they exist but enabled them simultaneously to seek, whenever needed, the intrusion of political entities to distort the market in their favor. Far from being a system of free competition of all sellers, it is a system in which competition becomes relatively free only when the economic advantage of upper strata is so clear-cut that the unconstrained operation of the market serves effectively to reinforce the existing system of stratification.

This is not to say that there are no changes in position. Quite the contrary. There is constant and patterned movement between groups of economic actors as to who shall occupy various positions in the hierarchy of production, profit, and consumption. And there are secular developments in the structure of the capitalist world-system such that we can envisage that its internal contradictions as a system will bring it to an end in the twenty-first or twenty-second century. . . .

To understand the issues, we must successively treat the structure of the world-economy, its cyclical patterns including the present conjuncture, and the ways in which the position of particular states may change within this structure. This will, I believe, explain the limited possibilities of transformation within the capitalist world-economy.

The structure of the world-economy as a single system has come increasingly in recent years to be analyzed in terms of a core-periphery image, an image which has been linked with the discussion of "dependence." And thus it has been argued, for example, that Third World countries are not "underdeveloped" nations but "peripheral capitalist" nations.[1] This is far clearer terminology, but it leads unfortunately to further confusion if the unicity of the world-system is not borne clearly in mind. Ikonicoff argues, for example, that peripheral capitalist economies "operate by economic laws and growth factors [that] are clearly different from those of the economies one might call the model of classic capitalism" (1972: 692). This is only so because our model of "classic capitalism" is wrong, since both in the sixteenth century and today the core and the periphery of the world-economy were not two separate "economies" with two separate "laws" but one capitalist economic system with different *sectors* performing different functions.

Once one recognizes the unicity of the system, one is led to ask if the conception of a bi-modal system is adequate. Clearly, it leaves much unexplained, and thus we have seen the emergence of such terms as "subimperial" states (see Marini, 1969) or "go-between nation" (see

Galtung, 1972: 128–9). Both of these terms seem an important one, but not in my opinion the key one. I prefer to call them semiperipheral countries to underline the ways they are at a disadvantage in the existing world-system. More important, however, is the need to explicate the *complexity* of the role which semiperipheral states play within the system as well as the fact that the system could not function without being *tri*-modal.

Before this explication, it is necessary to spell out one more fact. The capitalist system is composed of owners who sell for profit. The fact that an owner is a group of individuals rather than a single person makes no essential difference. This has long been recognized for join-stock companies. It must now also be recognized for sovereign states. A state which collectively owns all the means of production is merely a collective capitalist firm as long as it remains—as all such states are, in fact, presently compelled to remain—a participant in the market of the capitalist world-economy. No doubt such a "firm" *may* have different modalities of internal division of profit, but this does not change its essential economic role *vis-à-vis* others operating in the world market.[2] It, of course, remains to discuss in which sector of the world-system the "socialist" states are located.

The capitalist world-system needs a semiperipheral sector for two reasons: one primarily political and one politico-economic. The political reason is very straightforward and rather elementary. A system based on unequal reward must constantly worry about political rebellion of oppressed elements. A polarized system with a small distinct high-status and high-income sector facing a relatively homogeneous low-status and low-income sector including the overwhelming majority of individuals in the system leads quite rapidly to the formation of classes *für sich* and acute, disintegrating struggle. The major political means by which such crises are averted is the creation of "middle" sectors, which tend to think of themselves primarily as better off than the lower sector rather than as worse off than the upper sector. This obvious mechanism, operative in all kinds of social structures, serves the same function in world-systems.

But there is another reason that derives from the particular needs of this kind of social structure, a capitalist world-system. The multiplicity of states within the single economy has two advantages for sellers seeking profit. First, the absence of a single political authority makes it impossible for anyone to legislate the general will of the world-system and hence to curtail the capitalist mode of production. Second, the existence of state machineries makes it possible for the capitalist sellers to organize the frequently necessary artificial restraints on the operation of the market.

But this system has one disadvantage for the sellers. The state machineries can reflect other pressures than of those who sell products on the market, for example, of those who sell labor. What regularly happens in core countries is the operation of a guild principle which, in fact, raises wage levels. It is this to which Arghiri Emmanuel refers when he says: "The value of labor power is, so far as its determination is concerned, a magnitude that is, in the immediate sense, *ethical*: it is *economic* only in an indirect way, through the mediation of its moral and historical element, which is itself determined, in the last analysis, by economic causes" (1972: 120).

The rising wages of the workers in the core countries, combined with the increasing *economic* disadvantage of the leading economic producers, given constant technological progress, and heaviest investment in rapidly outdated fixed capital by precisely the leading producers, leads to an inevitable decline in comparative costs of production. For individual capitalists, the ability to shift capital, from a declining leading sector to a rising sector, is the only way to survive the effects of cyclical shifts in the loci of the leading sectors. For this there must be sectors able to profit from the wage-productivity squeeze of the leading sector. Such sectors are what we are calling semiperipheral countries. If they weren't there, the capitalists system would as rapidly face an *economic* crisis as it would a *political* crisis. . . .

How then can we tell a semiperipheral country when we see one? Even if we admit a tri-modal system, it would be an oversimplification not to bear in the front of our mind that each structural sector contains states of varying degrees of political and economic strength. Furthermore, each sector contains some states that are seeking to move (or *not* to move) from one structural position to another (and for whom such a move is plausible) and other states that for the moment are mired in the location where they find themselves.

Nonetheless, it is important to spell out some defining characteristics of a semiperipheral state, as opposed to a core or a peripheral state. If, we think of the exchange between the core and the periphery of a capitalist system being that between high-wage products and low-wage products, there then results an "unequal exchange" in Emmanuel's conception, in which a peripheral worker needs to work many hours, at a given level of productivity, to obtain a product produced by a worker in a core country in one hour. And vice versa. Such a system is *necessary* for the expansion of a world market if the primary consideration is *profit*. Without *unequal* exchange, it would not be *profitable* to expand the size of the division of labor.[3] And without such expansion, it would not be profitable to maintain a capitalist world-economy, which would then either disintegrate or revert to the form of a redistributive world empire.[4]

What products are exchanged in this "unequal exchange" are a function of world technology. If in the sixteenth century, peripheral Poland traded its wheat for core Holland's textiles, in the mid-twentieth-century world, peripheral countries are often textile producers whereas core countries export wheat as well as electronic equipment. The point is that we should not identify any particular product with a structural sector of the world-economy but rather observe the wage patterns and margins of profit of particular products at particular moments of time to understand who does what in the system.

In a system of unequal exchange, the semiperipheral country stands in between in terms of the kinds of products it exports and in terms of the wage levels and profit margins it knows. Furthermore it trades or seeks to trade in both directions, in one mode with the periphery and in the opposite with the core. And herein lies the singularity of the semiperiphery as opposed to both the periphery and the core. Whereas, at any given moment, the more of *balanced* trade a core country or a peripheral country can engage in, the better off it is in absolute terms, it is often in the interest of a semiperipheral country to *reduce* external trade, even if balanced, since one of the major ways in which the aggregate profit margin can be increased is to capture an increasingly large percentage of its *home* products.

This, then, leads to a second clear and distinctive feature of a semiperipheral state. The direct and immediate interest of the state as a political machinery in the control of the market (internal and international) is greater than in either the core or the peripheral states, since the semiperipheral states can *never* depend on the market to maximize, *in the short run*, their profit margins.

The "politicization" of economic decision can be seen to be most operative for semiperipheral states at moments of active change of status, which are two: (1) the actual breakthrough from peripheral to semiperipheral status and (2) strengthening of an already semiperipheral state to the point that it can lay claim to membership in the core.

The political economies of the various sectors of the world-economy show distinct differences in patterns at various moments of the long-run cycles of the world-economy. It was rather convincingly established by the price historians who began writing in the late 1920s that for a very long period the European world-economy (and, at least since the nineteenth century, the whole world) has gone through a series of systemic expansions and contractions (see a summary and synthesis of this literature in Braudel and Spooner, 378–486). It should be obvious that when the system as a whole is in economic crisis, some parts of it may have to pay a price in relative position as a result of the conflict engendered by the enforced redistribution that follows on economic contraction. But what does that mean for the nations of the periphery and the semiperiphery? Is world economic crisis their bane or their salvation? As one might guess, the answer is not easy. . . .

To be very concrete, it is not possible theoretically for all states to "develop" simultaneously. The so-called "widening gap" is not an anomaly but a continuing basic mechanism of the operation of the world-economy. Of course, *some* countries can "develop." But the some that rise are at the expense of others that decline. Indeed, the rest of this [chapter] will be devoted to indicating some of the mechanisms used by the minority that at given moments rise (or fall) in status within the world-economy. . . .

We must start with the clear realization that not all peripheral countries at any given time are in an equal position to lay claim to a shift in status. As Reginald Green somewhat depressingly puts it: "The attainment of a dynamic toward national control over and development of the economy must start from the existing structural and institutional position, both territorial and international" (1970: 277). We know, by looking backward in history, that among peripheral countries some have changed status and others have not. The Santiago meeting of UNCTAD in 1972 underlined among other things the differing *interests* of different Third World countries in various proposals. The United Nations has developed a list of "hard-core" poor nations, of which sixteen are in Africa (about half of all African states), eight in Asia and Oceania, and only one (Haiti) in Latin America. It is not clear that politico-economic decisions on the reallocation of world resources, such as those that have been favored by the Group of 77, would in fact do very much to alter the relative status of these "hard core" countries (see Colson, 1972, especially 826–30). . . .

Basically there are three strategies: the strategy of seizing the chance, the strategy of promotion by invitation, and the strategy of self-reliance. They are different, to be sure, but perhaps (unfortunately) less different than their protagonists proclaim.

By seizing the chance, we mean simply the fact that at moments of world-market contraction, where typically the price level of primary exports from peripheral countries goes down more rapidly than the price level of technologically advanced industrial exports from core countries, the governments of peripheral states are faced with balance-of-payments problems, a rise in unemployment, and a reduction of state income. One solution is "import substitution," which tends to palliate these difficulties. It is a matter of "seizing the chance" because it involves aggressive state action that takes advantage of the weakened political position of core countries and the weakened economic position of domestic opponents of such policies. It is a classic solution and accounts, for example, for the expansion of industrial activity in Russia and Italy in the late nineteenth century (see, for example, Von Laue,

1963) or of Brazil and Mexico (see Furtado, 1970, especially 85–9)—or South Africa (see Horowitz, 1967, chapter 15)—in the wake of the Great Depression of 1929. A war situation, providing destruction is somewhat limited, and "reconstruction," aggressively pursued, may provide the same "chance." Was this not the case for North Korea in the 1950s? (See Kuark, 1963).

In each of these cases, we are dealing with relatively strong peripheral countries, countries that had some small industrial base already and were able to expand this base at a favorable moment. . . .

"Seizing the chance" as a strategy has certain built-in problems, for industrial development leads these prospective semiperipheral countries to import both machines and manufactured primary materials from the core countries, essentially substituting new dependence for the old, from which "no dependent country has yet succeeded in liberating itself" (Dos Santos, 1971: 745). This problem is far more serious today than in the 1930s, and *a fortiori* than in earlier centuries because of the world level of technology. Merhav has argued that what he calls "technological dependence"

> inevitably leads, on the one hand, to the emergence of a monopolistic structure because the scales of output that must be adopted to introduce modern methods are large relative to the extent of the initial market; and on the other hand, these markets will be only practically expanded through income generated by investment, since a large proportion of the capital goods must be imported. In addition, the monopolistic structure itself will restrict the volume of investment. . . . So that the two effects reinforce each other.[5] . . .

Furthermore, such (national) monopolies are created "even in industries which in the advanced countries are more nearly competitive in structure . . . " (Merhav, 1969: 65). Thus, despite the industrialization "investment is less than what it could be with the existing resources."[6]

The national political alliance of "development populism" furthermore is subject to internal contradictions in countries based on private enterprise since it involves a temporary coming together of the industrial bourgeoisie and the urban workers to favor certain kinds of state action, but once these actions are engaged in, the two groups have opposite interests in terms of wage scales. . . .

The image thus far projected is of an attempt by an indigenous "developmentalist" sector in a peripheral country to "seize its chance" and strengthen its "industrial sector," thus becoming a "semiperipheral" country. Then, we have suggested, over time the combination of internal pressure (the "agricultural sector") and external *force majeure* ("technological dependence") leads to the recuperation of the rebel and the stabilization of the new economic structures such that the development of an "internal market" originally projected is abandoned[7] and a market is substituted, but one in which the semiperipheral country largely serves as a purveyor of products it is no longer worth the while of the core country to manufacture.

But have we not got beyond the "recuperated rebel" scenario? We may have, as the increasingly sophisticated techniques of the burgeoning multinational corporations seem to enable the world-system to arrive at the same result by means of what I am calling "semiperipheral development by invitation."

The whole system of direct investment across frontiers grew up in part because of the flowering of infant industry protectionism and in part because of some political limitations to growth of enterprises in core countries (such as anti-trust legislation). The multinational corporations quickly realized that operating in collaboration with state bureaucracies posed no real problems. For these national governments are for the most part weak both in terms of what they have to offer and in their ability to affect the overall financial position of the outside investor. As Hymer points out, governments of underdeveloped nations are roughly in the relationship to a multinational corporation that a state or municipal government in the United States stands to a national corporation. While the government of the metropolis can, by taxation, "capture some of the surplus generated by the multinational corporation," the competition among peripheral countries to attract corporate investment eats up their surplus (Hymer, 1972: 128).

Why then do the underdeveloped countries compete for this investment? Because, as the examples of the Ivory Coast and Kenya demonstrate, there are distinct advantages in winning this competition even at the disadvantageous terms such aided development is offered. For example, Samir Amin who has been one of the most vocal critics of the Ivory Coast path of development points out:

> Up to now [1971] every one has gotten something out of the Ivory Coast's prosperity via foreign capitalist enterprise: in the countryside, the traditional chiefs, transformed into planters, have become richer, as have the immigrant workers from [Upper Volta] who come out of a traditional, stagnant, very poor milieu; in the town, unemployment remains limited in comparison with what it is already in the large urban centres of older African countries (1971: 92).

No doubt, as Amin says, the Ivory Coast has gone from being "the primitive country that it was in 1950" to being a "veritable under developed country, well integrated, as its elder sister, Senegal, into the world capitalist system" (1971: 93). No doubt, too, as Amin suggests, only Nkrumah's pan-African proposals "would have made it possible to begin to resolve the true problem of development" (280). But Nkrumah did not survive, as we know. The effective choice of the Ivory Coast bourgeoisie may not, therefore, have been between the Ivory Coast path and that recommended by Nkrumah and Amin, but between the Ivory Coast path and that of Dahomey. Given such a choice, there seems little need to explain further why they chose as they did (see my discussion in Wallerstein, 1971: 19–33).

The path of promotion by invitation seems to have two differences with the path of "seizing the chance." Done in more intimate collaboration (economic and political) with external capitalists, it is more a phenomenon of moments of expansion than of moments of contraction. Indeed, such collaborative "development" is readily sacrificed by core countries when they experience any economic difficulties themselves. Second, it is available to countries with less prior industrial development than the first path but then it peaks at a far lower level of import-substitution light industries rather than the intermediate level of heavier industries known in Brazil or South Africa.

One might make the same analysis for Kenya, except that the neighbor of Kenya is Tanzania, and thus for Tanzania the path of *ujamaa* has survived and is indeed the prime example of the third road of development for a peripheral country, that of "self-reliance." Tanzania has been determined *not* to be a "complicit victim," in Sfia's trenchant phrase (see Sfia, 1971: 580).

A sympathetic analysis of Tanzania's attempts by Green (1970) starts with the assumption that "in Africa the closed-national strategy of structural change for development will be even harder to implement than Latin America" and that "economic decolonization and development will be agonizingly slow even with efficient policy formulation and execution and the best likely external economic developments" (284–5). Green terminates with the cautious conclusion that: "The Tanzania experience to date [1969] is that even in the short term a clearly enunciated and carefully pursued strategy of development including economic independence as a goal can be consistent with an accelerating rate of economic as well as social and political development" (324). Let us accept that Tanzania has done modestly well. We may applaud, but may we generalize the advice? One thing to consider is whether Tanzania's path has not been possible for the same reason as Kenya's and the Ivory Coast's, that it is a path being pursued not by all peripheral countries, but by very few. In this case, both Tanzania's poverty and her rarity among Africa's regimes stand her in good stead of thus far minimizing the external pressure brought to bear against her economic policies. Core capitalist countries calculate risks for Tanzania as well as Kenya. Tanzania's model of self-reliance would seem more convincing if Zambia were successfully to adopt it. . . .

To gauge the degree to which semiperipheral countries are able today to utilize the classic mechanisms of advancement in the world economy, we should review both how this classic mechanism worked and the role that wage differentials have played in the structuring of the world-economy. What in a national society determines the general wage level that so manifestly varies from country to country, and in particular seems always to be relatively high in core countries and relatively low in peripheral countries? Obviously, a given employer wishes to pay the least he can for the services he purchases, given the labor market, and the employee wishes to get as high a wage as he can. From the viewpoint of larger social forces, however, as mediated through the state, wage levels affect both sale of products externally (a motive pressing for lower wages) and sale of products internally (a motive pressing for higher wages). Furthermore, the collective organization of workers leads both to legislation and convention assuring at given times given minima, with the expectations socialized into the psyches of the members of the society. . . .

The problem of breakthrough for a semiperipheral country is that it must have a market available large enough to justify an advanced technology, for which it must produce at a lower cost than existing producers. Obviously, there are a number of elements involved in this which are interrelated in a complex way.

One way to enlarge a market for national products is to control access of other producers to the one market a given state politically controls, its own: hence, prohibitions, quotas, tariffs. A second is to expand the political boundaries thus affected via unification with neighbors or conquest. Or, conversely, instead of increasing the costs of imported goods, a state seeks to lower the costs of production, thus affecting simultaneously the home market and external markets. Subsidies for production in whatever form are a mode of reallocation of national costs, such that the effective price of others goods is raised relative to the item subsidized. Reducing costs of production by reducing wage levels is a two-edged sword since it increases external sales at the risk of lowering internal sales, and only makes sense if the balance is positive. A fourth way to increase the market is to increase the internal level of purchasing power which, combined with the natural competitive advantages of low or zero transportation costs, should result in increased internal sales. If this is done by raising wage levels, this is the converse two-edged sword of the previous one, increasing internal sales at the risk of lowering external sales. Finally, the state or other social forces can affect the "tastes," primarily of internal consumers, by ideology or propaganda, and thus expand the market for its products.

Obviously, in addition, it is critical not merely to have optimal costs levels, but to have a certain *absolute* size of the market. Furthermore, the steady advance of technology involving machinery with larger and larger components of fixed capital constantly raises the threshold. Thus, the possibility of a state passing from semiperipheral to core status has always been a matter of juggling elements that move in varied directions to achieve a nearly perfect mix.

For example, the mix that England achieved in the "long" sixteenth century involved a combination of a *rural* textile industry (thus free from the high guild-protection wage costs of traditional centres of textile production such as Flanders, southern Germany, and northern Italy), with a process of agricultural improvement of arable land in medium-sized units (thus simultaneously providing a yeoman class of purchasers with an evicted class of vagrants and migrants who provided much of the labor for the textile industry), plus a deliberate decision to push for the new market of *low*-cost textiles (the "new draperies") to be sold to the new middle stratum of artisans, less wealthy burghers, and richer peasants who had flourished in the expanding cycle of the European world-economy (see Wallerstein, 1974a, for this argument in detail). Germany, too, in the nineteenth century operated on the advantages of a medium wage level, based on the historic legacy of a declining artisan class to create a sufficiently large internal market, yet with a cost of production sufficient to compete with Britain especially in areas to the east and south, where it had transportation advantages. This is not, however, the only mix that can work. There is the "white settler" phenomenon where high wage levels *precede* industrialization and distance from world centers of production (providing the natural protection of high transportation costs for imports). Once again, Emmanuel pushes the point to clarify what is happening. He reminds us that of Britain's five colonies of settlement—the United States, Canada, Australia, New Zealand, and the Cape—the first four have today the highest per capita income in the world whereas South Africa is at the level of Greece or Argentina. Yet it had the same colonists, the same links to Britain. . . .

The high-wage route (that is, high in relation to the wages in the leading industrial countries of the world) is not likely to be easily repeated. First, it requires special political conditions (a settler population attracted in the first place by the immediately or potentially *high* standard of living) plus the technological level of a past era, where world distances mattered more and technological dependence (as discussed above) mattered less. . . .

If high wages are so advantageous in terms of unequal exchange, why doesn't everyone raise their wage levels, or at least every state? Obviously, because the advantage is a function also of low absolute competition (quite apart from price level). To be sure, capital will always flow to high profit areas, but it "flows." There is always a lag. The way it works, in fact, is that whenever some producer is undercut in the cost of production, there will be a tendency over time to uncover a new specialization requiring a momentarily rare skill, which "in the international division of labor at that moment, is free from competition on the part of the low-wage countries" (Emmanuel, 1972: 145). And this is possible because we socially legitimate the variety of products which are technologically feasible.

This process, however, can most easily operate in moments of economic expansion, when it is easier to create new markets for new products than to fight over old ones. But in moments of contraction, the calculus changes. As has become clear once again in the 1970s, core countries are quite willing to expend considerable energy fighting over old ones.[8]

What is the impact of such a fight on the possibilities of semiperipheral countries moving towards core status and peripheral ones moving towards semiperipheral status? I believe that the "slippage" of core countries offers, still today, opportunities for the semiperiphery but makes the outlook even more bleak for the periphery.

At moments of world-economic downturns, the weakest segment of the world-economy in terms of bargaining power tends to be squeezed first. The relative decline in world output reduces the market for the exports of the peripheral countries, and faster than it does the prices of their imports. Peripheral countries may even discover new protectionist barriers against their exports as other countries seek to "take back" areas of production once thought to be of such low profitability as to be worthy only of peripheral countries. To be sure, a few peripheral countries who have the relatively strongest technological base may use the impetus of the crisis to push forward with import substitution. But the bulk of the periphery simply "stagnates."

What happens in the semiperiphery is rather different. In an expanding world-economy, semiperipheral countries are beggars, seeking the "aid" of core countries to obtain a part of the world market against *other semiperipheral* countries. Thus, becoming the agent of a core country, the subimperial role, is if not a necessary condition of further economic gain at least the facile road to it. It is no accident, thus, that ideologically semiperipheral countries are often the loudest exponents of particular *weltanschauungen* and the strongest denouncers of evil practices—of other semiperipheral countries.

As long, therefore, as expansion continues, the mode of economic prosperity for producing groups in semiperipheral areas is via the reinforcement of dependency patterns *vis-à-vis* core countries. However, when world contraction comes, the squeeze is felt by core countries who proceed to fight each other, each fearing "slippage." Now the semiperipheral countries may be courted, as the outlets for core products become relatively rarer. The bargaining relationship of a core and semiperipheral country changes in exactly the way the bargaining relationship between seignior and serf changed in moments of economic contraction in the Middle Ages, in favor of the lower stratum, enabling the latter to get some structural and even institutional changes as part of the new exchange.

But will not the economic difficulties lead to increased strife among the core countries? Curiously, as we so clearly see, it does not. It leads them to limit their strife in order to face, each in its turn, the harder bargaining it must do with its dependent semiperipheral clients. Conversely, we may see new movements towards alliances between semiperipheral countries, which will take the political form of changes in regimes to place themselves in a position to make such alliances.

Notes

1. See, for example, the whole special issue of *Revue Tier-Monde 1972*, especially for the introduction by Ikonicoff.

2. I have argued this at length in my paper, *The Rise and Future Demise of the World Capitalist System: Concepts for Comparative Analysis* (1974b). [The remainder of this note is an extended quote of Samir Amin. The interested reader can refer to the original work.]

3. See Samir Amin (1972: 707–08). [For the remainder of this note see the original text.]

4. It would take us far astray to develop this here. What I mean by "redistributive world-empire" is defined in my *The Rise and Future Demise.* . . . It would be interesting to see if it were not such processes as these which account for the stifling of nascent capitalist elements in such ancient systems as the Roman Empire.

5. Merhav, 1969: 59–60. [For the remainder of the note, see the original text.]

6. Merhav, 1969: 59–60. "What it could be" reminds one of Paul Baran's concept of "potential economic surplus." (See Baran, 1957, chapter 2.)

7. See André Gunder Frank: "But this import substitute development did not create its own market, or at least its own internal market. This development if anything created a post-war internal market for externally produced and imported producer goods, and foreign investment . . . rather than raising internal wages. . . . Instead, to pay for the imports of producers goods required to sustain industrial production, as well as to sustain the latter's profitability, this dependent capitalism again resorted—perforce—to the increasing super-exploitation of labor, both in the export and the domestic sectors, as in Brazil and Mexico (and India?) (1972: 41).

8. Actually, the in-fighting began earlier. "When the U.S. balance of payments was strong, its reserves apparently unlimited, and its dollar untouched by any hint of possible devaluation, the government could face the massive outflow of capital by U.S. companies with equanimity. In today's conditions, this is no longer possible. Under President Johnson, the government was forced to introduce a number of measures to stem the tide of U.S. investmest overseas" (Tugendhat, 1971: 43).

References

Amin, Samir. 1971. *L'Afrique de l'Oues bloquée*. Paris: de Minuit.

Amin, Samir. 1972. "Le modele théorique d'accumulation et de développement dans le monde contemporain." *Revue Tiers-Monde*, 13: 52 (October– December).

Baran, Paul. 1957. *The Political Economy of Growth*. New York: Monthly Review Press.

Braudel, F. P. and F. Spooner. 1967. "Prices in Europe from 1450 to 1750." In E. E. Rich (ed.). *The Economy of Expanding Europe in the Sixteenth and Seventeenth Centuries*. Vol. IV of *Cambridge Economic History of Europe*. Cambridge: Cambridge University Press.

Colson, Jean-Phillipe. 1972. "Le groupe de 77 et le probleme de l'unité des pays du tiers-monde." *Revue Tiers-Monde*, 13: 52 (October–December).

Dos Santos, Theotonio. 1971. "Théorie de lat crise économique dans les pays sous-développés." In A. Abdel-Malek (ed.), *Sociologie de l'impérialsime*. Paris: Anthropos.

Emmanuel, Arghiri. 1972. *Unequal Exchange*. New York: Monthly Review Press.

Frank, André Gunder. 1972. "That the extent of the Internal Market is Limited by the International Division of Labor and the Relations of Production." Paper for IDEP-IDS-CLASCO Conference on Strategies of Economic Development: Africa Compared with Latin America, Dakar, 4–17 September, Mimeographed.

Furtado, Celso. 1970. *Economic Development of Latin America*. New York: Cambridge University Press.

Galtung, Johann. 1972. "Structural Theory of Imperialism." *African Review*, 1: 4 (April).

Green, Reginald. 1970. "Political Independence and the National Economy: An Essay on the Political Economy of Decolonization." In Christopher Allen and R.W. Johnson (eds.), *African Perspectives*. Cambridge: Cambridge University Press.

Horowitz, Ralph. 1967. *The Political Economy of South Africa*. New York: Praeger.

Hymer, Stephen. 1972. "The Multinational Corporation and the Law of Uneven Development." In Jagdish N. Bhagwati (ed.), *Economics and World Order*. New York: Macmillan.

Ikonicoff, Moises. 1972. "Sous-développement, tiers monde ou capitalisme périphérique." *Revue Tiers-Monde*, 13: 52 (October–December).

Kuark, Yoon T. 1963. "North Korea's Industrial Development During the Post-War Period." *China Quarterly*, 14 (April–June), 51–64.

Marini, Ruy Mauro. 1969. *Subdesarollo y revolución*. Mexico: Siglo XXI.

Merhav, Meir. 1969. *Technological Dependence, Monopoly and Growth*. Oxford: Pergamon Press.

Sfia, Mohamed-Salah. 1971. "Le systeme mondial de l'imperialisme: d'une forme de domination a l'autre." In A. Abdel-Malek (ed.), *Sociologie de l'imperialisme*. Paris: Anthropos.

Tugendhat, Christopher. 1971. *The Multinationals*. London: Eyre and Spottiswoode.

Von Laue, Theodore H. 1963. *Sergei Witte and the Industrialization of Russia*. New York: Columbia University Press.

Wallerstein, Immanuel. 1971. "The Range of Choice: Constraints on the Policies of Governments of Contemporary Independent African States." In

Michael F. Lofchie (ed.), *The State of Nations*. Berkeley: University of California Press, 19–33.

Wallerstein, Immanuel. 1974a. *The Modern World System: Capitalist Agriculture and the Origins of the European World-Economy in the Sixteenth Century.* New York and London: Academic Press.

Wallerstein, Immanuel. 1974b. "The Rise and Future Demise of the World Capitalist System: Concepts for Comparative Analysis." *Comparative Studies in Society and History*, 16: 4 (September), 387–415.

13

THE "NEW" SOUTH AFRICA: ASCENT OR DESCENT IN THE WORLD SYSTEM?

_____ *Patrick J. McGowan* _____

Patrick J. McGowan's chapter is an example of world systems theory in the postcommunist world. Defining the three tiers of the world system (the core, semiperiphery, and periphery) in terms reminiscent of Johann Galtung's "structural theory of imperialism," McGowan argues that core status is achieved through cultural, political/military, and economic strength. He then assesses South Africa's prospects for ascending from the semiperiphery to the core (or descending into the periphery). McGowan contends that in terms of culture, South Africa has a strong artistic and educational background. This success, especially compared with others in the region, is marred by the policies of apartheid, which caused educational spending to be directed toward the white minority, leaving nonwhites—particularly blacks—with low levels of education. Politically the state is weak and is plagued by periods of violence and instability. In the economic realm, South Africa has grown uncompetitive in the international arena. McGowan concludes by forecasting that South Africa will have a difficult time maintaining it semiperipheral status and may even sink into the periphery.

Introduction

With a 1990 national income per capita of $2,530 (R7,084), South Africa is an upper middle-income developing country according to the

Originally published in *The South African Journal of International Affairs* Vol. 1, No. 1 (Spring 1993), pp. 35–61. Reprinted with permission from the South African Institute of International Affairs.

World Bank's criteria.[1] It shares this zone in the world economy with 14 other such countries, including Mexico, Brazil, Hungary, Portugal, Korea and Greece. Between 1965 and 1990 GNP per capita grew at the annual rate of 2.8% for this group as a whole, whereas South Africa's average rate of growth was only 1.3% per year. In terms of this widely used index of national development, South Africa's relative position at the forefront of developing societies has declined since 1965.

In terms of international political-economy, South Africa is a classical semi-peripheral society,[2] exporting raw and semi-processed minerals and agricultural products to the core (advanced industrial societies in North America, the European Community, and Japan) and importing from these core societies machinery parts and, in times of drought, maize and other grains.[3] South Africa's exports to the core of the world-system are produced in the main by relatively low-wage black labour, although its mining and agricultural industries use relatively advanced technologies of production controlled by the white minority of its society. South Africa's imports from the core are generally technologically advanced, high-wage commodities.

In the intermediate zone of the world economy, semi-peripheral South Africa has historically dominated the peripheral southern African region. Its gross domestic product of some $90,720 billion in 1990 was nearly three times as large as Nigeria's $34,760 billion and seventeen times bigger than SADC's largest economy, Zimbabwe ($5,310 billion). . . . Long a supplier of labour to South Africa's mining industry, southern Africa's economic ties to the Republic increasingly involve providing energy products—electricity and petroleum—and water. Most importantly, South Africa dominates the region's infrastructure of transportation and communications.

As a semi-peripheral member of the world-system and a regional superpower, South Africa has played a role in the international political economy similar to the roles played by Mexico and Brazil in Central and South America, to Israel and Iran in the Middle East, and to Indonesia and Malaysia in Southeast Asia. As a relatively sophisticated industrial power, the Republic is often compared to the newly industrialised countries (NICs) of the world economy: Brazil, Chile, Mexico, Turkey, Hong Kong, the Republic of Korea (South Korea), Malaysia, Singapore, Taiwan, and Thailand.

Given that the world is organised as a political-economic hierarchy of *core states* (the 23 members of the OECD, led by the Group of 7), *semi-peripheral states and zones* (including Eastern Europe, the successor states of the former Soviet Union, the major oil-exporting countries, and the various NICs), and *large peripheral regions* in Latin America and the Caribbean, Africa, the Middle East and Asia, national development in modern times has involved ascent in this hierarchy (as happened to both Germany and the United States in the 19th century and to the Republic of Korea since 1960); and national decline has taken the form of semi-peripheralisation (as happened to Hapsburg and Bourbon Spain), and peripheralisation (as happened to tropical Africa between 1875 and 1914). The new South Africa is at an historical turning point today. Will it ascend from the semi-periphery into core status at least similar to minor core states like Greece, Ireland and Portugal, or will it descend into the African zone of the world's periphery?

A tentative answer to this vital question is to be found in the record of the recent past and in a hard-headed analysis of the present and near-term situation in the world and in South Africa. In undertaking such an analysis, it must be understood that ascent and descent are not merely a matter of economic performance. While long-term economic development forms the base for upward mobility in the world-system, leadership in international and regional affairs also depends upon cultural strength and impact, and on political stability and legitimacy in combination with sound public and foreign policies by the state (what is often spoken of as "state strength").

South Africa arrived at a similar turning point in the mid-1970s, and it did not respond well. 1973 saw the outbreak of major wildcat strikes in Durban's textile industry and the first oil price hike stemming from the October War in the Middle East. This was followed by the unexpected 25 April 1974 military coup d'etat in Portugal that resulted in political independence for Mozambique and Angola in 1975. Then, there was the Soweto rebellion beginning in June 1976 that soon spread country-wide and that was ruthlessly repressed, leading to the suppression of the Black Consciousness movement, the death of Steve Biko in late 1977, and a flood of young recruits for the exiled liberation movements. There were further oil price hikes in 1979 and the Wiehahn Commission's recommendations to legally recognize black trades unions. Finally, in 1980 Zimbabwe achieved independence under that arch foe of apartheid, Robert Mugabe.[4]

In retrospect, there was a fundamental change in South Africa's domestic and external environments in the years 1973–1980, with 1975–76 comprising the major breakpoint because of the independence of the former Portuguese colonies and the Soweto rebellion. Instead of recognizing the serious political-economic crisis it was facing because of the unsustainability of the apartheid paradigm both domestically and regionally and the shift in the balance of political-economic power in South Africa in favour of increasingly organised black labour and other organisations opposed to the apartheid regime, the Vorster and Botha governments responded by initiating what Giliomee and Schlemmer have called "reform apartheid" domestically and with the "total onslaught/total strategy" policy, both domestically and regionally.[5]

The results for South Africa of this intransigence in the face of these profoundly changing realities were disastrous. On the cultural front, the academic and cultural boycotts were intensified, further depriving many South African artists, intellectuals and technologists of useful international contacts and experiences and producing one of the most inward-looking intellectual cultures in the world. Politically, legitimacy and stability were not achieved by Botha's timid reforms which, in fact, were a principal cause of the renewed rebellions beginning in September 1984 which led to the imposition of crippling financial and economic sanctions in 1985 and 1986. Economically, the South African economy went into a nose dive from which it has yet to recover. As Table 13.1 shows, between 1919 and 1975 South Africa's annual real rate of growth in GDP at factor cost was impressive by world standards. In the period 1975–1990 this annual rate of growth fell to only 1.8%, well below the peak 3.0% per annum population growth reached in 1980 (it has fallen to "only" 2.4% in 1992). So far in the 1990s, South Africa has experienced negative economic growth in both absolute and per capita terms. The bottom line is that since 1975 South Africa has failed to maintain an adequate rate of economic growth; it has become poorer in per capita terms since 1980, and it has lagged seriously behind most other semi-peripheral societies and NICs since the mid-70s in aggregate economic growth.

Table 13.1   South Africa: Annualised Rates of Growth
(in real gross domestic product at factor cost, 1919–1993)

Period	Growth Rate (%)
1919–1929	5.0
1929–1939	5.8
1939–1949	5.8
1950–1960	4.4
1960–1965	6.0
1965–1970	5.4
1970–1975	4.0
1975–1980	2.8
1980–1985	1.1
1985–1990	1.4
1990	−0.5
1991	−0.6
1992	−2.1
1993 (projected)	0.0–0.5

Sources: 1919–1985, Stephen R. Lewis, Jr., *The Economics of Apartheid.* New York: Council on Foreign Relations Press, 1990, p. 24; 1986–1990, International Monetary Fund, *World Economic Outlook,* May 1993. Washington, DC: IMF, 1993, p. 135; 1991–1995, Michael McGrath and Merle Holden, "Economic Outlook: the 1993–1994 Budget," *Indicator South Africa,* 10, 2 (Autumn 1993), p. 19.

Particularly troubling in this record of economic decline are the relative impoverishment of the country's total population, as demonstrated in Figure 13.1, and the fact that this burden of increasing poverty has fallen mainly upon South Africa's already disadvantaged black population. . . . . According to South Africa's widely respected Reserve Book, annual per capita income peaked in 1975 and then in 1980 at R4,000 (as measured in constant 1985 prices); it has steadily declined since then to only R3,150 in 1992 because of the slowing up of aggregate economic growth in combination with continued inflation and population growth. Employment in the formal economy between 1981 and 1991 increased by only 186,000, while the economically active population grew by 3.3 million, resulting in a net increase in the unemployed and underemployed of more than 3.1 million persons (almost all blacks). Even more troubling is that the small increase in formal sector employment was solely due to an increase in government employment; the private sector, where most economically productive job creation and activity ordinarily takes place, saw a net decline of 47,000 jobs, and this employment situation has become worse since 1991.[6]

Figure 13.1   South Africa: Long-Term Trends in GNP, Population, and GNP per Capita, 1960–1991

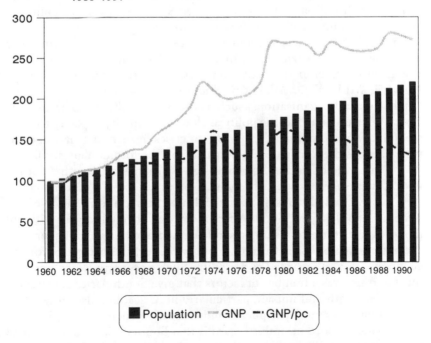

Source: South African Reserve Bank, *Annual Report 1992*, Pretoria: SARB, 1992, p. 10.

The "new" South Africa was born on 2 February 1990 with the urbanizing of the liberation movements and other anti-apartheid organisations. It is now more than three and one-half years later. Based upon what has happened since white South Africa unclenched its fist and on deeper structural features of the white South African and global political-economies, one must now ask whether or not the baby is growing or failing? In short, where is the new South Africa heading— toward the core, or continuing to survive in the semi-periphery, or gradually descending into Africa's periphery? Will it fail to respond to changing realities, as it did in the Vorster-Botha era?

The Components of (Inter)National Development

Cultural Strength

As the leading (hegemonic) power in the world, the United States illustrates well the interconnections of cultural, political/military and economic strength. While there is a vast literature concerning America's (relative) decline vis-à-vis rising economic competitors such as Germany and Japan, this literature too often ignores the impressive and growing "cultural" strength of the United States, as well as its enduring economic and military superiority over all other global powers.[7] In the cultural sphere, America combines "Coca Cola" culture, including such cult figures as the various members of the Jackson family and Hollywood, with such eminent institutions as its great research universities— Harvard, MIT, Yale, Michigan, Stanford, etc.—and its outstanding "high" cultural organisations, such as the Metropolitan Opera in New York. America alone has the political clout and military capacity to initiate military and diplomatic responses to crises in such distant and complex places as the Persian Gulf, Somalia, and the former Yugoslavia. . . .

In terms of cultural strengths and weaknesses, South Africa is generally misunderstood. The typical picture is based upon the country's massive and obvious linguistic, cultural, ethnic and racial diversity. According to this view, South Africa is a deeply divided society with but dim prospects for establishing a stable democracy.[8] As a consequence of the anticipated political instability and violence, the prospects for the economy are also regarded as very dim. Such a scenario is not impossible, but it ignores a number of factors that give South Africa remarkable cultural strength and impact, particularly in Africa, but also in terms of other competing semi-peripheral, industrialising societies.

Most important in this regard is that South Africa is a member of the English-speaking world. While mother-tongue English language speakers comprise only around 40% of the white population, or just over 5% of the total population in 1992, its use is widespread in other communities: most Afrikaners and educated Coloureds are bilingual, English is the dominant language in the Indian community, and urban and educated blacks generally prefer the language to Afrikaans. It is striking that whenever Mr. de Klerk or Mr. Mandela want to maximize the domestic and international impact of their statements, they make them in English. It is conceivable that a post-April 1994 government dominated by the ANC will elevate English to the *de facto* status of sole official language in the country and relegate Afrikaans and other languages to secondary, albeit protected statuses.

English, in its various national forms, is the only global language in business, science and technology, scholarship, and increasingly in mass entertainment and electronic communication, e.g., CNN and the BBC. South Africa therefore has a serious competitive advantage in its English language fluency that facilitates its commerce, technology transfers, scientific and technological research and development, and the impact of its artists globally. Among upper-middle income countries, only Trinidad and Tobago share this advantage, which promotes international competitiveness. English is also widespread in other NICs such as Hong Kong, Singapore and Malaysia. Nevertheless, South Africa's long-standing membership in the English-speaking world, and its likely renewal of membership in the Commonwealth of Nations, are distinct cultural advantages.

A second area of strength is South Africa's artistic and sporting prowess. The National Arts Festival held each winter in Grahamstown is surely the most impressive artistic feast in the Southern Hemisphere. . . . Increasingly, South Africans of all backgrounds are part of the English-speaking, global cultural mainstream.

In international sports individual South Africans have won the New York Marathon and hold world boxing titles, and through sporting ties established in the era of the British Empire, Springbok teams now regularly and effectively compete in football, cricket and rugby against countries as varied as England, France, Australia and Sri Lanka. It is therefore no wonder that the Republic has long (and inappropriately) been regarded as a "developed" country.

The relative attractiveness of South African culture and society is evidenced by the continuing legal and illegal migration flows to the Republic. . . . South Africa's hospitals, technikons and universities are presently flooded with international staff. In comparison to the rest of Africa and the former Soviet empire, South Africa remains an attractive country: climatically, culturally, and economically.

Another source of cultural strength is South Africa's 21 universities, 15 technikons, and selected areas of its research and development apparatus. . . . The quality of these universities and technikons varies from adequate to very good when compared to similar institutions in the Western world. . . . South Africa has more university agricultural and technical facilities than all the SADC countries combined.[9]

Less favourable are South Africa's research and development capabilities, which may be viewed either as a cultural or economic asset. Because of its international pariah status until the early 1990s, many of the country's leading capacities in R&D and technology have focused on beating sanctions, such as MOSSGAS and SASOL, and in fighting apartheid's opponents, for example, ARMSCOR and the recently admitted nuclear weapons programme. R&D in manufactured consumer durables and non-durables for the domestic and export markets is among the lowest in the industrial and industrialising world. In 1990, only 0.8% of South African GDP was spent on R&D in all areas in comparison to Japan's 3.0%, Germany's 2.8%, America's 2.8%, South Korea's 1.8%, and Taiwan's 1.4%. The country's largest manufacturing firm, Barlow Rand, spends only one-fifth of one percent of earnings on R&D, and the average R&D expenditure in industry as a whole in the early nineties was 1% of sales, whereas in Japan it was 6% and in the USA 3%.[10]

Nevertheless, South African capabilities in selected areas of technology, such as mining and civil engineering, railroad equipment, and telecommunications are impressive by world standards. These are competitive assets and could prove indispensable in infrastructure and mining projects, particularly elsewhere in Africa.

A distinct cultural disadvantage of South Africa is its highly skewed distribution and generally low level of skills and training. A direct result of apartheid and its Bantu Education philosophy, whites dominate all highly skilled areas of society, whereas as much as 60% of the economically active population are functionally illiterate. Fully 90% of the country's scientific and technological skills are drawn from the white segment of the population. Among the 21 largest companies in South Africa in mid-1991 only 3.3% of managers and senior managers were black, 3.3% were Indian, and 2.6% Coloured, leaving nearly 91% of all managerial positions occupied by whites (most of them men). According to estimates made by the Education Foundation, there will be a shortage of 500,000 skilled workers by the year 2000—professional, technical, highly skilled, executive and managerial—and a surplus of 2.4 million unskilled, mainly black workers.[11]

According to *Africa Confidential* "South Africa's lack of sufficiently skilled workers, as well as the lack of flexibility and technical capacity in industry will be a major economic constraint for the next decade at least, and is a major disadvantage in comparison with the industrialising countries of south-east Asia."[12] A senior economist in the World Bank's Southern African Department said in April 1993 that "[t]he South African labour force is relatively unskilled for a country at this stage of economic development. This is both a potential impediment to a growth revival in the economy and . . . a major source of inequality."[13] In the 1993 World Competitiveness Report on 15 industrialising, non-OECD economies, South Africa was down-graded from eighth place in 1992 to eleventh in 1993 largely because "[i]ts weak spot remained its human resources. It was at or near the bottom in worker attitudes, competitive values, educational structures and availability of skilled labour."[14] The most competitive societies were Singapore, Hong Kong, Taiwan and Malaysia in that order.

As is widely recognised, the deplorable level of skills and training in society stems from the legacies of Bantu Education and the continuing woeful state of black schooling and vocational training. . . . While the present government has committed itself to equalising spending among all schools and segments of the population and the ANC has called for ten years of free and equal education for all youth, both face daunting obstacles in achieving these goals. . . . The IMF reached the pessimistic conclusion that " . . . it is apparent that equalizing per capita spending on education even at the present Asian or Coloured levels . . . would be beyond the capacity of the budget."[15] Thus, it would appear that this profound cultural weakness of unacceptably low levels of skills and training for the majority of the population and the highly skewed nature of societal skills will be a feature of the South African political-economy for many more years to come.

South Africa's overall cultural balance sheet is therefore decidedly mixed. Cultural pluralism and gross inequalities in skills, education and opportunities are distinct handicaps to ascent in the world system. But the picture is not entirely bleak. The widespread use of English, entertainment and artistic achievement of a high order, sporting links, a tertiary education system of considerable quality, and competitive technology in certain endeavours are sources of genuine strength. Finally, as Adam and Moodley have persuasively argued, within South Africa's diversity there are unifying cultural forces such as Christianity and increasingly Western, materialistic values and lifestyles. The political struggles that have characterised the country for decades are not about non-negotiable matters such as religious faith, as in Bosnia or Northern Ireland, but about political power and socio-economic privilege, matters that can, and in fact are, bargained about.[16]

State Strength and Politics

Ascent in the international political-economy has always been associated with a "strong" state as in the Republic of Korea and Singapore, and descent often comes with a "weak" or disintegrating state as recently happened to the Soviet Union. Increasingly, toward the end of the 20th century ascent has been associated with democratisation, as in Portugal and Spain. It is not by chance that today's 23 core political-economies of the OECD are all capitalist democracies.

State strength does not rely on political form: the United Provinces of the Netherlands in the 17th century formed a stronger state than did most of the absolutist monarchies of the time. Whether the new South Africa is a unitary or a genuinely federal state does not relate directly to its state strength except as it will impact on the legitimacy of government, political stability, and the effectiveness of both the central and other levels of political authority. While it is true that strong states usually have important military capacities (one thinks of the British Royal Navy in the 19th century), strength is based ultimately on sound public finances; a system of government and politics that is legitimate in the eyes of both the public and key elites; the existence of a "hegemonic bloc" comprising political, economic and intellectual elites that provides direction and coherence to state policies; and, finally, because of these key features, the capacity to make and effectively carry out public policies promoting economic growth, equity, stability and security, both domestically and internationally.

These conditions did not obtain in the old South Africa, and as of September 1993 they also do not exist in the new South Africa. Since its creation in 1910, South Africa's successive governments have never been viewed as legitimate by the vast majority of the population. Feelings of illegitimacy are now stronger around the country than ever before and, for the first time since 1914, involve an apparently growing segment of the Afrikaans-speaking white community. The current constitutional negotiations at Kempton Park's World Trade Centre manifest wide divergences among the negotiating parties regarding what an acceptable new constitution should look like. Whatever principles are agreed to there and then enshrined in a new constitution drafted after the proposed 1994 all-persons election, significant portions of the Afrikaner, Zulu and Tswana communities may come to regard them as illegitimate. . . .

Public finance has long been another weakness of the South African state. Between the fiscal years of 1980/81 and 1991/92 general government current expenditure as a percentage of GDP grew from 20.5% to 33% and capital expenditure fell from 6% to 3.5% in the same period. This is a long-term trend, and it means that each year the state consumed a growing share of GDP in operations and salaries for its growing workforce, and invested a declining share of GDP in productive capital. These are politically driven patterns, as the South African state is the major employer of Afrikaners, and their generous treatment by the state has been used to secure their votes for successive National Party governments. Equally troubling is that general government revenues have been consistently below expenditures, resulting in a steadily growing public debt as a percent of GDP. Finally, the profligate foreign borrowings of government up to the financial sanctions of 1985 to finance such projects as SASOL and MOSSGAS have placed a heavy burden on the economy and balance of payments to manage and pay down this foreign debt. This has been achieved, but at the price of declining rates of real growth in the economy.[17] Minister of Finance Derek Keys and Governor of the South African Reserve Bank, Dr. Chris Stals, represent the best financial and economic leadership team since 1948, but they are working to counteract trends of more than four decades. Finally, at this point in time, one simply does not know what the fiscal, financial, and economic policies of an ANC-dominated government will be.

Thus, in terms of state strength and politics, South Africa would seem to be at a considerable competitive disadvantage in comparison to other similarly situated states such as Mexico, South Korea and Malaysia. While this is true, events since the late 1980s have produced two favourable trends. Most clearly, because of the accords in late 1988 over Namibia and Angola, the collapse of communism between 1989 and 1991, the domestic reforms begun in early 1990, and the independence of Namibia in the same year, South Africa's regional security situation has improved markedly. Problems exist on South Africa's borders regarding refugees and arms smuggling, but the country no longer has foreign "enemies," nor does it have any perceived or real external threats. This relatively tranquil international and regional environment contrasts sharply with the situation of certain East Asian NICs such as South Korea, Hong Kong and the Taiwan province of China.

Less certainly, South Africa is now clearly on the path towards establishing a non-racial, political democracy. How stable and legitimate this democracy will be remains an open question. Nevertheless, democratisation is today a necessary condition for upward mobility in the world-system as shown by the recent political liberalisations in Mexico, South Korea and Taiwan. Moreover, because South Africa is a microcosm of the world's ethnic and cultural diversity as well as its economic inequalities, the core powers, particularly the Group of Seven, may well promote South Africa's ascent in the system in order to "reward" a democratic South Africa, to help consolidate its new democracy, and to assist it to become an engine of economic growth for the southern African subcontinent.

On balance, then, state strength and politics as understood herein are another weak spot for South Africa in comparison to its competitors and comparators (although no state is free of domestic and international political problems). Yet, if an enduring democratic political settlement can be achieved by South Africans, growth should return to the economy, and ascent in the world system is entirely possible. Without such a political settlement, descent is certain.

The Economy

As stated earlier, long-term economic performance provides the material base for ascent or descent in the international political economy. Such performance cannot be studied in isolation, as all states are part of the same world economy. Poor performance might, therefore, reflect global economic downturns. For this reason, a series of comparative tables has been created to better understand South Africa's record over the past two decades. Analysis of these tables produces a dismal picture of the country's comparative economic performance and relative economic decline among semi-peripheral states.

The comparator countries represent three Latin American and three Asian NICs, two Mediterranean emerging economies, and Africa's second largest economy, Nigeria. In terms of the size of GDP and population the comparator states range from large ones—Brazil, Nigeria and Mexico—to quite small societies and economies—Chile, Greece and Malaysia. South Africa tends toward the middle of the spectrum, with a population the same size as South Korea, and an economy similar in size to Thailand and Turkey.

With the exception of Nigeria, these countries are at similar levels of economic development. While their 1990 GNPs per capita vary considerably, when GDP per capita is adjusted on a PPP basis, per capita incomes only vary from Thailand at $4,610 a year to Greece's high of $7,340. South Africa's PPP GDP per capita is similar to those of Brazil, Mexico, Malaysia and Turkey, indicating the comparability of the countries selected for detailed study.

The most important column in Table 13.2 is the last, where the average annual rate of growth in GNP per capita between 1965 and 1990 is given. On this basis of average long-term real economic growth, the ten countries fall into three groups: high growth economies—South Korea, Malaysia, and Thailand; moderate growth economies—Brazil, Mexico, Greece and Turkey; and low growth economies—Chile, Nigeria and South Africa. Why does South Africa find itself grouped with Nigeria and Chile, and not with South Korea and Malaysia?

One reason stands out immediately. In the period 1965–1990 Nigeria experienced a civil war and repeated military coups; Chile witnessed a divisive military coup in 1973 and an extended period of severe political repression thereafter; and South Africa saw major uprisings in 1976 and 1984–86 as well as other bouts of political violence and instability. While none of the countries in the Table were entirely free of

Table 13.2 South Africa and Nine Other Developing Countries: Economic Structure and Performance

	Population (millions) Mid-1990	GDP ($ millions) 1990	GDP per capita (Current Int. $)* 1990	GNP per capita	
				Dollars 1990	Average Annual Growth Rate (%) 1965–1990
Brazil	150.4	414,060	4,780	2,680	3.3
Chile	13.2	27,790	6,190	1,940	0.4
Mexico	86.2	237,750	5,980	2,490	2.8
South Korea	35.9	236,400	7,190	5,400	7.1
Malaysia	9.8	42,400	5,900	2,320	4.0
Thailand	55.8	80,170	4,610	1,420	4.4
Greece	10.1	57,900	7,340	5,990	2.8
Turkey	56.1	96,500	5,020	1,630	2.6
Nigeria	115.5	34,760	1,420	290	0.1
South Africa	35.9	90,720	5,500	2,530	1.3

*Purchasing Power Parity (PPP) average income, i.e., what one unit of the local currency would buy in the United States, whose Current International Dollar average income was $21,360.
Source: World Bank, op. cit., pp. 218–9, 222–3, 276–7.

instances of political violence and instability in these years—Mexico violently suppressed student protests in 1968 and also experienced episodes of rural unrest and Turkey has had to deal with urban terrorism and secessionist attempts by its Kurdish-speaking minority—Nigeria and South Africa have been politically most troubled of all the listed countries, and Chile has been at least as badly off as Brazil or Turkey. Both domestic and foreign investors prefer political stability and predictability, which did not exist for extended periods in the low-growth economies.

As Table 13.3 demonstrates, relative economic performance over the longer run is a function of macroeconomic and fiscal policies favouring savings, investment, and low inflation. In this table the real contrast is between the three high-growth Asian economies and the rest, including South Africa. In 1990 the high-growth Asian economies saved an average of 34.6% of their respective Gross Domestic Products and their GDI was fully 36% of GDP (the difference in GDS and GDI coming from foreign investment in their economies). Most importantly, they greatly increased their savings and investment ratios since 1965. South Africa's performance stands in sharp contrast to this record. In 1965 when its economy was still in a high growth mode (see Table 13.1), South Africa saved and invested a higher proportion of its GDP than any other country in Table 13.3. By 1990, it was only in the middle range in savings and near the bottom in GDI, with only Nigeria having a lower rate. Moreover, GDI had fallen to only 18% of GDP by

Table 13.3 **South Africa and Nine Other Developing Countries: Domestic Determinants of Economic Growth, 1980, 1990**

	Average Annual Growth Rate (%)				Distribution of GDP (%)			
	GDP	Industry	Manu.	Average Annual Rate of Inflation (%)	Gross Dom. Savings		Gross Dom. Investment	
					1965	1990	1965	1990
Brazil	2.7	2.1	1.7	284.3	22	23	20	22
Chile	3.2	3.4	3.5	20.5	16	23	15	20
Mexico	1.0	1.0	1.0	70.3	19	19	20	20
South Korea	9.7	12.2	12.7	5.1	8	37	15	37
Malaysia	5.2	7.1	8.8	1.6	24	33	20	34
Thailand	7.6	9.0	8.9	3.4	19	34	20	37
Greece	1.8	1.0	0.6	18.0	15	8	26	19
Turkey	5.1	6.2	7.2	43.2	13	18	15	23
Nigeria	1.4	-1.2	-1.0	17.7	10	29	15	15
South Africa	1.3	0.0	-0.1	14.4	26	25	27	19

Source: World Bank, *op. cit.*, pp. 218–21, 234–235.

1991, barely sufficient to replace depreciated plant and machinery, thus resulting in little net increase in South Africa's capital stock.[18] While there is no clear trend in saving behaviour in South Africa since the early 1980s, investment has fallen massively since 1985 as a consequence of political uncertainty and the financial sanctions imposed that year. (When GDS is greater than GDI, this difference is often used to service foreign debt, as in the Republic since 1985).[19]

All other things being equal, growing GDI should lead to growing GDP. In the case of the Asian NICs, this is the case as their high rates of GDI were associated with an average annual rate of increase in GDP between 1980 and 1990 of 7.5% a year in contrast to South Africa's 1.3%. Turkey approximates this pattern, although its levels of savings and investment are not as high. Very importantly, in the case of the Asian NICs and Turkey, high rates of economic growth in the 1980s were associated with even faster rates of growth per annum in both industry and manufacturing. As growth in industry and manufacturing was stagnant in South Africa, its modest overall GDP growth came from other sectors of the economy such as agriculture and services. One must ask why South African industry is not growing and what are the Asian NICs and Turkey doing right that South Africa is apparently doing wrong (in addition to the already noted differences in human capital, politics, savings and investment rates)?

Part of the answer is to be found in Table 13.3 regarding the comparative inflation rates between 1980 and 1990. Only the Asian

NICs maintained single-digit rates of inflation during these eleven years. Their average rate of inflation was similar to or less than their major trading partners in the Pacific Rim and North America. Now, while it is true that South Africa's inflation rate of 14.4% for this period is modest in comparison to the very high and hyper inflation rates in Latin America and Turkey, it was much higher than the average rates of its major trading partners in the Group of Seven. The annual average rate of inflation between 1975 and 1984 for the Group of Seven was 8.4%, whereas it was 12.7% for South Africa. Between 1985 and 1992, the rates were 3.7% for the Group, and 15.4% for the Republic, a much worse relative performance. And, while in mid-1993 inflation in South Africa was at an annual rate of just under 10%, the IMF has forecasted that it will only be 2.8% in the major industrial countries.[20] This makes exporting more difficult, and currency devaluations do not always help when manufactured products use a significant amount of foreign inputs as they do in South Africa.

Of course, fixed investment must be combined with other factors to create a given output. This is where productivity becomes so important, as it is nothing more than "the relationship between physical output and the capital, labour, materials and energy required to produce that output."[21] Increasing productivity means more output for constant inputs, or the same output from less inputs. In economic jargon, production functions symbolise how the factors of production combine with changing technology and productivity to produce a given output. Management combines the factors of production based upon their relative prices and available technologies of production to, in principle, produce output at the lowest possible marginal unit cost. Data compiled by the National Productivity Institute in Pretoria indicate that in South Africa's private economy excluding agriculture, production has become increasingly capital intensive and labour saving in the period 1970–1991.[22] This is a bizarre state of affairs, as South Africa is relatively labour abundant (see Table 13.2) and capital scarce, therefore labour should be cheap and capital dear. This has not been the case for years, however. Apartheid-induced skilled labour shortages, along with governmental policies that for years produced negative real interest rates and an overvalued Rand, have given industry signals to substitute capital for labour in the production process.

Even worse, while management has merely responded to market signals stemming from distorted relative factor prices created by wrong-headed government policies, it has combined these factors in an increasingly inefficient manner, generating few new jobs in the private sector. As Table 13.4 demonstrates, the productivity of labour has actually grown somewhat in the private economy between 1970 and 1989 and in manufacturing too, although labour productivity there has not

Table 13.4 Trends in South Africa Productivity, 1970–1991

	The Private Economy			Manufacturing		
	Multi-factor	Labor	Capital	Multi-factor	Labor	Capital
1970	100.00	100.00	100.00	100.00	100.00	100.00
1975	98.2	105.5	85.8	102.1	109.1	88.3
1980	99.9	114.2	78.1	109.1	124.6	78.5
1985	93.2	116.9	67.2	93.8	116.3	59.1
1989	98.2	125.5	69.6	104.1	124.3	68.5
1990	—	—	—	100.3	122.4	64.4
1991	—	—	—	97.6	122.1	60.8

Source: NPI, *Productivity Focus* 1993 *op. cit.*, pp. 28–9.

grown since around 1980. Shockingly, the productivity of capital has declined by over 30% in the private economy between 1970 and 1989, and by nearly 40% in manufacturing between 1970 and 1991. As a consequence, the South African economy was less productive overall (multifactor productivity) in 1989 than it was in 1970, and in manufacturing less productive in 1991 that it was in 1970! Stagnant or declining productivity is a prescription for relative descent in the world economy, and the comparisons are not positive for South Africa because its overall productivity has been declining since 1980 while productivity was growing elsewhere: annual rates of 6.5% in Taiwan, 5.4% in South Korea, and 2.9% in Japan.[23]

The culprit here is sharply declining capital productivity, indicating that management is not allocating a relatively scarce factor efficiently. In a massive understatement, the NPI has written that "Improving productivity is fundamentally a function which rests with management, for they decide what, how and how much should be produced with the resources at their disposal. Productivity growth [or the the lack thereof] can thus also be regarded as the result of managerial decisions . . . "[24] The situation in South Africa since the mid-1970s has been one in which apartheid has sharply distorted labour markets and maldistributed skills and opportunities, in which government policies have given the wrong signals to management, and in which management has failed miserably to make optimal decisions, to a large extent because another set of government policies going back to 1925 have sheltered South African industry from the chilling winds of change represented by international business competition.

Many studies have documented that since 1925 South Africa has followed an import-substitution industrialisation (ISI) policy, one that was adopted long before Latin American countries did the same after

World War II. The introduction of trade sanctions over the years, and particularly in the mid-1980s, served to intensify these policies. Since 1985 South African industry has been protected by a complex and opaque system of import surcharges, *ad valorem* duties, formula duties and an import-licensing system. According to GATT, the country's tariff walls were still high in 1993. The average level of protection in the industrial sector was no less than 27%—soaring over 60% in some pockets of manufacturing and to a staggering 90% or more in textiles, leather goods and automobiles.[25] The policy is designed to protect the domestic market against foreign manufactures and favour local South African industry. Total tariffs on primary product imports in mid-1990 were only 3.1%; processed primary products 14.5%; capital goods 20.2%; material-intensive goods 34.0%; and for manufactured products a very high 40.3%.[26] GATT is pressing government to reform this system so that it conforms to GATT rules and enables South Africa to participate in the Uruguay Round negotiations. Government has responded favourably with proposals that would during the rest of the 1990s seriously reduce present tariff levels and vastly simplify the present system. However, it is reported that the ANC has objected to the government's proposals to GATT because it was not consulted and because of the short- to medium-term possible loss of jobs as trade is liberalised.[27] Thus, it may be that an ANC-dominated government will retain protectionist, ISI trade and industrialisation policies.

The results for South Africa of its inward-looking growth strategy have, in general, been harmful. Industry has unquestionably developed behind tariff walls, but it often engages in unproductive rent-seeking behaviour appealing to the Board of Trade and Industries for special tariff protections (which in the past were usually granted). It is a high cost producer—in the manufacturing sector costs are 12.6% higher than they would be in a free trade regime because of the cost of protected, locally produced inputs.[28] South Africa's trade patterns have not changed in years. Exports peaked at 32.9% of GDP in the period 1956–1960, and were down to 25.1% in 1991. In 1991 gold still accounted for fully 30.0% of the value of the country's exports; and base metals, mineral products, and platinum added another 28.3%. Economist Stephen R. Lewis, Jr. has concluded that "[t]he most striking finding regarding the commodity composition of South Africa's exports is the early and continued dominance of gold." Moreover, " . . . the significance of the manufacturing sector as an export earner is lower in South Africa than in other upper-middle-income countries . . . manufactured exports per capita are lower in South Africa than in any of these countries except Brazil."[29]

This is a most dangerous situation, as gold is a finite and declining resource. In 1982 South Africa accounted for fully 64.6% of Western world gold production; by 1992 this had declined to 33.7%.[30] Between

1971 and 1988 South African manufactured exports increased by only 35% and were only 12.7% of total manufactured output. Similar figures for South Korea were a 64% increase, and 29.9% of output; and for Malaysia, a 336% increase, and 41% of output.[31] As a result of these policies, the industrial sector's share of South Africa's GDP was 21.3%, in 1946, it peaked at 30.0% in 1970, and had declined to just 28.0% in 1991 (this includes manufacturing, construction, electricity, water and gas production).

Table 13.5 puts this story in comparative perspective. In the high-growth economies of East and Southeast Asia exports are a significant proportion of GDP, although in the cases of South Korea and Thailand, not much greater than South Africa's 26.0%. The difference between the Asian NICs and Turkey on the one hand, and the other medium- and slow-growth economies, including South Africa, on the other hand, is the annual rate of growth in exports. The value of Nigeria's exports actually fell between 1980 and 1990, in part because of sharp declines in oil prices. Because of sanctions, but also because of its inward-looking policies, South Africa's exports were the second slowest growing among these ten comparator countries. And, although South Africa experienced a modest decline in its terms of trade between 1985 and 1990, largely because of declining commodity prices, Mexico and Malaysia saw even larger declines, yet they were able to expand their exports more rapidly than did South Africa.

Table 13.5 South Africa and Nine Other Developing Countries

	Merchandise Trade			Terms of Trade (1987 = 100)	
	Exports ($ million) 1990	Exports as % of GDP 1990	Annual Export Growth Rate % 1980–1990	1985	1990
Brazil	31,243	7.5	4.0	92	123
Chile	8,579	37.0	4.8	102	131
Mexico	26,714	11.2	3.4	133	110
South Korea	64,837	27.4	12.8	103	108
Malaysia	29,407	69.4	10.3	117	94
Thailand	23,002	28.7	10.2	91	99
Greece	8,053	22.0	3.8	94	105
Turkey	12,959	19.0	9.1	82	98
Nigeria	13,671	39.0	−1.6	167	100
South Africa	23,612	26.0	1.7	105	93

Source: World Bank, *op. cit.*, pp. 244–5, 234–5.
*Figures are for the Southern African Customs Union comprising South Africa, Namibia, Lesotho, Botswana and Swaziland; trade among the component countries is excluded.

In sum, the International Monetary Fund has assembled impressive data demonstrating that between 1974 and 1992 economies with a "strongly outward-oriented" trade strategy, where trade controls are either nonexistent or very low, experienced real GDP growth of 8.0% and real per capita GDP growth of 6.1% in the years of 1974–1985 and 7.5% and 5.9% between 1986 and 1992, despite a difficult international economic environment. Comparable figures for economies that were "strongly inward-looking," where the overall incentive structure strongly favours production for the domestic market, were 2.3% and –0.3% for 1974–85, and 2.5% and –0.1% for 1986–1992.[32] Since the mid-1970s trade has indeed been the engine of economic growth across widely varying global economic conditions. But South Africa has an "anti-export bias" in its trade policies, and this is a major reason why its economic growth has declined since the mid-1970s.[33]

More evidence could be provided, such as the vast sums, economic waste and corruption associated with the government's schemes to subsidise industrial development in and near its ten homelands and self-governing territories. But that is not needed. The performance of the South African economy since the mid-1970s has been terrible, and the causes are multiple: apartheid and its anti-development policies; political instability and, increasingly, a lack of clarity regarding the next government's economic policies; miserable macroeconomic and fiscal policies by past and present governments and public authorities discouraging investment, distorting relative factor prices, and producing inflation and a growing public debt; a terrible record in the development of human capital resources, comparable only to Brazil's failures; management and business leadership that is pampered, privileged and, on the evidence of declining productivity, inefficient and incompetent; and an inward-looking, ISI trade and development strategy that has denied South Africa the opportunity to use trade as an engine of economic growth, just as it ultimately did in Latin America. As a consequence, between 1980 and 1991 South Africa fell from the rank of the 16th largest exporting nation, in value terms, to 30th. Because the economy provides the material base for ascent in the world system, South Africa's economic performance over the past twenty years provides a sad story of absolute decline for most South Africans, and accelerating relative descent among other middle-income, semi-peripheral societies.

Conclusion

From the perspective adopted in this article, things began to fall apart in South Africa in the mid-1970s. Only a few positive trends such as enduring areas of cultural strength, growing regional security, political democratisation, and the fact that South Africa is the only serious industrial economy on the African continent, have been identified. Almost everything else of theoretical and practical importance has become worse since the crucial years of 1975–76. As much as one admires South Africa's wonderful and wonderfully diverse people and the country's exceptional beauty, this analysis leads to the conclusion that in global terms South Africa has declined since the mid-1970s, and at an accelerating rate. It is only when the Republic is compared with the rest of Sub-Saharan Africa that its strengths appear to be significant. We all now live in a global village, with one global economy. In this context, South Africa will be fortunate to retain a place among the world's semi-peripheral powers over the next twenty years. By 2013, the country is very unlikely to have achieved the status of a minor core power such as Spain. Rather more likely is relative descent, so that South Africa will increasingly resemble a big Zimbabwe, at the border between the periphery and semi-periphery.

Of course, forecasts are always problematic. Relative descent is not foreordained. Its prevention requires the collaborative efforts of all South Africans and all sectors of society. However, the many negative trends identified in this article suggest that South Africans cannot maintain their present position in the international political economy, much less enhance it, on their own. The collaborative efforts of South Africans and the international community led by the Group of Seven and the international organisations they dominate, particularly the IMF and World Bank, will be essential to the task. This said, it must be South Africans that take the lead. What needs to be done should be obvious from this analysis of what has gone wrong over the last two decades.

Notes

1. The World Bank, *World Development Report* 1992. New York: Oxford University Press, 1992, p. 219.

2. For an extended analysis along these lines see: Sergio Vieira, William G. Martin and Immanuel Wallerstein, *How Fast the Wind? Southern Africa, 1975–2000*. Trenton, NJ: Africa World Press, 1992, particularly chapters by Wallerstein and Vieira, "Historical Development of the Region in the Context of the Evolving World-System," pp. 3–15 and Darryl Thomas and William G. Martin, "South Africa's Economic Trajectory: South African Crisis or World-Economic Crisis?", pp. 165–196.

3. In 1991 only the Taiwan province of China was not a core society among South Africa's top ten trade partners. By order of the size of total trade, in that year, they were: Germany, U.S.A., Britain, Japan, Switzerland, Taiwan, Netherlands, Italy, France and Belgium. *The Star*, 18 January 1993.

4. In addition to Vieira, *et.al.*, *op.cit.*, this crucial period is well covered on the domestic side by James Barber and John Barratt, *South Africa's Foreign Policy: The Search for Status and Security, 1948–1988.* Cambridge: Cambridge University Press, 1990; Andre du Pisani, "Ventures into the Interior: Continuity and Change in South Africa's Regional Policy," pp. 188–232 in A. van Nieuwkerk and G. van Staden (eds.), *Southern Africa at the Crossroads.* Johannesburg: South African Institute of International Affairs, 1991; Tom Lodge, *Black Politics in South Africa since 1945.* Johannesburg: Ravan Press, 1983; Gail Gerhart, *Black Power in South Africa: The Evolution of an Ideology.* Berkeley and Los Angeles: University of California Press, 1978; and Robert M. Price, *South Africa: The Process of Political Transformation.* New York: Oxford University Press, 1991; and externally in Deon Geldenhuys, *The Diplomacy of Isolation: South African Foreign Policy Making.* Johannesburg: Macmillan, 1984.

5. Hermann Giliomee and Lawrence Schlemmer, *From Apartheid to Nation-Building.* Cape Town: Oxford University Press, 1989 and du Pisani, *op.cit.* See also Servaas van der Berg, "Long-term economic trends and development prospects in South Africa," *African Affairs*, 88 (April 1989), pp. 187–203.

6. *The Sunday Times (Business Times)*, 8 August 1993, p. 10. At least 200,000 formal jobs were lost between the fourth quarter of 1989 and the fourth quarter of 1992, including at least 85,000 in the mining industry. The South African formal economy is absorbing less than 10% of the 400,000 new job seekers who enter the market each year. Indeed, in late 1992, only 1 in 100 job seekers were finding jobs. According to Pretoria's National Productivity Institute, between 1980 and 1991 the private sector lost 67,100 jobs, government added 366,100 positions, for a net gain of only 299,000 jobs in the formal sector in 11 years! National Productivity Institute, *Productivity Focus* 1993. Pretoria: NPI, 1993, p. 22.

7. This debate was initiated by Paul Kennedy's pessimistic analysis of the prospects for the United States in *The Rise and Fall of the Great Powers.* New York: Random House, 1987. A major, more optimistic response, is Joseph S. Nye, Jr., *Bound to Lead: The Changing Nature of American Power.* New York, 1990.

8. See Donald L. Horowitz, *A Democratic South Africa?* Berkeley and Los Angeles: University of California Press, 1991, for a detailed and sophisticated argument in support of this view.

9. Donald Sparks, "The Peace Dividend: Southern Africa after Apartheid," *Indicator South Africa*, 10, 2 (Autumn 1993), p. 29.

10. Data are from Patrick J. McGowan, "The World Political-Economy Today and Tomorrow: Character, Trends, and Implications for Southern Africa," p. 46 in van Nieuwkerk and van Staden, op. cit., and National Productivity Institute, *Productivity Statistics* 1992. Pretoria: NPI, p. 107.

11. Data are from South African Institute of Race Relations, *Race Relations Survey 1992/93.* Johannesburg: SAIRR, 1993, pp. 581–2.

12. June 1992 issue, as quoted in *ibid.*, p. 581.

13. *The Star*, 29 April 1993.

14. *Business Day*, 29 June 1993.

15. D. Lachman and K. Bercuson, *Economic Policies for a New South Africa*, Washington DC: International Monetary Fund, January 1992, p. 23.

16. Heribert Adam and Kogila Moodley, *South Africa Without Apartheid: Dismantling Racial Discrimination.* Berkeley and Los Angeles: University of California Press, 1986.

17. The *Annual Reports* of the South African Reserve Bank describe these trends in detail.

18. South African Reserve Bank, *Quarterly Bulletin*, various issues.

19. Tamin Bayoumi, "Output, Employment and Financial Sanctions in South Africa," IMF Working Paper, WP/90/113. Washington, DC: IMF European Department, December 1990, pp. 2–3 and Howard Preece, "Investment Myth," *Finance Week*, 25 April 1993.

20. International Monetary Fund, *World Economic Outlook, May 1993*. Washington, D.C.: IMF, pp. 140–3.

21. *Productivity Focus 1993, op. cit.*, p. 1.

22. *Productivity Statistics 1992, op. cit.*, p. 43. With an index base year of 1980, real output between 1970 and 1991 grew from 69.3 to 103.7; labour input from 72.3 to 96.7; and fixed capital input an amazing 44.1 to 105.9. As a result, the capital/labour ratio in 1970 was 60.9, whereas it had grown to 109.6 by 1991.

23. *Sunday Times (Business Times)*. 25 July 1993, p. 6.

24. *Productivity Focus 1993, op. cit.*, p. 19.

25. *The Star*, 21 June 1993.

26. *Economic Policies for a New South Africa, op. cit.*, p. 36.

27. *Sunday Times (Business Times)*, 15 August 1993, p. 4.

28. Reg Rumney, "A Model Export Plan," *The Weekly Mail*, 26 March 1993.

29. S.R. Lewis, Jr., *The Economics of Apartheid*. New York: Council on Foreign Relations Press, 1990, pp. 57–8.

30. *Business Day*, 15 June 1993.

31. Brian Levy, "How Can South African Manufacturing Efficiently Create Employment? An Analysis of the Impact of Trade and Industrial Policy," Washington, DC: World Bank, Southern African Department, January 1992, Table 2.8.

32. *World Economic Outlook May 1993, op. cit.*, p. 76.

33. *The Citizen*, 2 June 1993, quoting from a GATT report.

PART 2

INTERNATIONAL
MONETARY RELATIONS

14

THE INTERNATIONAL MONETARY FUND

C. Roe Goddard and Melissa H. Birch

In this chapter C. Roe Goddard and Melissa H. Birch review the evolution of the International Monetary Fund (IMF) and the international financial system it tries to govern. The authors note that even though the IMF was originally created to provide only balance-of-payments financing, changing circumstances in the international economy have led to the expansion of the nature and scope of IMF lending. Under these changed circumstances, the IMF has designed new types of loans to deal with the special needs of heavily indebted, primary product–dependent countries. More recently, the International Monetary Fund has been working on strategies to aid countries undergoing a transition from centrally planned to market economies.

The International Monetary Fund (IMF) and the International Bank for Reconstruction and Development (World Bank) were created in July 1944. Delegates from forty-five countries attended the meeting in Bretton Woods, New Hampshire, at which the negotiations took place. The objective of the Bretton Woods conference was to establish the broad rules that would govern international economic relations and to design multilateral institutions capable of providing both stability to these relations and a check on the rise of economic nationalism, which was thought to have contributed significantly to the outbreak of World War II. Prior to the creation of the Bretton Woods institutions, there had been no permanent cooperative organizations to oversee the international economic system.

As a reaction to the problems of the times, the IMF's mandate was to stabilize and establish a clear and unequivocal value for each currency, encourage the unrestricted conversion of one currency into another, and eliminate practices such as competitive devaluations that had stifled investment flows and brought trade to a virtual halt in the 1930s. Attacking the problem piecemeal, the immediate postwar objective of the IMF was to restore exchange rate stability among the currencies of the countries that had fought in the war. Once that stability had been created and the basis had been set for the expansion of postwar trade, the IMF's charge shifted to ensuring exchange rate stability among all of the world's trading countries. Since its early history, the responsibilities of the IMF have grown as new and unforeseen challenges to international monetary stability have appeared. It is now entrusted with a wide array of responsibilities in the functioning of the international monetary system.

In their early years, the division of labor between the IMF and the World Bank was fairly clear. Only in the 1980s, when the World Bank began lending for balance-of-payments purposes and for the creation of structural adjustment facilities, did the line between the two institutions begin to blur. The Fund was to provide short- to medium-term financing for balance-of-payments problems. If a country was, for example, depleting its foreign-exchange reserves because imports were exceeding exports, the IMF would lend it money so it would not face an abrupt cutoff of imports when those reserves were depleted. By helping a country overcome its temporary liquidity problems, the IMF assists both the borrowing country, by maintaining its access to imports, and the country's trading partners, by maintaining a viable export market. This pivotal IMF role in maintaining national and international stability by ensuring a smoothly operating international monetary system was highlighted in Article 1, v, and vi of the original Articles of Agreement: "The Fund's primary financial purpose is to give confidence to members by making the general resources of the Fund temporarily available to them under adequate safeguards, thus providing them with the opportunity to correct maladjustments in their balance of payments without resorting to measures destructive of national or international prosperity and to shorten the duration and lessen the degree of disequilibrium in the international balances of payments of members" (Chandavarkar, 1984: 1).

The World Bank, as envisioned by its Bretton Woods creators, was intended to complement the IMF. Rather than providing short-term financing to help countries make the internal adjustments necessary to overcome temporary balance-of-payment deficits, it was to provide longer-term loans for specific development purposes. This division of responsibilities has remained broadly intact since World War II.

IMF Organization

The Articles of Agreement, which took effect in December 1945, outline the organizational structure of the IMF. They provide for a Board of Governors, an Executive Board, a managing director, a staff of international civil servants, and a Council.

The ultimate governing authority within the Fund is the Board of Governors, which presently consists of 179 governors. The individual board members represent the highest echelons of their governments' economic policymaking organizations, often having served as ministers of finance or as heads of the central banks. The Board of Governors meets biannually in the fall and the spring.

The Board of Governors delegates the authority to govern and to conduct the day-to-day business of the IMF to the Executive Board, which is the organization's locus of power and its permanent decision-making organ. It is composed of twenty-four directors, five appointed and nineteen elected, chosen by member countries or by groups of countries. At present, eight executive directors represent individual countries: China, France, Germany, Japan, Russia, Saudi Arabia, the United Kingdom, and the United States. The remaining positions are held by governors who represent groups of countries. The Executive Board selects as its chair the managing director of the IMF. The board usually meets three times a week to address a wide variety of policy, operational, and administrative matters, including surveillance of members' exchange rate policies, provision of financial assistance to member countries, consultations with members, and comprehensive studies on issues of importance to the membership. Decisions made by the board are based on consensus rather than a formal voting process, which minimizes confrontation and the potential politicization of lending decisions. Executive Board members and their voting power as of April 30, 1994, are listed in Table 14.1.

The managing director is the administrative head of the organization, whose responsibilities include chairing the Executive Board, participating in the combined annual IMF–World Bank meetings, advising the Group of Seven (G-7) leading industrialized countries, and overseeing the Fund's professional staff. Although the managing director is the official head of the organization, the position bestows the director no real power. The director cannot even cast a vote when chairing meetings of the Executive Board. In 1987, Michel Camdessus, former director of the French treasury, was appointed to a five-year term as managing director; his appointment was renewed in 1992. The managing director of the IMF has traditionally been European, and the president of the World Bank has been a U.S. citizen.

The managing director heads the IMF's international staff of around two thousand professional employees from 114 countries. The staff is made up mainly of economists, but it also includes professionals in taxation and public finance, statisticians, linguists, writers, research scholars, and support personnel. The staff carries out the policies and instructions of the Executive Board, including oversight of country

Table 14.1 IMF Executive Directors and Voting Power (as of April 30, 1994)

Director *Alternate*	Country for Which Votes Are Cast	Votes by Country	Total Votes[a]	Percentage of Fund Total[b]
Appointed:				
Karen Lissakers *Barry S. Newman*	United States	265,518	265,518	17.81
Stefan Schoenberg *Erika Wagenhoefer*	Germany	82,665	82,665	5.54
Hiroo Fukui *Toshihiko Fukuyama*	Japan	82,665	82,665	5.54
Marc-Antoine Autheman *Michel Sirat*	France	74,396	74,396	4.99
Huw Evans *John Dorrington*	United Kingdom	74,396	74,396	4.99
Elected:				
Willy Kiekens (Belgium) *Johann Prader* *(Austria)*	Austria Belarus Belgium Czech Republic Hungary Kazakhstan Luxembourg Slovak Republic Turkey	12,133 3,054 31,273 6,146 7,798 2,725 1,605 2,824 6,670	74,228	4.98
Godert A. Posthumus (Netherlands) *Oleh Havrylyshn* *(Ukraine)*	Armenia Bulgaria Cyprus Georgia Israel Moldova Netherlands Romania Ukraine	925 4,899 1,250 1,360 6,912 1,150 34,692 7,791 10,223	69,202	4.64
Roberto Marino (Mexico) *Gerver Torres* *(Venezuela)*	Costa Rica El Salvador Guatemala Honduras Mexico Nicaragua Spain Venezuela	1,440 1,506 1,788 1,200 17,783 1,211 19,604 19,763	64,295	4.31
Giulio Lanciotti (Italy) *Nikolaos Coumbis* *(Greece)*	Albania Greece Italy Malta Portugal San Marino	603 6,126 46,157 925 5,826 350	59,987	4.02
Douglas E. Smee (Canada) *Garrett F. Murphy* *(Ireland)*	Antigua and Barbuda Bahamas, the Barbados Belize Canada Dominica	335 1,199 739 385 43,453 310		

(continues)

Table 14.1   continued

Director *Alternate*	Country for Which Votes Are Cast	Votes by Country	Total Votes[a]	Percentage of Fund Total[b]
	Grenada	335		
	Ireland	5,500		
	Jamaica	2,259		
	St. Kitts and Nevis	315		
	St. Lucia	360		
	St. Vincent and the Grenadines	310	55,500	3.72
Jarle Bergo	Denmark	10,949		
(Norway)	Estonia	715		
Eva Srejber	Finland	8,868		
(Sweden)	Iceland	1,103		
	Latvia	1,165		
	Lithuania	1,285		
	Norway	11,296		
	Sweden	16,390	51,771	3.47
Muhammed Al-Jasser	Saudi Arabia	51,556	51,556	3.46
(Saudi Arabia)				
Abdulrahman A. Al- *Tuwaiijri (Saudi Arabia)*				
Ewen L. Waterman	Australia	23,582		
(Australia)	Kiribati	290		
Amando M. Tetangco Jr.	Korea	8,246		
(Philippines)	Marshall Islands	275		
	Mongolia	621		
	New Zealand	6,751		
	Papua New Guinea	1,203		
	Philippines	6,584		
	Seychelles	310		
	Solomon Islands	325		
	Vanuatu	375		
	Western Samoa	335	48,897	3.28
A. Shakour Shaalan	Bahrain	1,078		
(Egypt)	Egypt	7,034		
Yacoob Yousef	Iraq	5,290		
Mohammed	Jordan	1,467		
(Bahrain)	Kuwait	10,202		
	Lebanon	1,037		
	Libya	8,426		
	Maldives	305		
	Oman	1,444		
	Qatar	2,155		
	Syrian Arab Republic	2,349		
	United Arab Emirates	4,171		
	Yemen, Republic of	2,015	46,973	3.15
Konstantin G.	Russia	43,381	43,381	2.91
Kagalovsky				
(Russia)				
Aleksei V. Mozhin				
(Russia)				

(continues)

Table 14.1 continued

Director *Alternate*	Country for Which Votes Are Cast	Votes by Country	Total Votes[a]	Percentage of Fund Total[b]
J. E. Ismael	Fiji	761		
(Indonesia)	Indonesia	15,226		
Kleo-Thong Hetrakul	Lao People's Democratic			
(Thailand)	Republic	641		
	Malaysia	8,577		
	Myanmar	2,099		
	Nepal	770		
	Singapore	3,826		
	Thailand	5,989		
	Tonga	300		
	Vietnam	2,666	40,855	2.74
Daniel Kaeser	Azerbaijan	1,420		
(Switzerland)	Kyrgyz Republic	895		
Krzysztof Link	Poland	10,135		
(Poland)	Switzerland	24,954		
	Turkmenistan	730		
	Uzbekistan	2,245	40,379	2.71
Abbas Mirakhor	Afghanistan, Islamic State of	1,454		
(Islamic Republic	Algeria	9,394		
of Iran)	Ghana	2,990		
Mohammed Dairi	Iran, Islamic Republic of	11,035		
(Morocco)	Morocco	4,527		
	Pakistan	7,832		
	Tunisia	2,310	39,542	2.65
Alexandre Kafka	Brazil	21,958		
(Brazil)	Colombia	5,863		
Alberto Calderón	Dominican Republic	1,838		
(Columbia)	Ecuador	2,442		
	Guyana	922		
	Haiti	691		
	Panama	1,746		
	Suriname	926		
	Trinidad and Tobago	2,718	39,104	2.62
K. P. Geethakrishnan	Bangladesh	4,175		
(India)	Bhutan	295		
L. Eustace N. Fernando	India	30,805		
(Sri Lanka)	Sri Lanka	3,286	38,561	2.59
L. J. Mwananshiku	Angola	2,323		
(Zambia)	Botswana	616		
Barnabas S. Dlamini	Burundi	822		
(Swaziland)	Ethiopia	1,233		
	Gambia, the	479		
	Kenya	2,244		
	Lesotho	489		
	Liberia	963		
	Malawi	759		
	Mozambique	1,090		
	Namibia	1,246		
	Nigeria	13,066		
	Sierra Leone	1,022		
	Swaziland	615		

(continues)

Table 14.1 continued

Director *Alternate*	Country for Which Votes Are Cast	Votes by Country	Total Votes[a]	Percentage of Fund Total[b]
	Tanzania	1,719		
	Uganda	1,589		
	Zambia	2,953		
	Zimbabwe	2,863	36,091	2.42
Zhang Ming (China) *Wei Benhua (China)*	China	34,102	34,102	2.29
A. Guillermo Zoccali (Argentina) *Alberto F. Jimenez* *de Lucio (Peru)*	Argentina Bolivia Chile Paraguay Peru Uruguay	15,621 1,512 6,467 971 4,911 2,503	 31,985	 2.14
Corentino V. Santos (Cape Verde) *Yves-Marie T. Koissy* *(Côte d'Ivoire)*	Benin	703		
	Burkina Faso	692		
	Cameroon	1,601		
	Cape Verde	320		
	Central African Republic	662		
	Chad	663		
	Comoros	315		
	Congo	829		
	Côte d'Ivoire	2,623		
	Djibouti	365		
	Equatorial Guinea	493		
	Gabon	1,353		
	Guinea	1,037		
	Guinea-Bissau	355		
	Madagascar	1,154		
	Mali	939		
	Mauritania	725		
	Mauritius	983		
	Niger	733		
	Rwanda	845		
	Sao Tome and Principe	305		
	Senegal	1,439		
	Togo	793		
	Zaire	3,160	23,096	1.55
Totals			1,469,145[c]	98.52[d]

Source: IMF, Annual Report, 1991. Reprinted with permission.

Notes: a. Voting power varies depending on certain matters that pertain to use of the Fund's resources in the General Department.

b. Percentages of total votes (1,491,143) in the General Department and the Special Drawing Rights (SDR) Department.

c. This total does not include the votes of Cambodia, Croatia, the former Yugoslav Republic of Macedonia, the Federated States of Micronesia, Slovenia, Somalia, South Africa, and Tajikistan, which did not participate in the 1992 regular election of executive directors. The combined votes of these members total 21,998—1.48 percent of those in the General Department and the SDR Department. This total also does not include the votes of Sudan, which were suspended effective August 9, 1993, pursuant to Article XXVI, Section 2(b) of the Articles of Agreement.

d. This figure may differ from the sum of the percentages shown for individual directors because of rounding.

borrowers. The majority of staff members work at IMF headquarters in Washington, D.C.; however, a small number are employed in Paris, Geneva, and at the United Nations in New York.

The IMF and Surveillance in Exchange Arrangements

Methods of calculating the exchange value of individual countries' currencies have changed over time. Between 1947 and 1971, a fixed but flexible currency regime, known as the peg-and-band system, existed. Under this regime, members sought to keep daily fluctuations in currency value within 1 percent of the value at the beginning of the trading day. Although the system worked reasonably well, by the late 1960s countries were increasingly unable to contain valuation changes within the 1 percent rule, and breakdown occurred in 1971. Since that time a float regime evolved that was legitimized at the Jamaica conference in 1975. Today, the system includes three types of floats—market, managed, and "dirty" floats. Market, or free, floats exist when members' monetary authorities do not intervene in international currency markets for the purpose of influencing valuation. Managed floats exist when members intervene in international currency markets but only to offset "disorderly" conditions that may be characterized by, among other things, disruptive short-term movements in the exchange rates of their currencies (see Article IV of the Articles of Agreement). "Dirty" floats occur when a country is perceived to be manipulating the value of its currency to gain an unfair trading advantage and not because of an underlying economic rationale.

The Fund's responsibility is to monitor the exchange rate policies of members and, particularly, to alert the Executive Board in cases of "dirty floating." The process of consultation involves prompt, informal, and confidential meetings between the member and the managing director to identify whether a problem exists. Within four months of such meetings the managing director submits a report to the Executive Board, which reviews it and concludes whether the member's exchange rate policies are consistent with its obligations under Article IV. Under the float regime, then, the Fund no longer exercises its previous formal power to impose conditions when the value of a currency threatens to exceed the perimeters of the bank, and member compliance becomes essentially voluntary.

The collapse of the peg-and-band system also resulted in a delinking of currencies to gold or any other single standard. Each member now selects its own standard for evaluation, which offers flexibility in choosing a method of valuation. As of 1992, over thirty countries allowed their currencies to float independently, including Japan and the United States. Other countries pegged the value of their currencies to a key currency or group, or basket, of currencies. Seeking minimal fluctuation and maximum stability, many European countries, through coordinated intervention, strove to keep the relative value of their currencies within a narrow range, or, as it is known colloquially, the snake.[1] Chapter 17 of this book examines the European Monetary System in more detail. See Table 14.2 for a listing of countries' exchange arrangements.

The shift from the peg-and-band system to a float system changed the relationship of members with the IMF. It has increased IMF involvement in the formulation of member's economic policies that affect the exchange value of their currencies. Given that the exchange value of a currency is the final result of a broad range of economic policies, the IMF is intimately involved in monitoring and advising its members. This activity, known as surveillance, has been rather controversial because of the transparency required of the country, IMF encroachment on national sovereignty, and the social outcomes of IMF policies (Driscoll, 1994: 11). Contributing to the controversy surrounding IMF lending, in recent years the primary borrowers have been the less developed countries of the South. With the creation of new special lending facilities, many of these countries have become perpetual borrowers, operating continuously under IMF supervision. This has only heightened the perception that the IMF is an exploitative tool of the rich countries.

Sources of Funding Available to the IMF

Quotas

The IMF is, in effect, "owned" by its members, with ownership distributed in accordance with a system of quotas. The size of each member's quota is determined by a complex and often highly politicized formula that incorporates the size of the economy, the percentage of the economy involved in international trade, and the value of foreign-exchange holdings. This quota is the most fundamental element of a member's voting power in the IMF. The number of votes a country possesses is determined on the basis of one vote for each IMF 100,000 currency units (Special Drawing Rights, or SDRs) plus the 250 basic votes each member is automatically granted. Effectively, the system of quotas and voting heavily and favorably weighs power toward members with large gross national products (GNPs). In addition to determining voting power, a member's quota also determines the maximum amount of IMF

Table 14.2 Exchange Arrangements as of March 31, 1992[a]

		Pegged		
	Single currency		Currency composite	
U.S. dollar	French franc	Other	Special drawing rights	Other
Angola[d]	Benin	Bhutan	Burundi	Albania[d,e]
Antigua and Barbuda	Burkina Faso	(Indian rupee)	Iran, Islamic	Algeria
Argentina	Cameroon	Lesotho[d]	Republic of[d]	Austria
Bahamas, the[d]	Central African	(South African rand)	Libyan Arab	Bangladesh
Barbados	Republic	Swaziland (South	Jamahiriya[h]	Botswana
Belize	Chad	African rand)	Myanmar	Cape Verde
Djibouti	Comoros	Yugoslavia	Rwanda	Cyprus
Dominica	Congo	(Deutsche mark)	Seychelles	Czechoslovakia
Ethiopia	Côte d'Ivoire			Fiji
Grenada	Equatorial Guinea			Finland[j]
Iraq[d]	Gabon			Hungary
Liberia	Mali			Iceland[l]
Mongolia[d]	Niger			Jordan
Nicaragua[d]	Senegal			Kenya[d]
Oman	Togo			Kuwait
Panama				Malawi
St. Kitts and Nevis				Malaysia[k]
St. Lucia				Malta
St. Vincent and the				Mauritius
Grenadines				Morocco[n]
Suriname				Nepal[d]
Syrian Arab Republic[d]				Norway[p]
Trinidad and Tobago				Papua New Guinea
Yemen				Solomon Islands
				Sweden[q]
				Tanzania
				Thailand
				Tonga
				Vanuatu
				Western Samoa
				Zimbabwe

Source: *IMF Survey* May 1992.

Notes: a. Current information relating to Cambodia is unavailable.

b. In all countries listed in this column, the U.S. dollar was the currency against which exchange rates showed limited flexibility.

c. This category consists of countries participating in the exchange rate mechanism of the European Monetary System. In each case, the exchange rate is maintained within a margin of 6 percent.

d. Member maintains exchange arrangements involving more than one exhange market. The arrangement shown is that maintained in the major market.

e. The basic exchange rate of the lek is pegged to the European currency unit (ECU).

f. Exchange rates are determined on the basis of a fixed relationship to the SDR, within margins of up to ±10 percent on either side of a weighted composite of the currencies of the main trading partners.

g. The exchange rate is maintained within margins of ±10 percent on either side of a weighted composite of the currencies of the main trading partners.

Table 14.2 continued

Flexibility Limited Against a Single Currency or Group of Currencies			More Flexible	
Single currency[b]	Cooperative arrangements[c]	Adjusted according to a set of indicators	Other managed floating	Independently floating
Bahrain[f]	Belgium	Chile[d,g]	China[d]	Afghanistan[d]
Qatar[f]	Denmark	Columbia[d]	Ecuador[d]	Australia
Saudi Arabia[f]	France	Madagascar	Egypt	Bolivia
United Arab Emirates[f]	Germany	Mozambique[d]	Greece	Brazil[d]
	Ireland	Zambia[d]	Guinea	Bulgaria
	Italy		Guinea-Bissau[d]	Canada
	Luxembourg		India[d,i]	Costa Rica
	Netherlands		Indonesia	Dominican
	Spain		Israel[k]	Republic
	United Kingdom		Korea	El Salvador[d]
			Lao People's Democratic Republic	Gambia, the
			Maldives	Ghana
			Mauritania	Guatemala
			Mexico	Guyana
			Pakistan	Haiti
			Poland	Honduras[d]
			Portugal	Jamaica
			Romania	Japan
			Sao Tome and Principe	Kiribati[m]
			Singapore	Lebanon
			Somalia[d]	Namibia[d,o]
			Sri Lanka	New Zealand
			Tunisia	Nigeria[d]
			Turkey	Paraguay
			Uruguay	Peru
			Vietnam	Philippines
				Sierra Leone
				South Africa[d]
				Sudan
				Uganda[d]
				United States
				Venezuela
				Zaire

h. The exchange rate is maintained within margins of ±11 percent.

i. The exchange rate is maintained within margins of ±5 percent on either side of a weighted composite of the currencies of the main trading partners.

j. The exchange rate, which is pegged to the ECU, is maintained within margins of ±3.0 percent.

k. The exchange rate is maintained within margins of ±5.0 percent.

l. The exchange rate is maintained within margins of ±2.25 percent.

m. The currency of Kiribati is the Australian dollar.

n. The exchange rate is maintained within margins of ±3.0 percent.

o. The currency of Namibia is the South African rand, pending issuance of Namibia's own national currency.

p. The exchange rate, which is pegged to the ECU, is maintained within margins of ±2.25 percent.

q. The exchange rate, which is pegged to the ECU, is maintained within margins of ±1.5 percent.

financing to which the country has access. The 1995 U.S. quota was just under 18 percent of the total. Together, the industrial countries possess a majority of votes and thus dominate the decisions of the Executive Board.

Special Drawing Rights and International Liquidity

When the IMF was established in 1944, each member's quota was assumed to be adequate to provide access to enough international currencies to meet any balance-of-payments problems that might develop; however, the negotiators at Bretton Woods failed to anticipate the explosive growth in world trade flows that occurred after World War II. As trade has grown, particularly the tendency for increasingly larger surpluses and deficits, the financing needs of members facing balance-of-payments problems have also grown. To keep pace with the growth in world trade, to meet financing needs, and to maintain adequate international liquidity, the IMF has periodically increased members' quotas, a strategy that worked fairly well until the late 1950s. At that time, with quotas no longer providing adequate liquidity, a second source of funding known as the General Agreement to Borrow (GAB) was created, allowing the IMF to borrow from the G-10—a select group of governments and central banks. Finally, following a series of liquidity crises in the mid-1960s associated with a deteriorating balance of payments among the member countries, a new reserve asset, the Special Drawing Right, was created by the membership in 1969 to serve as an international unit of account, exchangeable among central banks, to supplement each member's reserve assets. The SDRs generated considerable critical commentary. In the words of Henry Hazlitt, "These SDRs were created out of thin air, by a stroke of the pen" (Hazlitt, 1984: 15). However, as of 1994, four IMF members had chosen the SDR as the standard for valuing their currencies (*IMF Survey*, 1994: 21).

Initially, the monetary authorities chose to base the value of SDRs on a weighted "basket" of sixteen currencies. In 1981, the basket was reduced to the currencies of the G-5 countries. As of May 31, 1993, the five currencies in the basket and their respective weights were the U.S. dollar (42 percent); Deutsche mark (19 percent), Japanese yen (15 percent), French franc (12 percent), and pound sterling (12 percent) (*IMF Survey*, 1993: 174). The precise value of the SDR is determined daily. Its value is more stable than that of any single currency in the basket, given that changes in the value of any of the basket currencies are somewhat offset by changes in the values of other currencies.

Other Sources of IMF Funding

Other sources of funding for IMF activities include selling the Fund's gold reserves, charging fees, and borrowing from member countries. Most such borrowing has occurred under the GAB, through which the IMF has borrowed from the governments and central banks of the ten wealthiest industrialized countries. By matching the interest rate and the maturity of its borrowing and lending, the IMF enhances international liquidity by serving as a conduit for the transfer of funds from countries that possess reserve assets to those that wish to borrow. A second source of liquidity came from Saudi Arabia and other oil-exporting countries. When oil prices quadrupled in 1973–1974, the IMF used assets from the surpluses of the oil-exporting countries to provide assistance to countries that faced a significant increase in the cost of energy imports.

Borrowing from the Fund

In its early years, IMF lending was limited to countries experiencing traditional balance-of-payment problems, but in the fifty years since its creation, the organization has met a number of disruptive challenges to the smooth operation of the international monetary system. These challenges have included periodic liquidity problems because of aggregate member needs exceeding available assets, the dislocation associated with oil price hikes in 1973–1974 and 1978–1979, and the debt crisis of the 1980s.

To address this array of anticipated and unanticipated contingencies, the Fund provides financial assistance to countries under three broad sets of programs. The first involves providing balance-of-payments financing through unconditional and conditional tranches. The second program provides funding under special facilities for countries that have specific needs and circumstances. The third program provides concessional financing for low-income member countries.

Regular Quota–SDR Facility

A member country approaches the IMF for financial assistance as a "lender of last resort" when it is earning insufficient foreign exchange from exports, from providing services such as banking or insurance, and from what tourists spend in the country to pay for its imports. The first source of IMF balance-of-payments financing is the country's gold or reserve tranche. The first tranche is a slice or a portion, up to one-quarter, of the country's quota denominated in a currency of its choosing or in SDRs. Because of the role the U.S. dollar has played as the world's key currency and the willingness of most trading partners to accept it in exchange, members often request, but are not limited to, the dollar. When another currency is purchased from the first tranche, the currency of choice or SDR is provided with minimal conditions. The only expectation is that the purchasing country will make a "reasonable effort" to overcome its balance-of-payments problems. According to John Williamson, "A member requesting a drawing limited to the first credit tranche was expected to have in place a program representing reasonable efforts to overcome its balance of payments difficulties, but what constitutes reasonable efforts is in practice left to the borrower's discretion, since a country applying for such a drawing is given the overwhelming benefit of the doubt in any difference of view between the member and the Fund" (Williamson, 1982: 65).

If the purchasing country fails to make the adjustments necessary to earn enough foreign exchange to balance its accounts after accessing the first tranche, it will purchase from the second, the third, and possibly the fourth tranches. Countries drawing on all four tranches can purchase up to 100 percent of their quotas.

Upper-conditional tranches. The first tranche is known as an unconditional tranche because of the minimal performance requirements placed on the borrower. The second, third, and fourth tranches are conditional tranches with progressively more rigorous requirements for borrowing. When a country seeks to borrow from these conditional tranches, it must comply with specific macroeconomic policies put forth by the IMF. By imposing conditions on borrowers, the IMF seeks to ensure that a country that purchases foreign currencies, SDRs, or both will be able to overcome its balance-of-payments difficulties and repay the borrowed amount in a timely manner, thereby preserving the revolving nature of IMF resources and ensuring that resources will be available to other countries in time of need. Before access to the upper tranches is granted, meetings are held between the country's economic leaders and IMF representatives to establish performance criteria. Following these meetings, a letter of intent is exchanged. The letter outlines the macroeconomic policies to which the country has agreed to alleviate its balance-of-payments problems and establishes the performance criteria to be used to measure the country's progress. Upper-credit–tranche drawings are made in installments and are released when the country has implemented those policies specified in the negotiated program and has reached performance targets.

The drawings on the conditional-credit tranches are known as standby arrangements, which typically cover a twelve- to eighteen-month period. Repayment of standby arrangements is to be made within three-and-one-quarter to five years of each drawing. As of August 31, 1994, twenty-two countries had standby arrangements from the IMF. Table 14.3 lists the countries that were under standby and other arrangements.

Fund conditionality. Fund conditionality is very controversial and has increasingly placed the IMF in the public spotlight. Critics argue that Fund programs are driven solely by ideology, specifically a singular commitment to liberal economic theory and its orthodoxy concerning the limitations of the state and the virtues of the market. As a corollary, critics charge that the IMF imposes a single policy framework, or "adjustment recipe," on all borrowers regardless of specific conditions that vary from country to country. Finally, the Fund is charged with encouraging the deterioration of social conditions and the physical environment.

The Fund has studied such charges and over the years has produced books, monographs, and articles that counter these criticisms. According to the Fund, the logic behind its recommendations is straightforward: A slightly undervalued currency lowers the cost of domestic goods, thus enhancing the competitiveness of the country's exports while simultaneously decreasing the demand for imported goods by making them more expensive. Reducing government spending and the money supply is intended to reduce inflation by limiting demand. The Fund argues that inflation, which decreases the price competitiveness of domestic goods, lowers exports, and lowers foreign earnings, must be addressed if a member is to balance its payments. Finally, the Fund supports the liberalization of foreign investment and trade restrictions to promote capital inflows and allow market forces to rationalize the economy. Whatever the truth, concerned nongovernmental organizations and borrowing-country elites continue to chafe under the discipline imposed by IMF programs, and demonstrations have erupted during recent meetings of the Board of Governors. Although it stands firm in its commitment to orthodox principles, the Fund has not been impervious to public concerns. During the 1980s, closer collaboration between the IMF and the World Bank permitted the latter to make loans designed, in part, to mitigate some of the adverse social consequences of Fund stabilization programs.

Special Facilities

In the fifty years since its creation, the IMF has periodically created special facilities to arrange for access to credit that extends beyond its traditional focus on short-term balance-of-payments adjustment. These facilities vary in terms of the nature or source of the problem they are designed to address and the terms and conditions of purchase or credit

Table 14.3 Standby, EFF, SAF, and ESAF Arrangements as of August 31, 1994
(in million SDRs)[a]

Member	Date of Arrangement	Expiration Date	Amount Approved	Undrawn Balance
Standby Arrangements				
Algeria	May 27, 1994	May 26, 1995	457.20	411.50
Bulgaria	April 11, 1994	March 31, 1995	69.74	46.49
Cameroon	March 14, 1994	September 13, 1995	81.06	59.15
Central African Republic	March 28, 1994	March 27, 1995	16.48	5.77
Chad	March 23, 1994	March 22, 1995	16.52	6.20
Congo	May 27, 1994	May 26, 1995	23.16	10.66
Ecuador	May 11, 1994	March 31, 1996	130.00	130.00
El Salvador	May 10, 1993	December 31, 1994	47.11	47.11
Estonia	October 27, 1993	March 26, 1995	11.63	9.30
Gabon	March 30, 1994	March 29, 1995	38.60	33.09
Hungary	September 15, 1993	December 14, 1994	340.00	283.30
Kazakhstan	January 26, 1994	May 31, 1995	123.75	111.38
Latvia	December 15, 1993	March 14, 1995	22.88	13.73
Lithuania	October 22, 1993	March 21, 1995	25.88	20.70
Moldova	December 17, 1993	March 16, 1995	51.75	30.00
Niger	March 4, 1994	March 3, 1995	18.60	7.49
Panama	February 24, 1992	September 23, 1994	74.17	19.60
Poland	August 5, 1994	March 4, 1996	545.00	545.00
Romania	May 11, 1994	December 10, 1995	131.97	94.26
Slovak Republic	July 22, 1994	March 21, 1996	115.80	100.38
Turkey	July 8, 1994	September 7, 1995	509.30	348.80
Vietnam	October 6, 1993	December 31, 1994	145.00	60.44
Total			2,995.58	2,394.33
EFF Arrangements				
Argentina	March 31, 1992	March 30, 1995	2,483.15	417.15
Egypt	September 20, 1993	September 19, 1996	400.00	400.00
Jamaica	December 11, 1992	December 10, 1995	109.13	45.75
Jordan	May 25, 1994	May 24, 1997	127.80	108.14
Pakistan	February 22, 1994	February 21, 1997	379.10	298.55
Peru	March 18, 1993	March 17, 1996	1,018.10	375.41
Philippines	June 24, 1994	June 23, 1997	474.50	438.00
Zimbabwe	September 11, 1992	September 10, 1995	114.60	46.80
Total			5,106.38	2,129.80
SAF Arrangements				
Ethiopia	October 28, 1992	October 27, 1995	49.42	14.12
Sierra Leone	March 28, 1994	March 27, 1995	27.02	—
Total			76.44	14.12
ESAF Arrangements				
Albania	July 14, 1993	July 13, 1996	42.36	25.42
Benin	January 25, 1993	January 24, 1996	51.89	27.18
Burkina Faso	March 31, 1993	March 30, 1996	48.62	30.94
Burundi	November 13, 1991	November 12, 1994	42.70	23.49
Cambodia	May 6, 1994	May 5, 1997	84.00	70.00
Côte d'Ivoire	March 11, 1994	March 10, 1997	333.48	273.93
Equatorial Guinea	February 3, 1993	February 2, 1996	12.88	8.28
Guinea	November 6, 1991	November 5, 1994	57.90	40.53
Guyana	July 20, 1994	July 19, 1997	53.76	44.80
Honduras	July 24, 1992	July 23, 1995	40.68	27.12

(continues)

Table 14.3 continued

Member	Date of Arrangement	Expiration Date	Amount Approved	Undrawn Balance
Kenya	December 22, 1993	December 21, 1994	45.23	22.62
Kyrgyz Republic	July 20, 1994	July 19, 1997	70.95	61.49
Lao People's Democratic Republic	June 4, 1993	June 3, 1996	35.19	23.46
Mali	August 28, 1992	August 27, 1995	79.24	44.19
Mauritania	December 9, 1992	December 8, 1994	33.90	8.48
Mongolia	June 25, 1993	June 24, 1996	40.81	22.26
Mozambique	June 1, 1990	June 14, 1995	130.05	14.70
Nepal	October 5, 1992	October 4, 1995	33.57	16.79
Nicaragua	June 24, 1994	June 23, 1997	120.12	100.10
Pakistan	February 22, 1994	February 21, 1997	606.60	505.50
Senegal	August 29, 1994	August 28, 1997	130.79	130.79
Sierra Leone	March 28, 1994	March 27, 1997	88.78	25.28
Sri Lanka	September 13, 1991	March 29, 1995	336.00	56.00
Zimbabwe	September 11, 1992	September 10, 1995	200.60	82.10
Total			2,720.10	1,676.96
Grand total			10,898.50	6,215.22

Source: IMF Treasurer's Department.
Note: a. EFF = extended Fund facility; SAF = structural adjustment facility; ESAF = enhanced structural adjustment facility. Figures may not add to totals shown because of rounding.

they make available. Four such facilities exist: the compensatory contingency financing facility (CCFF) (1963), the buffer stock facility (BSF) (1969), the extended Fund facility (EFF) (1974), and the systemic transformation facility (STF) (1993). Over the years developing countries and now the formerly socialist Soviet republics have made use of these special facilities.

Beginning operations in 1962, the CCFF was created to provide a member country with resources to help compensate for temporary shortfalls in export earnings and service receipts and temporary excesses in cereal import costs that arise from events largely beyond the country's control, such as price changes. Financial assistance is provided to cover unfavorable deviations in highly volatile and easily identifiable key variables that affect the member's current account, including main export or import prices and international interest rates. Resources under the buffer stock facility are provided to member countries to help finance their contributions to approved international buffer stocks. The BSF has been inactive for the past ten years.

The EFF provides assistance to member countries for longer periods and in larger amounts than are available under credit tranche policies. Financial assistance under the EFF is generally aimed at overcoming balance-of-payments difficulties stemming from structural problems that require a longer period of adjustment. Countries must repay EFF currencies within four-and-one-half to ten years of the drawing. As in the majority of IMF loans, specific conditions and performance criteria are similar to those of standby arrangements. As of August 31, 1994, eight countries had EFF arrangements.

The CCFF, BSF, and EFF are of particular consequence from the viewpoint of the nonindustrial members. First, borrowing through the CCFF and the BSF does not include conditionality. Second, their presence reflects an important adjustment in the institutional culture of the IMF in accepting the notion that members specializing in primary product exports may face special problems inherent in the global marketplace. These problems stem from imperfect supply-side responses to price cues and the extreme volatility and long-term decline of primary product prices relative to manufactures. These facilities legitimize the economic argument that questions the neutrality of market forces.

The systemic transformation facility was created in response to the needs of the countries of Central Europe, the Baltic countries, Russia, and the other countries of the Commonwealth of Independent States in making the transition from centrally planned economies to market economies. Under the STF, assistance is provided to members experiencing balance-of-payments difficulties as a result of severe disruptions in their traditional arrangements in trade and payments. Member countries experiencing a sharp fall in total export earnings or a permanent increase in import costs during the transition from significant reliance on trading at nonmarket prices to multilateral, market-based trade qualify for assistance under the STF. To provide assistance, the Fund must be satisfied that the country will cooperate in solving its balance-of-payments problems and will continue to reform its policies so the IMF can provide support under an upper-credit tranche arrangement. When requesting Fund assistance under the STF, the member must submit a written description of the objectives of its economic policies, its macroeconomic policy projections, and the structural, fiscal, monetary, and exchange measures it will implement over the next twelve months. The member must promise not to tighten exchange or trade restrictions or to introduce new restrictions or multiple currency practices.

In addition to the financial assistance available under the STF, the IMF has given countries in transition to market-based economies expertise to assist them in establishing the financial and economic structures viewed as critical for a market economy. IMF staff has played a crucial role in the creation of many of the basic institutions of a capitalist system, such as central banks, fiscal systems, and legal codes.

Concessional Facilities

The structural adjustment facility (SAF) (1986) and the enhanced structural adjustment facility (ESAF) (1987) were created in response to the debt crisis experienced by developing countries. Through these facilities, seventy-two low-income countries have access to concessional loans with terms up to ten years. The creation of these facilities by the Fund membership further legitimizes the argument that questions the neutrality and omnipotence of unbridled market forces.

The debt crisis is very complicated; it involves decisions by hundreds of international banks, dozens of borrowing countries, and the IMF. Although complex, a basic pattern has emerged in the process of debt renegotiation and management. With the onset of the debt crisis in 1982, the governments of the industrial world and the international banks made their rescheduling and additional lending agreements contingent on an agreement between the Fund and the debtor country. Negotiations focused on the terms for rescheduling short- and medium-term loans to long-term loans and for extending new loans. The new lending agreement would then be negotiated between the private banks and the borrowing country with the IMF acting as intermediary. Such renegotiations frequently stretched over many months and sometimes more than a year.

A difficult aspect of these renegotiations concerned new loans in the form of fresh funds as compared with new loans in the form of rolling over old debt. Naturally, many banks were hesitant to lend "good money after bad." Countries, on the other hand, were reluctant to accept new terms without fresh funds. The SAF and the ESAF provided the basis for a new source of fresh funds, thereby allowing the IMF, along with the World Bank Group (WBG), to extend such funds to heavily in-debted borrowers and thus facilitate the process of debt renegotiation. Countries that borrow under the SAF and the ESAF commit to a set of long-term conditions outlined in a policy framework paper (PFP), which includes the typical IMF policies outlined earlier as well as privatization, deregulation, and leveling the playing field for foreign investors. The PFP programs are outlined and implemented under the auspices of both the IMF and the WBG, which is also a source of fresh funds.

IMF Services for Member Countries

The IMF provides a number of services for its members in addition to its primary responsibilities of supervising the international monetary system and providing financial support. It operates training courses in Washington, D.C., and Vienna, Austria, and issues a wide variety of publications relating to international monetary affairs.

Training

Since its founding in Washington, D.C., in 1964, the IMF Institute has trained approximately nine thousand officials from its member countries, most of whom are employed in ministries of finance, central banks, and other government financial agencies. In addition to giving participants an understanding of the international monetary system and the role of the IMF within that system, the Institute through its training has helped to standardize methods of gathering and presenting monetary, balance-of-payments, and financial statistics. The Institute has also provided training in highly technical areas of public finance and central banking. Members have frequently relied on the IMF for assistance in such areas when domestic expertise was lacking, particularly in the 1960s and the 1970s when for the first time a large number of newly independent nations were establishing central banks, issuing new currencies, and devising tax systems (Driscoll, 1994: 21).

IMF Publications

The IMF is an important conduit of data on members' fiscal, monetary, and external debt positions. Since its early years, the IMF has issued statistical publications, such as *International Financial Statistics*, that keep members informed of the financial position of other members and provide an unmatched source of statistical information for the financial community, universities, research organizations, and the media. Other IMF publications include the semiannual *World Economic Outlook; Occasional Papers* on longer-term issues of finance and trade; *Economic Reviews* of countries; the *IMF Survey*, a biweekly publication featuring articles on international finance and national economies; a quarterly academic journal entitled *Staff Papers;* the joint IMF–World Bank quarterly *Finance and Development;* and a number of books on the international monetary system.

Conclusion

The IMF's relationship to member countries has changed dramatically since 1947. Its main purpose—serving as a lender of last resort in containing currency value fluctuations within the fixed but flexible peg-and-band system—evaporated with the breakdown of that system after

1971. Since then, the IMF has had the authority and the responsibility to monitor country compliance with the rules of the managed float system—that is, to exercise its surveillance power. In a potential expansion of the Fund's influence, since 1982 the IMF has participated in G-7 meetings, at which the managing director and staff members brief the G-7 regarding the short- and medium-term outlooks for the global economy. The IMF works with the G-7 in developing a set of indicators for possible coordination of macroeconomic policy. Nevertheless, IMF influence over industrial countries appears to have declined since 1971. Simultaneously, the Fund's involvement in and influence with the less developed countries of the South has increased as these countries have become increasingly dependent on Fund assistance in managing their heavy debt loads. This is particularly true in the case of the smaller countries with weak economies and very few exports. In such cases, the Fund has become a major policy influence and, together with the WBG, oversees the developmental strategies and trajectories of dozens of states.

Notes

The authors would like to thank John Conklin for his review of this manuscript and for his many helpful comments.

1. The arrangement by which members of the European Monetary System maintain their currencies within a narrow band is known as the Exchange Rate Mechanism and is often referred to informally as the European "snake" because of the shape of the fixed-width bank as it rises and falls against the dollar over time. For more details, see James C. Ingram and Robert M. Dunn Jr., *International Economics*. New York: John Wiley and Sons, 1993.

References

Chandavarkar, Anand G. 1984. *The International Monetary Fund: Its Financial Organization and Activities*. Washington, D.C.: International Monetary Fund.

Driscoll, David D. 1994. *What Is the International Monetary Fund?* Washington, D.C.: International Monetary Fund.

Hazlitt, Henry. 1984. *From Bretton Woods to World Inflation*. Chicago: Regnery Gateway Press.

IMF Survey. May 1992. Washington, D.C.: International Monetary Fund.

IMF Survey. May 31, 1993. Washington, D.C.: International Monetary Fund.

IMF Survey. August 1994. Washington, D.C.: International Monetary Fund.

Williamson, John. 1982. *The Lending Policies of the International Monetary Fund*. Washington, D.C.: Institute for International Economics.

15

THE CASE FOR
FLEXIBLE EXCHANGE RATES

—————— Milton Friedman ——————

Milton Friedman remains an important influence on both the study and the practice of political economy. Over the years Friedman has been a steadfast advocate of a system of flexible, or floating, rather than fixed, exchange rates. Here he addresses some of the major criticisms of floating regimes, many of which deal with the potential for relatively rapid fluctuations in the value of a country's currency and the way that impacts trade, further exchange market speculation, and the health of the domestic economy. In defending the flexible exchange rate regime, Friedman crafts a classic defense of free market exchange. With recent exchange market fluctuations and rising economic nationalist sentiments, proponents of a fixed exchange system have become more vocal, but this debate is far from settled.

The Western nations seem committed to a system of international payments based on exchange rates between their national currencies fixed by governments and maintained rigid except for occasional changes to new levels. This system is embodied in the statutes of the International Monetary Fund, which provides for changes in exchange rates of less than 10 per cent by individual governments without approval of the Fund and for larger changes only with approval; it is implicit in the European Payments Union; and it is taken for granted in almost all discussions of international economic policy.

Whatever may have been the merits of this system for another day, it is ill suited to current economic and political conditions. These

Reprinted with permission from the publishers of *Essays in Positive Economics* by Milton Friedman (Chicago: The University of Chicago Press, 1953): pp. 157–160, 161–164, 173–180.

conditions make a system of flexible or floating exchange rates—exchange rates freely determined in an open market primarily by private dealings and, like other market prices, varying from day to day—absolutely essential for the fulfillment of our basic economic objective: the achievement and maintenance of a free and prosperous world community engaging in unrestricted multilateral trade. There is scarcely a facet of international economic policy for which the implicit acceptance of a system of rigid exchange rates does not create serious and unnecessary difficulties. Promotion of rearmament, liberalization of trade, avoidance of allocations and other direct controls both internal and external, harmonization of internal monetary and fiscal policies—all these problems take on a different cast and become far easier to solve in a world of flexible exchange rates and its corollary, free convertibility of currencies. The sooner a system of flexible exchange rates is established, the sooner unrestricted multilateral trade will become a real possibility. And it will become one without in any way interfering with the pursuit by each nation of domestic economic stability according to its own lights.

Before proceeding to defend this thesis in detail, I should perhaps emphasize two points to avoid misunderstanding. First, advocacy of flexible exchange rates is *not* equivalent to advocacy of unstable exchange rates. The ultimate objective is a world in which exchange rates, while *free* to vary, are in fact highly stable. Instability of exchange rates is a symptom of instability in the underlying economic structure. Elimination of this symptom by administrative freezing of exchange rates cures none of the underlying difficulties and only makes adjustment to them more painful. Second, by unrestricted multilateral trade, I shall mean a system in which there are no direct quantitative controls over imports or exports, in which any tariffs or export bounties are reasonably stable and nondiscriminatory and are not subject to manipulation to affect the balance of payments, and in which a substantial fraction of international trade is in private (nongovernmental) hands. Though admittedly vague and subject to considerable ambiguity, this definition will do for our purposes. I shall take for granted without detailed examination that unrestricted multilateral trade in this sense is a desirable objective of economic policy. However, many of the arguments for flexible exchange rates remain valid even if this premise is not accepted.

Alternative Methods of Adjusting
to Changes Affecting International Payments

Changes affecting the international trade and the balance of payments of various countries are always occurring. Some are in the "real" conditions determining international trade, such as the weather, technical conditions for production, consumer tastes, and the like. Some are in monetary conditions, such as divergent degrees of inflation or deflation in various countries.

These changes affect some commodities more than others and so tend to produce changes in the structure of relative prices—for example, rearmament by the United States impinges particularly on selected raw materials and tends to raise their prices relatively to other prices. Such effects on the relative price structure are likely to be much the same whether exchange rates are rigid or flexible and to raise much the same problem of adjustment in either case and so will receive little attention in what follows.

But, over and above these effects on particular commodities and prices, the changes in question affect each country's balance of payments, taken as a whole. Holders of foreign currencies want to exchange them for the currency of a particular country in order to purchase commodities produced in that country, or to purchase securities or other capital assets in that country, or to pay interest on or repay debts to that country, or to make gifts to citizens of that country, or simply to hold for one of these uses or for resale. The amount of currency of a particular country that is demanded per unit of time for each of these purposes will, of course, depend in the first instance on the exchange rate—the number of units of a foreign currency that must be paid to acquire one unit of the domestic currency. Other things the same, the more expensive a given currency, that is, the higher the exchange rate, the less of that currency will in general be demanded for each of these purposes. Similarly, holders of the currency of the country in question want to exchange that currency for foreign currencies for the corresponding purposes; and, again, the amount they want to exchange depends, in the first instance, on the price which they can get. The changes continuously taking place in the conditions of international trade alter the "other things" and so the desirability of using the currencies of various countries for each of the purposes listed. The aggregate effect is at one time to increase, at another to decrease, the amount of a country's currency demanded at any given rate of exchange relative to the amount offered for sale at that rate. Of course, after the event, the amount of a particular currency purchased must equal the amount sold—this is a question simply of double-entry bookkeeping. But, in advance, the amount people want to buy need not equal the amount people want to sell. The *ex post* equality involves a reconciliation of these divergent desires, either through changes in the desires themselves or through their frustration.

There is no way of avoiding this reconciliation; inconsistent desires cannot simultaneously be satisfied. The crucial question of policy is the mechanism whereby this reconciliation is brought about. Suppose the aggregate effect of changes in the conditions affecting international payments has been to increase the amount of a country's currency people want to buy with foreign currency relative to the amount other people want to sell for foreign currency at the pre-existing exchange rate—to create an incipient surplus in the balance of payments. How can these inconsistent desires be reconciled? . . .

Changes in Exchange Rates

Two different mechanisms whereby exchange-rate changes may be used to maintain equilibrium in the balance of payments must be sharply distinguished: (1) flexible exchange rates as defined above and (2) official changes in temporarily rigid rates.

Flexible exchange rates. Under flexible exchange rates freely determined in open markets, the first impact of any tendency toward a surplus or deficit in the balance of payments is on the exchange rate. If a country has an incipient surplus of receipts over payments—an excess demand for its currency—the exchange rate will tend to rise. If it has an incipient deficit, the exchange rate will tend to fall. If the conditions responsible for the rise or the fall in the exchange rate are generally regarded as temporary, actual or potential holders of the country's currency will tend to change their holdings in such a way as to moderate the movement in the exchange rate. If a rise in the exchange rate, for example, is expected to be temporary, there is an incentive for holders of the country's currency to sell some of their holdings for foreign currency in order to buy the currency back later on at a lower price. By doing so, they provide the additional domestic currency to meet part of the excess demand responsible for the initial rise in the exchange rate; that is, they absorb some of what would have been surplus receipts of foreign currency at the former exchange rate. Conversely, if a decline is expected to be temporary, there is an incentive to buy domestic currency for resale at a higher price. Such purchases of domestic currency provide the foreign currency to meet some of what would have been a deficit of foreign currency at the former exchange rate. In this way, such "speculative" transactions in effect provide the country with reserves to absorb temporary surpluses or to meet temporary deficits. On the other hand, if the change in the exchange rate is generally regarded as produced by fundamental factors that are likely to be permanent, the incentives are the reverse of those listed above, and speculative transactions will speed up the rise or decline in the exchange rate and thus hasten its approach to its final position.

This final position depends on the effect that changes in exchange rates have on the demand for and supply of a country's currency, not to hold as balances, but for other purposes. A rise in the exchange rate produced by a tendency toward a surplus makes foreign goods cheaper in terms of domestic currency, even though their prices are unchanged in terms of their own currency, and domestic goods more expensive in terms of foreign currency, even though their prices are unchanged in terms of domestic currency. This tends to increase imports, reduce exports, and so offset the incipient surplus. Conversely, a decline in the exchange rate produced by a tendency toward a deficit makes imports more expensive to home consumers, and exports less expensive to foreigners, and so tends to offset the incipient deficit.

Because money imparts general purchasing power and is used for such a wide variety of purposes abroad as well as at home, the demand for and supply of any one country's currency is widely spread and comes from many sources. In consequence, broad, active, and nearly perfect markets have developed in foreign exchange whenever they have been permitted—and usually even when they have not been. The exchange rate is therefore potentially an extremely sensitive price. Changes in it occur rapidly, automatically, and continuously and so tend to produce corrective movements before tensions can accumulate and a crisis develop. For example, if Germany had had a flexible exchange rate in 1950, the crisis in the fall of that year would never have followed the course it did. The exchange rate would have been affected not later than July and would have started to produce corrective adaptations at once. The whole affair would never have assumed large proportions and would have shown up a relatively minor ripple in exchange rates. As it was, with a rigid exchange rate, the warning of impending trouble was indirect and delayed, and the government took no action until three months later, by which time the disequilibrium had grown to crisis dimensions, requiring drastic action at home, international consultation, and help from abroad.

The recurrent foreign-exchange crises of the United Kingdom in the postwar period are perhaps an even more dramatic example of the kind of crises that could not develop under a system of flexible exchange rates. In each case no significant corrective action was taken until large disequilibriums had been allowed to cumulate, and then the action had to be drastic. The rigidities and discontinuities introduced by substituting administrative action for automatic market forces have seldom been demonstrated so clearly or more impressively.

Official changes in exchange rates. These examples suggest the sharp differences between flexible exchange rates and exchange rates held temporarily rigid but subject to change by government action to meet substantial difficulties. While these exchange-rate changes have the same kind of effect on commodity trade and the like as those produced automatically under a system of flexible exchange rates, they have very different effects on speculative transactions. Partly for this reason, partly because of their innate discontinuity, each exchange-rate change tends to become the occasion for a crisis. There is no mechanism for producing changes in exchange rates of the required magnitude or for correcting mistakes, and some other mechanism must be used to maintain equilibrium during the period between exchange-rate changes—either internal price or income changes, direct controls, or monetary reserves.

Even though an exchange-rate change would not otherwise be the occasion for a crisis, speculative movements are highly likely to convert it into one, for this system practically insures a maximum of destabilizing speculation. Because the exchange rate is changed infrequently and only to meet substantial difficulties, a change tends to come well after the onset of difficulty, to be postponed as long as possible, and to be made only after substantial pressure on the exchange rate has accumulated. In consequence, there is seldom any doubt about the direction in which an exchange rate will be changed, if it is changed. In the interim between the suspicion of a possible change in the rate and the actual change, there is every incentive to sell the country's currency if devaluation is expected (to export "capital" from the country) or to buy it if an appreciation is expected (to bring in "capital"); either can be done without an exchange loss and will mean an exchange gain when and if the rate is changed. This is in sharp contrast with the situation under flexible exchange rates when the decline in the exchange rate takes place along with, and as a consequence of, the sales of a currency and so discourages or penalizes sales, and conversely for purchases. With rigid rates, if the exchange rate is not changed, the only cost to the speculators is a possible loss of interest earnings from an interest-rate differential. It is no answer to this argument to say that capital flows can be restricted by direct controls, since our ultimate objective in using this method is precisely to avoid such restriction.

In short, the system of occasional changes in temporarily rigid exchange rates seems to me the worst of two worlds: it provides neither the stability of expectations that a genuinely rigid and stable exchange rate could provide in a world of unrestricted trade and willingness and ability to adjust the internal price structure to external conditions nor the continuous sensitivity of a flexible exchange rate. . . .

Objections to Flexible Exchange Rates

Three major criticisms have been made of the proposal to establish a system of flexible exchange rates: first, that flexible exchange rates may increase the degree of uncertainty in the economic scene; second, that flexible exchange rates will not work because they will produce offsetting changes in domestic prices; and, third, that flexible exchange rates will not produce the best attainable timing or pace of adjustment. The first objection takes many different forms, and it will promote clarity to deal with some of these separately, even though this means considerable overlapping.

Flexible Exchange Rates and Uncertainty

Flexible exchange rates mean instability and uncertainty. On the naive level on which this objection is frequently made, it involves the already-mentioned mistake of confusing the symptom of difficulties with the difficulties themselves. A flexible exchange rate need not be an unstable exchange rate. If it is, it is primarily because there is underlying instability in the economic conditions governing international trade. And a rigid exchange rate may, while itself nominally stable, perpetuate and accentuate other elements of instability in the economy. The mere fact that a rigid official exchange rate does not change while a flexible rate does is no evidence that the former means greater stability in any more fundamental sense. If it does, it is for one or more of the reasons considered in the points that follow.

Flexible exchange rates make it impossible for exporters and importers to be certain about the price they will have to pay or receive for foreign exchange. Under flexible exchange rates traders can almost always protect themselves against changes in the rate by hedging in a futures market. Such futures markets in foreign currency readily develop when exchange rates are flexible. Any uncertainty about returns will then be borne by speculators. The most that can be said for this argument, therefore, is that flexible exchange rates impose a cost of hedging on traders, namely, the price that must be paid to speculators for assuming the risk of future changes in exchange rates. But this is saying too much. The substitution of flexible for rigid exchange rates changes the form in which uncertainty in the foreign-exchange market is manifested; it may not change the extent of uncertainty at all and, indeed, may even decrease uncertainty. For example, conditions that would tend to produce a decline in a flexible exchange rate will produce a shortage of exchange with a rigid exchange rate. This in turn will produce either internal adjustments of uncertain character or administrative allocation of exchange. Traders will then be certain about the rate but uncertain about either internal conditions or the availability of exchange. The uncertainty can be removed for some transactions by advance commitments by the authorities dispensing exchange; it clearly cannot be removed for all transactions in view of the uncertainty about the total amount of exchange available; the reduction in uncertainty for some transactions therefore involves increased uncertainty for others, since all the risk is now concentrated on them. Further, such administrative allocation of exchange is always surrounded by uncertainty about the policy that will be followed. It is by no means clear whether the uncertainty associated with a flexible rate or the uncertainty associated with a rigid rate is likely to be more disruptive to trade.

Speculation in foreign-exchange markets tends to be destabilizing. This point is, of course, closely related to the preceding one. It is said that speculators will take a decline in the exchange rate as a signal for a further decline and will thus tend to make the movements in the exchange rate sharper than they would be in the absence of speculation. The special fear in this connection is of capital flight in response to political uncertainty or simply to movements in the exchange rate. Despite the prevailing opinion to the contrary, I am very dubious that in fact speculation in foreign exchange would be destabilizing. Evidence from some earlier experiences and from current free markets in currency in Switzerland, Tangiers, and elsewhere seems to me to suggest that, in general, speculation is stabilizing rather than the reverse, though the evidence has not yet been analyzed in sufficient detail to establish this conclusion with any confidence. People who argue that speculation is generally destabilizing seldom realize that this is largely equivalent to saying that speculators lose money, since speculation can be destabilizing in general only if speculators on the average sell when the currency is low in price and buy when it is high. It does not, of course, follow that speculation is not destabilizing; professional speculators might on the average make money while a changing body of amateurs regularly lost larger sums. But, while this may happen, it is hard to see why there is any presumption that it will; the presumption is rather the opposite. To put the same point differently, if speculation were persistently destabilizing, a government body like the Exchange Equalization Fund in England in the 1930's could make a good deal of money by speculating in exchange and in the process almost certainly eliminate the destabilizing speculation. But to suppose that speculation by governments would generally be profitable is in most cases equivalent to supposing that government officials risking funds that they do not themselves own are better judges of the likely movements in foreign-exchange markets than private individuals risking their own funds.

The widespread belief that speculation is likely to be destabilizing is doubtless a major factor accounting for the cavalier rejection of a system of flexible exchange rates in the immediate postwar period. Yet this belief does not seem to be founded on any systematic analysis of the available empirical evidence. It rests, rather, I believe, primarily on an oversimplified interpretation of the movements of so-called "hot" money during the 1930's. At the time, any speculative movements which threatened a depreciation of a currency (i.e., which threatened a *change* in an exchange rate) were regarded as destabilizing, and hence these movements were so considered. In retrospect, it is clear that the speculators were "right"; that forces were at work making for depreciation in the value of most European currencies relative to the dollar independently of speculative activity; that the speculative movements were anticipating this change; and, hence, that there is at least as much reason to call them "stabilizing" as to call them "destabilizing."

In addition, the interpretation of this evidence has been marred by a failure to distinguish between a system of exchange rates held temporarily rigid but subject to change from time to time by government action and a system of flexible exchange rates. Many of the capital movements regarded as demonstrating that foreign-exchange speculation is destabilizing were stimulated by the existence of rigid rates subject to change by government action and are to be attributed primarily to the absence of flexibility of rates and hence of any incentive to avoid the capital movements. This is equally true of post-World War II experience with wide swings in foreign-payments positions. For reasons noted earlier, this experience has little direct bearing on the character of the speculative movements to be expected under a regime of genuinely flexible exchange rates.

Flexible exchange rates involve increased uncertainty in the internal economy. It is argued that in many countries there is a great fear of inflation and that people have come to regard the exchange rate as an indicator of inflation and are highly sensitive to variations in it. Exchange crises, such as would tend to occur under rigid exchange rates, will pass unnoticed, it is argued, except by people directly connected with international trade, whereas a decline in the exchange rate would attract much attention, be taken as a signal of a future inflation, and produce anticipatory movements by the public at large. In this way a flexible exchange rate might produce additional uncertainty rather than merely change the form in which uncertainty is manifested. There is some merit to this argument, but it does not seem to me to be a substantial reason for avoiding a flexible exchange rate. Its implication is rather that it would be desirable, if possible, to make the transition to a flexible rate at a time when exchange rates of European countries relative to the dollar would be likely to move moderately and some to rise. It further would be desirable to accompany the transition by willingness to take prompt monetary action to counter any internal reactions. A fear of inflation has little or no chance of producing inflation, except in a favorable monetary environment. A demonstration that fears of inflation are groundless, and some experience with the absence of any direct and immediate connection between the day-to-day movements in the exchange rate and internal prices would very shortly reduce to negligible proportions any increase in uncertainty on purely domestic markets, as a result of flexible yet not highly unstable exchange rates. Further, public recognition that a substantial decline in the exchange rate is a symptom of or portends internal inflation is by no means an unmixed evil. It means that a flexible exchange rate would provide something of a barrier to a highly inflationary domestic policy.

Very nearly the opposite of this argument is also sometimes made against flexible exchange rates. It is said that, with a flexible exchange rate, governments will have less incentive and be in a less strong position to take firm internal action to prevent inflation. A rigid exchange rate, it is said, gives the government a symbol to fight for—it can nail its flag to the mast of a specified exchange rate and resist political pressure to take action that would be inflationary in the name of defending the exchange rate. Dramatic foreign-exchange crises establish an atmosphere in which drastic if unpopular action is possible. On the other hand, it is said, with a flexible exchange rate, there is no definite sticking point; inflationary action will simply mean a decline in the exchange rate but no dramatic crisis, and people are little affected by a change in a price, the exchange rate, in a market in which relatively few have direct dealing.

Of course, it is not impossible for both these arguments to be valid—the first in countries like Germany, which have recently experienced hyperinflations and violently fluctuating exchange rates, the second in countries like Great Britain, which have not. But, even in countries like Britain, it is far from clear that a rigid exchange rate is more conducive under present conditions to noninflationary internal economic policy than a flexible exchange rate. A rigid exchange rate thwarts any immediate manifestation of a deterioration in the foreign-payments position as a result of inflationary internal policy. With an independent monetary standard, the loss of exchange reserves does not automatically reduce the stock of money or prevent its continued increase; yet it does temporarily reduce domestic inflationary pressure by providing goods in return for the foreign-exchange reserves without any simultaneous creation of domestic income. The deterioration shows up only sometime later, in the dull tables of statistics summarizing the state of foreign-exchange reserves. Even then, the authorities in the modern world have the alternative—or think they have—of suppressing a deficit by more stringent direct controls and thus postponing still longer the necessity for taking the appropriate internal measures; and they can always find any number of special reasons for the particular deterioration other than their internal policy. While the possibilities of using direct controls and of finding plausible excuses are present equally with flexible exchange rates, at least the deterioration in the foreign-payments shows up promptly in the more readily understandable and simpler form of a decline in the exchange rates, and there is no emergency, no suddenly discovered decline in monetary reserves to dangerous levels, to force the imposition of supposedly unavoidable direct controls.

These arguments are modern versions of an argument that no longer has much merit but was at one time a valid and potent objection to flexible exchange rates, namely, the greater scope they give for government "tampering" with the currency. When rigid exchange rates were taken seriously, and when the armory of direct controls over international trade had not yet been resurrected, the maintenance of rigid rates left little scope for independent domestic monetary policy. This was the great virtue of the gold standard and the basic, albeit hidden, source of its emotional appeal; it provided an effective defense against hyperinflation, against government intervention of a kind that had time and again led to the debasement and depreciation of once-proud currencies. This argument may still be a source of emotional resistance to flexible exchange rates; it is clear that it does not deserve to be. Governments of "advanced" nations are no longer willing to submit themselves to the harsh discipline of the gold standard or any other standard involving rigid exchange rates. They will evade its discipline by direct controls over trade if that will suffice and will change exchange rates before they will surrender control over domestic monetary policy. Perhaps a few modern inflations will establish a climate in which such behavior does not qualify as "advanced"; in the meantime we had best recognize the necessity of allowing exchange rates to adjust to internal policies rather than the reverse.

16

THE EFFECTS OF IMF PROGRAMS IN THE THIRD WORLD: DEBATE AND EVIDENCE FROM LATIN AMERICA

Manuel Pastor, Jr.

The International Monetary Fund (IMF) has long been criticized for its great concern with the health of an economy while all but ignoring the standard of living of the people working in the economy. Manuel Pastor reviews a series of critiques of IMF stabilization programs that assert that these programs cause recessions and suppress economic growth. After examining the response of IMF economists to these criticisms, Pastor presents the results of his study of eighteen Latin American countries. He redirects the criticism of what he calls the growth-oriented critique, which accuses the IMF of dampening conditions for economic growth, to the impact of stabilization programs on income inequality. In part, Pastor argues that IMF programs reduce the share of income received by labor, thus undermining the standard of living of domestic workers.

1. Introduction

Throughout the 1970s and 1980s, a debate has raged over the effects of the International Monetary Fund's (IMF) stabilization programs in the Third World. Many critics have offered a *growth-oriented critique* contending that Fund-supported stabilization programs have short-run recessionary impacts in the Third World setting and damage the prospects for long-run growth. Fund economists have challenged this view with cross-country studies of the actual effects of Fund programs

Reprinted with permission from the publishers of *World Development*, vol. 15, no. 2 (1987): pp. 249–262.

that demonstrate mixed impacts on growth rates coupled with significant success in achieving the IMF's supposed goals: current account and balance of payments improvements and inflation rate reduction.

In this article, I will briefly review the debate, paying particular attention to the studies noted above. I argue against the growth-oriented critique and recast the criticism of the Fund in terms of class and income distribution. I then present my own overview of the effects of IMF programs in 18 Latin American countries in the period 1965–81. The major findings are that: (1) program countries did experience significant balance of payments improvement but this may be mostly due to increased capital inflow induced by the IMF's "seal of approval" and not significant current account improvement; (2) in contrast to official IMF goals, fund programs in Latin America seem to be associated with accelerating inflation and not inflation rate reduction; (3) in contrast to the growth-oriented critique, fund programs had mixed impacts on growth rates; and (4) Fund programs were most significantly and consistently associated with declines in wage share.

I close the article by suggesting that a class-analytic approach is consistent with these results. Moreover, awareness of the profound redistributive consequences of Fund-sponsored programs may suggest some social limits to an IMF-directed resolution of the debt crisis of the 1980s.

2. The Debate

In the post–World War II era, the IMF has served as an international "lender of last resort" (Moffit, 1983: 124) by providing short-term financial assistance to member countries with balance of payments deficits. Such assistance is generally "conditional" upon member countries agreeing to a stabilization program that the Fund considers appropriate for correcting the deficits. The programs are often quite detailed, specifying both general policy measures and certain quantitative targets for various macroeconomic variables. To promote compliance, credit is doled out in installments as successive short-term quantitative targets are satisfactorily met.

What do Fund officials see as the goals of these programs? "For the Fund, the primary objective is balance of payments viability with weight given to a number of other goals, such as price stability . . ." (Eckaus, 1982: 774). Achieving these two objectives is frequently associated in the Fund perspective with a related goal of reducing government deficits and the consequent monetary emission. Another goal gaining prominence in the 1970s and 1980s has been "certifying" the ability to service external debt (Diaz-Alejandro, 1981; Gold, 1970: 39). In general, we can identify the major *official* macroeconomic goals of Fund programs as balance of payments amelioration and inflation rate reduction. To this end, a typical program in Latin America embodies a variety of policies: devaluation, limits on banking credit and public borrowing, removal of price subsidies, reduction of tariffs and elimination of some import controls, encouragement of foreign investment, and, finally resistance to nominal wage increases (Diaz-Alejandro, 1981; Lichtensztejn, 1983).

The specific impacts of Fund-supported stabilization programs have been debated at length. Fund economists argue that the overall intent of the sort of program outlined above is "to set the stage for sound and sustained rates of economic growth by improving the BOP (balance of payments) and bringing inflationary pressures under control" (Guitian, 1980: 25). Indeed, ". . . the full attainment of supply potential has always been the *ultimate* aim (of Fund policy)" (Guitian, 1981: 11). The main focus of the critics of the Fund has been that this is not true—that, instead, the Fund's goal and methods are fundamentally antithetical to economic growth and development in the Third World. This "growth-oriented critique" has been most associated with the so-called structuralist school.

(A) The Structuralist Critique

Structuralist economics is a broad term for those who take certain institutional specificities into account when discussing and modeling the economies of the "South." The usual "structural" characteristics considered include low productivity in agriculture, reliance on primary commodity exports (coupled with assumptions of an inelastic demand for and supply of these exports), and an underdeveloped system of financial intermediation. Formal models from this perspective have been offered by Krugman and Taylor (1978), Taylor (1979 and 1981), Arida and Bacha (1984), and many others.

In the debate over Fund policy, the structuralists begin by suggesting that balance of payments problems in the Third World often arise from the characteristics of the development process itself. They argue that there is a "development deficit" associated with the importation of capital goods to provide an industrial base, a strategy usually associated with import-substitution industrialization (ISI). Such a deficit can ultimately be reduced only by a "new phase of import substitution" (*profundizacion* or "deepening") (Serra, 1979: 114; Hirschman, 1979; 1968) in which backward linkages would be established and the capital goods being imported for early ISI would be increasingly produced domestically. Moreover, it is argued that such deepening will not only eliminate balance of payments problems but reduce inflation by easing the cost-push pressures from structural bottlenecks (see Diamand, 1978). In the meantime, "to try to 'correct' the development deficit is to halt the development effort itself." Instead, the "efficiency" of the deficit should be measured by its contribution to growth (Abdalla, 1980: 39–40).

Given this structural deficit, any of a series of *exogenous* changes —foreign debts coming due, a sudden plunge in primary commodity prices, a rise in the price of oil, a denial of aid—can easily and rapidly increase the existing payments deficits. Using this insight, structuralists argue that the deterioration in the current accounts of non oil-exporting developing countries (NODCs) through the 1970s and 1980s was "due entirely to factors beyond their control" (Dell, 1982: 600; Dell and Lawrence, 1980, and most recently Cline, 1985).

This is in sharp contrast to the IMF view that payments problems, in both North and South, have been caused by "expansionary financial policies mainly associated with large budgetary deficits and/or from a complex of cost-push factors and expectations" (Dale, 1983: 4; also see Wiesner, 1985).[1] For structuralists, the deficits are not primarily the result of countries "misbehaving" but are both endemic to the development process and aggravated mainly by external events. Given this, developing countries should not be "punished" for deficits with the monetary contraction and other measures embodied in Fund programs.

Moreover, structuralists argue, the sort of stabilization programs the Fund designs have perverse effects when implemented in the economies of the "South." In one important model, it is argued that "a deflationary impact from devaluation (a typical Fund policy) is more than a remote possibility; it is close to a presumption" (Krugman and Taylor, 1978: 446–447). Typically, IMF programs produce:

> " . . . in the short run mainly in a drop in domestic output; this drop in turn acts to discourage investment, which reduces the economy's long-run capacity to earn foreign exchange. . . . (Instead, IMF) economic policy should focus on removing supply bottlenecks and other structural rigidities, so that overall output capacity can be raised. In this way, excess demand would be reduced and resources generated for a balance of payments improvement. . . . " (Crockett, 1981: 55)

Thus, in the structuralist perspective, the IMF—in both its refusal to provide long-run financing and its short-run stabilization policies—is seen as a recession-inducing growth-wrecking agent. In the relevant literature (see, for example, Dell, 1982; Diaz-Alejandro, 1981; Foxley, 1983; Bacha, 1983; Girvan, 1980; Krugman and Taylor, 1978; Taylor, 1979; 1981), this argument is developed using theoretical models and case studies of Fund interventions.

(B) The Fund Responds

While some of the work cited above has also examined the distributional consequences of Fund programs, the IMF has until recently (see Sisson, 1986) primarily viewed its critics—both structuralist economists and Third World nations—as concerned with the growth issue. It has responded to this concern in two distinct ways. The first has involved changing some aspects of Fund operations to accommodate the critics. The structuralist notion of the development deficit led some to argue that the IMF should enlarge its resources and make payments financing available for long periods and with low conditionality (see Rweye-mamu, 1980: 85–91; Girvan, 1980: 72–74; Dell, 1982: 604–605). Through the 1970s, low conditionality facilities like the Oil Financing Facility and the Compensatory Financing Facility (both designed to deal with external shocks to a member country's terms of trade) were added or expanded. The Supplementary Financing Facility was developed in order to expand the credit available to member nations (Cutajar, 1980: 2). Finally, the Extended Fund Facility (EFF), with its two to three year programs, was created to allow longer adjustment periods and so avoid "unnecessary" output contraction.

Such policy changes did not come about merely because Fund economists are sensitive about the tarnishing of their image by academic critics. Rather, the new policies arose (1) to prevent an international financial collapse provoked by the increasing balance of payments deficits of developing countries, and (2) to overcome the Third World resistance to Fund advice and resources that led to the underutilization problem of the mid- to late-1970s.[2] Nonetheless, the Third World resistance, complaints about the inadequacies of the IMF, and calls for a new international monetary order were fueled by the growth-oriented critique.

This helps explain the second Fund response to its critics: a series of systematic cross-country studies of the effects of IMF-supported stabilization programs conducted by Fund economists and published in the IMF's *Staff Papers*. The two most important and general of the studies have been those by Donavan (1982) and Reichmann and Stillson (1978).[3] Unfortunately for the IMF's critics, both have demonstrated that the feared recessionary effects of IMF programs do systematically occur.

The Donavan study examines the effects of IMF programs in the non-oil developing countries (NODCs) in the period 1971–80 by looking at the behavior of various variables (current account, balance of payments, inflation, growth, etc.) in the periods before and after the introduction of a program. He considers both one- and three-year periods and measures the variable performance both absolutely and relative to a series for all NODCs. He concludes that: . . . in broad terms, program countries recorded significant reductions in their external deficits while they exhibited only marginal changes in their growth rates of real GDP and consumption—changes that were not significantly different from those experienced by non-oil developing countries in general (Donavan also demonstrates minor relative reductions in inflation). Thus, considering the group of program countries in the aggregate, the costs associated with the external adjustment effort appear to have been less severe than has sometimes been suggested by participants in the controversy on Fund conditionality (Donavan, 1982: 197).

Earlier work by Reichmann and Stillson (1978) looked at the effects of IMF programs in both developed and developing countries in the period 1963–72. To determine the effects of the programs, Reichmann and Stillson compare the behavior of various variables for the eight quarters before and the eight quarters after the beginning of an IMF-supported program.[4] The significance of the change in pre- and post-IMF observations is determined by using a non-parametric procedure known as the Mann-Whitney U-test. Such a non-parametric procedure is necessary because of the expectation that the variance as well as the mean of the variable in question will change in response to a Fund program: this likely change in variance violates the homoscedasticity assumptions strictly required for a simple t-test of the means of the two periods. Further, since the Mann-Whitney procedure is essentially a test of the medians of the two periods, the significance levels obtained are not biased by the presence of outliers. For all these reasons, I rely on such non-parametric procedures in my own study below.

Testing the change in net foreign assets (a balance of payments measure), Reichmann and Stillson find some indication that Fund programs tend to improve balance of payments positions: of 75 cases examined, 18 cases showed statistically significant improvement (at the 90% confidence level), four cases showed a statistically significant worsening of their net foreign assets position, and 53 exhibited no significant change in either direction (Reichmann and Stillson, 1978: 300–301). The record on inflation is less impressive: of the 29 cases where significant inflation (defined as an annual inflation rate in excess of 5.3%) occurred before the introduction of the IMF-supported program, seven showed a significant decrease in the inflation rate, six a significant increase, and 16 no significant change.

To perform the relevant quarterly tests on growth, Reichmann and Stillson examine the rate of change in either an industrial production index or an index of employment. For the 24 cases examined, two show a significant decline in growth, one a significant increase, and 21 no significant change. But this is not really an adequate refutation of the growth-oriented critique since much of this critique depends on the structural specifities of the LDCs and, as Reichmann and Stillson admit in a footnote:

> This group of programs (those where the above indices were available) is not representative of the programs considered in the other statistical tests since 7 of the 24 cases in this group were from developed countries. For the less developed countries included in this test, the growth of industrial production is not an adequate indication of the level of economic activity. (Reichmann and Stillson, 1978: 303)

Turning toward a yearly GDP-based growth rate, Reichmann and Stillson find that, of 70 cases examined, growth rates increased in the post-program year in 33 countries, decreased in 28 countries, and "showed practically no change" in nine countries (Reichmann and Stillson, 1978: 303). Thus, despite the different country set and different methodology, their research reveals a pattern similar to that noted by Donavan: significant balance of payments improvements matched by unimportant changes in inflation and mixed effects on growth. The results of both studies are briefly summarized in Table 16.1.

The Fund, then, has fired back. In response to demands for change, it has altered certain policies. Moreover, a series of studies by IMF economists have evidenced an association of Fund programs with balance of payments improvement and, at the least, no negative inflationary consequences. Most important to the refutation of the IMF's critics, systematic cross-country analysis has revealed no generally negative impacts on growth. While the Fund does not promote growth, neither can it be termed a growth-wrecker.

(C) Another Sort of Critique

Marxist economists have also criticized the Fund, with most working within the dependency paradigm pioneered by Frank (1967) and others. In general, this Marxist-oriented dependency approach argues that the international capitalist system involves a drain of economic surplus from the Third World (periphery) to the First World (core). Such a "surplus drain"—through trade (unequal exchange), profit repatriation, and other devices—ensures that the economies of the periphery (Third World) "remain underdeveloped for lack of access to their own surplus"

Table 16.1 Results of Studies by IMF Economists*

Variables	Donavan	Reichmann & Stillson
Current account as % of GNP (current account ratio)	Absolute and relative reduction†	Not examined
Balance of payments measure	Absolute and relative improvement	Significant improvement in 24% of cases; significant worsening in only 5%
Inflation	Absolute increase but relative reduction	Mixed impacts
Growth rates	Mixed impact	Mixed impact
Growth rate of real consumption	Absolute and relative reduction in a slight majority of cases	Not examined

*The results presented here are described in the text and explained in detail in Donavan (1982) and Reichmann and Stillson (1978).

†As noted in the text, Donavan's *absolute* comparisons look at the performance of a variable before and after an IMF program; his *relative* comparisons contrast the change in a variable for countries with programs to the change in the same variable for a set of all non-oil developing countries.

(Frank, 1967: 9). Since the IMF is a major institution of international capitalism, it is not surprising that it is viewed as maintaining foreign domination and so frustrating growth and "autonomous development" in the Third World.

Cheryl Payer's *The Debt Trap* (1974) has been considered by many observers as the dominant application of this sort of analysis to the topic of IMF-Third World relations. Like the structuralists, she argues the short-run stabilization policies recommended in a typical Stand-by Arrangement have negative consequences for growth since they "open" the economy and thus effectively destroy any basis that may have been carefully laid for "autonomous" development along, say, ISI lines. In addition, the Fund's general encouragement of export production reinforces dependency by locking Third World economies into the vagaries of markets in the core. Moreover, she argues that the IMF leads peripheral economies into a so-called "debt trap." Since an agreement with the IMF can open the door to new official and private sources of credit, this allows Third World countries to survive balance of payments crises through either increasing indebtedness or "auctioning" of domestic assets to foreign investors. In the process, the nations become "aid junkies"—lurching from crisis to crisis with infusions of private and official credit. As a result, their economies fall increasingly under the control of multinational corporations, international banks, and core governments; the latter phenomenon maintains surplus drain and so prevents development.

Thus, in Payer's analysis, the IMF is seen as dampening growth potential and increasing dependency; in addition, its policies have helped create the debt problem it is now attempting to manage. Unfortunately for Payer and the dependency critique, the Fund's demonstration of mixed growth impacts may be used to argue as well against this approach as against the structuralist framework outlined earlier.

But has the Fund really refuted the *Marxist* criticism? I think not. While output growth is important for economists of any persuasion, the unique Marxist contribution to the development literature is its *focus* on the class character of different development processes. For Marxists, the question is not whether the Fund frustrates development *per se*, but whether it promotes a particular kind of development with benefits accruing to certain social groups. Payer's early work has indeed contributed to the Marxist understanding of the IMF by suggesting that the Fund's general promotion of an open economy and its specific policies allow the relatively stronger (or more "efficient") capitals of the core to dominate the relatively weaker capitals of the periphery. But this core-periphery (or intra-capitalist) dimension is only one aspect of Fund policy.[5]

By promoting an open economy and using conditionality to enforce balance of payments "discipline," the Fund also helps secure the domination of labor by capital in the various member countries' economies. This is because: (1) "an open economy generally serves the interests of the capitalists in resisting working-class demands for improved wages and social services" (Block, 1977: 7), and, (2) even though "the Fund holds that distributional considerations are none of its business" (Williamson, 1983: 630), the specific policies of the IMF are designed to ensure that the burden of adjustment is placed onto non-elite classes. This is not merely because of the economic framework of the IMF but because securing the cooperation of local elites for the implementation of IMF programs involves sparing them the costs of adjustment.[6] As Williamson comments, "there must be a danger that the typical Fund mission will avoid suggesting cuts that impinge on the politically powerful" (Williamson, 1983: 63). As a result, the "austerity programs (of the Fund) favor the most powerful sectors of the (local) bourgeoisie as much as they favor imperialist powers" (Serulle and Boin, 1983: 128).[7]

Using this insight, we should expect Fund programs to be accompanied by a redistribution of power (and income) toward local ruling elites and away from working and popular classes. *Either* increasing or decreasing growth rates would be compatible with such a redistributive outcome: the actual movement of growth would depend on the relationship of income distribution to savings and consumption ratios, the relationship of savings to capital formation, and whether the economy is primarily demand- or supply-constrained in its growth prospects. The main point is this: the empirical demonstration of the Marxist thesis relies on showing a consistent negative "IMF effect" on some barometer of working class power and income. Below, I do exactly that.

3. The Experience in Latin America

In this section, I report on my investigation of the effects of IMF programs in Latin America. I begin by explaining the construction and methodology of the study. Subsequently, I present the results. A more detailed description of variable construction, data sources, the country set, and the statistical methods is included in an appendix available from the author.

(A) Variables, Domain, and Method

The variables examined include balance of payments measures, inflation rates, growth rates and dependency measures, and, finally, indicators of labor's share of income; each variable is briefly defined as it is presented. The country set studied was limited to 18 Latin American countries. The data cover the time period 1965–81, longer than that of any published study.[8] The study examined two sets of program countries: (1) those engaged in stabilization programs under *any* Stand-by Arrangement or any EFF (which I call Type I), and (2) only those countries engaged in an upper credit SB or EFF (which I call Type II).[9] To shorten my presentation, I will focus on the results for the upper credit (Type II) set. There was a similar pattern of results when all programs were considered; where there are important differences or where the results for the Type I set are otherwise relevant, this is noted in the text or footnotes.

The methods employed here are modeled after the techniques used in the Fund-sponsored studies of Donavan (1982) and Reichmann and Stillson (1978). Like Donavan, yearly absolute and relative comparisons are made.[10] Like Reichmann and Stillson, methods (both parametric and non-parametric) were used to attach statistical significance levels to the findings.

More specifically, absolute comparisons were made between the values of program country variables (or their rates of changes) in the year preceding the IMF program and in the year of the program.[11] The significance of the differences in pre- and post-program variables was determined through use of the paired sample *t*-test, the signs test, and the Wilcoxon ranked-sums tests. For clarity of presentation, only the results of the non-parametric signs tests are reported below. Of the cases where the assumptions required for the two parametric methods were met, most significance levels were similar to those obtained in the signs test; the exceptions are duly noted in the text or footnotes.

In Table 16.2, I report the one-tail significance levels of the signs tests for absolute comparisons. In Row 1, for example, I consider the current account as a percentage of GNP and test the simple alternative hypothesis, proposed by the IMF, that the level after an agreement exceeds the level before (post > pre); that is, that the current account deficit is reduced or a surplus is generated by an IMF-supported stabilization program. The significance level for this hypothesis is reported in the last column and will be discussed in the results section below.

Table 16.2 Absolute Comparisons (upper credit programs)

Variable	Alternative Hypothesis		Significance Level
Current account as % of GNP (current account ratio)	[IMF]	post > pre	(0.598)
Change in current account ratio	[IMF]	post > pre	(0.344)
Overall BOP as % of GNP (BOP ratio)	[IMF]	post > pre	(0.055)
Inflation rate (based on GDP deflator)	[IMF]	post < pre	(0.990)
Change in inflation rate	[IMF]	post < pre	(0.970)
Growth rate of GDP	[GOC]	post < pre	(0.500)
Change in growth rate	[GOC]	post < pre	(0.394)
Labor share of income	[MPJ]	post < pre	(0.043)
Change in labor share	[MPJ]	post < pre	(0.127)

Note: In all cases, the null hypothesis is that there was no change in the variable during the course of the IMF program (e.g., that post = pre); a low significance level indicates rejection of this null hypothesis in favor of the specified alternative.

Absolute comparison can be misleading, of course. To find, for example, that growth rates for the program countries decline is unimpressive if growth rates for the non-program countries are declining as rapidly or more rapidly in the same period of time. Thus, I broke the country set for each year into program and non-program groups to examine the *relative* performance of the program group. The significance of the difference between the two groups for each year was determined using both parametric (*t*-test) and non-parametric (Mann-Whitney) techniques. The significance levels reported below are based on the Mann-Whitney procedure; where the relevant assumptions were met, the parametric results followed a similar pattern.

The logic of the statistics summarizing these year-by-year relative comparisons can best be appreciated by means of a graphical analogy. Consider the trend lines depicted in Figure 16.1. There, the dotted and solid lines represent the mean change in labor's share of income for *all* (Type I) program and non-program countries, respectively.[12] We can ask two sorts of questions about the relative performance of program countries: (1) do program countries *consistently* do worse—that is, is the dotted line usually beneath the solid line?; and (2) are the differences in the experience of program countries *dramatic*—that is, are the lines occasionally far apart (given the appropriate variance and degrees of freedom)?

In Table 16.3, these two points—the consistency of the result and the extent of difference in any year—are summarized in the following manner. To gauge consistency, a summary significance level for a specified simple alternative hypothesis is calculated for the yearly relative comparisons; this calculation relies on the use of a cumulative binomial probability as explained in the appendix. For example, in row 1 of Table 16.3, the difference between this year's current account ratio and last year's is tested against the alternative hypothesis, held by the IMF, that program countries fare relatively better (experiencing either a larger improvement in their current account ratios or a lesser worsening). In the table, this is indicated in column 2 by the statement "program > non-program (+)." Column 3 reports the overall significance of the test statistic in light of this hypothesis. In column 4, years are listed in which the differences between program and non-program countries were "significant."[13] The sign of the difference (positive if the program countries had the greater variable value; negative if not) is also noted.

Before proceeding to the results themselves, a few more methodological notes are in order. Note that significance and not confidence levels are reported; thus, a significance level of, say, 0.001, indicates that there is good reason to reject the null hypothesis in favor of the specified alternative. All significance levels are reported since as Donavan (1982) points out in criticizing Connors' (1979) study of Fund programs, it is "helpful to know how close the test statistics were to the 95% level" (Donavan, 1982: 182).

Note further that except for the test statistics on the years of significant difference, all significance levels are one-tail. The justification for

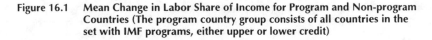

Figure 16.1   **Mean Change in Labor Share of Income for Program and Non-program Countries (The program country group consists of all countries in the set with IMF programs, either upper or lower credit)**

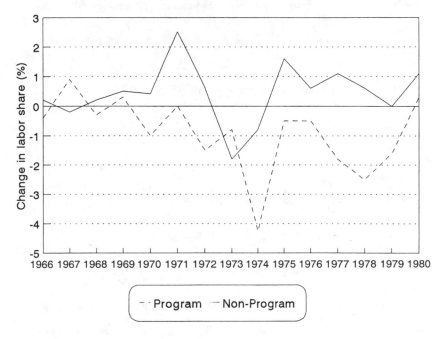

one-tails is rather simple: Each school of thought holds rather firm simple alternative hypotheses about the movements of various measures during an IMF-supported stabilization program. Moreover, one-tail tests are more powerful than two-tails in testing the simple alternative. They are, however, quite prone to the error of accepting the null hypothesis when, in fact, it should be rejected in favor of an absolutely opposing simple alternative. A significance level of, say, 0.990 is probably evidence of this latter situation.

Results of the Study

Balance of payments. Two basic balance of payments measures were examined: (1) the current account ratio (the current account as a percentage of GNP)[14] and (2) the overall balance of payments as a percentage of GNP.[15] The yearly percentage change in the current account ratio—the difference between this year's value and last year's—was also examined.

The Fund argues that its programs lead to improvement in both sorts of measures. In the absolute comparisons, I represent this IMF

Table 16.3 Relative Comparisons (upper credit programs)

Variable	Alternative Hypothesis	Overall Significance	Years of Significance Difference
Change in current account ratio	[IMF] program > non-program (+)	(0.402)	– + 1972(**), 1973(**), 1978(**)
Change in BOP ratio	[IMF] program > non-program (+)	(0.038)	– + 1976(**), 1978(**)
Change in inflation rate (based on GDP deflator)	[IMF] program < non-program (–)	(0.850)	– 1979(*) + 1970(*), 1974(*), 1980(*)
Change in growth rate	[GOC] program < non-program (–)	(0.697)	– 1975(**), 1980(**), 1981(**) + 1979(**)
Change in labor share	[MPJ] program < non-program (–)	(0.001)	– 1971(*), 1972(*), 1978(*) +
Growth rate of total real consumption	[MPJ] program < non-program (–)	(0.011)	– 1966(*), 1969(*), 1967(*), 1978(*), 1980(*) + 1973(*), 1974(*)

1) In each year, the null hypothesis is that the median of the variable for the program group is the same as the median for the non-program group; this hypothesis is tested using a Mann-Whitney rank test. An (**) by a "significant" year means that the difference between medians in that year ('+' if the program median is greater than the non-program median; '–' if it is less) was significant at a 10% *two-tail level*; (*) indicates significance at a 20% *two-tail* level.

2) In calculating overall significance, the null hypothesis is that the number of years in which the program median exceeds the non-program median is equal to the number of years in which the program median is exceeded by the non-program median; a low significance level indicates rejection of this null hypothesis in favor of the specified alternative.

position with the simple alternative hypothesis that current account ratios and the overall balance of payments improve concurrent with Fund programs. In the relative case, the IMF alternative hypothesis is that program countries experience more improvement (or less worsening) in these measures than non-program countries.

Looking at the absolute comparisons in Table 16.2, one finds no significant improvement in the current account ratios after an IMF program (as indicated by the 0.598 significance level); indeed, the results suggest that current account ratios worsened, albeit insignificantly. Did the worsening of the current account at least slow down? Looking at a measure for the change in the current account ratio one again finds results that are not significant at any reasonable level. However, turning to the overall balance of payments measure, we note an absolute improvement as indicated by the significance level of 0.055.

The relative comparisons described in Table 16.3 reveal that while there are a number of individual years in which the change in the current account ratio is larger (more positive) for program countries than for non-program countries, the overall significance level is very weak (at 0.402). In contrast, for the overall balance measure, the significance level is 0.038 and there are a few years in which the difference between program and non-program countries is significant.

What do these two sets of results indicate? One implication might be that the improvement in the overall balance of payments is coming not through the current account but rather through the capital account; at the least, it is the capital account improvement (perhaps in conjunction with current account improvement) which is essential to making the overall measure attain significance. Such capital account improvement might square with both the IMF's argument that Fund programs have a catalytic effect in attracting private funds (Killick, 1984: 230) and Payer's notion that the IMF's programs help to create a "debt trap." To investigate this and related issues, I examined absolute changes in various items in the balance of payments.

For the upper credit program countries, I found that the trade balance improved in only 49% of the cases; while this may be interpreted as lending credence to the structuralists' elasticity pessimism, it should be remembered that not all IMF programs recommend devaluation. On the other hand, the balance in other goods, services, and income *worsened* in 63% of the cases while the capital account *improved* in 65% of the cases.[16] Recall that this improved capital account *cannot* be occurring because of the IMF credit itself—official IMF assistance comes in "below the line" and so is not counted in the capital account.

Moreover, for the alternative hypothesis that capital account changes were larger (more positive) in dollar terms than changes in the balance of all goods, services, and income, the significance level was a strong 0.054 for the Type I countries but an anemic 0.315 for the upper credit group. This pattern of results is particularly interesting; the "stronger" significance when lower credit countries are included in the program set indicates that one reason for requesting Fund supervision of economic policy—even when balance of payments problems are not severe enough to require upper credit borrowing—might be to increase private capital inflows. Coupled with the evidence of general improvement in the capital account and overall balance, it seems that signing an IMF agreement amounted to a "seal of approval" that allowed program countries to obtain loans from private banks, attract foreign investors, and entice local capitalists to stay.[17]

Inflation. The Fund generally argues that its programs tend to reduce the rate of inflation or at least the rate at which it increases; in the absolute comparisons below, I consider this to be the Fund's alternative hypothesis. For relative comparisons, the Fund's alternative hypothesis is thought to be that the increase in inflation rates in program countries is less than the increase in non-program countries.[18]

For the IMF's alternative hypothesis that it lowers inflation rates, the results are abysmal. Indeed, the significance levels in Table 16.2 suggest that rather than being coincident with reductions in the inflation rate or with slowdowns in the rate of increase of the inflation rate, inflation rates increase and at a faster rate than they were rising before the introduction of the IMF-supported stabilization program.

Turning to the relative comparisons of Table 16.3, one finds a similar result: the overall significance level of 0.850 indicates that program countries may have been experiencing increases in their inflation rates larger than those experienced by countries without the "benefit" of Fund help and advice. A glance at the years of significant differences between program and non-program countries reinforces the notion of a lack of success in restraining inflation. In the years reported, there are more years of significantly greater inflation increases in program countries than years of significantly lower inflation increases. In Latin America at least, Fund programs probably tend to be coincident with an acceleration of inflation.

Why does inflation accelerate? I do not explore this here but refer the reader to a recent piece by Kirkpatrick and Onis (1985) that tackles this matter directly. Nonetheless, it is worth mentioning that in the face of the Fund's usual recommendation that the growth of nominal wages be restrained, inflation acceleration is consistent with the redistributive effects to be noted momentarily.

Growth. In examining growth, we consider the alternative hypothesis, "proposed" by the growth-oriented critique (GOC), that IMF programs dampen growth rates. A related hypothesis for the dependency framework is that the Fund promotes dependency (as measured, say, by exports and imports as a percentage of GNP). The IMF, of course, contends it has no such impact on growth and would see an increase in the dependency measure described above as evidence of increased international integration. Such integration, Fund economists would suggest, will ultimately promote growth and development.

Looking at the absolute comparisons of Table 16.2, one finds no evidence for the growth-dampening thesis. Significance levels for both the growth rate and the change in the growth rate (the difference between this year's growth rate and last year's) are 0.500 and 0.394, respectively. As the IMF has insisted, Fund programs have no consistent impact on growth.

How do program countries fare relative to non-program countries? In Table 16.3, we compare the change in growth rates in program countries relative to the change in those rates in non-program countries and find no evidence that the change in growth rates is relatively lower in program countries (i.e., either lower increases or greater decreases). While there are several years where the change in growth rates in program countries is significantly less (or more negative) than the change in non-program countries, there is at least one year in which the opposite is true.

These results on growth are even more mixed if we examine all (including lower-credit) arrangements.

While not reported in the tables, a standard "dependency" measure does increase relatively;[19] however, since this seems to have few growth costs, this provides more evidence for the open economy prescriptions of the IMF than for the usual autarkic remedies of the dependency school. In short, this study reaffirms the Fund's rejection of the generalizability of the growth-oriented critique.

Labor share. Finally, we turn to absolute and relative comparisons of labor's share of income (labor's share of the net domestic product; a discussion of its construction and theoretical appropriateness is in the appendix). As noted earlier, my simple alternative hypothesis (MPJ) is that there are reductions in labor's share of income during the course of Fund programs.[20]

Why would we expect evidence to reject the null hypothesis of no change in labor share in favor of this particular alternative? As argued before, the IMF's desire to secure the cooperation of local elites may lead them to design programs which place the burden of adjustment on workers and other "popular classes." In this vein, IMF programs have increasingly required nominal wage restraint at least for government employees (see Beveridge and Kelly, 1980: 240). Coupled with inflationary effects of devaluation and the removal of price controls and other consumer subsidies (which make up part of the "social wage"), workers will likely bear the brunt of adjustment.[21] If government deficit cutting hits basic social services (which would be likely in the case of an elite seeking to displace burdens), the "social wage" will decline further and the distributional consequences will be worse.

Turning to Table 16.1, we find that the alternative hypothesis that labor share is reduced obtains the strongest significance levels reported in *any* of the absolute comparisons (0.040). Further, it appears that this is not simply the result of a process that was already in place before the beginning of the program. Considering the relatively strong results (0.127) on the change in labor's share of income, one can conclude that even if labor share were declining at the beginning of a Fund program, that decline generally accelerates during the IMF program period. The results of parametric (t-test) absolute comparisons on these labor share measures are even stronger.

The results of relative comparisons also indicate strong evidence—an overall significance level of 0.001—in favor of the author's alternative hypothesis that the program group experiences smaller increases or larger declines in labor share.[22] Further, there are three years in which the change in labor share of income is significantly lower in the program countries and none in which the reverse is true; moreover, the number of years of significantly lower changes in labor share in the program group increases to six in the examination of all (including lower credit) arrangements. Indeed, for the upper credit programs, there is only one year (1967) in which the mean (or median) of the change in labor share in the program countries is even insignificantly greater than it is in the non-program countries.

This redistributive effect can also be confirmed by testing the rate of change of real total consumption, a measure Donavan (1982) uses: in addition, since this measure includes government consumption, it may also catch the reductions in social wage discussed above. The relative comparisons of Table 16.3 reveal that real consumption growth rates are lower in the program countries as indicated by an overall significance level of 0.011 and by the preponderance of years in which this measure was significantly lower in the program countries. Assuming that workers have a higher propensity to consume than elites and that cuts in government consumption fall most heavily on programs used by non-elite groups, this result squares with the earlier findings for labor share. In short, the single most consistent effect the IMF seems to have is the redistribution of income away from workers.

4. Conclusion

I have previously outlined the findings of the two IMF studies of the "effects" of Fund programs (Donavan, 1982: Reichmann and Stillson, 1978)—significant gains in reducing current account and balance of payment deficits, minor effects on the inflation rate (or its rate of increase), and few, if any, associated growth costs.

The profile that emerges from this study is somewhat different. For the time period and country set examined, we find: (1) insignificant improvement in current accounts accompanied by significant improvement in the overall balance of payments in general and the capital account in particular, (2) increases in both the inflation rate itself and its rate of increase, (3) mixed impacts on growth rates, and, (4) the strongest and most consistent effect of Fund programs: absolute and relative reductions in labor share of income.

Taken together, the results of this study provide ammunition for criticisms both of the Fund and of its traditional growth-oriented critics. For the Fund, it may be noted that rather than achieving their stated goals of inflation reduction and current account and long-term balance of payments equilibria, Fund programs—and the "seal of approval" they bestow—seem more effective at securing loans and other capital inflows for the program countries. This does not promote long-term balance of payments equilibrium for if the lending ever stopped (which it would in the early 1980s), balance of payments and debt crisis would emerge. Thus, as Payer (1974) suggested earlier, the debt crisis the Fund now purports to manage is, in part, of its own making.

The growth-oriented critique of the Fund also stands challenged. First, the argument that the Third World's balance of payments deficits should be financed rather than corrected (due to the development deficit, etc.) seems actually to have been addressed by the capital inflow secured by the Fund's programs. More important, this study—like those of the Fund and other researchers—reveals no evidence that Fund programs consistently lower growth rates. A standard dependency measure does rise relatively; however, since there are no growth consequences to this increase in international integration, it may be difficult to argue that this is a negative result (unless one makes the argument for relative autarky on different grounds).

In contrast, a class analytic or *distribution-oriented* critique can provide a successful explanation of the two major findings: labor share reductions and capital flow increases. The labor share reduction is not surprising in light of the Fund's role of providing a structure for the dual domination of periphery by core *and* labor by capital. The macroeconomic prescriptions of Fund programs lower labor share and increase the surplus available to dominant classes, tilting the balance of power to those already in power. This is partly because, as argued previously, the cooperation of local elites can be obtained by sparing them the burdens of adjustment. This rise in surplus—given no general effects on growth rates—should lead to an increase in profitability sufficient to attract the private capital inflows demonstrated.[23] This inflow may allow a rosy picture of balance of payments improvement, but beneath it lies worsening income distribution, exacerbated social tension, and little or no improvement in the inflation, current account, and growth fundamentals.

In the current period of IMF "management" of the debt crisis, the growth-oriented critique so belittled by Fund economists has reemerged. It is true that in the last few years, IMF programs have been associated with output declines; determining whether these are relatively worse in program countries requires further empirical work. It is likely, however, that the pattern of redistributive outcomes associated with Fund programs has continued.[24] It is these outcomes and the social conflicts engendered by them that impose social limits to debt management as "objective" as the standard full employment constraint .

After riots induced by IMF-recommended price increases left 60 dead, 200 wounded and 4,300 arrested, the planning minister of the Dominican Republic rejected (temporarily) the IMF pact commenting that "It is not that we are unwilling to put our own house in order. It is that we want to keep our house and not let it go up in flames." Economic policymakers both inside and outside the Fund should recognize that the inequitable apportionment of adjustment burdens demonstrated in this article cannot persist without letting societies "go up in flames." The design of stabilization policies to replace the unfair and often ineffective Fund policies should be the object of new research.

Notes

Many thanks go to Samuel Bowles, Carmen Diana Deere, Karen Pfeiffer, and Gerald Epstein for their help in developing both the empirical and theoretical projects this work embodies. I would also like to thank Ann Helwege and two anonymous referees for suggesting ways to improve the analysis and reorganize the paper.

1. A recent IMF study (Khan and Knight, 1983) argues and demonstrates empirically that both external and internal factors led to NODC current account deterioration in the 1970s. In their view, however, since at least some of the external factors are unlikely to be reversed (particularly movements in the terms of trade), adjustment required and continues to require shifts in domestic demand policies. Thus, in this view, the fault still lies with the internal policies of the NODCs.

2. For example, in 1978, the repayments of non-oil developing countries to the IMF exceeded their borrowing (or "repurchases") by 700.8 million SDR. In 1979, borrowing exceeded repayment by only 154.0 million SDR (Cline and Weintraub, 1981: 6).

3. A similar pattern of results is noted in Connors (1979). Killick (1984) provides a good review of all the various studies and conducts some of his own tests as well.

4. These comparisons are also made for four quarters before and four quarters after; the pattern of results was similar although less significant.

5. A similar Marxist criticism of Payer is offered by Phillips (1983).

6. In different terms, this point has been acknowledged by two Fund economists who write that often: ". . . those with the most to lose from a program whose distributional objectives are egalitarian tend to be those with the most power. Moreover, if not provided for in the design of the program, these interests will tend to assert themselves" (Johnson and Salop, 1980: 21).

7. Melo and Robinson (1982) provide a model of the distributional impact of trade adjustment policies for three different archetype economies. For our purposes, what is most interesting is their finding that elites will either

benefit or suffer less than other groups if they are able to maintain or create oligarchic (non-democratic) political regimes. The association of IMF-style policies with a turn to authoritarianism is discussed in Foxley (1983) and modeled more formally in Pastor (1987).

8. Killick's (1984) review of studies of IMF programs covers a similarly long period but his own empirical work only looks at the period 1974–79.

9. The distinction between lower and upper credit tranche Stand-bys for the whole time period of the study is not general public information. While IMF press releases and annual reports in recent years sometimes specify the nature of the credit tranches, this was not previously the practice. The information used here to distinguish SBs over the whole 1965–81 period for these particular countries was provided by the Public Relations Department of the Fund.

10. Such annual, rather than quarterly-based, comparisons are dictated by data limitations. While some of the series used below is available on a quarterly basis (specifically, *some* of the balance of payments variables from the International Financial Statistics series), critical variables, such as growth rates and wage shares are available only on an annual basis. For purposes of consistency, all the tests are for yearly changes.

11. The definition of what exactly constitutes a program period in both the absolute and relative comparisons more or less follows Donavan (1982). For clarification, see the available appendix. Comparisons were only for one-year periods since I believe that multiple-year comparisons hardly allow one to isolate the effects of the Fund programs.

12. The figure is constructed for all (Type 1) program countries to avoid a discontinuity in 1976 (when there were no upper credit programs in the country set used to test labor share). In addition, to "smooth" this graph of means and give a more realistic idea of the difference between program and non-program groups, I eliminated one country from consideration that had both positive and negative outliers: the country is included in the statistical tests reported in the text since the non-parametric procedures are not as sensitive to outliers. If the tests reported are done with the country excluded, the results follow a similar pattern.

13. The significance levels employed in these yearly comparisons are both dictated by the small number of observations per year and consistent with those used by Reichmann and Stillson (1978); for them, a confidence level of 90% was sufficient to characterize a variable's movement as "significant."

14. Following Donavan (1982), the current account was defined as total savings minus total investment. Results for another more direct measure (the balance of goods, services, and income as a percentage of GNP) followed a similar pattern but with slightly weaker significance levels for the IMF's alternative hypotheses.

15. Donavan (1982) does not use GNP as a base because of the problem of choosing the appropriate exchange rate to convert the local currency-denominated GNP into a measure that can be compared with the dollar-denominated reserve changes measure (which both he and I use in calculating the overall balance of payments). My method of calculation avoids this exchange rate problem as explained in the appendix. Tests on a measure identical to Donavan's follow a similar pattern on the relative comparisons but were weaker on the absolute comparisons. I also tested a net foreign assets measure like that used in Reichmann and Stillson (1978). While the results were similar, the problem of choosing the appropriate exchange rate to convert this measure to dollars renders the tests theoretically suspect.

16. The capital account measure included net errors and omissions since the latter is usually made up of rapidly moving short-term capital. Leaving out net errors and omissions yields similar results.

17. This "seal of approval" effect is discussed in Williamson (1983: 608–609). In 1983, the General Director of the IMF, Jacques de Larosiere, noted that each dollar of Fund credit led to four dollars in new commercial loans (Serulle and Boin, 1983: 1). Such "parallel financing" became common practice in the 1970s and has become particularly important in the debt crisis of the 1980s.

18. In testing inflation, I examined inflation rates based on both the Consumer Price Index and the GDP deflator. I report only the results on the deflator-based rate since the results were fairly similar and because Donavan argues that ". . . the GDP deflator might for some purposes be a better indication of the underlying inflation rate (than the CPI)" (Donavan, 1982: 182). In addition, I considered both the inflation experience in all countries and, following Donavan, in a country set that excluded countries with rates above 35%. Again, similar results lead me to economize and present the results for the examination of *all* countries.

19. Let the alternative hypothesis be that dependency (as measured by DEP, exports plus imports as a percentage of GNP) rises during the course of Fund programs. In absolute comparisons, this alternative hypothesis obtains a significance level of only 0.198 for the upper credit programs. However, relative comparisons on the rate of change of the dependency measure (CHDEP) for upper credit arrangements obtains an overall significance level of 0.038 for the alternative hypothesis and there is a preponderance of years in which CHDEP is significantly larger in the program countries.

20. For reasons of data availability the country set is slightly different for the tests on labor share. This is discussed in the appendix.

21. See Feinberg (1982) for a more detailed discussion of the likely distributional impacts of IMF programs. Duncan (1985) provides an excellent study of the impacts of Fund-sponsored stabilization in Costa Rica in the early 1980s.

22. 1981 is not included in these relative comparisons because of the low number of observations on labor share for that year.

23. This is acknowledged by two Fund economists who argue that during a stabilization program, "real wage rates may have to fall and real profit rates increase so as to encourage increased foreign capital inflow and private domestic capital formation" (Johnson and Salop, 1980: 23).

24. Working along the lines of the class analytic perspective developed in this paper, Duncan (1985) analyzed the effects of Fund stabilization in Costa Rica in the early 1980s. He, too, found that balance of payments improvement was mostly through the capital account. Most important, he argues that ". . . the findings of this study confirm the hypothesis that orthodox Fund stabilization policies tend to redistribute real income to agro-exporters, particularly agribusiness and larger landowners, at the expense of urban and most rural workers" (Duncan, 1985: 57).

References

Abdalla, Ismail-Sabri. 1980. "The inadequacy and loss of legitimacy of the International Monetary Fund." *Development Dialogue*. 2: 25–53.

Arida, Persio, and Edmar Bacha. 1984. "Balancao de Pagamentos: Uma Analise de Desequilibrio para Economias Semi-industrializadas." *Pesquisa e Planejamento Economico*. 14: 1–58.

Bacha, Edmar L. 1983. "Vicissitudes of recent stabilization attempts in Brazil and the IMF Alternative," in Williamson, pp. 323–340.

Beveridge. W. A. and Margaret R. Kelly. 1980. "Fiscal content of financial programs supported by stand-by arrangements in the upper credit tranches, 1969–78." IMF *Staff Papers*, 27: 205–244.

Block, Fred L. 1977. *The Origins of International Economic Disorder: A Study of United States International Monetary Policy from World War II to the Present*. Berkeley and Los Angeles, California: University of California Press.

Cline, William R. 1983. "Economic stabilization in developing countries: Theory and stylized facts," in Williamson, pp. 175–208.

Cline, William R. 1983a. *International Debt and the Stability of the World Economy*. Washington, D.C.: Institute for International Economics.

Cline, William R. 1985. "International debt: From crisis to recovery?" *American Economic Review*. 75: 185–190.

Cline, William R., and Sidney Weintraub (Eds.). 1981. *Economic Stabilization in Developing Countries*. Washington, D.C.: The Brookings Institution.

Collier. David (Ed.). 1979. *The New Authoritarianism in Latin America*. Princeton, N.J.: Princeton University Press.

Connors. Thomas A. 1979. "The Apparent Effects of Recent IMF Stabilization Programs." *International Finance Discussion Papers* No. 135. Board of Governors of the Federal Reserve System.

Crockett, Andrew. 1981. "Stabilization policies in developing countries: Some policy considerations." IMF *Staff Papers*. 28: 54–79.

Cutajar, Michael Zammit. 1980. "Background Notes on the International Monetary Fund." *Development Dialogue*. 2: 95–112.

Dale, William B. 1983. " Financing and adjustment of payments imbalances." in Williamson pp. 3–16.

Dell, Sidney. 1982. "Stabilization: The political economy of overkill," *World Development*. 10: 597–612.

Dell, Sidney, and Roger Lawrence. 1980. "The balance of payments adjustment process in developing countries." New York: Pergamon Press.

Diamand, Marcelo. 1978. "Towards a change in the economic paradigm through the experience of developing countries," *Journal of Development Economics*. 5: 19–53.

Diaz-Alejandro, Carlos. 1981. "Southern Cone stabilization plans," in Cline and Weintraub. pp. 119–147.

Donavan, Donald J. 1982. "Macroeconomic performance and adjustment under Fund-supported programs: The experience of the Seventies," IMF *Staff Papers*, 29: 171–203.

Duncan, Cameron. 1985. "IMF conditionality, fiscal policy, and the pauperizarion of labor in Costa Rica," Paper presented at the American Economics Association meetings, December.

Eckaus, Richard S. 1982. "Observations on the conditionally of international financial institutions," *World Development*, 10: 767–780.

Feinberg, Richard E. 1982. "The International Monetary Fund and basic needs: The impact of stand-by arrangements," in Margaret E. Crahan (Ed.), *Human Rights and Basic Needs in the Americas*. Washington, D.C.: Georgetown University Press.

Foxley, Alejandro. 1983. *Latin American Experiments in Neoconservative Economics*. Berkeley and Los Angeles: University of California Press.

Frank, Andre Gunder. 1967. *Capitalism and Underdevelopment in Latin America: Historical Studies of Chile and Brazil.* New York: Monthly Review Press.

Girvan, Norman. 1980. "Swallowing the IMF medicine in the Seventies." *Development Dialogue*, 2:55–74.

Gold, Joseph. 1970. *The Stand-by Arrangements of the International Monetary Fund* Washington, D.C.: International Monetary Fund.

Guitian, Manuel. 1980. "Fund conditionality and the international adjustment process: The early period, 1950–70," *Finance and Development*, 17 December.

Guitian, Manuel. 1981. *Conditionality: Access to Fund Resources, Pamphlet reprinted from Finance and Development*, Washington, D.C.: International Monetary Fund.

Hirschman, Albert. 1968. "The political economy of import-substituting industrialization in Latin America," *Quarterly Journal of Economics*, 82: 1–32.

Hirschman, Albert. 1979. "The turn to authoritarianism in Latin America and the search for its Economic determinants," in Collier, pp. 61–98.

Johnson, Omotunde, and Joanne Salop. 1980. "Distributional aspects of stabilization programs in developing countries," IMF *Staff Papers*, 27: 1–23.

Khan, Mohsin S., and Malcolm D. Knight. 1981. "Stabilization programs in developing countries A formal framework," IMF *Staff Papers*, 28: 1–53.

Khan, Mohsin S., and Malcolm D. Knight. 1982. "Some theoretical and empirical issues relating to economic stabilization in developing countries." *World Development*, 10: 709–730.

Khan, Mohsin S., and Malcolm D. Knight. 1983. "Determinants of current account balances of non-oil developing countries in the 1970's: An empirical analysis." IMF *Staff Papers*. 30: 819–842.

Killick, Tony. 1984. "The impact of Fund stabilization programmes," in Tony Killick (Ed.), *The Quest for Economic Stabilisation.* New York: St. Martin's Press.

Kirkpatrick, Colin. and Ziya Onis. 1985. "Industrialisation as a structural determinant of inflation performance in IMF stabilisation programmes in less developed countries," *Journal of Development Studies*, 21: 347–361.

Krugman, Paul, and Lance Taylor. 1978. "Contractionary effects of devaluation," *Journal of International Economics.* 8: 445–456.

Lichtensztejn, Samuel. 1983. "IMF-developing countries: Conditionality and strategy," in Williamson, pp. 209–222.

Melo, Jaime de, and Sherman Robinson. 1982. "Trade adjustment policies and income distribution in three archetype developing economies," *Journal of Development Economics.* 10: 67–92.

Moffit, Michael. 1983. *The World's Money.* New York: Simon and Schuster.

Pastor, Manuel Jr. 1987. *The International Monetary Fund and Latin America: Economic Stabilization and Class Conflict.* Boulder, Colorado: Westview Press.

Payer, Cheryl. 1974. *The Debt Trap: The IMF and the Third World.* New York and London: Monthly Review Press.

Phillips, Ron. 1983. "The role of the International Monetary Fund in the post–Bretton Woods era." *Review of Radical Political Economics.* 15.

Reichmann, Thomas M. and Richard T. Stillson. 1978. "Experience with programs of balance of payments adjustment: Stand-by arrangements in the higher tranches, 1963–72," IMF *Staff Papers.* 25: 292–310.

Rweyemamu, Justinian F. 1980. "Restructuring the international monetary system," *Development Diaglogue.* 2: 75–91.

Serra, Jose. 1979. "Three mistaken theses regarding the connection between industrialization and authoritarian regimes," in Collier, pp. 99–163.

Serulle, Jose, and Jacquelin Boin. 1983. *Fundo Monetario Internacional: Capital Financiero Crisis Mundial.* Santo Domingo: Ediciones Gramil.

Sisson, Charles A. 1986. "Fund-supported programs and income distribution in LDC's," *Finance and Development.* 23: 30–32.

Taylor, Lance. 1979. *Macro Models for Developing Countries.* New York: McGraw-Hill.

Taylor, Lance. 1981. "IS/LM in the Tropics: Diagramatics of the new structuralist macro critique," in Cline and Weintraub, pp. 465–503.

Wiesner, Eduardo. 1985. "Latin American debt: Lessons and pending issues," *American Economic Review.* 75: 191–195.

Williamson, John (Ed.). 1983. *IMF Conditionality.* Washington, D.C.: Institute for International Economics, pp. 605–660.

Williamson, John. 1983. "The lending policies of the International Monetary Fund," in Williamson. *IMF Conditionality.*

17

THE MARCH TOWARD MONETARY INTEGRATION: EUROPE AND THE MAASTRICHT TREATY

Beverly Springer

With the appearance and expanding agenda of regional economic associations such as the North American Free Trade Agreement (NAFTA), the Asia Pacific Economic Cooperation (APEC), and the European Union (EU), economic integration has become an important phenomenon in the study of international political economy. In this chapter, Beverly Springer examines the progress of the EU toward economic and political integration and superpower status. She notes that whereas the political and social dimensions of unification have tended to lag, economic integration has proceeded rapidly. However, completing the monetary union will not be easy because it involves a level of integration and a sacrifice of sovereignty that goes well beyond previous stages and programs of integration. With this in mind, in 1992 the EU member states drafted the Maastricht Treaty, which delineates a series of three steps to achieve monetary union and a single European currency based on a convergence of policies and economic indicators among the signatories. Although the treaty contains loopholes that allow members to delay and/or avoid full implementation, Springer asserts that the prospects for monetary integration are reasonably good.

In November 1993, the Treaty on European Union (the Maastricht Treaty) was ratified, opening a new era in integration for the twelve countries constituting the European Community (EC) (Belgium, Denmark, France, Germany, Greece, Ireland, Italy, Luxembourg, the Netherlands, Portugal, Spain, and the United Kingdom). The name *European Union* was adopted for the entity, which included new areas of authority such as foreign and security polices. The treaty came at the end of a remarkable period during which the member states achieved unprecedented levels of integration. The EC gained many of the attributes of a single economic entity—it made laws, gathered revenues, and dispersed funds. No other regional entity matched its level of authority. Many European leaders, however, believed more integration was needed to allow European firms to compete successfully with U.S. and Japanese firms in the global economy. The resulting treaty enables the European Union (EU) to assume some of the most cherished prerogatives of national sovereignty.

The member states of the EU are bound by the Treaty on European Union to create a single currency by the end of the twentieth century (UNCTAD, 1994). Work is in progress following a blueprint contained in the treaty. The success or failure of the work has major implications for the global economy as well as for European integration. An EU currency would introduce a major player into the world currency markets and would perhaps lessen the role of the dollar; it would also compel the governments of member states to formulate economic policy within parameters set by new European monetary actors. The story of European monetary integration is fascinating and important, combining economic forces and high and not so high politics that have fundamental philosophical differences.

Forecasts about the importance of an EU currency are based on the strength of the EU in the global economy. In 1990, the EU provided 47.6 percent of merchandise exports and 49.6 percent of the exports of commercial services in the global economy; the United States, by comparison, contributed 14.7 percent and 17.7 percent, respectively (UNCTAD, 1994). Three members of the EU—France, Germany, and the United Kingdom—play more important roles in exporting commercial services than does Japan, and they are surpassed only by the United States in global rankings. Japan, the United States, and the European Union make up the triad that dominates foreign direct investment (FDI) in the world, contributing approximately 80 percent of the total. The EU is the dominant supplier of FDI to the countries of Central and Eastern Europe, large sections of Africa, three countries in the Asia Pacific region, and three countries in Latin America (UNCTAD Programme on Transnational Corporations, 1993).

The European Union as a
Unique Actor in International Relations

Raymond Vernon (1994) recently described the EU as a historical aberration smuggled into the family of nations. An understanding of European monetary integration begins with his description. The EU is an aberration in the sense that it is neither an international organization nor a fully sovereign state. Attempts to compare it to a federal system, such as that of the United States, are as flawed as attempts to compare it to the North American Free Trade Agreement (NAFTA).

Vernon's remark is a picturesque way of stating that the EU has evolved from an obscure community for regulating coal and steel in the 1950s into a major actor in the global economy in the 1990s. Through the years, the EU has acquired attributes comparable to those of a powerful national government. In international negotiations its leaders are seated at the table with the leaders of Japan and the United States. The EU and U.S. leaders held hostage the recent General Agreement on Tariffs and Trade (GATT) negotiations until they settled their disputes. International politicians have added Brussels to their itinerary when on world tours. EU officials were entrusted by world leaders to guide the transition in Eastern and Central Europe following the end of the Cold War.

The transformation of the EU into its present status occurred incrementally and often imperceptibly. The founders of the EU believed member states should take small steps toward integration. The success of each step would encourage another step, and integration would grow piecemeal. They called such growth *functionalism*, which they set in motion through agreements on practical measures, such as tariffs. Member states agreed to transfer small amounts of sovereignty to new institutions that would have real but limited authority to legislate and adjudicate laws. Through the years, the free trade area (no internal tariffs) became a customs union (common external tariffs), eventually adopted the attributes of a common market (relatively free movement of the factors of production), and approached the status of an economic union with common economic policies. Today, EU directives set the parameters for national laws and regulations that deal with topics ranging from standards for machine tools to maternity leave for working women.

Despite the development of the EU, the leaders have never defined what they are building. People talk about a United States of Europe; others talk about a Europe of States. Some fear the transfer of sovereignty to the EU, and others advocate it. Some want economic but not political integration. For some, Europe is an ideal; for others, it is a convenience. Some hints about its objectives are found in the language of four of the treaties that form the basic laws of the EU. The Treaty Establishing the European Coal and Steel Community, signed in 1951, indicates that peace is the objective. The Treaty Establishing the European Economic Community (Treaty of Rome), which was signed in 1957 and is the most important of the treaties, provides the vague objective of "an ever closer union among the peoples of Europe" (UNCTAD Programme on Transnational Corporations, 1993: 18). The

Single European Act, signed in 1985, asserts that the states will transform their relations into a "European Union" but does not define the term. Participants in the discussion of the Treaty on European Union also failed to define the concept. Early drafts of the treaty include the phrase *federal union,* but the British delegation opposed the inclusion of the term *federal.* The final draft, which was signed in Maastricht in February 1992, retains European Union as the objective of European integration. It is an objective waiting to be defined.

Three Characteristics of the EU

The examination of three concepts—sovereignty, integration, and subsidiarity—provides some insights into the unique character of the EU (Vernon, 1994). The first two are familiar to students of the international political economy, but the third is more obscure.

Sovereignty

The EU is distinguished from international organizations by its claim to sovereign powers. Sovereignty, as defined in the EU, is divisible. Accordingly, member states can transfer or pool sovereignty to or with the EU or with other member states. The member states transferred limited amounts of sovereignty to the EU when they signed its basic treaties; they retain all other aspects of sovereignty. The EU has the authority to negotiate for the member states in trade talks such as the GATT rounds (UNCTAD, 1993). It can legislate on any topic assigned to it by the basic treaties, and its laws supersede national laws when the two conflict. Its court can declare a national law invalid when it conflicts with a legitimate act of the EU. Its laws can directly affect the member states. Corporations and individuals, as well as member states, are subject to EU law.

Many current articles about the EU refer to the "pooling of sovereignty," which occurs when the member states combine their power and authorize the EU to act for them to enhance the influence of them all. Pooling is occurring increasingly in international relations. Sovereignty, as traditionally defined, has limited relevance for member states in Europe today because of their mutual dependence; for example, what is the relevance of the sovereign authority of the Dutch or the Austrian government to control interest rates when the economy of each country is dependent on the German economy and when the Bundesbank (the German central bank) raises German interest rates? In such a case, effective authority rests in Germany, and the Dutch and Austrian governments have lost the power of independent control. Many authorities in Europe comment on the loss of monetary sovereignty and suggest that pooling sovereignty to create a single currency is preferable to the current situation in which the values of national currencies are held hostage to the major actors in the global market.

Integration

Integration is the second concept of importance in understanding the EU. It is a concept that has many facets—political, economic, legal, sociological—and the extent of European integration varies among these facets. Economic integration, not surprisingly, is the most highly developed facet. The United Nations Conference on Trade and Development (UNCTAD) treats the EU as a single (and major) actor in the global economy. According to UNCTAD, the EU constitutes, along with Japan and the United States, the triad that dominates the global economy (UNCTAD, 1993). Economic integration increased dramatically among the EU member countries during the 1980s and early 1990s. Such age-old national barriers as those to financial services crossing borders, to moving capital, and to regulating standards fell while the popularity of the 1992 program rode a surge of economic indicators.[1] As these barriers fell, enterprises began to restructure to take advantage of the single market. Mergers and acquisitions increased markedly, and distribution systems were redesigned. The most recent step in economic integration consists of a major program to integrate the transportation and communications systems of the member states. The program is contained in the White Paper on Growth, Competitiveness and Employment, which the EU adopted in December 1993.

Political integration is usually equated with the creation of a federal system.[2] Most scholars agree that political integration, as measured by the existence of a federal system, does not exist in the EU; however, many would argue that EU politics is more than international relations. Political life in the EU is organized around its major institutions: the commission, the council, the parliament, and the court. The institutions function within a complex network of interest groups, independent experts, and political groupings that links them to relevant stakeholders in a new form of supranational politics.[3] Major policy areas, such as that on the environment, have highly developed political regimes with norms and values, which distinctly separate the discourse from national politics.

Karl Deutsch pioneered the use of communications theory to study European integration (Deutsch et al., 1957). More recently, sociologists have studied social patterns and value systems to determine the extent of social integration. They want to know whether Europe is locked into a system of nation-states or whether the rudiments of a European society exist. Many agree that Europe is composed of overlapping social patterns that do not necessarily accord with national boundaries. The findings of the European Value Study led to the conclusion that "the underlying organization of values is remarkably unified . . . [and] transcends national and linguistic boundaries" (Harding and Phillips, 1986: 212–213). Polls conducted by *Eurobarometer* registered increased support for integration by residents of the member states until the mid-1990s, but then nationalism started to regain favor.[4] Given recent events, one can conclude that the level of social integration does not match that of economic or even political integration.

Legal integration vies with economic as the most advanced form of integration. EC law directly affects member states, providing rights and obligations for citizens and corporations, and has supremacy over national law, as noted earlier. Rulings of the European Court have been one of the most important forces behind European integration. According to a recent article, "The most striking feature of the Community, and that which distinguishes it most clearly from other international groups or organizations of states, is the essentially federal nature of its legal system" (Easson, 1994: 78).

Subsidiarity

Subsidiarity was mentioned in the Single European Act, a basic treaty of the EU signed in 1985, but it became a principle that guides all EU policy in the Maastricht Treaty. According to the treaty, "The Community shall take action, in accordance with the principle of subsidiarity, only if and insofar as the objectives of the proposed action cannot be sufficiently achieved by the Member States and can therefore, by reason of the scale or effects of the proposed action, be better achieved by the Community" (Title II, Article 3b). Subsidiarity forms a bulwark against the centralization of authority in Brussels and has reassured Europeans who became concerned by the rush to integration in the late 1980s. The juxtaposition of subsidiarity with sovereignty and integration, which have contrary connotations, is indicative of the complexity and ambiguity that characterize the EU.

The Maastricht Treaty and the European Monetary Unit

Preparing for the Treaty

When leaders of the EU began to draft the Maastricht Treaty, they believed they had a mandate to further European integration. Member governments, business groups, labor unions, and voters indicated a readiness for more integration. The 1992 program, the most ambitious in EU history, was on schedule. Capital markets had liberalized, financial services had begun to cross borders, and foreign direct investments soared as Japanese and other investors rushed to get inside the market. The economies of the member states were prospering, and Brussels claimed the credit. It was the high moment in popularity for integration and was an auspicious time for a new treaty to introduce a new era of integration.

Two groups prepared the new treaty. One dealt with a wide range of subjects, including foreign policy and European citizenship. The other, the relevant group for this study, had a specific task: to draft provisions for the creation of a single currency. The members of the group came from all of the member states and included leading authorities on the subject. They had the benefit of previous work by the Delors committee, which had prepared a report detailing three stages of transition to currency unification. They also had the support of the commission and influential business organizations. Unfortunately, however, the climate in which the group worked deteriorated throughout 1992, so the ambition of the proposal no longer accorded with the mood in Europe; nevertheless, a plan for full currency unification was set into EU law by the signing and ratification of the Treaty on European Union.

Background on Currency Unification

The EU has had a number of motives for currency unification. One is the belief that such unification is one of the essential attributes of European integration. This motive derives from a philosophical commitment to integration. Other motives have a more pragmatic basis. Some proponents of currency integration argue that it is a logical extension of the 1992 program to create a single market. They point to the transaction costs firms encounter as they do business across national boundaries. Other proponents believe the EU should create an island of stability to protect the integrated economies of the member states from the vicissitudes of volatile global exchanges. Still other proponents, motivated by conservative economic doctrines, advocate linking currencies in a fixed exchange rate system and eventually integrating currencies as a means of forcing governments to follow responsible economic policies. Opponents of currency unification also have a mixture of motives. Some fear the loss of national sovereignty. Others worry about the negative effect of unification on the poorer member states, which would lose the possibility of devaluing their currencies to be more competitive. Many are concerned about possible German domination of the new system and oppose the conservative economic philosophy they believe would thus dominate EU monetary policy.

Through the years, various national governments, individuals, and interest groups have led the initiative for monetary unification. The French government has been a consistent advocate, and the governments of the smaller member states have generally supported unification. The German government has supplied cautious leadership, demanding provisions to resist inflation and to ensure the independence of monetary authorities from politics. The Italian and Spanish governments have supported monetary integration as a part of general integration but have demanded compensation for the negative consequences on their weaker economies. Groups representing large corporations have been the most consistent advocates for currency unification among the numerous interest groups operating in Brussels. The British government and large segments of the British Conservative Party have been the main opponents, and the Danish government has also been reluctant. The public has generally supported the idea of integration but became fearful when confronted with the possible loss of national currencies during the recent recession.

Although currency unification came into prominence in the 1980s, its story begins much earlier and needs to be traced within the context of other European events as well as within the context of global monetary developments. When the Treaty of Rome was signed in 1957, currency unification was not an issue that needed to be considered. The common market envisaged by the drafters of the treaty could operate effectively despite the existence of different currencies because they had exchange rates that were fixed through the Bretton Woods system. During the 1960s, the EC became more integrated both economically and through new, more intrusive policies, while the global monetary system became more unstable. Intra-EC trade grew rapidly, making the economies of the member states more interdependent. The EC adopted a Common Agriculture Policy (CAP) based on common prices and the assumption of fixed exchange rates. Both the growth of intra-EC trade and the operation of CAP were threatened by growing pressures in the Bretton Woods system, and, consequently, leaders of the EC began to search for a more stable environment for intra-EC trade.

The Werner report of 1970 proposed a plan for currency unification. Economic and Monetary Union (EMU) was to be achieved in ten years by means of a program involving three stages in which the margin of fluctuation for the currencies of the participants would be narrowed and monetary authority would be centralized in Brussels. The project quickly ran into difficulty because of both economic and political failings (Papadia and Saccomanni, 1994). "The snake," as the program was called, never had the full support of the members of the EC and did not protect the EC from the monetary storms of the 1970s.

A more promising start was made in 1979 when the president of the commission, Roy Jenkins, and the heads of the two most powerful member states, France and West Germany, united to launch the European Monetary System (EMS). The system still exists, and it forms the basis for the latest attempt at currency unification. The core of the system is the ecu, a currency derived from the weighted average of the value of the currencies of all of the member states. If they so desire, member states can join the exchange rate mechanism (ERM). Each member of the ERM has a central rate with the ecu and thereby has a bilateral exchange rate with other member currencies. The members originally agreed to limit their fluctuation around the bilateral rates to 2.5 percent, except for Italy, which was allowed a 6 percent fluctuation rate. A system of divergence indicators was created, and central banks were committed to intervene when their currencies reached the divergence threshold. The system pressured member states to make exchange rate stability the objective of their economic policies and to keep inflation in check. The poorer ERM members were promised financial assistance from other programs to counter the negative consequences of the necessary economic policies. Despite the original skepticism of many, to most observers the EMS appeared to be a success after its first decade of existence (Kaufmann and Overturf, 1991). It had survived, other countries were interested in membership, and economic convergence was occurring among the participating states.

Because of this positive news, the EC leaders decided to prepare for currency unification. Before they finished their work, however, the situation changed, and currency unification appeared unrealistic and even dangerous. The story is complicated, but the outline can be briefly told. German unification is the crucial variable that precipitated the crisis, but deeper problems were involved as well (CEC, 1993). Many had warned even before German unification that stable exchange rates, free capital movement, and uncoordinated national monetary policies formed an incompatible triad (Boyer, 1994). Member states had recently adopted measures to liberalize the movement of capital in the EU. Most of these states were also linked to the narrow band in the ERM, but they still operated their monetary policies autonomously. When Germany adopted a policy to pay for unification that entailed high interest rates, other countries tried to match these high rates to avoid a flight of capital. The high rates were the opposite of what the weaker EC countries needed at a time of slow growth in the global economy and U.S. decline, and these weaker economies fell into recession. Divergence replaced convergence among the economies of the member states. The resulting strain on the ERM might have been alleviated if members had agreed to adjust the central ecu rate, but they did not do so. Speculators, empowered by the recent liberalization of capital markets, rightly assumed that the situation was ripe for them.

In the ensuing crises in 1992 and 1993, the United Kingdom and Italy left the ERM; France was almost forced out as well, and a number of members devalued their currencies. The crises ended the remnants of economic confidence, undermined the belief not only in monetary union but in integration in general, and exacerbated tense relations among the member states. In particular, the British government blamed the Germans for failing to support the pound as strongly as they had the French franc. The worst of the crises was ameliorated, however, in August 1993, when the remaining ERM members agreed to widen the margins of fluctuation to 15 percent, thus reducing the attraction for speculation. The agreement did not address the future of the system, but it provided time for the Maastricht Treaty to be ratified and for the recession to weaken.

The Maastricht Treaty Provisions for EMU

The Maastricht Treaty, which was finally ratified in late 1993, is the most complicated and controversial treaty in the history of European integration. It contains numerous provisions relevant to monetary union, both in the body of the text and in attached protocols. The EU gains the power of oversight for national economic policies to ensure that member states follow responsible policies. The EU now has the power to be rather intrusive. Member states are bound to follow economic policies that contribute to EU objectives and to accept a system of multilateral surveillance. The EU council can force compliance on member states that fail to adopt responsible policies. It can invite the European Investment Bank to reconsider loans to the member state, require a noninterest-bearing deposit from the member, and impose fines (Article 104c).

The treaty also establishes three new institutions that have important powers for the EMU.

1. The European System of Central Banks (ESCB) is composed of the central banks of the member states of the European Central Bank (ECB) and is responsible for maintaining price stability. Each member state is obligated to ensure that the statutes of its central bank are compatible with the ESCB requirements. (A number of member states have increased the independence of their central banks to meet this obligation.)

2. The European Central Bank will be created when the EU is ready to begin to use a single currency. The ECB shall have the exclusive

right to issue bank notes. It shall have the power to issue regulations and make policies necessary for the operation of an EU monetary policy and to punish entities that fail to comply. The ECB shall have a governing council composed of the governors of the national central banks and of the executive board of the bank. The members of the executive board will be selected from recognized authorities in the member states. Leaders of the commission and the council may participate in the work of the bank, but they cannot vote. The independence of the bank is similar to that of the German central bank.

3. The European Monetary Institute (EMI) is a temporary body that began operating in Frankfurt, Germany, in 1994 and that will be replaced by the ECB when a single currency is in place. It has a wide range of responsibilities in preparing for currency unification (Article 109f). Authority for monetary policy remains with the member states during the operation of the EMI, but the EMI ensures coordination among the actors.

The provisions for the transition to monetary unification appear simple and concrete, but they provide room for interpretation. The transition measures discussed in the treaty are to be introduced during the second of the three stages agreed to in the Delors Report that preceded the treaty (discussed earlier). Stage one was established by agreement of the European Council and began in July 1990. During this stage, all EU members were to join the ERM, and the margin of fluctuation was to be narrowed. As mentioned earlier, problems existing at the time prevented the objectives of stage one from being reached, but stage two began as scheduled in January 1994.

The work during the transition from stage two to stage three, when monetary unification will occur, will take place at two levels. At the European level, the EMI will prepare to introduce a single currency at the start of stage three. It will carry on the technical work associated with replacing the national currencies with the ecu, work closely with the commission and the member states to ensure coordination and agreement, and share with the commission the crucial task of recommending to the council the member states that are ready for monetary unification.

Convergence Criteria

In selecting the member states, the commission and the EMI are guided by a set of convergence criteria. The national governments agreed that economic convergence had to take place before a single currency could be introduced. They also agreed to four criteria that would serve as a measure of convergence. The criteria are explained in Article 109j of the treaty and are elaborated in an attached protocol. The council, acting unanimously on a proposal from the commission, can also adopt provisions that will replace those in the protocol. The four criteria are:

1. A high degree of price stability as measured by a rate of inflation that is close to the rates of, at most, the three member states whose economies have been the most stable
2. A sustainable government financial position as measured by a national budget for which the deficit does not exceed 3 percent of GDP and a public debt that does not exceed 60 percent of GDP
3. A stable exchange rate determined by remaining within the 2.25 margin in the ERM for two years before the decision
4. A durable convergence as measured by an average nominal interest rate on long-term government bonds that does not exceed by more than 2 percent that of the three best-performing member states

The list of criteria is not an infallible guide to which member states will participate in currency unification. The criteria may be strictly observed or may serve only as an indicator. In the latter case, a country in which the trends are moving in the right direction could be declared ready. Hans Tietmeyer, president of the German central bank, has demanded that the criteria be strictly observed, but other participants do not necessarily agree (Gawith, 1994). The language in the treaty allows for interpretation. It states that the commission and the EMI must "examine the achievement of a high degree of sustainable convergence by reference to the fulfillment by each Member State of the [aforementioned] criteria" (Article 109j). The phrases "high degree," "sustainable convergence," and "by reference to" are open to interpretation. The fact is that no decision by the EU could ever be made solely by referring to a list of economic criteria. This list gives a misleading appearance of inevitability to a decision that involves both economic and political judgments.

Critics attack the convergence criteria on a number of grounds. The criteria measure nominal convergence rather than real convergence in terms of living standards and levels of development. For example, Ireland and Luxembourg are the two countries that are eligible for integration in 1994 according to the criteria, but they differ markedly in terms of living standards. Governments that adopt the austerity policies necessary to meet the criteria could hinder economic development; for example, anti-inflation policies necessary for convergence can result in declining investments when interest rates are used as weapons. Slower modernization of the economy, less competitiveness, and increased unemployment are likely results of higher interest rates. Governments also lose the freedom to expand their economies in response to recessionary pressures. The political cost could be high for a government elected to end unemployment; in addition, governments cannot devalue their currency to gain a price advantage in the competition for trade. British critics of EMU point to the recovery of British exports and the de facto devaluation of the pound following Britain's exit from the ERM.

Another criticism of the criteria comes from persons concerned with the larger issue of European union. They fear that decisions based on economic criteria risk sidelining member states, such as Italy, that have given long and loyal support to the goals of union.

In summary, the critics cite both economic and political costs of the convergence criteria. They are not a cohesive group. Some are economists who have professional concerns about the validity of the criteria. Others are representatives of member states who fear the political costs. Some are motivated by a desire to preserve national sovereignty and others by the ideals of European union. Their existence gives evidence of the complex and unprecedented program to which the EU is committed by the Maastricht Treaty.

When the risks are considered, the question inevitably arises as to why all of the members, except the British, agreed to the convergence criteria when they signed the Maastricht Treaty. The answer is only partly economic. Policymaking in the EU involves tradeoffs among interests; it is not solely the sum of national interests. No policy stands alone. EMU has organic ties to the regional policy of the EU, which provides money to poor regions in the member states.[5] The Regional Fund was reformed and enlarged in the 1980s in tandem with the steps to EMU in that decade (Coombes and Rees, 1991). Further expansion of the Regional Fund was promised during the negotiations for the Maastricht Treaty, and a new Cohesion Fund was created to give more assistance to the four poorest member states (Springer, 1994). Cohesion is a principle of the treaty, and member states agree to make it an objective of their economic policies (Articles 2, 102a). The treaty also has a protocol on economic and social cohesion, which promises that EU policies will respect the different capacities of the member states. As a result of the provisions in the treaty, governments of the poorer member states know the regional policy serves as a compensatory mechanism for the possible harmful effects of EMU.

The Maastricht Treaty lists the steps that must precede stage three, when currency unification takes place. The commission and the EMI must report to the council on the progress of each member state regarding the convergence criteria and compatibility of national laws with the provisions for EMU. The council decides whether member states have fulfilled the conditions necessary for a single currency and whether a majority of member states meet the conditions. When the latter criterion has been reached, a council, composed of the heads of the governments and acting on the basis of a qualified majority vote, will decide by December 31, 1996, whether to start stage three and, if so, on what date. (The council must consult the parliament, but the parliament has only advisory power on the subject.) If the council finds that conditions are not ready at that time, EMU will start on January 1, 1999, among those countries that are qualified. At least every two years thereafter, the process will be repeated to reassess the member states not included in the currency union.

Following the agreement to establish stage three, the ECB and the ESCB will begin to operate under the provisions of the Maastricht Treaty, and the responsibilities for national monetary policy will be transferred to the new authorities. The council, composed only of the member states participating in EMU, shall, by unanimous vote, set the conversion rates at which the currencies will be irrevocably fixed and the fixed rate at which the ecu will be substituted for the national currencies. The treaty does not stipulate whether the conversion must take place as a "big bang" or whether the national currencies and the ecu will coexist for a time. This issue is still being debated.

Conclusion

Taken in its entirety, the EU has a carefully crafted blueprint for monetary unification. This blueprint has an aura of inevitability, but on closer examination it is less inevitable than it appears at first glance. Any forecast about the commencement of EMU must consider a number of disparate variables and not limit itself to economic indicators. The following key points have emerged from the discussion in this chapter.

First, EMU is a part of European integration. Decisions to advance or to retard its progress will be made, at least in part, on the basis of its contribution to integration.

Second, EMU is linked to other policies, such as regional policy, and the links serve to broaden its support. Political tradeoffs play an important role.

EMU entails the transfer of sovereignty on monetary matters to the EU by the member states. In reality, many member governments no longer control monetary policy and prefer to pool sovereignty in the EU to retain a role in shaping such policy.

A fourth point is that EMU is a major, unprecedented development with no model to guide it. Even when EMU is considered solely on economic grounds, experts do not agree on its potential costs and benefits.

The decision to start stage three is partly political, so political leadership is vital in both the commission and the council. The role of interest groups is also important. Interest groups that represent big business are among the strongest supporters of EMU.

Sixth, the convergence criteria to which member governments agreed provide a measure of readiness for monetary union. The criteria selected indicate broad acceptance of conservative economic doctrines. Conformance with the criteria may entail significant economic and social costs for the poorer member states.

Seventh, although subsidiarity is a popular doctrine in Brussels, it does not apply to EMU. Sovereignty and integration are the relevant concepts. EMU thus differs from other policies in Brussels in the post-Maastricht era because it preserves a role for national governments.

In conclusion, EMU is not inevitable, but it is probable. It is a choice that must be made according to a schedule and a procedure established by the Maastricht Treaty, but the outcome will be determined by numerous factors. A positive decision will be easier if economic recovery continues, but effective leadership is equally important. A successful outcome has enormous implications for the global economy; however, the process of creating EMU has been a uniquely EU exercise, and its future will be shaped by its existence within an integrating Europe.

Notes

1. See, for example, Loukas Tsoukalis, 1993. *The New European Economy*, 2d rev. ed. Oxford: Oxford University Press.

2. See, for example, Mark Tushnet, ed., 1990. *Comparative Constitutional Federalism: Europe and America*. New York: Greenwood Press.

3. For an excellent collection of articles on the politics of the EU, see Robert Keohane and Stanley Hoffman, eds., 1991. *The New Europe*. Boulder: Westview Press.

4. Commission of the European Community, *Eurobarometer*, a periodical publication of the commission. See, for example, number 41, July 1994.

5. For an excellent study of the politics of EMU, see Wayne Sandholts, 1993. "Monetary Bargains: The Treaty on EMU," in Alan Cafruny and Glenda Rosenthal, eds., *The State of the European Community*, vol. 2, pp. 125–142. Boulder: Lynne Rienner Publishers.

References

Boyer, Miguel. 1994. "Application of the Maastricht Treaty and the Experience of a Year of Crisis in the European Monetary System," in Alfred Steiner, ed., *Thirty Years of European Monetary Integration*, pp. 83–87. London: Longman.

Commission of the European Community (CEC). 1993. "Annual Economic Report for 1993." *European Economy*, no. 54 (Brussels): 11–23.

Coombes, David, and Nicholas Rees. 1991. "Regional and Social Policy," in Leon Hurwitz and Christian Lequesne, eds., *The State of the European Community*, pp. 207–228. Boulder: Lynne Rienner Publishers.

Deutsch, Karl, Sidney Burrell, Robert Kann, Maurice Lee, Jr., Martin Lichterman, Raymond Lindgren, Francis Loewenheim, and Richard Van Wagenen. 1957. *Political Community and the North Atlantic Area*. Princeton: Princeton University Press.

Easson, Alex. 1994. "Integration Through Law: The Court of Justice and the Achievement of the Single Market and the European Union," in Hans Michelmann and Panayotis Soldatos, eds., *European Integration: Theories and Approaches*, Lanham: University Press of America.

Gawith, Phil. 1994. "Tietmeyer Set Out Tough Line on Emu Convergence Criteria," *Financial Times* (November 6): 2.

Harding, S., and D. Phillips. 1986. *Contrasting Values in Western Europe*. London: Macmillan.

Kaufmann, Hugo, and Stephen Overturf. 1991. "Progress Within the European Monetary System," in Leon Hurwitz and Christian Lequesne, eds., *The State of the European Community*, pp. 183–205. Boulder: Lynne Rienner Publishers.

Papadia, Francesco, and Fabrizio Saccomanni. 1994. "From the Werner Plan to the Maastricht Treaty: Europe's Quest for Monetary Union," in Alfred Steinherr, ed., *Thirty Years of European Monetary Integration from the Werner Plan to EMU*, pp. 57–68. London: Longman.

Springer, Beverly. 1994. *The European Union and Its Citizens*. Westport, Conn.: Greenwood Press.

United Nations Conference on Trade and Development (UNCTAD). 1993. *World Investment Report, An Executive Summary*. New York: United Nations.

———. 1994. *Liberalizing International Transactions in Services*. New York: United Nations.

United Nations Conference on Trade and Development (UNCTAD) Programme on Transnational Corporations. 1993. *World Investment Report 1993*. New York: United Nations.

Vernon, Raymond. 1994. Speech to the Academy of International Business Conference, Boston, November 4.

PART 3

DEVELOPMENT AND THE WORLD BANK

18

THE WORLD BANK:
ITS FIRST HALF CENTURY

K. Sarwar Lateef

The role and impact of the World Bank on Third World development remain controversial. In this essay by the World Bank's K. Sarwar Lateef, a defense of the World Bank is presented. Drawing on aggregate social and economic indicators, Lateef argues that during the past fifty years the world has experienced unprecedented improvements in the levels of human material conditions, although poverty remains a major global problem. Lateef states that the Bank has assisted this process of improvement by making funds available to countries on terms that would never have been available through standard sources. He also credits the conditions the Bank places on loans for forcing countries to use the funds properly. Lateef concludes by pointing to shifts in the Bank's institutional culture toward a more holistic approach, an approach that expands the Bank's concerns to include matters of growth and poverty, people-focused investments, environmental protection, private-sector stimulation, and government-sector reorientation.

With the hardships of the Great Depression and the war years still a fresh memory, few people would have predicted in 1944 that the next fifty years would witness the most rapid growth in living standards the world had ever known. Certainly, few of the delegates from forty-four nations who gathered at a conference in Bretton Woods, New Hampshire, were thinking of such a future. Their goals were to reform a global economic system that had failed miserably during the Depression and, through a process of intergovernmental cooperation, to lay the foundation for a new era of stable growth. To oversee the birth of this new economic order, the conference established the World Bank (formally called the International Bank for Reconstruction and Development, or the IBRD) and the International Monetary Fund (IMF).

Parallel negotiations in Havana were coordinating the establishment of an International Trade Organization to complement the Bretton Woods institutions. The trade organization never came to fruition, although it survived in truncated form as the General Agreement on Tariffs and Trade (the GATT).

The past fifty years have seen dramatic, unprecedented gains for many developing countries. Some poor economies—Hong Kong, Singapore, and Taiwan (China)—have become richer than some former colonial powers, such as Portugal and Spain. Per capita income, after growing at a plodding 0.5 percent a year in Asia and Latin America in the period 1913–1950, shot up to 3.3 percent a year during the period 1950–1973 and 3 percent in 1973–1989. Only in Africa has progress come intermittently, with many setbacks.

Social indicators have improved greatly in developing countries, particularly in the past thirty years, and poverty has declined (most dramatically in East Asia). Between 1960 and 1990 average life expectancy increased by six months each year; infant mortality rates fell from 169 to 69 per 1,000 live births; food production increased 240 percent, much faster than population growth; the proportion of people chronically undernourished fell from 36 percent to 20 percent; adult literacy rose from 46 percent (in 1970) to 69 percent; and the share of households with access to safe water more than doubled, to 70 percent.

Although poor data cloud the trends in poverty, evidence suggests that "there has been considerable progress in reducing the incidence of poverty, a more modest reduction in the number of poor, and the achievement of somewhat better living standards for those who have remained in poverty."[1] The most dramatic gains have come in East Asia. Even as the region's population grew by 42.5 million, the number of absolute poor fell from an estimated 400 million in 1970 to between 170 million and 180 million in 1990. Progress was more modest but still impressive in South Asia, where the bulk of the world's poor live. Only in sub-Saharan Africa did poverty continue to spread as the number of poor increased. It is clear that without the impressive overall economic performance, hundreds of millions more people in the developing world would have slipped into poverty.

The reasons for this postwar miracle are numerous and varied—expanded international flows of capital, goods, services, and technology; development of efficient institutions and human resources; harnessing of entrepreneurship, from small farmers to large industry; higher levels of social spending; better infrastructure; and more investment. In some countries in the 1990s these trends have greatly accelerated, and developing countries have become a major source of growth in the world economy. The World Bank was one of many institutions that has tried to promote these trends, but the bulk of the credit goes to the countries themselves.

Progress has not been unbroken or universal, however. Since 1980, per capita incomes have stagnated or declined in Latin America and Africa. Development, it became clear, was not a one-way street. For many countries in those regions, the 1980s were a lost decade. But for developing countries as a whole, progress continued even during that bleak period. As Table 18.1 shows, per capita income accelerated from 2.6 percent a year in the period 1974–1980 to 3.4 percent in 1981–1993 (for gross domestic product [GDP] weighted by population). Improved performance in China and India (each more populous than sub-Saharan Africa and Latin America combined) and rapid growth in East Asia generally more than offset setbacks elsewhere.

Table 18.1 Population-Weighted Growth of Developing Countries' Real GDP Per Capita, 1965–1993

	% 1966–1973	% 1974–1980	% 1981–1993
Developing countries	3.5	2.6	3.4
East Asia	5.4	4.0	6.9
China	5.9	3.9	8.1
South Asia	0.9	1.6	2.9
India	1.1	1.5	3.0
Middle East and North Africa	3.5	2.8	–0.7
Sub-Saharan Africa	1.7	0.2	–1.2
Latin America and the Caribbean	4.3	2.5	0.0

Source: World Bank data.

But even with all the progress in the past fifty years, more than 1 billion people still live on one dollar a day or less, and many lack access to safe drinking water, schools, and health clinics. Environmental degradation threatens the sustainability of development in many areas. Gender bias and urban bias remain serious problems. Much has been achieved; much remains to be done.

The Role of the World Bank

The world has changed greatly over the past fifty years, and so has the Bank—in its membership, organizational structure, size of operations, and development agenda.[2] From 38 members in 1946 to 177 members today, the Bank has expanded to near-universal membership. New affiliates were established to complement the Bank's work and to address its new priorities. In 1956 the International Finance Corporation was formed to promote the private sector in member countries, and in 1960 the International Development Association (IDA) was established to address the needs of the poorest member countries. As foreign direct investment flows increased in size and importance, the International Centre for Settlement of Investment Disputes was established in 1966 to provide conciliation and arbitration services to foreign investors and host countries, and the Multilateral Investment Guarantee Agency was founded in 1988 to provide noncommercial investment risk insurance to foreign investments. The World Bank had become the World Bank Group. But throughout this period of change, the Bank's two principal roles remained the same: to mobilize financial resources from private savings and public sources and on-lend them for development and to help client countries address the "what" and the "how" of development. The Bank also responds selectively to shareholder requests for regional and global development initiatives.

The Financial Role

The World Bank was born of the conviction—strongly held by those assembled at Bretton Woods—that the twin disasters of depression and global war could be averted through international cooperation for mutual benefit, open trade, and full participation in the world economy by all nations. The conference delegates knew as well that open trade and full participation required healthy, functioning economies, recovered from the ravages of war and capable of providing a decent standard of living for all. It was clear then (as it is today) that domestic savings and investment alone could not do the job; for most of the world's developing countries, foreign financial flows—both private and official—would also be required. The World Bank was one of the financial intermediaries established to facilitate these flows.

The International Bank for Reconstruction and Development. Named formally the International Bank for Reconstruction and Development, the institution soon came to be known simply as the World Bank. Yet it is not a bank in any conventional sense. The IBRD accepts no deposits; has only governments as shareholders; lends to members that have limited access to capital markets, rather than to its richest, most creditworthy members; and limits its lending (by charter) to the value of its equity and callable capital—a 100 percent adequacy ratio against a normal banking ratio of 8 percent.

The IBRD was structured to rely on private sources to fund its operations and to promote private foreign investment. Indeed, the

IBRD has many of the characteristics of a private-sector institution. It is organized as a stock corporation, with voting rights proportional to equity investment. It finances itself in private capital markets through medium- and long-term bond issues on commercial terms, applying conservative financial policies that have earned and preserved a triple-A bond rating. The IBRD insists on disciplined lending, charges market-based rates of interest, and demands prompt payments of interest and principal. It has consistently earned a profit (over $1 billion in fiscal 1994), which its shareholders reinvest or direct to causes appropriate to its mission.

The IBRD has been remarkably effective in its financial inter-mediation. It borrows in capital markets at fixed rates (for maturities of thirty years and more) only a few hundredths of 1 percent higher than the rates paid by its largest government shareholders for their own bor-rowings. It passes this finance on to its members with a spread of 0.50 percent or less, from which it covers administrative expenses and gen-erates a profit. Such long maturities and low interest rates are available nowhere else to the IBRD's developing country members—not even to the most creditworthy. These terms represent a savings to developing countries of at least $3 billion a year (on loans outstanding of more than $100 billion). The IBRD has achieved all of this at a total cost to its shareholders of $10.7 billion in paid-in capital.

The International Development Association. The Bank's concessional arm, the International Development Association, is also a financial in-termediary. It is funded by grants from richer member countries, which it on-lends to the poorest and least creditworthy members. IDA funds are replenished every three years. The tenth and most recent IDA re-plenishment of $18 billion covers the period beginning July 1993. At this level of funding (around $6.5 billion annually), IDA accounts for about 12 percent of all concessional assistance worldwide. These replen-ishments are supplemented by IDA reflows (repayments) and transfers from IBRD's profits. IDA loans are interest-free (they are called cred-its) but carry a service charge of 0.75 percent a year. Until the mid-1980s, these loans were repayable over fifty years with a ten-year grace period before payments had to start. Recently, the maturity period was lowered to forty years for the poorest countries and thirty-five years for others.

IDA's membership and subscriptions (and hence its voting rights) differ from the IBRD's. But rather than create a new bureau-cracy, the Bank's shareholders decided that the Bank would carry out IDA's work, receiving a management fee in compensation. Today, a ref-erence to the World Bank includes both the IBRD and the IDA. In fact, there is no separate IDA staff, an arrangement that promotes the best possible coordination between the soft and hard lending areas and eases a country's transition from one to the other as its circumstances change. The arrangement also ensures that IDA-financed projects are subject to the same rigorous standards as IBRD-financed projects. The criteria for the allocation of IDA funds are agreed upon afresh in each replenishment. Current criteria focus on the strength of a country's efforts to reduce poverty in an environmentally sustainable manner and on its per capita income. There are guidelines on the amount of IDA resources that are made available to sub-Saharan Africa (46–50 percent) and to blend countries—that is, countries that are IDA eligible but that also borrow from the IBRD (30–35 percent).

The IDA replenishment process also provides a forum for the IDA donor countries to agree on the general uses of the resources provided. The consensus that poverty reduction is IDA's overarching objective has been translated into an increased operational focus on poverty reduction. In the 1990s, IDA has increased lending for basic human resource development and social services while emphasizing the importance of country policies in encouraging broad-based growth that increases the productivity and incomes of the poor.

Mobilizing resources from multiple sources. Through fiscal 1994, the Bank had lent over $330 billion for around six thousand operations, of which the IBRD accounted for about $250 billion and IDA for the rest. The largest growth in lending took place in the 1970s and the first half of the 1980s. Since then, IBRD lending has leveled off, reflecting poor policy environments in some cases and increased availability of private flows in others. IBRD and IDA lending has been relatively stable in real terms over the past several years, with total commitments currently running at about $21 billion.

To help ensure that loan funds are put to proper use, the Bank lays down conditions with its loans. Although these conditions are widely perceived as efforts to correct government failure, they are as often designed to correct market failures and imperfections. Because markets do not address income distribution or ensure that the poor receive basic services, the Bank also sees an important need for governance. It seeks to strengthen both markets and governments in the areas that are most appropriate for each.

The Bank addresses imperfections in global capital markets and in domestic markets of developing countries. Through its intermediation function, the Bank makes funds available on terms to which most countries would otherwise never have access, thereby addressing global market imperfections. The imperfections that affect developing country markets are as different as the countries themselves. Impediments range from inadequate roads, telecommunications, credit agencies, electricity, and agricultural extension services to underdeveloped human resources.

Before World War II, creditworthiness alone determined a country's access to market lending. For enterprise loans, banks conducted some rudimentary project appraisal, but they relied mainly on collateral and credit standing to ensure repayment. The World Bank devised a new lending paradigm by welding together the fragmentary concepts of project appraisal (to make sure the schemes it financed would be profitable enough to generate returns to repay the loan), competitive procurement procedures (to ensure the lowest project costs), monitoring of the end use of funds (to see that the project progressed as envisaged and to make midcourse corrections if necessary), and, beginning in the 1970s, evaluation after a project was completed (to see how well it had worked and to learn lessons for future lending). All of these elements improved the quality of lending, strengthened the chances of success, and built up the expertise of borrowing institutions in developing countries.

In addition to providing its own resources, the Bank helps catalyze resources from other sources: official bilateral and multilateral institutions, regional development banks, nongovernmental aid agencies, official export credit agencies, and the private sector. Roughly, for every dollar the Banks contributes, it mobilizes an additional dollar through such "cofinancing." Through more active use of Bank guarantees, greater efforts are being made to attract private-sector cofinancing, which helps borrowers gain access to syndicated commercial bank loans and international capital markets. These direct cofinancing efforts are supplemented by aid coordination groups for selected countries. The Bank currently chairs around forty consultative groups aimed at coordinating donor response to country needs.

The Advisory Role

In addition to its lending and cofinancing functions, the Bank takes advantage of its wealth of experience to help its members improve their policies, ideas, and expertise. Over time, this role has increased in importance relative to the financing role. It takes four forms.

1. The Bank engages in intensive dialogue with all of its borrowers on policies that influence the outcomes of investments it finances and on the overall macroeconomic environment, public expenditure policies, and institutional context that determines a country's economic performance. This dialogue is informed by regular and thorough analysis of economic and sectoral issues undertaken in close collaboration with borrowers. Frequently, the Bank's contribution to shaping its borrowers' policies, rather than the financing it provides, has the stronger

impact on the country's overall performance over the long term. Bank endorsement of borrower policies also catalyzes other funding for that country's development objectives. Examples of the effectiveness of this process range from Japan in the 1950s to Korea, China, Ghana, and Indonesia in the 1980s to Argentina, Mexico, and Poland in the 1990s.

2. The Bank promotes the use of the most effective practices in project preparation, technology choice, organizational structure, procurement, monitoring, and supervision. This helps to update and transfer continually the best available expertise to recipients.

3. To upgrade skills and to create new institutions or strengthen existing ones, the Bank has lent extensively for technical assistance, training, and institution building. The Bank's Economic Development Institute was established in 1956 to train developing country personnel, who then become trainers and institution builders at home. The Institute now provides about 150 courses annually for 4,400 participants.

4. As a development practitioner, the bank has a rich body of experience regarding effective development procedures, which it continually refines through research, publications, and seminars. Drawing on its own cross-country experience from fifty years in development and the analytical skills of its staff, seasoned by operational experience in the field, the Bank produces a formidable research output. Its many publications have elucidated the lessons of development. Its *World Development Report* is perhaps the most widely read annual economic report.

A Regional and Global Role

In addition to its principal financial and advisory roles, the Bank has addressed specific problems of regional or worldwide import. These endeavors have included the conquest of river blindness in West Africa, the amassing and dissemination of information on agricultural technologies through the Consultative Group for International Agricultural Research, and the funding of environmental projects of global importance with the UN Development Programme and the UN Environment Programme through the Global Environment Facility.

The Evolution of the Bank

As new challenges to sustainable growth and the equitable distribution of the benefits of growth have emerged over the past fifty years, the Bank has adjusted its strategies to respond to those challenges. The Bank began as a financier of postwar reconstruction in Europe in the 1940s, then shifted to conservative lending for what were considered

"bankable" projects in the early 1950s. In the 1960s, the institution became a full-blown development agency, broadening its sectoral coverage to the "soft" sectors and lending to poor countries on concessional
terms through a soft-loan affiliate. The Bank focused on improving living conditions for the poor in the 1970s and shifted its attention to policy reforms to improve the prospects for development in the 1980s.
Then, recognizing the range and depth of its activities and drawing on
the lessons learned from experience, in the 1990s the Bank embraced a
broad-based development strategy aimed at helping countries reduce
poverty and increase living standards by combining attention to sound
economic policies, human resources development, and environmental
sustainability. These goals were articulated in three *World Development
Reports*—in 1990 on poverty, in 1992 on the environment, and in 1993
on health reform.

The Bank's emphasis has shifted over time from individual projects to the policies, strategies, and institutions that help projects succeed. The changes in perspective were both large and small: from an
emphasis on the volume of investment to the productivity of investment; from physical capital to human capital; from infrastructure and
industry to developing poor rural areas; from a belief that the benefits
of economic growth would trickle down to the poor to an appreciation
that reducing poverty also requires extra measures targeted at the poor;
from a top-down to a bottom-up approach to projects that emphasize
beneficiary participation, client orientation, and market-determined
preferences; from state-led industrialization to the fostering of dynamic
private enterprise; and from exploitation of natural resources to ensuring sustainable development.

Toward a Holistic Approach: The 1990s

In many respects, as the Bank entered the 1990s the challenges facing
its borrowers remained the same as they had ever been. More than a
billion people lived in acute poverty. Rapid population growth and economic expansion were contributing to pressures on the environment. In
many countries the institutional infrastructure was an impediment to,
rather than a mechanism for, addressing these problems adequately. At
the same time, the context in which the Bank operates was becoming
more complex and more challenging and was changing rapidly.

There has been rapid integration in the global economy, with the
growth in trade outpacing growth in GDP. Developing countries are
leading this trend: They are the fastest component of the growth in trade.
Private capital flows to these countries have more than recovered from
the precipitous decline following the debt crisis and are now at record
levels. These flows were projected to reach between $157 billion and

$167 billion for 1993, consisting largely of foreign direct investments ($65 billion) and portfolio equity investments ($46.9 billion). This is three times the level of flows at the end of the 1980s, and it reflects the increasing integration of global financial markets. Implementation of the Uruguay Round agreements will keep these trends on an upward path.

Equally dramatic political developments have occurred, with the spread of democracy, the expansion of political participation, and the surge in the number of nongovernmental organizations. The most dramatic change, of course, has been the collapse of the former Soviet Union, which has contributed to the globalization of the Bank's membership.

The complexion and composition of the groups of countries that make up the Bank Group's clients have changed as well. There are now four such groups. Many countries are prospering in the new global environment; these include the most populous countries in the developing world (China and India), other countries in East Asia, and Latin America. These countries will progressively rely less on official development finance. At the other extreme are many countries, mostly in Africa, that have lagged behind. For them, poverty is increasing, and they risk being excluded from full participation in global markets and from the benefits such participation brings. In the middle are the countries that require further policy and institutional reforms and a more supportive international environment to join the ranks of the first group. Finally are the nations of Central and Eastern Europe and the former Soviet Union. These countries have abundant human capital but face obsolete and deteriorating physical capital and have seen massive declines in output. They are moving from command to market economies in a fluid political and institutional context. If successful in their reforms, they can look forward to restored growth that would provide a massive stimulus to the global economy. There are early signs of hope (notably in Poland and the Czech Republic), but for many the journey may be long and difficult.

Organizational Changes

To keep pace with changing demands, the Bank has created four new vice presidencies to strengthen internal capacity to take on new challenges as they arise: (1) a vice presidency for human resources and operations policy, to support a major emphasis on poverty reduction and human resource development; (2) a vice presidency for the environment and sustainable development, to bring a clearer focus on sustainability issues to all aspects of the Bank's work; (3) a vice presidency for finance and private-sector development, to enhance and support growth, private-sector development, and financial-sector reform; and (4) a vice presidency

for Europe and Central Asia, to assist new member countries of the former Soviet Union and Central and Eastern Europe in their transition to
market-based economies.

In addition, important changes are occurring in the World Bank
Group's institutional culture. There is greater concern for quality in the
performance of the project portfolio, more support for innovation and
cost consciousness, and more transparency and openness in external
dialogue.

Five development challenges. The Bank Group has renewed its commitment to help borrowers reduce poverty and improve living standards
by promoting sustainable growth and investing in people. Five major
development challenges, on which the Group will focus in the coming
years, face the Bank Group's clients:

- Pursuing economic reforms to enhance growth and reduce
  poverty
- Investing in people
- Protecting the environment
- Stimulating the private sector
- Reorienting government

New challenges

These five challenges are closely linked, and they reflect the Bank
Group's more holistic approach to development.

Six guiding principles. The agenda is large, and the Bank Group must
be agile and responsive while avoiding the danger of stretching itself
too thin. Six guiding principles have been adopted:

- Selectivity—identifying actions that will be the most helpful
  in improving a client's potential and the Bank's impact
- Partnership—seeking alliances with other development agencies (governments, international agencies, nongovernmental
  organizations, private-sector investors) to maximize the effectiveness of development assistance
- Client orientation—responding to the needs of clients and fa-
  cilitating their participation in the design and implementation
  of Bank-supported programs
- Results orientation—strengthening implementation of the
  projects and programs the Bank finances, thereby achieving
  better results "on the ground"
- Cost-effectiveness—ensuring that scarce resources are spent
  wisely

6 principles

- Financial integrity—maintaining the Bank's high standing in financial markets to ensure that it can provide finance to members on the best possible terms

Applying these guiding principles in the Bank Group's future work will require further changes in the way it conducts its business. Recent organizational changes have begun to strengthen internal capacities in human resource development, environmentally sustainable development, and financial- and private-sector development. They have also improved the Bank's ability to respond to new challenges presented by the countries in transition from centrally planned to market-oriented economies.

The consistent application of these six guiding principles and the new emphasis on efficiency, cost-effectiveness, and results mark the beginning of fundamental changes in the Bank Group's way of conducting business. The objective is clear: to create an institution that is leaner, more agile, more focused on priorities, and more responsive to changing client needs.

The Unfinished Agenda

The current rapid changes in the global environment are bound to influence the Bank's future, just as they have done in the past. Many successful countries in Asia may soon stop borrowing from the Bank, as European members did in the 1950s. The regional development banks, the European Union, and Japan are increasingly influential and financially important players on the development scene. Many borrowers are developing their own analytical skills and are using the resources of other agencies, both official and unofficial.

This increased competition offers new opportunities for the Bank to become even more responsive to the needs of its clients, demonstrating the flexibility that has helped it remain a relevant institution over time. Fifty years of evolution have achieved a great deal, but much unfinished business remains. History has shown that new challenges relentlessly follow old ones; history has also shown that the Bank has successfully changed with the times to serve its members more effectively. It is doing so again to help them eradicate poverty and ensure sustainable development.

If reforms are to succeed and take root, they must be "owned" by politicians and technocrats who believe in their efficacy and will direct their design. Experience has shown that reforms work when the Bank has supported local technocrats who are committed to the reforms and are able to tailor the new policies to local conditions. The borrower's commitment is the single most important factor in the success of Bank projects.

Conclusion

Several lessons stand out from the World Bank's development experience over the past fifty years. First, poverty reduction is best pursued through a direct assault on the conditions that perpetuate poverty. One way of doing this is to pursue rapid economic growth through strategies that make use of the most abundant asset of the poor—labor. This calls for policies that harness market incentives, social and political institutions, infrastructure, and technology to this end. The second method is to invest in people by providing basic social services to the poor. Primary health care, family planning, nutrition, and primary education are particularly important. These two strategies are mutually reinforcing; one without the other is insufficient.

Second, a prime requirement for rapid economic growth is a stable macroeconomic framework. Beyond a point, budget deficits, excessive government borrowing, and monetary expansion are quickly followed by inflation, chronic overvaluation of the currency, and loss of export competitiveness.

A third lesson is that integration with global markets for goods, services, finance, and technology yields major gains. Openness to trade, investment, and ideas is essential in encouraging domestic producers to reduce costs by adopting new technologies and improving existing ones.

Private enterprise and governments both have vital roles to play in development, and success lies in building on their complementarities rather than trying to choose between them. Competitive markets are the best way yet found to efficiently produce the goods and services consumers want. Such markets require a dynamic private sector motivated by adequate incentives and an environment conducive to savings, investment, and labor-intensive growth. But markets do not work in a vacuum—they require legal and regulatory frameworks governments need to provide efficiently. At other tasks, markets may be inadequate or may fail altogether, which is why governments must ensure adequate investments in infrastructure, provide essential services to the poor, and create safety nets to prevent others from slipping into poverty.

Fifth, for development to be sustainable, the environmental basis of production must be protected. Fortunately, many policies that encourage growth also protect the environment. These include removing subsidies that encourage excessive use of fossil fuels, irrigation, electricity, pesticides, and logging; clarifying rights to manage forests, fisheries, and land; and providing sanitation and drinking water to poor areas. Appropriate pricing and property rights are not enough in some cases, and strong institutions and clear rules may be needed to guard against degradation. Local participation can be of major assistance.

A sixth lesson is that rapid development requires good governance. Experience has shown that the way power is exercised for economic and social development is extremely important. Efficient legal and administrative structures, clear rules for economic actors and enforcement of contracts, speed and transparency in decisionmaking, and high standards of financial and political accountability are needed.

Participation is essential for economic development. Participation in project design and execution by beneficiaries can improve outcomes. Projects that give beneficiary communities a sense of ownership and a stake in their outcomes elicit grassroots support that protects projects from erosion by vested interests. Divesting power to local communities yields positive results.

Finally, investing in women is of vital importance to the economy, to households, and to children. The education of girls has a long-term impact on the productivity of women in the workplace and on fertility and infant and child mortality. Economic returns to education are often higher for women than for men.

Notes

K. Sarwar Lateef is economic adviser in the International Economics Department of the World Bank. The author is grateful for the substantial contribution made by Swaminathan S. Aiyar, a Delhi-based economist and journalist and a consultant to the World Bank, on which this chapter draws heavily, and for contributions and comments from numerous Bank colleagues.

1. The World Bank. 1990. *World Development Report*. New York: Oxford University Press.

2. The use of the term *Bank* refers to the International Bank for Reconstruction and Development and the International Development Association.

19

WORLD BANK/IMF:
50 YEARS IS ENOUGH

Bruce Rich

*In contrast to the previous chapter, Bruce Rich asserts that instead of con-
tributing to sustainable development, the World Bank and the International
Monetary Fund have actually undermined development. Rich finds fault with
the World Bank for taking a top-down approach to developmental policy. This
approach is a continuing feature of Bank operation, wherein developmental experts on the staff rather than the borrowers themselves determine what is best
for their countries. This policy has resulted in numerous ill-chosen projects that
have exacerbated developmental problems and left borrowing countries responsible for paying off loans for projects that have often been economically, financially, and managerially flawed. Rich also criticizes the Bank for ignoring the
environmental impact of its projects. The Bank has left in its wake extensive
ecological destruction as well as displaced persons. A third criticism concerns
Bank involvement with many of the world's most notorious dictatorships. More
recently, criticism has focused on the Bank's market-oriented approach to development with little regard for or assessment of negative social impacts.*

As the World Bank slouches toward its 50th anniversary, more and
more voices are questioning its credibility and its legacy. On May 27,
1993, 11 African heads of state gathered in Libreville, Gabon, where
they heard U.S. civil rights leader Jesse Jackson denounce the effects of
Bank policies on the poor in the developing world. "They no longer use
bullets and ropes. They use the World Bank and IMF," Jackson declared.

Reprinted with permission from the publishers of *50 Years Is Enough: A Case
Against the World Bank and the International Monetary Fund* edited by Kevin
Danaher (Boston: South End Press), pp. 6–13. Copyright © 1994.

In June, Republicans in the U.S. House of Representatives proposed an amendment to eliminate all U.S. funding of one of the Bank's two principal lending branches, the International Bank for Reconstruction and Development (IBRD). The motion was defeated by only two votes.

The past two years have been particularly difficult for the Bank. Its management defied the recommendations of the Morse Commission Report on India's Sardar Sarovar Dam and failed to develop meaningful measures to arrest the relentless decline of project quality documented in the Wapenhans report (the internal report found that more than one-third of Bank projects were essentially failing). A review of the Bank's past half-century shows that these problems are not new.

From Reconstruction to Development

The founders who gathered for the Bretton Woods Conference in July 1944 foresaw two primary functions for the Bank in the post–World War II era: first, reconstruction of Europe, and later, guaranteeing loans made by private banks for projects in poorer, developing countries. But as an agent of reconstruction, the Bank was stillborn. What war-torn Europe needed was not interest-bearing loans for specific projects that required lengthy preparation, but rapidly disbursing grants and concessional loans for balance of payments support and imports necessary to meet basic needs. In all, the Bank made only four loans for reconstruction, totaling US $497 million. It was the U.S.-initiated Marshall Plan, not the Bank, that was the engine of reconstruction, disbursing $41.3 billion by 1953.

Nor was there much demand for World Bank loan guarantees. When the World Bank took the next step and assumed its role as a direct lender for projects in developing countries, it ran into yet another problem. According to the Bank's third annual report for the years 1947–48, "the number of sound, productive investment opportunities thus far presented to the Bank is substantially smaller than was originally expected." Rather than question the need for the Bank's services, the report blamed the prospective borrowers for not borrowing, citing their lack of technical and planning skills and economic instability. The Bank's third president, Eugene Black, reiterated before the United Nations Economic and Social Council in 1950 that the reason the Bank had made so few loans was "not the lack of money but the lack of well-prepared and well-planned projects."

If there was insufficient demand for World Bank projects, the Bank decided, it would create sufficient demand. Warren Baum, who held positions in senior Bank management through the 1980s, admitted in 1970 that the Bank had to help design projects in a ceaseless struggle to keep the money flowing: "We do not get enough good projects to appraise unless we are involved intimately in their identification and preparation."

Distinguished economist Albert Hirschman reminisced about his experience in the early 1950s as an advisor to the newly created Colombian National Planning Council while he was working for the Bank, "which," he observed, "had taken an active part in having the Planning Council set up in the first place and then in recruiting me for it."

Hirschman recollected that he . . .

"wanted to learn as much as possible about the Colombian economy . . . in the hope of contributing marginally to the improvement of policy making. But word soon came from World Bank headquarters that I was principally expected to take, as soon as possible, the initiative in formulating some ambitious economic development plan that would spell out investment . . . and foreign aid targets over the next few years. . . . One aspect of this affair made me particularly uneasy. The task was supposedly crucial for Colombia's development, yet no Colombian was to be found who had any inkling of how to go about it. That knowledge was held only by a few foreign experts."

The Pressure to Lend

The Bank's sad record of supporting military regimes and governments that openly violated human rights began on August 7, 1947, with a $195 million reconstruction loan to the Netherlands. Seventeen days before the Bank approved the loan, the Netherlands had unleashed a war against anti-colonialist nationalists in its huge overseas empire in the East Indies, which had already declared its independence as the Republic of Indonesia. The Dutch sent 145,000 troops (from a nation with only ten million inhabitants at that time, economically struggling at 90 percent of 1939 production), and launched a total economic blockade of nationalist-held areas, causing considerable hunger and health problems among Indonesia's then 70 million inhabitants. In the United Nations, the World Bank was condemned for providing the Dutch government with the resources it needed to continue its economic recovery while waging full-scale war half-way around the world. Historians credit

threats by the U.S. Congress to cut off all bilateral aid to the Netherlands as critical in prompting the Dutch to halt the war and grant Indonesia independence in 1949. The Bank's intransigence was a marked
contrast and an ominous portent for the future.

In 1966, the Bank directly defied the United Nations, continuing
to lend money to South Africa and Portugal despite resolutions of the
General Assembly calling on all UN-affiliated agencies—including the
Bank—to cease financial support for both countries. Portugal's colonial
domination of Angola and Mozambique, and South Africa's apartheid
were, the resolutions declared, flagrant violations of the UN charter. But
the Bank argued that Article IV, Section 10 of its Charter, which pro-
hibits interference in the political affairs of any member, legally obliged
it to disregard the UN resolutions. As a result, the Bank approved loans
of $10 million to Portugal and $20 million to South Africa after the UN
resolution was passed. Even a personal plea from UN Secretary General
U Thant to Bank president George Woods was of no avail.

The 1960s also saw an increase in the Bank's pressure to lend, as
some of its borrowers began to pay back more annually to the Bank
than it disbursed in new loans. In 1963, 1964 and 1969 India transferred
more money to the World Bank than the Bank disbursed to it, despite
large cash infusions from the newly created International Development
Association (IDA). According to the 25-year history of the Bank written
by Edward Mason and Robert Asher, the increase in lending in the
1960s began by the 1970s to "create unmanageable demands for reverse
flows." Mason and Asher noted that "an institution limited to a zero net
transfer of capital can hardly be characterized as a development institution." To solve the problem, the Bank had two choices: forgive or write
down World Bank debt, or increase the volume of lending to the same
countries, thereby piling on more debt. The latter scenario would work
best if the Bank could obtain more funds to disburse as grants or concessional, low-interest loans.

On a Mission from McNamara

World Bank president Robert McNamara temporarily solved the
dilemma by increasing lending (IBRD and IDA combined) at a phenomenal rate, from $953 million in 1968 to $12.4 billion in 1981. If
ever there was an example of unsustainable growth, McNamara's World
Bank was it. His views on management help to clarify his legacy. In the
1960s, he proclaimed that "running any large organization is the same,
whether it's the Ford Motor Corporation, the Catholic Church, or the
Department of Defense. Once you get to a certain scale they're all the

same." But McNamara's master stoke wasn't in how he managed the Bank; it was in how he redefined its mission. It was McNamara who introduced the idea of the Bank as benevolent patron of the poor, and it was McNamara who gave the Bank its first environmental mandate.

McNamara's mission for the Bank to help the poor was couched in idealistic, moralistic terms. ("All of the great religions teach the value of each human life . . . The extremes of poverty and deprivation are simply no longer acceptable. It is development's task to deal with them," he exhorted in 1973 at the Bank/Fund annual meeting in Nairobi.) But the means were infused with a disquieting lack of accountability and with a structure of top-down control. As pressure to lend intensified, the immediate solution was to employ the same approaches and technologies everywhere, with predictable results: they were inefficient at best and often so environmentally and socially inappropriate that they were destined to fail.

At the 1972 Stockholm Conference on the Human Environment, McNamara claimed that the Bank's environmental office—which he had established in 1970—reviewed "each project processed by the Bank" and conducted "careful in-house studies" of the ecological components, using comprehensive environmental criteria embodied in checklists that "encompass the entire spectrum of development." In two years, he claimed, the Bank had established a formidable environmental record, which, he implied, was worthy of emulation: "While in principle the Bank could refuse a loan on environmental grounds . . . the fact is no such case has yet arisen. Since initiating our environmental review, we have found that in every instance the recommended safeguards can and have been successfully implemented."

But the statement had no basis in reality. In 1972, the environmental office consisted of one senior advisor and a recently hired assistant. The environmental review of every project and "successful implementation" of "safeguards" were, in any meaningful sense of the words, non-existent.

Some of the more egregious Bank environmental follies of the 1980s began in the 1970s as a major component of the "poverty" strategy: huge agricultural colonization and land-clearing schemes on poor soils in tropical forests in Latin America and Asia. The performance of Bank agricultural projects approved during the McNamara period was abysmal in the Bank's own terms of meeting appraised economic rates of return, avoiding huge cost and time overruns, and reaching the poor. The 1989 review of evaluation results produced by the Bank's Operations Evaluation Department examined 82 Bank agricultural projects, most approved between 1975 and 1982, the prime years for McNamara-style "poverty" lending. Nearly 45 percent were judged to be unsatisfactory.

Beyond the wasted money and the environmental devastation, there was an even more sinister side to the Bank during the McNamara years: the World Bank's predilection for increasing support to military regimes that tortured and murdered their subjects, sometimes immediately after the violent overthrow of more democratic governments. In 1979, Senator James Abourezk, a liberal Democrat from South Dakota, denounced the Bank on the Senate floor, noting that the Bank was increasing "loans to four newly repressive governments [Chile, Uruguay, Argentina, and the Philippines] twice as fast as all others." He noted that 15 of the world's most repressive governments would receive a third of all World Bank loan commitments in 1979, and that Congress and the Carter administration had cut off bilateral aid to four of the 15—Argentina, Chile, Uruguay and Ethiopia—for flagrant human rights violations. He blasted the Bank's "excessive secretiveness" and reminded his colleagues that "we vote the money, yet we do not know where it goes."

The Bank abandoned even the most cynical pretensions to intellectual integrity and rigor when, shortly after cutting off lending to the democratically elected Allende government in Chile in the early 1970s, it geared up to lend to Ceaucescu's Romania, one of the most centrally planned and repressive regimes on earth. Between 1974 and 1982, the period of Bank lending, Romania became even more centrally planned and repressive. Some Bank staff had trouble seeing the economic logic of lending to Ceaucescu. According to former Bank staff member Art Van de Laar, at one meeting, McNamara responded to questions about Romania with a statement that he had "great faith in the financial morality of socialist countries in repaying debts." At that point, a Bank vice-president ironically observed the "Allende's Chile had perhaps not yet become socialist enough."

A 1979 World Bank country economic study on Romania cites Ceaucescu's pronouncements and, under a section entitled, "Importance of Centralized Economic Control," concludes that "it remains probable that Romania will continue to enjoy one of the highest growth rates among developing countries over the next decade and that it will largely succeed in implementing its development targets."

In many ways, Romania was the ideal Bank borrower: policy dialogue and loan negotiations were streamlined and efficiently focused in the Executive Branch of the government, and the Bank's comparative advantage in lending huge amounts for gigantic infrastructure schemes was identical with the government's priorities for massive power projects, heavy industry, irrigation and large-scale agro-industrial schemes. By 1980, Romania was the IBRD's eighth-biggest borrower out of a total of 19; in 1982, it ranked eleventh in loan commitments out of a total of 43 borrowers that year.

New Ideologues and Policy-Based Lending

It is ironic that at the same time it was pushing money for centralized planning in Romania, new ideologues in the Bank were making their presence known, fervently pushing free-market solutions to all the world's ills. Partly because of the political unsustainability of the austerity measures imposed by the International Monetary Fund (IMF), the Bank entered into "policy dialogue" with Southern governments about appropriate "market oriented" policies, making its first structural adjustment loan in 1980. Although the Bank subsequently acknowledged that it had failed to assess the possible negative social impact of these loans, they nevertheless grew to a quarter of its portfolio by mid-decade and have remained near that level ever since. The policies associated with adjustment programs—export promotion, trade liberalization, privatization, deregulation, wage restraint and budget and credit cuts—led not only to a deepening and spreading of poverty around the globe, but also to intensified environmental damage.

During the 1980s, however, the Bank's environmental rhetoric remained very much the same. In 1981, Bank President A.W. Clausen claimed in one of his first speeches that "for a decade now, the Bank has required . . . that every project it finances be reviewed by a special environmental unit—nearly two thirds of the projects reviewed have raised no serious health or environmental questions, and I'm pleased to say that it has been possible to incorporate protective measures in all the projects we have financed over the past decade."

It was only after dozens of Congressional hearings and mounting NGO campaigns around the world that Clausen's successor, Barber Conable, admitted in 1987 that "the World Bank has been part of the problem in the past" as far as the environment was concerned. But a recent loan decision serves as a good example of how Conable's attempted reforms have failed to influence Bank practice.

On June 29th, the second to last day of the Bank's 1993 fiscal year, the Bank's Board approved a $400 million loan to India for coal-fired power generation over objections by Germany, the United States and Belgium on environmental, social and economic grounds. The representatives of these nations refused (in vain) to approve the loan because, among other things, the loan agreement fails to adequately rehabilitate 140,000 poor people displaced by previous Bank projects for coal-mining and coal-fired electricity production in India. It also fails to evaluate alternatives that could provide as much electricity at less economic and ecological cost (and less indebtedness) for India.

The Bank plans to pour money into coal-fired power production with half-billion-dollar loans to India every 18 to 24 months. If the whole program is realized it would add 16,000 megawatts of coal-burning power plants over the next decade in India alone, which would account for an estimated 2.5 percent of the world's increase in global warming and would increase CO_2 emissions over the same period.

Mission Accomplished?

Has the Bank succeeded in helping the poor or even the governments of the poor? Consider the figures in its 1992 Annual Report. In that year, the Bank (both the International Bank for Reconstruction and Development and the International Development Association) paid out $16.441 billion in gross disbursements to its borrowers. However, net disbursements (disbursements less the amount of money repaid to the Bank on outstanding loans and credits) totaled $6.258 billion. In the same year, the Bank's borrowers paid companies in rich Organization for Economic Cooperation and Development (OECD) nations $6.547 billion for procurement of goods and services on outstanding World Bank loans. In other words, when all is said and done, the nations that borrowed money from the World Bank paid $198 million more to OECD economies for Bank-associated procurement than the borrowing countries actually received from the Bank in 1992.

Meanwhile, the number of unemployed people has grown rapidly around the world (projected by the International Labor Organization to reach one billion in 1994), and wage levels have plummeted, often to levels half as low as at the beginning of the 1980s. Small producers have been displaced by larger-scale export schemes, and education and health-care systems have deteriorated. The result has been a rapid expansion of poverty and a concentration of national incomes: Brazil, Jamaica and Ghana are cases in point.

On this, the 50th anniversary of the birth of the World Bank, it is good to remember that, for most of its life, it has been a creature of the Cold War; geopolitically, the most consistent rationale for development assistance over the decades has been checking the advance of communism, or even that of non-communist regimes and systems friendly to the Soviet Union. For decades, the United States and other leading industrialized countries gave World Bank management a relatively free hand. They were not overly concerned whether the Bank was propping up particularly nasty regimes or traducing its purported poverty and environmental goals, since it was above all an invaluable institution for helping to win the Cold War—and on this last point they were right. But the Cold War is over.

The World Bank is an institution out of time and place. Fifty years of the Bank as we know it is enough. If, indeed, the role of multilateral institutions is an important one in the new world order, the World Bank must literally remake itself, open its files, end its secret ways and document and learn from its mistakes—not merely on projects, but in the foundations of its economic policy prescriptions. It needs to trade in the policies developed by old cold warriors and grasp the essential meaning of its favorite new phrase: sustainable development. The world (which, after all, provided the Bank with a name) has had enough lies and enough secrecy.

20

PRODUCTIVITY: GROWTH AND CONVERGENCE

J. Bradford De Long

Earlier chapters, such as the one by Peter Drucker, argued that the transfer of technology from the industrialized countries to the Third World was one of the prime causes of economic growth and the weakening of the state system. Convergence theory, J. Bradford De Long explains, was devised by economic historians to explain the impact of this technology transfer on global patterns of economic growth. Proponents of convergence theory argue that an inverse relationship exists between levels and rates of productivity. The lower the original level of productivity, the higher the potential for rapid growth. Over the long run this means the gap between rich and poor countries will close. De Long points out that one of the previous studies that found evidence of convergence had examined only countries that had subsequently converged. When De Long corrected the sample selection bias, convergence disappeared. He then analyzes other variables to determine whether the pattern of growth he found can be explained. The optimistic view that the gap between rich and poor countries is closing is not sustained by the data.

Economists have always expected the "convergence" of national productivity levels. The theoretical logic behind this belief is powerful. The per capita income edge of the West is based on its application of the storehouse of industrial and administrative technology of the Industrial Revolution. This storehouse is open: modern technology is a

Reprinted with permission from the author from the *American Economic Review*, vol. 78, 5 (1986): 1138–1148.

public good. The benefits of tapping this storehouse are great, and so nations will strain every nerve to assimilate modern technology and their incomes will converge to those of industrial nations.

William Baumol (1986) argues that convergence has shown itself strongly in the growth of industrial nations since 1870.[1] According to Baumol, those nations positioned to industrialize are much closer together in productivity now than a century ago. He bases this conclusion on a regression of growth since 1870 on 1870 productivity for sixteen countries covered by Angus Maddison (1982).[2]

Baumol's finding of convergence might—even though Baumol himself does not believe that it should—naturally be read to support two further conclusions. First, slow relative growth in the United States since World War II was inevitable: convergence implies that in the long run divergent national cultures, institutions, or policies cannot sustain significant productivity edges over the rest of the developed world. Second, one can be optimistic about future development. Maddison's sixteen all assimilated modern technology and converged; perhaps all developing nations will converge to Western living standards once they acquire a foundation of technological literacy.

But when properly interpreted Baumol's finding is less informative than one might think. For Baumol's regression uses an *ex post* sample of countries that are now rich and have successfully developed. By Maddison's choice, those nations that have not converged are excluded from his sample because of their resulting present relative poverty. Convergence is thus all but guaranteed in Baumol's regression, which tells us little about the strength of the forces making for convergence among nations that in 1870 belonged to what Baumol calls the "convergence club."

Only a regression run on an *ex ante* sample, a sample not of nations that have converged but of nations that seemed in 1870 likely to converge, can tell us whether growth since 1870 exhibits "convergence." The answer to this *ex ante* question—have those nations that a century ago appeared well placed to appropriate and utilize industrial technology converged?—is no. . . .

Maddison (1982) compiles long-run national income and aggregate productivity data for sixteen successful capitalist nations.[3] Because he focuses on nations which (a) have a rich data base for the construction of historical national accounts and (b) have successfully developed, the nations in Maddison's sixteen are among the richest nations in the world today. Baumol regresses the average rate of annual labor productivity growth over 1870–1979 on a constant and on the log of labor productivity in 1870 for this sample. He finds the inverse relationship of the first line of Table 20.1. The slope is large enough to erase by 1979 almost all initial income gaps, and the residual variance is small.

Table 20.1 Regressions Using Maddison's Sixteen

Independent Variable	Dependent Variable	Constant	Slope Coefficient	Standard Error of Estimate	R^2
Natural Log of 1870 Productivity	Annual Percent Productivity Growth	5.251	−0.749	.14	.87
			.075		
Natural Log of 1870 Income	Log Difference of 1979 and 1870 Income	8.457	−0.995	.15	.88
			.094		

Source: Data from Maddison (1982).

Regressing the log difference in per capita income between 1870 and 1979 on a constant and the log of per capita income in 1870 provides a slightly stronger case for convergence, as detailed in the second line of Table 20.1. . . . The logarithmic income specification offers two advantages. The slope has the intuitive interpretation that a value of minus one means that 1979 and 1870 relative incomes are uncorrelated, and extension of the sample to include additional nations becomes easier.

Baumol's regression line tells us little about the strength of forces making for convergence since 1870 among industrial nations. The sample suffers from selection bias, and the independent variable is unavoidably measured with error. Both of these create the appearance of convergence whether or not it exists in reality. Sample selection bias arises because any nations relatively rich in 1870 that have not converged fail to make it into Maddison's sixteen. Maddison's sixteen thus include Norway but not Spain, Canada but not Argentina, and Italy but not Ireland. . . .

The unbiased sample used here meets three criteria. First, it is made up of nations that had high potential for economic growth as of 1870, in which modern economic growth had begun to take hold by the middle of the nineteenth century. Second, inclusion in the sample is not conditional on subsequent rapid growth. Third, the sample matches Baumol's as closely as possible, both because the best data exist for Maddison's sixteen and because analyzing an unbiased sample close to Baumol's shows that different conclusions arise not from different estimates but from removing sample selection and errors in variables' biases.

Per capita income in 1870 is an obvious measure of whether a nation was sufficiently technologically literate and integrated into world trade in 1870 to be counted among the potential convergers. . . .

. . . The choice of cutoff level itself requires balancing three goals: including only nations which really did in 1870 possess the social capability for rapid industrialization; including as many nations in Baumol's sample as possible; and building as large a sample as possible. . . .

If the convergence club membership cutoff is set low enough to include all Maddison's sixteen, then nations with 1870 incomes above 300 1975 dollars are included. This sample covers half the world. All Europe including Russia, all of South America, and perhaps others (Mexico and Cuba?) were richer than Japan in 1870. This sample does not provide a fair test of convergence. The Japanese miracle is a miracle largely because there was little sign in 1870 that Japan—or any nation as poor as Japan—was a candidate for rapid industrialization.

The second poorest of Maddison's sixteen in 1870 was Finland. Taking Finland's 1870 income as a cutoff leads to a sample in which Japan is removed, while Argentina, Chile, East Germany,[4] Ireland, New Zealand, Portugal, and Spain are added.

All the additional nations have strong claims to belong to the 1870 convergence club. All were well integrated into the Europe-based international economy. All had bright development prospects as of 1870. . . . Argentina, Chile, and New Zealand were grouped in the nineteenth century with Australia and Canada as countries with temperate climates, richly endowed with natural resources, attracting large-scale immigration and investment, and exporting large quantities of raw and processed agricultural commodities. They were all seen as natural candidates for the next wave of industrialization.

Ireland's economy was closely integrated with the most industrialized economy in the world. Spain and Portugal had been the technological leaders of Europe during the initial centuries of overseas expansion—their per capita incomes were still above the European mean in the 1830s (Paul Bairoch, 1981)—and had retained close trading links with the heart of industrial Europe. Coke was used to smelt iron in Asturias in the 1850s, and by 1877 3,950 miles of railroad had been built in Spain. It is difficult to see how one could exclude Portugal and Spain from the convergence club without also excluding nations like Sweden and Finland.

Baumol's sample failed to include those nations that should have belonged to any hypothetical convergence club but that nevertheless did not converge. The enlarged sample might include nations not in the 1870 convergence club. Consider Kuwait today: Kuwait is rich, yet few would take its failure to maintain its relative standard of living over the next fifty years as evidence against convergence. For Kuwait's present wealth does not necessarily carry with it the institutional capability to turn oil wealth into the next generation's industrial wealth. . . .

The volume of overseas investment poured into the additional nations by investors from London and Paris between 1870 and 1913 tells us that investors thought these nation's development prospects good. Herbert Feis' (1930) standard estimates of French and British overseas investment [the interested reader should refer to Table 2, p. 1143 of the original article—*Eds.*] show the six non-European nations among the top ten[5] recipients of investment per capita from France and Britain, and four of the five top recipients of investment belong to the once-rich twenty-two.[6] Every pound or franc invested is an explicit bet that the recipient country's rate of profit will remain high and an implicit bet that its rate of economic growth will be rapid. The coincidence of the nations added on a per capita income basis and the nations that would have been added on a foreign investment basis is powerful evidence that these nations do belong in the potential convergence club.

Errors in estimating 1870 income are unavoidable and produce equal and opposite errors in 1870–1979 growth. These errors therefore create the appearance of convergence where it does not exist in reality. . . .[7]

From one point of view, the relatively poor quality of much of the nineteenth century data is not a severe liability for this chapter. Only if there is less measurement error than allowed for will the results be biased against convergence. A more direct check on the importance of measurement error can be performed by examining convergence starting at some later date for which income estimates are based on a firmer foundation. A natural such date is 1913.[8] The relationship between initial income and subsequent growth is examined for the period 1913–1979 in Table 20.2. . . .

Table 20.2 Maximum Likelihood Estimation for the Once-Rich Twenty-Two, 1913–1979

p	Slope Coefficient B	Standard Error of Slope	Standard Error of Regression	Standard Error of 1870 PCI
0.0	−.333	.116	.171	.000
0.5	−.140	.136	.151	.107
1.0	0.021	.158	.133	.133
2.0	0.206	.191	.106	.150
infinity	0.444	.238	.000	.167

Source: Data from Maddison (1982).

The longer 1870–1979 sample of Table 20.3 . . . is slightly more hospitable to convergence than is the 1913–1979 sample, but for neither sample do the regression lines reveal a significant inverse relationship between initial income and subsequent growth. When it is assumed that there is no measurement error in 1870 income, there is a large negative slope to the regression line. But even in this case the residual disturbance term is large. When measurement error variance is assumed equal to half disturbance variance, the slope is slightly but not significantly negative.

For the central case of equal variances growth since 1870 is unrelated to income in 1870. There is no convergence. Those countries with income edges have on average maintained them. If measurement error is assumed larger than the regression disturbance there is not convergence but divergence. Nations rich in 1870 or 1913 have subsequently widened relative income gaps. The evidence can be presented in other ways. The standard deviations of log income are given in Table 20.4. Maddison's sixteen do converge: the standard deviation of log income in 1979 is only 35 percent of its 1870 value. But the appearance of convergence is due to selection bias: the once-rich twenty-two have as wide a spread of relative incomes today as in 1870.

The failure of convergence to emerge for nations rich in 1870 is due to the nations—Chile, Argentina, Spain, and Portugal. In the early 1970s none of these was a democracy. Perhaps only industrial nations with democratic political systems converge. A dummy variable for democracy over 1950–80 is significant in the central ($p = 1$) case in the once-rich twenty-two regression in a at the 1 percent level, as detailed in Table 20.5.

But whether a nation is a democracy over 1950–80 is not exogenous but is partly determined by growth over the preceding century. As

Table 20.3 Maximum Likelihood Estimation for the Once-Rich Twenty-Two, 1913–1979

p	Slope Coefficient B	Standard Error of Slope	Standard Error of Regression	Standard Error of 1870 PCI
0.0	−.566	.144	.207	.000
0.5	−.292	.192	.192	.136
1.0	0.110	.283	.170	.170
2.0	0.669	.463	.134	.190
infinity	1.381	.760	.000	.196

Source: Data from Maddison (1982).

Table 20.4 Standard Deviations of Log Output for Maddison's Sixteen and the Once-Rich Twenty-Two

Sample	1870	1913	1979
Maddison's 16	.411	.355	.145
Once-Rich 22	.315	.324	.329

Source: Data from Maddison (1982).

of 1870 it was not at all clear which nations would become stable democracies. Of the once-rich twenty-two, France, Austria (including Czechoslovakia), and Germany were empires; Britain had a restricted franchise; Spain and Portugal were semiconstitutional monarchies; the United States had just undergone a civil war; and Ireland was under foreign occupation. That all of these countries would be stable democracies by 1950 seems *ex ante* unlikely. Table 20.6 shows that shifting to an *ex ante* measure of democracy[9] removes the correlation. Whether a nation's politics are democratic in 1870 has little to do with growth since. The elective affinity of democracy and opulence is not one way with democracy as cause and opulence as effect.

There is one striking *ex ante* association between growth over 1870–1979 and a predetermined variable: a nation's dominant religious establishment. As Table 20.7 shows, a religious establishment variable that is one for Protestant, one-half for mixed, and zero for Catholic nations is significantly correlated with growth as long as measurement error variance is not too high.[10]

Table 20.5 Democracy over 1950–1980 and Long-Run Growth for the Once-Rich Twenty-Two, 1870–1979

p	Slope Coefficient B	Standard Error of Slope	Coefficient on Democracy Variable	Standard Error	Standard Error in 1870 PCI	Standard Error of Regression
0.0	−.817	.277	.495	.085	.155	.000
0.5	−.744	.203	.476	.084	.154	.109
1.0	−.599	.208	.437	.090	.150	.150
2.0	0.104	.227	.248	.071	.131	.185
infinity	1.137	.019	.044	.003	.000	.198

Source: Data from Maddison (1982).

Table 20.6 Democracy in 1870 and Long-Run Growth for the Once-Rich Twenty-Two, 1870–1979

p	Slope Coefficient B	Standard Error of Slope	Coefficient on Democracy Variable	Standard Error	Standard Error in 1870 PCI	Standard Error of Regression
0.0	−.567	.342	.001	.091	.207	.000
0.5	−.272	.322	−.038	.094	.192	.136
1.0	0.164	.454	−.095	.115	.169	.169
2.0	0.742	.976	−.170	.180	.131	.155
infinity	1.231	.167	−.195	.022	.000	.194

Source: Data from Maddison (1982).

Table 20.7 Dominant Religion in 1870 and Long-Run Growth for the Once-Rich Twenty-Two, 1870–1979

p	Slope Coefficient B	Standard Error of Slope	Coefficient on Democracy Variable	Standard Error	Standard Error in 1870 PCI	Standard Error of Regression
0.0	−.789	.252	.429	.088	.166	.000
0.5	−.688	.225	.403	.088	.164	.116
1.0	−.470	.248	.347	.098	.158	.158
2.0	0.375	.232	.132	.061	.132	.187
infinity	1.199	.021	−.003	.004	.000	.197

Source: Data from Maddison (1982).

This regression is very difficult to interpret.[11] It does serve as an example of how culture may be associated with substantial divergence in growth performance. But "Protestantism" is correlated with many things —early specialization in manufacturing (for a given level of income), a high investment ratio, and a northern latitude, to name three. Almost any view—except a belief in convergence—of what determines long-run growth is consistent with this correlation between growth and religious establishment. Moreover, this correlation will not last: neither fast grower Japan nor fast grower Italy owes anything to the Protestant ethic. The main message of Table 20.7 is that, for the once-rich twenty-two, a country's religious establishment has been a surprisingly good proxy for the social capability to assimilate modern technology.

The long-run data do not show convergence on any but the most optimistic reading. They do not support the claim that those nations that should have been able to rapidly assimilate industrial technology have all converged. Nations rich among the once-rich twenty-two in 1870 have not grown more slowly than the average of the sample. And of the nations outside this sample, only Japan has joined the industrial leaders.

This is not to say that there are no forces pushing for convergence. Convergence does sometimes happen. Technology is a public good. Western Europe (except Iberia) and the British settlement colonies of Australia, Canada, and the United States are now all developed. Even Italy, which seemed outside the sphere of advanced capitalism two generations ago, is near the present income frontier reached by the richest nations. The convergence of Japan and Western Europe toward U.S. standards of productivity in the years after World War II is an amazing achievement, and this does suggest that those present at the creation of the post–World War II international order did a very good job. But others—Spain, Portugal, Ireland, Argentina, and Chile—that one would in 1870 have thought capable of equally sharing this prosperity have not done so.[12] The capability to assimilate industrial technology appears to be surprisingly hard to acquire, and it may be distressingly easy to lose.

The forces making for "convergence" even among industrial nations appear little stronger than the forces making for "divergence." The absence of convergence pushes us away from a belief that in the long run technology transfer both is inevitable and is the key factor in economic growth. It pushes us away from the belief that even the nations of the now industrial West will have roughly equal standards of living in 2090 or 2190. And the absence of convergence even among nations relatively rich in 1870 forces us to take seriously arguments like Romer's (1986) that the relative income gap between rich and poor may tend to widen.

Notes

1. Consider Baumol (1986): "Among the main observations . . . is the remarkable convergence. . . . [T]here is a strong inverse correlation between a country's productivity . . . in 1870 and its . . . productivity growth since then," and Baumol (1987): "Even more remarkable . . . is the convergence in . . . living standards of the leading industrial countries. . . . In 1870 . . . productivity in Australia, the leader, was 8 times . . . Japan's (the laggard). By 1979, the ratio . . . had fallen to about two."

2. Moses Abramovitz (1986) follows the behavior of these sixteen over time and notes that even among these nations "convergence" is almost entirely a post–World War II phenomenon. Abramovitz' remarks on how the absence of the "social capability" to grasp the benefits of the Industrial Revolution may prevent even nations that could benefit greatly from industrializing are well worth reading. Also very good on the possible determinants of the social capability to assimilate technology are Irma Adelman and Cynthia Taft Morris (1980), Gregory Clark (1987), and Richard Easterlin (1981).

3. Maddison's focus on nations that have been economically successful is deliberate; his aim in (1964), (1982), and (1987) is to investigate the features of successful capitalist development. In works like Maddison (1970, 1983) he has analyzed the long-run growth and development of less successful nations.

4. Perhaps only nations that have remained capitalist should be included in the sample, for occupation by the Red Army and subsequent relative economic stagnation has no bearing on whether the forces making for convergence among industrial capitalist economies are strong. There is only one centrally planned economy in the unbiased sample, and its removal has negligible quantitative effects on the estimated degree of convergence.

5. The foreign investment figures do provide a powerful argument for adding other Latin American nations—Mexico, Brazil, and Cuba—to the sample of those that ought to have been in the convergence club. Inclusion of these nations would weigh heavily against convergence.

6. Japan would not merit inclusion in the 1870 convergence club on the basis of foreign investment before World War I, for Japanese industrialization

was not financed by British capital. Foreign investors' taste for Japan was much less, investment being equal to about one pound sterling per head and far below investment in such nations as Venezuela, Russia, Turkey, and Egypt. Admittedly, Japan was far away and not well known, but who would have predicted that Japan would have five times the measured per capita GNP of Argentina by 1979?

7. By contrast, errors in measuring 1979 per capita income induce no systematic bias in the relationship between standard of living in 1870 and growth since, although they do diminish the precision of coefficient estimates.

8. The data for 1913 are much more plentiful and solid than for other years in the early years of the twentieth century because of the concentration of historians' efforts on obtaining a pre–World War I benchmark. Beginning the sample at 1913 does mean that changes in a country's "social capability" for development as a result of World War I appear in the error term in the regression. If those nations that suffered most badly in World War I were nations relatively poor in World War I, there would be cause for alarm that the choice of 1913 had biased the sample against finding convergence when it was really present. But the major battlefields of World War I lay in and the largest proportional casualties were suffered by relatively rich nations at the core of industrial Europe.

9. Defined as inclusion of the electorate of more than half the adult male population.

10. The once-rich twenty-two are split into nations that had Protestant religious establishments in 1870 (Australia, Denmark, Finland, E. Germany, Netherlands, New Zealand, Norway, Sweden, U.K., and United States), intermediate nations—nations that either were split in established religion in 1870 or that had undergone violent and prolonged religious wars between Protestant and Catholics in the centuries after the Protestant Reformation—(Belgium, Canada, France, West Germany, and Switzerland), and nations that had solid Catholic religious establishments in 1870 (Argentina, Austria, Chile, Ireland, Italy, Portugal, and Spain). This classification is judgmental and a matter of taste: are the Netherlands one of the heartlands of the Protestant Ethic or are they one of the few nations tolerant and pluralistic on matters of religion in the seventeenth century?

11. The easy explanation would begin with the medieval maxim *homo mercator vix aut numquam placere potest Deo:* the merchant's business can never please God. Medieval religious discipline was hostile to market capitalism, the Protestant Reformation broke this discipline down in some places, and capitalism flourished most and modern democratic growth took hold strongest where this breakdown of medieval discipline had been most complete.

But this easy explanation is at best incomplete. Initially the Reformation did not see a relaxation of religious control. Strong Protestantism—Calvin's Geneva or Cromwell's Republic of the Saints—saw theology and economy closely linked in a manner not unlike the Ayatollah's Iran. And religious fanaticism is not often thought of as a source of economic growth.

Nevertheless the disapproval of self-interested profit seeking by radical Protestantism went hand-in-hand with seventeenth century economic development. And by 1800 profit seeking and accumulation for accumulation's sake had become morally praiseworthy activities in many nations with Protestant religious establishments. How was the original Protestant disapproval for the market transformed? Accounting for the evolution of the economic ethic of the Protestant West from Jean Calvin to Cotton Mather to Benjamin Franklin to

Andrew Carnegie is a deep puzzle in economic history. The best analysis may still be the psychological account given by Max Weber (1958). Originally published in 1905.

12. One can find good reasons—ranging from the Red Army to landlord political dominance to the legacy of imperialism—for the failure of each of the additional nations to have reached the world's achieved per capita income frontier in 1979. But the fact that there are good reasons for the relative economic failure of each of these seven nations casts substantial doubt on the claim that the future will see convergence, for "good reasons" for economic failure will always be widespread. It is a safe bet that in 2090 one will be able *ex post* to identify similar "good reasons" lying behind the relative economic decline of those nations that will have fallen out of the industrial core.

References

Abramovitz, M. 1986. "Catching Up, Forging Ahead, and Falling Behind," *Journal of Economic History*, June, 46, 385–406.

Adelman, I. and C. T. Morris. 1980. "Patterns of Industrialization in the Nineteenth and Early Twentieth Centuries," in Paul Uselding, ed., *Research in Economic History*, Vol. 5, Greenwich: JAI Press, 217–46.

Bairoch, P. 1981. "The Main Trends in National Economic Disparities Since the Industrial Revolution," in P. Bairoch and M. Lévy-Leboyer, eds., *Disparities in Economic Development Since the Industrial Revolution*, New York: St. Martin's Press.

Baumol, W. 1986. "Productivity Growth, Convergence, and Welfare," *American Economic Review*, December, 76, 1072–85.

———. 1987. "America's Productivity 'Crisis'." *The New York Times*, February 15, 3:2.

Clark, G. 1987. "Why Isn't the Whole World Developed? Lessons from the Cotton Mills," *Journal of Economic History*, March, 47, 141–74.

Easterlin, R. 1981. "Why Isn't the Whole World Developed?," *Journal of Economic History*, March, 41, 1–19.

Feis, H. 1930. *Europe, The World's Banker*, New Haven: Yale.

Maddison, A. 1987. "Growth and Slowdown in Advanced Capitalist Economies," *Journal of Economic Literature*, June, 25, 649–98.

———. 1983. "A Comparison of Levels of GDP per Capita in Developed and Developing Countries, 1700–1980," *Journal of Economic History*, March, 43, 27–41.

———. 1982. *Phases of Capitalist Development*, Oxford: Oxford University Press.

———. 1970. *Economic Progress and Policy in Developing Countries*, London: Allen & Unwin.

———. 1964. *Economic Growth in the West*, New York: The Twentieth Century Fund.

Romer, P. 1986. "Increasing Returns and Long Run Growth," *Journal of Political Economy*, October, 94, 1002–37.

Weber, M. 1958. *The Protestant Ethic and the Spirit of Capitalism*, New York: Scribner's. Originally published in 1905.

21

CONVERGENCE AND DIVERGENCE IN THE POST–WORLD WAR II ERA

John T Passé-Smith

In this chapter John Passé-Smith takes stock of global economic growth between 1960 and 1985 for a sample of 112 countries. He argues that focusing on the long-term pattern of growth among only the richer countries in the world has caused proponents of convergence theory to lose sight of patterns established by the rest of the world. This error is compounded by the fact that convergence theory has found very little empirical confirmation. If countries are not moving to similar levels of productivity, then what is their pattern of growth? After discussing the post–World War II era, Passé-Smith examines the evidence for convergence. In comparing periods of global economic expansion (1960 to 1974) and contraction (1975 to 1985), Passé-Smith finds that during the expansionary period evidence for convergence strengthens, but during the global economic contraction the gap grows wider. In other words, instead of all countries gradually moving toward a similar level of output, the world economy followed a wavelike pattern. A longer time period needs to be examined, but this pattern of periodic convergence and divergence based on the health of the world economy could explain the lack of empirical support for convergence theory.

Although the gap between rich and poor countries has apparently widened in the post–World War II era, proponents of convergence theory, such as Moses Abramovitz (1986), assert and attempt to demonstrate that over time, countries at lower levels of growth will have higher rates of growth, thus narrowing the gap between rich and poor countries.[1] The essential advantage shared by latecomers to industrialization is that they have not incorporated new technologies developed in the richer countries. By integrating these new technologies into production, the productivity rate of workers increases, and higher rates of economic growth follow. As William Baumol put it, among economic historians "one central theme is that forces accelerating the growth of nations who were latecomers to industrialization and economic development give rise to a long-run tendency towards convergence of levels of per capita product or, alternatively, of per worker product" (1986: 1075).

Given these assertions, the poorest countries in the world should have the highest growth rates, followed by the middle-income and finally the rich countries. Convergence of all countries in the world would be in evidence. Unfortunately for its proponents, no empirical support exists for this pure convergence hypothesis. According to Baumol, only the wealthiest countries and the richest of the middle-income countries—which he calls the "convergence club"—have been shown to converge.

With these patterns of economic growth in mind, this chapter evolves three foci: (1) economic growth in the post–World War II era, (2) the evidence for convergence and the experience of "nonconvergence club" countries, (3) patterns of growth during periods of world economic growth and economic stagnation.

The first of the three foci surveys growth in the post–World War II era. Following Western Europe's rapid recovery after the war, the governments of the wealthy industrialized states turned to aiding Third World countries in their development efforts. In the 1950s and early 1960s, economic growth became the centerpiece of economists' development plans. To that end, the United Nations declared the 1960s the Development Decade and set a goal of 6 percent annual growth as necessary to raise the poverty-stricken to a decent standard of living (Dube, 1988: 2–3). Twenty-five years later David Morawetz (1977) was commissioned by the World Bank to take stock of what had been accomplished in the area of development. Morawetz evaluated the world's growth between 1950 and 1975, concluding that although the world as a whole had experienced relatively rapid growth, the gap between rich and poor countries in terms of per capita real gross domestic product (RGDP/pc) was growing wider. This chapter seeks to discover whether the characteristics of world growth established by Morawetz still prevail.

The second of the foci concerns convergence theory. Has convergence taken place in the post–World War II period? Although evidence of convergence has been offered for the period 1870 to 1979 (Abramovitz, 1986; Baumol, 1986), attempts to demonstrate the closing of the gap between rich and poor countries in the post–World War II epoch have fallen short (see De Long, 1986). However, convergence theorists argue that the period under examination is far too brief and allows short-term economic fluctuations or disturbances to cloud the long-term processes. Baumol's study (1986) covered the period 1870–1979, but when dealing with the depth of the convergence phenomenon he focused on the postwar years. Here he found that convergence has occurred among relatively wealthy countries, but this pattern does not extend to the poorer countries of the world. In this section I determine whether the data indicate that only the convergence club behaved as described and examine the experience of the nonconvergence club countries.

In the third section I compare the characteristics of growth during periods of world economic growth and stagnation. Convergence theorists discuss patterns of growth over very long periods of time, so the expectations that guide predictions for the long term no longer apply. They point out that the long-term tendency to cluster more tightly together is not always apparent because of short-term disturbances. The oil shocks and the extended world recession would certainly qualify as short-term disturbances. The question is, what patterns emerge during the downturns?

It would not be surprising to find that the convergence process was in abeyance during global economic slowdowns, but it is not clear what pattern would or should be expected during these periods. When convergence does temporarily fade, are the growth rates of countries at different levels of growth random, or does another predictable pattern emerge? Proponents point out that the convergence phenomenon is a long-term process and that examination of shorter periods could produce a distorted picture. However, if the brief periods in which convergence is not taking place are times of rapid, abrupt reversal that reestablishes or worsens the income gap for those countries that are not members of the convergence club, then focusing solely on the long-term picture could blur or hide a divergence phenomenon that is as important as the convergence phenomenon.

To answer these questions, three aspects of growth are examined here: rates of growth, levels of growth, and mobility. Rates of growth allude to the rapidity with which a country or the world has grown, whereas the level of growth refers to the wealth of countries as measured by the real gross domestic product per capita. The section on mobility evaluates the upward and downward movement of countries both in relation to each other and across the aggregated groups.

Economic Growth, 1960–1985

National accounts statistics were obtained from the work done by the International Comparisons Project (ICP) as reported in Robert Summers and Alan Heston's "A New Set of International Comparisons of Real Product and Prices: Estimates for 130 Countries, 1950–1985" (1988). Summers and Heston reported gross domestic products converted to 1980 constant U.S. dollars with a conversion factor that is supposed to reflect actual purchasing power. The result is what the authors call a real gross domestic product. Although the data run annually from 1950 to 1985, I have chosen a shorter period, 1960 to 1985, to allow inclusion of the newly independent countries of Africa in the sample. For the most part, these countries' data became available in 1960 upon their independence. The annual average growth rates reported here were then computed from the constant per capita RGDPs using the regression method described by the World Bank in the *World Development Report* (1988: 288–289).[2] The sample includes 112 countries for which there are data for every year during the 1960 to 1985 period.

Two types of country groupings are analyzed. The first is income groupings defined by the level of growth. Those countries with RGDP/pcs of $4,000 (1980 U.S. dollars) or greater are considered rich, middle-income countries have RGDP/pcs of $500 to $3,999, and the poor countries are those with RGDP/pcs of less than $500. One of the effects of using the purchasing power conversion factor is that it usually increases the apparent wealth or production of a society. Assuming that it is an accurate portrayal, many more countries than are normally considered middle income are placed into this category. Because of the lack of agreement over where to draw the cutoff points for the various income groups, none of the conclusions drawn here is based solely on analysis of groups. Too often the patterns of growth of the "rich," "poor," or "middle-income" countries are asserted or assumed, yet no one agrees on which country belongs where. I have not settled the issue, but I did define the cutoffs earlier in this paragraph, and I list the countries that belonged to each group in 1960 in the note to Table 21.1.

One group that was not defined by its RGDP/pc includes the communist and the former communist countries. The communist countries kept national accounts data that were not comparable to noncommunist national accounts statistics. The results of the ICP are only as good as the data that went into the conversion process, so these data should be read with care and have thus been placed in a sepaarate group.

World regional categories constitute the second type of grouping. The geographic categories were drawn from the distinctions made by the International Monetary Fund (IMF) and include Africa, Asia, the Middle East, Western Hemisphere, and the developed countries. I then borrowed the East Asia–Pacific category from the World Bank's *World Tables 1992* because it allowed for separate analysis of the Asian newly

Table 21.1   Economic Growth Rates by Income Groups and Region

	Annual Average Growth Rates, 1960–1985 (%)
World	2.16
Income Groups	
Rich[a] ($4,000 and more)	2.24
Middle income ($500–$3,999)	2.28
Poor ($500 and less)	1.30
Communist countries	3.33
Regions[b]	
Developed	2.98
Africa	1.05
Asia	.99
East Asia–Pacific	4.50
Middle East	3.01
Western Hemisphere	1.71

Source: Data computed from Summers and Heston (1988).
Notes: a. The income groups for 1960 are as follows.
Rich: Australia, Belgium, Canada, Denmark, Finland, France, Germany, the Netherlands, New Zealand, Norway, Sweden, Switzerland, Trinidad and Tobago, the United Kingdom, the United States, Venezuela
Middle income: Afghanistan, Algeria, Angola, Argentina, Austria, Benin, Bolivia, Brazil, Cameroon, Chad, Chile, Colombia, Congo, Costa Rica, Côte D'Ivoire, Dominican Republic, Ecuador, El Salvador, Gabon, Ghana, Greece, Guatemala, Haiti, Honduras, Hong Kong, India, Iran, Iraq, Ireland, Israel, Italy, Jamaica, Japan, Jordan, Korea, Madagascar, Malaysia, Mauritius, Mexico, Morocco, Mozambique, Nicaragua, Nigeria, Pakistan, Panama, Papua New Guinea, Paraguay, Peru, Philippines, Portugal, Senegal, Singapore, South Africa, Spain, Sri Lanka, Sudan, Syria, Taiwan, Thailand, Tunisia, Turkey, Uruguay, Zambia, Zimbabwe
Poor: Bangladesh, Botswana, Burundi, Central African Republic, Egypt, Ethiopia, Guinea, Kenya, Lesotho, Liberia, Malawi, Mali, Mauritania, Myanmar, Nepal, Niger, Rwanda, Sierra Leone, Somalia, Tanzania, Togo, Uganda, Zaire
Communist: Bulgaria, China, Czechoslovakia, German Democratic Republic, Hungary, Poland, Romania, USSR, Yugoslavia
b. The regions, including the Developed category, are the regional divisions used in IMF publications (IMF, 1984).

industrializing countries (NICS). Again, the communist and former communist regimes constitute a separate category.[3]

Over the twenty-six–year period 1960–1985, the annual average rate of RGDP/pc growth for the world as a whole was an impressive 2.16 percent (see Table 21.1). To put this achievement in perspective, one must realize that, according to Simon Kuznets (1972:19), the countries considered wealthy today began to experience a surge of economic activity around the mid-nineteenth century that lasted more than one hundred years. By the end of this century of unprecedented growth, these countries had achieved the world's highest average standards of living and were also several times wealthier than the rest of the world.

The growth rate that helped the presently industrialized countries achieve such a record was an annual average of 1.6 percent (Kuznets, 1972: 19). Not only does the present 2.16 percent annual rate surpass the earlier mark, but it is so impressive because it measures the annual growth of all 112 countries in the sample—rich, middle-income, poor, and communist countries—not just the fastest-growing countries.

For the period 1960 to 1985, the rich countries grew at an even more striking pace, 2.24 percent annually. As a group, the rich countries apparently widened the gap between themselves and the rest of the world. The middle-income countries grew the fastest during the twenty-six–year period, the rich followed relatively closely behind, and the poorest countries expanded at a 1.3 percent annual average. The most important factor is that all three income groupings experienced economic expansion between 1960 and 1985.

Regarding regional economic growth, East Asia, which contains the so-called Asian NICs (Hong Kong, Singapore, South Korea, Taiwan, and Thailand) had the fastest annual growth rate—4.50 percent (see Table 21.1). Following the NICs was the Middle Eastern group, with a rate of expansion just over 3 percent per year; the developed countries fell just short of the Middle East at 2.98 percent average annual growth. Asia and Africa's growth rates were the slowest, both hovering near 1 percent per annum.

Perhaps the most surprising outcome was the showing of the communist, many now formerly communist, countries. The nine communist countries for which the ICP project presented data reported the fastest growth rate among the income groups, averaging 3.33 percent, between 1960 and 1985. Given the demise of many of the communist countries in the late 1980s and early 1990s, it seemed logical that their growth rates would be a harbinger of impending doom. This was not the case. Indeed, all nine of the communist countries boasted relatively robust growth—Bulgaria 3.2 percent, China 5.2 percent, Czechoslovakia 2.2 percent, East Germany 3.0 percent, Hungary 2.3 percent, Poland 2.5 percent, Romania 3.9 percent, the USSR 3.1 percent, and Yugoslavia 4.6 percent.

Turning to the experiences of individual countries rather than income or regional groupings, Table 21.2 highlights the world's ten fastest- and slowest-growing countries between 1960 and 1985. One of the more striking features of Table 21.2 is the fact that middle-income countries dominate both lists: Eight of the ten fastest-growing countries were middle-income countries, whereas seven of the ten slowest-growing countries were middle income. Botswana was the only poor country to make the fastest-growing countries list. China, the ninth-fastest-growing country, was the only communist country on either list. As might be expected, Asian countries dominated the fastest-growing list, and African countries dominated the slowest-growing countries.

Table 21.2   Economic and Population Growth Rates, 1960–1985

Income Group (1960)	Country	Annual Average Growth Rates (%)		Ranking Among the 112 Countries	
		GNP/pc	Population	GNP/pc	Population
The Ten Fastest-Growing Countries:					
Middle	Singapore	7.74	1.71	1	77
Middle	Korea	6.96	1.97	2	70
Middle	Hong Kong	6.93	2.27	3	62
Middle	Taiwan	6.17	2.33	4	57
Middle	Gabon	6.02	1.32	5	83
Middle	Japan	5.75	1.07	6	86
Poor	Botswana	5.63	3.40	7	4
Middle	Malaysia	5.40	2.58	8	46
Communist	China	5.17	2.08	9	68
Middle	Brazil	4.84	2.50	10	52
The Ten Slowest-Growing Countries:					
Middle	Chad	−2.72	1.98	112	69
Middle	Angola	−2.31	2.36	111	56
Rich	Venezuela	−2.11	3.60	110	3
Middle	Mozambique	−1.94	3.27	109	9
Poor	Zaire	−1.77	2.62	108	42
Middle	Ghana	−1.69	2.72	107	33
Middle	Madagascar	−.93	2.53	106	48
Poor	Somalia	−.77	3.21	105	14
Middle	Sudan	−.68	2.81	104	26
Middle	Benin	−.63	2.72	103	34

Source: Data computed from Summers and Heston (1988).

Convergence in the Post–World War II Era

As the economic position of the United States appeared to deteriorate during the past twenty years or so, a debate formed concerning the ability of the United States to retain its leadership position. Some argued that from its position on high the United States had provided the fertile ground for world economic growth (see Gilpin, 1987). Although conditions for growth were positive for the United States as well, they were in fact less propitious for the United States than for some other countries. This pattern of growth and development made way for the rise of challengers to U.S. economic dominance.

Economic historians (Abramovitz, 1986; Baumol, 1986) surveyed the pattern and began to revisit the ideas expressed in convergence theory. Convergence theorists have long postulated that an inverse relationship exists between long-run economic growth and levels of per capita product. Baumol added that U.S. productivity had not in fact slowed but that other countries had taken advantage of a backlog of technology and caught up. He asserted that the "U.S. productivity growth rate has been surprisingly steady, and despite frequently expressed fears, there is no sign recently of any *long-term* slowdown" (Baumol, 1986: 1073). In fact, according to Baumol, U.S. productivity growth rates had been lower than those of Germany, Japan, and a number of other countries for the better part of a century, but this fact should not cause concern about U.S. decline because it was probably the convergence process in action (1986: 1073).

In an attempt to explain why the poorest countries have not been among the countries that have converged, Moses Abramovitz (1986) explained that they may have lacked the education, familiarity with industrial society, or sufficient management expertise—social capability—to take advantage of the potential for rapid growth. Countries with low social capability are most often the poorest countries, and they are the ones Abramovitz predicted will fall further behind because they lack the requisite experience to grow. As Baumol (1986) put it, the poorest countries belong to the nonconvergence club.

When a pattern of growth similar to that depicted in Table 21.1 was found by Robert Jackman in his 1982 study of world growth, he labeled it the "modified Matthew effect" (1982:175). In the Bible, the Book of Matthew contains a reference to the continued accumulation of wealth by the rich and the further impoverishment of the poor; by modified Matthew effect, Jackman meant that not only did the rich get richer but so, too, did the middle-income countries.

Although Jackman's article was not a test of convergence theory, his modified Matthew effect represents the weakened form of convergence. In his study, Jackman regressed growth rates on initial levels of growth, explaining that if the estimates for the regression were positive for the GNP/pc (logged) and negative for the squared term, this indicated that growth rates rose with initial levels of wealth until an apex was reached. Beyond the apex, growth rates declined somewhat, resulting in a plot that looks like an inverted "U."

Table 21.3 provides results from procedures similar to those used by Jackman and Baumol, with the time frame changed to the years 1960 to 1985. Equations 21.3A, C, and E show the results of the linear equations (the pure form of convergence) and 21.3B, D, and F the nonlinear results (the weaker form). If all countries in the world conformed to the pure, or simple, convergence hypothesis, as Abramovitz called it, a scatterplot of the relationship between levels and rates of growth would show a trend line sloping downward from left to right. The poorer countries would have the fastest growth rates, and the richer countries would have the slowest growth rates. The estimates for the RGDP/pc (logged) variable shown in Table 21.3 would be negative and

Table 21.3   Effects of Levels of Economic Growth on Rates of Growth, 1960–1985

Equation	Logged RGDP/pc	Logged Squared RGDP/pc	Adjusted R^2
	All 112 Countries in the Sample		
A	.011	—	.04
	$(2.32)^{**a}$	—	
B	.153	–.023	.06
	$(2.06)^{**a}$	$(-1.92)^{**a}$	
	The Sample Minus the 9 Communist Countries		
C	.011	—	.04
	$(2.17)^{**a}$	—	
D	.133	–.020	.05
	$(1.73)^{*a}$	$(-1.59)^a$	
	The 80 Rich and Middle-Income Countries		
E	.010	—	.01
	$(1.26)^a$	—	
F	.461	–.071	.10
	$(3.08)^{**a}$	$(-3.17)^{**a}$	

Source: Data computed from Summers and Heston (1988).
Notes: * $p \leq .05$; ** $p \leq .01$; a. t = ratio in parentheses

significant, and the fit as indicated by the adjusted R^2 should be better than that in the nonlinear equations.[4]

In fact, the estimates for the linear equations 21.3A and 21.3C are positive and significant, indicating divergence, or the opening rather than the closing of the gap. However, when the sample includes only the rich and middle-income countries, the pattern of divergence dissipates. This evidence, along with that presented in Table 21.1, reveals that the growth rate of the middle-income countries surpassed that of the rich while simultaneously an apparent gap opened between the rich and the nonrich. This apparent paradox is examined more closely below.

The estimates for the nonlinear equations, 21.3B, D, and F, show some evidence for the weaker form of convergence. In all three equations the logged RGDP/pc shows a positive and significant estimate, meaning that as countries grow richer their growth rates increase as well. The estimates for the logged squared RGDP/pc show that in Equations 21.3B and D the estimates are negative and significant. This evidence indicates that the gap between rich and poor was widening but that some countries in the upper reaches of the middle-income category and the lower reaches of the rich group were narrowing the gap. In equation 21.3D the nine socialist countries were removed from the sample, and the convergence relationship disappeared.

Because no clear pattern of convergence or divergence characterized the 1960 to 1985 period, in the remainder of this section I take a closer look at the gap to determine how it behaved over time and whether any countries could close the gap any time soon. One way to examine the gap is to analyze what is called the absolute gap. As defined by David Morawetz (1977), the absolute gap is the difference between the mean level of growth of a set of rich countries and that of poorer countries (or income groups). It reveals the extent of the gap in dollars, thus showing the increase in RGDP/pc a nonrich country must achieve to have an RGDP/pc equal to that of the rich countries.

Simon Kuznets (1972) reported that the mean per capita GNP of the rich countries was $1,900, whereas that of the poor countries was $120.[5] One of the major trends over the previous 100 to 125 years, Kuznets argued, was that the absolute gap widened very slowly up until World War II and then began to accelerate. Kuznets stated, "A reasonable conjecture is that, in comparison with the quintupling of the per capita product of developed countries over the last century, the per capita product of the 'poor' LDCs [less-developed countries] rose two-thirds at most" (1972:19). It seems fair to say that the large disparity between the world's rich and poor countries is a relatively recent phenomenon.

Morawetz found that between 1950 and 1975 the absolute gap between the Organization for Economic Cooperation and Development (OECD) and developing countries more than doubled (from $2,191 to $4,839 in 1975 U.S. dollars). The data presented in Table 21.4 show that for the 1960–1985 period, the absolute gap between the rich and middle-income countries grew from $3,970 to $6,917 in 1980 U.S.

Table 21.4   Absolute Gap by Income Group and Region, 1960–1985

	Absolute Gap (1980 U.S. dollars)	
	1960	1985
Income Group		
Middle income	3,970	6,917
Poor	4,920	8,381
Region		
Africa	4,082	8,643
Asia	4,065	8,624
East Asia–Pacific	3,683	5,867
Middle East	2,888	6,076
Western hemisphere	2,801	6,938
Communist countries	2,592	3,165

Source: Data computed from Summers and Heston (1988).

dollars, and the gap between the rich and poor countries grew from $4,920 to $8,381. The table also shows that the absolute gap for every region in the world widened during that period. Figure 21.1 graphically illustrates RGDP/pc for the three income groups and the communist countries; the absolute gap is the distance between the lines. The growth of the gap between the income groups is readily apparent. Again, the communist countries provide a surprise. The smallest of the absolute gaps between the rich and all other groups (either income group or geographic region) is that of the communist countries. In 1960 the gap stood at $2,592, increasing to $3,165 by 1985.

At the aggregate level, then, the gap between the rich and the other two income groups is growing. But does this prove the adage that the rich get richer while the poor get poorer? Figure 21.1 shows that although the gap opened, as groups the middle-income and poor countries did not get poorer. Nor does it provide a hint about what soon happened to the communist world. The information provided in Figure 21.1 and all of the tables thus leads to apparently incongruous conclusions: First, the absolute gap between the rich and the nonrich is growing

Figure 21.1   Gap Between Rich and Poor

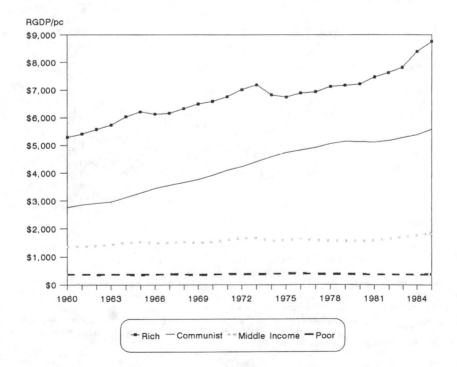

wider, much wider; second, the growth rates for the middle-income countries for the entire period under examination are higher than those of the rich countries. The same can be said for the communist countries: Their growth rates are higher, yet the absolute gap continues to widen. Assuming they maintain a faster growth rate for a sufficiently long time, they will eventually overtake the rich, but that could take a very long time.

The following discussion illustrates the extraordinary efforts needed to close the gap between the rich and the poor. As Table 21.5 shows, catching up could take some countries hundreds and even over a thousand years.[6] The number of years it would take a country to do so can be calculated by projecting current rates of growth into the future.[7] Only fifteen countries have achieved a rate of growth sufficient to allow them to catch up to the rich countries.

The results presented in Table 21.5 assume that countries will maintain the same growth rate as that achieved during the base period 1960–1985. As the table shows, South Korea will be the first to join the

Table 21.5   Closing the Absolute Gap

Country	1985 RGDP/pc (1980 U.S. dollars)	Annual Growth Rate, 1960–1985 (percent)	Number of Years Until Gap Will Close if 1960–1985 Growth Rates Continue
Rich[a]	9,040	3.24[b]	—
Korea	3,056	6.96	32
Taiwan	3,581	6.17	35
Gabon	3,103	6.02	42
Malaysia	3,415	5.40	50
Brazil	3,282	4.84	71
China	2,444	5.17	75
Botswana	1,762	5.63	75
Portugal	3,729	4.31	95
Syria	2,900	4.32	121
Thailand	1,900	4.44	148
Lesotho	771	4.81	175
Tunisia	2,050	4.22	176
Ecuador	2,387	4.02	205
Panama	2,912	3.45	1,053
Egypt	1,188	3.54	1,067

Source: Data computed from Summers and Heston (1988).

Notes: a. The rich countries in 1985 were Australia, Austria, Belgium, Canada, Denmark, Finland, France, Germany, Greece, Hong Kong, Ireland, Israel, Italy, Japan, the Netherlands, New Zealand, Norway, Singapore, Spain, Sweden, Switzerland, Trinidad and Tobago, the United Kingdom, the United States.

b. This growth rate represents the annual average for the countries that were rich in 1985. The growth rate reported in Table 21.1 represents the annual average growth rate for those countries that were rich in 1960.

rich countries—in thirty-two years—and the last of the fifteen countries will be welcomed over a millennium later. Growth rates achieved between 1960 and 1985 are unlikely to remain the same, but neither is catching up likely to become any easier.

David Morawetz (1977) noted that it might be easier for nonrich countries to narrow the relative gap than the absolute gap, making that achievement a more accessible development goal. The relative gap shows the RGDP/pc of the middle-income and poor countries as a percentage of that of the rich. Morawetz explained that between 1950 and 1975, the developing countries had actually narrowed the relative gap. Their RGDP/pc, measured in a relative way, rose from 6.7 percent of the RGDP/pc of the rich (OECD) countries in 1950 to 7.2 percent in 1975.

The relative gap, as reported in Table 21.6, indicates that the countries that had achieved middle-income status in 1960 were able to close the relative gap with the rich, albeit only slightly. The RGDP/pc of the middle-income countries expressed as a percentage of the RGDP/pc of the rich countries was 25 percent in 1960, improving to 27.9 percent by 1985. The relative position of the poor countries worsened, however. The RGDP/pc of the countries that were poor in 1960 was 7 percent of that of the rich; this had slipped to only 5.6 percent by 1985.

Only one of the geographic regions, East Asia–Pacific (the NICs), and the communist countries were able to narrow the relative gap. In 1960 the mean RGDP/pc of the East Asia–Pacific region was 21.2 percent of the rich countries' RGDP/pc, rising to an impressive

Table 21.6   Relative Gap by Income Group and Region, 1960–1985

	Relative Gap (percentage)	
	1960	1985
Income Group		
Middle income	25.0	27.9[a]
Poor	7.0	5.6
Region		
Africa	12.7	9.0
Asia	13.1	9.2
East Asia–Pacific	21.2	38.2[a]
Middle East	38.2	36.0
Western hemisphere	40.1	26.9
Communist countries	51.0	57.9[a]

Source: Data computed from Summers and Heston (1988).
Note: a. Closed the relative gap

38.2 percent in 1985. The communist countries' relative gap score was 51.0 percent in 1960, by 1985 this score had increased to 57.9 percent.

Comparing Periods of Economic Growth and Decline

Proponents of convergence argue that an examination of twenty-six years is too brief to capture evidence of the process. It allows short-term economic fluctuations and political disturbances to cloud the long-term processes that bring about the closing of the gap (Baumol, 1986). This may be true, but even the long-term phenomenon has been difficult to isolate. After removing sampling bias from Baumol's evidence, J. Bradford De Long discovered little indication of convergence (see Chapter 20 of this volume).

I do not mean to be critical of the fine work done by proponents of convergence theory, but their focus on the so-called convergence club has left the rest of the world—most of the world, in fact—out of the picture.[8] Also, a fixation on the long term ignores predictable patterns that may occur in the shorter term. Convergence might take place during periods of rapid growth, whereas for some countries the gap might be reproduced and perhaps even widened during periods of global economic contraction. It is logical that the rich countries have the economic depth and diversity to brace against hard times, whereas the nonrich do not. If this is the case, perhaps it is more logical to look for a rhythmic pattern, such as swells in the ocean, rather than a long-term linear pattern. Here, the ebb and flow of the swell refers to the gap between rich and poor, not to world growth. During world economic contractions the gap would grow, and during periods of rapid growth the gap would ebb.

In this section I am particularly interested in learning what happened to the rates of economic expansion of countries at different levels of growth when the world economy experienced the economic crises of the 1970s and 1980s. From the end of World War II until the first oil shock in the early 1970s, the world experienced tremendous economic growth. Then, beginning in the 1970s, a number of crises caused slow and even negative growth rates in many countries. The oil shock of 1974 was only the beginning. A second spike in the price of oil occurred in 1979, and energy prices rose again. The worldwide recession that struck in 1979 extended into the early 1980s, and in 1982 the debt crisis began when Mexico announced it had insufficient funds to meet its international obligations. The analysis here revisits the data presented earlier, except the period of economic expansion (1960–1974) is compared with the period of contraction (1975–1985).

As Table 21.7 shows, during the era of economic expansion the mean world growth rate was 2.96 percent. The countries that were middle income in 1960 grew slightly more slowly (3.16 percent) than the rich (3.18 percent). The poor countries, although they grew more slowly than the rich or middle-income countries, also took advantage of a positive global climate and grew at an average rate of 1.85 percent. Neither the poor nor the middle-income countries' rates of growth allowed them to close the gap with the rich, but their rates of growth were relatively healthy. Even the rate of expansion of the poor countries exceeded that experienced in the century of unprecedented growth discussed earlier. In terms of the geographic regions, every region had positive growth, and all except Asia grew in excess of 2 percent annually. The fact that the middle-income countries grew more slowly than the rich countries means the gap between the rich and middle-income countries grew wider, but the richer of the middle-income countries may have closed the gap, as suggested in Table 21.3.

The right-hand column of Table 21.7 shows growth rates during the period of global contraction. The mean world growth rate dropped to .75 percent. Thus, all three income groups suffered during the contraction, but it is also true that the groups' relative fortunes began to change. The era in which the economic expansion of the middle-income countries roughly equaled that of the rich drew to a close in 1974. During the contraction the rich countries were the best able to cope, growing at an annual rate of 1.67 percent. The middle-income countries

Table 21.7   Economic Growth Rates by Income Groups and Region, 1960–1985

	Annual Average Growth Rates (%)	
	1960–1974	1975–1985
World	2.96	.75
Income Groups:		
Rich ($4,000 and more)	3.18	1.67
Middle income ($500–$3,999)	3.16	.60
Poor ($500 and less)	1.85	–.86
Communist countries	4.08	1.94
Regions		
Developed	3.91	1.93
Africa	2.03	–.44
Asia	.50	1.70
East Asia–Pacific	4.53	4.14
Middle East	4.06	–.46
Western Hemisphere	2.68	–.30

Source: Data computed from Summers and Heston (1988).

fell well below 1 percent to .60 percent, whereas the poor countries *constricted* at an annual rate of .86 percent. During the era of global growth only 12 countries, mostly African, had negative growth rates, but during the global contraction 42 of 112 countries experienced economic reversal. Not one country in the rich category suffered a negative growth rate for the 1975–1985 period.

The gap between the rich and middle-income countries appears to have expanded very slightly during the initial period of rapid, worldwide growth, and the widening of the gap accelerated rapidly during the global economic contraction. Regression analysis provided in Table 21.3 showed some support (Equation 21.3B) for a weak form of convergence—the inverted "U" curve—which disappeared (Equation 21.3D) when the communist countries were removed. The information provided in Table 21.8 replicates this analysis for the periods of economic expansion and contraction.

As anticipated, the period of economic expansion offers some confirmation that the weak form of convergence was taking place. The estimates for Equation 21.8B (full sample, the nonlinear equation) show the inverted "U" pattern. The positive estimate for the logged RGDP/pc is evidence of the growing gap, and the negative estimate for the logged and squared RGDP/pc means a threshold was crossed beyond which the gap apparently closed—the weak convergence pattern. In other words, although not all of the middle-income countries participated in the closing of the gap, this evidence suggests that some of the richer of the middle-income group did so. If this pattern disappears during the global economic contraction, the wavelike pattern discussed earlier appears to be in place.

For the period of economic contraction, the picture changes dramatically. Not one of the three nonlinear equations is significant; in fact, the contrary is true. In Equation 21.8G, the total sample, the estimates indicate that divergence was occurring. During the contraction the gap was being reproduced. This was true of both the full sample (Equation 21.8G) and the sample with the communist countries removed (Equation 21.8I). However, when the communist and poor countries were removed (Equations 21.8K and L), there appears to be no relationship between levels and rates of growth.

In searching for convergence, Abramovitz analyzed the coefficient of variance, which is the standard deviation around the world mean per capita product divided by the mean (in this case the world mean RGDP/pc). The standard deviation is standardized because it would not be surprising to find that as the world grows richer, the increase in the standard deviation would also grow larger as a reflection of that overall increase. The coefficient of variation standardizes the deviation score for changing means so one can be relatively certain that an

Table 21.8   Effects of Levels of Economic Growth on Rates of Growth, 1960–1985

Equation	Years	Logged RGDP/pc	Logged Squared RGDP/pc	Adjusted R^2
		All 112 Countries in the Sample		
A	1960–1974	.015	—	.07
		$(3.04)^{**a}$	—	
B	1960–1974	.163	–.024	.09
		$(2.12)^{**a}$	$(-1.93)^{**a}$	
		The Sample Minus the 9 Communist Countries		
C	1960–1974	.015	—	.07
		$(2.86)^{**a}$	—	
D	1960–1974	.143	–.021	.08
		$(1.76)^{*a}$	$(-1.58)^{a}$	
		The 80 Rich and Middle-Income Countries		
E	1960–1974	.013	—	.03
		$(1.87)^{*a}$	—	
F	1960–1974	.543	–.082	.16
		$(3.75)^{**a}$	$(-3.66)^{**a}$	
		All 112 Countries in the Sample		
G	1975–1985	.015	—	.05
		$(2.69)^{**a}$	—	
H	1975–1985	.093	–.012	.05
		$(.99)^{a}$	$(-.83)^{a}$	
		The Sample Minus the 9 Communist Countries		
I	1975–1985	.015	—	.06
		$(2.67)^{**a}$	—	
J	1975–1985	.068	–.01	.05
		$(.70)^{a}$	$(-.54)^{a}$	
		The 86 Rich and Middle-Income Countries		
K	1975–1985	.011	—	.02
		$(1.54)^{a}$	—	
L	1975–1985	.036	–.004	.00
		$(.24)^{a}$	$(-.17)^{a}$	

Source: Data computed from Summers and Heston (1988).
Notes: * p ≤ .05; ** p ≤. 01; a. t = ratio in parentheses

increase in the coefficient of variation is not a relic of an increasing mean value.[9] Interpreting trends with the coefficient is straightforward: If the gap is closing, the coefficient of variance should grow smaller and vice versa.

Figure 21.2 displays the coefficient of variation for the RGDP/pc. As can be seen in the figure, in terms of convergence and divergence, the record during the period of global economic expansion was mixed. Divergence occurred during seven of the years, and convergence was seen during eight of the years. The trend line for the initial period as a whole tilts slightly downward, indicating slow progress toward convergence. In 1960 the coefficient of variance stood at 0.955,

Figure 21.2   Coefficient of Variance, 1960–1985

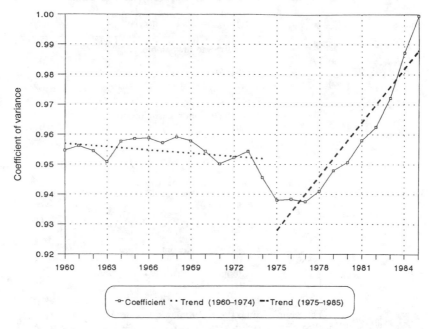

Note: The coefficient of variance is the standard deviation divided by the mean.

and for 1974 it was approximately 0.945. During the contraction the trend line tilts upward from left to right, indicating divergence. In 1975 the coefficient was 0.939, and by the end of the period under investigation the measure climbed to just below 1.0.

In terms of the ebb-and-flow pattern, the coefficient of variance performed much as predicted. There was a closing of the gap during the era of growth and a widening of the gap during the period of global contraction. During good economic times, the middle-income countries seem to be able to tap their potential and grow at tremendous rates, but when the world economy declines, middle-income countries are less able than the rich to protect themselves.

Conclusion

This chapter has examined three aspects of growth during the period 1960 to 1985. First, I analyzed economic growth for the entire period; then I reviewed the evidence for convergence as well as divergence and included the experience of the nonconvergence club countries; and finally, I compared the economic behavior of countries at different levels of growth when the world economy experienced both expansion and contraction. The major conclusions drawn from each of these sections are discussed here.

First, worldwide growth for the period occurred at an impressive 2.16 percent annually. If scholars such as Simon Kuznets (1972) and Michael Lipton (1977) are correct, this rate is phenomenal. Kuznets has demonstrated that between the mid-1800s and 1950 the countries considered rich in 1950 experienced economic expansion averaging 1.6 percent annually; he called this the century of unprecedented growth. What is truly amazing about the period under examination here is that the entire world (112 countries), not just the rich countries, grew at 2.16 percent annually.

The fastest-growing region in the world was East Asia–Pacific, which included the Asian NICs; this region grew at an average annual rate of 4.5 percent. Perhaps the largest surprise was the rate of growth experienced by the nine communist countries in the sample (3.33 percent). If a harbinger of doom were expected, it was not found in the economic performance of these countries.

These data also indicate that not everyone has shared in the growth. The absolute gap between rich and middle-income countries and between rich and poor countries has grown steadily since 1960. For the middle-income countries, the absolute gap during the period studied grew from $3,970 to $6,917, and the gap for poor countries fell from a deficit of $4,920 to a deficit of $8,381. On average, each year during this period the absolute gap widened by $113 for the middle-income countries and $133 for the poor countries. On the other hand, the middle-income group slightly improved in the relative gap. In 1960 the RGDP/pc of the middle-income countries was 25 percent of that of the rich countries; by 1985 that figure had climbed to 27.9 percent. The poor countries' RGDP/pc, however, sunk from 7 percent to 5.6 percent that of the rich countries. The only region to increase its RGDP/pc as a percentage of that of the rich countries was East Asia–Pacific, which improved from 21 percent to an impressive 38 percent of the RGDP/pc of the rich.

The second focus concerned convergence theory. I examined whether convergence of RGDP/pcs has taken place in the post–World War II period. Two types of convergence were noted: pure convergence and a weakened form. The pure type of convergence occurs when all countries move toward a common level of growth per capita. The weakened form is found when the RGDP/pc gap closes between the rich and the wealthier, more socially capable middle-income societies but the poor countries are left behind. No solid evidence of the pure form of convergence has been found. As stated earlier, one of the prime examples of the weakened form of convergence was provided by William J. Baumol (1986), but a subsequent study found Baumol's work to have been flawed by sample selection bias (De Long, 1986). When the bias was removed, so was convergence.

The evidence provided in this chapter indicates qualified support for the weakened form of convergence between 1960 and 1985. The first bit of evidence obtained was that the middle-income countries grew faster than the rich and the poor countries. The rich countries were the second-fastest group, and the poor countries grew at the slowest rate. This ranking of growth rates is favorable to the weakened form of convergence yet is insufficient evidence of convergence. Regression analysis (Table 21.3) showed that when the full sample of countries was included, the results indicated that convergence was taking place. The estimates showed that the richer the country, the faster the growth rate until a threshold was reached; beyond that point richer countries grew more slowly. This evidence was strengthened when the rich and middle-income countries alone were examined. However, when the nine communist countries were removed from the sample, the weakened form of convergence disappeared.

The last section of the chapter compared the growth of countries during the periods of economic expansion and contraction. Of particular interest was whether the convergence pattern held or whether another predictable pattern emerged. The proposition was that the richer countries have stronger economies that enable them to survive economic adversity to a much greater extent than the nonrich countries. Accordingly, during world economic downturns the gap between the countries was expected to grow, and during periods of rapid growth the gap was predicted to stabilize or even close.

The wave pattern did emerge, but, as with the support for the weakened form of convergence, it was not without qualifications. Three samples were analyzed: all 112 countries, all countries except the 9 communist countries, and the rich and middle-income countries. Two of the three samples demonstrated that the weakened form of convergence indeed occurred. The evidence of convergence disappeared, however, when the communist countries were removed. During the global economic downturn, the results indicated that the inverted "U" pattern had dissipated; all three samples were in agreement. Two of the three samples (all 112 countries and all except the communist countries) led to the conclusion that a positive linear relationship had taken the place of the convergence pattern. In other words, the gap was widening.

Figure 21.2 provided an illustrated version of the coefficient of variation. The figure showed that during the initial period of growth, weak evidence of convergence was present. The trend line showed a slightly downward trail. The path was reversed during the global downturn; the trend line showed a steep upward turn. This indicated that divergence was taking place, that the gap was growing.

Proponents of convergence theory point out that convergence is an excruciatingly slow process. The evidence of the century-long pattern presented by most theorists rests on a very few observations, and this is simply inadequate. The evidence suggests that the weakened form of convergence takes place during periods of economic growth and that the gap widens during periods of global contraction. This research points to the need to test previous periods of economic crisis to determine whether the rhythmic opening and closing of the gap was present during other crises such as the period around the Great Depression in the late 1920s and the 1930s. I do not mean to suggest that convergence theory is wrong but rather that the long-term pattern is more complex and perhaps even more interesting than a linear pattern broken by short-term random disturbances.

Notes

1. The convergence hypothesis in its purer form asserts that labor productivity rates close over time, but a common proxy used for productivity is GDP/pc. See, for example, Abramovitz, 1986; Baumol, 1986; and DeLong, 1986.

2. The growth rates are calculated by the regression method described in the *World Development Report 1988*. The least-squares method finds the growth rate by fitting a least-squares trend line to the log of the gross national product per capita. This takes the equation form of $x_t = a+bt+e_t$, where x equals the log of the GNP/pc, a is the intercept, b is the parameter to be estimated, t is time, and e is the error term. The growth rate, r, is the [antilog (b)] – 1. For further information, see World Bank, 1988: 288–289. For a discussion of different methods of computing growth rates, see Jackman, 1980.

3. For a brief discussion of the treatment of centrally planned economies in the ICP project, see Summers and Heston, 1988.

4. In examining only rich countries this negative coefficient showed up but was never significant. I did not report on more combinations of countries at different levels of development or in different income groups because none changed the basic conclusions drawn from Tables 21.3 and 21.8. Analysis of residuals (Cook's D) did not reveal influential cases.

5. Kuznets (1972) defined the rich countries as those with GNP/pcs greater than $1,000 (1965 U.S. dollars). A narrow definition of the poor countries set the GNP/pc cutoff point at $120 or less; for his more broadly defined poor category, Kuznets raised the cutoff point to $300. The middle-income group varied according to Kuznets's choice of the narrowly or the broadly defined poor group in any particular example. Kuwait and Qatar were excluded because their growth had been dependent upon a single commodity and was not diversified. Puerto Rico was excluded because its GNP/pc was so tightly

connected to the United States. Japan was included in the rich group even though its GNP/pc was below the cutoff point because it had achieved tremendous growth with very few natural resources; thus, its growth was achieved through diversified development of the economy. For further information on how Kuznets defined his income groups, see Kuznets, 1972.

6. A simple way to determine whether a nonrich country can close the gap with a rich country is to divide the growth rate of the rich country by the ratio of the nonrich country's GNP/pc to the rich country's GNP/pc. This equation yields the growth rate the nonrich country must exceed to begin to close the (absolute) gap. If, for example, the rich country has a mean GNP/pc of $8,000 and a growth rate of 2 percent, a nonrich country with a GNP/pc of $1,000 must exceed a growth rate of 16 percent to begin to close the absolute gap that year.

7. The projections are calculated from the following formula:

$$G_1 = G_0{}^*(1 + r)^t;$$

where G_1 is the parameter to be estimated, G_0 is the GNP/pc at the year of origin, r is the rate of growth, and t is the number of years.

8. Moses Abramovitz (1986) did offer a good hypothesis concerning social capability, yet there was no attempt to systematically test that hypothesis. The focus was still on those countries that had the potential to converge.

9. The coefficient of variation is the standard deviation divided by the mean.

References

Abramovitz, Moses. 1986. "Catching Up, Forging Ahead, and Falling Behind." *Journal of Economic History* 46, no. 2 (June): 385–406.

Baumol, William J. 1986. "Productivity Growth, Convergence, and Welfare." *American Economic Review* 76, no. 5 (December): 1072–1085.

De Long, J. Bradford. 1986. "Productivity Growth, Convergence, and Welfare: Comment." *American Economic Review* 78, no. 5: 1138–1153.

Dube, S. C. 1988. *Modernization and Development: The Search for Alternative Paradigms*. London: Zed Books.

Gilpin, Robert. 1987. *The Political Economy of International Relations*. Princeton: Princeton University Press.

International Monetary Fund (IMF). 1984. *International Financial Statistics: Supplement on Output Statistics*, no. 8. Washington, D.C.: IMF.

Jackman, R. W. 1980. "A Note on the Measurement of Growth Rates in Cross-National Research." *American Journal of Sociology* 86: 604–610.

———. 1982. "Dependence on Foreign Investment and Economic Growth in the Third World." *World Politics* 34: 175–197.

Kahn, H. 1979. *World Economic Development: 1979 and Beyond*. Boulder: Westview Press.

Kuznets, S. 1972. "The Gap: Concept, Measurement, Trends," in G. Ranis, ed., *The Gap Between Rich and Poor Nations*, pp. 3–58. London: Macmillan Press.

Lipton, M. 1977. *Why the Poor People Stay Poor: A Study of Urban Bias in World Development*. London: Temple Smith.

————. 1989. *New Seeds and Poor People*. London: Unwin Hyman.

Morawetz, D. 1977. *Twenty-Five Years of Economic Development: 1950–1975*. Washington, D.C.: World Bank.

Summers, R., and A. Heston. 1988. "A New Set of International Comparisons of Real Product and Prices: Estimates for 130 Countries, 1950–1985." *Review of Income and Wealth* 34, no. 1 (March): 1–25.

World Bank. 1988, 1990. *World Development Report*. New York: Oxford University Press.

————. 1992. *World Tables 1992*. Washington, D.C.: World Bank.

PART 4

INTERNATIONAL
TRADE RELATIONS

22

INTERNATIONAL TRADE
AND DOMESTIC POLITICS

——————— *Joan Spero* ———————

*In this chapter Joan Spero traces the evolution of the international trade sys-
tem, highlighting the important linkage between international trade and domestic politics. Spero also describes the way in which the role of the United
States has evolved and changed over time. In the 1940s free trade sentiments
dominated U.S. policy, but by the 1960s protectionist sentiments were growing. In the aftermath of the Kennedy Round (1967) of world trade talks, U.S.
protectionist forces became more effective at lobbying the executive and legislative branches of government. The result was an explosion of trade barriers that
were sometimes more difficult to identify as barriers (e.g., labeling requirements) than as quotas or tariffs. These barriers became known as the new protectionism. Spero notes that in the 1970s and 1980s Japan and the European
Union pursued their perceived interests in trade more forcefully because the
United States was less willing, or perhaps unable, to provide leadership in the
multilateral trade system. She concludes with a review of the Tokyo and
Uruguay Rounds and indicates the need for a new system of shared governance
of world trade.*

Trade policy is the stuff of domestic politics. Tariffs, quotas, and nontariff barriers are familiar issues for a broad range of economic groups,
from farmers to manufacturers to labor unions to retailers. Because
trade policy often determines prosperity or adversity for these groups,

it is also the subject of frequent and often highly charged domestic political conflict.

In the United States, the Constitution accentuates the political conflict over trade policy by giving Congress the power to levy tariffs and regulate foreign commerce while at the same time giving the president authority in foreign policy. Conflict within Congress and between Congress and the executive branch is a central characteristic of U.S. trade policy. Because members of Congress are responsible to their constituents and, therefore, responsive to their economic concerns, there is often pressure within Congress for a trade policy that protects those special interests. Furthermore, the demands of relatively few interest groups directed at Congress may snowball into national trade policy, as occurred with the Smoot-Hawley Tariff Act of 1930, the most protectionist law of the century.[1]

While Congress tends to link trade policy with particular domestic interests, the United States executive branch often links trade policy with larger foreign policy and foreign economic goals. Thus, for example, since the 1930s, U.S. presidents have advocated open trade as the preferred economic policy, for broad economic and strategic reasons. Presidents, however, must have congressional approval for any agreement to reduce trade barriers. Yet the very process of approval raises the threat of interest group opposition. Presidents have tried to overcome this legislative constraint by asking Congress to delegate authority to the President to conclude trade agreements without subsequent congressional approval. Since 1934, Congress has regularly delegated such power for specifically limited periods of time and with specific constraints.

Domestic politicization in the United States and throughout the world has been an important constraint on international management. In this chapter we shall examine the evolution of trade management in the face of domestic political constraints.

The Havana Charter

The same factors that led to the creation of a managed international monetary system after World War II also led to the first attempt to subject trade to systematic international control. Protectionism and the disintegration of world trade in the 1930s created a common interest in an open trading order and a realization that states would have to cooperate to achieve and maintain that order. The retreat into protectionism in the interwar period led not only to economic disaster but also to international war. In the postwar era, mechanisms for guarding against such economic nationalism and reducing and regulating restrictions on trade would have to be created. In the United States, policy was shaped by Secretary of State Cordell Hull, who was the major advocate of the liberal theory that open trade would lead to economic prosperity and international peace.[2]

The interwar experience also led to the willingness of the United States to lead the system. As the State Department explained:

> The only nation capable of taking the initiative in promoting a worldwide movement toward the relaxation of trade barriers is the United States. Because of its relatively great economic strength, its favorable balance of payments position, and the importance of its market to the well-being of the rest of the world, the influence of the United States on world commercial policies far surpasses that of any other nation.[3]

Despite the perception of a common interest in management and an open system and despite the willingness by the United States to lead the system, domestic political conflict made it difficult to translate the generally perceived common goals into an international order for trade. The conflict between domestic politics and international management began with the Havana Charter, the first attempt to build an order for international trade. The charter was an essential part of the plan to create a new, internationally managed economic system in the postwar era and, like the rest of that plan, was a product of strong U.S. leadership.

United States efforts to create an open system dated from the Reciprocal Trade Agreements Act of 1934, a product of Cordell Hull's liberal vision. Under that act, the United States concluded numerous agreements reducing the high tariffs of the early 1930s. During World War II, the United States obtained from its allies commitments to a postwar international commercial order based on the freeing of international trade. In 1945, the United States presented a plan for a multilateral commercial convention to regulate and reduce restrictions on international trade. The convention offered rules for many aspects of international trade—tariffs, preferences, quantitative restrictions, subsidies, state trading, international commodity agreements—and provided for an International Trade Organization (ITO), the equivalent of the IMF (International Monetary Fund) in the area of trade, to oversee the system. In 1946 the United States called for an international conference to discuss this U.S. proposal and to implement a new trading order.[4]

Agreement on a new international order for trade, however, was more difficult to achieve than was agreement on a monetary order. The process of negotiation was very different from that of Bretton Woods, in which the United States and the United Kingdom dominated the decision making and there was little disagreement on the features of the desired system. The United States clearly played a leadership role in the negotiation process, but because each participant faced important domestic political constraints, the United States was not able to impose its plan on others. Britain, for example, insisted on provisions for its Imperial Preference System; other Europeans insisted on safeguards for balance-of-payments problems; and the less-developed countries demanded provisions for economic development. The result was a long-delayed international negotiation. Discussion began in 1943, but the final negotiations did not take place until 1947. In the end, the Havana Charter was a complex compromise that embodied in some way the wishes of everyone, but in the end it satisfied no one.[5]

Nevertheless, the charter might have become operational had it not been for domestic politics in the United States. . . . After delaying for three years, the Truman Administration finally decided in 1950 that it would not submit the Havana Charter to Congress, where it faced inevitable defeat. Once the United States withdrew, the charter was dead.[6] Despite a prevailing norm of international cooperation and strong persistent U.S. leadership, an agreement on international control of trade proved elusive.

Multilateral Management Under U.S. Leadership

The demise of the Havana Charter meant that trade management would be more limited than was originally envisaged. The consensus for an international trading order survived, embodied in GATT (General Agreement on Tariffs and Trade), which had been drawn up in 1947 to provide a procedural base and establish guiding principles for the tariff negotiations then being held in Geneva. Intended to be a temporary treaty to serve until the Havana Charter was implemented, GATT, by default, became the world's trading organization.

GATT reflected the prevailing agreement on open trade: the economic consensus that open trade would allow countries to specialize according to their comparative advantage and thereby achieve higher levels of growth and well-being, and the political consensus that a liberal trading regime would promote not only prosperity but also peace. The major rule for implementing free trade was the GATT principle of nondiscrimination. All of the contracting parties, that is, member states, agreed to adhere to the most-favored-nation principle, which stipulated that "any advantage, favour, privilege or immunity granted by any contracting party to any product originating in or destined for any other country shall be accorded immediately and unconditionally to the like product originating in or destined for the territories of all other contracting parties."[7] The only

exceptions to this general rule of equal treatment were for existing preferential systems and future customs unions and free-trade associations.
A second element of nondiscrimination in the GATT was the provision
for national treatment designed to prevent discrimination against foreign products after they enter a country. Under GATT rules, a country must give imports the same treatment as it gives products made domestically in such areas as taxation, regulation, transportation, and
distribution.[8]

GATT also established an international commercial code with
rules on such issues as dumping and subsidies. The most important rule
prohibited the use of quantitative restrictions, such as quotas, except for
balance-of-payments or national security reasons. GATT also provided
a mechanism for resolving disputes under this commercial code.

There were, however, important departures from these rules.
Provisions in the original GATT treaty and amendments made in the
1950s established a separate regime for agricultural trade. GATT rules
on agriculture reflected the powerful political influence of agricultural
groups in the contracting parties of GATT and the resultant policies of
government intervention to protect domestic prices and producer incomes and to assure food security. . . .

There were also important gaps in the coverage of GATT as
compared with the Havana Charter. Provisions for economic development, commodity agreements, restrictive business practices, and trade
in services, for example, were not included. In addition, other topics not
of great concern at the time, such as relations with state trading countries, were left undeveloped in the code. These departures from GATT
norms and gaps in GATT coverage eventually became a major problem
for the management of international trade. Finally, GATT's institutional mechanisms had important weaknesses. The dispute settlement
mechanism was lengthy, allowed parties to delay or block decisions, and
was not binding.

In addition to establishing trade principles, GATT provided a
set of rules and procedures for what was to be the principal method of
trade management in the postwar period: multilateral trade negotiations. The agreement contained a commitment to enter into such negotiations and provided guidelines for them. The most important rule
was reciprocity, the concept that tariff reductions should be mutually
advantageous. Although not part of the original GATT, the principal
supplier procedure by which negotiations were to take place among actual or potential principal suppliers also became a negotiating rule of
GATT.

From a temporary treaty, GATT became not only an established
commercial code but also an international organization with a secretariat and a director general to oversee the implementation of its rules,

manage dispute settlement, and provide a forum and support for multilateral trade negotiations.

Whereas GATT provided the framework for achieving trade liberalization, the United States put that framework into action. With the coming of the Cold War, Cordell Hull's vision of trade liberalization took on new significance as a key to a prosperous West and Western security in the face of Soviet aggression. United States economic strength and the lure of foreign markets were a further reason for U.S. interest in leading trade liberalization. . . .

In the two decades following World War II, the United States led the system by helping Europe and Japan rebuild production and by pushing for trade liberalization. In the early years, the Marshall Plan, or the European Recovery Program as it was officially known, was the tool of U.S. leadership in Europe. As we have seen, the United States played a key role in financing international trade and encouraging long-term European trade competitiveness through the Marshall Plan. The United States also used the plan as a lever to encourage regional trade liberalization in Europe. During the war and the immediate postwar period, significant barriers to trade had been erected throughout Europe, which underscored the trade restrictions in effect since the 1930s. The United States pushed actively for the liberalization of trade and payments among Western European countries and, in some cases, made available the funds for such liberalization, even though this conflicted with the larger U.S. goal of nondiscrimination on an international basis and even though regional liberalization sometimes involved direct discrimination against the United States.[9]

The United States also took an important leadership role with Japan. During the Occupation, the supreme commander for the Allied forces and his administration directly controlled Japanese trade and the Japanese monetary system. Until the 1960s, the United States helped the recovery and development in Japan by keeping the U.S. market open for Japanese goods while at the same time accepting Japanese protectionist policies, many of which had been instituted under the Occupation. The United States also supported Japanese membership in GATT and urged the Europeans, unsuccessfully, to open their markets to Japanese exports.[10]

Finally, the United States took a leading role in multilateral trade negotiations. . . . In the postwar period, this procedure of bilateral negotiations based on reciprocity was expanded to a series of multilateral trade negotiations conducted by the members of GATT. The United States, with the world's largest economy and a huge share of international trade, was the essential motivating force in these negotiations. Because the United States was, in many cases, one of the world's principal suppliers, its participation was required under GATT's negotiating rules. Because the U.S. market was so important, there was little possibility of achieving reciprocity in tariff negotiations without the United States. Most importantly, without U.S. initiatives, the negotiations would probably never have taken place. Initiatives by the United States were responsible for the eight major trade negotiations from the Geneva Round in 1947 to the Uruguay Round, which began in 1986. The U.S. negotiators were necessary participants—mobilizing others, seeking compromises—in the actual negotiations.

Furthermore, throughout the 1940s and 1950s, the United States accepted limited benefits from the trade negotiations. Although tariffs were reduced on a reciprocal and mutually beneficial basis, U.S. trading partners gained more than the United States did. Because of European and Japanese exchange controls that persisted through the 1950s, the trade concessions had a limited effect on U.S. exports. Because the United States did not impose controls, Europe and Japan gained immediate benefit from the tariff reductions. The United States accepted such asymmetrical benefits because of a commitment to European and Japanese recovery, because it expected to benefit from the reductions when the exchange controls were removed, and because it sought to maintain the momentum of establishing a more open trading system.

The system worked very well for the developed countries. Most quotas and exchange rate barriers were eliminated. Although restrictions remained in agricultural products, there was substantial liberalization of trade in manufactured products.[11] The rapid growth of trade was an important source of economic prosperity. The high point of trade management of this period was the Kennedy Round, which culminated in 1967. Although states were unable to reach any significant agreement on agricultural trade, tariffs on nonagricultural products in the developed countries were reduced by about one-third.[12] After the Kennedy Round reductions, tariffs on dutiable, nonagricultural products were reduced to an average of 9.9 percent in the United States, 8.6 percent in the six EC (European Community) states, 10.8 percent in the United Kingdom, and 10.7 percent in Japan.[13]

Structural Change and Protectionism

After 1967, however, important changes in the international trading system began to emerge and to undermine the GATT system of management and the liberal international trading order created by GATT. Over the next two decades, structural changes led to domestic political challenges to international management of trade and to new forms of protection. Governments sought, with only limited success, to stem the tide of protectionism and to modernize the international trading regime. Thus, the conflict between national and international approaches to management—the same conflict we have seen in the international monetary system—came to plague international trade management.

As in the case of monetary relations, a central force for change was increased interdependence. Interdependence increased the level of political sensitivity to trade as trade came to affect more sectors and more jobs. After World War II, economic growth, trade liberalization, decreasing transportation costs, and broadening business horizons led to a surge in trade among the developed market economies.[14] Merchandise trade among the developed countries more than quadrupled between 1963 and 1973; increased over two-and-one-half times from 1973 to 1983; and grew almost one-and-one-half times again between 1983 and 1986.[15] From 1960 to 1986, the percentage of GDP derived from trade (exports plus imports) doubled to 14.4 percent in the United States, gained 40 percent to an average 63 percent in the original six EC countries, while remaining fairly constant at 17.3 percent in Japan.[16] The role of trade was even greater in certain sectors. For example, in 1979, 5.5 percent of U.S. consumer goods and 12 percent of U.S. business equipment purchases came from abroad. By 1987, the figures for consumer goods had grown to about 12 percent, whereas foreign business equipment outlays exceeded 40 percent.[17] Interdependence in certain sectors was reinforced by the emergence of the global company which sources parts from around the world. One example is the Boeing Company, which produces commercial jetliners. In 1980, imported parts accounted for 2 to 3 percent of airplanes produced by Boeing. By 1988, imported parts represented 28 percent of Boeing airplanes.[18]

Another dimension of trade interdependence was growing convergence of the developed countries' economies. The rapid accumulation of physical and human capital, the transfer of technology, and the growing similarities of wages narrowed the differences in factor endowments, which are the basis for comparative advantage and trade. In 1970, for example, labor costs in the United States and West Germany were over twice the labor costs in Japan. By 1986, the costs were roughly equal.[19] Similarly, in 1970, U.S. manufacturing productivity was 58 percent greater than West Germany and 105 percent greater than Japan in 1970. By 1986, these figures had fallen to 20 percent and 2 percent, respectively.[20] Convergence altered the nature of comparative advantage, leading to more complex specialization and fostering the global company and intraindustry trade. Also, because of economic convergence, small changes in factor costs led to large shifts in comparative advantage and thus in trade, production, and employment—and to political reaction to those shifts.

A second change that increased protectionist pressures was the shift in competitiveness worldwide. Changes in factor endowments altered the competitive positions of several industries in the developed countries, including autos, steel, textiles, shipping, and consumer electronics. In some sectors, the shift favored the developing countries. Lags in capital investment in the developed countries plus rising labor productivity, lower labor costs, and aggressive export policies in some of the LDCs led to a shift in comparative advantage toward the newly industrialized countries (NICs), such as Taiwan, Korea, and Brazil.[21] In other cases, because of differing levels of investment and research, of management effectiveness and labor productivity, as well as exchange rate changes, the shift occurred among the developed countries. The reasons for this shift in competitiveness among developed countries has become a subject of significant debate. In the United States, for example, debate has focused heavily on declining U.S. competitiveness vis-à-vis Japan, which has been evidenced by greater Japanese investment per employee, greater productivity growth, and greater average growth of total gross fixed capital formation.[22]

The main economic manifestations of the shift in competitiveness were serious competition from imports and surplus capacity—that is, a demand inadequate to maintain price, profit, and employment at politically acceptable levels—in industries that had been the mainstays of many economies.[23] The major political manifestation was pressure from these sectors for protection. The combination of interdependence and changes in competitiveness made national economies more sensitive to external events and provoked domestic producers to mobilize for protection from foreign competition.

A third change contributing to protectionism were disruptions in the economic system in the 1970s and 1980s. Trade management from the end of World War II until the end of the Kennedy Round took place in an environment of unprecedented growth and stability. From 1960 to 1970, growth in the OECD countries averaged almost 5 percent per year, unemployment stood at 2.7 percent, and the volume of world trade grew at an average annual rate of 8.5 percent.[24] Throughout this period, the U.S. trade balance was strongly positive, providing the basis for a national consensus for liberalizing trade. . . . In such an expanding world economy, economic groups were able to perceive the advantages of cooperation and trade liberalization.

In the 1970s and 1980s, these favorable conditions altered dramatically and contributed to the new protectionism. The 1970s was the era of stagflation, slow growth combined with rampant inflation. In the wake of the oil crisis, the developed countries' real GNP growth dropped to 2.7 percent between 1974 and 1979, while their inflation exploded to double digits, reaching a high of 13.4 percent in 1974.[25] Unemployment in the OECD countries increased to an average of 4.9 percent for the period 1974 to 1979.[26] Stagflation increased pressures on governments to adopt beggar-thy-neighbor policies such as trade restrictions.

The floating exchange rate system also contributed to growing protectionism. In the 1970s, monetary problems led to trade measures designed to protect payments balances such as exchange controls and special duties. The breakdown in the system of fixed exchange rates also complicated the process of trade negotiations. In a fixed rate system, negotiators had been able to estimate the impact of agreements on their trade and payments. Under floating rates, such calculations were much more difficult. As a result of these economic changes, world trade grew by only 5 percent between 1970 and 1980.[27]

In the early 1980s, deep recession put a brake on trade. Deflationary policies led to a steady decline in inflation from 12.9 percent in 1980 to 2.5 percent in 1986.[28] At the same time, growth ground to a halt. The years 1980 to 1982 witnessed the lowest average growth rate—0.73 percent per year—of any three-year period since the end of World War II.[29] Unemployment rose to levels once thought politically unacceptable. By the end of 1983, recession had pushed total unemployment in the OECD countries to a record 8.5 percent.[30] Significantly, unemployment was concentrated in those industries with the highest levels of foreign competition. For example, in December 1982, when total U.S. unemployment reached its peak of 10.6 percent, unemployment in the auto industry stood at 23.2 percent, and in the primary metals (steel) industry, it was 29.2 percent.[31] Because of the recession, world trade stagnated. The volume of world trade growth slowed to 1.2 percent in 1980, 0.8 percent in 1981, and actually fell by 2.2 percent in 1982.[32]

By the second half of the 1980s, the economic environment improved. Growth among the developed countries rose to 3.2 percent in 1985 and 2.8 percent in 1986, while inflation fell to 4.5 percent in 1985 and to 2.5 percent in 1986.[33] World trade also expanded, growing 3.5 percent in 1986 and 4.0 percent in 1987.[34] Because of labor market rigidities, however, unemployment remained high and persisted as a force for protection. In 1986, unemployment in the developed countries still stood at 8.3 percent, with U.S. unemployment at 7.0 percent, Japanese at 2.8 percent, and the EC at 11.2 percent.[35] In the 1980s, the exchange rate system emerged as a central problem for trade management. As we have seen, the misalignment of exchange rates was a major factor in the emergence of massive trade and payments imbalances. In particular, the overvaluation of the dollar and corresponding undervaluation of the yen and deutsche mark were a major cause of the U.S. trade deficit and the resultant rise in protectionism in the United States.

Pluralism

In the 1970s and 1980s, the rise of Japan and the European Economic Community and the relative decline of the United States complicated the system of trade management. Trade problems and a decline in power combined with growing protectionist pressures left the United States less willing and less able to lead the system. At the same time, the EC and Japan were not prepared to assume a leadership role. Absent strong leadership, management where power is more evenly shared proved a major challenge to the system. . . .

[O]ne of the most important developments in the 1970s and 1980s was the erosion of U.S. dominance of the international trading system and the related decline in U.S. support for a multilateral trade regime. While the United States remained the world's largest economy and largest trading power, it was no longer overwhelmingly preponderant as in the first two postwar decades. In 1950 the United States accounted for 26.1 percent of trade among developed market economies; by 1980 that figure had fallen to 18.3 percent.[36] Furthermore, after 1970 the United States began to experience what seemed to be chronic merchandise trade deficits. The huge and traditional (since 1893) U.S. merchandise-trade surplus turned in 1971 into a persistent and growing merchandise-trade deficit.[37] The United States traditional surplus with Japan turned into deficit in 1965, and its traditional surplus with Western Europe diminished and in 1983 became a deficit.[38] In the 1980s, U.S. trade deficits soared due to several factors: an overvalued dollar; strong U.S. economic growth in comparison with other developed countries; the declining rate of increase in U.S. productivity relative to other industrialized countries; lower demand for U.S. agricultural exports; the increased competitiveness of foreign companies in many traditional sectors even as the competitiveness of U.S. industry declined; the rise in the number of protectionist barriers; and the Third World debt crisis, which resulted in sharply reduced imports by debtor countries that had been important U.S. markets. In 1987 the U.S. merchandise-trade deficit reached its nadir of $167 billion.

. . . [D]omestic pressures for protection increased and became increasingly effective. As trade problems developed, more industries organized into special interest groups to put pressure on Congress and the executive for relief from foreign competition. Beginning in the late 1960s following the Kennedy Round, vulnerable industries, such as textiles, steel, electronics, and shoes, began to put strong pressure on Congress to alleviate import competition.[39] In 1970, organized labor officially shifted its policy from support for free trade to active lobbying for protection. Proposals for sectoral protectionist legislation increased in

Congress and put pressure on the President to negotiate bilateral agreements outside the GATT to avert legislated quotas and tariffs. At the same time, U.S. industries facing barriers to market access abroad increasingly turned to the U.S. government for help in breaking down foreign barriers. As markets became increasingly global, many high-technology, export-oriented industries, such as microelectronics and supercomputer industries, chafed under restrictions on access to foreign markets. Their goal was to use access to U.S. markets as bargaining leverage to open up foreign markets.[40]

As the trade problem deepened and spread from sensitive industries to the entire economy in the 1980s, many U.S. industry, labor, and political leaders came to believe the United States was no longer benefiting from the system and was being subjected to unfair treatment by its trading partners and by the trading regime. Japan, in particular, was singled out as a country that benefited from the liberal trading order and access to U.S. markets while maintaining barriers to its own market.[41] Proposals for broad-based protectionist legislation increased in Congress. In 1988, Congress enacted omnibus trade legislation, which tightened U.S. trade law to give the president less discretion in case of unfair trade practices by foreign competitors and to require the executive branch to identify and achieve changes in the policy of countries that have unfair trade practices.[42]

In response to persistent congressional pressures, the Reagan administration sought nonlegislative ways to resolve trade conflicts: negotiated voluntary export restraint agreements as in automobiles; negotiations to open overseas markets, such as the Market Opening Sector Specific (MOSS) talks between the U.S. and Japan; and aggressive use of the U.S. trade provisions, which authorizes the U.S. government to retaliate against countries deemed not to be allowing U.S. exports fair market access. Finally, the United States negotiated a broad-based bilateral trading agreement with Israel in 1986 and a more important agreement with Canada in 1987. The U.S.-Canada Free Trade Agreement reduced a number of trade and investment barriers between the two countries, established rules on trade in services, and put in place a new dispute settlement mechanism between the two countries. Although the free-trade agreement was described as a reinforcement of the multilateral regime and a model for future GATT agreements on investment and services, it was potentially a departure from the postwar U.S. policy of multilateralism in international trade.[43]

Despite the important shift in the domestic political consensus, the United States remained committed to the multilateral system. As it negotiated VRAs and bilateral free-trade agreements, the United States also continued efforts to reform the GATT system and to further trade liberalization through multilateral negotiations. United States initiatives launched both the Tokyo and the Uruguay Rounds of multilateral trade negotiations. And a key provision of the 1988 trade legislation authorized the president to enter into multilateral trade negotiations, which Congress agreed to approve under fast-track procedures.

The New Protectionism

The result of these structural changes in the global trading economy was a surge in protectionist policies in developed countries. The new protectionism took several forms.

One form was nontariff barriers (NTBs) to trade. In part, the NTB problem grew out of the very success of the GATT. GATT had been designed to liberalize trade by removing quotas and tariffs. With the success of such liberalization in manufactured products, the major remaining barriers to trade were nontariff barriers such as government procurement policies, customs procedures, health and sanitary regulations, national standards, and a broad range of other laws and regulations that discriminate against imports or offer assistance to exports. Regional policy, agricultural policy, and consumer and environmental protection are other examples of nontariff measures that have trade-distorting consequences.

Furthermore, the success of the GATT in trade liberalization actually increased the use of nontariff barriers. Because governments can no longer use tariffs and quotas as tools of national economic policy, they have tried to shape comparative advantage through a variety of national industrial policies. States have used subsidies and tax preferences to help ailing industries, such as steel and shipbuilding. They have provided a variety of incentives for the development of new, technologically sophisticated industries, such as airframes and computers. And they have used a combination of tax and financial incentives as well as requirements for local content, export performance, and technology transfer for foreign investors.

Countries now had to reduce nontariff trade barriers to maintain what had already been achieved, let alone continue the process of liberalization. However, the control of nontariff barriers is far more difficult than the regulation and removal of tariffs and quotas. Such policies are usually an integral part of national economic and social policies. Because they are often carried out for reasons other than trade protection, NTBs have traditionally been considered national prerogatives not subject to international negotiation. Nontariff barriers also pose practical negotiating problems. Because NTBs take many different forms and because many different governmental bodies have authority over them, it is not possible to conduct broad international negotiations, such as those over tariffs. The reduction of nontariff barriers requires international agreements to coordinate and harmonize a broad range of policies, for which GATT offers few guidelines.[44]

Another form of the new protectionism were voluntary restraint agreements (VRA), also known as voluntary export restraints (VER). VRAs were developed as a response to pressure for protection from import-sensitive industries. GATT provides three principal forms of recourse for industries hurt by imports. If foreign competitors are dumping, that is, selling goods abroad at prices below those in the home market, countries are allowed to impose a duty to offset the dumping. Although the anti-dumping law is well developed both domestically and internationally, action can take a long time, and proving dumping cases can be difficult. GATT also permits countries to impose duties to offset foreign subsidies of exported products. However, this is a remedy used only by the United States. Finally, GATT permits certain emergency measures known as safeguard actions. GATT permits governments to impose restrictions on fairly traded imports if an unforeseen surge in imports resulting from a trade concession causes or threatens serious injury to a domestic industry. Such safeguard actions must be applied to all countries; protection must be limited in time and be gradually removed; and importing countries must adopt meaningful adjustment policies. For several reasons, however, this GATT provision has rarely been invoked. It must be applied to all countries, whereas governments have preferred to target certain suppliers for import controls. GATT also requires the importing country to grant compensatory concessions to all affected exporting countries. Furthermore, GATT does not clearly define "serious injury" and offers inadequate guidance—for example, on consultative procedures, duration, and adjustment—for implementing and regulating safeguards actions. Thus, governments have turned increasingly to VRAs, which are outside the GATT framework.[45]

Under such agreements, which are usually bilateral and sometimes secret, low-cost exporters "voluntarily" restrict sales to countries where their goods are threatening industry and employment. There is a long history of such agreements. In the 1950s and 1960s, for example, the United States negotiated a number of voluntary export controls with Japan and many LDCs, under which exporters restricted their sales in the U.S. market. Two agreements—the Longterm Textile Arrangement of 1962 and the subsequent Multi-Fiber Arrangement of 1974—were negotiated multilaterally and within the GATT context. . . . These earlier agreements were unusual steps, exceptions to normal GATT procedures. In the recent period, however, VRAs have become an

accepted mode of trade regulation.[46] In the 1970s and 1980s, VRAs proliferated in various sectors—textiles, steel, automobiles, electronics, and
footwear—and covered trade among the industrial nations themselves.

In the United States, the typical pattern has been a surge of imports, followed by massive filings of unfair trade actions, followed by
pressure on Congress for protectionist legislation, followed, in turn, by a
negotiated voluntary export restraint agreement as a way to reduce imports without resolving the legal cases and without legislating protection.

Steel was the first major industry subjected to VRAs among developed market economies. In 1968, faced with surging imports and
under pressure from proposed legislation to limit steel imports, the
Johnson administration negotiated VRAs with the European Community and Japan, which set specific tonnage limits on each for their steel
exports to the United States.[47] In 1978, in response to new surges of
imports and a large number of anti-dumping cases, the Carter administration instituted the trigger price mechanism (TPM), which established a "fair value" reference price for steel based on Japanese production costs. All European and Japanese imports entering the United
States below that price were presumed to be dumped and were subject
to a fast-track anti-dumping investigation. By 1982, due to a rise in the
dollar and renewed import competition, the TPM was on the rocks.
Numerous trade actions against foreign producers and proposed legislation to cut imports forced the Reagan administration to negotiate
VERs with not only the EC, Japan, and Australia, but also Argentina,
Brazil, Mexico, Korea, and South Africa.[48]

In the 1980s, VRAs among developed countries grew. The most
important industry to be added to the list was automobiles, which account for 15 percent of world manufactured goods exports.[49] A surge in
Japanese exports led to legal and political pressure to keep Japanese automobiles out of Western Europe and the United States. The first VRA
on automobiles was in 1976 between the United Kingdom and Japan.
The following year, France negotiated an agreement with Japan. In
1981, in response to proposed legislation to limit Japanese imports, the
Reagan administration and Japan agreed to a VER. Agreements with
West Germany, Canada, the Netherlands, Belgium, and Luxembourg
followed.[50] By the latter half of the 1980s, VRAs had spread to high-
technology sectors.

The GATT regime became increasingly irrelevant in the face of
the new protectionism. GATT had been designed to manage import restrictions, especially quantitative restrictions and tariffs, not nontariff barriers and voluntary export controls. Furthermore, countries often preferred politically negotiated bilateral solutions to GATT's multilateral
rules and procedures. Finally, with increasing government intervention in
the economy, shifting comparative advantage and surplus capacity in

many sectors, and frequent departures from GATT rules, many policy-makers and analysts began to argue for a regime based on managed trade, not on the GATT principle of open trade. A managed-trade regime would recognize the reality, indeed the desirability, of government intervention in national economies to decide comparative advantage and intergovernmental agreements to shape international trade flows.[51] Proposals for such a regime ranged from an outright advocacy of tariff barriers as a tool of national policy[52] to proposals for global negotiations to allocate world production[53] to a set of regimes based on varying levels of government intervention, anywhere from managed trade in surplus sectors to free trade in the advanced sectors.[54]

New Issues

In addition to the new protectionism, trade management in the 1980s had to confront trade problems in sectors that had not yet been brought under GATT rules and process. One such challenge for GATT was both old and new protectionism in agriculture. As we have seen, agriculture was subject to a separate GATT regime and did not benefit from the liberalization process of the postwar era.

National agricultural policies of most developed countries remained interventionist and protectionist. Since the 1930s, the U.S. government has intervened in domestic agricultural markets to maintain agricultural prices and the income of U.S. farmers. It has supported domestic prices by purchasing surplus commodities, production controls, and deficiency payments, and further managed the domestic market through export subsidies and import quotas. Japan's government, led by a political party that has depended heavily on electoral support from farmers and also motivated by a deep concern for food security resulting from wartime shortages, has widespread import restrictions to maintain domestic agricultural prices above world price levels and to provide farmers with incomes comparable to nonfarmers.

The European Community maintains farm incomes through its Common Agricultural Policy (CAP). The CAP establishes common, artificially high internal prices, which it maintains through the purchase of surpluses and a flexible external tariff on agricultural imports, which ensures that imported products are more expensive than domestic products and that imported products can only assume the slack that the EC producers cannot fill. Because the CAP has no production controls, high prices for agricultural products have generated large food surpluses, which are exported with the help of export subsidies.

Although protection was extensive, the exemption of agriculture from the rules of international trade did not become a serious problem until the 1980s. Conflict was limited because agricultural trade grew steadily, driven by economic growth, rising incomes, and improved diets. However, in the 1970s, burgeoning populations, inappropriate agricultural policies in developing countries and the Eastern bloc, unfavorable weather conditions, and overall global inflation led to a dramatic rise in the demand for food imports and in the price of agricultural products. Rising prices and expected long-term food shortages led both importing and exporting countries to increase production.[55] Favorable market conditions combined with government encouragement resulted in soaring food production.[56]

. . . GATT was unable to restrain the agricultural trade war, because domestic agricultural programs and export subsidies received special treatment under its rules. The combination of trade war and budgetary costs led countries for the first time in the postwar period to consider seriously multilateral negotiations that would change the GATT regime for agriculture and lead to reform of domestic agricultural policies.

In addition to agriculture, other sectors not adequately covered by the GATT raised important management issues in the 1980s. As the structure of international production and trade evolved, the developed countries tried to adapt GATT to cover industries of increasing importance in international trade.

One challenge was posed by the growing importance of services in the national economies and international trade of the developed countries. Services, or invisibles, differ from goods in that they cannot be stored and, therefore, require some form of direct relationship between the buyer and seller. The international trade of services thus requires some form of commercial presence in foreign markets. Consumer services are provided directly to retail customers by such businesses as restaurants, hotels, and travel agencies and tend to be produced, sold, and consumed within the same market. Producer services—banking, securities trading, insurance, law, advertising, accounting, data processing—are used in the intermediate production of manufactured goods and other services and are more frequently traded internationally.

By the late 1970s, services in the United States accounted for two-thirds of the GNP and for more than 50 percent of the GNPs in twelve other developed countries. Within the service sector, producer services experienced particularly rapid growth. As the economies of the developed countries matured, services came to play an ever greater role in the production and distribution of goods.[57] During the 1970s and 1980s, services also became a major factor in international trade among developed countries.[58] The liberalization of goods and capital markets created business opportunities for firms trading in services, while the revolution in telecommunications and computer technologies made possible the rapid transmission of data at long distances and enabled services to be offered across national boundaries. By 1986, for example, U.S. exports of services amounted to $148.4 billion, equivalent to 39.8 percent of U.S. exports.[59] Because of problems both in defining services and collecting data, worldwide exports of services are difficult to quantify with any degree of certainty. Many estimates put this figure around $600 billion.[60] Services account for between 20 percent[61] and 30 percent[62] of world trade.

Services trade has grown despite widespread nontariff barriers. Many service industries, such as telecommunications, banking and insurance, and law and accounting, are highly regulated and often involve state-owned industry. Frequently, such regulation discriminates against foreign services providers by denying access to national markets or by imposing constraints on activities of foreign firms operating in domestic markets. Such barriers include discriminatory treatment of foreign firms in licensing and taxation; policies through which a section of the market is reserved for domestic industry; investment performance requirements; discriminatory government procurement; and government monopolies.[63] Barriers to trade in services have not been subject to the process of liberalization, because services are not covered by the GATT regime. Although there have been efforts to establish liberalizing rules for such services as insurance in the OECD, by and large services have been outside the international trade regime.

As services grew in importance in the developed countries, service industries, particularly those in the United States and the United Kingdom, began to organize to press governments for adaptation of the trading regime to cover services. In the United States, for example, the service industry successfully pressed for a change in U.S. trade law to make trade rules and remedies applicable to services as well as goods.[64] As a result, services barriers began to receive greater attention in bilateral U.S. trade relations. The service sector in the developed countries also sought to make the inclusion of services in the GATT a goal of the Uruguay Round of multilateral trade negotiations.

Intellectual property is another new trade issue.[65] The comparative advantage of many of the most competitive industries of the developed market economies has become increasingly dependent on their advanced technology, which is expensive and time consuming to develop. Such technology can sometimes be easily and quickly copied and used to produce products at a much lower cost than that incurred by the developer, thus undermining the competitive ability of the firm that developed the technology. The cost of computer software, for example, derives largely from developmental costs. Yet such software can often be easily copied and sold at a price far below the cost to the developer. Similarly, the cost of developing pharmaceutical products is high, while drugs can be easily copied, produced, and sold below the cost to the developer.

For this reason and to encourage the development of technology, most developed countries protect the developer of technology through patent, trademark, and copyright laws. However, intellectual property protection differs among the developed countries and frequently is nonexistent in developing countries. As high-technology firms have increased in importance in trade and as their concern about intellectual property has increased, they have argued that such pirating undermines their ability to compete internationally and, thus, disrupts trade. Because efforts to standardize and expand protection for intellectual property through the World Intellectual Property Organization (WIPO) have not led to common rules and dispute settlement procedures, they and their governments argued that GATT should be broadened to cover intellectual property.

Finally, some developed countries also pressed for GATT rules to eliminate trade-restrictive and trade-distorting effects of government investment policies and practices.[66] Trade-related investment measures (TRIMs) include local content requirements, which require domestic sourcing; licensing requirements, which stipulate that an investor license production locally and often limit the amount of royalties; product mandating requirements, which oblige an investor to supply certain markets with specific products; trade-balancing requirements, which mandate arbitrary export or import levels; and export-performance requirements, which oblige an investor to export a percentage of its production.

The Tokyo and Uruguay Rounds

The Tokyo and Uruguay Rounds—the seventh and eighth rounds of multilateral trade negotiations—attempted to respond to the changed international trading system, to reform the postwar system of trade management by developing rules in new areas, and by addressing nontariff barriers to trade. The Tokyo Round, begun in 1973 and completed in 1979, started the process of trade reform.

The Tokyo Round of Multilateral Trade Negotiations (MTN) was the result of a U.S. initiative launched after the dollar crisis of 1971. Begun in 1973 in the midst of the oil crisis, deep recession, and rising protectionism, it took place in an economic and political environment less propitious than that of earlier trade negotiations. Nevertheless, its goals were more ambitious than those of earlier rounds.

Previous negotiations sought to lower quotas and tariff barriers, primarily on nonagricultural products, and to implement GATT goals and rules. The Tokyo Round continued the pursuit of tariff reduction and also tried to regulate uncharted areas of international trade such as non-tariff barriers; safeguards (i.e., the use of unilateral measures such as voluntary export restraint agreements); tropical products, which were of interest to developing countries; agriculture; and several sectors in which there were still unresolved problems.

In April 1979—six-and-a-half years after the first meeting in Tokyo—the multilateral trade negotiations were concluded.[67] Some of the goals of the participants had been achieved: tariffs on manufactured products were reduced; codes on certain nontariff barriers (NTBs) were drawn up; and changes were made in the application of GATT rules to the LDCs. Other efforts collapsed, including the liberalization of trade in agriculture and, most critically, the effort to regulate safeguards.

The most important outcome of the Tokyo Round was the progress made on regulating nontariff barriers to trade. The Tokyo Round agreement included several new codes that significantly modified the GATT system by extending trade management to nontariff barriers to trade. For example, the Code on Subsidies and Countervailing Duties was a step toward dealing with national industrial policies. The code recognized subsidies on manufactured products (but not raw materials) as nontariff barriers to trade. It allowed countries unilaterally to impose countervailing duties when a subsidy led to a material injury in the importing country and, with authorization from the other signatories, to impose such duties if subsidies led to injury to exports in third markets. A dumping code established comparable rules for anti-dumping measures. The Code on Government Procurement recognized government purchasing policies as NTBs and set rules for giving equal treatment to both national and foreign firms bidding for contracts from official entities. Although the number of government agencies covered by the code was small, it established an important precedent. Other codes covering product standards and customs valuation and licensing established rules for regulating these NTBs. The NTB codes not only established rules but also provided for surveillance and dispute settlement mechanisms. Each code set up a committee of signatories, some of which had powers only to consult (i.e., to oversee) and some of which were given dispute settlement authority.[68]

Despite the new departure signified by the NTB codes, there remained important limits to their effectiveness. Because the NTB codes apply only to the signatories, they diverged for the first time from the GATT principle of most-favored-nation status (MFN) or nondiscrimination. Whereas the developed countries signed and ratified the MTN codes, most of the developing countries were not convinced of their value and chose not to sign, thus leaving themselves open to discrimination that is legal under GATT's rules. The codes are also incomplete. The Code on Subsidies and Countervailing Duties, for example, does not specify which forms of government intervention beyond direct export subsidies are to be considered trade barriers.[69] Even more serious was the failure to reach agreement on a safeguards code to bring rapidly proliferating VRAs under multilateral management. The pivotal, unresolvable issue in the safeguards negotiations was selectivity, the desire of some GATT contracting parties, most importantly the EC, to target safeguards measures instead of applying them on a MFN basis.[70]

The efforts to extend trade management to include agriculture also met with little success. The negotiations were unable to reconcile two opposing views of the purpose and nature of international control in agriculture. The United States, because of its competitive advantage in agriculture, advocated liberalization of agricultural trade including the modification of the European Community's CAP. The EC, on the other hand, urged the use of commodity agreements to stabilize world prices and long-term supply and refused to negotiate on the fundamentals of CAP. Japan was also unwilling to liberalize trade in agriculture. The result was thus minimal: an agreement to consult about certain agricultural problems, including those connected with meat and dairy products. The sectoral negotiations yielded only one important result: an agreement on civil aircraft that liberalizes trade in this industry. Finally, only limited progress was made on improving GATT's dispute settlement mechanism. Thus, although the MTN was an important step, it was only a limited one,[71] and it was to prove inadequate to stem the burgeoning protectionist pressures of the 1980s.

Following the Tokyo Round, pressures on the GATT system increased. Departures from GATT rules, such as voluntary export restraints, grew; the agriculture trade war erupted; and trade conflicts became more frequent and more heated. Nevertheless, the postwar political consensus supporting open trade remained alive, if not well. The leaders of the developed countries used summit and OECD meetings to reiterate their commitment to open trade principles and to resolving specific conflicts, even as they negotiated managed-trade agreements. New forms of international dialogue were tried. Bilateral meetings, most notably between the United States and Japan, were used to try to resolve specific trade conflicts, and multilateral meetings, such as regular quadrilateral meetings of the United States, Japan, the European Community, and Canada, were begun to try to resolve systemic issues.

The precarious nature of the multilateral trading regime was revealed in 1982, when GATT held its first ministerial meeting since the 1973 meeting that launched the Tokyo Round. The agenda of the meeting was ambitious: a review of the Tokyo codes on NTBs; action on GATT dispute-settlement procedures; continuation of the negotiations on a safeguards code; efforts to bring agriculture under the GATT regime; and consideration of new codes on trade in high technology and services. The meeting ended in failure. The ministers made virtually no progress on any issues under discussion and could pledge only to "make determined efforts" to ensure that their countries' trade policies were consistent with GATT's rules.[72] Perhaps the most positive result of the ministerial meeting was the widening recognition that the international trading system faced collapse.

The following year, the Reagan administration, aided by the economic recovery in the United States, supported by Japan and the GATT secretariat, began a campaign to launch a new round of multilateral trade negotiations. Initially the EC, confronted with severe unemployment and recession, argued that the time was not right. However, in 1985, the world's trade officials agreed to launch a new round of multilateral trade negotiations and established a committee to develop an agenda. In September 1986, a special session of the GATT contracting parties meeting in Punta del Este, Uruguay, officially launched the negotiations, which came to be known as the Uruguay Round and set a target date of 1990 for their completion. The Uruguay Round negotiations began in 1987.

The ministerial declaration issued at Punta del Este instituted a stand-still on new trade-restrictive or distorting measures and called for the elimination by the end of the Uruguay Round of measures inconsistent with the provisions of the GATT. The trade ministers also established fifteen negotiating groups that fell into four broad categories.

Some groups focused on issues that had been taken up in earlier negotiating rounds, including those (such as tariffs) that had long been on the GATT agenda as well as others (such as subsidies and safeguards) that had not been resolved satisfactorily in the Tokyo Round. Most important, and perhaps most difficult, among these issues was safeguards. As we have seen, GATT rules on safeguard actions have been ineffective and relatively easy to circumvent through new protectionist measures, such as voluntary restraint agreements (VRAs). The success or failure of the Uruguay Round on the safeguards issue will, in large part, determine whether the GATT will retain influence over the international trading system as protectionist measures continue to multiply outside of GATT disciplines. Although the 1986 ministerial declaration called for "a comprehensive agreement on safe guards," the political difficulty of reaching such an agreement remained significant. As in the Tokyo Round, the central conflict centered on selectivity. The EC insisted on the need for selectivity. The United States advocated safeguard actions taken either on a most-favored-nation or "consensual selectivity" basis. The developing countries—for whom the safeguards negotiations were a top priority in the Uruguay Round—strongly advocated the most-favored-nation position.

A second set of negotiations focused on concerns of developing countries, such as tropical products, natural resource-based products, textiles, and clothing. Due to the increasingly active role of the developing countries in the GATT, successful completion of these negotiations was essential to their continued involvement in the GATT system.

A third set of negotiating groups had mandates to reform existing GATT rules or mechanisms. Dissatisfaction with existing GATT dispute settlement mechanisms had been mounting for years. Countries were able to delay or block resolution of a dispute; there was no effective mechanism for enforcing decisions or overseeing their implementation; and protection of third countries affected by the dispute was inadequate. The ministerial declaration at Punta del Este instructed the negotiating group on dispute settlement to "improve and strengthen the rules and procedures of the dispute settlement process." Negotiations moved rapidly in this negotiating group due to broad agreement on the need to expedite dispute settlement procedures and to the absence of any significant North-South division. By the end of 1988, negotiators had agreed on several measures to streamline procedures and speed up decisions in the dispute settlement process. These reforms were implemented on a provisional basis in 1989.

The negotiations on the functioning of the GATT system (FOGS) were intended to strengthen the role of GATT as an institution. The negotiating group focused on ways to enhance GATT surveillance of trade policies and practices; to improve the overall effectiveness and decision making of the GATT by involving ministers; and to strengthen GATT's relationship with the IMF and World Bank. Because there was a significant degree of consensus on what needed to be done, negotiations on FOGS proceeded smoothly. By the end of 1988 agreement was reached on the establishment of a new trade policy review mechanism to examine and publicize national trade policies on a regular basis. Negotiators agreed to begin implementing this mechanism in 1989 rather than wait until the conclusion of the Uruguay Round.

Finally, some groups sought to broaden the scope of the GATT to cover nontraditional areas. One of the most significant and controversial decisions made at Punta del Este was the agreement to include the so-called new issues—services, intellectual property rights, and investment—in the round. The opposition to their inclusion was led by a small group of developing countries, which feared that GATT rules developed for the new issues could be used by the industrialized countries to overwhelm their fledgling industries and to undermine domestic policies that the developing countries considered critical to their national economic development. They argued that the Uruguay Round should concentrate instead on unfinished business from the Tokyo Round and on reform in areas where the GATT had clearly failed to impose adequate international discipline, such as safeguards, textiles, and agriculture. They also insisted that GATT was not the appropriate forum for the new issues that, they argued, came under the purview of other organizations, such as WIPO for intellectual property or the United Nations for investment.

The industrialized nations stressed the need to modernize the GATT by broading its scope to deal with new areas of trade. As in previous GATT rounds, the United States took the initiative in pushing aggressively for the inclusion of services, intellectual property rights, and investment in the Uruguay Round. The EC and Japan supported the U.S. position, but they were not entirely convinced of the wisdom of increasing the burden of the GATT at a time when so many long-standing problems had yet to be resolved. They also shared some of the concerns of the developing countries about the extent to which GATT rules in the new areas might impinge on their sovereignty in domestic regulation and government policy. In the case of investment in particular, they questioned the appropriateness of using GATT as the forum for management. Finally, while there was a consensus among the developed countries about the principles that would cover some of the new issues (especially services and intellectual property), it proved difficult to come to agreement on specific details of the application of those principles.

The issue that is most likely to determine the ultimate success or failure of the Uruguay Round, however, is not a new issue but an old one: agriculture. As we have seen, agriculture has been treated as an exception in the GATT. Agriculture remains a highly controversial issue, largely because it is so deeply imbedded in the domestic politics of most nations. Although the United States, the EC, and the key agricultural producers have agreed on the need for reform, there is no agreement on how to go about it. The United States ambitiously proposed phasing out all direct farm subsidies and farm trade protection within a decade. The Cairns group—a coalition of fourteen smaller producing nations (including Australia, Argentina, Hungary, and Canada among others)—advocated a similar approach. The EC accepted the need to reduce subsidies, but viewed the U.S. proposal as highly unrealistic, advocating instead an approach that would allow it to maintain its Common

Agricultural Policy. Japan was also unenthusiastic about the U.S. proposal, but generally tried to keep a low profile.

Conclusion

The Uruguay Round will thus be a major test for the multilateral trade regime. The challenge is great. New rules and techniques must be developed to constrain the new protectionism. GATT must be expanded to cover new sectors. In the process, GATT must be expanded from a fragile dispute settlement regime and periodic international negotiation to an effective international organization capable of resolving conflicts, containing protectionist pressures, and promoting liberalization in both old and new sectors. If the Round can make headway in achieving these goals, it will make possible the continued vitality of a multilateral, liberal system.

If it fails, the stage is set for increased reliance on managed trade and a breakdown into regional blocs. As we have discussed, the European Community is forming its own separate trading system that could turn inward. The United States and Canada have signed a free-trade agreement that is intended to complement the GATT but which, without a vital multilateral system, could become the basis for a separate North American market. If such regional systems begin to emerge, there will be severe pressure on Japan to secure market access. Some have proposed a free-trade agreement between the United States and Japan. Others conjecture that, instead, Japan may turn to Southeast Asia as its central trading system. Such managed trade and regionalism bear dangerous resemblances to the blocs of the 1930's.

The continued vitality of a multilateral liberal system will also depend on the development of plurilateral management. Economic power is now more evenly dispersed. The United States as the largest (although no longer the dominant member) will have to continue to provide leadership for the system. This will be possible only if the United States can redress its trade imbalance and revitalize its competitiveness. At the same time, Europe and Japan must define new, more active roles in trade management. Europe will have to find the appropriate balance between looking inward towards the creation of an internal market and its need to look outward to the multilateral trading system. Because of its size and its role in world trade, reestablishing a reasonable balance between Japan and its trading partners, as well as integrating Japan into the management of the international trading system, will be a central challenge for the remainder of the century. Finally, as development outside the developed market economies proceeds, all will need to address the new role, first, for the newly industrialized countries, and, then, for other developing countries.[73]

Notes

1. Schattschneider, E. E. 1935. *Politics, Pressures and the Tariff.* Englewood Cliffs, N.J.: Prentice-Hall. See also: Robert A. Pastor. 1976. *Congress and the Politics of U.S. Foreign Economic Policy, 1929–1976.* Berkeley and Los Angeles: University of California Press, and Stephanie Ann Lenway. 1985. *The Politics of U.S. International Trade: Protection, Expansion and Escape.* Marshfield, Mass.: Pitman Publishing

2. See, for example, Richard N. Gardner. 1980. *Sterling-Dollar Diplomacy in Current Perspective: The Origins and Prospects of Our International Economic Order.* New York: Columbia University Press, p. 9.

3. Ibid., p. 102.

4. Ibid.; Clair Wilcox. 1949. *A Charter for World Trade.* New York: Macmillan. The trade charter was not exclusively an American idea; British planners were also closely involved in the process. See E. F. Penrose. 1953. *Economic Planning for the Peace.* Princeton, N.J.: Princeton University Press.

5. See Gardner. 1971. *Sterling-Dollar Diplomacy,* Chaps. 8 and 17; Wilcox, *A Charter for World Trade;* Committee for Economic Development, Research and Policy Committee, *The United States and The European Community: Policies for a Changing Economy.* New York: CED, November.

6. Gardner. 1952. *Sterling-Dollar Diplomacy,* Chap. 17; William Diebold, Jr., *The End of the I.T.O.* Princeton, N.J.: International Finance Section, Department of Economics and Social Institutions, Princeton University.

7. Dam, Kenneth W. 1970. *The GATT: Law and International Economic Organization.* Chicago: University of Chicago Press, p. 392.

8. Ibid., pp. 396–397.

9. Diebold, Jr., William. 1952. *Trade and Payments in Western Europe: A Study in Economic Cooperation 1947–1951.* New York: Harper & Row; Robert Triffin. 1957. *Europe and the Money Muddle: From Bilateralism to Convertibility, 1947–1956.* New Haven, Conn.: Yale University Press.

10. Ozaki, Robert S. 1972. *The Control of Imports and Foreign Capital in Japan.* New York: Praeger, pp. 5–9; Warren S. Hunsberger. 1964. *Japan and the United States in World Trade.* New York: Harper & Row.

11. See, for example, Gardner Patterson. 1966. *Discrimination in International Trade: The Policy Issues, 1945–1965.* Princeton, N.J.: Princeton University Press; Karin Koch. 1969. *International Trade Policy and the GATT, 1947–1967.* Stockholm Economic Studies XI. Stockholm: Almquist & Wiksell.

12. Evans, John W. 1971. *The Kennedy Round in American Trade Policy: The Twilight of the GATT?* Cambridge, Mass: Harvard University Press, p. 282. For other studies of the Kennedy Round, see Ernest H. Preeg. 1970. *Traders and Diplomats: An Analysis of the Kennedy Round Negotiations Under the General Agreement on Tariffs and Trade.* Washington, D.C.: Brookings Institution; Thomas B. Curtis and John R. Vastine. 1971. *The Kennedy Round and the Future of American Trade.* New York: Praeger.

13. Baldwin, Robert E. 1970. *Non-Tariff Distortions of International Trade*. Washington, D.C.: Brookings Institution, p. 1.

14. Cooper, Richard N. 1968. *The Economics of Interdependence: Economic Policy in the Atlantic Community*. New York: McGraw-Hill, pp. 59–80.

15. General Agreement on Tariffs and Trade. 1987. *International Trade 1986–87*. Geneva: GATT, p. 158.

16. International Monetary Fund. *International Financial Statistics*. Washington, D.C.: IMF, January 1968 and April 1988, various pages; International Monetary Fund. *Direction of Trade Statistics Yearbook 1987*. Washington, D.C.: IMF, 1987, various pages; Organization for Economic Cooperation and Development, *Main Economic Indicators*. Paris: OECD, April 1988, p. 174.

17. Sinai, Allen. 1987. "The 'Global' Factor and the U.S. Economy," *Economic Studies Series*, No. 27, Shearson Lehman Brothers, October 6, p. 1

18. *New York Times*. May 5, 1988. p. 1.

19. Council on Competitiveness. 1988. *Competitiveness Index: Trends, Background Data and Methodology*. Washington, D.C.: Council on Competitiveness. Appendix II.

20. Ibid.

21. See Richard Blackhurst, Nicolas Marian, and Jan Tumlir. 1978. *Adjustment, Trade and Growth in Developed and Developing Countries*, GATT Studies in International Trade, No. 6. Geneva: General Agreement on Tariffs and Trade; William Diebold, Jr. 1978. "Adapting Economics Structural Change: The International Aspect," *International Affairs* (London) 54:4. October. pp. 573–588.

22. Krugman, Paul R., and Hatsopoulos, George N. 1987. "The Problem of U.S. Competitiveness in Manufacturing," *New England Economic Review*. January/February. 22; Organization for Economic Development and Cooperation, *OECD Economic Outlook 42*. Paris: OECD, December. pp. 41, 178.

23. See Susan Strange. 1979. "The Management of Surplus Capacity: or How Does Theory Stand Up to Protectionism 1970s Style?" *International Organization*, 33:3. Summer. pp. 573–588.

24. *Economic Report of the President*. 1988. Washington D.C.: GPO. pp. 373, 374; General Agreement on Tariffs and Trade, *International Trade, 1986–87*. Geneva: GATT, 1987, p. 10. Unemployment figures are for the G-7 countries.

25. Organization for Economic Cooperation and Development. 1987. *OECD Economic Outlook 42*. Paris: OECD. December. pp. 174, 184.

26. Ibid., p. 190.

27. General Agreement on Tariffs and Trade, *International Trade, 1986–87*, p. 10.

28. *OECD Economic Outlook 42*, p. 184.

29. Ibid., p. 174.

30. Ibid., p. 190.

31. U.S. Department of Labor, Bureau of Labor Statistics.

32. International Monetary Fund. 1987. *Annual Report 1987*. Washington, D.C.: IMF, p. 16.

33. *OECD Economic Outlook 42*, pp. 174, 184.

34. General Agreement on Tariffs and Trade. 1988. Press Release, GATT/1432, 29 February. p. 4

35. *OECD Economic Outlook 42*, pp. 5, 28.

36. *International Financial Statistics Yearbook 1985*. Washington, D.C.: IMF, 1985.

37. *Economic Report of the President.* 1988. Washington, D.C.: GPO, pp. 364–365.

38. Ibid., p. 367.

39. See U.S. Congress. 1968, House Committee on Ways and Means, Foreign Trade and Tariff Proposals, Hearings, 90th Cong., 2d Sess.

40. On the politics of supporters of free trade see: I. M. Destler and John S. Odell. 1987. *Anti-Protection: Changing Forces in the United States Trade Politics.* Washington, D.C.: Institute for International Economics, September; and Helen V. Milner. 1988. *Resisting Protectionism: Global Industries and the Politics of International Trade.* Princeton, N.J.: Princeton University Press.

41. Milner, Helen V., and Yoffie, David B. 1989. "Between Free Trade and Protectionism: Strategic Trade Policy and a Theory of Corporate Trade Demands," *International Organization,* 43, 2. Spring. pp. 239–272.

42. See Prestowitz, Clyde V. 1988. *Trading Places: How America Allowed Japan to Take the Lead.* New York: Basic Books.

43. PL100-418, Omnibus Trade and Competitiveness Act of 1988.

44. See Diebold, Jr., William. 1988. ed., *Bilateralism, Multilateralism and Canada in U.S. Trade Policy.* Cambridge, Mass.: Ballinger; Jeffrey J. Schott and Murray G. Smith. 1988. eds., *The Canada-United States Free Trade Agreement: The Global Impact.* Washington, D.C.: Institute for International Economics; Paul Wonnacott. 1987. *The United States and Canada: The Quest for Free Trade.* Washington, D.C.: Institute for International Economics.

45. Baldwin, Robert E. 1970. *Non-Tariff Distortions of International Trade.* Washington, D.C.: Brookings Institution; William Diebold, Jr. 1972. *The United States and the Industrial World: American Foreign Policy in the 1970s.* New York: Praeger, pp. 123–140; J. M. Finger, H. K. Hall and D. R. Nelson. 1982. "The Political Economy of Administered Protection," *The American Economic Review,* vol. 72. pp. 452–466; Stanley D. Metzger. 1974. *Lowering Non-Tariff Barriers: U.S. Law, Practice and Negotiating Objectives.* Washington, D.C.: Brookings Institution.

46. See 97th Cong., 2d sess. 1982. *The Mercantilist Challenge to the Liberal International Trade Order,* a study prepared for the use of the Joint Economic Committee, Congress of the United States, December 29. Washington, D.C.: U.S. Government Printing Office, pp. 8–31.

47. See Brian Hindley and Eri Nicolaides. 1983. *Taking the New Protectionism Seriously.* Trade Policy Research Centre, Thames Essay No. 34. London: Trade Policy Research Centre.

48. Walter, Ingo. 1986. "Structural Adjustment and Trade Policy in the International Steel Industry," in Cline, *Trade Policy in the 1980s,* pp. 497–500; Gary C. Hufbauer & Diane T. Berliner, Kimberly A. Elliot. 1986. *Trade Protection in the United States: 31 Case Studies.* Washington, D.C.: Institute for International Economics. pp. 156, 176; Ingo Walter, "Structural Adjustment and Trade Policy in the International Steel Industry," in Cline, *Trade Policy in the 1980s,* p. 489.

49. Hufbauer, pp. 170–173.

50. General Agreements on Tariffs and Trade, *International Trade 1986–1987,* p. 29.

51. See Robert B. Cohen. 1983. "The Prospects for Trade and Protectionism in the Auto Industry," in Cline, *Trade Policy in the 1980s.* Washington, D.C.: Institute for International Economics, pp. 527–563; Gary C. Hufbauer et al. 1986. *Trade Protection in the United States: 31 Case Studies.* Washington D.C.: Institute for International Economics, pp. 249–262.

52. See Paul R. Krugman. 1988. ed., *Strategic Trade Policy and the New International Economics*. Cambridge, Mass.: MIT Press.

53. This is the view of the Cambridge Economic Policy Group. See their journal, the *Cambridge Economic Policy Review*.

54. Bressand, Albert. 1983. "Mastering the World Economy," *Foreign Affairs*, 16:4. Spring. pp. 747–772.

55. Reich, Robert B. 1983. "Beyond Free Trade," *Foreign Affairs*, 16:4. Spring, pp. 773–804. See also Stephen S. Cohen and John Zysman. 1987. *Manufacturing Matters: The Myth of the PostIndustrial Economy*. New York: Basic Books for the Council on Foreign Relations.

56. See Raymond Hopkins and Donald E. Puchala. 1978. eds., "The Global Political Economy of Food," *International Organization*, 32. Summer, entire issue.

57. *Economic Report of the President*. 1988. Washington, D.C.: Government Printing Office. p. 144.

58. See Ronald Kent Shelp. 1981. *Beyond Industrialization*. New York: Praeger; Thomas M. Stanback, Jr., Peter J. Bearse, Thierry J. Noyelle, and Robert A. Karasek. 1981. *Services: The New Economy*. Totowa, New Jersey: Allanheld, Osmun.

59. Mowery, David C. 1988. *International Collaborative Ventures in U.S. Manufacturing*. Cambridge, Mass.: Ballinger; Geza Feketekuty. 1988. *International Trade in Services: An Overview and Blueprint for Negotiations*. Cambridge, Mass.: Ballinger; Steven S. Wildman and Stephen E. Siwek. 1988. *International Trade in Films and Television Programs*. Cambridge, Mass.: Ballinger; Lawrence J. White. 1988. *International Trade in Ocean Shipping Services*. Cambridge, Mass.: Ballinger; Ingo Walter. 1988. *Global Competition in Financial Services: Market Structure, Protection, and Trade Liberalization*. Cambridge, Mass.: Ballinger; Thierry J. Noyelle and Anna B. Dutka. 1988. *International Trade in Business Services: Accounting, Advertising, Law, and Management Consulting*. Cambridge, Mass.: Ballinger; Jonathan David Aronson and Peter E. Cowhey. 1988. *When Countries Talk: International Trade in Telecommunications Services*. Cambridge, Mass.: Ballinger; Daniel M. Kasper.1988. *Deregulation and Globalization: Liberalizing International Trade in Air Services*. Cambridge, Mass.: Ballinger.

60. *International Financial Statistics Yearbook 1987*, p. 701.

61. Coalition of Service Industries; British Invisibles Export Council. 1987. *Annual Report and Accounts 1986–87*. London: British Invisible Exports Council, p. 34.

62. U.S. Department of Commerce. 1986. *U.S. Trade: Performance in 1985 and Outlook* Washington D.C.: GPO. p. 2.

63. Coalition of Service Industries. Derived from IMF figures by Boston Economic Advisors, Inc.

64. See Spero, "Removing Trade Barriers"; William Diebold, Jr., and Helena Stalson. "Negotiating Issues in International Services Transactions," in Cline, *Trade Policy in the 1980s*, pp. 581–609.

65. U.S. Congress. 1984. *Trade and Tariff Act of 1984*, Public Law 98-573, October 30.

66. See Robert R. Benko. 1987. *Protecting Intellectual Property Rights: Issues and Controversies*. Washington, D.C.: American Enterprise Institute for Public Policy Research; R. Michael Gadbaw and Timothy J. Richards. 1988. eds., *Intellectual Property Rights: Global Consensus, Global Conflict?* Boulder, Colorado: Westview Press; Helena Stalson. 1987. *Intellectual Property Rights and U.S. Competitiveness in Trade*. Washington, D.C.: National Planning Association.

67. Business Roundtable, "Negotiations on International Investment in the Uruguay Round: A Preliminary Statement," March 1988; U.S. Trade Representative, Submission of the United States to the Negotiating Group on Trade-Related Investment Measures, June 1987.

68. See U.S. Senate, Committee on Finance. 1979. *Trade Agreements Act of 1979, Report on H.R. 4537 to Approve and Implement the Trade Agreements Negotiated Under the Trade Act of 1974, and for Other Purposes*, 96th Cong., 1st sess. Washington, D.C.: U.S. Government Printing Office; Stephen D. Krasner. 1979. "The Tokyo Round: Particularistic Interests and Prospects for Stability in the Global Trading System," *International Studies Quarterly*, 23:4, December, pp. 491–531; Thomas R. Graham. 1979. "Revolution in Trade Politics," *Foreign Policy*, 36. Fall. pp. 49–63.

69. See U.S. Senate, Committee on Finance. 1979. MTN Studies No. 4, *MTN and the Legal Institutions of International Trade*, report prepared at the request of the Subcommittee on International Trade, 96th Cong., 1st sess. Washington, D.C.: U.S. Government Printing Office.

70. See Gary C. Hufbauer, "Subsidy Issues After the Tokyo Round," in Cline, *Trade Policy in the 1980s*, pp. 327–361.

71. See Alan W. Wolff, "The Need for New GATT Rules to Govern Safeguard Actions," in Cline, *Trade Policy in the 1980s*, pp. 363–391.

72. See John H. Jackson, "GATT Machinery and the Tokyo Round Agreements," in Cline, *Trade Policy in the 1980s*, pp. 159–187.

73. GATT Press Release, No. 1328, November 29, 1982. See also Jeffrey J. Schott "The GATT Ministerial: A Postmortem," *Challenge* (May–June 1983). pp. 40–45.

23

FROM GATT TO THE WORLD TRADE ORGANIZATION: PROSPECTS FOR A RULE-INTEGRITY REGIME

John G. Conklin

The formation of the World Trade Organization (WTO) to replace the GATT raises anew the prospects for a multilateral trade regime founded on a system of effectively enforced rules—that is, a rule-integrity regime. The effectiveness of the old system was limited by its inability to enforce the rules of the trade game; the WTO moves toward addressing those institutional limitations. John Conklin reviews the GATT Accords and the negotiation process and outlines the reforms associated with the WTO, including strengthened member commitment to the organization; increased administrative capacity, particularly in dispute settlement cases; and enhanced status for trade negotiations in international economic forums. The WTO improves upon the GATT in each of these dimensions; however, the long-term commitment of the United States and the European Union, as well as that of other industrialized countries, to abide by the rules of the WTO system remains problematic.

The conversion of the formal and legal arrangements for the conduct of international trade negotiations and the oversight of the trade system from the General Agreement on Tariffs and Trade (GATT) to the World Trade Organization (WTO) will test the capacity of states to both abide by their trade commitments and press ahead with reducing trade barriers. Whatever the trade regime, state compliance with the rules is essentially voluntary, and the regime's effectiveness requires implementation by individual states. With the creation of the WTO, states have demonstrated a willingness to organize an institutional framework capable of guiding the trade system in a liberal direction. Whether states, in their individual and collective behaviors, will stay the liberal course at the international level remains an open question. The WTO improves upon the GATT, although its significance remains to be seen in the coming years as the WTO absorbs the old GATT system and new institutions and rules are tested in the multilateral flow of goods and services. Although the WTO enhances and empowers the institutional base of the multilateral trade system, it provides ample space for individual members to violate the rules of the trade game in both spirit and letter. The WTO exists only in documentary form. The precise meanings and uses of its institutional framework remain to be determined in the operation of the organization itself. Any discussion of the meaning of the evolution from the GATT to the WTO, therefore, is necessarily speculative (see, for example, GATT 1994; Jackson 1989, 1990; OECD 1993; Petersmann 1993; Root 1994).

The GATT Treaty

The GATT Accords consist of the original treaty plus approximately two hundred additional agreements that have been appended to the original document over the course of the organization's existence, including tariff reduction schedules. The original treaty is the core document drafted by the United States between 1945 and 1947 during the effort to organize the more ambitious but stillborn International Trade Organization. The core document specifies principles, procedures, and major substantive concerns, but it provides no organizational framework to administer and oversee trade agreements. The major structural features, pertaining to matters of governance and administration and giving life to the GATT Accords, were added as necessity dictated. The original GATT Treaty consists of three parts. Part 1 focuses on the nondiscrimination, or most-favored-nation (MFN), clause and obligations regarding tariff stabilization and reduction. Part 2 concerns the elimination of nontariff barriers (NTBs), essentially customs valuation, import licensing, subsidies, antidumping duties, and national treatment of foreign goods. Part 3 pertains to matters of governance and procedure, including dispute settlement mechanisms. Part 4, which waives the principle of reciprocity in negotiations between developed and less developed contracting parties, was added to this core in 1964.

Reciprocity is one of four principles underlying the formation of the GATT; the others concern the previously mentioned nondiscrimination, the tariff as the preferred form of protection, and the legitimacy of safeguards. Reciprocity refers to the notion that all trade concessions granted by one party must be matched by a concession of equivalent value by another party or parties. Nondiscrimination, or the MFN clause, states that any concession granted to one GATT member must be granted to all other members except in cases involving adjacent states, colonialist-colony agreements, and regional economic integration programs. The tariff is the preferred form of protection because of its transparency and more precise measurability relative to NTBs, which are opaque and for which the impact is difficult to measure. Safeguards define conditions under which members may legitimately introduce protectionist measures. GATT safeguards include the right of a country to adopt protection to retain the capacity to feed itself, to shield industries whose existence has reached a point of peril, to defend itself against dumping, or to overcome problems related to balance-of-payments disequilibria. Problems with the balance of payments are the most frequently used, some would say abused, safeguard in the GATT Treaty.

Particularly important to the operation of the GATT has been the diluted legal obligation of members regarding adherence to Part 2—the part concerned with NTBs. The enabling legislation, the Protocol of Provisional Application, requires members' full and strict compliance with Parts 1 and 3 without exception, but members are to implement Part 2, "to the fullest extent not inconsistent with existing [national] legislation" (Jackson, 1990: 13). This effectively provided states with a legal means to avoid NTBs as a topic of negotiation contraprotectionism for the first twenty-five years of the GATT's existence. NTBs constitute a pervasive and long-term problem for both the past and the future of the international trade system. Typical of the problem of NTB proliferation, the enabling legislation granted extensive grandfathering rights to members that have since been used by countries to argue for a waiver on the basis of the precedent of such a right.

All members must be signatories to the original, or core, treaty, but they need not be signatories to the approximately two hundred amendments and additions that have been appended. The status of these accords varies, with designations ranging from treaty to code to agreement to understanding. A member may choose to be signatory to such agreements, to be signatory with implementation deferred, or to be nonsignatory. The GATT Accords, therefore, are a cluster of treaties, codes, side agreements, and understandings with varying numbers and coalitions of members participating in each. Further confounding the situation, various treaties, codes, agreements, and understandings appear to be mutually contradictory or to conflict with the original core treaty to which all members are signatory. In this sense, no single GATT exists, and the letter and spirit of the accords are easily violated if the intent is there.

The GATT empowers members to organize periodic negotiating rounds, of which eight were held between 1947 and 1994. Usually named after the place of origin, the eight rounds are designated as Geneva (1947), Annecy (1949), Torquay (1950), Geneva (1956), Dillon (1960–1961), Kennedy (1962–1967), Tokyo (1973–1979), and Uruguay (1986–1994). The consistent need to extend the length of sessions reflects the increased difficulty and complexity of international trade negotiations. The early years, rounds one through four, involved twenty-three countries—essentially the Organization for Economic Cooperation and Development (OECD) countries—wherein began the dramatic reduction of tariff levels among those countries that has occurred over the past half century. With round five came an increase in membership to forty-five countries, bringing into the organization the semiperiphery, or newly industrializing countries (NICs). The addition of Part 4, which waived the rule of reciprocity in negotiations between less developed and developed members, removed the major barrier to broader participation. Ninety-nine countries participated in the Tokyo Round, and 125 were involved in the Uruguay Round. Currently, much of the former socialist bloc, along with China, is awaiting entry into the organization. Along with increased numbers of participants, the negotiating agenda has expanded dramatically, contributing to the lengthening of rounds from weeks and months to years.

Negotiations in rounds one through six involved relatively simple and straightforward reductions of tariff levels for manufactured products. Rounds seven and eight—Tokyo and Uruguay, respectively—involved a major substantive expansion of the negotiation agenda and the addition of governance and procedural matters. Agricultural goods, tropical products, and NTBs were added to the negotiation agenda in the Tokyo Round; and services, textiles, natural resources, and intellectual property were additions in the Uruguay Round. The inclusion of NTBs brought into existence seven new negotiating committees: subsidies and countervailing duties, trade-related investment measures, technical barriers, customs valuation, government procurement, import licensing, and safeguards. Included in the agenda of both rounds were the broader issues of GATT constitutional reform and procedures for dispute settlement. In essense, matters of governance, substance, and procedure—largely ignored or bypassed during rounds one through six—came to the fore at the Tokyo and Uruguay Rounds.

GATT Negotiations

GATT negotiations are organized around and driven by discussions between the two states that constitute the principal market and the principal supplier for a product. In the early years, the South did not participate; the United States was inevitably the principal market, and Japan or a European member was the principal supplier. The United States, Europe, and Japan continue to dominate the negotiating process, but the inclusion of both new members and new topics has slowly transformed the negotiation process and the ambiance. Since the early years, increasing numbers of southern states have joined the negotiations, and they now constitute a substantial majority—exceeding the two-thirds or three-quarters votes necessary to amend the treaty, pass waivers, approve budgets, accept new members, and approve dispute settlement reports. Legally, power in the GATT is distributed on the basis of one member having one vote; as of 1995, the membership included ninety-six southern and twenty-four northern countries. De facto, the GATT operates on the basis of unanimous consent, with each state possessing a virtual veto power. Vetoes exercised by large-market, wealthy members are more consequential for the operation of the international trade system, and the southern majority is rendered meaningless if the Triad or one of its members refuses to initial an agreement.

The expansion of the membership, along with the expansion of the trade agenda beyond the single consensus issue of tariff reduction, has resulted in coalitional behavior that crosses traditional North-South, the old East-West, and intra-Triad lines. The inclusion of agriculture, for example, has resulted in the formation of the Cairns Group (G-13), the members of which ally with the United States in agriculture negotiations.[1] The European Union (EU) and Lome South countries are frequently in coalition on NTB issues. Japan and various aggregations of southern countries often become a coalition on matters pertaining to services and property rights. The historical global division of trade negotiations between North and South, which has always been frayed at the edges, has eroded further along with intra-North and intra-South alliances.

The cozy relations and atmosphere that resulted from the exclusive North club that characterized the early years of negotiations have evolved to a more complicated, more universal club with new arenas of disagreement among old allies and of agreement among former antagonists. As negotiating issues and committees have proliferated, southern countries have become more active in the processes of decisionmaking. The southern shift to liberal, market-oriented development strategies has dramatically increased the relevance of the WTO for the South. Generally lacking significant market power to deal with northern protectionism, a recourse for the South has been to appeal to the principles and rules the North has built into the multilateral trading system—the WTO. It is the South that now presses for constitutional reform and for strengthening dispute settlement procedures.

The United States was not the only dominating member of the early years, although it remains the primary actor and played a lead role in expanding the agenda at the Tokyo and Uruguay Rounds. In the early years, the United States played a progressive leadership role in tariff negotiations and, in a limited sense, encouraged the formal and legal institutional development of the GATT. But the United States has chosen to avoid the GATT dispute settlement mechanism or to obstruct GATT processes, thus undermining the norm of compliance with the formal and legal rules. The United States further undermined the institutional development of the GATT by leading members in the use of import-licensing safeguards and making no effort to implement Part 2—the elimination of NTBs. Typically, as tariff reductions threatened individual manufacturing sectors—textiles, steels, automobiles, footwear, and the like—the United States organized import-licensing schemes in forms such as voluntary export restraints, orderly marketing agreements, and trigger price mechanisms.

Europe and Japan have followed the U.S. lead in organizing quota systems that allocate market shares among importers and protect domestic producers. The increasing competitiveness of southern product lines appears to have quickened this process. Among the Triad, Europe has been less supportive of the institutional development of the GATT than has the United States. In the opinion of one observer, Europe is the veto state that forces the lowest common denominator upon the dispute settlement regime (Jackson, 1990: 73). In recent years, Japan has appeared more committed to the institution than either the United States or the EU, particularly since the United States has increasingly sought to bilateralize U.S.-Japan negotiations. Japan uses the WTO as a reference point to blunt U.S. efforts to impose a managed guaranteed access regime, pointing to the inconsistency of numerically negotiated trade outcomes with GATT–WTO principles. Southern coalitions have taken the lead role to liberalize the international trade system through the GATT–WTO.

All members of the multilateral trading system are simultaneously engaged in negotiations at the international, regional, and bilateral levels. Negotiations are particularly dynamic at the regional level, and this will have important repercussions for the evolution of the WTO. From the liberal perspective, dynamism and growth in regional trade are consistent with a growing international trade system and merely precede the globalization of trade. From the nationalist perspective, intensification of regional trade ties presages more intense competition among regional poles and enhances the probability of greater conflict, including overt warfare. The documents that established the WTO include an understanding of the relationship between regional customs unions and free trade areas and the WTO that recognizes the contribution to the expansion of world trade that may result from closer integration of the economies of parties and regional agreements. Currently, numerous regional trade integration programs are in place. The evolution of regional trade poles will frame and shape the medium- and long-term possibilities for the WTO.

The World Trade Organization

The WTO institutionalizes the negotiating agenda that evolved during the Tokyo and Uruguay Rounds, replacing the provisional treaty that created the GATT with a permanent international trade organization that in a legal sense is equivalent to the International Monetary Fund (IMF) and the World Bank Group (Office of the U.S. Trade Representative, 1994). The WTO provides an ongoing negotiating forum for forging agreements and overseeing compliance. The organization draws together the disparate elements of the GATT into a single agreement with a uniform set of rules and procedures applicable to all members. It frames disputative substantive, procedural, and constitutional issues in a manner designed to reduce conflict over definitional matters and to provide guidance for future negotiations. The WTO institutionalizes sectoral negotiations in seven substantive areas—tropical products, natural resources, agriculture, services, textiles, intellectual property rights, and trade-related investment measures in addition to negotiations on tariffs and NTBs. Constitutional and procedural matters focus on matters of governance and dispute settlement, respectively. The WTO is an effort to empower the international trade system in three senses: (1) requiring more uniform and higher levels of commitment from members; (2) reforming the administrative capacity of the organization, particularly strengthening the dispute settlement mechanism; and (3) raising the status of trade as a topic of international economic negotiation.

Member Commitment

Membership in the WTO requires acceptance and ratification of the total results of the Final Act of the Uruguay Round—a 550-page compendium of documents signed by 125 countries at Marrakesh on April 15, 1994.[2] The document that created the WTO consists of sixteen articles, which essentially make permanent existing institutions and the norms of governance that evolved under the GATT. Each member has a single vote, and issues are to be determined by a consensus vote. When a consensus vote is not possible, supermajorities are required for passage of an agreement, a waiver, an amendment, or the accession of new members.

The essential governance feature that distinguishes the WTO from the GATT is that it initiates a process whereby all members are subject to the same rules of governance and procedure. The WTO specifies the obligation of members to adhere to the goals, processes, and procedures outlined in the Final Act and to move toward the reduction, elimination, or both of protectionist measures and practices. It commits all members to the single set of treaties, agreements, understandings, arrangements, and decisions that constitute the Final Act, giving a more permanent shape to matters of governance and dispute settlement, and to the topical agenda of trade negotiations. Under the GATT all members were committed to a set of common principles, but the administration and application of the agreement varied from state to state depending upon the willingness of individual states to accept, delay, or reject the treaties, codes, agreements, and understandings that constitute the GATT Accords. The WTO initiates the process of bringing the membership into a single organization with a common set of obligations and commitments.

The Final Act binds signatories to both specific and general commitments to reduce protectionism. Particularly important for monitoring the evolution of the WTO are specific obligations involving five arenas of negotiation—tariff reductions on manufactures, trade in the agricultural and textile sectors, the use of safeguards, and rules for government procurement (IMF, 1994: 2–4).

Tariffs on manufactures are to be reduced on average by at least one-third according to varying time schedules. This plan continues the evolution toward tariff reduction that is the major success of the GATT years; many southern members, particularly NICs, will make even larger cuts to better approximate the lower tariff levels characteristically found in the North. Tariff negotiations initially involved discussions of manufactured products on an item-by-item basis. Linear tariff negotiations, which involved a percentage reduction in the general level of tariff protection, were introduced during the Kennedy Round. The commitment to a minimum one-third general tariff reduction to join the WTO results from linear tariff negotiations. Tariff harmonization, bounding, rollback, and zero leveling are additional topics of these negotiations. In the WTO, northern countries are committed to zero tariff levels in a number of sectors, notably steel, pharmaceuticals, and wood products. Southern countries, particularly the periphery, have an extended time period for phasing in tariff reductions on manufactures.

Agreements on agricultural products involve three aspects. Members will convert NTBs to tariffs, reduce the volume of subsidized exports by 21 percent, and reduce tariffs on agricultural goods by 36 percent. Reductions are to be made over a period of six years for northern members and ten years for southern members. A special provision for periphery members ensures the availability of credits to finance necessary food imports in case the liberalization of agriculture results in rapid, short-term price increases. Textiles and clothing quotas currently in force under the most recent Multifiber Arrangement are to be progressively increased to allow greater market access, leading to their elimination by 2004 if they meet their goals.

Specific commitments related to NTBs concern safeguards and government procurement. Under the WTO all "gray-area" safeguards are to be prohibited, with a phasing-out period of four years. Gray areas include import-licensing measures, which represent the most pervasive problem in managing NTBs. The agreement also provides for discipline in the use of all safeguard measures, including time limits, investigative requirements, and multilateral application. The Agreement on Government Procurement, signed by the northern members at Tokyo, will be extended over time to the southern members. This agreement requires that all contracts for goods with a value greater than 195,000 Special Drawing Rights (SDRs) and not involving national security or tied to aid be open to international bidding. In the WTO, government procurement negotiations will expand to include services and levels of government subordinate to central governments.

Other negotiation arenas are framed more generally, without measurable targets and specific deadlines.[3] The most important of these arenas focus on services, intellectual property, and NTB-related issues—trade-related investment measures, subsidies, technical barriers, and antidumping rules. Services are the most rapidly growing component of international trade and will be a primary arena of negotiation in the WTO. They involve economic sectors strongly linked to domestic security issues, the cultural domain, and citizen treatment in foreign countries. Seven specific service sectors are included in negotiations—financial; telecommunications; transport by land, sea, and air; audiovisual; tourism; guest workers; and personal services. The negotiating framework commits members to move toward liberalization and nondiscrimination.

Negotiations on intellectual property provide for improved levels of protection for the rights of owners of all types of such property—copyrights, trademarks, patents, and trade secrets. WTO members are called upon to grant nonnational owners of intellectual property national treatment, as yet unspecified minimum levels of protection, and remedies under national laws to allow foreigners to enforce their rights. Trade-related investment measures that violate GATT–WTO principles, such as local content regulations and investment offsets, are to be eliminated. Subsidies, technical barriers, and antidumping rules are framed in considerable detail and in a manner designed to discipline their use by members. The effect of these policies on countries' behavior remains to be seen.

Administrative Capacity and Dispute Settlement Mechanism

Much of the framework for the governance and administration of the WTO is a cosmetic renaming of existing GATT structures. The fundamental organ of the membership is the Ministerial Conference, which, like its predecessor, the Annual Conference, will meet at least every two years. The General Council will replace the Council of Representatives as the membership organization to oversee the day-to-day operation of the WTO. The Interim Committee for the International Trade Organization, created in 1947 as the administrative arm of the GATT, will become the WTO Secretariat. The title of the head of the WTO will remain director-general.

The General Council is the locus of government power—working with the director-general, rendering decisions when necessary, managing member responsibilities on a day-to-day basis, and overseeing the administrative agent, the Secretariat. The General Council is responsible for the development of rules and procedures for the organizations created by the WTO. Legally, separate councils will govern three broad arenas of negotiation—trade in goods, trade in services, and trade-related aspects of intellectual property rights. This tripartite framework means disagreement in one of these arenas need not delay ratification of agreements in the other two. The General Council will make appropriate arrangements for effective cooperation with intergovernmental organizations that have responsibilities related to those of the WTO and for consultation and cooperation with nongovernmental organizations (NGOs). The council will oversee the organization of five additional permanent bodies and committees: a Dispute Settlement Body (DSB), which includes an Appellate Body (AB); the Trade Policy Review Body; and Committees on Balance of Payments Restrictions, Trade and Development, and Trade and the Environment. Participation in these organizations is open to all WTO members.

The DSB governs the use of the Dispute Settlement Mechanism (DSM), which involves five steps: consultations, panel formation, panel report, appeal process, and surveillance (see, for example, Dunoff, 1994; Pescatore, 1993; and Petersmann, 1994). The major features of each step are summarized in Table 23.1. The DSB approves panel composition, panel reports, and appellate reports, and it exercises surveillance. Two traditions inform the evolution of the DSM. The DSM began as a direct bargaining and conciliation process between or among parties to a dispute until reforms in 1955 outlined a formal-legal dispute process that introduced arbitration panels and interpreted dispute settlement as arbitration-rule application. Subsequent reforms in 1979 and 1988 were designed to make the DSM an arbitration-rule application process, and the WTO DSB continues this evolution. Smaller countries

Table 23.1   WTO Dispute Settlement Mechanism

	Initiation		Disposition
Consultation mechanism	Member complaint, Secretariat replies within ten days, consultations to begin within thirty days. If no settlement within sixty days, member may request panel arbitration.	Director-general provides good office, conciliation, and mediation services to resolve dispute without arbitration.	Parties must consult.
Panel formation	Parties to dispute agree on panel composition within ten days.	Director-general and chair of DSB select panel within ten days.	Consensus vote of DSB required not to establish a panel.
Panel report	Panel reviews documents to the dispute, meets twice with parties, submits interim report—including findings and conclusions—to parties. Panel reviews requests by parties and submits final report to members.	Schedule for arbitration final report: urgent case—three months general rule—six months No case should exceed nine months.	Consensus vote of DSB required for nonadoption of panel report (within sixty days). In appeal cases, no DSB vote.
Appeal process	Party or parties to dispute may appeal to AB.	Appellate body decisions rendered are confidential. AB may uphold, modify, or reverse panel report within sixty days and in no case beyond ninety days.	Consensus vote of DSB required for nonadoption of appellate report (within thirty days).
Surveillance	Within thirty days of DSB adoption of panel or AB report, member shall inform DSB of measures to be taken to implement ruling.	Implementation to begin within reasonable period, normally forty-five to ninety days, maximum fifteen to eighteen months.	The DSB shall report to members the compliance/noncompliance of parties under surveillance.

Source: Compiled from the Final Act of the Uruguay Round (1993).

tend to support the arbitration-rule application model, whereas larger countries tend to be either ambivalent or supportive of the bargaining-conciliation model. The evolution of the DSM and its effectiveness will be important for the future of the WTO.

The DSM improves upon the former system by creating a single organizational form for managing and arbitrating disputes, establishing timely schedules for concluding the five steps of the DSM, confirming and legitimizing the participation of the director-general in the dispute process, introducing a single AB for parties that appeal panel decisions, and, most important, eliminating the exercise of veto power by a single member. Under the GATT framework a single member could obstruct the dispute settlement process by vetoing either the formation of a panel or a panel decision. Under the WTO a consensus vote of all members of the DSB is required to obstruct the process at any stage in the proceedings. This is a significant empowerment of the DSM, but the text of the Final Act of the Uruguay Round includes language that allows for possible delay, and precedent exists for avoiding effective implementation of a DSM finding. The organization of a fixed period of time (nine months) for completing the arbitration process brings automaticity to the DSM and makes procedural obstructionism more difficult for members that want to delay or avoid dispute settlement. On the matter of surveillance, the maximum time for introducing compensatory measures is set at eighteen months, although in reality it "may be shorter or longer."[4] Moreover, members that lose arbitration proceedings have occasionally chosen to "note" rather than adopt panel reports, a precedent that undermines the effort toward effective implementation of the arbitration-rule application model, although no member has officially rejected an approved panel report. Members are enjoined to strengthen the multilateral trading system by respecting and adhering to the DSM, but key members—including the United States—continue to have recourse to domestic arbitrational institutions and unilateral decisionmaking. The operation and integrity of the DSM will apparently undergo an early critical test in the dispute between Japan and the United States over trade in automobiles and auto parts.

The Trade Policy Review Body, created in 1988, organizes the Trade Policy Review Mechanism (TPRM), the purpose of which is to contribute to improved adherence by all members to WTO rules, disciplines, and commitments. The frequency of member review varies according to three categories of WTO members based on their share of world trade. The Triad is reviewed every two years, the NICs every four years, and the periphery every six years. The study focuses on three areas: (1) domestic transparency of government decisionmaking on trade policy, (2) member compliance with multilateral trade commitments, and (3) impact of member policies on the functioning of the multilateral trade system. The TPRM is not designed to serve as a basis for the enforcement of WTO obligations, for dispute settlement, or to impose policy commitments on members. The review and publication of member trade policies and compliance with WTO commitments are aspects of an ongoing information flow between members and the Secretariat. A separate annual review of the major activities of the WTO and of significant policy issues that affect the international trade system are drafted under the direction of the director-general, whose annual review may evolve in a manner analogous to the IMF's World Economic Outlook, which does assess country policy and recommend policy changes.

The Committee on Balance of Payments Restrictions consults with members to review all restrictive import measures taken for balance-of-payments purposes. Members are to notify the General Council of any new restriction or of an extension of existing restrictions prior to or no later than thirty days following their announcement. Members that adopt import restrictions for balance-of-payments purposes are to enter into consultations with the committee within four months of adoption. Consultations include developing a plan for the elimination and progressive relaxation of remaining restrictions. The committee report on the results of consultations is the basis for a General Council determination as to whether a member is in compliance or noncompliance with its GATT–WTO commitments.

The Committee on Trade and Development was formed in 1964 and reflects the change introduced at the time that waived the rule of reciprocity for less developed members. It also reflects institutional acceptance of the notion that to be more just, the trade system required special treatment for southern members. The Final Act contains numerous references to the special needs of southern members and provisions for extending the timing of liberalization for the South. The issue of "graduation" from southern status, along with the usual matter of specifying "special provisions," will continue to be low-level arenas of conflict in multilateral trade negotiations.

The Committee on Trade and the Environment is a new organization that reflects the growing number of GATT–WTO disputes involving national environmental legislation and the impact of "green imperialism" and "green protectionism." Policy matters for the committee encompass institutional and external dimensions. First is the issue of the participation of environmental NGOs in the negotiation process. These NGOs participated in the Uruguay Round as observers that represented and presented the environmental viewpoint in open committee meetings that preceded executive sessions in which decisions were made. The way the environmental and other NGOs link to the Secretariat and the General Council can have important long-range implications for multilateral trade negotiations. Second, the committee will shape the broader WTO perspective on the link between trade and environmental issues, which are potentially volatile in both the South and the North. Third, the relationship between trade and sustainable development will be a matter of increasing concern for the WTO over the long term. This is potentially a major nexus in the relationship among the WTO, the International Monetary Fund, and the World Bank Group (WBG).

Status of the WTO: Strengths and Weaknesses

The WTO strengthens the international trading system in three important ways. First, members are involved more regularly and intensively with the WTO, sharing information when making decisions pertinent to the scope and rules of the multilateral trading system. Although member compliance remains voluntary, instances of violation are clearer, and pressures for compliance are greater. The DSM, the TPRM, and the Committee on Balance of Payments Restrictions all require that members communicate and work within the WTO framework when designing trade policy and making trade-related decisions. Moreover, the expansion of the trade agenda to include services, intellectual property rights, and trade-related investment measures greatly broadens areas of WTO concern. These areas link into the particularistic dimensions of society and have potential repercussions for national laws and industries that are politically controversial. Such matters as leveling the national marketplace for all investors, providing equal access in telecommunications for all producers of music and film, and devising rules for the treatment of expatriate and guest workers provoke concerns about national language, culture, and the very character of society. Negotiations in these areas require a more permanent, ongoing process for reaching and implementing agreements. With the enlargement of the agenda, relations between the WTO and members will deepen, and the WTO's domain will expand.

Second, the WTO will be structured as a thoroughgoing international institution along the lines of the IMF and the WBG. The WTO will be linked more clearly and closely with these two groups to upgrade its status in international economic forums. All three bodies are enjoined by their memberships to work to bring greater coordination and cohesion to global economic policymaking. These and other substantive responsibilities will require a considerable expansion of the WTO Secretariat, including the formalization of a permanent DSM, the implementation of membership-reporting systems, oversight of balance-of-payments safeguards, and the formation of offices for relations with NGOs from environmental and other sectors.

Third, the WTO adds a significant body of substantive law, particularly regarding NTBs, and clarifies articles, sentences, clauses, and phrasings that have proven troublesome and delayed conflict definition and resolution. Technically, the WTO does not resolve all issues of language, and unfortunate phrasings remain, but overall the WTO is much superior to the GATT. The Final Act includes seven understandings and three agreements that seek to resolve long-standing interpretative disputes in the articles of the GATT. It includes agreements that bring greater specificity to contentious issues, particularly technical barriers to trade, rules of origin, import-licensing procedures, subsidies and countervailing measures, and safeguards. The WTO marks a considerable advance in the institutionalization of the rules of trade, both substantively and procedurally. A comparison of levels of institutionalization in the WTO, the IMF, and the WBG is presented in Table 23.2.

Although the WTO improves on the GATT, important challenges remain. The WTO continues the traditional mode of reform that has characterized the evolution of the multilateral trade system—minimalist and incremental. This is a reflection of the GATT–WTO

Table 23.2   Comparison of Multilateral Economic Institutions

	GATT–WTO	IMF	WBG
Membership (pending)	125 (22)	179	178
Professional staff and knowledge base	Mathematics Economics 250	Economics—macro Monetary and financial 2,000	Economics—macro Sectoral and developmental 6,000
Administrative budget	$80.5M	$257.3M	$1,238.3M
Level of institutionalization[a]	Low	High	High
Level of autonomy[b]	Low	High	High
Policy scope and leverage with members	Narrow Low with borrowers	Broad High with borrowers	Narrow to moderate Moderate with borrowers
Origin	1947/1995	1947	1947

Source: Data compiled from various issues of the annual reports of the IMF, WBG, and GATT.

Notes: a. Institutionalization—adaptability, complexity, coherence, universality of membership, capacity to implement organizational goals and principles (see Huntington, 1968)

b. Autonomy—impact of internal forces, history, tradition, and culture of organization as influences on policy decisions and actions system of governance, which favors the lowest common denominator, the sensitivity of domestic political processes to multilateral trade, and the overarching concern of some members with matters of sovereignty. The WTO reflects what was politically possible in the early 1990s; it is not a holistic instrument for governing and managing multilateral trade.

The overriding issue for the future of the WTO concerns member compliance and rule integrity, particularly in the use of the DSM. The evolution of the DSM has generally been positive. As shown in Table 23.3, approximately 233 cases have been initiated, with about half resulting in a panel report. A quantitative study of the dispute mechanism found an 88 percent success rate between 1948 and 1989. However, the number of unadopted panel reports has increased, and the four-year extension of the Uruguay Round resulted in a blockage of the process. Throughout the 1980s a dramatic increase in noncompliance occurred, notably by the United States, Canada, and the EU (Petersmann, 1994: 1203). Recent strident and even petulant postures by the United States suggest potential difficulties. During spring 1994, the United States threatened to withdraw from the WTO if ratification was delayed. Most recently, the United States has warned that it will pull out of the WTO if it suffers three adverse, unfair rulings within five years (*Rapid*, January 28, 1995). The United States will determine what constitutes "fairness." Regardless of whether these are negotiating ploys or real threats, they are not encouraging for the institutionalization of a rule-integrity regime.

The United States has also pressed for an examination of the relationship between trade and internationally recognized labor standards. The South views this as an effort to undermine one of the few areas of comparative advantage enjoyed by the semiperiphery and the periphery. The U.S. insistence on forcing the labor issue onto the agenda has led southern members to add a series of issues for consideration by the Prepatory Committee that will be defining the future duties of the WTO. This list includes the relationship of trade to immigration, competition policy, export financing, restrictive business practices, financial and monetary stability, debt, company law, political stability, alleviation of poverty, and the extra-territoriality of national law.

Table 23.3   Dispute Settlement Cases, 1947–1988

Total Dispute Cases	Successful Consultations	Withdrawn, No Resolution, or Pending	Panel Reports Approved	Approved Panel Report Not Implemented
233	42 (18 percent)	101 (43 percent)	90 (38 percent)	8 to 10 (3–4 percent)

Source: Compiled from data in John H. Jackson (1990, 66–67).

With an expanded negotiation agenda, an expanded relationship with members, and formal ties to the IMF, the WBG, and NGOs, the WTO will be a more active and involved participant in global economic policymaking. This enhanced role is empowering and raises the visibility and status of the multilateral trade system. But empowerment in the sense of rule integrity remains problematic. If the past is a guide for understanding the future, the short and medium forecast is for continued "muddling through" when the rules are bent to oblige power realities. Issues of process and procedure will continue to inform negotiations and dispute settlement. Country behavior will likely continue to be erratic and self-serving at critical junctures. Two key members, the United States and the EU, appear unlikely to lead in the effort toward a trade regime based on rule integrity. Moreover, Japan and the South lack the capacity, let alone the long-term will, to lead effectively. For functionally specific transnational institutions, prospects for significant rule-integrity empowerment will likely either dissipate or improve under conditions of crisis. When national political leaderships of larger states recognize the international trade system and the WTO as important for managing contemporary problems of domestic economic duress, WTO prospects will be more favorable. Assuming we have moved beyond dissolution in the case of crisis, the WTO is a significant step forward for a more timely and adept management of that eventuality.

Notes

1. The Cairns Group of 13 includes Argentina, Australia, Brazil, Canada, Chile, Colombia, Hungary, Indonesia, Malaysia, New Zealand, the Philippines, Thailand, and Uruguay.
2. The total documentation of agreements made during the Uruguay Round equals approximately 26,000 pages.
3. This is not always the case; talks on telecommunications and maritime transport, for example, are scheduled to conclude in April 1996. Such deadlines, where talks remain in the earlier stages, are likely to be difficult to meet.
4. Understanding on Rules and Procedures Governing the Settlement of Disputes, Final Act, p. 14.

References

Dunoff, Jeffrey L. 1994. "Institutional Misfits: The GATT, the ICJ, and International Trade Disputes." *Michigan Journal of International Law* 15 (Summer): 1042–1078.
GATT. 1994. *GATT Activities in 1993*. Geneva: GATT.

Huntington, Samuel P. 1968. *Political Order in Changing Societies.* New Haven: Yale University Press.

International Monetary Fund. 1994. "Trade Agreement Mandates Broad Changes." *IMF Survey* 10 (January): 2–4.

Jackson, John H. 1989. *The World Trading System.* Cambridge: The MIT Press.

Jackson, John H. 1990. *Restructuring the GATT System.* New York: Council on Foreign Relations.

OECD. 1993. *Assessing the Effects of the Uruguay Round.* Paris: OECD.

Office of the U.S. Trade Representative. 1994. *Final Act Embodying the Results of the Uruguay Round of Multilateral Trade Negotiations* (Version of 15 December, 1993). Washington, D.C.: U.S. Government Printing Office.

Pescatore, Pierre. 1993. "The GATT Dispute Settlement Mechanism—Its Present Situation and Prospects." *Journal of International Arbitration* 10 (March): 27–42.

Petersmann, Ernst-Ulrich. 1993. "International Competition Rules for the GATT-WTO World Trade and Legal System." *Journal of World Trade* (December): 35–68.

Petersmann, Ernst-Ulrich. 1994. "The Dispute Settlement of the WTO and the Evolution of the GATT Dispute Settlement System Since 1948." *Common Law Market Review* 32 (December): 1157–1244.

Root, Franklin. 1994. *International Trade and Investment*, 7th ed. Cincinnati: South-Western Publishing.

24

EVALUATING THE OPTIONS

— Robert Z. Lawrence and Charles L. Schultze —

As Joan Spero mentioned in Chapter 22, support for free trade was waning in the 1960s. Today, a consensus regarding free trade no longer exists. Lawrence and Schultze trace the growing dissatisfaction with free trade dogma among policymakers, economists, and the citizenry, as well as the rising interest in the notion of a strategic trade policy. According to strategic trade theory, trade policy should be designed to promote long-term strategic goals linked to national competitiveness in high-technology sectors. This could easily be interpreted as a modern version of the types of policies advocated by Alexander Hamilton in the Report on Manufactures. *Lawrence and Schultze reject strategic trade policy and propose that the United States should reassert its commitment to multilateralism and the General Agreement on Tariffs and Trade (GATT).*

During the first four decades after the Second World War, the U.S. government and a clear working majority of both political parties espoused an international economic policy whose principal component was the promotion of a regime of multilateral free trade. It was widely agreed that trade among sovereign nations should be conducted with the minimum of tariff or other economic barriers and that the rules of the game should be developed in an international forum, the General Agreement on Tariffs and Trade (GATT). Practice did not always live up to principle. Industries beleaguered by stiff foreign competition sometimes managed to secure protection of one kind or another; and

Reprinted with permission of publisher from *An American Trade Strategy—Options for the 1990s* edited by Robert Z. Lawrence and Charles L. Schultze (Washington, D.C.: The Brookings Institution). Copyright © 1990 pp. 1–6, 10–17, 18–33, 35, 38, 39.

governments were not above providing subsidies or other aids to favored export industries. Nevertheless, through most of the period, practice was as close to principle as it was in other areas of public life.

Over the years, periodic rounds of multilateral negotiations succeeded in greatly reducing the protection inherited from earlier periods. Importantly, in the United States there was fairly broad agreement not only that the principle of multilateral free trade was a desirable one, but that it was also at least approximately achievable in practice. The legislative battles were waged over securing exceptions to the principle rather than over its legitimacy. In economic theory, agreement that a regime of multilateral free trade was the best approach for promoting economic welfare was so universal as to be almost a prerequisite for membership in the association of professional economists.[1]

No longer. Times have changed. An increasing number of politicians, especially Democratic members of Congress, numerous business executives, and even some former trade officials of the Reagan administration, while still giving lip service to the potential advantages of multilateral free trade in an ideal world, have come to view the real world as one in which the machinations of other governments, or the particular economic structure of some countries (read, Japan), have rendered the principle unachievable in practice. Further, it is argued, continued pursuit of that unachievable ideal by the United States harms its economic interests and, in particular, leaves some of the most essential and dynamic U.S. industries vulnerable to erosion and incursion by foreign firms whose societies do not play by the rules of free trade.

Simultaneously, back in academia, some highly respected economists have been developing new concepts of international trade that provide a possible, theoretical rationale for active intervention by government to pursue a "strategic trade policy," benefiting its own citizens at the expense of other countries. Unlike classical trade analysis, these theories apply to a world in which there are sometimes large gains from "getting there fastest with the mostest," especially with specialized, high-technology products. If one or a few firms can gain a foothold in a new market, through protection at home and favorable credit terms or subsidies for expansion, they may then be able to take advantage of economies of large-scale production and gain a sizable share of the world market. They can, for a significant period of time, exploit the market to earn high incomes to be split among workers and owners.

In a related vein, some other academics have argued that the electronics and other strategic, high-technology industries produce knowledge and technological advance critical to the expansion of technology and productivity in this country. The expansion of those industries should be promoted by the federal government, and they should be protected against the policies of other countries who are seeking the dominance of their own strategic industries in world markets.

The Sources of Dissatisfaction with Free Trade

Traditionally, the main political threats to free trade have arisen because of a fear of loss of jobs. The infamous Smoot-Hawley tariff was passed during the early stages of the Great Depression. And in the first truly deep recession of the postwar years, 1974–75, the Organization for Economic Cooperation and Development (OECD) felt it urgent to get a pledge of no new trade restrictions from its member governments. Fears of job loss in weak and declining industries threatened with increased competition from abroad have long been the main source of selective pressures for protection during periods of prosperity. But while today's currents of dissatisfaction with a policy of multilateral free trade have many roots, they now seem to stem from new sources and to call for types of government intervention different from the older forms of protection.

For more than seven years now, job growth in the United States has been good, and the unemployment rate has been steadily pushed down to low levels. Today's dissatisfactions arise not so much from fear of unemployment as from a growing concern about the stagnant growth of real wages and incomes in the United States, the availability of "good jobs at good wages," and an identification of that problem largely with international pressures on the U.S. economy. Correspondingly, the pressure on government has been not only to protect older, declining industries but to push aggressively for a wider opening of foreign markets to American exports and to insulate newer, high-technology, U.S. industries from real or alleged predator practices of industries in other countries.

American productivity growth slowed sharply after 1973 and recovered only a little of that loss in subsequent years. The slowdown in productivity growth together with a sharp run-up in oil prices—which in real terms are still well above their pre-1973 levels—virtually halted the growth in the real wage of the average American worker over the past fifteen years. Moreover, the slowdown was not evenly distributed. In particular, younger, adult, male workers with a high school education or less have done especially poorly; their real wage in recent years has been well below what it was in the early 1970s. In earlier decades these principally blue-collar workers benefited from relatively high wages in the tradable-goods manufacturing industries. Recent research has shown that much of the decline in the relative wages of unskilled or semiskilled workers was not because of the disappearance of high-paying manufacturing jobs and their replacement with low-paying service jobs, but rather because of an almost universal decline in the relative wages of unskilled and semiskilled workers in all industries. Nevertheless, the widespread belief persists that the problem of lagging real wages, especially among blue-collar workers, is because of the disappearance of "good" manufacturing jobs.

Coincident with the developments that produced a stagnation of real wage growth were several other developments that tended to single out the international trade sector of the economy as the problem area. With the overseas value of the dollar rising sharply after 1982, the United States began to run a large and mounting trade deficit; imports swelled and exports stagnated. Although the dollar reached a peak in 1985 and the trade deficit, after some delay, declined, that deficit remains huge by earlier standards. And within that overall picture the bilateral trade deficit of the United States with Japan stands out sharply. In 1989 the trade deficit with Japan was $49 billion, and even that deficit was held down by the U.S. surplus of agricultural trade; in manufacturing the trade deficit with Japan stood at $66 billion, virtually undiminished from its peak in 1987. Partly because of this fact, partly because Japan has been so successful at displacing highly visible American goods—in traditional industries such as automobiles and consumer electronics and in the newer industries such as semiconductors—and partly because Japan imports a smaller share of manufactured goods consumption than any other advanced country, it has become a particular focus of the dissatisfaction.

At a popular level, concern began to grow that American goods were being frozen out of many foreign markets. At a more analytic level even some academic economists became fearful that barriers to imports in other countries, especially Japan, would require the United States to undergo an excessive depreciation of the dollar and a consequent unwarranted lowering of living standards in order to balance its international accounts. A more desirable outcome, involving a smaller depreciation of the dollar, would be a wider opening of Japanese markets to imported goods.

Another trend, parallel with these developments, reinforced the feeling among a number of influential people that U.S. trade policy needed serious changes. In the earlier postwar decades the United States was the unchallenged technological leader of the world. But as the countries of Europe and Japan, and later the dynamic smaller countries around the Asian rim, began to close the technological gap—most of them devoting large shares of their national income to gap-closing investments in modern plants and equipment—the technological edge began to narrow, and in many sectors to disappear. Never mind that the recovery of Europe and Japan, and the rapid growth of other smaller countries had long been a prime objective of farsighted American policy. The hard fact was that many Americans began to sense a big slippage in American competitiveness and to believe the nation needed a more activist government policy to compete successfully in the world market and more generally to keep American industry from falling behind in the creation and adoption of modern technology.

While all of this ferment was going on, the defenders of traditional trade policy were not silent. The Reagan administration yielded on several occasions to political pressures for protection, usually of the traditional kind to help older industries such as steel or autos, but occasionally of the newer variety to protect high-technology industries such as semiconductors. And some members of the Reagan and Bush administrations made it clear they had joined the camp of those calling for more fundamental changes in trade policy. Nevertheless, despite the slips and the intramural debates, the two administrations tried hard to hew to the traditional American policy of multilateral free trade and vigorously fought against congressional efforts during the last several years to impose a shift in the trade policy stance.

Academic defenders of multilateral free trade have not been wanting in numbers or in articles critical of the new strategic trade theories. The criticisms did not so much dispute the theoretical possibility that carefully calibrated government trade intervention might, in certain circumstance, bring gains to the United States, but principally argued that the potential gains were small; that intervening in a productive way would pose impossible information requirements; and that political pressures would convert an initially well-meaning intervention policy into a boondoggle for special interests.

These political, economic, and intellectual developments have combined to bring national trade policy to the political forefront in a way it has not been for many years. The legislative result of this ferment was the Omnibus Trade Act of 1988, a compromise among the many viewpoints. Its most noted innovation, Super 301, straddles the issue. It provides a mechanism through which U.S. trade negotiators can threaten the eventual imposition of special surcharges on a country's imports if that country does not agree to modify its "unfair" trade practices (as unilaterally defined by the United States), but gives the president great flexibility in determining whether or how far to apply the sanctions. Enactment of this legislation has not settled the issue. If the growth of American productivity and real wages remains low, and, as is likely, the U.S. trade deficit and bilateral deficit with Japan remain high, trade policy will continue to be at the forefront of the political dialogue.

Anne O. Krueger presents the case that the United States should continue to espouse a policy of multilateral free trade. She argues that the United States should deal with the problems and shortcomings of the current world trading system not by abandoning it for something new but through a vigorous campaign to open markets further in the ongoing multilateral negotiations under the GATT.

Rudiger W. Dornbusch describes and defends a policy of aggressive bilateralism. He diagnoses America's trade problems as stemming principally from formal and informal barriers to American imports in several foreign countries, especially Japan, the consequence of which is to force down the value of the dollar and depress American real wages and living standards. He proposes to meet this problem in two ways: set numerical targets for American imports into Japan (or any other country with unreasonably low imports), using sanctions like those provided in Super 301 as a threat to induce the offending country to meet the targets; and negotiate free trade areas with other countries, as the United States has done recently with Israel and Canada.

Laura D'Andrea Tyson offers quite a different version of a new U.S. approach to international trade. Essentially she argues that the United States needs a government policy that, in contrast to current laissez-faire attitudes, actively promotes the development of high-technology industries. The rapid development of those industries sets in motion, she believes, forces that indirectly strongly benefit the rest of the American economy. Especially because other governments actively support their high-technology industries in carving out a share in world markets, the United States cannot afford to leave their development to market forces alone. As part of a broader effort to foster development of its high-technology industries, the United States needs a new policy of managed trade that would recognize this imperative. Among other elements, her proposals envisage the negotiation of a series of international agreements recognizing that governments do subsidize, protect, and otherwise support their high-technology industries and codifying rules of the game for such intervention. If such agreements cannot be reached, Tyson argues that the United States should then set numerical targets for foreign exports to the United States or U.S. exports to other countries (applied to certain industries rather than globally as Dornbusch proposes) and use the threat of various sanctions to enforce those outcomes.

What a National Trade Policy Can and Cannot Accomplish

It is widely believed that, whatever their other consequences, protectionist measures to restrict imports can increase domestic employment.

Under most circumstances, that belief is wrong. The United States has for some years been operating at or near full employment, and the Federal Reserve consistently takes action to try to ensure that the United States does not seriously deviate from this path with either too much or too little spending for goods and services. Imposing a wide range of protectionist measures may indeed increase employment in the protected industries as a larger fraction of demand is satisfied from domestic production rather than from imports. But with the economy already at or near full employment, the new surge in the demand on the nation's capacity will threaten inflation, and the Federal Reserve will have to step in with higher interest rates to restrict economic activity elsewhere in the economy to prevent overheating. Job gains in the newly protected industries will be offset by job losses in the industries depressed by the higher interest rates, chiefly construction, machinery and equipment, and exports. In brief, trade restrictions can change the composition but not the overall level of national employment.

Similarly, a country cannot, except in the very short run, change its trade balance—the excess of exports over imports—by changing its trade policy. Whether a country runs a trade deficit or a trade surplus, and how large, is determined by its saving and investment propensities not its trade policies. If, for example, a country insists on saving less than it wants to invest domestically, it will set in motion a train of events that will cause it to run a current account deficit. The best illustration is what happened in the United States during the 1980s. The national saving rate fell substantially. Both private households and the government increased their spending relative to their incomes; indeed, the federal government began to run an unprecedentedly large budget deficit, simultaneously reducing its income with tax cuts and increasing its spending for defense.

To prevent the surge of spending from leading to an overheated boom and renewed inflation, the Federal Reserve permitted and actively helped engineer a sharp rise in real interest rates. The high interest rates did somewhat reduce domestic investment spending, but another important effect was to attract a lot of foreign funds into the United States to take advantage of the high returns. The "normal" foreign demand for dollars to buy U.S. exports was supplemented by the demand from foreigners wanting dollars with which to buy American securities and otherwise invest in this country. This rise in the foreign demand for dollars drove up its overseas value sharply and made exports very expensive for foreigners to buy while lowering the price of foreign imports for American buyers. As a result the United States began to run a large trade deficit, and a net inflow of goods and services into the United States was created to match the net inflow of foreign investment funds. In short, a country like the United States with a basically good credit rating can spend more than it produces by importing more than it exports and setting interest rates high enough to attract sufficient foreign funds to finance the resulting trade deficit. The converse is true of a country like Japan. It saves a good bit more than enough to finance its domestic investment opportunities. The excess of domestic saving drives down interest rates, Japanese funds flow abroad seeking the higher returns available there, the yen falls, and Japan runs a balance-of-payments surplus. It is the relationship between saving and investment in Japan and the United States, not trade policies or practices, that is responsible for balance-of-payments surpluses or deficits.

As another illustration of the inability of trade policy to have serious effects on the balance of payments, consider what would happen if, by whatever means, Japan greatly increased its propensity to buy imported (let's say American) goods, while neither Japan nor the United States changed its domestic saving and investment habits (leaving interest rates in the two countries unchanged). The demand for American exports by Japanese buyers would surge, leaving fewer surplus dollars potentially available for Japanese investors. But with interest rates in the United States remaining higher than in Japan, Japanese investors would continue to be interested in purchasing U.S. assets. The potential scarcity of American dollars relative to Japanese yen would lead to an appreciation of the dollar and a depreciation of the yen. The demand for American exports to Japan would fall back somewhat, and Japanese exports to the United States would rise, until the American trade deficit and the supply of dollars available to Japanese investors was restored to more or less its original level.[2] But notice that in the process Americans would be better off. U.S. currency would appreciate and terms of trade improve; that is, the United States would be buying more Japanese imports at lower prices (while the trade deficit would be no worse than it was before). The buying power of American wages would be greater and living standards consequently higher.[3] And, of course, if the United States simultaneously succeeded in getting the Japanese to open their markets wider and raised its own national saving rate, the nation could have both a lower trade deficit and a higher living standard.

Clearly, there is wide agreement that the choice among alternative trade strategies has nothing to do with how best to lower the American trade deficit or to increase American output and employment. Trade policy cannot achieve either of those goals.

Although economists generally agree that trade policy measures cannot alter employment, an increasing number of people have been arguing that trade policy can and should do two other things. First, to the extent American trade policy can induce other countries to increase their demand for American-made goods, the United States can improve its terms of trade, that is, it can exchange its exports for other countries' goods on more favorable terms. Each hour of American labor spent in producing exports will buy more imports, thus improving American living standards. Dornbusch's [work] . . . is built upon this theme, especially as it applies to Japan. Second, even if trade policy cannot raise American output and employment, it can change their composition, favoring some industries at the expense of others. . . . Few economists anywhere, favor traditional protectionist measures that seek to preserve jobs and output in declining American industries that face successful foreign competition in domestic markets. Virtually all agree that in the long run, such protectionist policies reduce American living standards. But lately, some business executives, former trade policy officials, and economists have argued that governmental trade measures can and should be used to improve the fortunes of America's high-technology, high-profit, and high-wage industries and defend those industries against the predatory policies of other governments—Japan is usually named as chief culprit—thereby raising American productivity and incomes.

At its core, therefore, the modern trade debate is not about jobs but about incomes.

The Axes of Debate

Though the modern debate about trade distinguishes itself from earlier controversy because of its concentration on wages and living standards rather than jobs, the simplicity of characterization ends there. . . . Recent proposals for changes in American trade policy together with their rationales, reveals three different dimensions or axes along which the protagonists divide themselves. Any particular set of proposals may differ from any other set not just by one differentiating characteristic, but by three.

First, as noted earlier, proposals differ according to which of two principal goals they seek: improving America's terms of trade, a traditional objective of an activist trade policy; or the more novel and controversial proposals for a strategic trade policy, designed to aid industries considered essential to the advance of technology.

Second, proposals may be distinguished by the means or tools they would use to achieve their goals. There are several alternatives. Some proposals would abandon or modify America's postwar reliance on multilateral arrangements and substitute bilateral deals and the establishment of free trade zones with one or more trading partners. Other proposals are grounded in the view that in some countries—usually Japan is held out as the chief offender—there exist strong barriers to trade, as well as other trade practices inimical to U.S. interests. Such obstacles are not amenable to being fixed by agreements about governmentally determined rules of trade, and hence agreements that stipulate quantitative outcomes for sectoral or even aggregate import or export flows among countries are needed.

Finally, the various trade proposals can be differentiated by whether their rationale is, or is alleged to be, essentially offensive or defensive in nature. Thus, Dornbusch would threaten Japan with a tariff on its imports as a device to widen its markets for American goods because, he argues, the barriers to imports that exist tilt the terms of trade between the United States and Japan unfairly in favor of Japan. His policy proposals are urged as defense against the consequences to the United States of Japanese customs and market structures.[4] Tyson would favor certain strategic U.S. industries, principally the high-technology electronic and communications industries, both on positive grounds, because she believes their expansion will confer special productivity-improving advantages on the U.S. economy, and on defensive grounds to avoid what she believes would be a shrinkage in their markets under the onslaught of the aggressive trade practices of other countries (again, Japan).

The current public debate about these issues has been confused because the various protagonists often use the term "managed trade" to describe different kinds of trade policy whose only common feature is some form or other of governmental intervention in international trade flows. Before proceeding, it will be useful to try to clear up the confusion.

The term managed trade has at least three different meanings. . . . Some authors use the term to denote results-oriented measures—the establishment of quantitative targets for imports or exports, along the lines just described. In this definition managed trade policies are contrasted with rules-oriented policies, under which governments establish the rules of the trading game, whether they be protectionist or free trade in spirit, and then let the market determine the outcome. In this use of the term, Dornbusch's proposal to establish quantitative targets for American exports into Japan represents a managed trade policy.

Tyson uses the term managed trade in a different manner, namely, to describe her strategic trade policies that, in turn, are a subset of a broader national industrial policy designed to promote the high-technology industries. She would have the U.S. government use both results-oriented and rules-oriented trade measures to help achieve this end.

More loosely, the term managed trade is sometimes used simply to describe an overall trade policy characterized by frequent and specific governmental intervention in trade flows, through tariffs, import quotas, quantitative targets for American exports into specific countries, the active use of antidumping laws, and so forth.

In view of this confusion, we will not use the term managed trade in the remainder of this chapter. Rather we will describe Tyson's overall approach as strategic trade policy and denote measures that would establish quantitative targets of various kinds as results-oriented policies.

In evaluating the various arguments and proposals for a new American trade policy we first evaluate the two chief objectives—improvement in the terms of trade and strategic industrial policy—and then turn to the various means suggested for their attainment. When relevant, we will identify the offensive or defensive nature of the proposals and what that implies for their validity.

Objective 1: Terms of Trade

As Krueger elaborates, traditional economic analysis suggests that free trade is the best approach to raise global welfare. But this traditional analysis has long recognized that a country like the United States, with the world's largest market, could try to exploit its monopoly power by using the threat of taxing imports or exports to extract from other countries agreements that would expand American exports (or limit imports) so as to improve U.S. terms of trade, and thus the United States would do better than under free trade. This so-called optimal tariff policy could backfire, however, if other countries retaliated with tariffs of their own.[5] Indeed, given the importance of the United States in the global economy, U.S. actions are likely to have systemic consequences. Protectionist policies by the United States will inevitably lead other countries into defensive actions or even into policies that outdo the United States with yet more aggressive measures. In the long run, therefore, a protectionist United States would leave all countries, including the United States, worse off.

Although it would be risky for the United States to try to exploit its monopoly power, the same logic suggests it could be foolhardy to ignore the protectionist actions of others. Foreign protection or export subsidies can reduce the U.S. terms of trade. If, for example, foreigners subsidize aircraft exports, U.S. exporters have to charge lower prices to match the competition. Similarly, if foreigners erect barriers against some U.S. exports, then to achieve a given U.S. export level, more exports of other products will be required. To induce greater sales of those exports, they will have to be more attractively priced. As long as other nations help companies that produce goods the United States imports, the United States gains. But if countries subsidize their exports to third markets or protect domestic firms against U.S. exports, they can lower U.S. living standards.

As already noted, Dornbusch believes that the informal, mainly nongovernmental, barriers to manufactured imports into Japan have biased the terms of trade against the United States. He seeks to increase aggregate U.S. manufactured exports to Japan because that would improve the terms of trade. Similarly, he argues that the negotiation of additional free trade areas with other U.S. trading partners would do likewise and might have the additional advantage of putting extra pressure on Japan to agree to trade concessions in the form of increasing its imports of U.S. goods. (If the United States entered into a number of free trade agreements with countries who were Japan's export competitors, the Japanese might lose some of their U.S. markets.) But Dornbusch is not explicitly concerned about the specific composition of U.S. exports; one dollar's worth of exports is as good for the United States as any other dollar's worth. In particular he does not argue that priority be given to high-technology or any other strategic group of industries. Thus, when he proposes the negotiation of numerical targets for the expansion of imports into Japan, he envisages an aggregate target for manufactured goods and sees no reason to look beneath the total.

Strategic Objective 2: Promoting Industries

Tyson is concerned about high-technology products. She and other proponents of industrial policies argue some industries are more important than others. They voice two concerns: that market forces left to their own devices will not channel sufficient resources into the critical high-technology industries; and that the trade and industrial policies of other countries will drive U.S. producers out of these key sectors and thus lower U.S. living standards.[6] But why do the proponents of industrial policy and managed trade believe that all industries are not created equal? What special characteristics do these high-technology industries have that warrant the government favoring them at the expense of others? If market forces were operating well, they would automatically arrange matters so that the last (that is, the marginal) dollar of resources allocated to each industry yielded the same benefit to the economy. The next dollar invested in making hamburgers would yield both the same economic returns and the same social benefits as the next dollar invested in computers. Otherwise, firms could increase profits simply by shifting resources from the low-yield to the high-yield use with national living standards being improved in the process. And the same reasoning applies to world trade; in world markets operating well, the marginal dollar of imports or exports would yield the same benefit in every line of business.

According to the advocates of managed trade and industrial policy, however, there are three principal kinds of departures from the world of efficiently functioning markets that make some industries "more equal than others" and that warrant interventionist policies.[7]

One, because of the nature of their products and production processes, some markets are necessarily imperfectly competitive and can generate, for a limited number of firms in the world market, surplus profits (rents)—profits higher than necessary to induce investment in the sector. If a country can somehow secure a place for its firms in such markets, it can earn surplus profits—its capital investments would earn more than could be earned in other uses. Two, some industries pay workers surplus (premium) wages, more than their experience and skills could earn elsewhere in the economy. Expansion of those industries will increase real wages and living standards. Three, the production of certain goods produces "spillover" benefits for the rest of the economy; that is, the benefits to the economy from the production of the goods in question are greater than the revenues earned by the producers, so that private incentives alone will not call forth as much output of those kinds of goods as it would be beneficial for society to have. It is argued, for example, that high-technology firms do an unusually large amount of research and development (R&D), many of whose benefits cannot be kept within the originating firm through patents and secrecy. These and related benefits spill over from high-technology industries into the rest of the economy in the form of free knowledge and faster technological advance.

Let us consider each of these three market imperfections in turn. How important are they, and to what extent do they warrant special governmental intervention, either at home or in foreign trade flows, to correct the resource allocation of the marketplace?

Surplus Profits

In recent years the analysis of trade has moved beyond the assumption that competition is perfect, to take account of the existence of economies of scale (that is, the tendency of average production costs to fall as the scale of production rises) and of the widespread reality of imperfect competition.[8] In industries that produce very specialized products, and in which the fixed costs of research and development, investment, and market development are high, the world market may have room for only a limited number of firms producing at low unit costs. The high fixed costs, and perhaps a long period of learning, may make it possible for the firms in the industry to go on for some time earning surplus profits. The new trade theories suggest that in such imperfectly competitive situations a country may be able to use government intervention strategically, to enrich itself at the expense of other nations. In particular, a direct export subsidy or one provided indirectly through protection in the home market could discourage foreign competitors and shift profits toward domestic producers.[9]

Though theoretically interesting, however, the circumstances under which these monopoly-promoting policies might pay off are extremely difficult to detect in practice. They depend crucially on behavioral features in the market, the degree to which other countries retaliate, and the supply responses of other firms to the government intervention.[10] Moreover, it is not enough for government to know the consequences of its policies on the favored firms. It must also know the full consequences in the industries from which the resources are drawn. Redirecting scarce scientific and engineering resources into a particular sector could create losses elsewhere in the economy that outweigh the gains in the sector being promoted.[11] The literature has also shown how fairly minor modifications in various elements of the problem can radically change the nature of the optimal policy, for example, from subsidizing trade to taxing trade.[12] Thus Avinash Dixit studied the U.S. automobile industry and concluded the optimal policy for the United States was a tariff on imports and a subsidy to domestic production.[13] But Kala Krishna, Kathleen Hogan, and Phillip Swagel demonstrated that with relatively minor changes in specifying the industry demand curve, the optimal policy changed to a subsidy on both imports and domestic production.[14]

Since economists' ability to estimate demand and costs' curves with precision is very low, to predict the response of other firms to the market changes induced by government intervention is lower still, and to calculate the general equilibrium effects from the drawdown of resources elsewhere in the economy "is virtually nil," there is very little chance that government could know in advance whether any particular beggar-my-neighbor policy of subsidy or protection will add to or subtract from national income. In any case, profits are usually a relatively small share of overall value added. And the evidence suggests that in industry, rents in the form of surplus profits usually range from small to nonexistent.[15] Wages, however, are another story. They are a larger share of value added, and rents in the form of premium wages are potentially a larger source of benefits.

Surplus or Premium Wages

Several recent studies of the U.S. wage structure suggest that some industries systematically pay premium wages (rents)—wages that are higher than workers with the same skills and other easily observable characteristics could earn in other industries.[16] Unionization may be one reason for the premium, but the studies suggest that there may be other "efficiency wage" reasons for the premiums. In some industries—importantly those with high capital intensity—it is very costly to firms if employees have a high absenteeism rate or shirk on the job. Such firms pay premium wages as a means of maintaining productivity at high levels, giving employees an incentive to keep absences and shirking at a minimum—get caught and you lose your premium wage job. But many workers with the requisite skills and other characteristics who are working in low-wage industries could be equally productive at such jobs if only the output for the premium wage industry could be expanded.[17]

Some have advocated using trade policies to enhance employment in sectors with premium wages.[18] One study argues that American export industries tend to be high-wage industries and that export promotion would raise national productivity and real wages.[19] But there are problems with this analysis and the associated trade policies. Statistically, it is difficult to distinguish between wage rents and payments that reflect skills, abilities, and attitudes of workers and characteristics of the job such as the disutility of certain types of labor. One critique has noted that the studies may be overestimating the size of the premium.[20] If what appear to be rents are in fact payments for skills, abilities, or other characteristics of workers or jobs, a governmental policy that subsidized the expansion of these industries could have damaging consequences. And policies that supported high-wage industries would encourage unions to claim even higher wages, while the distributional impact of such policies could be perverse.[21] Also, many high-wage industries—autos, steel, primary nonferrous metals, oil refining, glass, cans, paper and pulp mills, coal mining, tobacco—are not high-technology industries. On the other hand, several of the most prominent high-technology industries—computers and electronic components and accessories—while paying at or a little above the manufacturing average, are not at the top end of the wage scale. A policy of supporting the highest-wage industries would not be fully congruent with a policy of supporting high-technology industries. Finally, the distributional impact of using taxes to support high-wage sectors is regressive.

Spillover Benefits

The view that some industries, usually the high-technology ones, provide productivity-enhancing spillover effects to the rest of the U.S. economy lies at the heart of the arguments of many proponents of policies for managed trade. Tyson is among this group. Her paper recognizes the difficulties and dangers a country faces in trying to manipulate trade policy to capture surplus profits in imperfectly competitive industries. And she does not rely on the existence of premium wages as the mainstay of her arguments for favoring certain industries. But the existence of spillover benefits from one set of U.S. industries to other ones is critical to her conclusions.

It is not sufficient for the argument that certain goods or activities generate spillover benefits—the spillovers must be of more benefit to the country in which they originate than to the world at large. Otherwise the United States (or any other country) could sit back and gain the full advantage of other countries' spillover-generating activities—one wouldn't need to worry about where the world's high-technology production was located. And though some spillovers may be confined to one location or one country, most are not. Innovations by U.S. companies allow foreigners to improve their technology through reverse engineering. Similarly, foreign consumers could benefit from intensified competition.

The power and the wide diffusion of spillovers affecting consumers in a single economy is well known. It is striking, for example, that the wage of workers in high-technology industries rise little if any faster than the wages of workers in the rest of the economy. The real buying power of barbers, whose productivity has shown almost no improvement, will rise at the same rate as that of people producing semiconductor chips because the benefits of innovation in chips are passed on to all consumers through lower prices. What matters for living standards is the overall rate of innovation, not the rate in the sector in which a worker is employed.

Spillovers diffuse not only within a country, but across its borders, especially in the modern world where information, goods, and capital move so much more freely than they did in earlier eras. The chief explanation for the convergence in incomes among developed economies in the world economy during the postwar period is precisely that U.S. innovations spilled over to the rest of the world. Moreover, the fact that incomes in small countries (such as Switzerland, Sweden, Austria, Denmark), which have highly incomplete industrial structures, are no lower than incomes in large countries suggests that global spillovers are powerful. What matters for living standards, therefore, is not only what a country produces but also the access it has to the innovations and products of others.[22]

Nonetheless, not all spillovers are fully diffused outside a country's borders. The tendency of companies from the same industry to locate near one another, for example, Silicon Valley, does suggest some role for geographically confined spillovers. In principle, the existence of geographically confined spillovers could deprive a country of important benefits because market forces would not generate the appropriate amount of output from the spillover-creating industries. But even then it does not follow straightforwardly that government policies to promote these industries are called for. As Paul Krugman has pointed out, even where there are external economies (that is, spillovers), "If additional resources of labor and capital are supplied elastically to the industry, the external benefits of larger production will not be confined to the promoting country. Instead they will be passed on to the consumers around the world."[23]

Even granted that specific industries do generate spillover, and that some of those spillovers are not diffused on a global basis, how are those industries to be identified and favored? Industries in Washington are like children in Lake Wobegon—they are all above average. If no consistent set of principles exists to determine which industries the government should support, who will decide? An industry committee with a vested interest in cheap financing is scarcely the appropriate arbiter of how society's scarce resources should be spent. To choose among claims, the government would need a consistent and defensible set of principles on which to base its choices; adequate information to determine if claims are justified; and adequate restraint to avoid political pressures to provide aid where it is not justified.

Proponents of an industrial policy, for example, have advocated support for sectors that are high technology, pay high wages, have high value added per worker, are intensive in research and development, have strong links to other industries, or show rapid growth in productivity. Indeed, Tyson generally talks of high-technology sectors rather than specifying the ones meeting the precise conditions required to warrant government intervention. But almost any industry can make a claim under one or another of these headings. Basically, proponents of industrial policy and strategic trade intervention ignore the principle that intervention and the associated costs are worthwhile only if those measures yield a higher return than would other uses of the same resource; people often forget that in a fully employed economy, resources redirected by the government into high-definition television or steel or any other favored industry will reduce output elsewhere in the economy. Nor is there any reason to think government officials can predict market outcomes better than private businesses can.

In theory, economists may agree that market failures exist, resulting in rents and spillovers, which may justify government intervention. In the real world of scarce information, uncertainty, and pervasive rent seeking, policymakers will inevitably miss the crucial and subtle distinctions between profits that are high because of rents and those that are high because of risk; between wages that are high because of rents, and those that are high because of skills; and between sectors that provide inputs, and those that result in spillover externalities. Moreover, policymakers would find it extremely difficult to identify appropriate sectors and confine public largesse to sectors meeting such criteria.

Although these considerations suggest that the benefits to the United States from such strategic trade policies are likely to be highly uncertain, it does not follow that the costs to the United States from its trading partners who pursue such policies are negligible. Even though the United States might benefit little from its own strategic policies, it is possible that the strategic policies of others could seriously hurt the

United States—however misguided such policies may be in the interest of those other countries. To be sure, foreign policies to induce innovation or subsidize exports are not necessarily bad for the United States, but they can be. Those directed at lowering the costs of goods the United States can import will raise American living standards. But those directed at U.S. export industries could hurt. Foreign targeting must be taken more seriously as foreign economies become more competitive with the United States. Similarly, as long as the U.S. market was much larger than those abroad, the scale economies provided to foreign firms from domestic protection could be ignored. But as foreign markets have expanded, these considerations have become more significant. Before discussing appropriate defensive strategies against potentially harmful trade measures of other countries, however, consider first the various means or instruments of trade policy.

The Means and Instruments of Policy

Krueger stresses the advantages of the traditional U.S. strategy of negotiating multilateral (as opposed to bilateral) rules-based procedures (as opposed to quantitative targets) as the vehicle for accomplishing American trade objectives. But increasingly this view is being challenged. Indeed, while the proponents of a change in American trade policy would add some new policy objectives to the traditional ones, the big disagreements in this volume turn more on differences over means than on differences over ends.

One thrust of the challenge to traditional policy comes from those who maintain multilateralism is too weak and should be replaced or supplemented with unilateral and bilateral approaches. This view is stressed by Dornbusch. U.S. trade policy has already shifted in this direction. In the 1980s the United States concluded bilateral free trade agreements with Israel and Canada. In 1990 it entered into serious negotiations for a free trade area with Mexico and stated a long-term goal of a free trade area with Latin America. In 1988 the United States enacted legislation containing the famous Super 301 clause, which uses the threat of denying access to the U.S. market to back up the U.S. position in bilateral negotiations aimed at removing or modifying foreign trade practices the United States deems inappropriate.[24]

A second challenge comes from those who question the feasibility of securing through multilateral negotiations and multilateral rules the enlarged objectives they propose for American trade policy. Thus many proponents of a more interventionist U.S. trade policy, while tipping their hat in the direction of the desirability of multilateral rules for trade behavior, argue that in a world in which most major countries pursue industrial policies, it will sometimes be necessary to influence trade flows through the establishment of numerical targets for trade outcomes. This is essentially the position taken by Tyson; multilateral rules to manage competing industrial policies would be the best result, but until all the chief players become genuinely committed to free trade, multilateral rules probably cannot be successfully negotiated. Thus, quantitative targets will often be a necessary fallback.

Of course, bilateralism and results-oriented agreements are not mutually exclusive. Indeed, Dornbusch combines bilateralism with quantitative targets, while Tyson advocates a more multilateral approach to the establishment of such targets. Nonetheless, it is useful to discuss these notions separately.

Bilateralism

It is tempting for the United States to try to solve its trade problems with particular trading partners on a bilateral basis. As the world's largest economy, the United States appears in a particularly strong position when it confronts smaller and weaker economies one-on-one. Bilateralism allows the United States to press its case forcefully.[25]

But bilateralism has numerous disadvantages. It may be costly politically. In many countries the notion of submitting to American economic influence is not popular. U.S. actions under Section 301 have sparked Koreans to burn the U.S. flag and a Thai cabinet to resign. Bilateral approaches may also increase friction with excluded third parties. The improvements in trade with some countries could come at the expense of broader relations with others.

Bilateralism also may not lead to the best economic results. Multilateralism can increase the number of potentially liberalizing deals. To take a simple case, the United States might make a concession that favors Germany, who agrees to something that is particularly important to South Korea, who in turn liberalizes in an area of special importance to the United States. Indeed, in an interdependent global economy many problems simply cannot be solved bilaterally. A multilateral deal brings all interested parties to the table simultaneously. This is a great simplifying device compared with piecemeal discussions that occur under much greater uncertainty when several bilateral negotiations are implemented. Concessions made in one bilateral deal may undermine concessions made to another trading partner in an earlier deal. A sequence of bilateral deals may not be readily transformed into a multilateral system. There is the important danger that proceeding piecemeal will result in a complex, crazy-quilt system in which U.S. trade with different partners is subject to different regulatory regimes.

Bilateral arrangements in the form of free trade areas are sometimes beneficial, but their proliferation could pose serious problems. In particular, free trade agreements, like the recent U.S. one with Canada, usually do not solve the really sticky problems, such as U.S. antidumping practices, partly because the absence of other negotiating countries ruled out the multicornered bargains necessary to make progress in reducing such long-standing barriers. In the case of Canada these problems were left to be dealt with by a special Canadian-U.S. commission. This might be fine for one or two free trade agreements, but their multiplication could introduce a frightening array of separate trade barriers, each with its own administrative committee, rules, and temptation to give in to special pleaders.

These problems with bilateral approaches suggest the United States should give its highest priority to multilateral arrangements. The GATT should be used whenever possible to settle bilateral disputes and to negotiate new trade rules.

Bilateralism that is used to gain concessions only for the United States should be distinguished from bilateralism to achieve most-favored-nation (MFN) concessions for all members of the GATT. For the most part the United States has used bilateral negotiations to demand MFN concessions. Thus while the semiconductor agreement was negotiated between the United States and Japan, it set targets for purchases of semiconductors from foreign—and not just U.S.-owned firms. Similarly, the United States negotiated a more open Japanese market for imports of beef and citrus from all producing countries.

Indeed, bilateral approaches need not always undermine GATT processes and rules. The GATT allows the suspension of the MFN principle in the case of free trade areas that lower barriers across a broad range of products among participants. As long as the United States conforms to GATT laws, seeks MFN concessions, and objects to practices that violate international agreements, bilateral approaches may have some merit. Indeed if the United States is able to conclude a free trade agreement with Mexico, it would be well worth pursuing. But it is always tempting to use these bilateral approaches to gain special advantages for the United States. It is also tempting to withdraw concessions granted under the GATT to persuade countries to agree to practices not covered by the GATT. An egregious example was the raising of tariffs bound under the GATT against Brazil in a 301 case on intellectual property rights.[26] And finally, as enshrined in the Super 301 legislation, it is tempting to use bilateral responses not only with countries who have violated commitments made in international agreements (unjustifiable practices) but also those who engage in practices that the United States unilaterally deems unreasonable.

It is one thing to use carefully articulated bilateral initiatives to reenforce MFN and GATT rules. But it is quite another to pursue aggressively short-term national advantages that are counter to the letter and the spirit of a multilateral trading system. If the United States were indeed to declare that the "GATT is dead," the consequences for the global trading order could be disastrous.

On a broader scale, a regional Western Hemisphere free trade area, as recently proposed by President George Bush, could be a trade-liberalizing component of the GATT if it incorporated several essential characteristics. First, it should be negotiated simultaneously among all, or at least most, of the countries in the hemisphere—piecemeal negotiations would be much less likely to achieve substantial liberalization, and early signatories might well resist the loss of preferences they would suffer as others sought entry. Second, it should provide, for all the members, a substantial phased-in reduction of the high tariffs and nontariff trade barriers among the Latin American countries and a significant liberalization of the United States' principal selective barriers, such as quotas on steel, textiles, and sugar and U.S. use of the anti-dumping laws. Third, those countries that entered the agreement with especially high trade barriers against outside GATT members should reduce them, thus tending to ensure that the formation of the regional free trade area was consistent with GATT's article XXIV and did not end up injuring the rest of the trading world.[27] It is not obvious that such an agreement could be negotiated, but if it should prove possible, it could be a pathbreaking complement to the GATT system by demonstrating the scope for multilateral liberalization between developed and developing countries.

Results-Oriented Trade Policy: Quantitative Targets

U.S. trade policy has generally been directed at improving the rules that govern trade. This has been true both in negotiations at the GATT and in bilateral negotiations with trading partners.

Increasingly, however, there are calls for the United States to shift its demands from equal opportunity—a level playing field—to affirmative action. Some argue that Asian countries such as Japan and Korea will never play by Western rules.[28] Indeed, given the outstanding performance of the Japanese economy, the outside world has no right to demand that Japan change some of its internal practices that have served it so well; long-term stable relationships between industrial firms and their suppliers are an example. Instead of trying to change these countries, the outside world should simply negotiate quantitative import targets and allow their governments, which best understand their economic system, to ensure these targets are attained. The new slogan is, therefore, "results rather than rules."

But exactly what kind of outcome should the United States be seeking? One key principle of economic policymaking is that policy instruments should be precisely targeted to policy goals. A serious difficulty in designing and negotiating results-oriented trade measures is that there must be a precise agreement on goals so that the quantitative results are appropriately specified. Indeed, because advocates of such measures do not share the same goals, they differ over the countries they would include in their arrangements and the numerical targets they would define.

The list of goals sought by the various proponents of results-oriented trade policy includes avoiding needless frictions that arise from detailed discussions about institutional differences; improving the U.S. terms of trade; increasing U.S. domestic production; increasing production by U.S.-owned multinational companies; improving the U.S. defense industrial base; obtaining spillovers for the U.S. economy; maintaining the technological capacity of U.S.-owned firms; avoiding unfair trade practices; and saving jobs.

Because their goals differ, there are noteworthy differences in the outcomes that advocates of results-oriented trade policy would like to ensure. Targets include aggregate trade balances, bilateral trade balance, aggregate exports, aggregate imports, exports of specific products, and imports of specific products. Some would confine their approaches to countries, usually Japan and sometimes other Asian nations such as Korea, whose economic systems are seen as operating by rules that are too different from the United States.[29] Others advocate global, sectoral, quantitative arrangements, patterned, for example, after the Multifiber Arrangement.[30] Some would set bilateral numerical targets (for example, imports from the United States), others multilateral targets (imports from the world), some would allow only purchases from U.S.-owned firms to qualify, others would include foreign-owned firms. Finally, there are differences in the number of parameters proponents would like to have negotiated, for example, simple dollar value or quantitative targets or more complex sharing agreements encompassing sales volumes, prices, and other relevant competitive parameters. Clyde Prestowitz, for instance, believes international trade generally should be managed like IAATA—the international airline cartel.[31]

But setting numerical targets is rarely an effective mechanism for achieving specific goals.

Aggregate export targets. Dornbusch is concerned that protection of the Japanese market by nontariff and invisible barriers restricts U.S. exports to Japan. Accordingly, he seeks to increase the quantity and price of U.S. exports and to raise U.S. living standards by demanding that Japan increase the volume of manufactured goods it imports from the United States by 15 percent a year for the next decade. In the absence of such a response, Dornbusch advocates the imposition of a tariff on Japanese exports to the United States.

The advantage of this approach is that it would avoid the dollar devaluation that would otherwise be necessary to induce Japan to buy more U.S. products. Dornbusch argues that what is important from a U.S. perspective is "good jobs at good wages."

This proposal cannot be faulted on logical grounds. Forcing Japan to buy more products produced in the United States would have a favorable impact on employment and profits in U.S. export-producing firms. It should be stressed, however, that it would have several other, deleterious effects.

In the absence of a shift in saving and investment behavior, more imports into Japan would entail more exports from Japan. Indeed the motive behind the approach is to achieve a weaker yen. It would imply increased competition for American industries who compete with the Japanese here at home or in third markets abroad. Moreover, as advocated by Dornbusch, the approach would entail trade diversion from other countries. Dornbusch's target is for imports from the United States and this would sharply increase frictions with other countries.

Dornbusch argues it is irrelevant whether an American or a Japanese firm in the United States produces the exports for the Japanese market. An increased demand by Japan for imports from the United States raises the demand for American labor. However, if, as is the current practice, most of the imports are brought in by Japanese firms, the official and private practices that limit the degree to which newcomers can contest the Japanese market could continue. Although the Japanese market might have more imported products, these could still be priced to maximize the profits of Japanese firms with monopoly power. Japanese consumers would not necessarily enjoy the full benefits of access to cheaper imported products.

Although such a results-oriented approach might raise the volume of Japanese trade, it could actually lead to a market with more rather than less government and corporate control. Import targets can only be enforced if the Ministry of Trade and Industry (MITI) is powerful enough to guide Japanese firm behavior in great detail. MITI would be forced to organize and monitor numerous buying cartels. Firms would be forced to collude on how imported products are to be handled. Instead of encouraging Japan in the liberal direction urged in its own official Maekawa report, the policies would be driving it back toward precisely the system the world finds so difficult in the first place. Such an approach gives up on the idea that the Japanese economy will ever be genuinely open. It settles for making sure that at least Japan buys a certain amount of imports as a quid pro quo for its exports. By insisting Japan implement such a system, the United States would severely limit Japan's ability to become a genuinely liberal economy, and slow or halt the current movement in that direction. Although these arrangements are sometimes justified as an interim step toward a more liberal trading system, they represent a movement in the opposite direction.

Even acting in good faith, the Japanese government could not carve up many of its markets for U.S. goods. And when it did succeed, it could be counterproductive. Forcing the Japanese to buy goods by government edict is scarcely the way to enhance the reputation and the long-term future of American products in Japan.

High-technology competition. Tyson is particularly concerned about the fate of high-technology U.S. industries. Accordingly she supports the use of so-called voluntary import expansions to boost the sales of U.S. high-technology firms in Japan.[32]

In principle, Tyson believes in a rules-based international regime for high-technology trade, but in the short run she defends results-oriented trade measures such as the Semiconductor Trade Agreement (STA), which set minimum prices for Japanese chip exports and required Japan to boost purchases of foreign chips. Tyson argues that without such interim, results-oriented measures, the U.S. economy will lose strategic key sectors. She points out that in some industries knowledge does not easily spill over across national borders. Such knowledge accumulates in firms in the form of skilled workers, proprietary technology, and difficult to copy know-how. "The goal of intervention, therefore, is not simply to improve the trade balance or to address external barriers abroad, but to secure a share of world production and employment in such industries with the local knowledge, skills, and spillover benefits that they generate."[33] While the promotion of beneficial spillovers within the U.S. economy may be Tyson's goal, it is far from clear that the STA helped produce these advantages. Indeed, having sharply raised the price of semiconductor chips to most U.S. computer manufacturers, it may have discouraged some production from some industries that presumably have beneficial spillovers. It is a good example of the weaknesses both of the general proposition that trade policy should be managed to favor specific industries and of the use of quantitative targets as a mechanism to achieve that goal.

It is striking that the sideletter to the semiconductor agreement, which was negotiated between the United States and Japan, called for the products of non-Japanese companies to achieve 20 percent of domestic sales in Japan by 1991. It reflects concerns for the interests of U.S.-owned companies rather than for U.S. domestic production. The semiconductors that Texas Instruments produces in Japan or Korea, with Japanese or Korean labor and spillovers benefiting those countries, qualify for this quota, while the semiconductors that NEC or Fujitsu produce in the United States with U.S. labor and spillovers, do not. As it has been implemented, therefore, this initiative certainly does not encourage spillover effects on the domestic structure of production in the United States.

Japanese semiconductor firms, it is argued, gain a strategic advantage because their home market is protected. This enables them to enjoy rents not available to U.S. firms. The semiconductor agreement settles for giving foreign-owned firms 20 percent of that business, but it does not fundamentally undermine the basis of the rents. Indeed, because the semiconductor agreement has actually cartelized the global market for DRAMs (dynamic random access memory), it has dramatically increased the profitability of Japanese chip firms while raising the price of chips and the cost of production to U.S. computer manufacturers and other high-technology chip users. The agreement has done much more to boost the profits of Japanese firms who dominate world production than those of its U.S. competitors.

Tyson argues that mandatory shares for foreign firms will liberalize the Japanese market. But they are more likely to institutionalize a cartelized distribution system for semiconductors in Japan.[34] Moreover, the agreement has thus far not been successful in raising the share of foreign chips in Japanese consumption close to its target. Thus Japanese firms continue to enjoy the scale economies from their strong domestic position.

One of the key problems with sector-specific, managed trade solutions is that they will be dominated by industry participants whose interests do not necessarily coincide with those of the United States as a whole. This is particularly true in a key linkage sector such as semiconductors. The cartelization of the global market for DRAMs is certainly not in the interests of those U.S. computer firms who are not vertically integrated. Indeed this is a critical weakness of the whole concept of strategic industry trade measures like the Semiconductor Trade Agreement. Since a large fraction of so-called high-technology products serve as parts and components in other high-technology products, the United States can easily undermine itself by propping up the prices and restricting the production of items whose cheap availability is a boon to U.S. high-technology industries. Instead of favoring so-called linkage industries for these cartellike arrangements, the United States should be particularly reluctant to include them.

In sum, the semiconductor agreement is a clear demonstration of the pitfalls of the managed trade approach to strategically important sectors.[35] The precise specification of its goals reflects a capture of public policy by a subset of U.S. firms whose interests are not coincident with those of the U.S. economy as a whole. The semiconductor agreement affords more financial benefits to U.S. competitors than it does to U.S. firms. It has established, in the name of saving the U.S. consumer from foreign price gouging, a cartel that can gouge its customers. As David Mowery and Nathan Rosenberg have noted, if the Semiconductor Trade Agreement is an example of successful strategic industry trade policy, it is hard to know how one would define failure.[36]

Conclusion. Strategic industry trade policy is simply a bad approach, and results-oriented trade measures are poor tools to employ. They replace competition among firms with competition among bureaucrats. Conceivably, in the Japanese political system, the choices of which industries to favor, which to let decline, and what means to use in pursuing those goals might be made on the basis of cold economic logic and calculations of what is best for the national economy. But the division of powers in the U.S. political system is ill-suited to managing the details of the economy. In the United States any attempt to divide the pie would be based not on strategic economic and trade criteria, but on political trade-offs that would reflect lobbying skills and masquerade under the rubric of "fair shares."

. . . U.S. trade policy for most of the past fifty years has been amazingly successful not only defensively in fending off special interests, but offensively in achieving round after round of trade liberalization. One of the keys to this success—which flies in the face of cynical interpretations of democratic politics—was precisely the fact that the United States adopted a doctrine of adherence to a regime of multilateral free trade, a "standard to which honest men could repair." The numerous special pleaders could be told that however heartrending their problem, their plea for protection was completely inconsistent with basic and longstanding U.S. policy. It didn't always work, but it was successful far more often than not. Under a regime of managed trade, however, where the name of the game is precisely to use trade policy to foster the interests of particular industries, and where any lobbyist can buy a study attesting to the dynamism, technological potential, and strategic character of his or her client, the barrier against special interests would crumble rapidly. It is not that the U.S. political system is necessarily a patsy for special interests. There are many examples to the contrary. But the United States does have to be careful in designing policy instruments that have serious economic effects to make sure that they are shaped with the special nature of U.S. political institutions in mind. A policy of strategic trade intervention and results-oriented agreements does not meet that test.

When results are being managed, clearly the devil lies in the details. Unless there is a clear rationale for the policy, the specifics could make the results disappointing. For some purposes, for example, enhancing the welfare of U.S. workers, it may suffice to emphasize greater import volumes; for other purposes, for example, enhancing the profits of U.S. firms, it may suffice to seek increased participation by U.S. firms in Japan. But these approaches should not be confused with policies that aim at increasing global welfare by achieving a market that is open in the most fundamental sense, that is, a market that can be readily contested by new firms, both foreign and domestic, who chose to supply products made at home and abroad.

Finally, sector-specific agreements are always justified as transitional measures. But their history suggests that once established, they expand, become institutionalized, and extremely difficult to eliminate. Thus the voluntary export restraint in cotton textile exports from Japan to the United States in 1955 became the Multilateral Short-Term Arrangement in cotton textiles in 1960, then the Long-Term Cotton Arrangement in 1962, and eventually the Multifiber Arrangement in 1973, which has been renewed and tightened and is still in force today.[37] Today, many developing countries who objected to its establishment have acquired a vested interest in its perpetuation.

By the same token, those U.S. firms who are given guaranteed access to a market will be unwilling to give up those guaranteed market shares. Though a results-oriented trade arrangement may make the numbers look better in the short run, it is likely to be a step away from, rather than toward, the open, free trade regime the United States would like to see established.

Trade Policies for the 1990s

We have outlined some of the problems associated with bilateralism, strategic industrial policy, and results-oriented agreements. But that does not mean that the issues raised by advocates of these measures can be ignored. The United States needs policies to counter foreign practices that worsen its terms of trade. It also needs responses to policies of foreign governments that promote favored industries at the expense of otherwise competitive U.S. industries. In this section, we outline briefly what we believe are appropriate U.S. policies to deal with these questions.[38]

Open Markets

U.S. companies need open global markets. The United States has seldom used trade policies to protect its high-technology products, and it should continue this restraint. But as long as the United States provides foreigners with the ability to profit from sales here, it is justified in demanding similar access for its own firms and its own exports to markets abroad. Because scale economies are critical in the development of many high-technology products, a protected home market can give domestic firms an unfair advantage. A protected home market like Japan can also provide domestic firms with surplus profits they can use to accelerate their technological development.[39] The United States must insist that mature industrial economies not adopt infant industry approaches. This would mean establishing several trade policies.

First, with respect to firms operating abroad, the United States should demand that all countries treat high-technology companies of all nations identically. If programs for research and development are organized in the European Community, Japan, or the United States, foreign-owned firms should be allowed to participate. The United States should make participation by the firms of other countries in U.S. government-funded research programs and institutions contingent on the granting of "national treatment" to U.S. firms operating abroad, that is, they should be given equal treatment with domestic firms.

Second, if foreigners protect high-technology sectors with barriers against imports, the United States should impose tariffs on the sale of products developed that way. The key lies in putting foreign countries on notice during the development phase of such programs, rather than in waiting until U.S. importers have become dependent on such products as was the case with Japanese semiconductors. Carrying out such a policy will require the use of actions under Section 301 of the Trade Act of 1974, which are directed at targeted programs in their initial stages.

Two changes need to be made in U.S. antidumping policy. First, it needs to be retargeted. The current emphasis on preventing firms from selling below "full costs" is normally an unwarranted interference with normal business practices and needlessly costly to American consumers.[40] The definitions of predatory pricing for foreigners should conform to those for domestic firms.[41] Emphasis should be shifted to preventing classical price discrimination, that is, selling abroad at lower prices than are charged in the home market, which is universally recognized as an unfair trade practice. But second, the retargeted antidumping laws should be promptly and strictly enforced. As Michael Borrus has argued, antidumping laws have no "teeth" since the remedy is only to restore a fair market value.[42] A more severe penalty for discriminatory dumping should be applied.

The United States should not succumb to the temptation to negotiate a market share for its firms. This approach will not solve the essential problem, which stems from the fact that the foreign market is not open. Indeed, it is likely to reinforce foreign monopoly powers. How then should the United States deal with the well-established fact that the Japanese market effectively restricts the volume of imports?[43] Japan continues to import an unusually small percentage of manufactured goods from all countries; it has an extremely small amount of intraindustry trade.[44] Japanese firms abroad account for unusually high shares of Japanese imports; a large share of U.S. exports to Japan, for example, pass through the hands of the ubiquitous Japanese trading firms. The prices of imported products are much higher in Japan than elsewhere, and foreign investment levels are unusually low. Japanese producers abroad show strong preferences for buying Japanese materials, parts, and components.[45] While some of these characteristics may be partially explained by fundamental economic factors such as Japan's poor natural resource endowments and its distance from its trading partners, a variety of official and unofficial barriers also play a role. Other barriers reflect particular Japanese business practices that have been successful in raising Japanese industrial efficiency—the close and long-term relationships between particular producers and their suppliers is a key example. Nevertheless, if Japan is to play the leading role it sees for itself in the world economic community, and, more to the point, if it is to continue as a principal world exporter, it must be prepared to modify those practices and institutions that keep out imports.

Unfortunately, there is no simple solution to removing the barriers to imports and foreign investment in Japan. Neither simple numerical targets nor free trade agreements will do the trick. Detailed sector-specific negotiations to change the rules are inevitable.

While the United States has pursued sector-specific goals, it put too much emphasis on unilateral threats and bilateral negotiations— Japan is able to divert attention from legitimate complaints when they are made under U.S. Super 301 by arguing those complaints simply reflect U.S. "unilateralism." When Japan is criticized by the United States alone, it rebuts the argument by pointing to internationally recognized U.S. weaknesses, fiscal policy, the poor state of productivity growth, and the low level of saving and investment. But these are not the point. The case for a more open Japan can be made most compellingly and convincingly precisely when it is made at the multilateral level. Indeed the agreements opening the markets for beef and citrus have come precisely when Japan found the GATT was going against it. Instead of using 301 as a first resort and multilateralism second, the United States should have recourse to multilateral channels first, whenever they are available.

Although most Americans would in principle favor the use of multilateral pressures and reliance on market-oriented trade measures, the number of voices calling for the abandonment of those remedies has been increasing. The so-called revisionists claim that such measures will not work in relation to Japan, that Japanese trade is not responsive to macroeconomic adjustment pressures through exchange rates, and that Japanese markets are not made more open through rules-oriented negotiations. But neither of these claims is correct. In the three years after

1985, as the dollar weakened against the yen, U.S. exports to Japan increased by almost 70 percent, from $22.6 billion to $37.7 billion. Similarly, U.S. exports of manufactured goods increased from $12.3 billion to $22 billion—a rise of almost 80 percent in a period of relative price stability.[46] During this same period, the volume of Japanese imports from all countries increased by 39.4 percent, and the overall volume of Japanese imports of manufactured goods increased by 78.3 percent. By the first quarter of 1989, Japan was importing twice the volume of manufactured goods it had in 1985. Those who claim exchange rates do not change Japanese buying patterns have simply not examined the data.

This is not to say that all reliance should be placed on exchange rate adjustments. Negotiations for market opening are still necessary. But here also the traditional methods have paid off. Particularly rapid growth in U.S. exports has occurred in those sectors in which negotiations to change the rules have been concluded. Ironically, the widely cited report of the Advisory Committee for Trade Policy and Negotiations (ACTPN), which made headlines with its advocacy of sectoral import targets, also documented the success of the traditional negotiations. Thus, after ten years of pressure, virtually all barriers to the importation of tobacco into Japan have fallen.[47] The four sectors that were singled out for negotiation under the maligned Market-Opening, Sector-Specific (MOSS) talks in the mid-1980s have shown impressive growth in Japanese imports. According to the report, from 1985 to 1987, U.S. exports to Japan in the four product categories combined increased by 46.5 percent, well above the 24.8 percent increase in total U.S. exports to Japan over the same two-year period. The report dismisses this performance because the total increase in exports of the products (of $1.3 billion) was small relative to the entire bilateral trade imbalance. But no one expected negotiations in a few sectors to turn the entire imbalance around. The problem may not be the approach, that is, emphasizing rules and concentrating on certain import-limiting practices, but the limited resources and narrow focus of the number of sectors brought into consideration. The United States needs not only tough, persistent, sectoral negotiations but enough patience to let the results begin to build.

Trade Policy as Antitrust Policy

Unlike the situation in the first three decades after the Second World War, the United States is no longer the overwhelming source of technological advance and industrial innovation in the world. Quite naturally, indeed partly because of successful, U.S. postwar policies, other countries have joined the United States at the frontier of technology. As long as the United States remains a vigorous economy, the fact that the nation now has more nearly equal partners is a healthy, and, in any event, inevitable development. One consequence is that the United States cannot expect to be a chief player in every new industrial and technological specialty. And so, the United States is likely to become dependent on foreign supplies for some important high-technology products. Foreign countries also face a changed climate in world competitiveness. In earlier decades, when the United States was the technological leader in virtually all fields, the competitive environment in U.S. industries ensured that dependence on a foreign source of supply for a technological advanced product would not subject them to monopolistic exploitation. An effective U.S. antitrust policy offered substantial, de facto protection to the rest of the world against monopoly in any sector of traded goods. That is no longer true. These changed circumstances have important implications for both trade and antitrust policy, here and abroad.

Especially in the United States, but also abroad, it will be tempting to subsidize domestic production on the grounds that dependence on foreign suppliers (and owners) renders the country vulnerable to foreign pressures, political and economic. Occasionally this argument will be compelling. But not all dependence is bad, while the policies that would seek to avoid all instances of dependence would be. If foreign suppliers are geographically diverse and compete vigorously, countries have little to fear from dependence on foreign ownership or supplies. Or, to put it more precisely, in the United States and abroad, the problem of the relationship between foreign suppliers should be viewed from the standpoint of antitrust policy. All countries are potentially harmed if takeovers threaten undue concentration of the global market. Indeed, whatever the route by which one or a few firms come to dominate an important global market, all countries should be concerned. And so, both the United States and other industrial countries have an interest in beginning to negotiate a set of internationally applicable antitrust rules. But even if ultimately successful, this task will be thorny and protracted. In the meantime the United States may have no option but to use its antitrust laws to deal with economic threats from global monopolies and cartels.

When foreign takeovers threaten undue concentration of the global market, they should be stopped. Similarly, antitrust authorities must be vigilant if the United States relies on a few foreign suppliers for a vital input. Antitrust policies should be used to ensure the rapid diffusion of foreign products to the United States. If, for example, a few foreign firms in control of the market for DRAM semiconductors were to engage in monopolistic practices that denied access to U.S. users, or if they engaged in price fixing, U.S. antitrust policies should be invoked. Those damaged by these practices should be entitled to the normal treble-damages compensation.[48] This is also the context in which one should view foreign suppliers who sell in the United States at prices well below costs. If the world industry is reasonably competitive the United States should not use its antidumping laws to deprive American buyers of low prices. But if it is a foreign monopoly or cartel doing the selling, driving out U.S. producers in the process, then the United States should treat it just as it might predatory practices in the United States that might bring about a monopoly.

Like any set of antitrust policies, carrying these recommendations out in practice will involve many sticky questions and much argument over how the principles apply in particular cases. Moreover there will always be a temptation to be much more aggressive in applying the antitrust approach against foreign firms than against domestic ones. Nevertheless, formulating U.S. trade policies on the basis of such principles offers the best hope of walking the appropriate line between seeking the advantages of free trade and protecting the U.S. economy against real—as contrasted with trumped-up—dangers from unfair foreign trade practices.

Global Harmonization

In the early postwar period, tariffs and quotas obstructed trade, and capital movements were severely restricted. When economic interdependence was limited, trade policy needed to deal only with policies, such as tariffs and quotas, that directly affected trade in goods.

Economic interdependence has now expanded so much that serious differences and inconsistencies among government policies in much broader areas can no longer be readily tolerated. As border barriers have been eliminated, national differences in such areas as antitrust, regulation, tax, financial, and technology policy can now seriously distort trade and investment flows. Critics are correct, therefore, when they argue the GATT must extend its purview beyond tariffs and quotas. Indeed, the agenda of the current GATT negotiations, which includes areas such as services, agriculture, intellectual property rights, trade-related investment measures, and subsidies, indicates that the majority of GATT members feel the need for improvements in the global rules on these issues. Improved mechanisms for surveillance and dispute settlement are also needed.

In 1990, in particular, with negotiations reaching a critical point, U.S. trade policy should place its highest priority in achieving progress through GATT reform. Unilateral policy measures that might conflict vith this goal should be studiously avoided. However, subagreements within the GATT that promote trade, combined with conditional MFN treatment in their application, may well be appropriate when a significant bloc of countries refuses to participate in agreements that would be beneficial to a large number of other countries.

Over the medium term, U.S. trade policy should strive for an open, global trading system governed by common rules. This regime should be implemented through a vastly strengthened and extended GATT apparatus.

Once the GATT negotiations are concluded and the mechanisms for creating a single internal European market are achieved in 1992, the next step should be a multilateral effort to achieve a single OECD market for goods, services, and capital by the year 2010.[49] The approach should use the example of the initiative for Europe 1992. The European governments decided they needed to complete the internal European market by removing all remaining obstacles to the free movement of goods, labor, and capital within the Community by 1992. In a 1985 White Paper they laid out the 300 measures required to achieve this goal. The OECD should similarly be given the task of formulating measures to create an integrated market for goods, services, and capital. Of course, it would be impossible and undesirable to obtain identical practices across all nations. But this should not be necessary. Indeed, some competition among regulatory regimes could be beneficial. The difficult task will be to determine those issues on which harmonization will be essential, and those in which principles such as national treatment and mutual recognition of technical standards will suffice.

Participating countries would agree to procedures for handling allegations of unfair trade as well as measures to provide safeguards. Ideally, they could go further and establish a multinational tribunal to rule on whether allegations of unfair trade practices were supportable. As an interim approach, the findings of the tribunal would prevail unless explicitly overruled by the chief executive of the complaining country. Participating countries would also agree to rules to encourage innovation. These would include provisions for nondiscriminatory government procurement and national treatment for foreign firms. Similarly, an international entity would supplement national antitrust policies.

It is striking that most proponents of bilateralism and managed trade still believe that ultimately a single world market with a rules-based regime should be established. They advocate their approaches as more effective means for achieving these objectives. Sometimes it is necessary to take one step backward to take two steps forward. But in this case, the steps toward bilateralism and managed trade are steps in the wrong direction.

Notes

1. Of course, during this period international trade economists were developing theorems and arguments about the possible conditions under which a nation's welfare might, or might not, be improved by infant industry protection, by optimal tariffs, by regional customs unions, and the like. Nevertheless, on a broad combination of theoretical, practical, and political grounds, most Western economists strongly advocated a system of multilateral free trade as the most desirable overall regime for international trade, certainly among developed countries.

2. Indeed, the temporary export boom would force the Federal Reserve to raise U.S. interest rates, which would make dollar investments even more attractive and hasten the transition back to the "old," higher trade deficit.

3. The consequences for Japan might go either way. If the original barriers to trade had indeed been keeping tbe Japanese consumers from exercising their basic preferences, then the more open access to imports would improve their well-being. But they would have suffered a loss in their terms of trade—they would be paying more for the old level of imports. Another way of saying the same thing is that to the extent that Japan has artificial barriers to imports, those barriers are both helping and hurting its citizens and it's impossible to say, in the abstract, what the net balance is.

4. Interestingly enough, his argument implies that the effective prices of Japanese goods to U.S. consumers are too high and that the United States does not import enough from Japan, given the overall saving and investment position of the two countries.

5. See Harry G. Johnson, *International Trade and Economic Growth* (Harvard University Press, 1967), pp. 31–55.

6. Even if other countries were not promoting the expansion of their high-technology industries in world markets, Tyson and other supporters of industrial policies, who believe that high-technology industries are critical to economic growth, would presumably favor government policies that especially promoted the expansion of those industries. But in that case, the relevant policies need not be oriented to foreign trade (although they would surely have effects on trade).

7. The emphasis given each of the three departures differs among the various theories underlying proposals for managed trade.

8. For excellent introductions, see Elhanan Helpman and Paul R. Krugman, *Market Structure and Foreign Trade: Increasing Returns, Imperfect Competition, and the International Economy* (MIT Press, 1985), and *Trade Policy and Market Structure* (MIT Press, 1989).

9. Barbara J. Spencer and James A. Brander, "Intemational R&D Rivalry and Industrial Strategy," *Review of Economic Studies*, vol. 50 (October 1983), pp. 707–22. See also Paul R. Krugman, "Import Protection as Export Promotion," *Monopolistic Competition and International Trade*, Henry Kierzkowski, ed. (Clarendon Press, 1984); and Paul Krugman, "Is Free Trade Passe?" *Journal of Economic Perspectives*, vol. I (Fall 1987), pp. 131–44.

10. Subsidies may drive foreigners out of the market, but they could also induce entry by domestic firms. The added competition, as Horstmann and Markusen have emphasized, could ultimately dissipate the potential rents into the pockets of foreign consumers through lower prices. See Ignatius J. Horstmann and James R. Markusen, "Up the Average Cost Curve: Inefficient

Entry and the New Protectionism," *Journal of International Economics*, vol. 20 (May 1986), pp. 225–48.

11. See Avinash K. Dixit and Gene M. Grossman, "Targeted Export Promotion with Several Oligopolistic Industries," *Journal of International Economics*, vol. 21 (November 1986), pp. 233–50.

12. Thus Eaton and Grossman have shown that in the same duopoly model used by Brander and Spencer, if firms react to prices rather than quantities, the optimal policy is taxing rather than subsidizing exports. See Jonathan Eaton and Gene M. Grossman, "Optimal Trade Policy under Oligopoly," *Quarterly Journal of Economics*, vol. 51 (May 1986), pp. 383–406.

13. Avinash Dixit, "Optimal Trade and Industrial Policy for the U.S. Automobile Industry," in Robert C. Feenstra, ed., *Empirical Methods for International Trade* (MIT Press, 1988), pp. 141–65.

14. Kala Krishna, Kathleen Hogan, and Phillip Swagel, "The Non-Optimality of Optimal Trade Policies: The U.S. Automobile Revisited, 1979–1985," Working Paper 3118 (Cambridge, Mass.: National Bureau of Economic Research, September 1989).

15. Katz and Summers have found, for example, that "shareholders in American firms receive only very small monopoly rents. The weak, available evidence suggests the same for Japan." Lawrence F. Katz and Lawrence H. Summers, "Industry Rents: Evidence and Implications," in *Brookings Papers on Economic Activity, Microeconomics 1989*, p. 269.

16. See, for example, Katz and Summers, "Industry Rents."

17. Market forces alone won't generate enough output for these industries, since payment of the premium wage keeps the price of the output high. A subsidy could lower prices and expand output; the industries that would be displaced would have lower productivity and lower wages, so the economy would gain from the transfer.

18. See William T. Dickens and Kevin Lang, "Why It Matters What We Trade: A Case for Active Policy," in Laura D'Andrea Tyson, William T. Dickens, and John Zysman, eds., *The Dynamics of Trade and Employment* (Ballinger, 1988), pp. 87–122; and Katz and Summers, "Industry Rents."

19. Katz and Summers, "Industry Rents."

20. See Charles L. Schultze, "Comment" in Katz and Summers, "Industry Rents."

21. See, for example, the report on Victor Norman and his paper, "Imperfect Competition and General Equilibrium Aspects of Trade," in *Centre for Economic Policy Research Bulletin* (London, October 1989), pp. 5–6.

22. Indeed, because of spillovers, a particular country (and the world) could be better off if it does less innovation and allows other countries with a comparative advantage in innovation to do more. See Gene M. Grossman and Elhanan Helpmann, *Comparative Advantage and Long-Run Growth*, Working Paper 2809 (Cambridge, Mass.: National Bureau of Economic Research, January 1989).

23. Kingsman, "Is Free Trade Passe?" p. 140.

24. For an extensive discussion, see Jagdish N. Bhagwati and Hugh Patrick, eds., *Aggressive Unilateralism* (University of Michigan Press, 1990).

25. For a more complete treatment see Robert Z. Lawrence's discussion of Dornbusch in [the original] volume.

26. For a critical view of Super 301, see Jagdish N. Bhagwati, "U.S. Trade Policy at Crossroads," *World Economy*, vol. 12 (December 1989), pp. 439–79.

27. This third point is a suggestion made by Jagdish Bhagwati, "Multi-lateralism at Risk," The Harry Johnson Memorial Lecture, London, July 11, 1990. See p. 24 for a discussion of the role of regional free trade associations within a GATT framework.

28. See the writings of Pat Choate, Clyde Prestowitz, James Fallows, and Karl von Wolferen.

29. See, for example, Pat Choate and J. K. Linger, *The High-Flex Society: Shaping America's Economic Future* (Alfred A. Knopf, 1986), pp. 63–77.

30. See Robert Kuttner, *Managed Trade and Economic Sovereignty* (Washington: Economic Policy Institute, 1989).

31. Clyde V. Prestowitz, *Trading Places: How We Allowed Japan to Take the Lead* (Basic Books, 1988), p. 324.

32. The Advisory Committee for Trade Policy and Negotiations (ACTPN) also suggested that U.S. Trade Representative Carla Hills should set sector-specific targets for Japanese imports. But it advised choosing sectors in which the United States was competitive rather than simply those that were high technology.

33. See Tyson's "Managed Trade Is the Best Trade: Making the Best of the Second Bests" in [the original] volume.

34. Tyson argues that such a quota pressures Japanese semiconductor users to design sophisticated foreign chips into their products. Perhaps, but the global shortage of DRAMs (dynamic random access memory) has also enabled Japanese DRAM producers to insist on the purchase of their more sophisticated chips as a condition for obtaining DRAM supplies.

35. For further discussion see Kenneth Flamm, "Policy and Politics in the International Semiconductor Industry," paper presented at the SEMI ISS Seminar, January 1989; and Flamm, "Semiconductors," in Gary Clyde Hufbauer, ed., *Europe 1992: An American Perspective* (Brookings, 1990), pp. 225–92.

36. David C. Mowery and Nathan Rosenberg, "New Developments in U.S. Technology Policy: Implications for Competitiveness and International Trade Policy," *California Management Review*, vol. 32 (Fall 1989), pp. 107–24.

37. See William R. Cline, *The Future of World Trade in Textiles and Apparel* (Washington: Institute for International Economics, 1987), chap. 6.

38. We do not discuss programs to deal with the trade deficit because we believe these should be dealt with through macroeconomic measures. Nor do we discuss the problems of the domestic dislocation owing to foreign competition. For more complete treatments of these questions, see Robert E. Litan, Robert Z. Lawrence, and Charles L. Schultze, *American Living Standards: Threats and Challenges* (Brookings, 1988); and Robert Z. Lawrence, "Protection: Is There a Better Way?" *American Economic Review*, vol. 79 (May 1989, Papers and Proccedings, 1988), pp. 118–22.

39. Especially for newer industries, capital markets are far from perfect. Access to large amounts of internally generated funds does provide an important advantage for expansion and technological gains.

40. There are exceptions, however; see the discussion in the following pages on antitrust policy.

41. As Ostry has noted, "Logically the principle of national treatment under domestic competition policy should replace antidumping regulation. The same definition of undesirable pricing behavior that is applied to domestic firms should apply to foreign firms entering into the domestic market." See Sylvia Ostry, *Governments and Corporations in a Shrinking World* (New York: Council on Foreign Relations, 1990), p. 91.

42. Michael G. Borrus, *Competing for Control: America's Stake in Micro-electronics* (Ballinger, 1988), p. 247.

43. See Robert Z. Lawce, "How Open Is Japan?" paper prepared for NBER; Conference on "The United States and Japan: Trade and Investment," October 1989.

44. See Edward J. Lincoln, *Japan's Unequal Trade* (Brookings, 1990).

45. Mordechai E. Kreinin, "How Closed Is Japan's Market? Additional Evidence," *World Economy*, vol. 11 (December 1988), pp. 529–42.

46. Department of Commerce, *United States Trade Performance in 1988* (September 1989), pp. 83–84.

47. Advisory Committee for Trade Policy and Negotiations, "Analysis of the U.S.-Japan Trade Problem," Report to Carla Hills, Washington, February 1989.

48. For an application of the antitrust principles to the issue of foreign inputs for defense, see Theodore A. Moran, "The Globalization of America's Defense Industry: What is the Threat? How Can It Be Managed?" in *Industrial Organization* (forthcoming).

49. For similar proposals see Gary Clyde Hufbauer, *The Free Trade Debate*, background paper for a report of The Twentieth Century Fund Task Force on the Future of American Trade Policy (New York: Priority Press, 1989); and Ostry, *Governments and Corporations*.

PART 5

TRANSNATIONAL ENTERPRISES AND INTERNATIONAL PRODUCTION

25

THEORETICAL PERSPECTIVES ON THE TRANSNATIONAL CORPORATION

Rhys Jenkins

Rhys Jenkins reviews the fundamental tenets and policymaking implications of four major perspectives—neoliberal, global reach, neoimperialist, and neofundamentalism—on transnational corporations (TNCs). According to Jenkins, the neoliberal perspective emphasizes the relative efficiency of the TNC and its capacity to rectify market imperfections, particularly in the South where such imperfections are more pervasive and extreme. The global reach perspective emphasizes the oligopolistic nature of TNCs, which possess the power to create and benefit from market imperfections. Proponents of this perspective warn that governments need to be cautious in their relations with TNCs and to use regulation to ensure that the host state benefits from the presence and economic activities of TNCs. The neoimperialist perspective views the TNC as an obstacle to the socialist transformation of society. TNCs drain host-state resources, create monopolistic structures within the host state, and eviscerate the national bourgeoisie. The result in the South has been perpetual underdevelopment. Neofundamentalists are Marxists or neo-Marxists who view TNCs as positive and progressive agents of social change. Like Marx, they believe only the dynamic processes of capitalist production are capable of providing the material base for socialism. Analytically, the neofundamentalists have much in common with the neoliberals but with a different outcome.

Reprinted with permission by the publisher of *Transnational Corporations and Uneven Development*, by Rhys Jenkins. New York, Routledge Press, 1987, pp. 17–37.

Introduction

Not surprisingly, the intense debate over the impact of TNCs in the Third World has generated a vast literature and throws up a large number of conflicting arguments and positions. In order to bring some order to this literature, a number of writers have attempted to identify different approaches to the TNCs (Lall, 1974; Hood and Young, 1979, ch. 8). It is obviously useful to distinguish between those writers whose main emphasis is on the positive benefits which TNCs bring to Third World countries and those who adopt a more critical approach, stressing the disadvantages of TNC activities (although in practice there is a continuum with many writers discussing both costs and benefits and differing primarily over the degree to which state intervention is necessary to ensure that the benefits outweigh the costs). Although some writers have been content to adopt a twofold classification along these lines (e.g. Biersteker, 1978) this fails to recognize the very real methodological differences between Marxists and non-Marxists writers, which have important implications for their analysis of the TNC. Since Marxists and non-Marxist alike adopt different positions *vis-à-vis* the TNC, it is appropriate to start with a fourfold classification of approaches towards the TNC.

	Pro-TNC	TNC Critics
Non-Marxist	Neo-classical (Reuber, Meier, Vernon, Rugman, Balasubramanyam)	Global Reach (Barnet and Muller, Streeten, Lall, Vaitsos, Helleiner, Newfarmer)
Marxist	Neo-fundamentalist (Warren, Emmanuel, Schiffer)	Neo-imperialist (Baran, Sweezy, Magdoff, Girvan, Sunkel, Frank)

The above table identifies four main perspectives on the transnational corporation—the neo-classical, the Global Reach, the neo-fundamentalist and the neo-imperialist—and some of the leading exponents of each approach amongst writers concerned with the impact of TNCs in the Third World. . . . The purpose of this chapter is to sketch in broad outline the main features of each perspective.

Neo-Classical Views

Most advocates of the benefits of foreign investment by TNCs base their arguments on neo-classical economic theory. Although the neo-classical case has developed considerably over the past twenty-five years, a common theme runs through all these writings. It is that the TNCs act as efficient allocators of resources internationally so as to maximize world welfare. The distribution of the benefits from TNC operations is either assumed to accrue to both home and host countries, or is not addressed directly. . . .

Internalization

In the last ten years a new neo-classical synthesis for analysing trade and investment by TNCs has emerged. . . . It has become the approach adopted by most pro-TNC writers in recent years. The major proponents of internalization are quite specific in seeing it as a general theory within which previous contributions can be incorporated (Buckley and Casson, 1976; Rugman, 1981), regarding it as a synthesis not only of earlier neo-classical contributions but also of some of the critical studies discussed below.

The central argument of this approach is that TNCs exist because of market imperfections. If all markets operated perfectly there would be no incentive for firms to go to the trouble of controlling subsidiaries in different countries and to internalize markets between them, rather than engaging in arm's length transactions with independent firms. Internalization then is a way of bypassing imperfections in external markets.

Imperfections in a number of areas are regarded as being important in explaining the existence of TNCs. Markets for intangible assets such as technology or marketing skills are notoriously imperfect because of their public good nature, imperfect knowledge and uncertainty. This makes it difficult for the seller to appropriate fully the rent from such assets through external market transactions and creates an incentive to internalize. Similarly in vertically integrated industries such as oil or aluminium there are gains from internalization because of the existence of small numbers of oligopolistic firms and large investments which take a long time to mature. Internalization avoids the difficulties of determining market prices and the uncertainties associated with arm's length transactions in such a situation. A further important source of market imperfections internationally is government intervention. The existence of trade barriers, restrictions on capital movements or differences in tax rates between countries provide a further incentive to internalize since intra-firm prices can be set to minimize the effects of such controls.

The analysis of the consequences of the growth of TNCs follows from the view that they are essentially an efficient means of overcoming market failure. They therefore act to increase efficiency in the world economy. As with the product cycle theory, technology or information plays a central role in internalization theory. In analysing the gains to host countries these are not primarily related to the transfer of capital, as in the traditional neo-classical model, but to transfers of technology which would not otherwise take place because of external market imperfections (Casson, 1979: 5). More generally it is argued that the activity of TNCs makes both goods and financial markets more efficient than they would otherwise be (Rugman, 1981: 36). It has even been suggested that since market imperfections are more pervasive in the Third World than in the advanced capitalist countries, Third World countries are in a position to gain even more through TNC operations which circumvent such imperfections (Agmon and Hirsch, 1979).

A crucial assumption of this application of internalization theory to TNC operations is that market imperfections are exogenous, either "natural" or government induced, and that TNCs do not themselves generate such imperfections. As Rugman (1981: 33) points out:

> The multinational firm is able to circumvent most exogenous market imperfections. Concerns about its alleged market power are valid only when it is able to close a market or generate endogenous imperfections. In practice these events rarely occur.

It is here that the contrast between internalization and the Global Reach approach derived from Hymer's work with its emphasis on the creation of market imperfections by TNCs (see below) is most apparent.

Policy Implications

Although internalization theory provides a considerably more sophisticated analysis of TNCs than the earlier neo-classical theories of foreign investment, the policy prescriptions of both approaches are extremely similar. Any problems which TNC operations create are generally ascribed to misguided government policies. Thus a major recommendation is the removal of government induced distortions such as high protective tariffs (Reuber, 1973: 247–8; Rugman, 1981: 138). Such tariffs may give rise to a situation where direct foreign investment reduces income in the host country but the TNCs themselves are not to blame for this.

It follows that since there is, in the absence of misconceived government policies, a net gain to the host country from direct foreign investment (whether through inflows of capital or technology or through more efficient allocation of resources as a result of the elimination of market imperfections) host countries should generally encourage foreign investment, providing a "favourable climate for investment" (although not to the extent of introducing new distortions by granting large subsidies). In some cases the use of cost-benefit analysis to evaluate major projects is advocated but there should be in general a minimum of red tape. Government efforts to regulate the operations of TNCs are strongly discouraged. "Regulation is always inefficient. Multinationals are always efficient," as Rugman puts it (1981: 156–7). Reuber (1973: 248–9) agrees that government attempts to control TNCs probably do more harm than good.

Conclusion

A common thread which runs through the pro-TNC approaches to foreign investment is a primary concern with efficiency in resource allocation. This is of course quite explicit in internalization theory and is the underlying value premise of neo-classical analysis. A second common thread is the belief that direct foreign investment by TNCs is superior to all feasible alternatives. Here one faces the problem of the counterfactual which is at the heart of many of the debates about TNCs, i.e. what would have happened in the absence of direct foreign investment. The assumption of most neo-classical thinking on the subject is that the alternative to DFI is the complete absence of local production. Internalization theory on the other hand emphasizes local licensing as an alternative. Both of these alternatives are generally regarded as inferior to foreign investment.

Global Reach

A sharply contrasting view of the impact of TNCs is given in the writings of those authors who emphasize the oligopolistic nature of the TNCs. This approach has again been given different labels, for example the "nationalist approach" (Lall, 1974). . . . A rather more snappy title which captures the essence of this perspective is "Global Reach," after the title of the best seller on TNCs by Richard Barnet and Ronald Müller (1974).

Central to this approach is the view that foreign investment should be seen as part of the strategy of oligopolistic firms and not simply as a resource flow. Its roots can be traced back to industrial organization theory and the U.S. anti-trust tradition which was first applied to the analysis of DFI by Steve Hymer in the early 1960s. Hymer (1976) identified two major reasons leading firms to control subsidiaries in foreign countries: (i) in order to make use of a specific advantage which the firm enjoys over foreign firms; (ii) in order to remove competition between the firms concerned and to eliminate conflict. While most recent orthodox writings on TNCs have accepted the first point, it is only the Global Reach approach that has continued Hymer's emphasis on foreign investment as a means of restraining competition.

The main focus of attention of this approach is the market power of TNCs. This is seen as deriving from a number of oligopolistic advantages possessed by TNCs particularly access to capital (both internal to the firm and external); control of technology (both product and process technology); marketing through advertising and product differentiation; and privileged access to raw materials. (See Lall and Streeten, 1977: 20–9, and Hood and Young, 1979: 48–54, for a fuller discussion of these advantages.)

The existence of oligopolistic markets means that firms enjoy considerable discretionary powers rather than being the atomistic firms of neo-classical theory which respond to market conditions. Consequently much of the Global Reach literature focuses on the TNCs as *institutions*, their strategies and tactics. A leading proponent of this approach, Constantine Vaitsos, brings this out clearly in discussing the provision of "collective inputs" (i.e. a package) as a means of preserving monopoly rents. He concludes, "Thus a technological monopoly is transformed into an *institutional* one. *Viewed in this light the product cycle theory is seen as a theory of monopoly cycles*" (Vaitsos, 1974a: 18; emphasis in the original).

Whereas for neo-classical writers on the TNCs, particularly internalization theorists, market imperfections are exogenous, arising from government intervention or the nature of certain products such as technology, for the Global Reach view the TNCs are themselves major factors creating imperfect markets. Far from TNCs increasing global efficiency through overcoming market failure, they reduce efficiency by making markets less perfect as a result of their oligopolistic strategies.

The Global Reach approach has highlighted a number of consequences of the market power of TNCs for host countries. . . .

Market structure. TNCs have tended to invest in oligopolistic markets in host Third World countries and it has been suggested that they tend to contribute to increased concentration.

Monopoly profits. The market power of TNCs enables them to earn monopoly profits in host countries. These profits, however, do not always appear in the tax returns of the foreign subsidiaries because of various accounting procedures used by TNCs, particularly transfer pricing. There is also the question of how such monopoly rents are distributed between the TNCs and the host countries in which they operate.

Abuse of market power—restrictive business practices. Individually and collectively TNCs act in order to restrict competition in various ways. Individually they impose restrictive clauses on subsidiaries and licenses through technology contracts. These include tying inputs of raw materials, machinery, etc., to the technology supplier or restricting exports in order to divide world markets. Collectively they form cartels or engage in informal collusion through market sharing agreements or the allocation of spheres of influence.

Demand creation. TNCs use their market power to create demand for their products rather than responding to consumer preferences expressed through the market. This leads to "taste transfer" via the TNC and the expansion of the market for products which are inappropriate for local conditions.

Factor displacements. The package nature of DFI and the monopoly power of the TNCs leads to situations where at least part of the package displaces local inputs (Hirschman, 1969). Importing technology which is not available locally and hence supplements local resources could also bring with it imports of capital and management which displace local capital and entrepreneurship. This has led to concern over the denationalization (i.e. the extension of control by foreign subsidiaries) of local industry, which is seen as a reflection of the market power of TNCs rather than their inherently greater efficiency compared to local firms.

Policy Implications

A major implication of this view of foreign investment is the need for state control of TNCs. These controls may be imposed either on a national or international basis. The areas which have been particularly emphasized as requiring regulation are transfer pricing and restrictive business practices. Governments in a number of countries have set up agencies to control foreign investment and technology transfer since the early 1970s, with a view to eliminating practices such as export restrictions and tied inputs, and monitoring TNC behavior. There have also been steps to develop codes of conduct on TNCs and technology transfer by various international agencies.

The emphasis on TNCs as oligopolists which generate monopoly rents in their activities has also led to the view that the state in the Third World should actively intervene in bargaining with TNCs in order to ensure that a greater share of such rents accrue to the host country. There are two areas in which such an emphasis on bargaining has been of particular significance. First in the extractive industries where host governments have negotiated with TNCs to increase their share of revenue through taxation of profits, royalties, share ownership, etc. Secondly in technology transfer where government agencies have intervened in negotiations often between two private parties in order to reduce the level of royalty payments and hence the outflow of foreign exchange.

A corollary of this emphasis on monopoly rents and the scope for bargaining is that foreign investment projects cannot be analysed along the "take-it-or-leave-it" lines of conventional cost-benefit analysis. Any such project will itself be subject to bargaining over the distribution of returns with a range of possible outcomes. Thus government policy should not be directed primarily at evaluating whether a proposed foreign investment project has a positive net present value, but rather at getting the best possible terms from the foreign investor.

In so far as the packaged nature of DFI is seen as an important source of monopoly rents for TNCs, there is a case for "unpackaging" direct investment into its constituent elements. In other words rather than acquiring capital, technology, intermediate inputs, brand names, management skills all from the same TNC supplier, efforts can be made to acquire each component individually. This would permit each to be obtained at the lowest possible cost and for those elements for which domestic substitutes exist to be acquired locally. Such a call for unpackaging has become common in recent discussion of TNCs and technology transfer.

 A further implication often drawn from this approach is that the state should give preferential treatment to national capital, e.g. in terms of access to local sources of credit. This derives from the view that TNCs tend to displace local firms primarily because of their market power rather than because of greater productive efficiency. The state should therefore attempt to redress the balance in favour of local capital. Indeed it provides a theoretical rationale for forms of bourgeois nationalism as well as greater state intervention in the economy.

Conclusion

The overall framework of this approach contrasts with the pro-TNC writings discussed above in a number of key respects. First, TNCs are seen as important creators of market imperfections rather than as competitive firms or as an efficient response to exogenous imperfections. Secondly, TNCs often substitute rather than complement local factors. In other words the alternative of production under local control is more feasible than pro-TNC authors admit. Thirdly, there is a greater concern with the distributive effects of TNCs both internationally and internally.

Neo-Imperialist Views

The best known Marxist or neo-Marxist approach to TNCs is that represented by the Monthly Review School (especially Baran, Sweezy, O'Connor and Magdoff) and those writers on dependency most influenced by the Monthly Review approach (for example Frank and Girvan). These authors view the TNCs as a major mechanism blocking development in the Third World and an important obstacle to socialist transformation.

The origins of this approach can be traced back to the classical Marxist writings on imperialism in the early twentieth century with their stress on the concentration and centralization of capital and the link between monopolization of industry, capital export and imperialism (Lenin, 1917; Bukharin, 1917). A central element in the argument was that the monopolization of industry led to a growing mass of profit in the major capitalist countries, while at the same time limiting the possibilities of accumulation at home because of the restrictions imposed on expansion by cartels and trusts. This led capital to seek outlets for this relative surplus of capital overseas (see Olle and Schoeller, 1982 for a critique of this view). Furthermore Lenin particularly emphasized the parasitic nature of imperialism stressing that the development of monopoly inhibits technical progress and leads to a tendency to stagnation and decay (Lenin, 1917, ch. viii).

This leads to the question of the impact of capital export or more generally imperialism in the countries on the receiving end. Marx himself had stressed the progressive nature of these processes and this view was accepted (although only mentioned in passing) by the major Marxist authors writing on imperialism. However, as Warren (1980: 81–3) has stressed, the implication of this view of a parasitic, decaying monopoly capitalism was that imperialism could no longer play a progressive role in the colonies. It was not surprising therefore that imperialism was recognized as a major obstacle to industrialization of the colonies at the 1928 Congress of the Comintern.

The recent neo-imperialist literature continues Lenin's and Bukharin's emphasis on the rise of monopolies as a cause of TNC expansion, either by reference to the classical theories of imperialism or through the new version of the surplus capital theory proposed by Baran and Sweezy (1966). They argued that a major characteristic of U.S. capitalism was the tendency for the economic surplus, defined as the difference between total output and the socially necessary costs of producing total output, to rise over time. The major cause of this rising surplus was the growth of monopoly and the consequent decline of price competition with the result that increases in productivity did not lead to falling prices as under competitive capitalism, and that the gap between prices and production costs tended to widen. While the surplus tended to rise, the monopolization of the economy limited the opportunities for investment because of the need to maintain monopoly prices (Sweezy and Magdoff, 1969: 1). There is therefore a chronic tendency to underconsumption and stagnation under monopoly capitalism.

One of the possible outlets for the surplus identified by Baran and Sweezy was foreign investment. (Others discussed were advertising, government expenditure and militarism.) Thus, although only alleviating temporarily the problem of the rising surplus, because the return flow of profits and dividends to the United States soon exceeded the outflow of new investment, capital export and the overseas expansion of U.S. firms was seen as primarily a consequence of the existence of large monopoly profits and the need to go slow on expanding productive capacity directed at existing markets. Two solutions offered themselves— international expansion or conglomerate expansion (i.e. diversification into new industries in the domestic market) (Sweezy and Magdoff, 1969; O'Connor, 1970).

It is worth noting in passing that this emphasis on monopoly and the tendency to underemphasize the competitiveness of the oligopolies (cf. Barratt Brown, 1974: 217) was also accompanied by the view that the United States enjoyed undisputed hegemony within the international capitalist system. This view characterized by Rowthorn (1975) as "super-imperialism" plays down the increasing competition between the United States, Western Europe and Japan, both politically and economically which underlies the alternative "inter-imperialist rivalry" view of international relations. The downplaying of conflicts between capitals and between advanced capitalist states also tended to go hand in hand with a "Third Worldist" view which stressed that the struggle against capitalism and imperialism would primarily take place in the underdeveloped countries.

Foreign investment in the Third World is seen as contributing to the "blocking development" (Amin, 1977) or the "development of underdevelopment" (A.G. Frank, 1969). Three principal mechanisms link foreign capital to underdevelopment. Considerable emphasis is placed on the so-called "drain of surplus" from the underdeveloped countries in direct opposition to the claim of neo-classical economists that foreign capital supplements foreign exchange earnings and local savings. Thus surplus transfers which add to the problems of surplus absorption in the advanced capitalist countries at the same time deprive the countries of the Third World of the necessary resources for economic progress. The TNCs are viewed as a "vast suction-pump" for obtaining resources from the periphery. At the same time they are a major part of the balance of payments problems which are so chronic in most Third World countries.

While much of the empirical analysis of the impact of TNCs concentrated on the outflow of capital from the Third World, equal or even greater importance was attached to the impact of foreign investment on the economic and social structures of the underdeveloped countries. As Baran puts it

> The worst of it is, however, that it is very hard to say what has been the greater evil as far as the economic development of underdeveloped countries is concerned: the removal of the economic surplus by foreign capital or its reinvestment by foreign enterprise (Baran, 1973: 325).

The extension of TNC operations to the underdeveloped countries has also led to the extension of the monopolistic or oligopolistic structures of advanced capitalism to these areas (Dos Santos, 1968 on Brazil; Caputto and Pizarro, 1970: ch. 11.5 on Chile). Given the association of monopoly with stagnation in the United States, it is unlikely that monopolistic subsidiaries of U.S. firms operating in the periphery will be a major dynamic force. Thus monopolistic firms with high profit rates will tend to repatriate profits, intensifying the drain of surplus and limiting the rate of capital accumulation within the host economies.

In so far as TNCs do reinvest profits locally, they are likely to expand by displacing or acquiring local competitors or moving into new areas of activity (diversification). Thus the twin spectres arise of denationalization (i.e. increasing foreign control over the economy) and the reduction of the spheres available to local capital which is confined to the most competitive and least profitable sectors of the economy. This brings us to a central point of the argument against foreign capital, namely that it reduces the local bourgeoisie in the Third World to the subordinate status of a "comprador" or "dependent" bourgeoisie which is consequently incapable of playing its historical role in promoting capitalist development. Baran writing in the 1950s emphasized the strengthening of local merchant capital by foreign capital which was mainly directed towards the export sector, and the consequent blocking of the development of industrial capitalism (Baran, 1973: 337). Latin American dependency writers in the 1960s argued that a local industrial bourgeoisie did exist in the region but that its interests were closely tied to those of foreign capital and that it would not provide the basis for a strategy of national development. The crucial decisions on production and accumulation would be made in the light of the global interests of the parent companies of the foreign subsidiaries, and not in the interest of local economic development, a situation which local capital would be unwilling or powerless to alter.

While the drain of surplus, the creation of monopolistic structures and the emergence of a dependent bourgeoisie were the three main
ways in which foreign capital contributed to underdevelopment, they
were by no means the only consequences of TNC expansion. A common
argument is that a foreign capital far from supplying basic goods for the
mass of the population tends to concentrate on the production of luxu-
ries for a small élite. The extensive activities of the car TNCs are often
cited as an example (Frank, 1969: 168–9). The tendency for foreign subsidiaries to generate links primarily with the parent company or other affiliates and only to a very limited extent with local suppliers, leads to the
development of an economic structure which is not integrated at the
local level (Sunkel, 1972). Moreover, the TNCs are able to use their political influence in order that public expenditure is allocated to support
their investment through the provision of infrastructure.

Political Implications

The political conclusion that generally follows from this analysis is the
need to break out of the capitalist system in order to transcend underdevelopment. Hostility to TNCs is directed at them as the prime representatives of capitalism in the post-war period. In any case the lack of
an authentic national bourgeoisie capable of leading the process, renders national capitalist development in the Third World impossible.
Thus only through a socialist revolution can the situation of the periphery be fundamentally altered. Such a socialist transformation will
however inevitably have to face the hostility of the TNCs and their
home states.

Conclusion

Although many of the neo-imperialist arguments concerning the impact
of TNCs in the Third World are similar to those of the Global Reach
approach, and the two groups of writers are sometimes considered together (for example by Biersteker, 1978), the political conclusions
drawn are quite different. This derives from a very different evaluation
of the role of the local bourgeoisie in Third World countries and the
possibility of state action to control the TNCs.

Neo-Fundamentalist Marxists

In the last decade some Marxists have begun to develop a very different view of the TNCs to that discussed in the last section, arguing that

their impact on the Third World is overwhelmingly positive. This is presented as part of a more general picture of the progressive role played by capitalism in developing the forces of production and providing the material basis for a socialist society. These authors trace their roots back to Marx's view (for example in some of his writings on India) that the impact of imperialism in destroying pre-capitalist structures and laying the basis for the development of capitalism was progressive. The clearest exponent of such a position was Bill Warren (1973, 1980; see also Schiffer, 1981).

Warren stresses the continued competitive nature of the capitalist system going as far as suggesting that competition internationally has intensified since the loss of Britain's position of world hegemony, despite the rise of oligopolistic market structures within individual countries (Warren, 1980: 79–80). Thus he rejects the Leninist view of surplus capital as a cause of capital export and implicitly sees the geographic extension of capitalism as a consequence primarily of the competition of capitals (for a succinct presentation of this view see Cypher, 1979).

The main thrust of his thesis is to argue that the impact of imperialism on the Third World is progressive, in the sense that it is developing the productive forces in these areas. As part of this thesis he argues that "private foreign investment in the LDCs is economically beneficial irrespective of measures of government control" and "must normally be regarded not as a cause of dependence but rather as a means of fortification and diversification of the host countries. It thereby reduces 'dependence' in the long run" (Warren, 1980: 176).

The arguments on which he bases this thesis reproduce virtually point by point the claims made by bourgeois advocates of the TNCs discussed above. The three major assumptions of the neo-classical view of foreign investment are all accepted by Warren. First, foreign capital is seen in the main as complementary to local capital rather than displacing indigenous efforts (Warren, 1973: 37). Secondly, he points to increasing international competition particularly amongst manufacturing TNCs (Warren, 1980: 175), which has increased the bargaining power of Third World states enabling them to reduce the monopoly rents earned by the companies and to obtain technology on more favourable terms. Finally, Warren accepts the neo-classical view that TNCs not only supplement existing local resources but also generate additional local resources or utilize resources previously unutilized (Warren, 1980: 173, n. 31).

Not only does Warren share the main assumptions of pro-capitalist TNC advocates, but even on points of detail he reproduces the same arguments. Thus for instance TNCs are seen as playing a major role in opening up advanced country markets for Third World exports (Warren, 1973: 26–8), while the "drain of surplus" view of foreign investment is criticized on exactly the same grounds used by neo-classical economists (Warren, 1980: 140–3).

While Warren's position is an extreme one amongst Marxists, other writers who wish to stress that the problem of underdevelopment is a consequence of capitalism and not of TNCs *per se*, and that the foreign or local ownership of capital is not a major factor, come close to his position. Thus Emmanuel in pursuing this line of argument states that "Whenever we find . . . that in any particular aspect the behavior of the MNC differs from that of the traditional capitalist undertaking, the specific character of the MNC is generally to its (i.e. development's) advantage" (Emmanuel, 1976: 763). Emmanuel stresses primarily the technological contribution of TNCs emphasizing particularly the low cost of imported technology and rejecting arguments of the "inappropriate technology" variety (Emmanuel, 1976, 1982).

Political Implications

A major explicit political conclusion of this analysis is the need to distinguish carefully between anti-TNC rhetoric used to serve the interests of an expanding local bourgeoisie in the Third World, and true anti-capitalist struggles. As Warren (1973: 44) concludes, "Unless this distinction is clearly grasped the Left will find itself directly supporting bourgeois regimes which, as in Peru and Egypt, exploit and oppress workers and peasants while employing anti-imperialist rhetoric." However, the implicit conclusion to which Warren's analysis points is that capitalist development in the Third World should be actively supported since it is removing many of the internal obstacles to growth, and that the TNCs are playing a significant role in this process.

Conclusion

In recent years Marxist views of the TNCs have polarized around two positions which are, in terms of many of their arguments, not very different from those found amongst non-Marxist writers. The neo-imperialist view stresses the qualitative transformations which have taken place within capitalism with the rise of monopoly, and emphasizes the regressive nature of imperialist expansion, particularly the appropriation of surplus value from the peripheral areas. In contrast the neo-fundamentalist view stresses the essentially competitive nature of capitalism despite the concentration and centralization of capital and sees the international expansion of capital as playing a predominantly progressive role in breaking down pre-capitalist structures, and laying the basis for capitalist development.

The Internationalization of Capital

Although most of the current literature on TNCs and the Third World falls more or less neatly into the four categories discussed so far, and this exhausts the typology laid out at the beginning of this chapter, it is my view that none of these approaches offers a completely satisfactory treatment of the TNCs. . . .

Each of the approaches discussed so far is partial in that it emphasizes one level of analysis. The neo-classical, Global Reach and neo-imperialist approaches all focus on the sphere of circulation, that is on relations of exchange and distribution. Obviously this is the case with the neo-classical view of the firm responding to market forces, but it is also true of the Global Reach concern with *market* power and with income distribution both nationally and internationally. Similarly the neo-imperialist approach has also been described elsewhere as exchange-based (Cypher, 1979) in view of its emphasis on surplus transfer. On the other hand, the neo-fundamentalist view is a "productionist" approach (Jenkins, 1984b; Hoogvelt, 1982: 188–9). Its main concern is with the development of the forces of production and in so far as social relations are considered at all these are derived in a highly mechanistic way from the level of development of the forces of production. None of these approaches is able to successfully integrate the spheres of circulation and production.

Not only are these approaches partial in failing to take account of both the sphere of circulation and the sphere of production, but they also fail to integrate the analysis of TNCs as institutions with a broader analysis of the capitalist system. For both the neo-classical and the neo-fundamentalist approaches with their focus on markets and the forces of production respectively, structural and institutional concerns are largely absent. On the other hand, critics of the TNCs reacting against this neglect "have gone too far in lodging the laws with which they are concerned in firms as institutions, rather than treating the latter as the forms through which the laws of the market are manifested" (Murray, 1972). It is the failure to do this which has led to the position of many Marxist critics of the TNCs who "having first isolated the MNC as the characteristic evil of the century, they study it concretely as an excrescence of the system" (Emmanuel 1976: 769) which logically should lead them to the conclusion that a reformed capitalism without the TNCs would be perfectly acceptable.

A further unsatisfactory aspect of these approaches is their tendency to reduce a contradictory reality to one or other side of a false dichotomy. TNCs are regarded as either competitive or monopolistic.

In the Third World they either contribute to development or increase dependence. TNC-state relations are either harmonious or conflictual and the Third World state is either "nationalist" or "comprador." The dominant tendency in the world economy is either towards greater internationalization or the strengthening of nation states.

. . . The point that needs to be emphasized here is that these polarities around which the debate on TNCs has often revolved can lead to a misunderstanding of the real issues.

Some writers, however, notably Palloix and Murray, have attempted to develop a Marxist framework for analysing TNCs which overcomes these three limitations. Although the term is often used very loosely, I shall refer to this as the "internationalization of capital approach." It is far less well represented in the literature on TNCs than any of the other approaches except the neo-fundamentalist position. . . .

In contrast to other critical writings on the TNCs, the starting point of this approach is not the TNCs *per se* but the self-expansion of capital which can be traced through the circuits of capital discussed by Marx in Volume II of *Capital* (see Fine 1975, ch. 7 for a brief exposition of the circuits of capital). The different aspects of the internationalization of capital are identified with the internationalization of the three circuits of capital. The circuits of commodity capital, money capital and productive capital were for Marx three different aspects of the process of self-expansion of capital. In the context of the internationalization of capital these three circuits have been identified with the growth of world trade, the growth of international capital movements, and the growth of the operations of TNCs and the international circulation of products within such firms, respectively (Palloix, 1975). The circuits of capital comprise both the sphere of circulation and the sphere of production.

The growth of TNCs therefore is seen not as a phenomenon in its own right, but as an aspect of a broader process of internationalization of capital which tends to create a more integrated world economy. The driving force which underlies international expansion is capitalist competition (Cypher, 1979). It is important to stress that despite concentration and centralization of capital, the TNCs remain subject to the compulsion of competition. . . .

This approach stresses the highly uneven nature of development brought about by TNC expansion. Foreign investment has tended to be heavily concentrated in a relatively small number of Third World countries (Weisskopf, 1978). Moreover, far from the underdeveloped countries representing a homogeneous block, there is a process of increasing economic differentiation within the Third World with some countries emerging as "newly industrializing countries" or forming the intermediate "semi-periphery" (Marcussen and Torp, 1982: 28–30; Evans, 1979: 291).

Despite the highly uneven nature of its impact, the internationalization of capital is leading to an ever more integrated capitalist world economy. This implies transformations in the relations of production as new areas are incorporated into the circuits of capital. In some cases this involves the extension of fully capitalist relations of production and a corresponding growth of the working class. In other areas it involves modifications to or the reinforcing of existing social relations. The impact of the growth of transnational agribusiness on the relations of production in agriculture provides many examples of such processes as does the incorporation of petty-commodity producers through the use of sub-contracting in manufacturing. Social relations at the periphery are neither frozen into the existing mould by TNC expansion, nor can they be totally neglected. Rather they are being continuously transformed and redefined by the internationalization of capital, but not in any simple or universal way. The creation of a unified capitalist world economy is accompanied by the extension of the competitive process of standardization and differentiation on a world scale. In other words there is a growing tendency for the products and production techniques of TNCs to become similar, while at the same time as part of the competitive struggle capital seeks to differentiate itself attaining super profits through the introduction of new products or new techniques, or taking advantage of different local and national conditions.

A feature of these analyses of the internationalization of capital and dependent development is the role attributed to the Third World state. There is an emphasis on the alliance created between the state, TNCs and local capital which is central to the dynamic expansion of certain Third World economies (Evans, 1979; Weisskopf, 1978). However, it is also recognized that such an alliance is inherently unstable because of the contradictory position both of the local state and the local bourgeoisie.

Political Implications

The analysis of the internationalization of capital focuses attention on two crucial areas of struggle. One is the need to develop international links between workers so that labour is able to combine internationally in order to limit the power of international capital to divide it along national lines (Picciotto and Radice, 1971). The second area for struggle is the state itself. In dependent development the state has come to play a central role not only in regulating but also participating directly in the accumulation process. The alliance of foreign capital, local capital and the state is by no means immutable and both internal and international developments put it under stress.

Conclusion

The key features of the internationalization of capital approach are its attempt to locate the TNCs within a broader framework of capitalist development and its integration of the spheres of circulation and production. This enables it to provide a more comprehensive view of the TNC phenomenon which like capitalism itself is recognized as being contradictory in many respects.

Further Reading

The typology of theories concerning TNCs and the Third World used in this chapter is not the only possible one by any means. Other attempts to classify different approaches to the TNCs can be found in Lall (1974), Emmanuel (1976), Hood and Young (1979, ch. 8) and Biersteker (1978). The most useful short summary of the neo-classical view of TNCs in relation to the Third World which takes account of the most recent developments is Balasubramanyam (1980). More detail summaries of all the neo-classical theories discussed can be found in Hood and Young (1979, chs. 2 and 5). A useful critique of the neo-classical approach and particularly of Reuber (1973) can be found in Lall (1974). Rugman (1981) is recommended on internalization theory because it goes beyond the tedious discussions found in some of the earlier literature to bring out the normative implications of the approach.

For the Global Reach approach, the book of that name by Barnet and Müller (1974) is very readable and Chapters 6 and 7 are relevant to the discussion in this chapter. For a more academic presentation of this view, Lall and Streeten (1977; chs. 2 and 3) is particularly recommended. For criticism of this approach generally and of Lall and Streeten in particular see Lal (1978).

The best critical summary of the neo-imperialist position as exemplified by the works of Baran and Sweezy is Brewer (1980, ch. 6). See also Cohen (1973, ch. IV) for a critical account from a different perspective. Sweezy and Magdoff (1969) provide a short analysis of the TNCs. Sunkel (1972) discusses the impact of TNCs in the Third World, particularly Latin America.

The neo-fundamentalist position is summarized in Emmanuel (1976). It is also found in scattered discussion of the TNC in Warren (1973) and (1980, chs. 6 and 7).

Few of the writings of Palloix are available in English and they are in any case extremely dense and difficult to follow. See for example his article in Radice (1975). Cypher (1979) is useful in some respects in contrasting the internationalization of capital with what he terms the Monthly Review School, although he includes Warren in the former. For the contradictory impact of the internationalization of capital on the periphery see Weisskopf (1978) and Cardoso (1972).

References

Agmon, T. and S. Hirsch. 1979. "Multinational Corporations and the Developing Economies: Potential Gains in a World of Imperfect Markets and Uncertainty," *Oxford Bulletin of Economics and Statistics*, November.

Amin, S. 1977. *Imperialism and Unequal Development*, Hassocks: Harvester.

Balasubramanyam, V. N. 1980. *Multinational Enterprises and the Third World*. London: Trade Policy Research Center, Thames Essay no. 26.

Baran, P. 1973. *The Political Economy of Growth*, Harmondsworth: Penguin.

Baran P. and P. Sweezy. 1966. *Monopoly Capital: An Essay on the American Economic and Social Order*, Harmondsworth: Penguin.

Barnet, R. and R. Müller. 1974. *Global Reach: The Power of Multinational Corporations*. New York: Simon and Schuster.

Barratt Brown, M. 1974. *Economics of Imperialism*, Harmondsworth: Penguin.

Biersteker, T. J. 1978. *Distortion or Development? Contending Perspectives on the Multinational Corporation*. Cambridge, MA: MIT Press.

Brewer, A. 1980. *Marxist Theories of Imperialism: A Critical Survey*. London: Rutledge and Kegan Paul.

Buckley, P. and M. Casson. 1976. *The Future of Multinational Enterprise*. London: Macmillan.

Bukharin, N. 1917. *Imperialism and World Economy*, London: Merlin.

Caputto, O. and R. Pizarro. 1970. *Desarrollismo y Capital Extranjero*, Santiago de Chile, Ediciones de la Universidad Tecnica del Estado.

Cardoso, F. H. 1972. "Dependency and development in Latin America," *New Left Review*, 74.

Casson, M. 1979. *Alternatives to the Multinational Enterprise*, London: Macmillan.

Cohen, B. 1973. *The Question of Imperialism: the Political Economy of Dominance and Dependence*. London: Macmillan.

Cypher, J. 1979. "The Internationalization of Capital and the Transformation of Social Formations: A Critique of the Monthly Review School," *The Review of Radical Political Economics*, 11: 4.

Dos Santos, T. 1968. "Foreign Investment and the Large Enterprise in Latin America: The Brazilian Case," in J. Petras and M. Zeitlin (eds.), *Latin America: Reform or Revolution?* Greenwich: Fawcett Publications.

Emmanuel, A. 1976. "The Multinational Corporations and Inequality of Development," *International Social Science Journal*, XXVIII.

Emmanuel, A. 1982. *Appropriate or Underdeveloped Technology?* Chichester: Wiley/IRM Series on Multinationals.

Evans, P. 1979. *Dependent Development: The Alliance of Multinational State and Local Capital in Brazil.* Princeton University Press.

Fine, B. 1975. *Marx's Capital.* London: Macmillan.

Frank, A. G. 1969. *Capitalism and Underdevelopment in Latin America.* New York: Monthly Review Press.

Hirschman, A. O. 1969. "How to Divest in Latin America and Why," *Essays in International Finance,* 76, Princeton University Press.

Hood, N. and S. Young. 1979. *The Economics of Multinational Enterprise,* London, Longman.

Hoogvelt, A. 1982. *The Third World in Global Development.* London: Macmillan.

Hymer, Stephen H. 1976. *The International Operations of National Firms: A Study of Direct Foreign Investment.* Cambridge, MA and London, England: MIT Press.

Jenkins, R. O. 1984b. "Divisions over the international division of labor," *Capital and Class,* 22.

Lal, D. 1978. "On the multinationals," *ODI Review,* 2.

Lall, S. 1974. "Less-developed Countries and Private Foreign Direct Investment: A Review Article," *World Development,* 2, 4 and 5.

Lall S. and P. Streeten. 1977. *Foreign Investment, Transnationals and Developing Countries,* London: Macmillan.

Lenin. V.I. 1917. *Imperialism: The Highest Stage of Capitalism,* Moscow, Progress Publishers.

Marcussen, H. and J. Torp. 1982. *Internalization of Capital: Prospects for the Third World.* London: Zed Books.

Murray, R. 1972. "Underdevelopment, the international firm and the international division of labor," in *Society for International Development, Towards a New World Economy.* Potterdam University Press.

O'Connor, J. 1970. "International Corporations and Economic Underdevelopment," *Science and Society,* 32.

Olle, W. and W. Schoeller. 1982. "Direct Investment and Monopoly Theories of Imperialism," *Capital and Class,* 16.

Palloix, C. 1975. "The internationalization of capital and the circuit of social capital," in Radice (ed.) *International Firms and Modern Imperialism.* Harmondsworth: Penguin.

Picciotto, S. and Radice, H. 1971. "European integration, capital and the state," *Bulletin of the Conference of Socialist Economists.* 1: 1.

Reuber, G. L. 1973. *Private Foreign Investment in Development.* Oxford: Clarendon Press.

Rowthorn, B. 1975. "Imperialism in the 1970s—Unity or Rivalry?", in H. Radice (ed.), *International Firms and Modern Imperialism.* Harmondsworth: Penguin.

Rugman, A. M. 1981. *Inside the Multinationals: The Economics of Internal Markets.* London: Croom Helm.

Schiffer, J. 1981. "The Changing Post-War Pattern of Development: The Accumulated Wisdom of Samir Amin," *World Development* 9: 6.

Sunkel, O. 1972. "Big Business and 'Dependencia': A Latin American View." *Foreign Affairs.* 50: 517–31.

Sweezy, P. and H. Magdoff. 1969. "Notes on the Multinational Corporation," *Monthly Review,* 22, 5 and 6.

Vaitsos, C. 1974a. *Inter-Country Income Distribution and Transnational Enterprises.* Oxford: Clarendon Press.
Warren, B. 1973. "Imperialism and Capitalist Industrialization," *New Left Review*, 81.
Warren, B. 1980. *Imperialism: Pioneer of Capitalism.* London: Verso.
Weisskopf, T. 1978. "Imperialism and the economic development of the Third World." in R. G. Edwards, M. Reich and T. Weisskopf (eds.). *The Capitalist System.* Englewood Cliffs, N.J.: Prentice Hall.

26

THE WAY FORWARD

John Stopford and Susan Strange
_____ with John S. Henley _____

*Stopford and Strange address the relationship of states and transnational cor-
porations (TNCs) in the contemporary world. They feel dramatic shifts have
occurred in the international system since the mid-1980s. States are increasingly adopting democratic forms of government and choosing economic policies
that can best be described as liberal or neoliberal. Given these preferences, the
authors argue that the TNC can no longer be considered a secondary force following in the wake of the nation-state. Indeed, as a group states have lost
power to TNCs. In terms of the categories described by Rhys Jenkins in the
previous chapter, this argument fits comfortably in the neoliberal school.*

We now draw together the strands of argument . . . to indicate the
types of new questions we believe should be asked both by those who
study international relations or international political economy and by
those whose main concern is with corporate strategy and management.
[Research] suggests that many of the conventional frameworks of analysis fail to deal adequately with the contemporary dynamism of change.
The most common reason why they fail is that they do not take sufficiently into account either the broad structural changes in the global
political economy, nor the highly differentiated conditions of individual
states, where social, cultural and political forces often clash with economic imperatives. In looking at host-state/foreign firm relations we
see governments typically perceiving themselves as caught between the
upper millstone of structural change that forces them to compete for

Reprinted with permission from the publishers of *Rival states, rival firms—Competition for world market shares* (Cambridge: Cambridge University Press, 1991),
pp. 203–235.

world market shares and the nether millstone of their dependence for survival both on foreign investors and on local political support. We also see foreign investors feeling caught between the same upper millstone of structural change and the nether one of the rooted resistance of third world governments to more accommodating policies.[1]

In suggesting new questions to be asked, we also attempt to provide some advice for both governments and managers. That task is extraordinarily difficult, for there are few generalisations that hold up to scrutiny in particular circumstances. Advice that might be appropriate for Brazil may be wholly inappropriate for Kenya. Moreover, changing circumstance means that specific lines of policy appropriate for any one country will inevitably have to be altered over time. The same is evidently true for firms. How then to draw together the strands of the argument? We approach the task with a healthy dose of humility, yet we believe that there are some basic policy approaches of general validity. . . .

The evidence, however partial, strongly suggests that there is a growing possibility for new forms of collaboration between states and firms in the pursuit of shares of world markets. We recognise that this hope for a world of less adversarial bargaining will not be realised as a generality: mutual suspicion remains strong. Nonetheless, our conclusions reflect the belief that dilemmas can be resolved, but only over time and in a series of small steps, not giant leaps. They can and will be embraced by the more forward-looking states and firms. As that happens, many of the conventional frameworks of analysis will need substantial adjustment to deal adequately with the dynamism of change. New research issues that require perspectives much broader than in the conventional literatures are being thrown up and followed the whole time.

Basic Premises

Our initial propositions can be re-stated as three basic premises. The first is that the primary influences on the behaviour of firms and states are found within the international political economy. Changes in the world system are, to be sure, the product of a myriad of actions by all actors, whether individuals, firms, states or intergovernmental bodies. Taken together, their actions have limited the independent options for states during the last two decades or so.

The second is that most states have become more directly engaged in the competition for shares of the world's wealth, and not solely concerned in their foreign policy with power. They have therefore adjusted their frameworks of thought and priority for allocating national resources in ways that promote the accumulation of wealth-creating resources. These shifts suggest the basis of possible cooperation and partnership in production.

The third premise concerns the means to achieving the desired ends, namely that there are growing interactions between national strategies designed to achieve rising levels of social and economic aspiration and the global strategies of the firms. . . .

These three premises are fundamental to the conclusions we draw. For readers who may not be convinced, we offer some further amplification of all three.

Global Shifts

The crucial structural changes in the international political economy have been both political and economic. The most dramatic of the political changes occurred in the latter half of the 1980s: the melting of the Cold War between the superpowers; the liberation of Eastern and Central Europe from the Soviet Union; the drive for multiparty democracy and national self-determination not only in Europe but in many developing countries. Less dramatic, but equally important, have been the drives towards deregulation in developed countries and towards privatisation in most countries around the world. Such economic changes were primarily in the financial structure, where the mobility of capital increased, and in the production structure, where the diffusion of existing technologies also increased. In turn, these changes fuelled the exponential growth of FDI during the later 1980s and affected the forms of global competition among firms.

Taken together, these structural changes have often been loosely lumped together under the generic label of "Interdependence." But this is too vague and value-laden a label to tell either policy makers in government or corporate strategists how best to respond. Each has its own impact.

No political change was confined within a single nation state. The collapse of the Berlin Wall in 1989 reverberated throughout the world. The lack of any Western consensus, akin to the Marshall Plan, about how to assist the reforms in the East sent a clear message to firms; it would be each for himself. Firms, in the West and in the East, would have to use corporate diplomacy to get the best possible deal from their home and potential host governments. Where appropriate, they would have to seek corporate allies among banks at home and the formerly state-owned enterprises in the East.[2]

The reverberations also served to put economic concerns more centrally on states' international agendas. All developing countries now face the advent of new competitors for government aid, bank credit and FDI. Many fear that reconstruction aid for central Europe will divert scarce development funds from other areas. As Noordin Sopiee, the director-general of Malaysia's Institute for Strategic and International Studies and a former editor of the *Straits Times*, succinctly put it, "In the long run, more for Eastern Europe must mean less for everyone else" (*World Link*, 1990: p. 87). Vehemently though donor governments have denied it, the conviction remains in the developing countries that for them, too, political change in the Soviet bloc will sharpen the competition among them for market shares and for the multinationals' capital and technology.

Growing economic interdependence, however simplistically it is defined, creates other limits to national options. The proportion of the economy that is subject to external influence has been growing for almost all nations, except perhaps the smallest, poorest states. Failure to manage the external account constrains domestic policy, for balance-of-payments deficits can seldom be financed for long. The classic example in recent times has been the effect on the French government of such deficits in 1983. Mitterrand's socialist government was forced by the external deficits and the exhaustion of foreign credit into a major U-turn in policy away from state-owned enterprises and organised labour and toward productivity in export industries.

When combined with internal pressures induced by individuals' knowledge of events in Eastern Europe, external economic pressures can have an even more far-reaching local impact. An extreme example was the almost complete U-turn attempted by the former communist (since 1975) state of Laos in 1989. Laos allowed private trade to take over from state-controlled enterprises by abolishing all currency controls and removing all import controls on consumer goods. Past ideology was set aside. Elections were planned and foreign investment—most of it from Thailand—welcomed. Quite clearly, the role model was Thailand, not its other neighbour, Myanmar (Burma). . . .

More generally, the shifts in the global system have linked together agendas that were previously kept separate. The debate over the future of GATT illustrates the problems that have been created. Though the debate had not been resolved at the time of writing, the agenda was clear. Trade issues are increasingly and inextricably bound up with FDI and the behaviour of the multinationals. The use of the so-called trade-related investment measures (TRIMs) that tie government incentives to a broad range of trade, investment and financial policies provides one contested agenda.

Our evidence suggests strongly that, when linked to policies of import-substitution, TRIMs can be self-defeating by requiring the ineffective use of second-best local resources and so inhibiting the exports the policies are designed to create. They can cause the foreign firm great aggravation, especially when the local supplies are sub-standard so that the firm has to lower the quality of its product, risking the loss of market shares. With import substitution, it did not matter too much if, say, Filipino-made pencils were lower in quality than imported American ones. But if they are designed for export, it matters both to the firm and the host government. The moral is that policy should be directed to helping local suppliers to upgrade the quality of their inputs, rather than forcing inferior inputs on the manufacturer. And to give the suppliers time *and* incentive to do so, an advertised timetable of reducing proportions of required local content can be an effective compromise—as in the case of Nissan-built cars in Britain.

Similarly, the debate over trade-related intellectual property measures (TRIPs), muddied by polemics over "theft" and "piracy," fails to recognise that there are perfectly valid reasons for different calculations of the socially optimal length of time for protecting a patent. These differences are important, for they affect investors' perceptions of likely project returns and trading possibilities. Italy, for example, corrected many of its deficiencies in patent protection about a decade ago. The consequence has been a growing inflow of FDI, stimulating local creativity, employment and exports. By contrast, India, under pressure from its local producers, has opposed inclusion of intellectual property rights in GATT. Like Brazil until recently, India does not officially recognise the impact of such policies on future flows of technical transfers and exports.

Without resolution of the TRIPs and TRIMs debates for all sectors, including services, the multinationals' full potential for assisting export-led growth will not be harnessed. All too many developing countries hide behind Clause XVIII (b) that allows them to use balance-of-payments difficulties as an excuse to deny firms access to their markets. Equally, developed countries undermine the discipline of international competition by limiting market access in agriculture and textiles and by invoking Voluntary Exports Restraints for their troubled industries. . . .

That multinationals' interests are directly concerned by the outcomes of such debates seems incontrovertible. Yet few of them speak out on the issues. One exception is British Petroleum, which has issued a series of policy statements. In 1990, BP came out with unequivocal support for GATT: "as an international company, BP's commercial success is crucially dependent on the health of the world's economy, which in turn is based on the maintenance and enhancement of the GATT-based multilateral trading system." BP's statement recognised that progress on each of the specific issues depends on progress on the others. Multinationals need to become more directly concerned with the public debates about how progress might be achieved in practice and how the corrosive influence of unwise side payments may be avoided. . . .

We repeat: an obvious but vital lesson from all these changes is that the global trends for change now set the context within which national changes are attempted. Purely national frameworks of analysis, for political risk analysts as much as for sociologists, are outgrown. The dominant structural changes in the world of today and tomorrow are likely to be global, perhaps regional, but not national or local. These changes directly affect national options and the feasible forms of adjustment within states. They have heightened the importance of the two new dimensions of diplomacy—the bargaining between governments and firms, especially multinationals, and bargaining among firms. The importance of the new "triangular" diplomacy has been revealed in every project we reviewed.

The Pursuit of Wealth

Our second premise is that among their multiple goals, governments now accord greater priority to the accumulation of wealth-creating resources. This has direct implications for the study of international relations. Hitherto, students of international politics started from the presumption that, in an anarchical, Hobbesian international society, in which each state claims sovereignty and there is no superior ruling authority over them, the over-riding concern of every state was for its security (Bull, 1978; or, for a shorter and clearer statement of the realist view, Miller, 1982). This view assumed that governments, as guardians of the national interest, pursued power as a means of securing their independence from interference by others. International relations was therefore about the pursuit of power as a means of self-defence; wealth was needed primarily to provide that state with the revenue with which to match the offensive military capability of predatory neighbours. Now, many argue, wealth is needed to preserve the state more from internal rather than external threats to its cohesion and survival. Without wealth or the prospect of future sources of wealth, even if there is no external security threat, the state begins to fall apart.

Of course, this pursuit of wealth is part of a long, secular change that began in the Middle Ages with the spreading concern for raising the conditions of material life. It is still not finished. For decades to come, there will still be reversions to the old form of inter-state conflict. States will continue to be threatened by their neighbours with coercive violence, especially when there are scarce resources such as access to water at stake (Myers, 1989). . . .

Figure 26.1   Human Development Precedes Wealth Creation

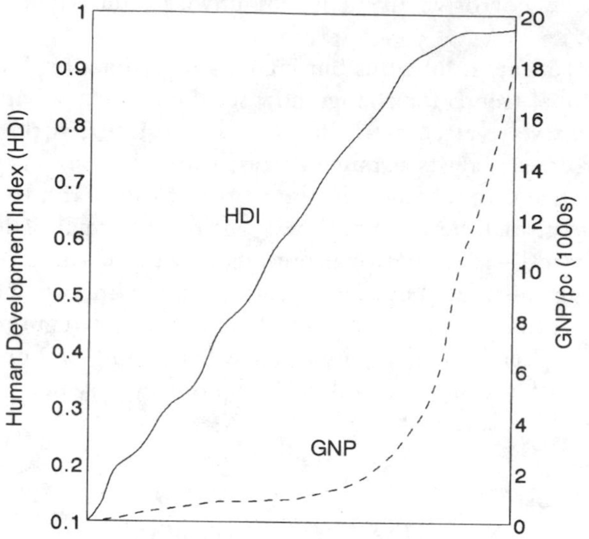

130 countries ranked by human development index and by GNP per capita

Source: Adapted from UNDP, *Human Development Report, 1990.*

Many states, however, now appear to regard security more broadly, as meaning more than defending territory against invasion. Wealth, too, is needed for political stability; and wealth can demonstrably be achieved by success in the new contest for world market shares. A helpful analogy might be to envisage governments as gardeners, each with his patch of ground. The gardener's prime concern used to be the fencing: to protect the plants, it had to be secure enough to keep marauders out. Even today, fences are not totally obsolete; many gardens still need them. But most gardeners now pay more attention to husbandry, to improving the water supply, to enhancing the fertility of the soil, and to keeping a proper balance of sun and shade so that small plants grow bigger and established plants produce more and better flowers and heavier crops. Forward-looking gardeners are now learning about becoming good husbandmen rather than effective fence-keepers. . . .

Partners of a Kind

The third of our premises is that politicians are already acutely aware of the high stakes for which the game is being played. By wooing multinationals into their territory, they are learning that the firms demand more than simple accommodation within the existing policy framework:

that framework often needs major adjustment if the benefits of the investments are fully to be captured. This premise challenges the conventions of international relations. In most textbooks, discussion of the multinationals comes as an afterthought at the end. They are described as "non-state actors" in a secondary category behind states as the main players.

All our evidence shows clearly that the multinationals are not secondary at all. They are increasingly indispensable allies, whether liked or not. They too are competing for world market shares as a means to wealth and survival. But whereas the state needs the production for the world market to be located on its territory, no matter who is oranizing it, the firm needs the production for the world market to be under its ultimate control no matter where it is located—and in many cases, no matter who possesses title to ownership.[3]

These are conditions that lead to both co-operation and conflict. There is a complementarity of interest when the state can secure the location and the firm can establish the control. There is conflict when the firm decides that it prefers another location (and can overcome the exit barriers) or when the state seeks to restrict how the firm exercises its control.

The qualities and assets needed to succeed in the new competition among states differ from what it was assumed, until recently, they were. In the traditional International Relations conception, it was the foreign policy of the state, and its defence policy, that was crucial for survival and success. Belgium failed and was occupied in 1940 at least partly because, clinging to neutrality, it had refused to join France in extending the Maginot Line to the coast. Sweden succeeded in surviving the same war at least partly by being "neutral" in favour of the Allies after Stalingrad. And so one could go on, drawing on the interpretation of the past experience of states by historians and scholars in international relations. Nowadays, however, traditionally defined foreign policy is relatively less important. Ministries of Finance, Trade or Economic Development offer more interesting and ultimately more rewarding careers. These and related ministries are where decisions will be taken about making the country a more or a less attractive location for multinationals and where new alliances will be fashioned between the state as host and the multinational as a welcome, though perhaps temporary, guest.

The multinationals' growing role in shaping internal policy has become a central issue in understanding the dynamics of the interactions between states and firms. As investment has matched or overtaken trade as the driving force in international economic relations, so the nature of the external policies and the appropriate weapons to be used by states have changed. . . .

Such conditions make it increasingly difficult for states explicitly to manage all the interrelationships among general policies as they apply to the specifics for building new sources of wealth-creating assets. Rather than attempt to forecast the outcomes when forming policy, some states are now turning to the possibility of ensuring progress by choosing partners that are capable of providing a stream of future benefits. In other words, forming alliances with particular firms is one way of dealing with the problem of enforcing the side payments. It is the choice of partner that can prove decisive. . . .

So Who Has Gained Power?

Before we go on to offer some advice to either side in these partnerships, we cannot pass over this crucial question. For a partnership between equals in power is obviously very different from a partnership of unequals. And the outcome of bargaining in the real world—as distinct from bargaining in game theory models—depends on who holds the whip hand, on who has the balance of bargaining power. We cannot dodge the question, how has the intensified competition between states and between firms for world market shares affected the balance of bargaining power between states *as a group* and multinationals *as a group*? Are governments now less able to influence outcomes including their own economic growth and development, while firms have more influence? Is that why, in the 1990s, "Welcome" is written on the mat in so many more developing countries than it was in 1975? Not because of any great love that developing country governments have for the foreign firm, but because they fear their growing power to help or hinder national economic development?

Our conclusion is that governments *as a group* have indeed lost bargaining power to the multinationals as the possibilities for collective action have diminished. Intensifying competition among states seems to have been a more important force for weakening their bargaining power than have the changes in global competition among firms. This is not to deny that governments can maintain considerable power in their dealings with any one foreign firm. The reasons lie in the nature of the competition for world market shares.

That competition is of two kinds. One is for access to the factors of production: whoever commands the critical factors has advantage for import-substituting investment. The other is for command of the profits and rents to be derived from selling the product or service on the world market. Command over *both* factors is a necessary condition for participation in export-led competition.

It seems to us that the changes in the production structure . . . have altered the relative importance of those factors over which states had most control, as compared with those over which firms had most control. States control access to land and to labour living on that land. Firms control capital and technology, or at least have better access to both. They can raise both debt and equity capital on international markets, whereas through most of the 1980s governments had severely limited access to capital. Firms' control of technology has increased as the accelerated pace of technological change has reduced the power of the patent system. Despite, or perhaps because of, the TRIPs debates, many firms increasingly rely on unpatented "know-how." . . .

Given that the relative importance of labour and the raw materials derived from land has fallen dramatically in determining competitiveness, while that of capital and technology has risen, does it follow that firms *as a group* have increased their bargaining power over the factors of production? Here the argument becomes complex, for the power of the individual firm may be regarded as having also fallen as competition has intensified. New entrants have altered the rules and offer governments new bargaining advantage.

One needs to separate the power to influence general policy from the power to insist on specific bargains. Multinationals can act collectively to exercise considerable influence over government choices. The role of big business in spurring Brussels towards the 1992 objective by pointing out the costs of "non-Europe" is one example. Commerce, firms also play a central role in shaping international standards on a wide range of issues, from bilateral tax treaties to environmental standards. Equally important in many sectors is the control developed by firms in some sectors over transnational advertising and marketing networks. Or, in other sectors, the global networks of communications and access to data which, with the aid of new technologies, have made them independent of governments while linking up their own managers scattered across the globe.[4]

Another variable factor in the power relationship that has impressed us is the time factor. Often we see a state constrained by social or political factors it cannot ignore to slow the pace of adjustment. A government may be convinced for instance that its autonomy requires public ownership of natural resources. Yet state-ownership may make it more difficult to market the country's oil or copper or bauxite on the world market than if it were privately owned by a transnational corporation with its own internalized access to foreign markets. Similarly, a state monopoly of power-generation may over-invest in new capacity, or be inefficiently managed, so that energy costs for users are raised above that of their competitiors. In labour relations, the welfare concerns of government may give rise to policies that protect workers against summary dismissal. But when policy is directed to winning world market shares, manufacturers, whether national or foreign, may need to have more flexibility in employing labour, increasing output to take advantage of rising demand or cutting back when orders slacken.

Quite clearly these dilemmas cannot be resolved in one giant leap forward: they can only be resolved over time. Indeed, we have shown repeatedly that change in one agenda without change in others is ineffective and that simultaneous change on all agendas is beyond the capacity of either a firm or a state to manage properly . . .

Continuing the Inquiry

The Nationality of the Firm

This is an important question for further research, more perhaps for the study of international relations than for international business. For the dominant realist paradigm in international relations theory assumes that the international system consists essentially of states as the dominant units; that we know what we mean by "a state"; and that all states share "functional sameness"—that is, they all perform the same functions with regard to society and economy (Waltz, 1979). Thus, when people refer to "the United States" or "Britain" or "Japan," these words are a comprehensive short-hand meaning both government, territory, people and economic enterprises. The pluralist, or liberal, paradigm in international relations does not fundamentally challenge this characterisation of the international system. It merely adds that there are transnational actors like multinationals who play a part in the system, but do not fundamentallly alter the state-based nature of authority in the international system. These are thus extras in the scenario, supercargo in the ship. They do not change the name of the game. It is tacitly assumed in both paradigms that US multinationals "belong" to the United States, French ones to France and so on. If they are not actually an additional instrument of foreign policy, a "tool of American imperialism," their fundamental association with the United States government is not seriously questioned.

By contrast, marxist, structural or radical paradigms—and, implicitly, much management literature—do however question the closeness of the association of state and enterprise. A common explanation sums it up by saying that the logic of accumulation is different for the nation, and for the firm. The nationalist logic of accumulation demands that value-adding operations be conducted and the profits retained, within the territory of the state. The global logic of accumulation demands that the firm manages and locates its value-adding operations wherever it decides this will maximise profit and minimise risk. It would therefore be illogical, according to this interpretation, to assume that the interest of the firm and the state—even its home state—will always and necessarily coincide. If they do, the theory would claim that it is merely coincidental.

A recent policy-oriented exposition of this logic by Robert Reich of the Harvard Business School has suggested that countries like the United States that ignore its practical implications do so at the risk of losing, instead of gaining, competitiveness to others (Reich, 1990: pp. 59, 64).

> Because the American-owned corporation is coming to have no special relationship with Americans, it makes no sense for Americans to entrust our national competitiveness to it. The interests of American-owned corporations may or may not coincide with those of the American people. . . . Corporations that invest in the United States, that build the value of the American work force, are more critical to our future standard of living than are American-owned corporations investing abroad.

But while Reich argues that Sony, Thomson, Philips and Honda contribute more to the US than do IBM, Motorola, Whirlpool or General Motors, popular—and indeed, political—opinion in the United States and in other developed countries is not so sure. Although governments have generally decided to take a more liberal attitude to foreign firms, most of them still reserve the right to forbid them to make some acquisitions. The German government refused permission to Kuwaiti interest to buy Krupp; the British government would not let a Hong Kong bank take over the Royal Bank of Scotland. There was an outcry in the United States when Japanese interests bought the freehold of the Rockefeller Center in New York.

Xenophobic emotion apart, there are two kinds of reasons for such reactions. One is that the foreign interest will be less responsive to or considerate of local social *mores* or national interests than a native owner. This is patently weak in logic, precisely because the rights which government keep in reserve inevitably put the foreign firm more at risk of being thrown out than the local one, and therefore more strongly motivated to avoid giving offence to local national susceptibilities.

The second reason is more substantial. It is that, however great the global reach of their operations, the national firm does, psychologically and sociologically, "belong" to its home base. In the last resort, its directors will always heed the wishes and commands of the government which has issued their passports and those of their families. A recent study of the boards of directors of the top 1,000 U.S. firms, for example, shows that only 12 per cent included a non-American—rather fewer, in fact, than in 1982 when there were 17 per cent (*Economist*, August 11, 1990). The Japanese firm with even one token foreign director would be hard to find. Even in Europe, with the exception of bi-national firms like Unilever, you do not find the top management reflecting by their nationality the geographical distribution of its operations.

It is precisely on this point concerning the relation of national identity and corporate identity that conflict has arisen in international relations concerning the management of international trade and investment. For there is a clear perception that this relation is closer in some states than in others, and that this affects the competition between states for market shares, both at home and abroad. It is felt in America that U.S. firms, perhaps because they are "older" multinationals, having anticipated the Japanese in moving production offshore, are somehow more truly "multinational" than the Japanese—and suffer for it.[5]

This has led to confrontation between governments, especially those of the U.S. and Japan. The Americans argue that if the competitive game between states is to be played fairly, with everyone observing the same rules of the game, then there should be a measure of symmetry in the relations of each home government towards its nationally-based firms. And there should be a measure of reciprocity in each government's treatment of foreign firms, whether banks, stockbrokers or manufacturers. "If you won't let ours in, we won't let in yours!" has been said to the Japanese by both the Americans and the Europeans. Both are convinced that not merely are some Japanese companies more efficient and better managed, but that, in addition, they enjoy significantly closer relations to their government and to government-influenced banks. Moreover, there is a conviction that the relationship is symbiotic; in return for state support, the firm more readily adapts its strategies to accommodate national political (including economic security) goals. It is on the basis of such conviction that pressures are put—especially by Washington and the USTR's office—on Tokyo to open up on a more level playing field as the American say, to foreign firms as well as to foreign goods—or else to face even greater barriers to Japanese exports to the American market.

Yet American policy has not been without its own kind of bias. Ever since the passing of the Buy American Act in the 1950s, the government has been statutorily obliged to give preference to U.S. firms when it came to defence and other government procurement. Its trade agreements, with the USSR, for instance, habitually insisted on the preferential use of U.S.-owned shipping. A provision of the U.S. Canadian Free Trade Agreement gives preference to cars produced in North America with a high minimum local content. If there is a "special relationship" between the government of Japan and Japanese firms, so is there between the government of the United States and U.S.-owned firms. One way, however, in which U.S. policies are more visibly even-handed as between domestic and foreign firms is that the U.S., as

compared to some European and developing countries, has relatively
few state-owned enterprises under its direct control; and its financial
and commercial intermediaries are less suspect than either German or
Japanese banks and sogo shosha (trading companies) of favouring their
home teams (Spindler, 1984). These are the two grounds on which, although the evidence is contested by Japanese scholars, retaliatory U.S.
trade measures have been justified.[6]

The other major difference between the US and other industrialised countries including Japan arises from its special role in the international security structure. While other states—the USSR and China
excepted—have to accept the dependence of their defence forces in
whole or in part on foreign suppliers, the Americans see their security
at risk if US forces are dependent for militarily vital weapons or parts of
weapons on firms based in other countries, especially those which could
conceivably be neutral or enemies in time of war. This has led to proposals for elaborate new statutory rules to prevent any such vulnerability. For instance, it was suggested that security is threatened if supply
comes from only four countries or from four firms producing more
than half total world supply.[7] But the American experience with the
Strategic Defense Initiative suggests that no rules can entirely avoid
technological dependence of foreign firms. The question is only how to
manage the dependence. Moran (1990) concluded that the choice lies
between relying on sub-optimally efficient US producers or recognising
the inevitability of reciprocal security dependence. The latter would
mean working towards a multilateral code by which all states would give
up the right to claim extraterritorial jurisdiction over the use by others
of military or other technology. Just what sanctions might be contem-
plated to give credibility to such a code is one of many unanswered
questions.

The political debate has generated quite a substantial literature
on Japanese corporate management practices, and on the political economy of Japanese trade and industry (Inoguchi and Okimoto, 1988;
Ohmae, 1982; Abegglen and Stalk, 1985; Clark, 1979 and Johnson,
1982). It has also given rise to much discussion, especially in the United
States, of what is called strategic trade policy (Krugman, 1986; Grossman and Richardson, 1985; Stern, 1987; Zysman and Cohen, 1988;
Rosecrance, 1986; Milner, 1988; Richardson, 1990 and Cohen; 1990).
Yet the empirical evidence for the allegation of asymmetry in state-firm
relations is patchy at best. More detailed firm-level and plant-level data
need to be collected. It is all very well for Cohen to say that economists
need to broaden their horizons from industrial organisation theories
and "help to build a formal structure to the interactions between market and politics" so that the nature of functional relationships between
political authority and economic enterprise can "be modeled in ways

that are theoretically robust and empirically generalizable" (Cohen, 1990). That is a lot easier said than done and the bricks for building such formal structures and making such models are just not available at present . . .

Notes

1. One example where the squeeze was felt by both sides was the dispute that broke out in 1988 between the Indonesian government and its Japanese partners in the largest aluminium smelter in South-East Asia at Asahan. The Indonesians, squeezed by rising domestic demand both for alumina for local industry and for water for irrigating farms, stopped the shipments to the Japanese who had been taking nearly 60 per cent of the smelter's output. The stand-off was finally broken when the Japanese offered new cash and a rescheduling of past debt. In return, the Indonesians resumed shipments of alumina, and through a debt-equity swap increased their share of the equity from 25 to 41 per cent.

2. One striking example of such corporate diplomacy was the initiative taken by the chairman of Deutsche Bank to enlist the support of both the German and Soviet governments for a deal whereby the latter agreed to the setting-up of an export zone at Kaliningrad—formerly Konigsberg in East Prussia—while the latter gave 90 per cent guarantees to commercial loans extended mainly to German suppliers hit by the foreign credit famine in the USSR. *Financial Times*, July 25, 1990.

3. Political debate still rages over how governments should promote, or discriminate in favour of, national (or "European") champions. Public opinion is still slow to adapt the idea that "foreign" corporations can be acting more in the local national interest than home-bred ones, as we discuss later on. Similarly, as we discussed in chapter 5, corporate boards still debate when and how a firm has to exert its control through ownership rather than by contract.

4. Small wonder that the debates over the control of trans-border data flows are now assuming heightened saliency in many countries. See, for example, Sauvant (1986).

5. It was an American firm, incidentally—IBM—that was credited with the first use of this euphemistic adjective in the early 1960s.

6. For a useful summary of various interpretations and explanations of the superior competitive performance of Japanese firms, see Best (1990: chapter 5).

7. For example, *Holding the Edge: Maintaining the Defense Technology Base*, U.S. Office of Technology Assessment, 1989; Senators Bingaman and McCain, *Deterrence in Decay: The Future of the U.S. Defense Industrial Base*, 1989; and other congressional studies, quoted in Moran (1990).

References

Abegglen, J. C. and Stalk, G., Jr. 1985. *Kaisha: The Japanese Corporation*, New York: Basic Books.

Best, M. 1990. *The New Competition: Institutions of Industrial Restructuring*, Cambridge: Polity.

Bull, H. 1978. *The Anarchical Society: A Study of Order in World Politics*, London: MacMillan.

Clark, R. C. 1979. *The Japanese Company*, New Haven: Yale University Press.

Cohen, B. J. 1990. "The Political Economy of International Trade," *International Organization* Vol. 44, no. 2, pp. 261–81.

———— 1990. *Economist*, August 11.

———— 1990. *Financial Times*, July 25.

Grossman, J. M. and Richardson, J. D. 1985. *Strategic Trade Policy: A Survey of Issues and Early Analysis*, Princeton, NJ: International Finance Papers.

Inoguchi, T. and Okimoto, D. (eds.) 1988. *The Political Economy of Japan: Vol. 2. The Changing International Context*, Stanford: Stanford University Press.

Johnson, C. 1982. *Miti and the Japanese Miracle: the Growth of Industrial Policy, 1925–1975*, Stanford: Stanford University Press.

Krugman, P. R. (ed.) 1986. *Strategic Trade Policy and the New International Economics*, Cambridge, MA: MIT Press.

Miller, J. D. B. 1982. *The World of States*, London: Croom Helm.

Milner, H. V. 1988. *Resisting Protectionism: Global Industries and the Politics of International Trade*, Princeton, NJ: Princeton University Press.

Moran, T. H. 1990. "The Globalization of America's Defense Industries: Managing the Threat of Foreign Dependence," *International Security*, Vol. 15, No. 1, pp. 57–99.

Myers, N. 1989. "Environment and Security," *Foreign Affairs*, No. 74, Spring, pp. 23–41.

Ohmae, K. 1982. *The Mind of the Strategist*, New York: McGraw-Hill.

Oman, C. 1984. *New Forms of International Investment in Developing Countries*, Paris: OECD.

Reich, R. 1990. "Who is US?" *Harvard Business Review*, Vol. 68, No. 1, January–February, pp. 53–64.

Richardson, J. D. 1990. "The Political Economy of Strategic Trade Policy," *International Organization*, Vol. 44, No. 1, pp. 107–35.

Rosecrance, R. 1986. *The Rise of the Trading State: Commerce and Conquest in the Modern World*, New York: Basic Books.

Sauvant, K. P. 1986. *International Transactions in Services: The Politics of Transborder Data Flows*, Boulder, CO: Westview Press.

Sharp, M. and Holmes, P. (eds.) 1989. *Strategies for New Technology: Case Studies from Britain and France*, London: Philip Allen.

Spindler, A. 1984. *The Politics of International Credit: Private Finance and Foreign Policy in Germany and Japan*, Washington, DC: Brookings Institution.

Stern, R. (ed.) 1987. *U.S. Trade Policies in a Changing World*, Cambridge, MA: MIT Press.

United Nations Development Programme (UNDP). 1990. *Human Development Report 1990*. Oxford: Oxford University Press.

United Nations Industrial Development Organisation (UNIDO) 1986. "Industrial Policies and Strategies in Developing Countries: an Analysis of Local Content Rules," *Industry and Development*, No. 18 (UN sales no. E86.II.B.2).

Waltz, K. 1979. *The Theory of International Politics*, Reading, MA: Addison Wesley.

Zysman, J. and Cohen, S. 1988. *Manufacturing Matters*, New York: Basic Books.

PART 6

CONCLUSIONS
AND FUTURE WORLDS

27

FORGING A NEW
GLOBAL PARTNERSHIP

Hilary F. French

During the past twenty years environmental issues have emerged as an important aspect of international political economy. If environmental degradation and resource depletion continue, as many anticipate they will, competition over resources could escalate economic rivalries and ultimately promote conflict. Hilary French reviews the current status of institutional and policy evolution in the management of global environmental problems. States have organized around eight hundred treaties and accords in response to environmental concerns and problems; the challenge now focuses on organizing political will at the domestic level for more effective treaty-accord implementation. Success has characterized some agreements, such as the Montreal Protocol, but most have failed to spark needed changes in state policies (e.g., the Climate Change and Biodiversity megapolicy). One of the more recent environmental plans, which emerged from the Rio Summit, is Agenda 21, which according to French, provides a blueprint for moving toward sustainable development. However, Agenda 21 merely exhorts countries to move in ecologically sound directions and places no binding responsibilities on the signatories. French proposes revamping and strengthening existing international social and economic organizations to press on with the implementation of Agenda 21.

In June 1992, more than 100 heads of state or government and 20,000 nongovernmental representatives from around the world gathered in Rio de Janeiro for the U.N. Conference on Environment and Development (UNCED). The event was widely heralded as historic. It resulted

Reprinted with permission from the publishers of *State of the World 1995* (Washington: Worldwatch Institute), pp. 170–189.

in the adoption of Agenda 21, an ambitious 500-page blueprint for sustainable development. If implemented, this would require far-reaching changes by international agencies, national governments, and individuals everywhere. In addition, Rio produced treaties on climate change and biological diversity, both of which over time could lead to domestic policy changes in all nations (Hinrichsen, 1992; Guruswamy, Palmer and Weston, 1994).[1]

The Earth Summit marked the coming of age of "sustainable development"—the point at which this concept moved from the environmental literature to the front page, and from there into the lexicon of governments and international agencies. Significantly, the Rio conference pointed to the need for a global partnership if sustainable development was to be achieved.[2]

Since Rio, a steady stream of international meetings has been held on the many issues that were on its agenda. Governments, for instance, have been preparing for the first Conferences of the Parties of the biological diversity and the climate conventions, where the real work of getting these agreements actually implemented will begin. Similarly, the U.N. Commission on Sustainable Development (CSD), created to oversee follow-through on Agenda 21, had met twice by mid-1994 and is starting to get its feet on the ground. And the September 1994 International Conference on Population and Development (ICPD) in Cairo put the spotlight of world attention on the inexorable pace of population growth—and on the need to respond to it through broad-based efforts to expand access to family planning, improve women's health and literacy, and ensure child survival ("Lack of Concrete Action," 1994; Pitt, 1994; UN-NGLS, 1994; Rensberger, 1994).

Unfortunately, though, the pace of real change has not kept up with the increasingly loaded schedule of international gatherings. The reality is that the initial burst of international momentum generated by UNCED is flagging, and the global partnership it called for is foundering due to a failure of political will. Though a small, committed group of individuals in international organizations, national and local governments, and citizens' groups continues trying to keep the flame of Rio alive, business as usual is largely the order of the day in the factories, farms, villages, and cities that form the backbone of the world economy.

The result is that the relentless pace of global ecological decline shows no signs of letting up. Carbon dioxide concentrations are mounting in the atmosphere, species loss continues to accelerate, fisheries are collapsing, land degradation frustrates efforts to feed hungry people, and the earth's forest cover keeps shrinking. Many of the development and economic issues that underpin environmental destruction also continue to worsen. Though some social indicators, such as global life expectancy and literacy rates, have improved in recent years, other key trends are headed in the wrong direction: income inequality is rising, Third World debt is mounting, human numbers keep increasing at daunting rates, and the absolute number of poor people in the world is increasing (Brown, Kane and Roodman, 1994; UNDP, 1994; World Bank, 1994a).

Fortunately, 1995 will bring a number of golden opportunities to strengthen the global partnership called for at Rio. In March, world leaders will gather in Copenhagen for the World Summit on Social Development—an effort to generate for social ills the same high level of attention the Rio conference garnered for environmental ones. And in September, the World Conference on Women will be held in Beijing, providing an opportunity for the international community to take concrete steps toward removing gender bias as a roadblock to alleviating poverty and arresting ecological decline (UN World Summit for Social Development, 1994; "Draft Platform," n.d.).

Throughout the year the world will celebrate the fiftieth anniversary of the founding of the United Nations. This will be a time to reflect on how the world has changed in 50 years—and on how the U.N. must evolve if it is to remain relevant. In addition, members of the Group of Seven (G7)—the major industrial powers—are devoting their July 1995 Economic Summit in Nova Scotia to the framework of institutions required to ensure "sustainable development with good prosperity and well-being of the peoples of our nations and the world" in the twenty-first century. The summit will consider both adaptations to existing institutions and the possible need to build new ones ("50," 1994; Commission on Global Governance, 1994; "Summit Communique," 1994).

The global partnership that is needed will have several distinct features. As suggested in Rio, it will involve a new form of relationship between the industrialized North and the developing South. Another feature will be a new division of responsibility between different levels of governance worldwide: Problems are best solved at the most decentralized level of governance that is consistent with efficient performance of the task; as they transcend boundaries, decision making can be passed upward as necessary—from the community to the state, national, regional, and in some rare instances the global level. A third requirement is the active participation of citizens in village, municipal, and national political life, as well as at the United Nations.

Above all, the new partnership calls for an unprecedented degree of international cooperation and coordination: the complex web of ecological, economic, communication, and other connections now binding the world together means that no government can build a secure future for its citizens by acting alone. As US inventor and statesman Ben

Franklin said as the 13 colonies in America declared their independence from the British crown: "We must indeed all hang together, or most assuredly we will all hang separately" (Browning, 1989).

Protecting the Global Environment

One of the primary ways the world community has responded to the environmental challenge is through the negotiation of treaties and other types of international agreements. Nations have now agreed on more than 170 environmental treaties—more than two thirds of them since the U.N. Conference on the Human Environment in Stockholm in 1972 first put the environment on the international agenda (see Figure 27.1). If other, less-binding types of accords are included in the total, the number of international environmental instruments on the books tops 800. Some important additions to these lists appeared in 1994: the climate and biological diversity conventions as well as the long-languishing Law of the Sea treaty all received enough ratifications to enter into force. In addition, governments signed a new accord on desertification and land degradation (UNEP, 1993; Labelle, 1994;

Figure 27.1   International Environmental Treaties, 1921–94

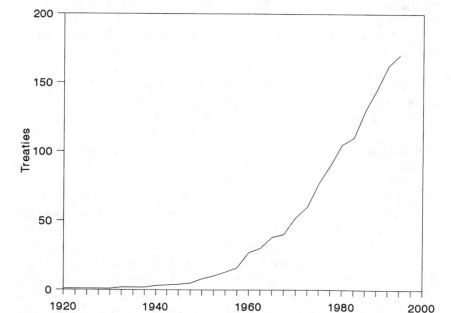

Weiss, Szasz and Magraw, 1992; "Climate Change Treaty," 1994; Pitt, 1994; Goodman, 1993; UN, 1994).[3]

These agreements have led to some measurable gains. Air pollution in Europe, for instance, has been reduced dramatically as a result of the 1979 treaty on transboundary air pollution. Global chlorofluorocarbon (CFC) emissions have dropped 60 percent from their peak in 1988 following the 1987 treaty on ozone depletion and its subsequent amendments. The killing of elephants has plummeted in Africa because of the 1990 ban on commercial trade in ivory under the Convention on International Trade in Endangered Species of Wild Flora and Fauna. And mining exploration and development have been forbidden in Antarctica for 50 years under a 1991 accord (Levy, 1993; Ryan, in Brown, Kane and Roodman, 1994; "Africa's Elephants," 1992; Porter and Brown, 1991).

Though some treaties have been successes, many more have failed to ignite the needed changes in domestic policies. All too often, environmental accords are written in such vague terms that they commit signatories to little. Monitoring of compliance with agreements is generally cursory at best, and sanctions are rarely imposed even when violators have been identified. Developing countries are often impeded in their efforts to comply with international accords by industrial countries' failure to deliver on promises of financial and technological assistance (French, 1994a; US General Accounting Office, 1992).

The broad framework of international agreements needed to protect the global environment is now in place. The challenge for the future is thus to see that existing agreements are translated into action around the world.

The hallmark of international environment governance to date is the Montreal Protocol on the Depletion of the Ozone Layer. First agreed to in September 1987 and strengthened significantly two times since then, the protocol now stipulates that the production of CFCs in industrial countries must be phased out altogether by 1996. It also restricts the use of several other ozone-depleting chemicals, including halons, carbon tetrachlorides, methyl chloroform, and hydrochlorofluorocarbons. Developing countries have a 10–year grace period in which to meet the terms of the original protocol and its amendments (Guruswamy, Palmer and Weston, 1994; UNEP, 1994).[4]

In a remarkably short period of time, the Montreal Protocol has become the international law of the land. More than 100 countries have ratified the original protocol, and both amendments have received enough approvals to enter into force. Because of the quick and dramatic reduction in global CFC emissions as a result of the pact, computer models suggest that if all countries comply with their commitments, chlorine concentrations will begin to level off soon (see Figure 27.2).

Figure 27.2   Atmospheric Chlorine, 1975–93, With Four Projections to 2055

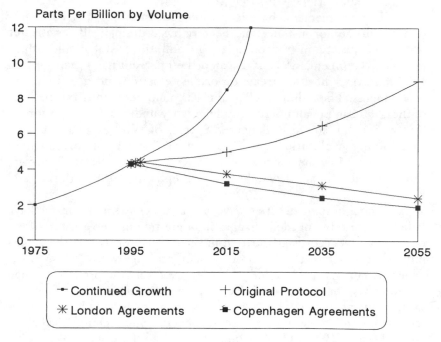

Parts Per Billion by Volume

- Continued Growth   + Original Protocol
- ✳ London Agreements   ■ Copenhagen Agreements

Though this will be a momentous international achievement, the world will nevertheless have paid a heavy price for earlier inaction: dangerous levels of ultraviolet radiation will be reaching the earth for decades to come, which scientists estimate will stunt agricultural productivity and damage ecological and human health (Smirnov, 1994; UNEP, 1994; Ryan, 1994; UNEP, WMO, US NASA, and NOAA, 1994; "Synthesis of the Reports," 1991).[5]

The lessons learned in the ozone treaty are now being put to a severe test, as the international community begins to confront a more daunting atmospheric challenge—the need to head off climate change. Less than two years after it was signed in Rio, the Framework Convention on Climate Change entered into force in March 1994 after the fiftieth country (Portugal) ratified it. Unfortunately, the speed with which the treaty was ratified was in part a reflection of the fact that it contains few real commitments.

The climate treaty's deliberately ambiguous language urges but does not require industrial nations to stabilize emissions of carbon—the primary contributor to global warming—at 1990 levels by the year 2000. Developing nations face no numerical goals whatsoever, though all signatories must conduct inventories of their emissions; submit detailed reports of national actions taken to implement the convention; and endeavor to take climate change into account in all their social, economic, and environmental policies. But no specific policy measures are required.

As of late 1994, most industrial countries had established national greenhouse gas targets and climate plans, but they vary widely in effectiveness. Among the most ambitious and comprehensive plans are those of Denmark, the Netherlands, and Switzerland, none of which have powerful oil or coal industries to contend with. Through the use of efficiency standards, renewable energy programs, and limited carbon taxes, these plans are likely to limit national emissions significantly (OECD, 1994; "IEA Reviews," 1994).

According to independent evaluations by nongovernmental organizations (NGOs), most of the climate plans issued so far will fall short of stabilizing national emissions and the other goals they have set for themselves. Germany and the United States, for example, two of the largest emitters, have each issued climate plans that take important steps but fail to tackle politically difficult policies—the reduction of coal subsidies in Germany and the increase of gasoline taxes in the United States. Neither country is likely to meet its stated goals. Reports from Japan suggest that it, too, is unlikely to meet its stabilization target. In another failure of will, long-standing efforts by the European Union to impose a hybrid carbon/energy tax have so far failed, despite strong support from the European Commission (Climate Action Network, 1994; Cushman, 1994; "Japan Will Substantially," 1994; "EU Ratifies Climate," 1993).

Even if the goal of holding emissions to 1990 levels in 2000 is met, this falls far short of reaching the broader aim of the Rio climate treaty: stabilizing atmospheric concentrations of greenhouse gases, which according to scientists will require bringing carbon emissions 60–80 percent below current levels. As a result, several European countries and the United States have voiced cautious support for strengthening the treaty to promote stronger actions, though they have not said exactly how (Evans, 1994; Intergovernmental Panel on Climate Change, 1994; IPCC, 1990; Cushman, 1994).

The first major opportunity to update the climate convention will come in March 1995, when the initial Conference of the Parties to the convention convenes in Berlin. Environmental groups urge that this meeting adopt a target of a 20-percent cut in carbon emissions by 2005. A caucus of small island states has tabled a similar proposal. Prospects are uncertain, but there is a good chance that governments will at least consider goals for emissions levels after 2000, which the current treaty is noticeably silent on. Other possible innovations include stipulating joint actions aimed at revamping policies in critical sectors such as energy, forests, and transport. Requiring that participating countries establish appliance efficiency standards, for example, could make a sizable contribution toward slowing the growth in global carbon emissions (US Climate Action Network, 1994; "Small Island Nations," 1994; Wirth, 1994).

Work is also slowly getting under way to implement the other major treaty agreed to in Rio—the Convention on Biological Diversity. Signed by 160 countries in Rio, this treaty entered into force on December 29, 1993. As of September 1994, 89 countries had ratified it, including many in both the North and the South. The first Conference of the Parties to the convention was scheduled for November 1994 (Pitt, 1994; Labelle, 1994).

As with protecting the atmosphere, preserving biological diversity is something that all countries have a stake in and that no one country can effectively do alone. Ironically, however, one of the convention's most important achievements was its rejection of the notion that biological diversity is the "common heritage of mankind," and—conversely—its recognition that biological resources are the sovereign property of nation-states. The reason: when countries can profit from something, they have an incentive to preserve it.

Genetic diversity is worth a lot. The protection that genetic variability affords crops from pests, diseases, and climatic and soil variations is worth $1 billion to US agriculture. Overall, the economic benefits from wild species to pharmaceuticals, agriculture, forestry, fisheries, and the chemical industry adds up to more than $87 billion annually—more than 4 percent of the US gross domestic product. Though international pharmaceutical companies have been extracting genes from countries for free for years, the biological diversity convention says that gene-rich countries have a right to charge for access to this valuable resource, and encourages them to pass national legislation to set the terms (Reid, 1992; World Resources Institute, World Conservation Union, and UNEP, 1992).

One widely publicized model of this is a 1991 agreement between Merck & Co., the world's largest pharmaceutical company, and Costa Rica's National Institute of Biodiversity (INBio). Merck agreed to pay the Institute $1 million for conservation programs in exchange for access to the country's plants, microbes, and insects. And if a discovery makes its way into a commercialized product, Merck has agreed to pay INBio a share of the royalties. Discussing how to replicate such agreements will likely be a high priority for countries that have signed the convention (Reid, 1992).

Besides providing a forum for future negotiations, the convention calls for a number of actions by governments to preserve biological wealth, including national plans and strategies for preservation and detailed biological inventories and surveys. Work on strategies has begun in a number of countries, including Canada, Chile, Indonesia, the Netherlands, Norway, Poland, and the United Kingdom; the United States and Costa Rica are in the process of conducting biological surveys. Possible actions in the future include discussions of a protocol on biotechnology, as well as deliberations on international standards for biodiversity prospecting agreements (Lanou, 1994; World Resources Institute, 1994; "Parties to Biodiversity," 1994; Reid et al., 1993).

The oceans are another natural resource whose protection requires international collaboration. Not only did the Law of the Sea receive sufficient ratifications to enter into force in 1994, but agreement was also reached on modifications to the original agreement that are likely to mean that the United States and other industrial countries will join in. The recent rebirth of this treaty comes just in time for the world's oceans and estuaries, which are suffering from overfishing, oil spills, land-based sources of pollution, and other ills (Canute, 1994; Fowler, 1994).

The Law of the Sea contains an extensive array of environmental provisions. For instance, though countries are granted sovereignty over waters within 200 miles of their shores (called exclusive economic zones, or EEZs), they also accept an obligation to protect ecological health there. The treaty also serves as an umbrella for scores of existing international agreements covering the oceans, including the London Dumping Convention, the MARPOL agreement regulating shipping, and numerous international fisheries agreements and regionally based initiatives. All countries that are members of the Law of the Sea are obligated to adhere to these various oceans conventions. In addition, the treaty contains pathbreaking compulsory dispute resolution provisions, under which countries are bound to accept the verdict of an international tribunal (Weber, 1993; UN, 1983).

Just as the Law of the Sea is coming into force, however, its rules are already being overtaken by events in one important area—overfishing. In particular, the original treaty failed to resolve the problem of fish stocks that straddle the boundaries of EEZs and of fish species that migrate long distances. The United Nations has convened a series of meetings to discuss possible international action to deal with a situation that has seen seafood catch per person fall 8 percent since 1989 . . . ("Summary of the Third Session," 1994; UNFAO, various years, 1993).

The latest addition to the international repertoire of environmental treaties is a convention intended to curb land degradation, adopted in Paris in June 1994 and signed by 87 countries as of October of that year. The idea for this came up in Rio, as a response to developing-country concerns that the issues most relevant to them were largely left off the table. According to the U.N. Environment Programme (UNEP), the livelihoods of at least 900 million people in some 100 countries are threatened by such degradation, known to many as desertification, which affects about one quarter of the earth's land area. The degradation—caused by overgrazing, overcropping, poor irrigation practices, and deforestation, and often exacerbated by climatic variations—poses a serious threat to efforts to raise agricultural productivity worldwide (UNEP, 1993; "Summary of the Fifth Session," 1994; Labelle, 1994).[6]

The desertification treaty supplies a framework for local projects, encourages national action programs, promotes regional and international cooperation on the transfer of needed technologies, and provides for information exchange and research and training. It will also create a global mechanism to coordinate funds from various sources. The convention encourages the creation of national desertification trust funds that incorporate extensive provisions for public participation.

Meeting Human Needs

Protecting the environment and combating poverty are now widely recognized to be interlinked priorities, a reality reflected in the decision to focus UNCED on both environment and development. Similarly, the Cairo conference looked at the complex interconnections among population growth, deteriorating social conditions, gender inequity, environmental degradation, and a range of other issues. As these landmark international gatherings both underscored, a sustainable future cannot be secured without an aggressive effort to combat poverty and meet basic social needs.

Trends during the last several decades suggest a mixed record on improving human welfare. Though impressive progress has been made in boosting immunization rates, reducing infant mortality, and increasing life expectancy, one in three children remains malnourished, more than 1 billion people lack safe water to drink, and about 1 billion adults cannot read or write. The share of the world's population living in "absolute poverty" has steadily declined, but the actual numbers continue to grow, with more than 1 billion people—a fifth of humanity—consigned to this state. Rather than shrinking, the gap between the rich and the poor is growing: in 1960, the richest 20 percent of the world earned 30 times as much income as the poorest 20 percent; by 1991, the richest fifth was appropriating 61 times as much wealth as the poorest (UNDP, 1991).

A crucial first step toward turning these statistics around was taken in Cairo, when more than 160 countries approved a World Population Plan of Action aimed at keeping human numbers somewhere below 9.8 billion in 2050. It covers a broad range of issues, including the empowerment of women, the role of the family, reproductive rights and health, and migration. The plan calls for expenditures on population programs to more than triple by 2000—from today's $5 billion to some $17 billion. Of the total, $10 billion is intended for family planning programs, $5 billion for reproductive health, $1.3 billion for the prevention of sexually transmitted diseases, and $500 million for research and data collection. Industrial countries are expected to come up with $5.7 billion, with the remainder from domestic resources in the developing world. The action plan also calls for accelerating existing U.N. initiatives aimed at expanding women's literacy and improving their health—though it curiously fails to provide spending targets for doing so (UN General Assembly, 1994; Cowell, 1994).

Vatican opposition to proposed language on abortion rights captured headlines during the Cairo conference, but the real news was the remarkable consensus forged between the industrial and developing worlds and among representatives of population, women's, and human rights groups during two years of preparation for the meeting. Key elements of this include a recognition that slowing population growth and making progress on a range of social fronts are inextricably linked challenges. It follows from the new consensus that reaching population stabilization goals will require a far different approach than in the past. In particular, family planning programs alone will be insufficient to meet the population challenge. Equally important are investments in changing the conditions that generate demand for large families—such as illiteracy and the low status of women. In addition, there was widespread agreement that family planning efforts must be noncoercive and integrated broadly with reproductive health programs (Bongaarts, 1994; UN General Assembly, 1994).

Cairo provided a vivid demonstration of what U.N. conferences can accomplish when they are skillfully prepared for and when the political climate is ripe for progress. US leadership was widely credited with making the ICPD a success, a factor that has all too often been lacking at past gatherings. These meetings make an important contribution simply as international consciousness-raising events. In addition, they provide a unique forum where countries can share experiences and plot joint strategies on issues of common concern. In one exciting initiative that emerged from the Cairo conference, 10 diverse developing nations representing Muslim, Buddhist, and Christian religious traditions joined together in a program to share their experiences with others. Each has achieved considerable success in recent years in bringing fertility rates down. In Indonesia, for instance, the birth rate dropped from 5.6 births per woman in 1971 to 3.0 in 1991. And in Colombia, it declined from 7.1 children per women to 2.9 over 30 years (Crossette, 1994).[7]

Following quickly on the heels of Cairo, the Social Summit has a mandate to take on poverty, unemployment, and social integration. . . .

Revamping International Institutions

Achieving sustainable development requires protecting the rights of local people to control their own resources—whether it be forests, fish, or minerals. Yet nations and people everywhere are also discovering that if we are to master today's transnational challenges, a wider role for international institutions is inevitable. It is thus a paradox of our time that effective governance requires control being simultaneously passed down to local communities and up to international institutions (Korten, 1991–92; Broad and Cavanagh, 1993; Colchester, 1994).

To respond to this need, considerable reforms are needed in the United Nations to prepare it for the world of the future. The U.N. Charter, for instance, was written for a different era. Neither "environment" nor "population" even appear in the document. And though the need for more effective international institutions is clear, people the world over are justifiably worried by the prospect of power being centralized in institutions that are remote from democratic accountability (Office of Public Information, n.d.).

Many different U.N. agencies are involved in the quest for sustainable development. To date, the U.N. Environment Programme is the primary environmental organ in the system (see Table 27.1). Created after the 1972 U.N. conference in Stockholm, it is charged with catalyzing environmental work throughout the U.N. But many other agencies have active environmental programs: the World Health Organization (WHO), for instance, promulgates air and water pollution guidelines that are considered the international norm, and the World Meteorological Organization has made important contributions to better understanding of the complexities of climate science. The U.N. Food and Agriculture Organization (FAO) is at the front line of efforts to boost agricultural productivity and protect dwindling fisheries. UNDP launched a Capacity 21 initiative after Rio, which has so far raised $30 million to help countries integrate environmental considerations into their development plans, and has also recently strengthened its natural resources unit (Sand, in Matthews, 1991; UNDP, n.d. a).

Table 27.1   Estimated Expenditures and Staffing of Various U.N. Agencies, 1992–93[1]

Agency	Professional Staff	Expenditure
	(number)	(million dollars)
U.N. Development Programme	1,571	2,235
UNICEF	1,179	1,810
Food and Agriculture Organization	2,659	1,557
World Health Organization	1,833	1,372
Int'l. Labour Organization	1,373	676
UNESCO	1,056	662
Int'l. Atomic Energy Agency	699	535
U.N. Industrial Devel. Organization	660	491
U.N. Population Fund	166	333
U.N. Environment Programme	303	214
World Meteorological Organization	182	145
Int'l. Maritime Organization	122	82

[1]Budget figures are for biennium 1992-93 (which includes both years), but staff size figures are for 1990 except for UNEP 1993 and UNFPA 1994.
   Source: Budget figures from United Nations, *Programs and Resources of the United Nations System for the Biennium 1992–1993;* staff sizes from Erskine Childers with Brian Urquhart, "Renewing the United Nations System," *Development Dialogue* (Dag Hammarskjöld Foundation/Ford Foundation), 1994:1, except for U.N. Population Fund (UNFPA) staff from Bikash Shrestha, Administrative Assistant, Personnel Office, UNFPA, New York, private communication, October 18, 1994, and UNEP budget and staff size from Sergei Khromov, communications programme officer, UNEP, Nairobi, private communication, October 31, 1994.

Numerous agencies contribute to the broader social development agenda. The U.N. Population Fund is instrumental in encouraging family planning programs worldwide, and will play a crucial role in overseeing follow-through on the Cairo conference. And UNICEF has achieved impressive successes in its efforts to improve children's welfare worldwide.

The Bretton Woods institutions—GATT, the IMF, and the World Bank—are all also critical players in the sustainable development challenge. GATT, which will be subsumed into a new World Trade Organization once the Uruguay Round of negotiations is ratified, lays down the rules of world trade and procedures for enforcing them. The agreement has been widely criticized as being environmentally insensitive, although governments are now discussing ways to green GATT rules at a newly created Trade and Environment Committee. The World Bank has also come in for heavy criticism in recent years. It has increased its spending on environmental programs as a result, though it continues to have a poor record on enforcing many of its own environmental and social policies. Finally, the IMF is an influential source of macroeconomic policy advice, particularly in the developing world.

Unfortunately, it has so far been reluctant to incorporate tools such as natural resource accounting and environmental taxation into its recommendations (French, 1993; "Decision on Trade," 1994; French, in Brown et al., 1994; World Bank, 1994b; Reed, 1992; Cruz and Repetto, 1992).

Governments took a number of steps at UNCED to make the United Nations system a stronger force for sustainable development. Perhaps most significant, they created the Commission on Sustainable Development with 53 members of the United Nations to provide an international forum where governments could review progress in implementing Agenda 21, share information about what works and what does not, and discuss impediments such as inadequate financial resources or access to innovative technologies (Kimball, 1994, 1993; Sessions, 1992).

To try to improve coordination and cooperation between various U.N. agencies on the sustainable development agenda, governments decided to create an Inter-Agency Committee on Sustainable Development (IACSD), composed of representatives of several relevant U.N. agencies. In addition, an organizational shake-up at the U.N. Secretariat in New York resulted in the creation of a new Department for Policy Coordination and Sustainable Development, headed by Under-Secretary-General Nitin Desai. Among its vast array of responsibilities, this office provides staff support to the CSD and the IACSD, and serves as a high-level focal point for promoting sustainable development throughout the United Nations (Kimball, 1994, 1993).

By mid-1994, the CSD had met twice—with mixed results. On the positive side, it has provided a forum where governments and nongovernmental participants can share information about successes and failures in implementing the Rio accords. Already, there is quite a bit to discuss. Agenda 21 called on all nations to devise national sustainable development strategies. By May 1994, 103 had created national commissions charged with implementing Agenda 21. Beyond this, at least 36 countries have devised strategies based on their deliberations. China, for instance, has recently published a lengthy national Agenda 21 plan designed to reorient both national policies and international assistance. Encouragingly, there is also a growing movement worldwide to create sustainable cities and communities. The Toronto-based International Council for Local Environmental Initiatives is spearheading a campaign to promote the adoption of local Agenda 21s. Cities already participating include Buga, Colombia; Quito, Ecuador; and Lahti, Finland (Earth Council, Natural Resources Defense Council, and World Resources Institute, 1994; Earth Summit Watch, 1994; UNDP, n.d. b; Gildred and Kelly, 1994; International Council for Local Environmental Initiatives, 1994).

Governments are also increasingly using the CSD to exchange views on difficult and sometimes contentious issues related to sustainable development that cut across traditional sectoral lines. For instance, at the May 1994 session the Commission took up the role of trade in sustainable development as well as the controversial question of changing unsustainable production and consumption patterns. Among the issues on its lengthy agenda for the 1995 session are an evaluation of the adequacy of existing international actions to protect biodiversity, forests, and mountains and to combat desertification and drought (Khor, 1994; "Summary of the Second Session," 1994; UN-NGLS, 1994).

Despite these hopeful signs, the CSD suffers from certain structural defects that impede substantive progress. For one, its mandate is so broad that priorities are often not clear. In addition, the official process for reporting information has not proved altogether satisfactory. The initial suggested format was long and unwieldy, with little concrete guidance on what information is sought. Changes have recently been made to simplify the process. Participation has also been unsatisfactory, with fewer than half the CSD members and only 10 non-CSD members submitting reports for the May 1994 session. Because governments are reporting on their own actions, the documents tend to be long on self-congratulation and short on substantive analysis of remaining challenges (Interaction Council, 1994; "Reporting System," 1994).

To overcome these problems, a high-level panel convened by the Interaction Council (an independent group consisting of former heads of government) recommended that instead of relying on national reports, the CSD should request studies by independent experts. . . .

In addition to creating the CSD, the Rio conference gave a shot in the arm to a newcomer on the international stage—the Global Environment Facility (GEF). Countries created this in 1991 to finance investments in preserving the global commons—specifically international waterways, the atmosphere, and biological diversity. Under the joint management of UNDP, UNEP, and the World Bank, the GEF had as of July 1994 committed $742 million in grants—43 percent for biological diversity preservation, 38 percent for global warming-related initiatives, 16 percent to protect international waters, 2 percent for overarching projects, and 1 percent for projects aimed at heading off ozone depletion. After Rio, GEF was designated as the "interim funding mechanism" for the climate and biodiversity treaties (Global Environment Facility, 1991, 1994b).

In March 1994, after months of arduous negotiations, governments agreed to replenish GEF with $2 billion in new resources to be spent over the next three years. They also agreed to make the fund permanent, and to change the way it is governed. For instance, the GEF secretariat will be more independent from the World Bank than it was during the pilot phase. A new and innovative voting system has been devised for GEF: decisions will require two consecutive majorities—the first through a one-nation, one-vote system similar to that used at the United Nations, and the second by a one-dollar, one-vote system comparable to that of the Bretton Woods institutions. This is intended to make the fund more broadly representative of its members ("Agreement Reached," 1994; GEF, 1994a).

These changes were made in response to questions from various quarters about GEF's performance during the pilot phase. Its close association with the Bank had been a source of concern both to developing countries, who resent the fact that donor countries have disproportionate clout there, and to many NGOs, whose long experience with the Bank has made them skeptical that it is the right institution for the job—particularly given its penchant for secrecy and the difficulty it has working closely with local peoples. An independent evaluation of GEF called for by its member-governments in the course of the replenishment negotiations confirmed that there were reasons to worry. Given the recent changes, however, the parties to the climate and biological diversity conventions are likely to make GEF their permanent funding arm (UNDP, UNEP and World Bank, 1994).

GEF has a much-needed role to play as a provider of what amounts to venture capital for the global environment, but the far more critical task is to reorient all financial flows to developing countries in support of sustainable development. It should ideally help catalyze broader actions by international funding sources and national governments. At the moment, the good done by a small GEF grant is all too often overwhelmed by larger, poorly conceived World Bank projects. For instance, small loans for solar energy in India, though desirable, pale in significance for the global environment next to massive planned investments in coal-fired power plants there that are expected to become one of the single largest sources of carbon emissions during the next decade (World Bank, 1993a; Environmental Defense Fund, 1993).[8]

If the Bank and other donors would develop policies aimed at implementing major environmental conventions such as the climate and biodiversity treaties in their lending programs, it would help avoid such anomalous situations. This would be in keeping with a Bank policy that prevents lending in violation of international treaties. In one small step in this direction, the Bank has initiated a program that will begin to integrate global considerations into some national environmental action plans, country assistance strategies, and other documents. The G7 Summit in 1995 provides an opportunity to push the whole process forward. In addition, governments can promote greater attention to global priorities in multilateral lending through the conventions themselves. Parties to the climate convention, for example, could call for the World Bank to report on the greenhouse gas emissions projected to result from proposed projects (Global Environmental Operations, World Bank, 1994; Rosebrock, 1994; Greenpeace International, 1994; Barratt-Brown, Velasco, and Hajost, 1994).

As the fiftieth anniversary of the U.N. approaches, many ideas are being floated for changes to prepare the world body for the future. Some proposals concern the need to expand membership on the Security Council to make it more broadly representative of today's world. Others focus on the economic and social side of U.N. operations. UNDP, for instance, is advocating an Economic Security Council—a body of 22 members to promote the cause of "sustainable human security" at the highest levels (Crossett, 1994; UNDP, 1994; Childers and Urquhart, 1994: 1).[9]

While these proposals are debated, one other idea merits consideration: the creation of a full-fledged environment agency within the U.N. system. UNEP has contributed a great deal for an organization its size—its limited budget is smaller than that of some private U.S. environmental groups. But it does not enjoy the stature within the U.N. system of a specialized agency. This means it has few operational programs of its own. Though it is charged with coordinating the U.N. response to environmental issues, it has little ability to influence the programs of other agencies with much larger budgets. The fiftieth anniversary of the United Nations is an appropriate time either to upgrade UNEP to specialized agency status or to create a new U.N. environment agency (Benedick, 1991; Khromov, 1994; National Wildlife Federation, 1993; Leonard and Hoffman, 1990).[10]

Some will disagree with this suggestion, citing the need to integrate environmental policymaking throughout the system rather than isolating it in one, marginalized agency. But such integration is equally important at the national level as well, yet few would dispute the need for strong domestic environmental ministries. What is needed in both cases is a watchdog group. . . .

Finally, the time has come for governments to create some form of dedicated funding mechanism to finance investments for the transition to a sustainable society—including environmental expenditures, social initiatives, and peacekeeping costs. Among the possibilities for such a fund are a levy on carbon emissions, on international air travel, or perhaps on international flows of money. To discourage destabilizing currency speculation, Nobel-laureate James Tobin has suggested that a 0.5-percent tax be placed on foreign-exchange transactions. This would raise more than $1.5 trillion annually. But even a far smaller levy would raise sizable funds. A tax of just 0.003 percent of current daily currency transactions would raise $8.4 billion—more than four times the recent replenishment of GEF. The Social Summit would be an opportune time to launch such an initiative (UNDP, 1994; Walker, 1993; Childers with Urquhart, 1994).

Involving People

Even in the best of circumstances, the slow pace of international diplomacy and the rate at which environmental and social problems are growing worse are difficult to reconcile. The best hope for improving the process of global governance lies with people. Just as national policymaking cannot be considered in isolation from public pressure, so international policymaking increasingly must consider an organized and influential international citizenry.

The most familiar role for NGOs and grassroots groups is within national borders. Around the world, there is an encouraging growth in such activities. In addition to this critical work, citizens' groups are also beginning to make their influence felt in international forums. In Rio, the 20,000 concerned citizens and activists who attended from around the world outnumbered official representatives by at least two to one. Similarly, more than 4,000 NGOs participated in the Cairo conference, where they were widely credited with helping to shape the terms of the debate. Some of the organizations represented at these meetings—such as Friends of the Earth, Greenpeace, the International Planned Parenthood Federation, and the World Wide Fund for Nature—are themselves international, meaning they represent global constituencies rather than parochial national interests. Taken together, all this activity adds up to the creation of a bona fide global environmental movement (Salamon, 1994; Fisher, 1993; Hinrichsen, 1992; Randolph, 1994; Clough, 1994).

Working through international coalitions such as the Climate Action Network and the Women's Environment and Development Organization, these groups are a powerful force. Daily newsletters produced by citizens' groups, including *Eco* and the *Earth Negotiations Bulletin*, have become mainstays of the international negotiating process. Widely read by official delegates and NGOs alike during international meetings, they reveal key failures in negotiations and prevent the obscure language of international diplomacy from shielding governments from accountability for their actions.[11]

The participation of the international scientific community also is critical. International panels of scientists convened to study both ozone depletion and climate change played instrumental roles in forging the scientific consensus needed to push these political processes forward. The treaties on these two problems created scientific advisory groups that now meet regularly and offer advice on whether the agreements need to be updated in light of new scientific information.

The interests of the business community can also sometimes be harnessed to positive effect. For instance, U.S. industry came to support strongly the Montreal Protocol because it saw U.S. legislation as inevitable and did not want to be at a competitive disadvantage as a result. The Business Council for Sustainable Development, some 50 chief executives from the world's largest corporations, were active in the lead-up to the Earth Summit. Though the Council opposed language in Agenda 21 that would have advocated developing standards to regulate multinational corporations, it argued persuasively in its report *Changing Course* that sound environmental policies and sound business practices go hand in hand. More recently, the U.S.-based Business Council for a Sustainable Energy Future—a coalition of energy efficiency, renewable energy, and natural gas companies that favor taking action to avert global warming—has begun to participate in international climate negotiations, where they counterbalance the lobbying efforts of oil and coal companies (Benedick, 1991; Greenpeace International, 1992; Zarocostas, 1992; Schmidheiny with the Business Council for Sustainable Development, 1992; "Constructive Industry," 1994).

Despite the impressive contributions they make, citizens' groups working at the global level face formidable obstacles. International law has traditionally functioned as a compact among nations, with no provisions for public participation comparable to those that are virtually taken for granted at the national level in democracies around the world. There is nothing yet resembling an elected parliament in the United Nations or any of its agencies. Though the U.N. has begun to experiment with occasional public hearings on topics of special concern, these continue to be rare events. No formal provisions are made for public review and comment on international treaties, nor is there a mechanism for bringing citizen suits at the World Court. International negotiations are often closed to public participation, and access to documents of critical interest to the public is generally highly restricted (Wirth, 1992; Shepard, 1994; Leonard and Hoffman, 1990).

Agenda 21 encourages the democratization of international lawmaking by devoting a lengthy section to the important role of "major groups" (including citizens' groups, labor unions, farmers, women, business interests, and others) and by endorsing the need to make information freely and widely available. In an important precedent, the Commission on Sustainable Development has based its rules for NGO participation on the liberal regulations that were in effect for the Rio conference. As a result, more than 500 groups are accredited to observe CSD deliberations and make selective interventions. An international NGO Steering Committee has recently been created to help promote collaboration among these groups from diverse corners of the globe, and to facilitate interaction with the secretariat of the CSD and with governments (UN, 1992; Sessions, 1993; Ayoub, 1994; NGO Steering Committee, 1994).

One interesting NGO initiative at the CSD is Earth Summit Watch, a project of the U.S.-based Natural Resources Defense Council and CAPE 21 (a coalition of U.S. environmental groups). This effort has led to two reports based on in-depth surveys of actions taken to put Agenda 21 and other Rio initiatives into practice around the world. *Four in '94*, prepared for the 1994 CSD session, asked governments to list concrete actions taken in four of the portions of the agenda up for review that year—health, human settlements, fresh water, and toxic chemicals and hazardous waste. Among the findings: 34 of 67 countries surveyed had taken steps to reduce lead exposure by moving toward lead-free gasoline and through other means; 45 reported some initiatives to promote clean water; 61 of the 178 countries at Rio have ratified the Basel convention on trade in hazardous wastes, and 74 have imposed national bans on hazardous waste imports; yet only 10 of 67 countries surveyed have taken steps to protect rivers. For the time being, most countries are simply reporting on actions they were planning to take anyway. But over time, the "peer pressure" process may induce them to move forward on new policies. A *Five in '95* report is planned for this year (Earth Summit Watch, 1993, 1994).

Another way in which NGOs participate in the Rio follow-up process is through their participation in some national sustainable development commissions. These bodies take different forms in different countries. Some are composed only of government representatives; others are "multistakeholder" forums composed of a range of interested parties, including government, NGOs, and the business sector. In 1987, Round Tables on the Environment and the Economy in Canada pioneered the concept of bringing diverse parties to the table. This has since been widely replicated, including the Philippine Council on Sustainable Development, and by the President's Council on Sustainable Development in the United States (Earth Summit Watch, 1994; Earth Council, NRDC, and World Resources Institute, 1994).

The U.N. Economic and Social Council is currently reviewing the rules for the participation of citizens' groups in the U.N. system at large. Some of those involved in the debate advocate making it easier for groups to be involved, taking the Rio experience as their guide. Others resist this view, worrying about the system being overwhelmed by sheer numbers, or about whom the citizens' groups are accountable to. The outcome of these deliberations remains to be seen, but it seems likely that the UNCED process has set a new standard for participation that the U.N. system will have difficulty backing away from (Ni with Burns, 1994; The Stanley Foundation, 1994).

The Bretton Woods institutions pose the greatest challenge when it comes to openness and accountability. To an even greater extent than at the U.N. itself, information and documents at these institutions are a tightly guarded secret, and negotiations between governments are completely closed to observers, with no NGO newsletters offering blow-by-blow accounts of who says what to whom.

GATT has been subject to particularly strong criticism for its secretive procedures. When a national law is challenged as a trade barrier under GATT, the case is heard behind closed doors by a panel of professors and bureaucrats steeped in the intricacies of world trade law, but not in the needs of the planet. Legal briefs and other critical information are generally unavailable to the public, and there is no opportunity for citizens' groups to testify or make submissions. Governments are currently discussing rules on public participation for the Trade and Environment Committee of GATT's successor, the World Trade Organization. Preliminary reports suggest that the fight for public access will be a long and hard-fought battle (Charnovitz, 1994; Zaracostas, 1994).

Despite a checkered history regarding openness, the World Bank recently instituted two new policies that others would do well to emulate. Under a new information policy, more Bank documents will be publicly available than before, and an information center has been established to disseminate them. The second change—the creation of an independent inspection panel—will provide an impartial forum where board members or private citizens can raise complaints about projects that violate the Bank's own policies, rules, and procedures. Though both initiatives were watered down in the negotiating process, they nonetheless represent sizable chinks in the World Bank's armor. It will be up to the concerned public to test the limits of these new policies and to press for them to be strengthened—and replicated elsewhere (World Bank, 1994c, 1993a; Hunter and Udall, 1994; Bramble, 1993).

Besides access to information, the public needs to become a fuller partner in the development process itself. All too often, "development" has served the purposes of a country's elite, but not its poorest members. A growing body of evidence suggests that for a project to succeed, its planning process must include the people it is supposed to benefit. In other words, aid should be demand-driven rather than imposed from above. Several bilateral aid agencies have developed new ways of fostering widespread participation in the development planning process, and the World Bank has also recently come up with a new strategy along these lines. The challenge, as always, will be moving from words to action (Operations Evaluation Department, 1993; Bhatnagar and Williams, 1992; Alexander, 1994; World Bank, 1994b; Griesgraber, 1994).[12]

Securing the Future

Just over 25 years ago, photographs of the earth taken from space by Neil Armstrong helped launch the modern environmental movement, indelibly impressing on all who saw them that although the earth is crisscrossed by political boundaries, it is united by ecological systems. Today, we know the condition of the earth and of those who live on it to be more fragile than ever.

Though the planet's health has deteriorated markedly in the last 25 years, the same period has witnessed the rise of an impressive number of international initiatives designed to stabilize ecological support systems. Some of the agreements amounted to just words, but many have led to measurable actions, proving that when the conditions are ripe for it, international collaboration can work. The urgent task now facing the world community is to accelerate dramatically the international political response to the challenge of ecological deterioration and social disintegration before they become irreversible. . . .

Surveys indicate that most people would support such changes: a recent groundbreaking Gallup Survey found that public concern about environmental problems is uniformly high around the world—dispelling the myth that only rich countries can afford to care about these issues. In the Philippines, 94 percent of those polled said they cared about environmental problems a "great deal" or a "fair amount"; in Nigeria, 87 percent responded in this way, as did 85 percent of those questioned in the United States and 66 percent of people in Japan. Interestingly, the survey found little inclination toward global fingerpointing. When asked whether rich or poor countries were more responsible for global environmental harm, everyone accepted some share of the blame. Support for international cooperation to solve shared problems was also high: majorities in both industrial and developing countries favor establishing an international agency with a mandate for global environmental protection (Dunlop, Gallup, Jr. and Gallup, 1993).

Yet despite public support for far-reaching changes, the international response to the interlinked threat of ecological collapse and social disintegration remains seriously inadequate. Fifty years ago, with large parts of Europe and Asia in ruins in the wake of World War II, the world community pulled together with an impressive period of institution-building that set the tone for the next half-century. The time has come for a similar burst of innovation to forge the new global partnership that will enable the world to confront the daunting challenges that await it in the next millennium.

If the changes called for in this chapter are made, and if the power of public commitment to sustainable development is unleashed, we can head off global ecological collapse and the social disintegration that would be sure to accompany it. But if complacency reigns and international forums generate lots of talk and paper but little action, the future does not look bright. The choice is ours to make.

Notes

1. United Nations Framework Convention on Climate Change and Convention on Biological Diversity included in Guruswamy, Palmer and Weston, 1994.

2. Call for a global partnership is in Article 7 of the Rio Declaration on Environment and Development, included in Guruswamy, Palmer, and Weston, 1994.

3. Figure 27.1 based on U.N. Environment Programme (UNEP), 1993; and Labelle, 1994. Figure of 800 from Weiss, Szasz, and Magraw, 1992. "Climate Change Treaty Comes Into Force," 1994; Goodman, 1993. Information Program on Sustainable Development, 1994.

4. Montreal Protocol and subsequent amendments from Guruswamy, Palmer, and Weston, 1994; UNEP, 1994.

5. As of August 30, 1994, 140 countries had ratified the Montreal Protocol, from Smirnov, 1994. Figure 27.2 from Ryan, based on data from Prather and McFarland; UNEP, World Meteorological Organization, U.S. National Aeronautics and Space Administration, and National Oceanic and Atmospheric Administration, 1994; "Synthesis of the Reports of the Ozone Scientific Assessment Panel . . . ", 1991.

6. UNEP estimate from Information Program on Sustainable Development (UNEP, 1993).

7. The countries are Bangladesh, Colombia, Egypt, Indonesia, Kenya, Mexico, Morocco, Thailand, Tunisia, and Zimbabwe (Crossette, 1994).

8. Indian renewables project described in World Bank, 1993b.

9. For a number of recommendations on needed reforms, see Childers with Urquhart, 1994.

10. On the achievements of UNEP, see, for instance, Benedick, 1991; budgets from Khromov, 1994, and from National Wildlife Federation, 1993.

11. *Eco* is produced regularly by NGOs at major international negotiations. The *Earth Negotiations Bulletin* is published by the International Institute for Sustainable Development of Winnipeg, Manitoba.

12. For a discussion of the GATT dispute resolution procedure, see Charnovitz, 1994, and Zarocostas, 1994.

References

"Africa's Elephants Could Soon Be Under the Gun Again." 1992. *Christian Science Monitor*. February 2.

"Agreement Reached on Funding GEF; Program to Receive More than $2 Billion." 1994. *International Environment Reporter*. March 23.

Alexander, Nancy. 1994. *Bread for the World Institute*. Private communication. October 20.

Ayoub, Ferita (Chief of NGO Section). 1994. Private communication. Department of Policy Coordination and Sustainable Development. New York: United Nations. August 24.

Barratt-Brown, Liz, Kando Velasco, and Scott Hajost. 1994. "Financial Reform and the Climate Convention," *Eco* (NGO Newsletter at the Intergovernmental Negotiating Committee). September 2.

Benedick, Richard Elliot. 1991. *Ozone Diplomacy*. Cambridge, Mass.: Harvard University Press.

Bhatnager, Bhuvan, and Aubrey C. Williams, eds. 1992. *Participatory Development and the World Bank: Potential Directions for Change*. Washington, D.C.: World Bank Discussion Papers.

Bongaarts, John. 1994. "Population Policy Options in the Developing World." *Science*, February 11.

Bramble, Barbara. 1994. "CSD Needs a Better Structure." *Newsletter of the Citizens Network for Sustainable Development*. Bolinas, Calif. Summer.

———. 1993. "World Bank Reforms: The Beginnings of Accountability." *Newsletter of the Citizens Network for Sustainable Development*. Bolinas, Calif. October/November.

Broad, Robin and John Cavanagh. 1993. "Beyond the Myths of Rio: A New American Agenda for the Environment," *World Policy Journal*. Spring.

Brown, Lester R., Hal Kane, and David Malin Roodman. 1994. *Vital Signs 1994*. New York: W.W. Norton & Company.

Browning, D. C. 1989. *Dictionary of Quotations and Proverbs*. London: Cathay Books.

Canute, James. 1994. "Oceans Set to Yield Up Their Treasures." *Financial Times*. July 7.

CAPE 21/Citizens Network for Sustainable Development. 1994. Procedural recommendations to Klaus Töpfer, Chairman of the Commission on Sustainable Development. October.

Charnovitz, Steve. 1994. "Dolphins and Tuna: An Analysis of the Second GATT Panel Report." *Environmental Law Reporter*. October.

Childers, Erskine, with Brian Urquhart. 1994. "Renewing the United Nations System." Development Dialogue (Daj Hammarskjöld Foundation/Ford Foundation).

Climate Action Network. 1994. *Independent NGO Evaluations of National Plans for Climate Change Mitigation*. Brussels.

"Climate Change Treaty Comes Into Force." 1994. *International Environment Reporter*. March 23.

Clough, Michael. 1994. "Grass-Roots Policymaking: Say Good-Bye to the 'Wise Men'." *Foreign Affairs*. January/February.

Colchester, Nicholas. 1994. "Goodbye, Nation-State. Hello . . . What?" *New York Times*. July.

Commission on Global Governance. 1994. "Our Global Neighbourhood: Commission Report Nears Completion," *Update*. Geneva. September.

"Constructive Industry Hits INC 10." 1994. *ECO*. Climate Negotiations, Geneva. August 26.

Cooper, Helene. 1994. "Sub-Saharan Africa is Seen as Big Loser in GATT's New World Trade Accord." *Wall Street Journal*. August 15.

Cowell, Alan. 1994. "The Hidden Population Issue: Money." *New York Times*. September 12.

Crossette, Barbara. 1994. "A Third-World Effort on Family Planning." *New York Times*. September 7.

Cruz, Wilfredo and Robert Repetto. 1992. *The Environmental Effects of Stabilization and Structural Adjustment Programs: The Philippines Case*. Washington, D.C.: World Resources Institute.

Cushman, John H. 1994. "Clinton Wants to Strengthen Global Pact on Air Pollution." *New York Times*. August 16.

"Decision on Trade and Environment." 1994. General Agreement on Tariffs and Trade. Marrakesh, Morocco. April 15.

"Draft Platform for Action." Undated. Fourth World Conference on Women.

Dunlop, Riley E., George H. Gallup, Jr., and Alec M. Gallup. 1993. "Of Global Concern: Results of the Health of the Planet Survey." *Environment*. November.

Durning, Alan Thein. 1972. *Guardians of the Land: Indigenous Peoples and the Health of the Earth*. Worldwatch Paper 112. Washington, D.C.: Worldwatch Institute. December.

Earth Council, Natural Resources Defense Council (NRDC), and World Resources Institute. 1994. "Directory of National Commissions on Sustainable Development." Washington, D.C. May.

Earth Summit Watch. 1994. *Four in '94. Assessing National Actions to Implement Agenda 21: A Country-by-Country Report*. Washington, D.C.

———. 1993. *One Year After Rio: Special First Edition*. New York: NRDC. June.

Environmental Defense Fund. 1993. "Memorandum: IBRD, NTPC Loan Global Warming Implications." Washington, D.C.: EDF, June.

Esteva, Gustavo. 1994. "Mexican Indians Say No to Development." *People-Centered Development Forum*. New York. May 20.

Esty, Daniel C. 1993. "GATTing the Greens." *Foreign Affairs*. November/December.

———. 1994. "The Case for a Global Environmental Organization," in Peter B. Kenen, ed., *Managing the World Economy: Fifty Years After Bretton Woods*. Washington, D.C.: Institute for International Economics.

"EU Ratifies Climate Convention Without Carbon/Energy Tax." 1993. *Energy, Economics, and Climate Change*. December.

Evans, Robert. 1994. "UN Conference Says New Cuts in Emissions are Needed." *Journal of Commerce*. February 22.

"*50.*" The Newsletter of the 50th Anniversary of the United Nations. 1994. New York, Summer.

Fisher, Julie. 1993. *The Road from Rio: Sustainable Development and the Nongovernmental Movement in the Third World*. Westport, Conn.: Praeger.

Fowler, Rebecca. 1994. "Law of the Sea: An Odyssey to U.S. Acceptance," *Washington Post*. July 29.

French, Hilary F. 1993. "GATT: Global Menace or Potential Ally?" *World Watch*. September/October.

———. 1994a. "Making Environmental Treaties Work." *Scientific American*. December.

———. 1994b. "Rebuilding the World Bank," in Lester R. Brown et al., *State of the World 1994*. New York: W.W. Norton & Company.

Gildred, Kathleen and Sheila Kelly, Citizens Network for Sustainable Development. 1994. "Sustainable Communities Working Group Paper." Unpublished. July 21.

Global Environment Facility (GEF). 1991. Brochure. Washington, D.C. December.

———. 1994a. "Instrument for the Establishment of the Restructured Global Environment Facility." *Report of the GEF Participants Meeting*. Geneva, Switzerland. March 14–16.

———. 1994b. "Quarterly Operational Report." Washington, D.C. August.

Global Environment Operations, World Bank. 1994. "Business Plan. Fiscal Year 1995." Washington, D.C.

Goodman, Anthony. 1993. "UN's Law of the Sea to Take Effect Next Year." *Journal of Commerce*, December 8.

Gosovic, Branislav. 1992. *The Quest for World Environmental Cooperation*. London and New York: Routledge.

Greenpeace International. 1994. "Lending for the Climate: MDBs and the Climate Convention." Prepared for the 10th Session of the *Intergovernmental Negotiating Committee for a Framework Convention on Climate Change*. Geneva, Switzerland. August 22–September 2.

———. 1992. *Beyond UNCED*. Amsterdam.

Griesgraber, Jo Marie, ed. 1994. *Rethinking Bretton Woods: Toward Equitable, Sustainable, and Participatory Development*. NGO Addendum. Washington, D.C.: Center of Concern.

Guruswamy, Lakshman D., Sir Geoffrey W. R. Palmer and Burns H. Weston. 1994. *International Environmental Law and World Order* (A Problem-Oriented Coursebook). Supplement of Basic Documents. St. Paul, Minn.: West Publishing Co.

Hinrichsen, Don. 1992. "The Earth Summit." *The Amicus Journal*. Winter.

Hunter, David and Lori Udall. 1994. "The World Bank's New Inspection Panel: Will It Increase the Bank's Accountability?" Center for International Environmental Law, Brief No. 1, Washington, D.C. April.

"IEA Reviews Energy Policies in Germany, UK, and Denmark." 1994. *Energy, Economics, and Climate Change*, August.

Information Program on Sustainable Development. 1994. "Legal Agreement to Curb Desertification is Concluded." Press Release. New York: United Nations. July.

Interaction Council. 1994. Report on the Conclusions and Recommendations by a High-Level Group on "The Future Role of the Global Multilateral Organizations." The Hague, Netherlands. May 7–8.

Intergovernmental Panel on Climate Change (IPCC). 1994. "Draft Summary for Policymakers of the 1994 Working Group I Report on Radiative Forcing of Climate Change." Executive Summary. Maastricht, The Netherlands. September 15.

International Council for Local Environmental Initiatives. 1994. "Local Agenda 21 Network News." Toronto. June.

IPCC. 1990. *Climate Change: The IPCC Scientific Assessment*. New York: Cambridge University Press.

Jacobson, Jodi L. 1992. *Gender Bias: Roadblock to Sustainable Development*, Worldwatch Paper 110. Washington, D.C.: Worldwatch Institute. September.

"Japan Will Substantially Overshoot Year 2000 CO_2 Emissions Target, Report Says." 1994. *International Environment Reporter*. August 10.

Joyce, James Avery. 1980. *World Labor Rights and Their Protection*. London: Croom Helm.

Khor, Martin. 1994. "CSD Still Alive, But Not Yet Kicking Into Action." *Third World Economics*. June 1–15.

Khromov, Sergei. 1994. Private communication. UNEP, Nairobi. October 31.

Kimball, Lee A. 1994. "International Institutional Developments" in *Yearbook of International Law 1993*. Oxford: Oxford University Press.

———. 1993. "International Institutional Developments: The U.N. Conference on Environment and Development," *Yearbook of International Law 1992*. Boston/Dordrecht: Graham & Trotman/Martinus Nijhoff.

Korten, David C. 1991–92. "Sustainable Development." *World Policy Journal*. Winter.

Labelle, Mark. 1994. Treaty Office, United Nations. Private communication. New York. September 27, October 17.

"Lack of Concrete Action at Talks Decried by NGOs but Backed by Industry as Not Needed," *International Environment Reporter.* September 7, 1994.

Lanou, Steven M. 1994. "National Biodiversity Planning Activities: Overview." World Resources Institute. Unpublished matrix. Washington, D.C. June 7.

Leonard, Pamela and Walter Hoffman. 1990. *Effective Global Environmental Protection: World Federalist Proposals to Strengthen the Role of the United Nations.* Washington, D.C.: World Federalist Association.

Levy, Marc. 1993. "European Acid Rain: The Power of Tote-Board Diplomacy." *Institutions for the Earth: Sources of Effective International Environmental Protection.* Cambridge, Mass.: MIT Press.

Nash, Nathaniel C. 1994. "Latin Economic Speedup Leaves Poor in the Dust." *New York Times.* September 7.

National Wildlife Federation. 1993. *1993 Annual Report.* Washington, D.C.

"The NGO Steering Committee to the Commission on Sustainable Development." 1994. Memorandum. New York. June 5.

Ni, Yolanda Kakabadse with Sarah Burns. 1994. "Movers and Shapers: NGOs in International Affairs." *International Perspectives on Sustainability.* Washington, D.C.: World Resources Institute. May.

Office of Public Information. "Charter of the United Nations and Statute of the International Court of Justice." New York: United Nations.

Operations Evaluation Department. 1993. *Evaluation Results for 1991.* Washington, D.C.: World Bank.

Organization for Economic Cooperation and Development (OECD). 1994. International Energy Agency. *Climate Change Policy Initiatives—1994 Update, Vol. 1, OECD Countries.* Paris.

———. 1993. "Assessing the Effects of the Uruguay Round." *Trade Policy Issues,* No. 2. Paris.

"Parties to Biodiversity Treaty to Discuss Possible Protocol on Biotechnology Safety." 1994. *International Environment Reporter.* July 13.

Pitt, David E. 1994. "Biological Pact Passes Into Law." *New York Times.* January 2.

Porter, Gareth. 1994. "Multilateral Agreement on Minimum Standards for Manufacturing and Processing Industries." Environmental and Energy Study Institute. Washington, D.C. July.

Porter, Gareth and Janet Welsh Brown. 1991. *Global Environmental Politics.* Boulder, Colo.: Westview Press.

Prather, Michael and Mack McFarland, E.I. Du Pont de Nemours.

Randolph, Kate. 1994. NGO Planning Committee for ICPD. Private Communication. October 18.

Reding, Andrew. 1994. "Chiapas is Mexico: The Imperative of Political Reform." *World Policy Journal.* Spring.

Reed, David, ed. 1992. *Structural Adjustment and the Environment.* Boulder, Colo.: Westview Press.

Reid, Walter. 1992. World Resources Institute, Hearings on Convention on Biological Diversity. Committee on Foreign Relations, U.S. Senate. Washington, D.C. April 12.

———. et al., ed. 1993. *Biodiversity Prospecting: Using Genetic Resources for Sustainable Development.* Washington, D.C.: World Resources Institute.

Rensberger, Boyce. 1994. "Cairo Conference Ends With Broad Consensus for Plan to Curb Growth." *Washington Post.* September 14.

"Reporting System on Environmental Progress Needs Simplification, Groups Tell CSD Session." 1994. *International Environment Reporter.* June 1.

Rosebrock, Jens. 1994. Private communication. World Bank: Washington, D.C. October 20.

Ryan, Megan. 1994. "CFC Production Continues to Drop." in Brown, Kane, and Roodman, 1994.

Salamon, Lester M. 1994. "The Rise of the Nonprofit Sector." *Foreign Affairs.* July/August.

Sand, Peter H. 1991. "International Cooperation: The Environmental Experience," in Jessica Tuchman Mathews, ed. 1991. *Preserving the Global Environment: The Challenge of Shared Leadership.* New York: W.W. Norton & Company.

Sanford, Jonathan E. 1993. "African Debt: Recent Initiatives and Policy Options for Multilateral Bank Debt." Washington, D.C.: Congressional Research Service (CRS), U.S. Library of Congress. July 9.

Schmidheiny, Stephan with the Business Council for Sustainable Development. 1992. *Changing Course.* Cambridge, Mass.: The MIT Press.

Sessions, Kathryn G. 1992. "Institutionalizing the Earth Summit." UNA-USA Occasional Paper, Washington, D.C.: United Nations Association of the United States of America (UNA- USA). October.

————. 1993. "Options for NGO Participation in the Commission on Sustainable Development." UNA-USA Background Paper. Washington, D.C.: UNA-USA. May.

Shepard, Daniel J. 1994. "UN Seeks Experts' Testimony in Series of Extraordinary Hearings on Development." *Earth Times.* June 15.

"Small Island Nations Protocol Proposes 20 Percent CO_2 Cut for Developed Nations." 1994. *International Environment Reporter.* October 5.

Smirnov, Valery. 1994. *Multilateral Fund for the Implementation of the Montreal Protocol.* Private communication. Montreal, Canada. October 6.

The Stanley Foundation. 1994. "The UN System and NGOs: New Relationships for a New Era?" *Report of the Twenty-Fifth United Nations Issues Conference.* Harriman, N.Y. February 18–20.

"Summary of the Fifth Session of the INC for the Elaboration of an International Convention to Combat Desertification 6–17 June 1994." 1994. *Earth Negotiations Bulletin.* June 20.

"Summary of the Second Session of the Commission on Sustainable Development 16–27 May 1994." 1994. *Earth Negotiations Bulletin.* May 30.

"Summary of the Third Session of the UN Conference on Straddling Fish Stocks and Highly Migratory Fish Stocks 15–26 August 1994." 1994. *Earth Negotiations Bulletin.* August 29.

"Summit Communique." 1994. Naples, Italy. July 9.

"Synthesis of the Reports of the Ozone Scientific Assessment Panel, Environmental Effects Assessment Panel, Technology and Economic Assessment Panel." 1991. Prepared by the Assessment Chairs for the Parties to the Montreal Protocol. November.

Thrupp, Lori Ann. 1994. "Challenges in Latin America's Recent Agroexport Boom." *Issues in Development.* Washington D.C.: World Resources Institute. February.

United Nations. 1992. *Agenda 21: The United Nations Program of Action From Rio.* New York: U.N. Publications.

————. 1983. *The Law of the Sea: United Nations Convention on the Law of the Sea.* New York: United Nations.

United Nations Development Programme (UNDP). 1994. *Human Development Report 1994*. New York: Oxford University Press.

————. 1991. *Human Development Report 1991*. New York: Oxford University Press.

————. 1993. "Heading for Change: UNDP 1993 Annual Report." New York, undated.

————. 1993. *Implementing the World Bank's Strategy to Reduce Poverty: Progress and Challenges*. Washington, D.C.

————. Undated a. "Capacity 21: Management Report on the First Year of Operation." New York.

————. Undated b. "Formulating and Implementing China's Agenda 21," Capacity 21 Program information sheet.

UNDP, UNEP, and World Bank. 1994. *Global Environment Facility: Independent Evaluation of the Pilot Phase*. Washington, D.C.: World Bank.

UNDP, UNFPA, and UNICEF. Undated. "The 20/20 Initiative: Achieving Universal Access to Basic Social Services for Sustainable Human Development." New York.

U.N. Environment Programme (UNEP). 1993. *Register of International Treaties and Other Agreements in the Field of the Environment 1993*. Nairobi: UNEP.

UNEP. 1994. "Copenhagen Amendment on Ozone Layer to Enter Into Force." Press Release. Nairobi, March 22.

UNEP, World Meteorological Organization, U.S. National Aeronautics and Space Administration, and National Oceanic and Atmospheric Administration. 1994. "Scientific Assessment of Ozone Depletion: 1994." Executive Summary. Washington, D.C. August 19.

U.N. Food and Agriculture Organization (FAO). 1993. *Fishery Statistics: Catches and Landings* (Rome: various years), and from FAO, Rome. Private communications. December 20.

U.N. General Assembly. 1994. "Programme of Action of the United Nations International Conference on Population and Development" (draft), New York. September 19.

United Nations Non-Governmental Liaison Service (UN-NGLS). 1994. *E & D File*, Briefings on UNCED follow-up. June.

"United Nations World Summit for Social Development." 1994. Fact Sheet. New York. May.

U.S. Climate Action Network. 1994. Letter to the Hon. Timothy E. Wirth, U.S. Undersecretary of State for Global Affairs. July 28.

U.S. General Accounting Office. 1992. *International Environment: International Agreements Are Not Well Monitored*. Washington D.C.

Walker, Martin. 1993. "Global Taxation: Paying for Peace." *World Policy Journal*. Summer.

Weber, Peter. 1993. *Abandoned Seas: Reversing the Decline of the Oceans*. Worldwatch Paper 116. Washington, D.C.: Worldwatch Institute. November.

Weiss, Edith Brown, Paul Szasz, and Daniel Magraw. 1992. *International Environment Law: Basic Instruments and References*. Transnational Publishers, Inc.

Wirth, David A. 1992. "A Matchmaker's Challenge: Marrying International Law and American Environmental Law." *Virginia Journal of International Law*. Winter.

Wirth, the Hon.Timothy E. 1994. U.S. Undersecretary of State for Global Affairs. "Next Steps on International Climate Policy." Speech to *Next*

Steps on Climate Change: A Public Consultation. Washington, D.C.: U.S. Department of State. August 3.

World Bank. 1994a. *Implementing the World Bank Strategy to Reduce Poverty: The Progress and Challenge.* Washington, D.C.: World Bank.

———. 1994b. *Making Development Sustainable: The World Bank Group and the Environment, Fiscal 1994 Report.* Washington, D.C.

———. 1994c. "The World Bank Policy on Disclosure of Information." Washington, D.C.: World Bank. March.

———. 1993a. "Operations Inspection Function: Objectives, Mandate and Operating Procedures for an Independent Inspection Panel."

———. 1993b. *The World Bank and the Environment, Fiscal 1993 Report.* Washinton, D.C.: World Bank.

"The World Bank and Participation." 1994. Report to the Board of the World Bank. August 25.

World Resources Institute, World Conservation Union, and UNEP. 1992. "Global Biodiversity Strategy: Policy-makers' Guide." Washington, D.C.

World Resources Institute. 1994. *World Resources 1994–95.* New York: Oxford University Press.

Zarocostas, John. 1992. "Earth Summit Nations at Odds Over Issue of Multinationals." *Journal of Commerce.* April 6.

———. 1994. "Environmental Proposal for WTO Met Coolly." *Journal of Commerce.* September 19.

28

THE FUTURE OF THE GLOBAL POLITICAL ECONOMY

Barry B. Hughes

Barry Hughes concludes this volume with the argument that the evidence seems to suggest that international political economy is moving in the direction anticipated by (neo)liberal theory. Hughes reviews the most recent contributions to the three dominant paradigms and concludes that the technology and knowledge revolution will shape the broad parameters of international political economy for the foreseeable future. He contends that the knowledge revolution will affect all facets of social, economic, and political organization. He also notes that the growing cross-national interconnectedness of interests and the intrusion of ideas from abroad challenge the state-centric system. Like Lester Thurow, Hughes asserts that the European Union will likely provide global leadership, although the Triad will lead cooperatively and collaboratively through the Organization for Economic Cooperation and Development. The great challenge to the neoliberal vision is to balance individual and collective needs and interests, particularly regarding distributional and ecological issues.

Cicero reportedly suggested to the Roman Senate that "no soothsayer should be able to look at another soothsayer without laughing." Although modern soothsayers seldom rely on reading entrails, unfortunately many in society still search for their fates in the stars. The art and credibility of the futurist have little advanced.

Admitting this fact provides a solid basis for great modesty. Speculation about the future proceeds here in two steps. First, I turn once again to the stars, in this instance to those authors who have previously sought to divine the future of the global political economy. Specifically, I seek to identify the primary questions they have raised and the range of answers provided. Second, I expose some admittedly very uncertain groping with the same questions.

Key Questions: The Agent-System Question

Although it is sometimes asked and answered implicitly, the most basic question of political-economic analysis is, What are the key political-economic actors, and in what systems do they interact? At least a tentative answer to the "agent-system" question logically precedes investigation of how the system is structured or the rules by which the actors interact.

Robert Gilpin (1975) provided an early but influential answer to the agent-system question in international relations. He labeled his "Three Models of the Future" the sovereignty-at-bay model, the dependencia model, and the mercantilist model, borrowing the first two titles from Raymond Vernon (1971) and from Latin American authors. To only somewhat oversimplify, the three models, respectively, identified agents and systems as multinational corporations interacting in a global market system, classes interacting in a global class system, and states interacting in a global state system. Although Gilpin seriously considered the arguments that control of trade and financial flows by corporations might undercut the autonomy of states or that the structuring of economic and political relationships by classes might dictate the patterns of interstate relations, he concluded that for the foreseeable future states will use their overwhelming power to pursue domestically defined agendas, to organize the global economy around them, and to define the structure and behavior of any transnational actors—such as international organizations—that might seek to establish more independent paths.

A decade later, K. J. Holsti (1985) concluded that there were only three serious contenders for the status of separate paradigms in the study of international relations: the classical state-centric one, world or global society models, and dependency–world capitalist-system theories. Nearly twenty years after Gilpin's article, in a comprehensive review of the theories and perspectives of political economy, James Caporaso (1993: 451) argued that three metaphors organize the approaches to the field: "the market, the polity, and class processes." Given such consistency of agent-system definition over time, it should not surprise us that the theoretical section of this volume similarly divides selections into those that focus on mercantilism and nationalism, those that look at liberalism and interdependence, and once again those that discuss dependency and world systems theory.

Some readers will have noticed, however, that in contrast to the relative uniformity of characterization by different authors of the state-centric and class-centric models, the multinational corporation (MNC), global society, market, and liberal labels appear less clearly cotermi-nous. In fact, Caporaso, after identifying the three metaphors, pro-ceeded to discuss four major approaches: realist (state-centric), Marxian (class-centric), neoclassical (market-centric), and liberal (with roots "more in domestic than international politics") (1993: 465). Increas-ingly, the "third model" in such typologies is not Gilpin's model of strictly economic actors, such as MNCs interacting in a market, but one of a plurality of political and economic actors interacting in an open and adaptive (or *liberal*) global political-economic system.

The collapse of the former Soviet Union and the end of the Cold War have directed additional attention to the liberal model. After all, it was the Western liberal democracies, with their relatively open economies, that won the Cold War and that now appear, through the continued deepening and widening of the European Union and the maintenance of collaborative spirit throughout the Organization for Economic Cooperation and Development (OECD), to be consolidating their victory.

E. H. Carr (1939) correctly warned an earlier generation that its new-found fascination with an idealistic liberalism would soon run aground on the hard rocks of fascism in a fundamentally state-centric world. In spite of this, Francis Fukuyama (1989) boldly proclaimed both the value of idealist (as opposed to materialist) understandings of his-tory and the culmination of historic change in the triumph of liberal-ism.[1] Fukuyama not only dismissed both fascism and communism as vanquished foes of liberalism but similarly downplayed the contempo-rary challenges of religion and nationalism.

Whereas Fukuyama's article simply asserted the victory of liber-alism as an idea, substantial academic enterprise has elaborated and de-veloped liberalism as an analytical framework for understanding global political economy. Five theoretical traditions cumulatively add dimen-sions of complexity to liberal theory (Caporaso, 1993: 466–467; Keo-hane, 1990: 175–180; Zacher and Matthew, 1995: 120–137):

1. Cognitive liberalism, which places the personal development of the individual at the center of sociopolitical progress in the tradition of the Enlightenment
2. Republican liberalism, which emphasizes the importance of democratic, constitutional institutions and process
3. Commercial liberalism, focused on the interaction of self-interested economic agents (the strand of liberalism that en-compasses Vernon's sovereignty-at-bay model)

4. Sociological liberalism, which stresses group life within and across modern, pluralistic political economies
5. Institutional neoliberalism, which investigates both the origins and the role of formal and informal international institutions

In the footsteps of Immanuel Kant's 1795 essay *Toward Eternal Peace*, many contemporary authors have elaborated the linkages between republican liberalism and peaceful international interaction (see Doyle, 1986 and 1995). Others have investigated the connections between international cooperation and either commercial liberalism (Schumpeter, 1955; Rosecrance, 1986) or sociological liberalism (Keohane and Nye, 1970). Still others have emphasized the linkages between republican and commercial liberalism (Friedman, 1962).

Although it lacks the parsimony and hence the clarity of assumption and proposition that characterize both realism and dependency–world systems theory, liberalism can claim growing theoretical sophistication. The liberal framework identifies a confusing plurality of actors and interactions, but it is fundamentally individual-centric. Empowered modern citizens pursue their interests through a wide range of secondary and tertiary agents, including MNCs, domestic and transnational interest groups (nongovernmental organizations), domestic governments, international organizations, and international regimes. In so doing, citizens seek to create and sustain an environment in which they are simultaneously (1) protected from the predations of others in that environment; (2) supplied with material goods adequate to guarantee not only survival but some comfort; (3) free of substantial coercion, repression, and limits to action; and (4) sufficiently connected to others to allow mutually beneficial interaction. For the most part, a global political economy of peacefully and actively interacting democracies satisfies these demands.

There are, of course, observers less certain than Fukuyama and other liberals that all idealistic challengers to liberalism have lost. Samuel Huntington (1993), for example, presented an alternative argument based on the clash of civilizations. His agent-system model is one of multiple cultures interacting in a world of competing civilizations. The protection of identity is fundamental (even fundamentalist). This interest supplements and interacts with competitive interests in territory and economic well-being in ways Huntington did not really elaborate but that implicitly draw on the zero-sum theories of state-centric political economy.[2]

Some of the popular press has filled the vacuum left by the collapse of East-West tension with complementary speculation about the future of conflict between Christian and Islamic worlds (for instance, the *Economist*'s extended survey in August 1994). In general, however, forecasts of continued and violent nationalistic battles centered on the definition of state boundaries and governance have rung truer for most observers of the post–Cold War world than have forecasts of intercivilizational conflict.

The agent-system question has a corollary, to which discussions of liberalism, clashes of civilizations, and resurgent nationalism draw our attention. Specifically, what are the roles of interests and ideas, and what is their relative importance, in motivating key political-economic agents? The state-centric model has always stressed interests over ideas. Hans Morgenthau, a founding father of realist thought, was adamant that states should not be motivated by ideals. Similarly, dependency and world systems theory stressed the motivation of political-economic actors by their self-interest in economic well-being and political control. Simple commerical liberalism, including the sovereignty-at-bay model, did the same.

In contrast, broader liberalism has long reached for ideas, such as pursuit of individual human rights and freedom of action, as at least a partial explanation of agent behavior (and hence it has been tarred by realists as "idealistic"). Yet attention to ideas can be heavily analytical rather than prescriptive. For example, John Ruggie (1982) and Judith Goldstein (1993) have explained how ideas, what Ruggie labels "embedded liberalism," undergird liberal trading orders and foreign policy orientations. More generally, these and other authors (Goddard, 1993; Goldstein and Keohane, 1993) have directed attention to the importance of ideas and to the complex interaction of ideas and interests in all political-economic paradigms, even in state-centric explanations of international politics.

The System Structure–Dynamics Question

Once scholars have answered the agent-system question to their satisfaction—something that was much easier when the state-centric model dominated the study of international relations—the next logical step is to ask, How do actors interact, and how does system structure both shape that interaction and result from it? Attention to the system structure–dynamics question accounts for much of the post–World War II progress in international political economic theory and analysis.

Structural or neorealists began to move beyond traditional realists (who restricted their attention primarily to individual actors or dyads) by discussing systemic polarity and its imposition of certain behavior patterns, including the classical balance of power, on states (Kaplan, 1957;

Waltz, 1979). When they began to accord economic power distributions as much or even greater significance as military ones, they also moved to systemic theories of hegemonic stability (Keohane, 1980) and transition (Kennedy, 1988). In contrast, dependency and world systems theory began at the level of the systemic structure because the center of their theoretical content lies in explaining how the global system structures the world into core and periphery (Frank, 1969; Wallerstein, 1976). The institutional strain of liberals, as represented by functional and neofunctional theories (Haas, 1964; Mitrany, 1966) and by the regime theory of neoliberal institutionalism (Keohane, 1989; Krasner, 1983) has gradually elaborated a liberal understanding of global structures, both formal and informal.

Two corollary questions can help us organize theoretical perspectives on system structure and dynamics. First, to what degree and in what way do cycles and progressive change characterize the structural dynamics of political-economic systems (Hughes, 1994; Puchala, 1994)? A secondary question is difficult to address in isolation from the first: What is the role of technological change?

Cyclical dynamics are pervasive in state-centric and class-centric perspectives. In structurally oriented state-centric models, the most common cycle is that of the rise and fall of great powers (Gilpin, 1981; Kennedy, 1988). Most analysts look for the driver of the dynamic primarily in the phenomenon of imperial overstretch. Countries expand the geographic scope of the formal or informal empire and of the domestic resources devoted to it until committed resources exceed the benefits obtained from the empire. Payment of the excess costs thereafter drains the strength of the expansive country until some other power surpasses it.

Many variations on this theme attribute more importance to the role of technological-economic leadership (Modelski, 1978; Modelski and Thompson, 1987; Rasler and Thompson, 1989). A technologically innovative state can maintain an economic or a military advantage based on that innovation for many years, but diffusion of technology generally occurs more rapidly than technological innovation. Thus, other states overtake the leader, and some newly dynamic innovator will ultimately surpass it.

Because technological innovation is inherently cumulative, it would be logical to overlay these repetitive cycles of technological leadership on an underlying assumption of progressive technological change. John Herz (1957) did so with respect to military technology and concluded that the modern state is no more viable in the face of nuclear weapons than was the feudal unit in the face of gunpowder. Curiously, however, state-centric theorists remain more likely to speculate on the alternating advantages of offensive and defensive military technology (Quester, 1977) than to analyze the implications of the progressive expansion of explosive power and its delivery capability. Even Herz revisited and, in part, recanted his earlier argument (Herz, 1969).[3]

Although the dependency theory elaboration of a class-centric model suffers from the same inattention to dynamics that classical realism does, world systems theory places front and center a cyclical dynamic of global economic expansion and contraction (Braudel, 1979; Wallerstein, 1976 and 1980). Portrayal of this dynamic can reach back to Marx to build on the growth of social conflict between factor-controlling and factor-dependent classes, in which periodic failures of social adjustment mechanisms result in conflict (or crises) that fundamentally reorganize the system. Cyclical world systems theories can and do, however, also build on the intermittent impact of a wide range of other variables, such as demographic (surges, migrations, plagues), agricultural (new crop technologies, changed climate and therefore production patterns), and technological variables (the industrial revolution).

World system theorists (both class-centric and more eclectic ones) almost invariably portray a cyclical dynamic as an overlay on a secular or progressive trend, one important manifestation of which is the fairly steady historic expansion in the geographic size of the world economy. Immanuel Wallerstein attributes this secular trend in substantial part to technological change, particularly in transportation and communication technologies (1976: 231). Class-centric theories also remain essentially committed to the progressive belief that some ultimate crisis of capitalism will transform the system to socialism.

Liberal theory obviously recognizes the reality of historic cycles in the size of empires or state systems, the wealth of political entities, and the peacefulness of human interaction. Yet the gaze of its theorists tends to look through these cycles and to focus on what it sees as a progressive, albeit at times a glacially slow, trend beneath them. Although its appeal as an explanation of development in Africa or Latin America has waned, a modernization theory arguing that all good things eventually go together (specifically that technological advance, economic growth and transformation, and political-social liberalization reinforce each other) provides at least the implicit base of most liberal thought.

Explicitly optimistic liberals such as Herman Kahn (Kahn, Brown, and Martel, 1976), Alvin Toffler (1980), Julian Simon (1981), and Allan Goodman (1993) commonly put progressive technological advance at the center of their thought. In particular, liberals most often see modern communications and information technologies (informatics) as a critical foundation for the prosperity of economies and the openness (with high levels of interaction) of political-social systems.

Some liberals pay much less attention to technology; they might focus their attention on the linkage of economic transformation and social-political change (Rosecrance, 1986) or solely on secular trends in more strictly social-political variables, such as the spread of democratic institutions around the world or the waning of warfare among great powers (Mueller, 1989). Although these orientations are sometimes derived from the belief that social and political progress can be made in the absence of fundamental technological or economic transformation (Ray, 1989), most liberal theorists at least implicitly root the dynamics of their understandings in technological change.

Liberals obviously engage in debates about this progressively better future with state-centric and class-centric theorists. Yet because of the importance of technological advance in much liberal theory, liberals also often see their fundamental challenge in environmentally pessimistic perspectives. The environmental pessimists (or ecopessimists), such as the Worldwatch Institute's Lester Brown, argue that humanity has by no means risen above its environmental constraints; instead, it has used the technological advance of recent decades (perhaps centuries) to extend the overshoot of environmentally unsustainable agricultural and energy systems. It is only a matter of time, they argue, until environmental limits re-emerge with a vengeance, undercutting economic and political gains that only appear firmly based. Dennis Pirages (1978, 1983) and Nazli Choucri and Robert North (1975) tied ecopessimism back to realism by arguing that "ecoconflict" is both past and future.[4] Interestingly, when Paul Kennedy (1993) moved beyond his thinking on the historical rise and fall of powers to speculate about the future, he drew upon a regionally differentiated environmental pessimism for his ongoing attachment to cycles.

Groping with the Future

This review of perspectives suggests two great dangers in speculating about the future of the global political economy. The first is the danger of joining the ranks of those who have mistakenly and repeatedly argued that we have reached a critical historic juncture—of arguing that the future will be increasingly less constrained by interstate or interclass conflicts or by environmental limitations and will therefore be less subject to cyclical patterns of hope and despair. The second great danger is of underestimating the power of underlying progressive technological advance, economic transformation, and social-political development —of arguing that the future will be very much like the past but with technology that is more destructive of both humans and the environment (Orwell, 1949). Avoiding both dangers is possible only by succumbing to a third: being mealymouthed.

The horn of this dilemma with which I choose to gore myself is that of optimism, some will say wishful thinking. It should be obvious from the wording of the choice that I do not choose to focus on progressive change with the certainty of a Kahn or a Toffler. My choice instead reflects a belief that the weight of evidence, but by no means an overwhelming preponderance of it, rests on the side of optimism.

For a technologically optimistic liberal, the sequence of questions presented in the first half of this chapter is wrong. Identifying the dominant contemporary actors and the system of their interaction risks attributing too much longevity (even permanence) to their dominance. Moving then to investigate their patterns of interaction and, finally, asking about the impact of technological change on those patterns can relegate the real dynamics of change to an afterthought. Instead, we should identify the most important long-term technological trends, consider how they are reshaping the economies of countries and the world, and investigate the ways these technologies and economies are reshaping social and political life.

This bold statement of priorities for forecasting may suggest the mentality of a strict materialist, one who believes that ideas about social and political organization are only the superstructure and that the material world fully defines the social-political possible. In reality, I *do* believe social and political ideas can vary with considerable independence of the underlying technological and economic system. Anthropologists have shown that traditional societies exhibit considerable variation in external aggression in the face of similar environmental conditions. In Greek and Roman history it was possible at times to introduce both liberal economies and democratic forms in world systems at a very low level of per capita economic well-being.

Yet externally peaceful societies in a world of scarcity are interesting in large part because they are anomalous (they are much more common in the richer modern world). Although one could argue that liberal economies and democratic forms build on systemic "top-dog" status, rather than on absolute economic advance, both historically and in the modern world, the reality is that they are also much more common today than ever before (and the democracy is "deeper" among the top dogs; for instance, it is not built on slavery). I must plead guilty to a fundamentally materialistic orientation.

I suggested earlier that individuals seek to create and sustain an environment in which they are simultaneously (1) protected from the predations of others in that environment; (2) supplied with material goods adequate to guarantee not only survival but some comfort; (3) free of substantial coercion, repression, and limits to action; and (4) sufficiently connected to others to allow mutually beneficial interaction. Modern technology provides the capability for some of this, particularly the material goods and the connections.

The Technological Foundation

Knowledge is the ultimate resource. The knowledge base of human beings is not only expanding, it is exploding. Although we are positioned early in the information age, we have clearly entered it. In the United States that emerged from the Revolutionary War, 80 percent of the population needed to farm to supply the food needs of the total population. Now only 3 percent need to work the land in a country that is a substantial net exporter of food. After World War II, nearly 40 percent of U.S. workers labored in industry; in 1993 20 percent produced enough to have made the United States the world's largest exporter of manufactured goods. The remaining workforce labors in service industries, increasingly in the "quatenary" economy, the knowledge or information sector. Structural transformation continues around the world at such a pace that there is less and less concern with the physical ability to provide adequate supplies of goods to global populations—rather, there is almost universal concern with providing sufficient employment so purchasing power can be distributed through the employment market rather than by way of governmental redistribution.

Driving the information revolution are technologies of information development, storage, and communication. Innovations in computers and telecommunications (together, informatics) continue to advance at exponential rates. It may sound like science fiction, but it also seems perfectly sensible to forecast that in the next century the continued advance will produce a future in which nearly every human can (1) possess, at relatively modest cost, computing power well beyond the supercomputers of today, (2) access volumes of information that exceed the capacities of most or all contemporary libraries, (3) apply artificial intelligence algorithms to the processing of that information, and (4) instantaneously communicate with any other human.[5]

Humanity will need to translate this incredible information revolution into greater freedom from disease, renewable energy for its transportation and goods-producing systems, adequate food supplies for all parts of the globe, and a sustainable relationship with its environment. None of these efforts will be easy, but it appears reasonable to forecast that humans will make progress on each front.

1. AIDS has reminded us that plagues are possible. Yet we continue to understand all life better, to catalog the human genome, and to push average life expectancy upward.

2. The ultimate exhaustion of some fossil fuels, specifically oil and gas, could threaten the steady rise in average energy available to humans. Yet coal is far from exhaustion, and it appears that advances in solar and nuclear energy technologies will free us in the next century from our dependence on fossil fuels.

3. It is true that global production of food per capita ceased to advance in the mid-1980s, that the per capita availability of land is declining, and that the oceans are overexploited. Perhaps more than any other problem, we should worry about overpopulation relative to our ability to produce food. The good news is that global population growth rates began a now-accelerating decline in the early 1970s, that after the 1990s the absolute number of people added to the global total each year will also begin to decline, and that the continent with the greatest contemporary food problems—Africa—also has the largest midterm potential for both slower population growth and advance in food production.

4. Finally, humans continue to increase the scale of their negative impacts on the physical and biological world. For instance, our assault on the ozone layer and on rain forests proceeds, and the addition of carbon dioxide to the atmosphere continues to accelerate. Unfortunately, none of these behaviors will change quickly. Environmental damage will increase throughout most or all of the next century until the global population stabilizes and, more important, until fundamental transformations create sustainable energy and agricultural systems.

Even to state the problems is to reiterate that success is far from certain. Moreover, the challenges are so great that there is a certain moral hazard in attempting to convince others that they will be overcome and thereby perhaps invite complacency; I feel ethically more comfortable supporting those who draw our attention to the problems and emphasize the substantial efforts we need to make in addressing them. Nonetheless, success appears probable.

The Domestic Economic and Social-Political Superstructures

For the past three hundred years global industrial production has grown fairly steadily at a rate that has almost always substantially exceeded population growth. Yet the industrial revolution is far from over. The substitution of machines for human labor continues, and by the end of the twenty-first century it would be surprising if more than 10 percent of the labor force of economically advanced countries were employed in industrial production (what some still, anachronistically, call *manu*facture). The diffusion of industrial production to Asia and Latin America is well underway, despite the image of these regions only a generation ago as the global haulers of water and hewers of wood. We should probably now label China and India newly industrialized economies; African countries will have their turn.

Marx and many others have long recognized that production systems have specific characteristics that heavily influence, if not fully structure, broader social-political relationships. In the early phases of the industrial era, production employed much of the workforce in factory jobs (supported by raw materials–extraction jobs) that were often dirty, dangerous, dull, and meanly paid. It sharply divided the owners of capital from those who worked in their factories and mines. This division spilled over from hostile economic relationships to hostile political ones, both domestically and internationally. It also provided a basis for the mass mobilization of society (Kornhauser, 1959) in economic activities (including communism's mass reproduction of large-scale industry), political movements (including fascism's campaigns of hate against minorities or outsiders), and military forces (including the military-industrial complexes of all types of governments).

Internationally, the industrial economy also supported growth in both trade and capital flows. Although two world wars and a global depression greatly set back the sharp rise that had characterized the nineteenth century, growth in the movement of goods and capital restarted after World War II and climbed to new peaks in the 1970s and 1980s.

Obviously, some states and some individuals or groups have felt they could secure at least a temporary and relative advantage by interfering with the free movement of goods and capital. Yet the logic of systemic economic advantage from free trade and capital movement, stated early in the industrial era by Adam Smith and David Ricardo, proved powerful not just for the richest and most influential states but also for the dragons and tigers and sloggers that entered the industrial era later. Thus most states supported the establishment in the 1940s, and the strengthening thereafter, of global institutions that helped trade and capital flows resume and grow.

What will be the essential characteristics of the knowledge- or information-based economy, and how will they influence broader society? The industrial revolution never fully vanquished the feudal opposition between the owners of land and their workforce. Instead, by reducing the importance of agriculture and opening other opportunities to economic advancement, it pushed that opposition into an economic and social backwater. Somewhat the same thing is already happening to the opposition between the owners of capital and those who are paid to work with it. Ownership has diffused from robber-baron entrepreneurs to shareholders and coupon clippers, and, as John Galbraith (1973) explained before Peter Drucker did, management has become divorced from ownership. In fact, the workers increasingly own the capital through pension plans and employee stock ownership plans. Modern societies often exhibit greater lines of conflict between workers inside and outside of the large corporations than between management and workers within those corporations.

In the knowledge economy, the fundamental division may be between those who hold executive, administrative, managerial, and professional jobs (the "suits") and those who do not. In 1990, the Department of Labor placed 38 percent of the U.S. labor force in the former category (and only 27 percent into broad production and laborer categories). Those at the top of the information economy hierarchy use various education credentials and professional certification requirements to help protect their positions (such as Ph.D.s and tenure for professors).

Yet key characteristics of the modern information economy are its pluralism and mobility. On top of the older divisions, left over from the feudal and industrial economies, is a confusion of job categories and work descriptions that makes identifying economic fault lines extremely difficult. Individual and especially intergenerational mobility, based in substantial part on education, appears even greater than was true in the industrial economy (in which it was *much* greater than in the feudal system).

To emphasize the pluralism and mobility of the information economy is not to be blind to significant problems. Those displaced from industrial jobs in midlife find movement to information positions nearly impossible. Also, not all entrants to the labor force possess the intellectual or social skills required to be effective in the information economy. Both unemployment and income distribution will remain substantial problems, especially during the period when industrial jobs continue to be eliminated in large numbers (as agricultural jobs were rapidly eliminated between the 1920s and 1950s). Income distribution is at the least a transitional problem for the information economy as transformation destroys earlier jobs. It could prove a longer-term problem. Whereas the labor unions of the industrial economy forced redistributive action both within the economy and through the political system, the complex pluralism of the information economy undercuts solidarity among those at the bottom of the economic hierarchy.

The implications of the modern information economy for the strength of democracy are mixed but are generally positive. First, democracy thrives in environments of economic and social pluralism rather than in those with sharp us-versus-them cleavages. Second, highly centralized, directive governments can be fairly effective in mobilizing capital and reproducing giant industrial plants, but the governments of Eastern Europe and the former Soviet Union proved nearly incapable of incubating a rapidly changing and diffusely organized information economy. Global recognition of that situation helped lead a rush away from such governments. Third, stable and effective democracy also appears to require both a reasonable level of economic well-being and a fairly equitable distribution of that well-being. As discussed, the early information economy does have some difficulties with distribution, but it offers a high level of average well-being.

We should also not forget or underestimate the direct linkages that exist between advanced information technology and democracy (in contrast to those that operate through intermediating economic variables). Fax machines, VCRs, satellite-delivered television (including CNN), copy machines, computer disks, and e-mail connections all facilitate the flow of information that helps to undercut authoritarian and totalitarian regimes. They support democratization around the globe.

Between 1800 and 1960 the gap in living standards, as measured by gross national product (GNP) per capita, between the industrializing European countries and the rest of the world steadily increased, perhaps from 2-to-1 to more than 15-to-1 (Hughes, 1994: 342–344). Since 1960 that gap has grown relatively little (although sharp differences have emerged among countries in what was once called simply the Third World, and inequality has increased within many of those countries). In purchasing power terms, the North-South gap is much less than 15-to-1, and World Bank data show that as many countries have increased their GNP per capita relative to the United States since 1970 as have lost ground (a large portion of the losers are in Central Europe and the former Soviet Union and may therefore in part reflect improved measurement). Moreover, the North-South gap in living standards, as measured by life expectancy, access to calories, literacy rate, and access to safe water, has narrowed significantly. We appear to have passed the peak of global inequalities. Although Africa promises to be a laggard, populations in the rest of the less developed world should substantially narrow the gap in incomes between themselves and the world's wealthy in the early twenty-first century. These trends suggest yet another supporting basis for global democratization: that of improved living conditions in countries that continue to industrialize and that will not for a considerable time become primarily information economies.

Freedom House (1993) data do show that democratization, in terms of both formal political rights and actual respect for civil liberties, is a worldwide phenomenon. Between 1981 and 1983 an average of 43.4 percent of the world's people lived in "not-free" societies. Taking a longer view, Michael Doyle (1995) counted three "liberal" societies in the eighteenth century, eight in the first half of the nineteenth century, twenty-nine in the first half of the twentieth century, and fifty-four since 1945.

Again, I must conclude with an admission of uncertainty and with an assertion that it will require great effort to overcome dangers. Advances in global economic well-being were sharply interrupted for much of the world, especially developing countries, in the 1980s, which were the "lost decade" for Latin America. And only a few years ago perhaps the dominant interpretation of the implications of exploding information was that central governments would use it to control their citizenry. Democratization has periodically suffered great reverses globally, not the least within a few years of World War I, the "war to make the world safe for democracy" (Huntington, 1991, traced a wave phenomenon in democratization). Yet in a world in which citizens become fairly steadily more wealthy, in which global literacy now grows by 5 percent per decade and considerably exceeds 50 percent, in which communications channels and media forms proliferate wildly, and in which pluralistic populations mobilize quickly to protect their interests, those who still aspire to be our "big brothers" face significant obstacles.

The Global Economic-Political System

How might state-level and regional economic-political developments affect global ones? The future of global politics, of global governance, will depend primarily on the interests of key actors (material forces), but we will also see change at the idealistic level. I therefore consider first some likely developments in global interaction patterns, returning later to the place of ideas.

Commercial Interaction

Trade and capital flows are the most important and general global exchanges. In contrast to the industrial era, domestic knowledge economies clearly favor capital and technology flows over trade and favor service trade over merchandise trade. Advances in telecommunications and computing only marginally reduce the cost of goods transport, but they dramatically lower the cost of transferring financial capital and technology.

In the short run, the ability to transfer capital and technology faciliates the movement of production to low labor-cost areas and is thus now increasing goods trade. It appears possible, however, that over time, especially with equalization of labor costs, these technologies might actually reverse the long post–World War II increase in goods trade as a percentage of GNP—that a wide variety of goods will be produced nearer their markets.[6]

Many data suggest that the shift to a global economy driven by capital flows rather than trade is well underway. Between 1960 and 1988, global trade in manufactured goods increased at a rate more than twice that of production. Since 1970, however, foreign bank deposits in economically advanced countries have climbed from half the level of annual exports to twice their level, and a wide range of other financial flows (including portfolio investments) have similarly grown at rates far above those in trade. The attention the United States insisted be focused on intellectual property and services in the Uruguay Round of the General Agreement on Tariffs and Trade (GATT) recognized this transformation. Over time, the new World Trade Organization will become more a general agreement on trade in services and less GATT. The world's primary financial institution, the International Monetary Fund, will need to take on new obligations, ultimately becoming more of a global central bank.

Possible developments in energy trade merit special comment because that trade looms large in the physical volume of world trade and because global dependence on Middle Eastern oil in the post–World War II world has so greatly affected many political interactions. I have argued repeatedly that humanity must move toward a renewable energy system, based on solar and nuclear energy, or global economies will flounder as oil and gas supplies run down in the twenty-first century (following the pattern of exhaustion that has characterized U.S. oil resources since 1960). It is unclear whether the movement to new technology will preceed exhaustion or follow it. Given the rapid growth in energy demand in the newly industrialized countries, the latter seems probable. If so, we can expect an interim period with new global energy price shocks and a seeming rebirth of Organization of Petroleum Exporting Countries strength. Given inevitable zero-sum conflict among states over oil supplies, this period will considerably strain the alliance of developed democracies.

Noncommercial Interaction

Historically, global interactions on environmental issues have been of low importance, very much low politics. This situation began to change with the 1972 Stockholm conference on the environment. Events such as the Montreal Protocol on CFCs and the Rio Conference on the global environment accelerated the change. Overexploitation of ocean fisheries has made fishing an increasingly important and contentious interstate issue. Because the world must move toward sustainability in the twenty-first century, and because this can happen only through collective agreements to restrain individual state interests in using the global commons as resource sources and pollution sinks, the growth in the number of global environmental organizations, conferences, and agreements should considerably exceed that in trade or security even if the effort at cooperation eventually fails.

Ultimately, global interactions occur among people, not among corporations or states. By many accounts, global tourism (which is normally measured so broadly as to include business and diplomatic trips, not just recreational ones) has become the world's largest industry. Even in the face of higher liquid fossil fuel prices, that growth will continue. Another component of interpersonal contact, not always face-to-face, is membership in nongovernmental organizations (NGOs), especially the transnational social movements that have become global interest groups. For example, Greenpeace grew from a handful of members in 1977 to 350,000 members in 1994 (*Economist*, August 13, 1994: 49). NGO growth has greatly exceeded that of either states or international organizations during the post–World War II era. This trend will continue and is clearly tied to global democratization.

Although the threat of mutual destruction certainly contributes to an explanation of the long-standing peace among great powers, democratic or not (Gaddis, 1987), and although changes in norms and beliefs about war may contribute as well, it is impossible to ignore the phenomenon of peaceful interaction among democracies. The absence of war between democracies for over two hundred years and the dramatic transformation of the U.S.-Russian relationship as the Russian government has moved toward democracy are striking. As Kant predicted two hundred years ago, a zone of peace has developed among Western democracies, and it continues to spread. This phenomenon, rooted in the technological and economic developments that underlay democratization (and, admittedly, in the fear of war with modern technology), is one of the most positive in the modern world.

The Clash of Ideas

We return to ideas. It is sometimes argued that Western ideas have reached the limit of their expanding influence globally and that the growing strength of other parts of the world and their reaction against the West mean universalistic interpretations of global ideals are wrong (Huntington, 1993; Puchala, 1994). Western concepts of human rights and democracy and Western commercial liberalism, it is argued, have reached their zeniths.

On materialistic grounds, I disagree. Interests have become more interconnected, and community in ideas will follow. Moreover, the cousin of community, both linguistically and practically, is communication.

The extensiveness and intensity of face-to-face communication around the world have increased dramatically. The extensiveness and intensity of communication through electronics have exploded, and the web of communication ties will almost certainly continue to tighten even more rapidly throughout the twenty-first century.

There are reactions in all parts of the world against the growing interconnectedness of interests and the intrusion of ideas from abroad—not the least in the developed Western world, where citizens tire of seeing the faces of starving children and nationalistic soldiers on television every day. There are efforts to staunch the flow of these external influences—not the least in the developed world, where immigrants threaten the supposed homogeneity of communities. Yet the increase in interaction and the interchange of ideas are unstoppable. In the clash of ideas, those of material progress, of liberal societies, and increasingly of sustainable economies dominate.

Many Middle Eastern scholars question whether this is true in the face of Islam (Cantori, 1994). Islamic societies often resist the social liberalization that is required if they are to control population growth, mobilize the creative energies of their citizens (including their women) for economic growth, and reconcile their modern secular and religious sides. They will gradually and unsteadily liberalize, however, because the citizens of these societies already embrace commercial liberalism— they already clearly understand one source of the greater economic prosperity of the West. Moreover, and even more fundamentally, advances in education and literacy are laying the base for cognitive liberalism. Because anything like the coherence the Soviet Union once imposed on communist countries is unlikely across Islamic ones, the liberalization of Islam will happen without the full-scale intercivilizational clash Huntington predicts.

Confucian societies will continue to adopt economically and, ultimately, politically liberal policies because their focus on this life rather than the next predisposes them to economic liberalization. Yet another predisposition, however, that toward governmental leadership of economic transformation, will create some continued difficulties in interaction both with less centrally directed Western economies and among themselves. For instance, the ongoing buildup of both economic and military capabilities in Asia, and the inevitable overtaking of Japan by China, will lead to tension and even overt conflict.

The Difficult Transition

Although liberalism is winning, it has not won. State-centric analyses of the twenty-first-century world will continue to be sharp and insightful.

That world will rely on the Bretton Woods institutions and the UN system for assistance with *interstate* cooperation. States will strengthen these institutions in many ways and will add new ones (such as the World Trade Organization). Although nongovernmental organizations will continue to proliferate, to draw increased membership at rapid rates, and to assert themselves more stridently on the world stage, almost all international organizations will continue to be state-based rather than citizenry-based, and they will respect the vetoes of states.

There is much to be done before a liberal vision of citzenry-based global governance becomes a reality. The processes of industrialization and transformation to information societies need to run their courses. Ecologically sustainable energy and agricultural systems must emerge. Democratization and respect for human rights need to diffuse globally. Income gaps within and across countries must close substantially.

Large-scale environmental crises will occur both regionally and globally. They will continue to plague Africa especially. Wars, limited mostly to developing countries and in large part civil conflicts, will not disappear. An economic crisis of the magnitude of the Great Depression could even threaten the democratic gains of the economically advanced countries and set the stage for conflict among them. Such a situation appears much less likely, however, than it did at the peak of their industrialization.

A Model of the Future

To see the longer-term global political-economic future, we must especially watch Europe and the North Atlantic community. This region was the womb of the modern nation-state and the nation-state system, of modern free trade, and of modern democracy. It is now giving birth to a new pattern of governance. State-centric models provided clear predictions for the region after the Cold War. Because those models understood the European Community to be fundamentally a counter-weight—against the Soviet Union through the North American Treaty Organization (NATO) and against the United States within NATO and the Western economy—they forecast that the end of the Cold War would lead to the collapse of NATO, the withdrawal (or even expulsion) of the United States from Europe, the weakening of the European Community (especially as a reunited Germany began to assert an independent role on the global stage), and the intensification of trade conflict.

Not only has none of these events happened, the early indicators suggest that many of the trends are in much the opposite direction. The mission of NATO has in essence been redefined and expanded: It continues to serve as a guarantor against external threat, as uncertain as that might be; it is also now to serve as the collective security organization of the advanced democratic states, helping them to maintain their own cooperative relationships; and it is to serve as an agent for the solidification of democracy and peaceful relations in Central and Eastern Europe through its new Partnership for Peace.

The European Community has not only largely attained its goals for finalizing the common market through the Single Act, it has set new goals at Maastricht and redefined itself as the European Union. It has become even more of a magnet for prospective members than before. In state-centric terms, the best candidate to replace the United States as the global economic hegemon in the twenty-first century appears to be the European Union. Yet even more important, the community of developed Western democracies, led by the United States and the European Union in cooperation and with associated membership of a more state-bound Japan, has continued to struggle with periodic trade disputes but also continues to exhibit deeper and wider cooperation.

A pattern of complex governance, in which large numbers of overlapping institutions facilitate cooperation in various issues areas (the environment, economics, and defense), will continue to assign a fundamentally important role to the historic state. Yet what Marx foresaw as the withering of the state, or what the functionalists more accurately saw as the progressive creation of an enveloping and sovereignty-limiting web of ties, will continue. Because the Organization for Economic Cooperation and Development essentially represents the core states in this evolving governance entity, and because through its admission of Mexico the OECD has proven capable of growing and adapting, we should watch it, as well as the European Union, for evidence of the widening of complex governance. Similarly, the powers of the European Parliament will say much about the deepening of the process.

Conclusion

I continue to worry that readers will misunderstand this statement of optimism as a denial of continuing problems. Unlike Fukuyama, who foresaw the end of (interesting or conflictual) history and lamented it, I foresee the continuation of very interesting and conflictual history and fear it.

Clashes among big ideas are not over. Humanity has exhibited a resilient ability to perceive what may earlier or later appear insignificant differences of opinion, understanding, or belief to be of the greatest consequence, worth taking the lives of others or giving one's own. Big ideas are, in large part, a matter of definition.

Even as liberalism is winning, one very important internal contradiction (Bell, 1976) grows within it—one that will require substantial internal transformation, perhaps facilitated by interaction with Confucian societies. It is the tension between the sometimes extreme individualism encouraged by liberalism and the communitarianism required to protect individuals both from each other and from themselves (that is, to organize necessary collective action for individual goals). Reconciling self-interest with the collective good is perhaps *the* great issue of the day. Liberal societies must somehow compensate for the pressures of modern society on families and other structures of social integration if they are to overcome growing economic inequalities and develop sustainable relationships with the environment. Success in balancing individualistic and collective needs is by no means certain.

In retrospect, the twentieth century has advanced liberalism considerably. Within the century a belief in the ability of technology to sustain human progress spread from its European origins to essentially the entire world. Similarly, within the period average economic and material well-being increased sharply. The average life expectancy of a male at birth in 1900 was only forty-eight years in the United States; it is now seventy-two in the United States and sixty-three years globally. The primary institution of liberalism, democracy, spread from a handful of countries early in the century to become, fully or in part, the governmental reality for two-thirds of the world's population (and the official form for nearly all of humanity). These transformations took place in a world that simultaneously experienced some of the greatest wars and famines in history—that pitted states and classes in dramatic interest and ideological conflicts.

In prospect, the twenty-first century will continue liberalism's advance. It will be the century in which humanity grapples with the issue of sustainability and ultimately wins the battle to reshape its technology to protect the physical and biological environment. It will be the century in which the recent great widening in economic conditions around the world substantially reverses. It will be the century in which democracy within the state becomes democracy across groupings of states, following the model being developed in the North Atlantic region. Unfortunately, these transformations will not occur without reverses and without trauma.

Notes

My appreciation to Mark Zacher for his useful suggestions.

1. Interestingly, Fukuyama's elaboration of his liberal argument (1992) was a more materialistic rendition, portraying a world of ideas driven substantially by underlying technological change.

2. Huntington may have presented the clash-of-civilizations argument in part to generate debate about post–Cold War politics rather than from full conviction. In an only slightly earlier book on democracy, he strongly questioned whether Islamic and Confucian cultures "pose insuperable obstacles to democratic development" (Huntington, 1991: 310).

3. More specifically, he recanted the prediction of the disappearance of the state but not the forecast that nuclear weapons would reduce international violence.

4. At the same time, some neoliberal internationalists use global environmental issues to pursue an activist's agenda of global cooperation and institution building. Those who do so, however, are fundamentally optimistic about overcoming environmental problems.

5. Although he cautions against exclusive attention to communications technology (at the expense, for instance, of military technology), Ronald Deibert skillfully developed propositions concerning the interaction between dominant communications media and international relations.

6. This could, of course, support renewed localism and even ethnocentrism. The obvious benefits of remaining open to flows of capital and technology should most often be a stronger force.

References

Bell, Daniel. 1976. *The Cultural Contradictions of Capitalism*. New York: Basic Books.

Braudel, Fernand. 1979. *The Perspective of the World*. Vol. 3 of *Civilization and Capitalism: 15th–18th Century*. New York: Harper and Row.

Cantori, Louis J. 1994. "Democracy, Islam, and the Study of Middle Eastern Politics," a Symposium of Seven Middle Eastern Scholars. *P.S.: Political Science and Politics* 27, no. 3 (September): 507–519.

Caporaso, James A. 1993. "Global Political Economy," in Ada W. Finifter, ed., *Political Science: The State of the Discipline II*, pp. 451–481. Washington, D.C.: American Political Science Association.

Cardoso, Fernando H., and Enzo Faletto. 1978. *Dependency and Development in Latin America*. Berkeley: University of California Press.

Carr, Edward Hallett. 1964 [1939]. *The Twenty Years' Crisis, 1919–1939*. New York: Harper and Row.

Choucri, Nazli, and Robert C. North. 1975. *Nations in Conflict: National Growth and International Violence*. San Francisco: W. H. Freeman.

Deibert, Ronald J. "*Typographica*: The Medium and the Medieval to Modern Transition." Unpublished manuscript.

Doyle, Michael W. 1986. "Liberalism and World Politics." *American Political Science Review* 80, no. 4: 1151–1169.

———. 1995. "Liberalism and World Politics Revisited," in Charles W. Kegley Jr., ed., *Controversies in International Relations Theory*, pp. 83–106. New York: St. Martin's Press.

Frank, Andre Gunder. 1969. *Capitalism and Underdevelopment in Latin America*. Rev. ed. New York: Modern Reader Paperbacks.

Freedom House. 1993. *Freedom in the World 1992–93*. New York: Freedom House.
Friedman, Milton. 1962. *Capitalism and Freedom*. Chicago: University of Chicago Press.
Fukuyama, Francis. 1989. "The End of History?" *National Interest*, no. 16 (Summer): 3–18.
———. 1992. *The End of History and the Last Man*. New York: Free Press.
Gaddis, John Lewis. 1987. *The Long Peace: Inquiries into the History of the Cold War*. New York: Oxford University Press.
Galbraith, John Kenneth. 1973. *Economics and the Public Purpose*. Boston: Houghton Mifflin.
Gilpin, Robert. 1975. "Three Models of the Future." *International Organization* 29, no. 1: 37–60.
———. 1981. *War and Change in World Politics*. New York: Cambridge University Press.
Goddard, C. Roe. 1993. *U.S. Foreign Economic Policy and the Latin American Debt Issue*. New York: Garland Press.
Goldstein, Judith. 1993. *Ideas, Interests, and American Trade Policy*. Ithaca: Cornell University Press.
Goldstein, Judith, and Robert O. Keohane, eds. 1993. *Ideas and Foreign Policy: Beliefs, Institutions, and Political Change*. Ithaca: Cornell University Press.
Goodman, Allan E. 1993. *A Brief History of the Future*. Boulder: Westview Press.
Haas, Ernst B. 1964. *Beyond the Nation-State: Functionalism and International Organization*. Stanford: Stanford University Press.
Herz, John H. 1957. "Rise and Demise of the Territorial State." *World Politics* 9, no. 4 (July): 473–493.
———. 1969. "The Territorial State Revisited," in James N. Rosenau, ed., *International Politics and Foreign Policy*, rev. ed., pp. 76–89. New York: Free Press.
Holsti, K. J. 1985. *The Dividing Discipline: Hegemony and Diversity in International Theory*. Boston: Allen and Unwin.
Hughes, Barry B. 1994. *Continuity and Change in World Politics: The Clash of Perspectives*. 2d ed. Englewood Cliffs, N.J.: Prentice-Hall.
Huntington, Samuel P. 1991. *The Third Wave: Democratization in the Late Twentieth Century*. Norman: University of Oklahoma Press.
———. 1993. "The Clash of Civilizations?" *Foreign Affairs* 72, no. 3 (Summer): 22–49.
Kahn, Herman, William Brown, and Leon Martel. 1976. *The Next 200 Years*. New York: William Morrow.
Kaplan, Morton A. 1957. *System and Process in International Politics*. New York: John Wiley and Sons.
Kennedy, Paul. 1988. *The Rise and Fall of Great Powers: Economic Change and Military Conflict from 1500 to 2000*. New York: Random House.
———. 1993. *Preparing for the Twenty-First Century*. New York: Random House.
Keohane, Robert O. 1980. "The Theory of Hegemonic Stability and Changes in International Economic Regimes, 1967–1977," in Ole R. Holsti, Randolph M. Siverson, and Alexander L. George, eds., *Change in the International System*, pp. 131–162. Boulder: Westview Press.
———. 1989. *International Institutions and State Power*. Boulder: Westview Press.
———. 1990. "International Liberalism Revisited," in John Dunn, ed., *The Economic Limits to Modern Politics*, pp. 165–194. Cambridge: Cambridge University Press.

Keohane, Robert O., and Joseph S. Nye Jr., eds. 1970. *Transnational Relations and World Politics*. Cambridge, Mass.: Harvard University Press.

Kornhauser, William. 1959. *The Politics of Mass Society*. New York: Free Press.

Krasner, Stephen D., ed. 1983. *International Regimes*. Ithaca: Cornell University Press.

Mitrany, David. 1966. *A Working Peace System*. Chicago: Quadrangle.

Modelski, George. 1978. "The Long Cycle of Global Politics and the Nation-State." *Comparative Studies in Society and History* 20, no. 2 (April): 214–235.

Modelski, George, and William R. Thompson. 1987. *Seapower in Global Politics: 1494–1993*. London: Macmillan.

Mueller, John. 1989. *Retreat from Doomsday: The Obsolescence of Major War*. New York: Basic Books.

Orwell, George. 1949. *1984*. New York: New American Library.

Pirages, Dennis. 1978. *Global Ecopolitics*. North Scituate, Mass.: Duxbury Press.

———. 1983. "The Ecological Perspective and the Social Sciences." *International Studies Quarterly* 27, no. 3 (September): 243–255.

Puchala, Donald J. 1994. "The History of the Future of International Relations." *Ethics and International Affairs* 8: 177–202.

Quester, George H. 1977. *Offense and Defense in the International System*. New York: John Wiley.

Rasler, Karen, and William R. Thompson. 1989. "Ascent, Decline and War." Paper delivered at the annual American Political Science Association meeting, Atlanta, Georgia.

Ray, James Lee. 1989. "The Abolition of Slavery and the End of International War." *International Organization* 43 (Summer): 405–440.

Rosecrance, Richard N. 1986. *The Rise of the Trading State: Commerce and Conquest in the Modern World*. New York: Basic Books.

Ruggie, John Gerald. 1982. "International Regimes, Transactions, and Change: Embedded Liberalism in the Postwar Economic Order." *International Organization* 36: 379–415.

Schumpeter, Joseph. 1955 [1919]. *Imperialism and Social Classes*. Cleveland: World Publishing.

Simon, Julian. 1981. *The Ultimate Resource*. Princeton, N.J.: Princeton University Press.

Toffler, Alvin. 1980. *The Third Wave*. New York: William Morrow.

Toynbee, Arnold. 1972. *A Study of History*. New York: Weathervane Books.

Vernon, Raymond. 1971. *Sovereignty at Bay*. New York: Basic Books.

Wallerstein, Immanuel. 1976. *The Modern World System*, Vol. 1. New York: Academic Press.

———. 1980. *The Modern World System*, Vol. 2. New York: Academic Press.

Waltz, Kenneth N. 1979. *Theory of International Politics*. New York: Random House.

Zacher, Mark W., and Richard A. Matthew. 1995. "Liberal International Theory: Common Threads and Divergent Strands," in Charles W. Kegley Jr., ed., *Controversies in International Relations Theory: Realism and the Neoliberal Challenge*, pp. 107–150. New York: St. Martin's Press.

INDEX

About the Book and Editors

This anthology introduces and places in context a collection of the most important contributions to our understanding of international political economy.

Designed for classroom use, the text begins with a series of chapters on the various ideologies of political economy. This section—made up of classic contributions, as well as chapters reflecting the timely application of the ideologies—provides each student with an enriched theoretical framework from which to interpret state and market behavior.

Subsequent sections critically examine the history and current tenor of international monetary and trade relations, the evolution and character of development assistance, and the role of the transnational enterprise in IPE. The inclusion here of chapters examining the functions and evolution of the major multilateral institutions is a distinctive feature of the book.

The final section draws conclusions about the likely constraints current trends foretell and the efforts of the global community to address environmental degradation.

C. Roe Goddard is associate professor and chair of the Department of International Studies at Thunderbird, the American Graduate School of International Management. He is author of *U.S. Foreign Economic Policy and the Latin American Debt Issue* and is managing editor of *International Studies Notes*. **John T Passé-Smith** is assistant professor of political science at the University of Central Arkansas. He coauthored *The Unionization of the Maquiladora Industry* and coedited *Development and Underdevelopment: The Political Economy of Inequality*. **John G. Conklin** is associate professor of international studies at Thunderbird and is organizing an environmental institute there.